MOON HANDBOOKS

ECUADOR

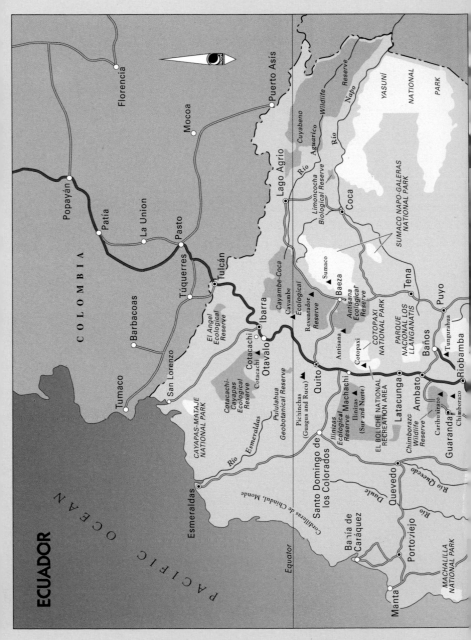

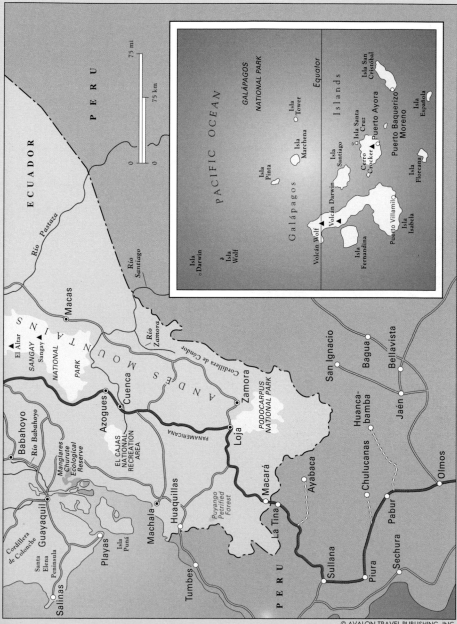

PERU

ECUADOR

PACIFIC OCEAN

GALÁPAGOS
NATIONAL PARK

Equator

Galápagos Islands

Isla
Darwin

Isla
Wolf

Isla Pinta

Isla
Marchena

Isla
Tower

Isla
Santiago

Isla Santa
Cruz

Cerro
Crocker

Puerto Ayora

Isla San
Cristóbal

Puerto Baquerizo
Moreno

Isla
Española

Volcán Darwin

Volcán Wolf

Isla
Fernandina

Puerto Villamil

Isla
Isabela

Isla
Floreana

75 mi

75 km

Río Pastaza

Río
Santiago

Macas

Río
Zamora

SANGAY
NATIONAL
PARK

El Altar

Sangay

Cordillera de Cóndor

ANDES MOUNTAINS

Cuenca

Azogues

EL CAJAS NATIONAL
RECREATION
AREA

Zamora

Loja

PANAMERICANA

PODOCARPUS
NATIONAL PARK

San Ignacio

Bagua

Bellavista

Huanca-
bamba

Jaén

Babahoyo

Río Babahoyo

Manglares
Churute
Ecological
Reserve

Guayaquil

Machala

Huaquillas

Macará

La Tina

Puyango
Petrified
Forest

Ayabaca

Chulucanas

Olmos

Pabur

Cordillera
de Colonche

Santa
Elena
Peninsula

Isla
Puná

Playas

Tumbes

Sullana

Piura

Sechura

Salinas

PERU

MOON HANDBOOKS

ECUADOR

SECOND EDITION

JULIAN SMITH

AVALON
TRAVEL

MOON HANDBOOKS: ECUADOR
SECOND EDITION
By Julian Smith

Published by
 Avalon Travel Publishing
 5855 Beaudry St.
 Emeryville, CA 94608, USA

Text and photographs © Julian Smith, 2001
 All rights reserved.
Cover,illustrations, and maps
 © Avalon Travel Publishing Inc., 2001
 All rights reserved.
 Some photos and illustrations are used by permission
 and are the property of the original copyright owners.

ISBN: 1-56691-338-1
ISSN: 1533-4333

Editor: Angelique S. Clarke
Series Manager: Erin Van Rheenen
Copy Editor: Ginjer L. Clarke
Proofreader and Indexer: Leslie Miller
Graphics Coordinator: Erika Howsare
Production: Darren Alessi, Karen McKinley, Marcie McKinley
Map Editor: Naomi Dancis
Cartography: Kat Kalamaras, Michael Balsbaugh, Mike Morgenfeld

Front cover photo: *Market, village of Zumbuhua, Ecuador* © 1995 Robert Fried

Distributed in the United States by Publishers Group West

Printed in China through Colorcraft Ltd., Hong Kong

Please send all comments,
corrections, additions,
amendments, and critiques to:

**MOON HANDBOOKS: ECUADOR
AVALON TRAVEL PUBLISHING
5855 BEAUDRY ST.
EMERYVILLE, CA, USA
e-mail: info@travelmatters.com
www.travelmatters.com**

Printing History
1st edition—1998
2nd edition—August 2001
5 4 3 2 1

Although every effort was made to ensure that the information was correct at the time of going to press, the author and publisher do not assume and hereby disclaim any liability to any party for any loss or damage caused by errors, omissions, or any potential travel disruption due to labor or financial difficulty, whether such errors or omissions result from negligence, accident, or any other cause.

CONTENTS

NORTHERN SIERRA . . . . 149~194

CENTRAL SIERRA . . . . 195~246

MAPS

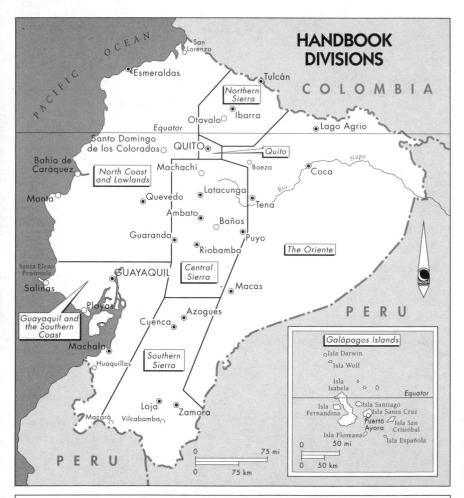

HANDBOOK DIVISIONS

PACIFIC OCEAN

COLOMBIA

San Lorenzo
Esmeraldas
Tulcán

Northern Sierra

Otavalo   Ibarra

Equator   Lago Agrio

Santo Domingo
de los Colorados   QUITO   Quito

Bahía de
Caráquez   Machachi   Baeza   Coca

North Coast
and Lowlands   Río Napo

Manta   Latacunga

Quevedo   Tena

Ambato

Guaranda   Baños
              Puyo
        Riobamba   The Oriente

Santa Elena
Peninsula   Central
Salinas   Sierra

GUAYAQUIL   Macas

Playas   PERU

          Azogues
Guayaquil and
the Southern   Cuenca
Coast

Machala
         Southern
Huaquillas   Sierra

                              MOON

Loja   Zamora

Macará   Vilcabamba

PERU

0   75 mi
0   75 km

Galápagos Islands

Isla Darwin
Isla Wolf

Isla
Isabela   Equator

Isla
Fernandina   Isla Santiago
             Isla Santa Cruz
             Puerto
             Ayora   Isla San
                     Cristóbal
Isla Floreana   Isla Española

0   50 mi
0   50 km

MAP SYMBOLS

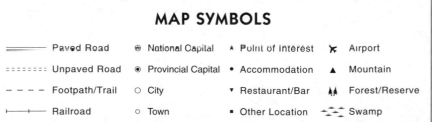

Paved Road	National Capital	Point of Interest	Airport
Unpaved Road	Provincial Capital	Accommodation	Mountain
Footpath/Trail	City	Restaurant/Bar	Forest/Reserve
Railroad	Town	Other Location	Swamp

IS THIS BOOK OUT OF DATE?

Sometimes writing guidebooks seems as inherently futile as buying clothes for children: no sooner do you commit yourself than your efforts become obsolete. Inevitably, kids grow, hotels close, cooks change recipes, and prices oscillate. We'd like to keep this book as accurate as possible and have made every effort to do so, but we could still use a little help in the ongoing struggle against inaccuracy.

We'd love to hear from you, whether it be a new place you'd like to recommend, a rant against an undeserved omission, or just a funny story that happened on the way to the bullfight. Be as specific as you can, and include any relevant diagrams, details, or punchlines. Map comments are especially appreciated. All contributions will be acknowledged, and thanks ahead of time.

Address all correspondence to:

Moon Travel Handbooks: Ecuador
Avalon Travel Publishing
5855 Beaudry St.
Emeryville, CA 94608, USA
email: info@travelmatters.com

ABBREVIATIONS

km—kilometers
kg—kilograms
Pana—Panamericana (Pan-American Highway)
IGM—Instituto Geográfico Militar
SAE—South American Explorers
IYH—International Youth Hostel
ppd—postage paid
4WD—four-wheel drive
ISIC—International Student Identity Card

pp—per person
GMT—Greenwich mean time
Av.—Avenida
Ave.—Avenue
Ed.—*edificio* (building)
Of.—*oficina* (office)
C.C.—*centro commercial* (mall)
Apdo.—*apartado* (post office box)
s—single occupancy
d—double occupancy

ACKNOWLEDGMENTS

I'd like to thank the readers who sent in recommendations for the second edition of *Moon Handbooks: Ecuador* including Martin Allen, Diane Bergeron, Andrew & Wai Cheng, Simon Davies, Lee Hutt, David Jenish, Ron Keesing, Tom Kilpatrick, Julia Krasevec, Dan Lipson, Sumana Reddy, Rick Rhodes, Angelika Schwabl, Stephanie Spivack, Jim Stewart, Lawrence Tirino, Brent J. Wexler, and S. L. Wyatt.

In Ecuador, invaluable help came from Wolfgang Boerchers, Caz Boynton, Jean Brown, Iain Campbell, Edward Cox, Maria Crespo, Andy Hammerman, Michelle Kirby, Jan Lescrauwaet, Margarita and Gaby Lugo, Diana Morris, Alfredo Neira, Steve Nomchong, Edmundo Paredes Proaño, and Galo Proaño.

Thanks also to Tim Bewer, Deb Davidson, Gretchen Maneval, Jeff Baker, Magnus McGlashan, Cheryl Wilson, and Emma Sutton.

Since leaving Cabool, we had slept in our clothes, where we could seldom or ever change them. We had halted among mud, waded through rivers, tumbled among snow, and for the last few days been sunned by heat. These are but the petty inconveniences of a traveler; which sink into insignificance, when compared with the pleasure of seeing new men and countries, strange manners and customs, and being able to temper the prejudices of one's country, by observing those of other nations.

—Alexander Burns

PREFACE

Ecuador, all in all you are one hell of a country.

—Henri Michaux

On one of my most recent trips to Ecuador, I made the mistake of leaving the Andes on Sunday afternoon for a Monday-morning flight from the Amazon. I didn't have much choice—the road downhill, under construction since the Crusades, was only opened two nights a week—but I'd been in the country long enough to know better.

Our bus pulled away from Baños' dripping green backdrop as the sun faded over the black church steeple. It started to rain. At the mouth of the first tunnel we waited three hours, with the roar of the Devil's Cauldron waterfall off in the darkness, until someone, somewhere, decided we could proceed.

The next thing I know I'm on a streetcorner in Puyo at 2 A.M., waiting for a connecting bus and holding my backpack over my head to keep from drowning. It arrives, we leave, and I fall back asleep. Suddenly I'm jostled awake to find our bus stopped and almost empty. "We're there!" I think, in a confused stupor. But it's still dark, and the noises outside are of the night rainforest, not a jungle city.

I follow my fellow travelers outside to find everyone lugging their bags over a swaying wooden bridge in the misty darkness. Apparently the main span was washed out in a flood: another bus waits for us on the other side to continue to Macas. What else could happen? I wonder, as water drips down the back of my neck. Halfway across, the clouds part and I halt in wonder. More stars than the sky can hold blaze down from above, turning the wide, lazy river into an ocean of light. On either side the dark forest echoes with alien cries, filling the air with the rich scent of earth and life. I barely make the connecting bus, and my flight later that morning.

Writers are always looking for metaphors, and sometimes they fall into your lap. Whether it's the gorgeous flowers poking over the broken glass atop a high brick wall, or the peasant placidly watching his herd in an airy Andean field as European cars zip by on the highway, Latin America in particular seems to lend itself to them.

I choose to look at this experience instead as just one more example of the sheer beauty of this place that crops up daily. It's almost too good to be true, really—this tiny country so lush that orchids grow like weeds along the road and entire rows of fenceposts take root and sprout leaves. In one handy package, Ecuador wraps up South America's big three attractions—the snowy Andes, the steamy Amazon, and endless miles of beaches—along with one attraction no other South American country has—the Galápagos Islands. And everything is within a day's travel of the capital, and it's cheap, and the government is reasonably stable, and on, and on.

So I'll leave my moment over the river as it is, without dressing it up, along with the countless others I've accumulated over the years I've spent traveling in Ecuador: the underwater swerve of a penguin past my face mask in the Galápagos, the smell of eucalyptus from the top of a bus in the thin air of the mountains, the ghostly roar of a howler monkey in the Amazon. Along with those go the memories of the stink of bus exhaust, the sting of sunburn, and the dull taste of potatoes again. I'm leaving room for more in the decades to come.

And next time, I'm flying to the jungle.

This book is dedicated to my parents,
who made the first edition possible
and have never faltered
in their support and patience.

BOB RACE

INTRODUCTION
THE LAND

Tucked up on the northwestern shoulder of South America, Ecuador is really three countries in one—four, if you count the Galápagos Islands. The Andes run like a great, knobby spine down the middle of the country, with the Pacific coast to the west and the Amazon jungle to the east. Each region is distinct from its neighbors, but all are so close that you can easily travel from one to another in under a day. At 269,178 square km, Ecuador is the second smallest country in South America—about the size of Colorado. Colombia lies to the north, Perú to the east and south, and the equator skewers the country just north of Quito.

THE SIERRA

All of us here smoke the opium of the upper altitude
Voices low, short steps, short breath

— *Henri Michaux,*
Ecuador, A Travel Journal

The Andes and their foothills fill about a quarter of Ecuador's land area, thrusting 10 of the country's 21 provinces skyward. Two parallel mountain ranges run north to south to form the country's backbone. The Cordillera Occidental (Western Range) and Cordillera Oriental (Eastern Range) together support 22 peaks over 4,200 meters. The result is one of Ecuador's scenic treasures: an easy drive south of the capital lies Alexander von Humboldt's "Avenue of the Volcanoes," where a dozen snow-capped volcanoes loom on either side of the Pan-American Highway.

Intermountain basins called *hoyas* are divided by east-west foothills called *nudos.* The 10 main basins average 50 km wide and 2,100 meters high. Almost every one supports its own large city, including the capital Quito, and altogether they contain half the country's population. Farms reach as high into the foothills as possible, surrounded by forests, grassy slopes, and rocks. Even higher are the harsher climates of the *páramo* and bare, icy mountaintops. Meltwater and rain feed the headwaters of rivers heading east and west.

THE COAST

One quarter of the country descends west to the Pacific Ocean, which meets the land in 2,237 km of coastline. The only thing between the

THE ORIENTE

Ecuador's Amazon takes up the other half of the country, spilling east from the gentle eastern slope of the Andes into lush northern Perú. The rainforest continues all the way to the Atlantic coast of Brazil, at such a gentle slope that the rivers drop less than 500 meters over the entire 2,200 km. The Andes give a few last gasps before giving up completely, sending up peaks like Sumaco (3,732 meters), east of Baeza. To the south the rugged Cordillera del Cóndor was the center of a long-running border dispute with Perú.

The Oriente's rivers are its highways. In the north the Ríos Coca and Aguarico feed into the Río Napo, Ecuador's longest river at 855 km. The Río Pastaza drains Pastaza province and lies just north of the Río Zamora, which becomes the Río Santiago in Perú.

western lowlands and the sea are a few low mountain chains: the Mache and Chindul near the middle, and the Colonche near Guayaquil. None climb higher than 1,000 meters. Tropical rainforests cling to the western slope of the Andes, fading into dry, thorny scrublands toward the south. Mangrove-choked estuaries and sandy beaches—some lined with palms, others with cliffs—face the water.

Two main rivers drain the lowlands. To the north the Río Esmeraldas flows for 320 km before emptying into the Pacific. Farther south the Río Guayas—only 60 km long between its genesis at the junction of the Ríos Babahoyo and Daule and its mouth at the Gulf of Guayaquil—is the widest river on the Pacific coast of the Americas. The Isla Puná sits at the base of one of the richest deltas in the hemisphere.

GEOLOGY

Ecuador's gorgeous mountain scenery comes with a high price. The country sits smack on the Pacific "Rim of Fire," where two tectonic plates grind together: the Nazca Plate, supporting the east Pacific, is slowly shoving itself under the American Plate that supports mainland South America. The result is the upthrust of the Andes, as well as a host of unpleasant side effects.

Approximately 30 of Ecuador's peaks began as **volcanoes,** and five or six are still smoking. Cotopaxi last erupted in 1877, but it's still considered the highest active volcano in the world. Sangay is one of the most active on earth, with a constant pool of lava burbling in its crater. Antisana, El Altar, and the Pichinchas were all active in the 20th century, and both Guagua Pichin-

*view while climbing
Imbabura*

JULIAN SMITH

cha and Tungurahua erupted in the late 1990s. Most cities in the highland, for some reason, are built within range of an active volcano. Ecuador's history books are filled with horror stories of entire cities being leveled in a heartbeat by lava and mudslides.

Along with the creeping magma and scalding smoke, most volcanic eruptions are accompanied by **earthquakes.** A major tremor in 1987 destroyed 40 km of the oil pipeline from the Oriente to the Sierra, killing hundreds of people, and Bahía de Caráquez is still reeling from a 1998 quake that measured 7.1 on the Richter scale.

It gets worse: **lahars**—catastrophic avalanches of melted ice, snow, mud, and rocks—can reach 80 kph when careening downhill. A heavy rain is often enough to induce a **landslide,** particularly in the muddy Oriente. "The approach of rain is enough to make the hair stand up on any countryman's neck," wrote Henri Michaux, "knowing as he does how rain can make a mountain split and go under."

CLIMATE

Seasons on the equator have a whole different meaning than in temperate latitudes. Here there are only two "seasons": a hot and wet period called *invierno* (literally, "winter"), and a dry and cool time called *verano* ("summer"). Temperatures often vary more in a single day than they do from month to month, especially at higher altitudes. (For information on weather in the Galápagos, see "Climate" under "Introduction" in The Galápagos Islands chapter.)

Sierra
The mid-Andes climate strikes a balance between the icy reaches of volcanic peaks and the sweltering extremes of lower altitudes, resulting in a pleasant, comfortable "eternal spring." Days warm quickly and lose the heat just as fast at night, varying as much as 15°C between day and night. Daytime temperatures

PRECIPITATION CHART

JAN	FEB	MAR	APR	MAY	JUNE	JULY	AUG	SEPT	OCT	NOV	DEC
Quito average precipitation (inches)											
4.7	5.2	5.9	6.8	5.2	1.9	0.8	0.9	1.9	5.1	4.1	4.0
Oriente average precipitation (inches)											
12.2	12.2	15.7	17.4	16.9	18.3	13.0	12.3	15.2	17.1	15.1	14.1

SIGHTSEEING HIGHLIGHTS

Sierra

High among the twin rows of the Andes, you'll find pastoral scenes of colorfully dressed indigenous herders watching sheep and llamas graze in windswept fields of grass. Indigenous markets like those in Otavalo and Saquisilí offer crafts for tourists and household goods and food (some squawkingly alive) for locals. A full-blown animal market—a PETA activist's nightmare—is an unforgettable sight. After a hike among the snow-capped peaks of Cotopaxi National Park or the alpine lakes of Las Cajas National Recreation Area, enjoy a soak in the hot springs of Baños or Papallacta.

Ancient steam trains run down the Avenue of the Volcanoes—at least for the time being—before squirming through the Devil's Nose below Alausí on their rattling way to the coast. A rooftop ride on one of these trains can be combined with a visit to Ingapirca, Ecuador's premiere Inca ruins. Farther south is the colonial center of Cuenca, which rivals Quito itself in its profusion of churches, convents, and museums.

The Coast

Ecuador's long Pacific coastline shelters kilometers of fine sandy beaches, unspoiled because easy access roads simply don't exist. Fishing villages like Súa and Montañita cater to budget travelers looking for surf and sun. High-end tourists, foreign and Ecuadorian alike, head for the gleaming highrises of the Santa Elena Peninsula west of Guayaquil. And in between there's the treehouse architecture of the Alandaluz Ecological Tourist Center.

Remnants of once-widespread mangrove estuaries are protected near San Lorenzo and in the Manglares Churute Ecological Reserve near Guayaquil. Machalilla National Park contains dry coastal hills and the richest archaeological sites of Ecuador's pre-Inca past, as well as the "poor man's Galápagos" of the Isla de la Plata. Birding in the western lowlands is excellent at places like Tinalandia and the Río Palenque Research Station.

Oriente

Head east for the green expanse of the Amazon rainforest, stretching all the way to Brazil and the Atlantic, to a luxury jungle lodge like La Selva, Kapawi, or the converted paddleboat of the Flotel Orellana. Budget trips are easy and inexpensive to arrange from the gateway cities of Baños, Tena, Coca, and Misahualli. Many visits stop by indigenous communities, where groups of Lowland Quechua, Huaorani, and Cofán still hold onto many of the old ways practiced by their ancestors.

Galápagos Islands

Everyone's heard about this archipelago off the shoulder of South America, where doe-eyed sea lions, birds with blue feet, and tortoises as large as armchairs roam free and fearless. A lucky few (including yourself, I hope) actually get to go and swim with puppy-sized penguins or walk past an eagle close enough to touch. The islands are one of the world's natural treasures, and a visit here will be a highlight of your trip—guaranteed.

---

average around 21°C year-round, with nights between 7–8°C.

The rainy season occurs Oct.–May, with overcast skies and precipitation peaking near April. The dry season runs June–Sept., with a short resurgence around December. Daily rainfall is mostly confined to brief afternoon showers.

Coast

The wet and dry seasons are more sharply defined on the coast, and ocean currents influence weather patterns more than anything else. The Perúvian (Humboldt) Current flowing up from Chile brings cool, dry weather May–Dec.—the best time to travel but the worst time for sunbathing at the beach, since skies are usually cloudy. Dominated by the warmer Ecuatorial Countercurrent from the north, Jan.–April is hot and rainy with daily downpours. Roads are often flooded and impassible. When it's not raining, though, the sun blazes and daytime temperatures average 31°C. For half the year, hardly any rain falls in southern coastal Ecuador at all.

Every few years the famous **El Niño** weather pattern brings abnormal amounts of rain from the end of the year to April or May, causing flooding and landslides all along the coast and wreaking havoc with wildlife dependent on stable ocean temperatures. See "Climate" under "Introduction" in the Galápagos chapter for more details on this phenomenon.

Oriente

Weather forecasters in the Amazon have it easy: "Hot and wet today, with continued hotness and wetness through this time next year." Rainy and rainier seasons pretty much sum things up. The most precipitation falls June–Aug., and Sept.–Dec. is drier. Daily highs average 30–32°C, with nighttime lows reaching 20°C.

Up to five meters of rain fall annually in certain spots, usually arriving in the afternoon in one of the country's most dramatic climatic displays: around 1 or 2 P.M. the air grows quiet suddenly, heavily, as the sky starts to gray. Temperatures drop quickly just before you hear a muted roar approaching. Then, *boom!*—it's time to break out the scuba gear. After half an hour or so of brutal downpour, the sky quickly clears, preparing for another spectacular sunset.

THE NATURAL WORLD

For a country with only two thousandths of the earth's surface, Ecuador's landscape is almost unbelievably lush and varied. The numbers alone can get overwhelming: 10 percent of all plant species on earth make their home here, including nearly 5,000 species of orchids alone. South America boasts one-third of the world's estimated 9,000 species of birds, and of these, roughly half live in Ecuador—meaning this tiny country is home to one-sixth of all bird species on the planet. On the whole, Ecuador is rightly considered one of the most species-rich countries in the world.

Along with the stunning range of habitats described as follows, however, Ecuador has an equally impressive list of threats to its natural world. Some ecosystems are close to disappearing completely, and far too many once-plentiful species are down to only a handful of individuals. If done right, tourism can help as much as anything else to preserve the country's wildlife, but in the end the only true solutions will germinate among those who live with the natural world every day.

CLOUD FOREST

The rainforest's lofty cousin covers the transition zone between the high Andes and lowland jungle. Nicknamed the *cejas de las montañas* (eyebrows of the mountains), cloud forests have a delicate, misty appearance, with trees draped in Spanish moss set along icy, rushing streams. Annual precipitation comes in the form of clouds and fog as often as it does in raindrops, and temperatures drop much lower here than in the Amazon.

Flora

Cloud forest vegetation is similar to that of the rainforest but sparser, more sturdy than lush. Up to 60 percent of all plants are **epiphytes,** which can live off airborne moisture and nutrient particles alone as they grow attached to the trunks of other plants, far above the soil. Many of these are **orchids,** which thrive at moist moderate to high altitudes. The largest family of flowering plants (with

In the upper plateau country, the people have a saying, and it's close to the truth—the four seasons in one day:

Morning summer. Noon springtime. The sky is beginning to get overcast. 4 p.m. rain. Freshness. A night cold and luminous like winter. For this reason, clothing is a problem if you must be out for more than a few hours. You watch the accursed setting forth, armed with straw hat, canvas, furpiece, and umbrella.

—*Henri Michaux,*
Ecuador, A Travel Journal

JULIAN SMITH

waterfall, near Aldea Salamandra

more than 30,000 identified species), orchids range in size from pinhead-sized buds to three-meter monsters with gaudy, pungent flowers 10 cm across. The woody trunks of **tree ferns** reach heights of five to eight meters, topped by a crown of giant fronds. Huge stands of **bamboo** go to seed and die all at once, and every available surface is covered with **mosses, lichens,** and **brachens.**

Fauna

Iridescent red feathers make the **Andean cock-of-the-rock** a birder's favorite. These birds prefer vertical cliffs and gather in courtship clearings called *leks.* **Golden-headed quetzals** have bright turquoise plumage and live in tree cavities next to vivid **tanagers** and top-heavy **toucans.** Dozens of species of **hummingbirds** have the best names of all: Collared Inca, Gorgeted sunangel, and the Green violetear, to name a few.

Nighttime temperatures in the cloud forest are too low for most large mammals. **Mountain**

tapirs, one of three Ecuadorian species and the largest land mammals in the country, have elongated snouts that betray their relation to the rhinoceros. Most likely, all you'll see is their brown rear ends crashing off into the underbrush and their tracks in the mud—three toes on the rear foot and four toes on the front.

The **Andean spectacled bear,** named for white patches around its eyes, is the only bear native to South America. Males can grow two meters long and range through the cloud forest and *páramo* from Venezuela to Bolivia. Ecuador has one of the largest populations of this highly endangered animal, which is poached for its meat and supposed medicinal value—the paws are said to protect one from evil, and its fat is used as a healing ointment.

PÁRAMO

These high-altitude grasslands stretch between the temperate montane valleys and the inhospitable snows of the highest peaks. Chill mists, dark lakes, and tussocks of sharp grasses make the *páramo* a surreally beautiful place to explore.

Flora

Thick, waxy leaf skins covered with fine, insulating hairs help the low, spongy *páramo* ground cover to survive high levels of ultraviolet light and wet, often freezing, conditions. Plants stick low to the ground to escape the wind and temperature variations, and often grow their leaves in a circle to make sure none shade any of the others.

The distinctive *frailejón (Espeleta hartwegiana),* is characteristic of the northern *páramo* near the Colombian border. With its crown of bright yellow leaves covered with insulating down, the plant is actually a member of the daisy family. *Frailejónes* range through the Andes from Ecuador to Venezuela, just as their namesake friars did in colonial times. At higher altitudes, frailejónes grow closer together for mutual protection against the elements.

The thistlelike **chuquiragua** *(Chuquiragua insignis)* has jagged leaves and orange flowers, and is used by *indígenas* as a cough suppressant. Its name means "sword of fire" in Quechua, and it's one of the few flowers found at this altitude. The **lycopodium** *(Lycopodium crassum)* club-moss also brightens the dreary landscape with its tubular red and orange stalks. **Caspivela** plants have flat, bushy branches that resemble evergreens. Also called candlewood, this waxy bush is so flammable that it can be lit in the rain. Spectacled bears love to break open the center of the thorny **achupalla** plant *(Puya hamata)*, which is also edible by people.

Fauna

Hummingbirds *(colibrís* in Spanish) are characteristic of Ecuador's higher altitudes. Blurring wingbeats allow them to hover and move backward, and at night most can enter a state of semi-hibernation called "torpor," in which their body temperatures and metabolism drop significantly. Their iridescent feathers were once sewn into cloaks for Inca rulers. Listen for the buzz of the coffee-colored *Cafe colibri,* the endemic Ecuadorian hillstar, or the *Chimborazo colibrí* with its blue head and white breast. *Royal colibrís* nest among the sharp leaves of araucaria plants, and the *sword-beak colibrí* totes around a 12-cm snout.

Torrent ducks, white-capped dippers, and **torrent tyrannulets** gather near running water. **Andean lapwings** have an unmistakable grate of a call and a gaudy white-and-brown-striped wing pattern. Cotopaxi National Park is the best place to see **Carunculated cararas,** the largest member of the falcon family with a bright red face, yellow bill, and black body.

Cotopaxi is also a good place to spot the **Andean condor,** which is related to the California condor and almost as endangered. Actually a vulture *(Vultur gryphus),* the condor is the world's largest flying bird, with a wingspan of more than three meters. Mature condors have glossy black plumage, a fuzzy white neck ruff, and a hooked beak. The red head and neck are naked of feathers to keep the bird clean as it digs into its meal of choice—carrion. Fewer than 100 mating pairs remain alive because of habitat destruction and a mistaken fear among *campesinos* that the giant scavengers will carry off livestock and children.

South America's high-altitude relatives of the camel—**llamas, vicuñas,** and **alpacas**—were once domesticated by the Incas for meat, wool, and hauling cargo. With the arrival of the Span-

ish, the animals have become extinct in the wild, but reintroduction programs in the Chimborazo Fauna Reserve and Cotopaxi National Park are promising. Chances are slim that you'll spot an **Andean stag, puma,** or small *páramo* **cat.** Wild **guinea pigs, opossums,** and **rats** live among the rocks and bushes.

COASTAL FORESTS

Tropics

Northwestern Ecuador falls within the Chocó bioregion, which extends from the Andes to the Pacific and into Colombia. The forests in this area are some of the most biologically diverse on earth, in part because they acted as warmer refuges during various Ice Ages, saving countless species of plants and animals from extinction. They're also incredibly wet, thanks to the union of the warm Panama and cold Humboldt Currents just offshore. Up to one-fifth of the plants in some areas are endemic (found nowhere else in the world). Sadly, less than 5 percent of the original tree cover has survived colonization, agriculture, and the timber industry.

Dry Areas

Even less of the tropical dry forests remain undisturbed—as little as 1 percent by some estimates. These forests stretch from the middle coast of Ecuador south to the Perúvian border, a region with well-defined wet and dry seasons. Machalilla National Park and the Chongón Hills west of Guayaquil shelter some of the largest tracts of this increasingly rare ecosystem.

Plant life consists of species more suited to the desert: water-stingy varieties include the palo santo bush common to the Galápagos, ceiba and balsa trees, and the tagua palm, the nuts of which can be carved like ivory. Birds such as the vermilion flycatcher, Pacific pygmy owl, and long-tailed mockingbird make their homes among the dry hills, accompanied by armadillos, opossums, and small cats called *tigrillos.*

Mangroves

Large groves of these tangled trees grow in brackish conditions where fresh water meets the ocean. The red mangrove is the most common, each with an extensive network of stilt limbs sent up from roots and down from branches. Mangroves are good colonizers, providing homes for seabirds in their branches and sea creatures among the roots. Once again, protected areas such as Manglares Churute near Guayaquil are all that stands between this ecosystem and the spread of civilization. Here, the main threat is the shrimp industry, which bulldozes mangrove swamps to build shrimp ponds.

RAINFOREST

"Epithet after epithet was found too weak to convey to those who have not visited the intertropical regions, the sensation of delight which the mind experiences . . . "

—**Charles Darwin,**
Journal of the Voyage of the Beagle

Compared to the common preconception of the jungle—an impenetrable Tarzan backdrop filled with strange cries in the sweltering mist—the reality is often surprising. It's surprisingly quiet, cooler than you would expect, and spacious, with little undergrowth below the high, closed canopy. During the day, the hum of insects and the occasional cry of a bird overhead are the only sounds in the still ocean of green. At night, both bugs and stars come out in astonishing profusion.

Rainforests are defined by low altitude (up to 1,000 meters), high temperatures (25–28°C), and daily rainfall that varies widely over the year. Two to three meters of rain is the annual norm, with no dry season—just wet and wetter. The result is a warm, humid environment as perfect for unbridled growth as any on earth. Among the oldest of all ecosystems, rainforests are also among the least known because of difficult access and scientific interest that has only recently blossomed. Large percentages of Ecuador's Amazonian plants and animals were only discovered within the last few decades.

Species Richness
Scientists are just beginning to understand the incredible biological diversity of Amazon forests, where 3,000 different types of beetles have been found in study plots of 12 square meters. Aside from having near ideal conditions for life, rainforests have also had time on their side. In some cases, plants and animals have had hundreds of millions of years to evolve into each one's particular **niche,** a vague ecological term that basically means an individual's role in the overall grand production of life—the space it occupies, the food it consumes, the ecological elbow room it needs. Over the eons, species become more and more specialized, leaving room for other species to find equally narrow, but slightly different, niches often only a few millimeters to one side.

The theory of Pleistocene forest refugia holds that during cool, dry periods far in the past, isolated patches of rainforest served as islands in the midst of huge expanses of grasslands. These refuges eventually reconnected, complete with thousands of new, unique species that had evolved in isolation. Most of eastern Ecuador falls within the Napo Refuge, which has been one of the largest and most stable refuges over history, and thus one of the most biologically diverse.

Shallow Basement
As any Amazon settler who's tried to start a farm will tell you, rainforest soil is surprisingly thin and poor. In contrast to temperate forests and their rich, deep layers of humus, rainforests have most of their nutrients suspended in the vegetation itself—in both living and dead matter—instead of the ground. In fact, less than 1 percent of forest nutrients are thought to penetrate deeper than five cm into the soil. As a result, when rainforests are cleared, the thin topsoil washes away in a few years to reveal an impenetrable layer of clay on which nothing can grow.

Death takes on a whole new importance in an ecosystem where so little is siphoned away through the ground. Countless bacteria, fungi, and insects are crucial in breaking down dead matter quick enough to return the nutrients to the pool of life. Jungle lodges that recycle often find their organic garbage pits completely empty within a week. Thriving fungi give the rainforest its characteristic rich, organic odor.

Hydrology
Blackwater rivers, unique to tropical forests, get their tealike color from **tannins,** the substances

used in winemaking and leather tanning, which are all that's left after tree roots and fungi absorb all the water's nutrients. Even algae can't grow in these highly acidic waters. Look near the shallows for the beautiful reddish-brown color, common to places such as the Cuyabeno Wildlife Refuge. Sediment from the Andes gives **white-water rivers** their milky appearance and neutral pH. When the two meet, they often flow side by side before mixing like cream in coffee.

Oxbow lakes are formed when a bend of a meandering lowland river is cut off from the main flow. The resulting U-shaped *cocha* (lake) slowly fills in with a succession of plants until it becomes indistinguishable from the rest of the forest.

Flora

"Tropical vegetation has a tendency to produce rhetorical exuberance in those who describe it," says Paul Richard in *The Tropical Rainforest.* It's easy to see why, with such a varied tangle of green surging upward toward the precious sunlight. Ecuador is home to more than 20,000 species of vascular plants, more than in all of North America, and most of them live in the Amazon. Although temperate forests in North America may contain six tree species in abundance, a plot of rainforest 10 meters on a side may shelter 25 different species.

Primary forest, undisturbed by man, has a high, tight canopy layer that blocks out most sunlight, keeping undergrowth to a minimum. This is where you'll find the best example of **emergent trees,** up to 50 meters high and five meters across at the base. Roots like rocket fins keep the towering giants upright—most of the time—and are used by indigenous tribes to signal over long distances (bang on one to see why). The smooth branches on the **ceiba**—whose buoyant cottony fibers were used to fill World War II lifejackets—look more like upsidedown roots, each covered with characteristically thick, smooth, oval leaves with tapered ends to shed heavy rainfall.

Each large tree in the rainforest supports a veritable zoo of aerial plant life, starting with huge, woody **lianas** that climb host trees to reach the sun. One kind of liana, contrary to all plant logic, initially grows toward darkness to find the base of the largest nearby tree to start climbing. Large lianas can loop several trees together, so that if one tree falls, several neighbors follow.

Epiphytes, aerial plants that get all their nutrients and water from the air, include **bromeliads,** which resemble the tops of pineapples. Inside each bromeliad's leafy crown, a small puddle of rainwater can support hundreds of insects, amphibians, and even other epiphytes. Epiphytes grow aerial roots to trap dust and falling debris for food, which can accumulate to half a meter thick on the tops of larger branches.

Supporting so much life has its drawbacks. **Strangler figs** of the *Ficus* genus are called *matapalos* (tree-killers) in Spanish for good reason. Starting as a small airborne seed, the fig eventually sends down woody roots that can encircle the host tree completely and squeeze it to death. By then the fig, a tree in its own right, has established roots of its own. Their wood isn't good for lumber, so figs are often the only trees left standing in cleared plots, but birds and animals love the sweet fruit.

All this added weight can easily cause even a large tree to collapse, so the hosts have developed several defensive strategies. The *capirana* tree sheds its outer bark periodically, leaving a smooth surface that epiphytes can't cling to. Other plants produce repulsive chemicals. Nonetheless, **tree falls** are surprisingly common (even if no one is there to hear them) and actually serve a crucial role in the life of the forest. Every large tree in a patch of forest can fall in as little as 100 years, each one producing a vital light gap that allows smaller plants to spurt upward in the hope of becoming canopy members themselves.

Other defensive strategies are more ingenious. One type of tree has worked out an arrangement with a particular type of ant that clears the branches and the surrounding forest floor of competing plants, and attacks any creature foolish enough to take a bite of a leaf. In return, the ants (which taste like lemon) get to make their home in special hollow stems. Stinging spines on the roots and trunks of other trees discourage larger creatures from climbing, scratching, or otherwise hurting the tree.

Chemical defenses often have beneficial side effects for humans. An incredible array of **medicinal plants,** long known to native cultures, have only recently begun to be appreciated by modern science. Many substances you're already familiar with were discovered this way—among them nicotine, caffeine, strychnine, novocaine, and quinine, the first effective medicine against malaria.

Pollination strategies can be just as complex. Because other plants of the same species may be situated kilometers away, wind and luck may not be enough to get seeds or pollen to a receptive host. Large, white nocturnal flowers attract bats with their rich pollen, and hummingbirds love small, reddish flowers filled with sugar-rich nectar. In both cases, pollen (microscopic male seeds) is attached to the unwary creature and transported to the next plant. Seeds hidden inside tasty fruit are designed to pass through the digestive systems of monkeys, rodents, fish, and birds unharmed and grow wherever they are dispersed—some won't germinate otherwise.

Insects are the most common pollinators and are deceived to no end by plants, often gaining little or nothing in return. Some orchids have parts that mimic female tachnid flies to lure males, or provide fragrances that male orchid bees collect and store to lure females. Fig wasps lay their eggs in fig flowers, from which the larvae eventually eat their way out and emerge covered in pollen. Some flowers smell like rotting meat to attract scavengers, whereas others mimic a mammalian ear, down to reddish veins and a musky odor, in order to lure mosquitoes.

Birds

It's said that 80 percent of the animal life in the rainforest lives above eye level, and most of that, it seems, is on the wing. Birds are by far the most abundant animal life you'll see: Ecuador rainforests alone have more than 1,500 identified species, compared to 700 in the forests of the United States and Canada combined. They can be difficult to observe in the upper canopy. You'll have better luck along the border of clear-cut areas and rivers, or near a fruiting tree. Different species often forage together in mixed flocks for added protection from predators.

Of the thousands of different species, a few stand out. **Hoatzins** are unmistakable with their Mohawk crest, ungainly body, and prehistoric squawk. These beauty-school dropouts have been called a missing link between birds and reptiles, since chicks are born with claws on the tips of their wings to help them climb back into the nest after they fall or jump out to escape predators. The hoatzin is one of the few birds that actually eats leaves, which it digests in a large, heavy crop that makes it almost impossible for the bird to fly gracefully. The smell of decomposing leaves gives these birds the nickname "stinky turkeys."

The liquid call of an **oropendula** is unmistakable—like a large drop of water falling into a deep well—and their long, woven nests are commonly seen dangling from tree branches. Oropendula chicks are a favorite prey of botfly larvae, so the birds often hang their nests near the nests of wasps to help keep the flies away. Parasitic species such as cuckoos lay their eggs in other birds' nests, leaving the unwitting parents to raise chicks that are often larger than themselves.

Every species of **kingfisher** found in South America lives in Ecuador, including the ringed, green, Amazon, and the rare green-and-rufous and American pygmy. **Harpy eagles** use their daggerlike claws to snatch monkeys out of tree branches. These eagles, which are South America's largest bird of prey, are revered by indigenous tribes.

Twenty species of **toucans** each have huge, hollow bills for reaching and opening fruit and seeds in the canopy. Forty-five species of **macaw,** including the blue-and-yellow and the chestnut-fronted, each mate for life.

Mammals

Large mammals are rare, partly because so many plant defenses have prevented the evolution of large herbivores that would have served as prey. Seventeen species of **monkeys** belong to the arboreal New World group (Platyrrhina) as opposed to the ground-dwelling Catyrrhina of the Old World (which include ourselves). Capuchins have white and black coats and faces like angry little old men. Red howlers are named after the roaring call, which is audible for kilometers, that males produce with a specialized bone in their throat. Squirrel monkeys follow the larger species to fruiting trees and lack a prehensile tail. At the bottom of the scale are silky-furred pygmy marmosets, who eat tree sap and are one of the smallest primates in the world.

Adorable **sloths** come in two- and three-toed varieties. Both hang from branches with their long claws and move so slowly that algae grows in their matted hair. A host of insect species also nest in sloth fur, including one type of moth that only lays its eggs in sloth feces (carefully deposited once a week at ground level). More than 100 species of **bats** flit through Ecuador's jungles in search of insects, small animals, fruit, and blood.

Piglike **tapirs** and **peccaries** root among leaves for tasty morsels, accompanied by the dog-sized **capybara,** the largest rodent in the world. Hunted for their coats, nocturnal jungle cats such as the **jaguar,** the aquatic **jaguarundi,** and the **ocelot** are rarely seen. Murky waters hide endangered **manatees** and pink **river dolphins,** descendants of Pacific species cut off from their ancestors by the upward thrust of the Andes. These rare dolphins often feed where rivers join to produce clashing currents that confuse fish.

Reptiles and Amphibians

Close to 400 species of **frogs and toads** fill the night with their clicks, whoops, and buzzes. Poison-arrow frogs raise their tadpoles in cups of water trapped in bromeliads. Their neon reds, blues, and greens warn potential predators of some of the most potent toxins in the animal kingdom. Indigenous groups use the frogs' poison on their arrow and dart points to bring down large game.

Semi-aquatic **anacondas** can grow up to 10 meters long, but even trained experts find it hard to locate most snakes. Flashlight beams will catch the glittering eyes of *caimans,* the smallest crocodilians in the New World.

Fish

Amazon catfish, called *bagre* in Ecuador, are the largest freshwater fish in the world, often topping 200 kg. Fear of **piranhas** shouldn't keep you out of the water completely; these small fish do have a potent set of choppers, but they rarely attack an animal that isn't bleeding already. Some species feed solely on fruit. Tales of "feeding frenzies" probably come from occasions when large groups of piranhas, trapped in small pools of water, are driven wild by the scent of blood.

Take care for **stingrays,** though, who hide in muddy shallows and can inflict an excruciating sting with a barb on the end of their whiplike tail. Shuffle your feet when you can't see the bottom. Even more fearsome is the **candirú catfish,** a narrow little fish with a propensity for warm, dark openings. After following a warm water current into the gills of fish, they attach themselves to feed by extending a sharp dorsal spine. A stream of urine can attract these little guys as well, so don't swim naked.

Insects

Some estimates say insects make up 80 percent of *all* animal species in Ecuador (and most of these are ants). Because they reproduce so often, insects can evolve quickly; scientists estimate that the thousands of species they've already cataloged are still only a small fraction of what's out there. Insects are also easier to spot than most other creatures—just turn on a light after dark and you'll be swarmed within minutes.

Some insect species have evolved close relationships with certain plants to the point that each couldn't survive without the other, an arrangement called **obligatory mutualism.** *Heliconius* butterflies live months instead of weeks when they eat the nutritious vine pollen of the cucumber vine *(Psiguria),* which in turn gets cross-pollinated as the insects travel from one plant to the other. **Leafcutter ants** live in huge colonies of up to several million individuals. Small bits of leaves carried back to the nest are chewed up, fertilized with ant feces, and set in carefully tended gardens to grow a particular type of fungus the ants then eat. The fungus can't survive on its own, and the ants can't eat anything else.

Other times the relationship isn't so mutual. The same *heliconius* butterflies love the vine leaves of the passionflower, which tries to discourage them by growing barbed hairs, changing the shape of its leaves, and sprouting warts that deceive female butterflies into thinking that another butterfly has already laid eggs on the leaves. But the butterflies keep adapting, covering the lethal hairs with soft webs and learning to detect the plant by its scent instead of its appearance. The result is the continual evolution of new species of butterfly and plant.

The papery nests of **termites** are a common sight, made of digested wood cemented together with droppings. Termites play a crucial recycling role in the rainforest by digesting dead wood with the help of microbes living in their gut. Inexorable columns of **army ants** are followed by antbirds, who eat the insects the army ants scare up. Three-centimeter **conga ants** forage alone for other insects and plant nectar. These horror-movie extras are known as *veinte-quatros* (twenty-fours) for the day-long pain of their potent bite. Electric-blue **morpho butterflies** are one of the most eye-catching creatures in the forest, drifting lazily through patches of light on their way down forest trails or waterways.

ENVIRONMENTAL ISSUES

Problems

Ecuador has the second-highest rate of deforestation in Latin America. Every year more than 323,000 hectares of forest—close to 2.5 percent of the country's total—are cut down, including almost 81,000 virgin hectares from the half of the rainforest that remains undisturbed.

Population pressure is the clearest reason for the massive deforestation. More and more people need land for cultivation and cattle grazing and wood for cooking, heating, and building. A short-term economic vision encourages Amazonian settlers to "improve" their land by clearing and planting it, and pays timber harvesters according to sheer volume, not the amount of useful wood cut.

Meanwhile, the Galápagos Islands are in danger of being loved to death. Organized tourism, which began with 4,500 visitors in 1970, had blossomed to 63,000 in 1997—a 700 percent increase in two decades. Immigration rates are soaring to 10 percent annually in response to unemployment on the mainland and a common misconception that life is easier on the islands. In the Oriente, nature reserves are also feeling the strain of overcrowding. Cuyabeno National Park saw 5,000 visitors in 1996, as compared to 500 10 years before, and more than 12,000 settlers received title to Amazon lands between 1964–1982. Oil companies tap the country's economic jugular but in so doing push entire indigenous tribes out of their ancestral homelands and leave thousands of hectares polluted by crude oil spills. Overgrazing on the coast encourages erosion, washing precious soils into the ocean.

Solutions

In the face of all these problems, there is hope. Reforestation programs in the Andes have left entire hillsides sprouting with fast-growing Monterey pines. It's hoped that this species will fit the ecosystem better than the ubiquitous Australian eucalyptus introduced under President García Moreno. The eucalyptus grew like a weed and soon took over large swaths of Andean countryside.

Another positive move are debt-for-nature swaps, in which foreign conservation groups buy off part of the country's foreign debt in exchange for the protection of threatened areas. In a 1989 swap, The Nature Conservancy, the World Wildlife Fund, and Ecuador's Fundación Natura joined forces to raise $10 million, enlarging the Cotacachi-Cayapas and Cayambe-Coca Ecological Reserves. Environmental groups can also outbid logging companies for forest concessions—an expensive but effective arrangement. The nonprofit Fundación Jatun Sacha is currently trying to raise money to buy a section of the Mache-Chindul coastal rainforest. The group purchased 1,400 hectares in 1994 and 1995 but would need another $100,000 to buy the rest.

Sustainable Development

Economists and settlers have both recently begun to realize that a tract of forest can be more valuable left alone than stripped for lumber and agriculture. The key is renewable rainforest products that can bring in as much or more money over the long haul than logging, farming, oil drilling, or cattle ranching can in the short term. Along the way, environmentalists must debunk the age-old belief that the only good forest is a cleared forest, and make sure that the profits go directly back to the people who generate them, so they'll continue what they're doing.

Conservation International's Tagua Initiative is an excellent model of sustainable development. The oblong white seeds of this palm (sold as

ENVIRONMENTAL ORGANIZATIONS ACTIVE IN ECUADOR

All of the organizations below accept (and appreciate) donations, and some of the Ecuadorian ones can place volunteers.

FOREIGN

Conservation International, 1015 18th St. NW, Suite 1000, Washington, DC 20036, 202/429-5660, fax 202/887-5188, website: www.conservation.org. A field-based, nonprofit organization that protects the Earth's biologically rich areas.

The Ecotourism Society, P.O. Box 755, North Bennington, VT 05257-0755, 802/447-2121, fax 802/447-2122, e-mail: ecomail@ecotourism.org, website: www.ecotourism.org. Dedicated to socially and environmentally responsible tourism.

The Nature Conservancy, 4245 North Fairfax Drive, Suite 100, Arlington, VA 22203-1606, 800/628-6860, website: www.tnc.org. Protects habitats and species by buying and setting aside critical lands and waters.

Wildlife Conservation Society, 185 1st St. and Southern Blvd., Bronx, NY 10460, 718/220-5100, e-mail: feedback@wcs.org, website: www.wcs.org. Works to save wildlife and wild lands worldwide.

World Wildlife Fund, 1250 24th St. NW, P.O. Box 97180, Washington, DC 20037, 202/293-4800, 800/CALL-WWF (225-5993), fax 202/293-9211, website: www.worldwildlife.org. The world's largest independent conservation organization, dedicated to protecting nature and biological diversity.

ECUADORIAN

Accion Ecologia, Alejandro de Valdez 24-33 y La Gasca, Casilla 17-15-246C, Quito, tel./fax 2/230-676, e-mail: verde@hoy.net. Environmental activism.

Comite Ecologico del Litoral, Numa Pompilio Llona No. 146, Barrio Las Peñas, Casilla 09-01-8354, Guayaquil, e-mail: cel@gye.satnet.net, website: www3.satnet.net/cel/. Coastal conservation projects near Guayaquil.

Corporación de Defensa de la Vida (CORDAVI), Casilla 17-12-309, Quito, e-mail: elaw@ ecnet.ec, website: www.igc.apc.org/elaw/ americas/ecuador/ cordavi.html. Environmental law.

Corporación de Conservación y Desarrollo (CCD), Apdo. 1716-1855, Quito, tel. 2/252-1645, fax 2/255-2614. Environmental conservation and development.

Ecuadorian Ecotourism Association (ASEC), Victor Hugo E10-11 y Isla Pinzón, Sector Jipijapa, tel. 2/466-295, fax 2/245-055, e-mail: asec@accessinter.net, website: ute.edu.ec/~mjativa/ce/ aseceng.html. Working to develop ecotourism opportunities in Ecuador.

Fundación Antisana, Apdo. 17-03-1486, Quito, tel. 2/433-851, fax 2/433-851, e-mail: correo@ funam.ecxec. Conservation in Antisana region.

Fundación Sinchi Sacha, Apdo. 17-07-9466, Quito, tel. 2/230-609, fax 2/567-311, e-mail: sinchisacha@ecuadorexplorer.org. Helping the indigenous population of Ecuador by encouraging self-directed development and fair trade.

Fundación Natura, Av. Rio Guayas 105 y Amazonas, Quito, tel./fax 2/434-449, e-mail: natura@ natura.ecuanex.net.ec. Ecuador's largest environmental organization, with biodiversity and ecology projects in Sangay National Park and the Galápagos.

FUNEDESIN, Casilla 17-17-92, Quito, tel. 2/541-862 or 543-851, fax 2/220-262, e-mail: info@yachana. com, website: www.yachana.com. Long-term community development and rainforest protection.

Oilwatch Secretariat, Alejandro de Valdez N24-33 y La Gasca, Casilla 17-15-246-C, Quito, tel. 2/230-676, 9/700-712, e-mail: oilwatch@uio.sat net.net. A watchdog group focusing on the petroleum industry.

Rainforest Rescue, Apdo 17-12-105, Quito, tel. 2/343-725, e-mail: mlgambo@uio.satnet.net.

Brazil nuts in North America) are soft enough to carve when raw but become hard as ivory when dried. They once accounted for one out of every five buttons made in the United States, but demand plummeted after the advent of plastics. Today, the Tagua Initiative is trying to resurrect this trade in Perú, Bolivia, Colombia, and Ecuador, where artisans are being trained to carve buttons, jewelry, and figurines for export. One community in Ecuador employs more than 1,000 workers and exports enough raw material for the production of 25 million buttons.

Other sustainable rainforest-friendly products include chocolate, manioc, quinine, and natural rubber from trees. In this age of patent medicine, the health benefits alone from rainforest products can be worth their weight in gold. It's become almost a cliché to say that a cure for cancer may be hiding in the last representative of a rainforest plant species right in the path of a bulldozer, but with all the medicines that have been found here already, it's probably not pure hyperbole. International pharmaceutical companies are sending expeditions into the rainforest to tap the wealth of native healing knowledge, and even cosmetics firms are studying the possible uses of local fruits in shampoos.

Agroforestry, in which native species are left growing among introduced food crops, anchors the soil and ensures a wider mix of nutrients for all plants involved. Indigenous tribes have been doing this for years—just visit any Achuar *chakra*—but modern farmers often still try to grow just one crop, quickly exhausting the soil of key nutrients.

Ecotourism

Defined by The Ecotourism Society as "responsible travel that conserves natural environments and sustains the well-being of local people," ecotourism has been called the travel trend of the 1990s. Andy Drumm of Tropical Ecological Adventures in Quito points out the difference between ecotourism and simple "nature tourism," in which the natural world is used only as a draw; true ecotourism promotes conservation among travelers and locals alike, educating and inspiring both to continue conservation efforts even after the tour.

Some purists claim that even ecotourism is too much, arguing that any amount of traffic

erodes trails, compacts soils, leaves litter, and disturbs animals. They pinpoint Costa Rica as an example of ecotourism gone awry, where famous reserves have become Disney-esque attractions for huge charter flights of tourists from Europe and North America. Imagine jet skis buzzing around the Galápagos.

In fact, the islands are a good example of both the pluses and the minuses of ecotourism in Ecuador. Early management plans were well-intentioned but set somewhat arbitrary limits on the number of visitors per year. A second airport was built as more and more concessionaires and tour operators vied for part of the pie, gradually bumping the visitation limits higher and higher. Worst of all, the animals began to suffer. Today, Galápagos tourism treads a fine line between conservation and exploitation. More visitors arrive than ever before, but the park service is doing its best to strictly supervise the impact of tour groups and the legality and qualifications of tour operators. The wildlife, meanwhile, watch quietly.

The **Ecuadorian Ecotourism Association** (ASEC), Calle Victor Hugo, E10-111 and Isla Pinzon, Ciudadela Jipijapa, Quito, tel. 2/245-055, 466-295, e-mail: asec@accessinter.net, is a federation of tour operators, hotels, and government agencies that are happy to provide a list of ecofriendly tour operators in Ecuador. On the Internet, try the award-winning **Planeta.com** (www.planeta.com), which is a great starting point for information on ecotourism in Latin America. Their "Eco Travels in Ecuador" page can be found at www2.planeta.com/mader/eco travel/south/ecuador/ecuador1.html.

Parks and Reserves

Since the Ecuadorian park service INEFAN disbanded, the 16 different conservation units have fallen under the administration of the Ministerio del Ambiente (Ministry of the Environment) in Quito. Not all is rosy in these protected areas, which cover an estimated 11 percent of the country. Parks are often understaffed and underfunded, and squatters, poachers, and mineral exploitation are very real threats.

On a hopeful note, in January 1999, President Jamil Mahaud declared Cuyabeno-Imuya and Yasuní National Parks off-limits to oil drilling, mining, lumbering, and colonization. The 2.7

million protected acres, twice the size of the state of Delaware, are home to at least 10,000 members of tribes like the Huaorani, who have violently but often futilely resisted the encroachment of modern society. Government sources reported that "friendly tourism" will still be allowed.

A host of private reserves, often associated with private lodges, have their own legal right to administer the land, buy more, and interact with local communities. Many of these reserves are seeking official national protected status.

HISTORY

History—what do the French say of it again?—is a fable agreed upon. Here, the fable is bloody and colorful, with violent incident, with gold, Incas, treachery, and a scoundrel unmatched—at least until recently unmatched—I am speaking of Pizarro. But we also have handy things, lovely memories, good names, and deeds to remember.

—Ludwig Bemelmans,
quoting an Ecuadorian in
The Donkey Inside

EARLIEST CULTURES

The first humans to gaze on the "New" World were nomadic hunter-gatherers who wandered across the Bering land bridge from Siberia anywhere from 15,000–50,000 years ago. They gradually made their way south, arriving in South America 12,000–15,000 years ago. Close to the Panamanian isthmus, Ecuador was one of the first areas to be settled. In fact, the oldest pottery yet found in all of the Americas was unearthed in Ecuador, dating to the **Paleoindian period** (11,000–4,000 B.C.), when small family groups roamed the area.

Andean

Coastal merchants found a new market for salt in three major kingdoms that had developed in the Sierra. The **Cara** got their start on the coast near A.D. 900, conquering the Bahía de Caráquez area before following the Río Esmeraldas upstream to settle near Quito. The Shyri family dynasty ruled this sun-worshiping culture, built observatories to track the seasons, and believed

that people inhabited the moon. Around A.D. 1300, a prince of the Puruh, a famous warrior tribe, married a Shyri princess to unite the groups into the **Quitu** kingdom, which dominated the Sierra until the arrival of the Incas and spawned many of today's indigenous groups, including the Otavaleños.

A loosely organized federation of 25 tribes formed the **Cañari** nation in the southern Sierra and coastal lowlands. These ferocious fighters would prove to be the Incas' toughest opponents in centuries to come. Even after many of them were relocated to Perú, the rest allied with the Spanish to fight against their former Inca overlords. According to oral history, the Cañari sacrificed 100 children every year to the god of corn and buried their chiefs with an entire retinue of wives and servants put to death for the purpose.

Coastal

Cultivation of corn, pumpkins, and beans began around 6,000 B.C. near the Santa Elena Penin-

---

CAÑARI ORIGIN MYTH

Two survivors of a great flood, they say, two young brothers, took refuge on top of a hill. Every day they left their shelter to look for food. One day they returned to find a hot meal waiting for them, but no one around to claim credit. The brothers decided to find out who had helped them. The next morning one left as usual but the other hid himself near their home and waited. Soon a pair of female macaws entered, cooked a meal, and flew off. That evening he told his brother what he had seen, and the two ambushed and caught the macaws the next day. From those two brothers and the macaws descended the Cañari people.

sula. By the **Formative period** (4,000–300 B.C.), organized settlements had begun growing crops, making pottery, and trading goods in earnest. The shiny red shell of the spiny oyster *(Spondylus princeps),* still a traditional material in the necklaces of Otavalan women, was especially valued as a symbol of fertility. The **Valdivia** culture thrived along the dry coastline of Manabí and Guayas province during the early part of the period, followed by the **Machalilla** and **Chorera** cultures.

The period of **Regional Development** (300 B.C.–A.D. 700) saw more coastal cultures build *tolas,* huge pyramids of earth topped with wooden temples. Hierarchical societies such as the **Jama-Coaque** and **Bahía** in Manabí grew into communities of thousands clustered around ceremonial centers such as San Isidro and Isla de la Plata. The **La Tola** culture, which spread from La Tola island in northern Esmeraldas into southern Colombia, was the first in history to work platinum, a complex technique requiring temperatures of 1,000°C that wasn't discovered in Europe until the 19th century. Bizarrely beautiful feline images became a trademark of the La Tola, and their sun-mask emblem is the symbol of the Banco Central.

Coastal cultures reached their peak during the period of **Integration** (A.D. 700–1460). The **Manteña-Huancavilca** civilization, stretching from the Bahía de Caráquez to the Perúvian border, counted 20,000 members by the time the Spanish arrived. Master seamen took advantage of favorable winds and currents as they piloted balsa rafts as far as Mexico to trade precious metals, mother-of-pearl, textiles, and ceramic figurines.

Some scientists think the similarities between ancient Ecuadorian pottery and pottery found in Japan from the same time period (called the Jomon period) are too striking to ignore. Various theories of balsa rafts crossing the Pacific Ocean from Asia or points in between have been proposed, but the idea has not gained general acceptance yet. The crossing has been attempted in modern times, most notably by Thor Heyerdahl aboard the famous *Kon-Tiki* in 1947, although he sailed from South America to Polynesia, proving that, in theory at least, settlement could have happened in reverse.

Oriente

With a lack of major archaeological sites and an environment better suited to burying the past than preserving it, the Amazon region was once thought to be historically infertile. Recently, historians have started to change their tune, theorizing that large settlements well into the thousands populated the jungle and the eastern slopes of the Andes almost as early as the coast and Sierra were originally settled. Manioc root, still a jungle staple, is known to have been domesticated at least 8,000 years ago and may have been instrumental in supporting Andean and coastal societies along with corn imported from Central America. Clay pottery began to make an appearance around 4,000 B.C.

THE RISE AND FALL OF THE INCAS

Conquest

The empire of the "Children of the Sun" began ignominiously near the shores of frigid Lake Titicaca, between Perú and Bolivia, in the 11th century. Soon the Inca empire began to expand exponentially from its capital in Cuzco, Perú. By the 14th and 15th centuries, the empire they called *Tahuantinsuyo* stretched from northern Chile to the edge of Ecuador.

In 1463 the ruling Inca Tupac Inca Yupanqui began the push into Ecuador from Perú. As they advanced into the Sierra, Inca armies met fierce resistance from local tribes. Spears, slingshots, and war clubs flew in screaming melees where combatants wore cloth armor or nothing at all. The Cara were defeated only after 17 years of resistance. Thousands were slaughtered in retribution, including thousands who were killed at the edge of Lago Yahuarcocha (Bloody Lake) north of Ibarra. A new northern Inca outpost called Tomebamba, decked out in enough splendor to rival Cuzco itself, was built on the ruins of the Cañari capital in present-day Cuenca.

By 1500 Ecuador was under the thumb of Huayna Capac, son of Tupac and a Cañari princess. Huanya grew up in Ecuador and spent most of his time putting down local uprisings.

Life Under the Incas

Ecuador's new overlords ruled for less than half a century but managed to change things from

JULIAN SMITH

could be used to keep track of populations, seasons, and food supplies. Buildings in the famous Inca masonry style—blocks weighing tons fit together so perfectly that a piece of paper can't fit between them even today—housed collections of intricately woven textiles, utensils made of precious metals, and musical instruments made of clay, shell, and human bones.

Tying everything together was an incredible network of roads, perhaps the Incas' most impressive achievement. Eight meters wide and paved with stone, the highways boasted trees planted for shade and a ditch of fresh water running alongside. Teams of runners could make the 2,000-km journey from Cuenca to Quito along the Capacñan (Inca Highway) in eight days, crossing suspension bridges over at least 100 rivers and resting in roadhouses along the way. A second highway ran 4,800 km along the coast from Santiago, Chile to Guayaquil, and was connected to the Inca Highway by roads climbing into the Sierra.

Things Fall Apart

The Inca Huayna Capac died suddenly in 1526, leaving a power vacuum contested by Huáscar, the legitimate heir in Cuzco, and Atahualpa, the offspring of Huayna and a Quitu princess. Civil war began almost immediately, as Atahualpa established his headquarters in Cuenca after defeating Huáscar's finest general and making a *chicha* cup out of his skull. That same year, an exploratory mission led by Spaniard Bartolomé Ruiz de Estrada waded ashore in northern Ecuador.

The drama began in earnest in 1532 when Atahualpa defeated his half brother and took him prisoner, after a major battle near Riobamba that still gives Ecuadorians a mild dose of nationalistic pride (Atahualpa, after all, was the *Ecuadorian* Inca). The Inca empire was thus completely divided and ravaged by war when the conquistador Francisco Pizarro arrived that same year, ushering in an even more violent phase.

the ground up with surprising speed. The Inca emperor, revered as a living god, imposed an iron fist on the Quitosuyo—as the section of the empire from Ecuador to Cuzco was known—from his base in Cuzco. Ongoing local resistance made military rule a necessity. Fortifications called *pucarás* were erected at dozens of strategic lookouts, bridges, and mountain passes. Populations that refused to pay tribute to the divine authority of the Incas were moved in their entirety as far as Chile, and a *mita* system of collective work and annual tribute fueled the empire's expansion and filled the coffers in Cuzco with riches.

The Incas imposed the Quechua language (not to be confused with the Quechua people who spoke and continue to speak it) on conquered cultures. Agriculture was collectivized under the watchful eye of the state, as new crops such as sweet potatoes and peanuts were grown on terraced fields watered by complicated systems of irrigation. Spring plowing was forbidden until the ruling Inca had broken the ground at Cuzco with a ceremonial golden hand-plow.

Records were kept through an intricate system of knotted, colored cords called *quipus,* which

THE *CONQUISTADORES* ARRIVE

The Spanish Conquest Begins

Most *conquistadores* (conquerors) were low-ranking Spanish noblemen looking for wealth, fame, and adventure (in that order) in the New World. Francisco Pizarro, the central figure in the conquest of the Incas, was an illiterate and illegitimate fortune-seeker from the Extremadura region of southern Spain. A decade after he accompanied Vasco Nuñez de Balboa across the Panamanian isthmus to discover the Pacific Ocean, Pizarro received permission from the Crown to explore the west coast of South America with fellow adventurer Diego de Almagro.

Two voyages in 1524 and 1526 failed miserably, but the next year Pizarro, against royal orders, landed in northern Perú with 13 men. After returning to Spain to plead for money and authority from King Charles I for another voyage, Pizarro once again arrived in the New World with the title of Governor and Captain-General of Perú and embarked on another exploratory mission. In 1531 Pizarro landed in the Bay of San Mateo near Manabí with Almagro (who was jealous of Pizarro's title and authority), 180 men, 27 horses, his two brothers Gonzalo and Juan Pizarro, and two half brothers.

Atahualpa's Fate

In November of 1532, Atahualpa, having just captured his half-brother Huáscar, met with Pizarro's group in Cajamarca in the mountains of northern Perú. The ensuing scene would have been fascinating to witness: two leaders meeting in the sun-baked central plaza under the eyes of hundreds of terrified Spanish soldiers and thousands of implacable Inca warriors, tension resonant in the air. Accounts about the events that followed differ, but most witnesses agree that Atahualpa refused the Spanish chaplain's order to submit to Spain and the Catholic God, throwing a Bible to the ground in disgust.

At a prearranged signal, Spanish soldiers fired cannons and charged their horses into the heart of the astonished Inca garrison. Within two hours, 7,000 Inca soldiers lay dead, the Sun King had been taken captive, and the fate of South America's greatest empire had been sealed. Among

Inca leader Ahatualpa

the Europeans, only Pizarro was wounded as he rushed to grab Atahualpa. For the record, Atahualpa later admitted that he had had a similar plot in store for the conquistadors. They just beat him to it, adopting the headlong-charge tactic that would prove so effective against native foot soldiers in the years to come.

During the nine months of his imprisonment, Atahualpa learned Spanish, chess, and cards while retaining most of his authority (attendants still dressed and fed him, burning everything he touched). Thinking that Pizarro planned to depose him in favor of Huáscar, Atahualpa ordered his captive halfbrother killed. When it became clear that his own life hung in the balance, Atahualpa offered to buy his freedom with the wealth of his entire kingdom. He is said to have reached high on the wall of a room five meters wide by seven long, offering to fill it once with gold and twice with silver. The ransom—one of the largest the world has ever known—was actually assembled and on its way to the capital when Atahualpa was strangled on August 29, 1533, after being baptized Francisco and put through a sham trial in which he was accused of polygamy, idolatry, and crimes against the Crown. The ransom, quickly hidden en route from Cuzco, has never been found (see the special topic, "The Inca's Ransom" in the Central Sierra chapter).

The Conquest is Completed

In November 1533, Cuzco fell to Pizarro and Hernando de Soto, and the Inca empire was finished. The victors were welcomed as liberators by many native tribes, who had resented and fought against the yoke of the Incas. A few battles remained to be fought: in May 1534 Sebastian de Benalcázar (Pizarro's second-in-command) found himself facing 50,000 Inca warriors under the guidance of Rumiñahui, the greatest Inca general, who had deserted and burned Quito rather than surrender it to the invaders. Benalcázar, aided by Cañari soldiers, defeated "Stone Face," whose capture, torture, and exe-

BOB RACE

cution signaled the end of organized native military resistance.

By 1549 fewer than 2,000 Spanish soldiers had defeated an estimated 500,000 natives. Although these numbers seem unbelievable—someone surely must have left off some zeros—they can be explained by a combination of factors. In the 16th century, Spanish soldiers were among the best in the world, almost invulnerable to attack from the ground when mounted on their fierce war horses in full battle armor. A dozen mounted soldiers could hold off and even defeat hundreds of Inca foot soldiers. In addition, European diseases, to which natives had no immunity, killed by the thousands.

As much as anything, the incredible timing of the conquest sealed the Incas' fate. If the Spanish had arrived as little as a year or two earlier or later, things might have worked out much differently. As it happened, though, they arrived exactly when the Inca empire was critically vulnerable, split by a civil war that already had many local tribes itching to throw off their newly acquired masters. The conquistadors, especially Pizarro, manipulated the situation brilliantly, installing puppet rulers to pacify the masses and always acting with brutal decisiveness as if they weren't actually months from reinforcements and thousands of miles from home.

The End of the Conquistador Era

Infighting among the Spanish began as soon as the Incas were out of the picture. In 1538, Diego Almagro contested Pizarro's right to govern the new territory of Perú. Almagro was defeated, tried, and sentenced to death in Lima. Francisco himself was assassinated in 1541 by remnants of Almagro's rebel army.

The Spanish Crown tried to step in by imposing the New Laws of 1542, aimed at controlling the unruly *conquistadores* and ending the enslavement of the indigenous peoples, already a widespread practice. A new viceroy sent to oversee the budding colonies was fought and killed by Gonzalo Pizarro near Quito in 1544, who was in turn defeated by royal troops in 1548 and hung for treason. By this point the chaotic period of the *conquistadores* was mostly over, but their violent legacy lived on in the countries their descendents inherited.

THE COLONIAL PERIOD

From 1544–1720 Ecuador existed as part of the Viceroyalty of Perú, one of the divisions of Spain's New World colonies. During two centuries of relative peace, settlers replaced the *conquistadores* and female immigrants evened the balance of the sexes.

Farms and Slaves

Without the mineral wealth of Perú or Bolivia, Ecuador had to earn its keep with the products of its soil. Soon the rich volcanic earth of the Andean highlands bore bumper crops of wheat, corn, and potatoes, which thrived in the mild climate. Cattle, horses, and sheep grazed on endless fields of grass.

The most common form of land tenure was the *encomienda* system, in which Spanish settlers were given title to tracts of the best land, along with the right to demand tribute from any indigenous people who happened to live there. In exchange, the *encomendero* agreed to develop the land and convert its inhabitants to Christianity. The Spanish Crown strove to impose strict rules governing the treatment of the *indígenas,* but the system was hard to regulate and usually resulted in virtual slavery. By the early 17th century, about 500 *encomenderos* controlled vast tracts of the Sierra.

Another important source of income was textile *obrajes* (workshops), where *indígenas* were forced to turn out cotton and wool cloth from dawn to dusk, often chained to their looms. Agriculture along the coast was hampered by rampant tropical diseases like malaria and a frustrating lack of natives to enslave. Bananas, cocoa, and sugarcane filled lowland plantations, as shipping and trade kept ports such as

---

Hail is falling
Lightning strikes
The sun is sinking
It has become forever night.

—epic lament composed to mourn
the death of Atahualpa

MEASURING THE EARTH

By 1735 most people agreed that the earth was round. Another question remained: *how* round was it? Some scientists held that the rotation of the earth caused it to bulge outward slightly in the middle. Others thought the idea ridiculous. And with explorers setting out daily to the far corners of the globe, it was becoming more and more important to determine how much, if any, the earth bulged in the middle, since navigational charts off by a few degrees could send ships hundreds of miles in the wrong direction.

To answer the long-standing debate, the French Academy of Sciences organized two expeditions to determine the true shape of the earth. One team headed north to Lapland, as close to the arctic as possible. The other left for Ecuador on the equator. Each team would measure one degree of latitude (about 70 miles) in its respective region. If the degree at the equator proved longer than the degree near the arctic, then the earth bulged. If not, it didn't.

The Ecuadorian expedition was the first organized scientific expedition to South America. At the time, Ecuador was part of the Spanish territory of Upper Perú and was chosen because of its easier accessibility than alternative locations along the equator—the Amazon basin, Africa, and Southeast Asia. The Ecuadorian expedition was led by Academy members Louis Godin, Pierre Bouguer, and Charles-Marie de La Condamine. With them came seven other Frenchmen, including a doctor/botanist, Godin's cousin, a surgeon, a naval engineer, and a draftsman.

Tensions hampered the expedition from the start, as Bouguer and La Condamine quickly learned they did not get along. Bouguer was stern, stoic, and accused of being paranoid of competitors, whereas La Condamine, a protégé of Voltaire's, was easygoing. This personal rivalry sparked numerous quarrels along the way as the extroverted, enthusiastic La Condamine became the effective leader of the expedition.

The group arrived in Cartagena, Colombia, in 1735. There they were joined by two Spaniards, both naval captains under secret orders from the King of Spain to report back on the French expedition and on conditions in the Spanish territories. In March 1736 the party sailed into Ecuador's Pacific port of Manta, and soon traveled by way of Guayaquil to Quito. Quiteños received the earth measurers with delight. Dances and receptions filled the days following the arrival. As the festivities continued, Pedro Vicente Maldonado Palomino, an Ecuadorian mapmaker and mathematician, was chosen to join the historic expedition.

Eventually the group got down to business. For the sake of accuracy it was decided that the measurements would be made in the flat plains of Yaruquí, 12 miles north of Quito. As the work progressed, troubles mounted. The French and Spanish, unused to

Guayaquil in business. The coast north of the Manta area received the most of the few African slaves that were imported to Ecuador. They intermarried with indigenous tribespeople and occasionally escaped into fortified communities of runaways called *cimmarones.*

A sweltering climate, impassable terrain, and fierce indigenous groups kept most settlers out of the Oriente, beyond a few brave (and often martyred) missionaries.

The Holy Scorecard

The Catholic Church was a cornerstone of life during the colonial period, for natives and immigrants alike. By a majority vote, the Vatican had decided that indigenous peoples actually did have souls, making their conversion a worthwhile endeavor. Every town had a church operated by either Franciscans, Jesuits, or Dominicans, all competing for souls like soccer teams vying for points. A strict tithe system made the Church the largest landowner in the colonies. Jesus and the Virgin Mary were blended with the old gods of the sky and mountains in ceremonies in remote villages.

The Racial Pot Simmers

Over everything lay the subtle but pervasive gauze of race. Purebred Europeans, born in Spain *(peninsulares)* or the New World *(criollos),* stood at the top of the social ladder. They ran the sweatshops and owned the *haciendas* (farm estates), raking in the money as others labored in the sun.

Mixed-blood *mestizos* were in the middle, keeping the urban machinery going as shop-the altitude and the cold of the Sierra, began to fall ill. Soon the group suffered its first casualty: the nephew of the Academy's treasurer, one of the youngest team members.

As the mourning scientists wandered about the plains with their strange instruments, local residents grew suspicious. Rumors began circulating that they had come to dig up and steal buried treasure, maybe even Inca gold. The situation became so tense that La Condamine and a fellow member of the expedition were forced to travel to Lima to obtain the viceroy's support. They finally returned in July 1737 with official papers supporting their story. The measurements continued, and by 1739 the goal of determining the true shape of the earth was in sight. Then disastrous news arrived from the Academy: the Lapland expedition had succeeded. The earth was flattened at the poles. The verdict was already in.

As La Condamine tried to keep the expedition from disintegrating, bad luck seemed to strike from every side. The party surgeon Juan Seniergues became involved in a dispute over a Cuencan woman, and was beaten and stabbed to death at a bullfight in the Plaza de San Sebastian by an angry mob sympathetic to his local rival, the woman's former fiancée. The rest of the group sought refuge in a monastery. In the confusion, the team botanist, Joseph de Jussieu, lost his entire collection of plants representing five year's work, a loss that eventually cost him his mind as well. The team draftsman was killed in a fall from a church steeple near Riobamba.

La Condamine had to fend off accusations from the Spanish crown that he had insulted Spain by omitting the names of the two Spanish officers from commemorative plaques he had already erected at Yaruquí.

Finally, in March 1743, the remaining scientists made the last measurements, confirming the Lapland expedition's findings and bringing the expedition to an end. Even though they had come in second, the group's efforts did lay the foundation for the entire modern metric system. Some members decided to stay on in Ecuador—two had already married local women—while others traveled to other South American countries. Most went back to Europe. La Condamine, accompanied by Maldonado, rode a raft down the Amazon for four months to the Atlantic Ocean. From there the pair sailed on to Paris, where they were welcomed as heroes. With them they brought the first samples of rubber seen in Europe. Maldonado died of measles in 1748, while La Condamine enjoyed the high life in Paris until his death in 1774.

In 1936, on the 200th anniversary of the expedition's arrival in Ecuador, the Ecuadorian government built a stone pyramid on the equator at San Antonio de Pichincha in honor of the explorers and their work. This pyramid was eventually replaced by the 100-foot monument that stands today. Busts along the path leading to the monument commemorate the 10 Frenchmen, two Spaniards, and one Ecuadorian who risked their lives—and sanity—for science.

keepers, craftsmen, and skilled laborers. This middle class, aspiring to wealth and status as they looked down on the native masses, was politically unstable and easily provoked by fiery rhetoric—a ready source of fuel for the spark of independence later.

The indigenous peoples that remained after the Spanish conquest made up most of colonial society, ranging in number from 750,000 to 1 million by the 16th century. Countless had died of imported diseases such as smallpox, measles, cholera, and syphilis to which they had no natural immunity, especially on the coast. Others were herded onto *reduciones*, hastily assembled townships that made collecting taxes and labor easier for the Spanish.

Forced labor systems had *indígenas* working months to build roads and buildings. Debts ac-

cumulated along the way far outweighed the pittance they earned, if anything, resulting in a system of peonage in which debt was handed down through the generations, each one unable to work off the burden in turn. For what it's worth, things could have been worse—much of the land inhabited by indigenous groups was inaccessible or otherwise of little interest to the Spanish.

INDEPENDENCE

First Sparks

Just as things had settled into a comfortable pattern in the colonies, a series of events unfolded that would eventually shake the continent to its foundation. First, scientific visitors started to bring news of the outside world and new ideas in science and philosophy. From 1736–1745 the French mission to measure the equator (see the special topic, "Measuring the Earth") spread ideas of rational science and personal liberty, courtesy of the Enlightenment. In the early 19th century, German explorer and scientist Alexander von Humboldt and aspiring naturalist Charles Darwin both helped diffuse the latest scientific findings around this mostly forgotten corner of the globe. Uprisings in other South American countries (Perú in 1692 and 1730, and Venezuela in 1749) set the stage for revolutions in the United States (1776) and France (1792).

In Ecuador the physician and writer Eugenio Espejo was born in 1747, growing up to become a famous liberal humanist who demanded freedom and a democratic government for the colonies. Thrown in jail repeatedly and even exiled for his books and articles, Espejo died in Quito in 1795, hailed as one of the fathers of independence. Elsewhere in the country, uprisings among both *indígenas* and *mestizos* protested colonial treatment at the hands of Spain and her regime in the New World.

The final straw came in July 1808 when Napoleon invaded Spain, deposed King Ferdinand VII, and installed his brother Joseph Bonaparte on the throne. Monetary demands on the colonies—always a source of friction—skyrocketed as Spain sought funds to fight for the de-

EL LIBERTADOR

Revered and despised, triumphant and frustrated, El Libertador (The Liberator) embodied all of the contradictions and potential of the continent he helped to set free from the colonial yoke of Spain. One thing is true: whether as the heroic liberator of South America or the tyrannical despot chasing an impossible vision of continental unity, Simón Bolívar made his mark on history. At his death his dream remained half-fulfilled; he could free his beloved land, but he couldn't unify it.

Born in Caracas on July 24, 1783 to a wealthy family of planters, Simón Antonio de la Santisima Trinidad Bolívar y Palacios saw both his parents die before his 10th birthday. Relatives and friends helped raise him in the cultured circles of the New World upper class. "His chest was narrow," according to a friend, "his legs particularly thin, his hands and feet were small—a woman might have envied them." There was more, however: "His expression, when he was in good humor, was pleasant, but it became terrible when he was aroused. The change was unbelievable."

Bolívar's early teenage years were spent in military school, where his records sheets revealed his innate martial talent. His studies continued in Europe; he divided his time between aristocratic parties and studies of history, art, and the classics. His attention was soon captured by the rising star Napoleon Bonaparte, who had just crowned himself emperor of France for life. As he soaked up the rhetoric of philosophers such as Rousseau and Voltaire, advocating the sacred duty of a monarch to protect the common man by means of the law, Bolívar was solidifying his own ideas for South America.

From his European experiences Bolívar came to believe that the best way to organize the struggling republics would be through a strongly centralized, even dictatorial government. At the helm would preside a lifetime ruler with limitless power who would labor for the greatest good instead of abusing his power: a "moralistic monarch."

By 1807 he was back at his estate in Caracas and a member of the growing independence struggle. Napoleon's deposition of Ferdinand VII of Spain gave the revolutionaries their chance; Venezuela proclaimed its independence on July 5, 1811 and declared war on Spain soon after. Although the campaign did not fare well initially, Bolívar soon established his military reputation, and two years later ecstatic crowds greeted him in Caracas, where he was formally titled El Libertador and given complete dictatorship over the country.

Spain struck back with crushing force, occupying Caracas in 1814. Ironically, the defeat of his political role model at the battle of Waterloo provided crucial aid to Bolívar's revolution. Having declared "war to the death," Bolívar quickly snapped up the surplus arms and soldiers and turned them to his cause. Meanwhile he was busy organizing the Congress of Angostura, which in 1819 made his dream of Gran Colombia real, with Bolívar as dictatorial president.

Nowhere else did Bolívar's contradictions seem

posed Ferdinand, and the colonists decided enough was enough.

Early Uprisings

On August 10, 1809 a group of Quito's elite threw the president of the Quito *audencia* (colonial government) in jail and seized power in the name of the deposed king of Spain. Ironically, the Quiteño Rebellion, one of the first revolts in the Spanish colonies, was in *support* of the Spanish king, and ended abruptly. All the main players were executed by troops loyal to Bonaparte. In December 1811 a junta declared the *audencia* independent and sent troops off to fight the Spanish, who mauled them to a man. In October 1820 the city of

Guayaquil declared its own independence, under a junta led by poet José Joaquín Olmedo.

The Heat of Battle

By then the New World fight for independence was in full swing. Two main armies were led by Venezuelan Simón Bolívar (see the special topic, "El Libertador") in Colombia and Venezuela, and Argentine José de San Martín to the south. The fight for Ecuador began in earnest in May 1821, when brash young general Antonio José de Sucre arrived in Guayaquil at Bolívar's orders. After winning the first few battles, Sucre's army was whipped by loyalist troops near Ambato. Fourteen hundred fresh soldiers sent from Perú

more apparent than in his political philosophy. The same man who admired the United States and its government so much that he described the North American democracy as "a government so sublime that it might more nearly benefit a republic of saints," also wrote to a friend how he was "convinced that our America can only be ruled through a well-managed, shrewd despotism." Perhaps Bolívar was demonstrating a ruthless practicality. Latin America, in his eyes, was quite simply not ready for democracy. "Do not adopt the best system of government," he said, "but the one that is most likely to succeed."

Spain's hold over Venezuela was finally broken, but the battle for a united South America was far from won. Even before Bolívar freed Ecuador and Perú, finally eliminating the Spanish threat to the New World, his dream of Gran Colombia began to falter. Bolívar knew the worst was yet to come. And it was in peace that the newly freed nations would eventually disappoint him. His noble-minded revolution soon dissolved into a bloody struggle between disparate political, regional, and racial factions. In a last-ditch attempt to reconcile the warring populations, Bolívar organized a peace congress in Panama in 1826. His effort was in vain—only four countries showed up.

Bolívar succumbed to tuberculosis early in the afternoon of December 17, 1830 in a small town on the Colombian coast. He never answered the question of whether a South America unified under a monarch would have prospered or if he simply would have recreated in the New World the system he fought to dispel. Shortly before he died, the fiery general seethed with bitterness at what he saw as the be-

trayal of both himself and his dream: "There is no good faith in America, nor among the nations of America. Treaties are scraps of paper; constitutions, printed matter; elections, battles; freedom, anarchy."

Even on his deathbed, though, his thoughts were full of hope for his beloved federation: "Colombians! My last wishes are for the happiness of our native land."

Simón Bolívar

by San Martín soon put them on another winning streak, which culminated on 24 May 1822 at the Battle of Pichincha, a decisive victory on the slopes above Quito. Within hours the *audencia* belonged to Sucre, and Ecuador was free.

A pair of further victories in Perú sealed South America's independence. The Battle of Junín on August 7, 1823 was fought by so many cavalrymen that it was called the "battle of the Centaurs." The night before the Battle of Ayacucho in 1824, men from both sides crossed into the opposing camps to bid farewell to friends and brothers. The next day less than 6,000 patriots defeated more than 9,000 royalists who had them outgunned by a factor of 10. Spain was beaten and withdrew its administrative apparatus with its tail between its legs.

Ecuador Is Born

In August 1830 Ecuador withdrew from Gran Colombia, Bolívar's ill-fated confederation that had succumbed to regional rivalries. Suddenly 700,000 people found themselves citizens of a new country, with nowhere to go but up.

EARLY YEARS OF THE REPUBLIC

Ecuador's childhood as a nation was marked by power struggles among *criollo* elites, in particular aristocratic conservatives from Quito and free-enterprise liberals from Guayaquil. Meanwhile the new republic had little effect on most of the country—the poor, in other words, stayed poor.

Juan José Flores held power from 1830–1845, either directly as president or through puppet figures. Most of his power came from Quito, but widespread discontent by 1845 forced him to flee the country. The period from 1845–1860 saw 11 governments and three constitutions come and go as the economy stagnated and the military's influence in politics grew. By 1860 the country was on the brink of chaos, split by provincial rivalries and tense over border disputes with Perú and Colombia.

The Moreno Era

In 1860 a new player rose to the top. Gabriel García Moreno embodied devout Sierra conservatism, so much so that some historians have dubbed his regime a theocracy. He grew up during the chaos of the preceding decades and was determined that that kind of anarchy would never happen in his Ecuador, not if he and the Church had anything to say about it.

Conservatives loved him, citing his many social programs as proof that he saved the country from disaster. An improved school system now accepted women and *indígenas,* new roads connected the coast to the highlands and Quito to the rest of the country, hospitals and railways were built, and exports jumped from $1 million to $10 million in 1852–1890. Liberals saw him as a religious nut who consecrated the country to the Sacred Heart of Jesus, renamed army battalions "Guardians of the Virgin" and "Soldiers of the Infant Jesus," and established Roman Catholicism as the official state religion, with membership a prerequisite for citizenship and voting. Free speech was tightly controlled and political opposition squelched.

In 1875, six years after establishing the official Conservative Party, Moreno was assassinated on the steps of the Capitol by a machete-wielding Colombian. Liberal Ecuadorian journalist Juan Montalvo rejoiced from his exile in Colombia: "My pen has killed him!"

INTO THE 20TH CENTURY

Two decades of jousting between the Liberal and Conservative parties ended with the ascension to power of General José Eloy Alfaro. In two terms as president, 1897–1901 and 1906–1911, Alfaro embodied the Radical Liberal Party as much as Moreno once typified conservatism. Alfaro toppled the Church from its pinnacle at the top of daily life by seizing Church lands, instituting freedom of religion, and secularizing marriage and education. But sure enough, on January 28, 1912, Alfaro was killed by a government-instigated crowd in Quito. His body was dragged through the streets and burned in the Parque El Ejido.

Musical Presidents

Between 1925 and 1948, Ecuador had no fewer than 22 heads of state, each of whom tried to ride out a series of economic slumps that culminated in the 1929 Wall Street crash, which caused exports to fall by two-thirds. In 1934 began the celebrity of José María Velasco Ibarra, who said, "Give me a balcony and I will be president again!" as he was elected over and over. The first to appeal to both liberals and conservatives, Ibarra was nonetheless overthrown four times during his five terms between 1934 and 1961.

Early Border Struggles

The border between Ecuador and Perú, outlined only roughly by the colonial *audencia* in Quito, has been a bone of contention since Ecuador became a country. Boundary talks broke down into skirmishes in 1938, and three years later Perú launched an all-out invasion of Ecuador's easternmost provinces. Fearing a coup, president Carlos Alberto Arroyo del Río kept the best troops in Quito during the border fighting, but a cease-fire was arranged within two months.

The January 1942 Protocol of Peace, Friendship and Boundaries (also known as the Río Protocol because it was signed in Río de Janeiro) quickly became a national disgrace to Ecuadorians. Not only did Ecuador have to sign away more than 200,000 square km of jungle territory rich in oil and gold deposits to her hated larger neighbor, but it also lost the Amazon river port Iquitos, her river access to the Atlantic, in the bargain. Ecuadorians quickly looked for someone to blame beyond the guarantor countries of the United States, Chile, Argentina, and Brazil, who were more interested in the recently erupted World War.

Ups and Downs

A period of relative political stability in the mid-20th century proved too good to last. After siding with the Allies in World War II (during which the United States built a naval base in the Galápagos and an airport at Salinas), Ecuador enjoyed a resurgence of democracy and its attendant freedoms. Even old Velasco Ibarra was finally able to finish a full term in 1952, his third (he was ousted from his second term by his minister of defense in 1947).

When a wave of disease ravaged Central America's banana crop, Ecuador stepped in to supply the huge U.S. demand, with the help of the United Fruit Company. Exports jumped from $2 million in 1948 to $20 million in 1952, and Ecuador's position as world banana king became official.

By the late 1950s, the banana boom was over. Ibarra, who was reelected in 1960, began a proud Ecuadorian political tradition by renouncing the Río Protocol in his inaugural address, to the delight of the crowd. His left-leaning policies proved ill-timed, however, coming as they did at the height of the Cold War. A gunfight in the Congressional chamber proved how bad things had gotten at the top. In November 1961 the military removed Ibarra from power, and two years later replaced his successor with a four-man junta.

Ecuador's first experiment with outright military rule was short-lived, barely managing to pass the well-intentioned but ultimately ineffectual Agrarian Reform Law of 1964 before succumbing to concerns over another economic slump. Ibarra was reelected in 1968 for the fifth time with barely one-third of the popular vote. For two years he enjoyed military support as he dismissed Congress and the Supreme Court, suspended the Constitution, and dictated harsh but necessary economic measures designed to get the country back on its feet.

By 1972—the same year it was discovered that Ecuador had the third-largest petroleum reserves in Latin America—another military junta was back in power. In response to widespread concern that the newfound wealth would be squandered by a corrupt civilian government, the junta instituted a firm strategy of modernization. Industrialization leapt forward, and the middle class grew in numbers and power, but further attempts at land reform met the stone wall of the landholding elite. Not surprisingly, the poor suffered from the oil boom inflation without reaping the attendant benefits.

Democracy at Last

Coups in 1975 and 1976 caused splits within the military, and in January 1978 a national referendum voted for a new constitution, universal suffrage, and guaranteed civil rights. Jaime Roldós took office in 1979, finding himself at the wheel of a country unfamiliar with democracy but with a government budget and per capita income increased more than 500 percent from the oil windfall. His center-left government began programs of improving rural literacy and housing, but less than two years later the president was killed in a plane crash along with his wife and minister of defense. Mild public suspicion fell on Perú (border hostilities had recently heated up, and the plane crashed near the border) and the United States (the president of Panama, no friend of the United States, had been killed in a similar crash three months earlier).

RECENT HISTORY

The early 1980s brought a cluster of crises. Border fighting with Perú flared up in January 1981, December 1982, and January 1983, and the disastrous 1982–1983 El Niño weather phenomenon caused $640 million in damage from drought and floods, ruining rice and banana crops along the coast. Sudden declines in petroleum reserves left the country with a foreign debt of $7 billion by 1983, when inflation hit an all-time high at 52.5 percent.

The Trials of León

Conservative León Febres Cordero beat out eight other candidates for the presidency in 1984. A pro-U.S. foreign policy and economic austerity plan brought him into conflict with Congress and the country. Petroleum workers in two northern provinces organized strikes and sabotage that led to the declaration of an 11-day state of emergency. This situation led to more strikes, resulting in hundreds of arrests and a few deaths.

January 1987 was not Cordero's month. First he was kidnapped by air force troops under orders from a mutinous general in prison. Only by granting the general amnesty was Cordero able to secure his own release after 11 hours in captivity. Then an earthquake in Napo province killed hundreds and ruptured the all-important oil pipeline, causing Ecuador to suspend interest payments on its $8.3 billion foreign debt.

Sixto Duran Ballón

In 1992 another Christian Socialist assumed the presidency. Further economic austerity measures, including a privatization law that left 100,000 public employees without jobs, helped curb inflation but prompted widespread demonstrations, bombings, and a general strike in May 1993.

Ballén's administration was also clouded by a scandal involving vice-president and economic guru Alberto Dahik, who fled to Costa Rica in a private plane after being accused (correctly, as it turned out) of embezzling millions of dollars in state funds. A government cover-up, which involved the seizure of Central Bank vaults that held incriminating microfilms, led to ministers resigning and the impeachment of one Supreme Court judge. Later polls showed that 80 percent of Ecuadorians believed the president had covered up evidence to protect his second-in-command. This action convinced many that the country would be better off under an authoritarian regime like that of Perúvian president Alberto Fujimori.

Tensions with Perú erupted into outright war in January 1995. Six weeks of combat over the headwaters of the Río Cenepa ended only after the intervention of a multinational team of observers. Ecuador lost $250 million in damage, plus untold more in lost commerce and tourism—but Ballén's popularity rating soared more than 90 percent.

El Loco

In 1996 the biggest political circus in Ecuador's history began with the presidential election of Abdalá Bucarám Ortiz, former mayor of Guayaquil and one of the least boring politicians in recent memory. Of Lebanese descent, Bucarám campaigned under the moniker "El Loco" (The Crazy One) and promised to lead Ecuador's vast army of the poor to newfound prosperity and influence and bring inflation to zero by stabilizing the sucre and selling off state-owned enterprises. The campaign worked; the urban poor vote propelled Bucarám to victory in the second round of elections.

From the start it was clear that El Loco wasn't firing on all cylinders, just as he claimed. Bucarám's inaugural address was described as a two-hour "hysterical diatribe." One day he was raising $742,000 for charity by shaving his moustache on live TV; the next he was having lunch with Ecuadorian-American Lorena Bobbitt of tabloid-surgery fame. The president released a rock album entitled *A Madman in Love* (including a prophetic Spanish-language version of "Jailhouse Rock") and crooned at a Miss Banana beauty contest.

Shortly after the election, accusations of corruption and political favoritism began to surface, including Bucarám's appointment of his brother to the post of Minister of Social Welfare. Soon voters began to remind themselves of Bucarám's unflattering résumé—as mayor of Guayaquil in 1985, he had fled to Panama to escape embezzlement charges (Guayas province was the only one Bucarám failed to carry in the election).

A strict austerity package passed in January 1997 proved to be his undoing. Electricity and gas rates doubled overnight, bus fares rose by 60 percent, and telephone rates leapt 600 percent. A general protest strike paralyzed the country, and on 6 February Congress surprised even themselves by voting the president "mentally incompetent" and unfit to govern by a 44–34 margin. It was just before the four-day Easter holiday weekend, and the fireworks began at once. Bucarám holed up in the presidential palace, calling the ruling a "de facto coup" and saying he'd rather die than step down in disgrace. Congress appointed its own leader, Fabian Alarcon, as interim president, as vice-president Rosalia Arteaga simultaneously laid claim to the office.

The military stayed nervous but neutral, sending a reassuring signal of noninterference. "This situation, which is extremely grave for our life as a nation, has caused uncertainty and a terrible sense of unease in the democratic-minded armed forces," read a statement issued by military chiefs, causing some to wonder about their true intentions.

Arteaga stepped into the presidency, becoming Ecuador's first female leader ever—for the moment. Meanwhile thousands of demonstrators surrounded the presidential palace, demanding that Bucarám leave office. Rocks and Molotov cocktails began to fly as troops tried to use tear gas to disperse the mob, leaving one protestor dead. When the military formally withdrew its recognition of him as Ecuador's commander in chief, Bucarám found himself all alone. He retreated to his traditional power enclave of Guayaquil and then left the country, pointing out that he had never been given the opportunity to defend himself in an official impeachment trial ("Congress is not a psychiatrist," he fumed). Bucarám promised to run for reelection soon after the year 2000—a proposition that political analysts say isn't all that *loco*.

When the smoke cleared, Alarcon had assumed the title of president from Arteaga, wasting no time in repealing the austerity measures that got the ball rolling in the first place.

Into the Millennium

Ecuador rode into the 21st century on a wave of upheaval. Another round of El Niño hit the country badly in 1998, washing out roads, devastating the country's farming and fishing industries, and killing off wildlife in the Galápagos. In August an earthquake measuring 7.1 on the Richter scale hit near Bahía de Caráquez, knocking out water and electricity supplies and even more roads.

Meanwhile, former Quito mayor Jamil Mahaud claimed the presidency by a margin of less than 5 percent in a hotly contested election over Alvaro Noboa. The Harvard-educated political centrist took office in August, just in time to lay to rest the long-standing border dispute with Perú.

On other fronts, Mahaud probably wasn't as eager to take over. A mounting economic crisis (see following "Economy" section) was causing the sucre to slide drastically in value. To make things worse, in October 1999, Guagua Pichincha broke a 340-year silence and belched a seven-mile-high cloud of ash over the capital, forcing the closure of the airport and the evacuation of 2,000 citizens. Luckily, the volcano seems to have quieted down before going into an all-out eruption. Ash clouds continued to clog sewers and force citizens to wear facemasks into the next year.

Two weeks later, louder rumblings from Tungurahua Volcano near Baños forced the evacuation of *that* entire city. Gases, steam, and ash spewed forth from the "Neck of Fire," as the volcano's name translates from Quechua. As of late 2000, some residents had returned to their homes, but life in the country's premier resort town was still far from normal.

The economy continued to crumble, causing Mahaud to liken it to "the sinking of the Titanic" in a state-of-the-nation speech in January 1999. He may not have been surprised, then, when 10,000 mostly indigenous protestors shut down much of the country one year later in a general strike to protest one of Ecuador's worst financial crises in history. Opponents charged that the president's plan to make Ecuador the first country in Latin America to adopt the U.S. dollar as its official currency would further impoverish poor citizens who have their savings in sucres, instead of stabilizing the economy.

On January 21, two weeks after Mahaud declared a state of emergency, hundreds of indigenous protestors occupied the Congress and Supreme Court buildings in Quito and declared a new government. Violent protests in Guayaquil followed, and Mahaud was deposed by a three-man military junta in a bloodless coup. Protesting that the military was angry because he had cut its budget and ended border skirmishes with Perú, Mahaud had no choice but to hand over the reins to his vice-president Gustavo Noboa Be-

jerano, a 61-year-old university professor from Guayaquil, on January 23.

Noboa, who had made a name for himself while supervising the rebuilding of Ecuador's devastated coast following the disastrous 1998–1999 El Niño season, pledged to continue Mahaud's economic stabilization policies and to complete his predecessor's term, which ends in 2003.

No sooner had Ecuador faded from the global spotlight than an oil spill in the Galápagos Islands in early 2001 focused world attention on the country once again. See "History" in the Galápagos chapter for more details.

GOVERNMENT AND ECONOMY

POLITICS

For much of its history, Ecuador has been anything but politically stable. The first 160 years after independence saw 86 governments and 17 constitutions come and go. Of the few administrations that resulted from popular election, not many were free of fraud. Citizens became understandably disenchanted with the system. In his book *The Donkey Inside,* written in the 1940s, Ludwig Bemelmans quoted one Ecuadorian as saying, "We have a revolution here every Thursday afternoon at half-past two and our government is run like a nightclub."

At the same time, Ecuador has managed to avoid many of the pitfalls its neighbors have fallen into. Democracy has been in place in name since 1948, and in reality since the end of military rule in 1979. Recent political fireworks have shaken many Ecuadorians' faith in the system and scared away a few tourists, but in the end the message has been reassuring: the military doesn't seem to want to take over, as it occasionally has in other Latin American countries, and political problems are corrected with surprising speed and little, if any, bloodshed. Ecuador was one of the first countries in Latin America to return to democracy after a wave of dictatorships in the 1960s and 1970s, and the system seems more entrenched every day.

The traditional rivalry between liberal, trade-happy coastal residents and conservative, land-

holding Sierra elites has spilled over into politics, with the presidency often alternating between the two interests. Sometimes the transition isn't smooth: in 1988, outgoing president Febres Cordero, a Guayaquileño, refused to hand over the presidential sash to his successor Rodrigo Borja, from Quito.

Organization

Under the 1979 constitution, Ecuador is a representative democracy, with compulsory suffrage for all literate citizens over age 18. An executive branch consists of 14 ministers, a vice-president, and a president elected by majority vote every four years. Presidents must be elected by at least a 50 percent majority, leading to frequent runoff elections. They cannot be reelected.

The Congreso Nacional (National Congress) has 121 seats filled by national and provincial deputies who serve four-year terms. Congress in turn appoints 16 justices to form the judiciary branch of the Corte Suprema (Supreme Court).

Twenty-two *provincias* (provinces)—the newest, Orellana, was formed in 1998—are ruled by governors who oversee 103 *cantones* (municipalities) and 746 *parroquias* (parishes). The Galápagos Islands are administered by the Ministry of Defense.

Parties

Almost 15 different political parties keep elections interesting. The traditional extremes of the

Conservative Party (PC) and the Radical Liberal Party (PLR), with power bases in Quito and Guayaquil, respectively, have grown stale through the 20th century. Today the left is the realm of the Democratic Left (ID), formed in 1977 by Rodrigo Borja and supported by younger reform-minded professionals. The Social Christian Party (PSC) and the Ecuadorian Conservative Party (PCE) claim the center-right. The populist left is the domain of the Roldosist Party (PRE), the Popular Democratic Movement (MPD), and the Concentration of Popular Forces (CFP).

No one party is strong throughout the country, making coalitions an important factor in national elections. The conservative Church's political strength has waned, and the military usually chooses to stick to the sidelines. Student unrest flared in the 1960s, causing military crackdowns on university campuses, but has since mellowed considerably.

ECONOMY

Ecuador's economy balances between relatively small agricultural enterprises, businesses in the Sierra, and monster export projects along the coast. Natural resources abound, but a large foreign debt hampers development, and unemployment and inflation are both high. Informal craftspeople and vendors make up close to 40 percent of the workforce.

Like many developing countries, Ecuador's wealth is concentrated in a few people at the top of the social ladder, with little trickling down to the rest. A large gap separates the haves from the have-nots; the sight of a Range Rover driving past a dirt hut is always jarring. In 1994, 35 percent of the country's population was estimated to live below the poverty line, and the monthly minimum wage ($183) stood well below the cost of living for a family of four ($383).

Agriculture
The *conquistadores* never realized it, but Ecuador's true wealth lies in its soil and the people who work it. Agriculture is the primary industry in the Sierra, followed by livestock trading and crafts. Despite agrarian reform laws in 1964 and 1974, the land remains unevenly distrib-

uted; three-quarters of all farms work less than 10 percent of the arable land. Tiny farms of under two hectares can't support families, leading many people to emigrate to the cities and the coast in search of work.

The rich river bottoms on the coast have seen their share of booms and busts. At the turn of the century, cocoa beans provided funds for the Quito-Guayaquil railway, and coffee and rice took off in the 1930s. Today coffee is the nation's second most valuable crop, grown in 20 percent of all farms. Bananas slid onto the scene in the 1940s, becoming Ecuador's leading export crop by 1947. Rich shrimp farms along the coast made Ecuador the world's largest shrimp exporter in 1986.

Industry
One-quarter of Ecuador's gross national product (GNP) has some catching up to do—the country still leans toward the export of raw materials and the import of finished products—but the situation is better than in many other developing countries. Factories process food and manufacture textiles, wood products, chemicals, plastics, metal goods, and timber. In 1997, Ecuador's $3.4 billion in exports were split between petroleum (30 percent), bananas (26 percent), shrimp (16 percent), cut flowers (2 percent), and fish (2 percent).

Recent mining strikes, including 700 tons of gold discovered in the Nambija region in southern Zamora Chinchipe, have some experts predicting that Ecuador will soon become the biggest gold producer in Latin America. Large international companies are already vying for mining permits to over one-sixth of the country.

The biggest moneymaker, though, is oil—the "black gold" that brought the Oriente into the national economy and Ecuador to the attention of the world. Natives in the Amazon once dug pits that filled with a dark, sticky substance, which they would let evaporate and use to caulk canoes and make torches. Modern drilling in the Amazon had to wait for decades after the invention of the internal combustion engine because most of the Oriente was still inaccessible.

Major strikes in 1967 near Lago Agrio got the sticky black ball rolling. In 1971, a pipeline was built from Lago Agrio through Quito to Esmeraldas, and Ecuador began to export petroleum.

One year later, Ecuador was found to have the third-largest reserves in Latin America, and a symbolic barrel of oil was paraded around the country. "People would put their hands in it," recalled one tour operator. "The idea was that everyone was now rich." At least a few were, anyway. Ecuador joined OPEC (the Organization of Petroleum Exporting Countries) in 1974, and the economic focus of the country began to shift away from agriculture. The government's coffers filled, allowing the construction of new roads and factories. Foreign countries began to see Ecuador as a creditworthy nation, and export earnings quintupled between 1971–1975.

Today Ecuador is the sixth-largest producer and fourth-largest exporter of oil in South America. Oil accounted for 11 percent of its gross domestic product (GDP) in 1994 and 30 percent of its export earnings in 1997. But along with the economic windfall, a downside has appeared. Such a dependence on oil makes the country highly subject to fluctuations in world oil prices. Government borrowing against future revenues and increased subsidies led to economic instability in the 1980s and ran the foreign debt up to $12 billion by 1993, leaving continued oil production as the only hope to avoid bankruptcy. A major earthquake in 1987 disrupted the pipeline, momentarily severing the source of Ecuador's lifeblood. The damage to the Amazon's ecosystems and indigenous groups by foreign oil companies is only beginning to be understood. Current reserves are estimated to be exhausted by 2005, forcing the underdeveloped country to further expose itself to international oil firms with the ability to search for more deposits.

Recent Turmoil

A dependence on world oil prices recently dragged Ecuador into its worst recession in almost a century. A period of economic stagnation and labor trouble in the mid-1990s followed several government privatization measures and austerity programs aimed at compensating for depressed oil prices. The $2.6 billion in damages caused by the 1997 El Niño season dug the pit deeper. When citizens began draining their bank accounts for fear that their dollar-based accounts would be confiscated, the government shut down much of the banking system.

In 1998 the government radically devalued the sucre, sparking widespread demonstrations, strikes, and protests and undermining public confidence in the country's economy. By 1999 the economy had shrunk by more than 7 percent, making it one of the worst performers in Latin America. The inflation rate is the highest in the region, topping 60 percent at one point. Foreign reserves were drained and foreign debt mounted until it equaled 110 percent of Ecuador's GNP, sparking fears of default.

President Mahaud's emergency measures, including cutting the budget, raising taxes, and declaring emergency bank holidays with limited withdrawals, only made things worse. Massive strikes and protests—many led by marginalized indigenous groups—brought the country to a halt repeatedly as residents protested rising gas and utility prices that weren't reflected in stagnant salaries. In late 1999 the government announced that it would default on hundreds of millions of dollars in Brady Bond and Eurobond debt.

Mahaud's dollarization plan in early 2000 was his undoing. By freezing the sucre at 25,000 to the U.S. dollar and making the dollar Ecuador's official currency, he hoped to halt inflation and stabilize the economy. His opponents, however, charged that the move would only further impoverish the country's poor, who have their savings in sucres. A bloodless coup soon replaced Mahaud with his vice-president Gustavo Noboa.

The early day's of Noboa's presidency have given some hope for recovery. While he saw his predecessor's dollarization plan set into effect, Noboa also pledged to repay deposits lost in the recent bank failures and to restructure the country's $13 billion external debt. As of late 2000, confidence in the economy was rising along with oil prices, cocoa exports, and tourism, and inflation was slowing. While only 10–20 percent of businesses paid taxes before the crisis, now the government is cracking down on tax collection to the point of shutting down establishments that are slow in paying. A free trade zone declared in Esmeraldas is the first of a series; others are planned for Manabí, Cuenca, and Riobamba.

PEOPLE

POPULATION

Ecuador's 12.5 million inhabitants are packed tight; even with large, empty tracts of Amazon rainforest, the country still has the highest population density in South America—40 people per square km. This overcrowding situation is visibly apparent along the coast and in the Sierra, where most of the land outside of parks, reserves, and jagged mountains is built on, planted, or otherwise occupied. The country doesn't feel that crowded—you can drive for kilometers through hills and fields without seeing more than a handful of people—but they're here, and the land strains to support them.

Growth

Ecuador's population is growing despite government attempts at family planning. It's a Catholic country to the core, so birth control is frowned upon (when an option at all). Large families are preferred for several reasons: more hands to help in daily labor, a sign of the father's virility, and proof of God's favor. Women marry young and have children quickly. A 1987 survey found that more than half of rural women were married and pregnant by age 20 (compared to about 40 percent of urban women).

Death rates are decreasing, especially infant mortality, which has been cut by more than half in the last three decades.

On the other hand, there are signs of slowing growth. Family planning efforts have begun to bear fruit—at least in the awareness of contraceptives, if not their use—and more women are working outside the home, making it more difficult to have and support a large family. The direct relationship between education and a lower birth rate is becoming apparent. Women (and men) who finish their basic schooling have fewer children than those who do not. Ecuador's annual birth rate fell from 33 per 1,000 in 1990 (versus a world average of 27.4, and second only to Bolivia in South America) to 22 per 1,000 in 1999, giving it an overall population growth rate of 1.8 percent. Fertility rates have dropped from almost seven children per woman in the early 1960s to 2.5 in 1996.

Nonetheless, Ecuador has a steep hill to climb. The cone-shaped population curve, with 35 percent of all Ecuadorians under 15 years old in 1999, foreshadows a boom in women at childbearing age and huge pressures on the already strained school systems and job market. The country's population is estimated to double every 27 years.

Distribution

Until the middle of the 20th century, the Sierra was Ecuador's most populated area. Between 1950 and 1974, though, a large shift to the coast in response to a land crunch in the highlands and an expanding coastal economy left the populations of the two regions roughly equal. Another countrywide shift from rural areas to the cities resulted in millions of people stranded in slums ringing urban centers. Ecuador's eastern forests still support only 3–5 percent of the country's population, despite a large increase to the area from 1950 to 1982 in response to government land incentives and the discovery of

JOAN KROLL

GRAFFITI

Few things betray a country's inner workings better than what's spray-painted on its walls, and Ecuador has a particularly rich variety of graffiti. (When was the last time you saw Goethe quoted in spray paint?) If the following examples pique your interest, look for Makarios Oviedo Reire's book *La Muralla, El Papel de Los de Agalla (The Wall, the Paper of Those With Guts)* at bookstores in Quito.

¿Es posible matar el tiempo sin herir a la eternidad?
Is it possible to kill time without hurting eternity?

La idea del suicidio me está matando.
The idea of suicide is killing me.

El amor es una enfermedad que nos tiene solo en la cama.
Love is a sickness that leaves us alone in bed.

Las mujeres son como el freno—que no avisan cuando se van.
Women are like car brakes—they don't warn you when they go.

Este país es el sueño de un díos cobarde.
This country is the dream of a cowardly God.

---

oil. Immigration into the Río Napo region was so heavy that in 1989 it was split into two provinces, Napo and Sucumbíos. The new Amazonian province of Orellana was created in 1998.

Racial Breakdown

With such a subtle spectrum of racial mixtures, numeric divisions are always off by more than a few percentage points. Mestizos—people of mixed Spanish and indigenous heritage—make up the largest sector (40–65 percent), with pure indigenous citizens coming in second at 25–40 percent. The remainder of Ecuadorians are Caucasians of direct Spanish descent, a small population of blacks descended from colonial slaves (about 500,000), and immigrants from the Middle East, Asia, Europe, and elsewhere in Latin America.

Emigration

Ecuador's recent political and economic troubles have prompted between one and three million of the country's inhabitants to try their luck elsewhere. Most live in the United States, Spain, and Italy, and many of them are there illegally. Lines for passports stretch around the block in Quito, and high-quality fake documents are often caught, along with their owners, at the transit sections of the Miami and Houston airports.

One result of this exodus is flotillas like those leaving Cuba, Haiti, and China. U.S. officials estimate that 1,500–2,000 Ecuadorians head north per month in boats carrying up to 200 passengers each. Smugglers of this human cargo grow rich on fees of more than $10,000 per migrant, who disembark in Guatemala to be smuggled over the U.S. border on land. Those that do manage to eke out a living in their new home send back millions of dollars to relatives and families in Ecuador every year.

INDIGENOUS GROUPS

Ecuador's traditionally downtrodden masses, most of whom scrape by on less than $1,000 per year (if they're lucky enough to have jobs), have recently begun a continent-wide movement toward better treatment and political recognition. Dozens of indigenous organizations have developed; their mission is political empowerment, usually in regard to land issues, and the preservation and promotion of native culture and languages.

In a march on Quito in May 1990, 1,000 people representing 70 indigenous organizations petitioned for recognition of indigenous land rights. The next month an uprising organized by CONAIE (the National Confederation of Indigenous Peoples of Ecuador) paralyzed seven Andean provinces as 500,000 participants blockaded roads, occupied haciendas, and took hostages. This protest, seeking land reform and compensation for the ravages of petroleum exploration, led to formal talks with the government and eventual title to more than one million hectares of Amazon land.

In an April 1992 protest, several thousand *indígenas* marched from the Oriente to the capital to demand recognition of their rights to two million hectares of historical homeland in the face of continued drilling. Finally, in May 1996, a decade of political organizing paid off. Seventy-six candidates backed by CONAIE, mostly *indígenas,* won more than 100 local and national elections throughout the country. The list of victors includes Luis Macas, the first ever indigenous member of Ecuador's Congress.

Sierra

Most of Ecuador's indigenous population inhabit the northern and central Andes. About 800,000 of the **Runa,** or "the people," as the Quechua-speaking descendants of the Incas call themselves, live in tightly knit communities where kinship bonds are paramount and everyone helps in voluntary communal work events called *mingas.* The *cabildo* (town hall), which is run by the *alcade* (mayor), keeps things running smoothly. Artisan work and subsistence agriculture brings in the most money, with private and community-owned plots planted with maize, barley, and potatoes as high as 4,000 meters. Festivals of Catholic patron saints are combined with ancient Inca harvest ceremonies.

Imbabura province is home to the famously successful **Otavaleños,** as well as smaller groups of **Caranquis, Natabuelas,** and **Salasacas.** Traditional dress persists here, with different groups represented by different colors and patterns. Cotopaxi province is home to special celebrations of Corpus Christi, along with important pilgrimages to sanctuaries in Baños and El Quinche.

Many indigenous men from Bolívar province descend to the coast for work. Back home, the number of bands on their felt hats tells their marital status: two means single, three married. Chimborazo province has more highland *indígenas* than any other province, while Loja is home to the successful cattle-raising **Saraguros.**

Coast

The **Tsachilas,** also known as the Colorados, inhabit the western foothills of the Andes near Santo Domingo de los Colorados. A handful of small communities contain about 2,000 members who make their living farming tropical crops and raising livestock. Modern clothing has replaced the traditional dress and red hair-painting, which the Colorados now do only for paying visitors. They are famous for their knowledge of natural medicine—the governor-general is also the head *pone* (curer), who is adept in the use of medicinal plants as well as ceremonies to drive

INDIGENOUS ORGANIZATIONS

Abya Yala Fund for Indigenous Self-Development in South & Meso America, P.O. Box 28386, Oakland, CA 94604, 510/763-6553, fax 510/763-6588, e-mail: abyayala@earthlink.net, website: ayf.nativeweb.org. This organization seeks to support indigenous peoples in economic, social, cultural, and spiritual ways, including the publication of a journal on Indian rights.

Confederation of Indigenous Nationalities of Ecuador (CONAIE), Av Granados 2553 y 6 de Diciembre, Casilla 17-17-1235, Quito, tel. 2/248-930, fax 2/442-271, e-mail: conaie@ecuanex.net.ec, website: conaie.nativeweb.org. Formed in 1986, the largest indigenous organization in Ecuador serves as a political mouthpiece for its members, focusing on ecology, land rights, education, and indigenous culture.

Confederation of Indigenous Nationalities of the Ecuadorian Amazon (CONFENIAE), Av. 6 de Diciembre 159 y Pazmino, of. 408, Apdo. 17-01-4180, Quito, tel. 2/543-973, fax 2/220-325, e-mail: confeniae@applicom.com, website: www.applicom.com/confeniae. The Shuar, Achuar, Huaorani, Siona-Secoya, Cofan, Zaparo, and Lowland Quichua groups banded together in 1980 to defend and legalize their historical territories in the Ecuadorian Amazon. Their umbrella organization seeks to promote the social, political, and economic development of indigenous communities.

Indigenous and Peasant Federation of Imbabura (FICI), M. Jaramillo 608 y Morales, P.O. Box 65, Otavalo, tel./fax 6/920-976, e-mail: fici@uio.satnet.net, website: fici.native web.org

Scientific Institute of Indigenous Cultures (ICCI), Buenos Aires 1028 y EE.UU, Casilla 17-15-50B, Quito, tel. 2/229-093, e-mail: icci@waccom.net.ec, website: icci.nativeweb. org. This private, nonprofit institution works toward the organization and preservation of different indigenous groups.

Union of Indigenous Peasant Organizations of Cotacachi (UNORCAC), González Suárez 2038 y Quiroga, Cotacachi, tel. 6/915-602, fax 6/915-977, website: unorcac.nativeweb.org

away evil spirits, attract good fortune, and look into the future. A rich oral tradition includes tales of Diochi, the creator and caretaker of the universe, who lives in a golden cloud guarded by thunder and lightning.

The tropical river country of the western Cotacachi-Cayapas reserve is home to the **Chachis,** also called the Cayapas. Tradition holds that they came from Quito in a series of migrations under pressure from Spanish settlers. Today the Chachis number about 4,000 and practice slash-and-burn agriculture, fishing, and hunting. Traditional open-sided, one-room homes covered by a thatched roof are built by entire communities. Three-man tribunals are overseen by a governor or *uñi,* who is assisted by two lesser governors called *chaitalas,* and every village has its own *brujo* (witch doctor). The Chachis have traditionally clashed with neighboring Afro-Ecuadorians over limited resources.

About 1,6000 **Awá-Kwaiker** live between the Mira and San Juan Rivers in the province of Carchi near Colombia, as well as in Imbabura province. The Awá owe their continued existence to a flagship program begun by Ecuador and Colombia in 1986, in which three protected areas, including 100,000 hectares in Ecuador, are being managed for environmental and cultural longevity.

Oriente

Of the 17 distinct ethnic groups that lived in the Amazon before European contact, only six are left today. Most subsist on wild fruits, nuts, and roots as well as by practicing slash-and-burn agriculture. Amazon *indígenas* also hunt (harder now because game levels have dropped) and fish, either by spear, hook and line, net, or stunning fish trapped in rock pools with the crushed leaves of the narcotic *barbasco* plant.

Animistic religions practiced in the Oriente center around the idea of transmigration of souls from one form to another—the animal you kill today was probably a person in another life, and you may come back as a plant, so treat them all with equal respect. Shamans serve as intermediaries between the terrestrial and spiritual world, curing diseases, overseeing initiation ceremonies, and preserving oral traditions. The hallucinogenic *ayahuasca* vine

INDIGENOUS MARKET DAYS

Sunday: Cuenca, El Quinche, Machachi, Peguche, Pujilí, Santo Domingo
Monday: Ambato
Tuesday: Latacunga
Wednesday: Pujilí
Thursday: Cuenca, Riobamba, Saquisilí, Tulcán
Friday: Latacunga
Saturday: Latacunga, Otavalo, Peguche, Riobamba

(Banisteriopsis caapi), traditionally used to enter the world of the soul, has since been patented and included on package tours of the jungle. Crafts include basket-weaving, pottery, and colorful ornaments of wood, feathers, beads, and insect parts. Tourist demand for souvenirs has encouraged native groups to kill endangered species.

Although contacted much later than groups in the highlands and coast, Oriente tribes have had to deal with tens of thousands of settlers because of a huge push from the Ecuadorian government to populate the area, as well as the pollution and development that have accompanied oil exploration. Disease, clear-cutting, and slaughter of game animals are all part of the mess, which has encouraged the formation of strong-willed tribal groups to fight for indigenous rights.

Lowland Quechuas, descendants of Andean groups that migrated from the Sierra soon after the Spanish conquest, are the largest group of Amazonian *indígenas,* counting 30,000–40,000 members. Two distinct subgroups, the Napu (Quijos) and the Canelos, fill western Napo and northern Pastaza provinces. Patrilineal groups of extended families called *ayllus* live in widely dispersed, permanent settlements that raise cattle and grow crops in communal *(llactas)* and family *(carutambo)* plots. Men hunt, fish, clear the land, and tend the cattle, while women weed, harvest, and care for the home *(huasi)* and garden plot *(chakra).*

Women also make the famous lowland Quechua pottery, an art that is passed down from mother to daughter. One subgroup, the Sarayacu, are especially well-known for creating striking white, red, and black images of gods such as Quilla Runa, the moon, who was banished to the sky for committing incest with his sister, and Pasu Supai Huarmi, the beautiful forest goddess with long dark hair, black lips, and teeth stained red from drinking the blood of her enemies. *Bancos,* or shamans, have adapted the Andean pantheon to the jungle, where spirits interact with humans in this world—called Yacu Pacha (the Dry World) with the Jahun Pacha (the sky, the World of Loneliness) above, and a world of water below.

The second-largest indigenous group in the Ecuadorian Amazon was once two separate tribes. Related by language with each other and tribes across the border into Perú, the **Shuar-Achuar** once sent fear into the hearts of children worldwide when they were known as the Jivaro, "Savages" who shrunk the heads of their enemies. For centuries the two closely related tribes have earned their tough reputation by protecting their rugged, isolated territory between the Pastaza and Marañón Rivers east of Cuenca. Their resistance started in 1527, when they sent Huayna Capac packing after his attempt to invade the Amazon—the Inca was forced to buy time with gifts as he fled. Soon after the first contact with the Spanish, the Achuar decided that the Europeans' thirst for gold was a disease. After capturing the town of Logroño, they poured molten gold down the governor's throat to satisfy his thirst for the metal.

Salesian missionaries helped the Shuar-Achuar found the first ethnic federation in the Ecuadorian Amazon in 1964. Today the groups, under the Shuar Federation and the Organization of Ecuadorian Achuar Nationalities, are among the best organized in the country. One reason for this was the ongoing border war with Peru, which pitted indigenous battalions against members of their own tribes across the border. They're still no one to be trifled with; a survey of the Achuar in 1993 found that 50 percent of tribe members' male ancestors had died from gunshot blasts—usually administered by other members. This gives them one of the highest murder rates of any population group in the world and helps explain the traditional Achuar greeting *Pujamik:* "Are you living?"

Many Shuar-Achuar still live in the traditional oval house called the *jea,* separated into male *(tankamash)* and female *(ekent)* zones. Crops such as yucca, papaya, sweet potato, and pineapple fill the gardens. The ceremonial process of creating *tsantstas* (shrinking heads) has faded, although the occasional unlucky sloth is still targeted. The fine-tuned Achuar calendar predicts everything from the rainy season to the breeding time of jungle insects. It's timed around the movement of the Pleiades, which they view as seven mythical orphans called the Musach who fled their despotic father for the heavens. The Pastaza river serves as the axis of the traditional Shuar world-view of the earth as hemispheres of earth and sky surrounded by water.

The **Huaorani** (Waorani) have recently entered the headlines in their fight against oil exploration, a struggle chronicled in Joe Kane's book *Savages.* They were one of the last groups contacted in the Ecuadorian Amazon and remain one of the least Westernized. Most of the tribe's 1,300 or so members live in a special reserve created for them in the shadow of Yasuní National Park, from the Napo to the Curaray Rivers. The Huaorani have started to abandon their nomadic ways and settle in small enclaves grouped by clan.

Men once wore only a *komi,* a small cord tying the penis to the belly, but Western clothing has

---

ANDEAN DREAM INTERPRETATIONS

When someone who is married dreams about shoes, they will be widowed soon.

If you dream of walking upward, it means your spirit is healthy and untroubled, and business matters are going well.

When one dreams of a house falling down, the owner of the house will die from disease or accident.

Dreams of large quantities of water mean acquaintances from far away will be visiting soon.

To dream of lizards is bad luck; to dream of corn is good luck.

Corpus Christi festival in Pujili

TIM BEWER

become popular. Both sexes still stretch their earlobes with balsa plugs called *dicago* up to five cm around. The Huaorani, once known by the pejorative Quechua term *aucas* (savages), have a reputation for defending their isolated autonomy with a fierceness equaled only perhaps by the Shuar. They are most well known for spearing five Summer Institute of Linguistics missionaries to death in 1956. As recently as 1987, a Roman Catholic bishop, who was visiting the tribe on a mission of friendship, was found with 17 spears in his body.

About 1,000 **Siona-Secoya** live a seminomadic existence along the Ríos Aguarico, Eno, Shushufindi, and Cuyabeno in Sucumbíos and eastern Napo province. The two groups, related in language and history to neighboring tribes across the border in Colombia, merged during the 20th century but have recently begun to maintain distinct ethnic identities. After oil exploration began to devastate their territory, the Sionas and Secoyas sued Texaco in 1993 for more than $1 billion for environmental abuses.

The **Cofán** (A'I), are the smallest remaining group, with about 600 members left from 20,000 at the Spanish conquest. They live along the Bermejo River in western Sucumbíos province. Randy Borman, son of an American missionary couple, grew up among the tribe and has become their de facto headman, leading them in their fight against oil exploration and encroachment by settlers. He also runs tours of the villages and the area.

RELIGION

Since the first conquistador planted a cross in honor of God and the King of Spain, Roman Catholicism has been a linchpin of Latin American culture. Where it once rivaled the government in its wealth and control of daily life, especially in education, however, the Church's role has moderated somewhat.

One of the most significant shifts occurred in the 1960s when the wave of Liberation Theology swept through Latin America. Priests who once encouraged the poor to accept their lot in life and hope for better treatment in heaven began to urge them to better themselves instead. Missionaries instituted literacy campaigns and helped fight for land reforms and social justice, to the horror and opposition of the more conservative elements of society.

Aside from Mass and annual festivals, the Church's influence is still felt in education, social services, and important occasions such as marriage, funerals, baptisms, and *quinceañeras,* a girl's coming-out celebration on her 15th birthday.

Protestantism continues to make inroads, particularly evangelical sects in the more remote areas of the country. Missionaries have been instrumental in contacting isolated tribes in the Amazon and recording their language and cultures—at the same time inevitably altering them. Indigenous religions are still firmly entrenched, although usually mixed with Catholicism, creating an intriguing combination of faiths. Other religions such as Mormonism (Latter-Day Saints), Judaism, and Baha'i have small enclaves.

EDUCATION

Primary schooling up to the age of 14 is free and compulsory, in theory. Many children in rural areas, however, lack the money for school supplies, without which they can't attend school (making pencils a good present to hand out to begging children if you must give something). Secondary schools are often private and/or religious, exist only in urban centers, and focus on foreign languages. A dozen state universities along the coast and in the Sierra are free, and there's a Catholic University in Quito. Private universities and technical schools have a tighter focus.

Ecuador has the highest literacy rate in South America—compulsory schooling was introduced here even before it was in Great Britain. In 1995 Ecuador's literacy rate was 90 percent, helped by government programs in rural areas where Spanish is often secondary to indigenous languages such as Quechua. Government spending on education has increased over the last few decades, and enrollment and retention rates have followed. Still, a frighteningly small percentage of rural children complete even primary schooling—only about one-third in some areas. Despite a tenfold increase in the number of professors from 1960–1980, qualified teachers are still in demand. Many Ecuadorians seek higher education abroad.

CUSTOMS AND CONDUCT

"There are three ways of doing things: the right way, the wrong way, and the South American way."

—Anonymous

Visitors from North America and Europe will sense it right away, although perhaps unconsciously at first: the slight undercurrent of looseness, bordering anarchy, that lies just beneath the surface in Latin American culture. It's the feeling of *"es la vida"* ("that's life"), emphasizing going with the flow even if things aren't always on your side, in contrast to the stubborn gringo reliance on rules and regulations.

Punctuality isn't nearly as ingrained here as it is in northern cultures. Showing up for an 8 P.M.

TEN GUIDELINES FOR TRAVEL IN EXOTIC PLACES

1. **Take more time to see less.** Get to know a few places and their inhabitants, instead of continually racing to your next destination.

2. **Don't surround yourself with a bubble of your own culture.** As tempting (and occasionally necessary) as it may be, you didn't come all this way to speak English and eat hamburgers, did you?

3. **Never leave home without:** Pepto-Bismol tablets, ear plugs, and a Swiss army knife.

4. **Take pictures of everyday life and people**—not just landmarks and scenery. Faces and daily details fade from memory the quickest.

5. **Learn at least some of the language of the place you're going, and use it.** It's the best way into a culture, and most people worth talking to appreciate any effort at all.

6. **Bring less than you think you should.** If you just might need it, you probably won't.

7. **Read about the history of your destination before you go.** One of the best ways to truly understand a culture is to learn how it became what it is.

8. **Take a break every so often.** Traveling is hard work—physically and mentally draining. Stay fresh and you'll enjoy it more.

9. **Bargain, if it's expected, but keep things in perspective.** Don't ruin anyone's day over a pittance, but don't leave the impression that tourists are easy prey, either.

10. **Every once in a while, put down the guidebook and just wander.** Pick a spot on a map that sounds interesting and go there. Welcome the unexpected.

POLITENESS, ECUADORIAN STYLE

Ludwig Bemelmans relates a story in *The Donkey Inside* that illustrates the humorous nature of the Latin American concern with politeness. An Armenian minister, after having a few too many drinks at a party, showed up at a nightclub wearing no pants. When a policeman tried to take him home, the minister started swinging. The next day the chief of police visited him at home with his hat in his hands.

The chief said: "I am a very busy man, I am perhaps too serious. So many things happen, stupid things, and everybody comes to me with their troubles. I think there was some trouble last night—I do not go out much, I do not know much of these places—I hear in a place called the Ermitage, and somebody—I have not heard the name—I think with perhaps a little too much to drink, comes there, without proper dress and there is a fight. Nothing's important—it happens all the time, it happens everywhere—but I wish people would not hit our policemen; it is so bad for the morale of the natives."

Then he left.

dinner date at 9:30 is common, and business hours owe more to the whim of the proprietor than the numbers written in the window.

Bureaucracy, usually in the form of the arbitrary enforcement of rules by some petty official, is the biggest downside of the South American way. Even Edward Whymper noticed it in the 19th century: "It is indeed true that nearly everything may be obtained in Ecuador. It is also true that we often had great difficulty obtaining anything." And Richard Poole in *The Inca Smiled* delivers a gratifying rant on the problem in eloquent British form. Ecuador, he states, is "divided into two clearly defined groups, those with authority and those without, and the former instinctively abuse the latter. . . . The tyrant behind the counter can only be appeased. He cannot be reasoned with, much less challenged."

It's true that the less authority someone has, the greater the potential he or she will abuse it, and usually at the worst possible time. But blowing your top won't help—in fact, it will often make things worse. As with playground bullies, the best strategy is to ignore the larval bureaucrat if possible and play along if you must. But be warned that even this diplomatic approach might not do any good. Poole continues: "Legitimate queries and claims are dismissed with callous disregard, in government offices they feed you the wrong information deliberately, and then insult you for bringing in the wrong papers and wasting their precious time. Then they instruct you to come back the next day knowing full well that the office will be closed."

The window of opportunity can work in your favor, though, if you know how to take advantage of it. "Ecuadorians find it hard to put regulations above people's needs," concedes Poole, and it's true. If you find yourself up against a wall, be patient, smile, and say, "Well, what can we do about this?" (*¿Pues, qué podemos hacer?*), and you might be surprised to find things shift in your favor.

Politeness

Latin Americans are much more physical in day-to-day interactions than their northern neighbors. Although public pawing is looked down on, you'll soon get used to the *abrazo*, a platonic hug and peck on the cheek when being introduced to people of the opposite sex. Even complete strangers are always given an *Hola* (hello), *¿Como está?* (how's it going?), or *Buenos días/tardes/noches* (good day/afternoon/night) when passed on the street.

Latin American politeness is very nonconfrontational, occasionally to the point of suppressing personal feelings (see the special topic, "Politeness, Ecuadorian Style"). You'll rarely see one Ecuadorian asking another to stop smoking, turn down a radio, or control a rampant child.

Hospitality

Henri Michaux said it best: "The Ecuadorian is not simply hospitable in an unheard-of style. He actually enjoys giving. On a boat the Ecuadorian will treat the whole ship to a drink. And it hurts him very much not to be able to invite by radio all the ships going in his direction to draw up alongside." The trick for foreigners is determining when the invitation is "real," or firm in a non-Latin sense. Ecuadorians will ask you left and right to come to their homes, meet their families, stay for as long as you like, and if you show up they'll make good on the offer. But this doesn't always mean they expect you to, which can lead to a slight social strain when offers are taken too literally. You'll have to feel out and set your own limits for accepting hospitality, and try to think of the offers as polite rather than false.

The Sexes

Latin American culture is very sexually polarized. Men are still the traditional head of the household, bringing home the bacon and laying down the law. Women manage the home and raise the children, which simultaneously earns them the highest respect and keeps them chained to the kitchen sink. Recently, though, Latin American women have begun to realize the power inherent in this position and are breaking into new freedoms in work and daily life.

Feminism came late to Ecuador: in 1979 president Jaime Roldos' wife Martha was the first prominent Ecuadorian feminist and the first woman ever to serve in the country's cabinet. The challenges women face are clear. Female beauty is overwhelmingly emphasized (an attractive woman can turn every male head within 100 meters faster than a traffic accident), women receive lower salaries than men and none at all for housework, and male dominance runs through society from top to bottom. Women find themselves in a split position in Latin society—both elevated on a platform as the saintly wife/mother figure and looked down upon and protected as the "weaker sex." Equal rights, recognition of the value of running the household, and advancements in family planning and reproductive choice are among the many goals of feminism.

The culprit? *Machismo,* the cartoon version of masculinity that gives rise to sayings such as *Mas gana el hombre silbando que la mujer hilando* ("There's more profit in a man whistling than in a woman spinning"). And whistle they do, although obviously not all men—mostly those suffering from a sense of socioeconomic impotence. *Machismo* manifests itself in ways ranging from subtle to blatant. Whistles and catcalls are seen as "harmless"; a double standard of marital fidelity accepts sneaking around by men but condemns it for women; and spouse abuse is often swept under the carpet. Men find themselves having to prove their manhood in their posturing, driving, womanizing, and extreme events such as Sangolqui's bullfight, where something's missing until someone gets seriously hurt.

Dealing with *machismo* as a foreigner can be tricky. Realize that it's a part of the culture, but don't let it pass unchallenged. Women may be frustrated that silence is often the best weapon, whereas men will find that confronting another man about his sexist ideology may provoke a thoughtful response.

IS THERE A TRASH CAN AROUND HERE?

The sign on the bus reads "Please throw garbage out the window." Trash cans are about as rare as short lunch breaks in Ecuador. Ticket sellers in the Quito bus terminal laugh when asked for a *basurero* (garbage can): "This is Ecuador!" Just because many Ecuadorians think nothing about tossing garbage on the floor or out the window, it doesn't mean you have to follow suit. Hold on to your *basura* (garbage) until you find a waste receptacle, and try to minimize your output of disposable packaging. Don't take a *bolsita* (little bag) with every purchase, though you'll be offered one, and drink the next soda from a recycled glass bottle instead of a plastic one.

BOB RACE

ON THE ROAD
SPORTS AND RECREATION

MOUNTAINEERING

There aren't many countries where you can reach the base of an ice-capped volcano in a day from the capital, make it to the summit by the next morning, and be back in your hotel by nightfall. In Ecuador you can do that with eight of the country's ten highest peaks, including one over 20,000 feet, as long as you're prepared and lucky with the weather. It's a great country to gain experience in high-altitude mountaineering without the usual toll in sweat and tears. Guiding services are numerous, and competition keeps prices down. With plenty of easy routes, several difficult ones, and even a few new routes waiting to be tackled, Ecuador is a climber's playground.

One magazine article based on Ecuador's mountain routes is titled "High and Mild," which sums up the country's mountaineering well. Many of the towering, ice-topped volcanic peaks are relatively easy to climb. Beginning mountaineers will find the country an excellent training ground for even higher, more difficult ascents elsewhere, but there's still enough challenging climbing to keep veterans busy for years.

Most of the major peaks along the Avenue of the Volcanoes have roads leading close to or even partway up their bases, and the ascents themselves are usually straightforward. Modest technical gear will do for the Big Three—Chimborazo, Cotopaxi, and Cayambe—whose huts and summits overflow with climbers during busy weekends in the peak season.

Other peaks aren't as welcoming. El Altar, probably the most difficult in the country, wasn't climbed until 1963. Even the "easy" ones can turn deadly in an instant. An avalanche on Easter Sunday in 1996 buried the shelter atop Cotopaxi, killing 11 visitors. Never underestimate the mountains.

In the end, though, there is no substitute for **up-to-the-minute information** and the services of a **trained guide.** An overwhelming majority of climbers killed in Ecuador were climbing without a locally trained guide. Conditions and routes vary drastically from year to year, even day to day. If you're hesitant, heed the voice and hire a qualified guide, or at the very least arm yourself with the latest reports on the mountain you plan to tackle. Remember: As many climbers fall victim to not knowing when to turn back as anything else.

Climbing History

Indigenous people undoubtedly climbed a few of Ecuador's peaks long before the advent of crampons, helmets, or even the printing press. Incan *pucaras* (stone forts) were built as high as 4,075 meters. José Ortiguerra's 1582 ascent of Guagua Pichincha was Ecuador's first official peak-bagging, and in 1735 the French expedition led by Charles-Marie de La Condamine concluded that Chimborazo was the highest peak in the world—probably when they decided to turn around at about 4,700 meters. The equator-measuring team surveyed many of the highest volcanoes and managed to climb Guagua Pichincha and Corazón.

Alexander von Humboldt's 1802 visit made Ecuador synonymous with volcanoes. The German naturalist made it to 5,900 meters on Chimborazo before being turned back by crevasses. The snow-covered giant also shrugged off many expeditions in the 19th century, including one in 1822 that brought Simón Bolívar to the snowline. Most of Ecuador's toughest mountains fell in 1879 and 1880 to Edward Whymper and a pair of Italian cousins named the Carrels. The trio made it to the summits of Cayambe, Antisana, Iliniza Sur, Cotacachi, and Chimborazo, and Whymper topped Cotopaxi twice for good measure. Along the way he conducted scientific studies on geology, natural habitats, and acclimatization.

Ecuador's first great mountaineer, Nicolás Martínez, was the first to stand atop Iliniza Norte in 1912. In the 10 years previous, he had become the first national to climb Tungurahua, Antisana, Cotopaxi, and Chimborazo. All-weather refuges (see the special topic, "Mountain Refuges") began appearing in the 1960s as climbing's economic (and danger) potential was realized.

Climbing Weather

Although climatic conditions differ among regions, December and January are generally the best months to climb. Coastal weather patterns influence the Western Cordillera, making June–Sept. dry and clear and perfect for climbing. December and January tend to see good snow conditions and weather as well. Feb.–May are the wettest months in the Western Cordillera.

Warm air from the Oriente brings heavy precipitation to the Eastern Cordillera, including El Alter, Antisana, Sangay, Tungurahua, and Cayambe, from June–Aug. This side of the Andes is driest in December and January, and occasionally passable as early as October and as late as February.

MOUNTAINEERING SPANISH

altitude sickness... *soroche*
ascent/ascend .... *subida/subir, escalar, ascender*
avalanche .... *avalancha, torrente*
bivouac .... *vivac*
boots .... *botas*
carabiner......... *mosqueton*
crampons .... *grampones*
crevasse .... *grieta*
descend.......... *descendir, bajar*
east .... *este/oriente*
evacuate,
evacuation........ *evacuar, evacuación*
fall .... *caer*
gaiters .... *polainas*
glacier .... *glaciar*
guide .... *guía*
harness .... *arnés*
hut .... *refugio*
ice axe........... *piolet*
ice screw......... *tornillo*
knot .... *nudo (to tie: amarrar)*
ledge .... *repisa*
moraine.......... *morena*
mountaineer ...... *andinista*
mountaineering.... *andinismo*
needle .... *aguja*
north .... *norte*
overhang......... *techo*
pass............. *paso*
peak............. *pico*
rappel .... *rapelar*
rope .... *cuerda*
route .... *ruta*
self-arrest .... *frenar en la nieve*
sling............. *cinta*
south .... *sur*
summit........... *cima, cumbre*
tent............. *carpa*
west............. *oeste/occidente*

ECUADOR'S MOUNTAIN HIGHS

Opinions differ on the exact heights of many of Ecuador's loftiest peaks. The following figures come from the most trustworthy source—1979 Instituto Geográfico Militar (IGM) surveys.

MOUNTAIN	HEIGHT (METERS)	VOLCANIC ACTIVITY	SNOW
Chimborazo	6,310	No	Yes
Cotopaxi	5,897	Yes	Yes
Cayambe	5,790	No	Yes
Antisana	5,704	Yes	Yes
El Altar	5,319	Yes	No
Iliniza Sur	5,263	No	Yes
Sangay	5,230	Yes	Yes
Iliniza Norte	5,126	No	No
Carihuairazo	5,020	No	Yes
Tungurahua	5,016	Yes	Yes
Cotacachi	4,939	No	Little
Guagua Pichincha	4,794	No	No
Corazón	4,788	No	No
Chiles	4,768	No	Occasional
Rumiñahui	4,712	No	Occasional
Rucu Pichincha	4,700	No	Occasional
Atacazo	4,410	No	No
Pasachoa	4,200	No	No

Training Climbs

Several peaks are good starters for acclimatizing and getting into shape with a minimum of special equipment or training. Pasachoa, Guagua Pichincha, Imbabura, Cotacachi, Corazón, and Atacazo can all be done in a day. Iliniza Norte requires a night in the refuge but can often be done in hiking boots (take an ice axe and crampons if it has snowed recently). Rumiñahui occasionally requires snow-climbing equipment as well and may involve spending the night on the way up, depending on whether you have your own transportation or not. Tungurahua is similar in difficulty to Rumiñahui, but don't even think about tackling it until the eruption alert is lifted.

Equipment

Specialized mountain gear, such as hard plastic boots, crampons, rope, helmets, and ice axes, can be rented from various shops in Quito. An ice hammer, ice screws, and snow stakes are necessary for the snowier peaks. Refuges make tents unnecessary, but bring your own sleeping pad and a 20°C sleeping bag. For warmth, a down jacket can't be beat when combined with a balaclava, gloves, and thermal underwear. Waterproof outer layers, gaiters, and dark climber's glasses with side light guards complete the outfit.

Because snow climbing is done at night, when the snow is hardest, a headlamp is essential, as are ski poles for balance and support and a camp stove for cooking in huts without stoves. A medical kit should include a low-reading thermometer for hypothermia, glacier cream or zinc oxide for the high-altitude sun, and inflatable splints or at least Ace bandages for falls and sprains. Topographical maps are available from the Instituto Geográfico Militar in Quito.

Guides

An experienced, responsible guide can make the difference between success and failure—and life and death—in the thin air and unpredictable conditions of Ecuador's highest peaks. It's easy to underestimate the task at hand or overestimate your own abilities, twin errors that kill novice and veteran climbers alike around the world. A guide is essential for your first few ascents of snow-capped mountains.

Guided climbs typically include any necessary equipment, transportation to the base, an overnight and meals in a hut, and a guide who will take you to the peak or decide if conditions merit a hasty retreat. For this you'll pay anywhere from $90–320 pp, depending on the mountain, the season, and how many people are in the group. Inexpensive operators may not have the skills, experience, or motivation to deal with extreme situations such as crevasse rescues or emergency evacuation for altitude sickness. All guides should be licensed by the ASEGUIM, Ecuador's official mountain-guide association, which also organizes emergency rescues. Smaller groups are better because large groups increase the odds of someone succumbing to altitude sickness or injury, in which case everyone has to turn around. A ratio of two or three clients per guide is recommended. See individual city listings for local guides (nationwide operators are listed in the Quito chapter).

Foreign Climbing Guides
Earth Treks, 7125-C Columbia Gateway Drive, Columbia, MD 21046, 800/CLIMB-UP, 410/872-0060, fax 410/872-0064, e-mail: etreks@ charm.net, ww.earthtreksclimbing.com, have been leading highly recommended climbing trips to Ecuador since 1992. A two-week trip up Cotopaxi, Antisana, and Chimborazo is $2,400 pp, and a one-week climb of Cotopaxi is $1,450. The **American Alpine Institute,** 1515 12th St., Bellingham, WA 98225, 360/671-1505, e-mail: info@aai.cc, www.mtnguide.com, offers climbs of Cayambe, Cotopaxi, Chimborazo, Antisana, Iliniza Sur, and El Altar ranging from 10–15 days and costing $1,690–4,460 pp, not including airfare.

A 12-day trip up Cotopaxi and Chimborazo with **Timberline Mountain Guides, Inc.,** P.O. Box 1167, Bend, OR 97709, 541/312-9242, fax 541/312-9225, e-mail: info@timberlinemt guides.com, www.timberlinmtnguides. com, costs $2,800 pp. **Southwest Adventures,** P.O. Box 3242, Durango, CO 81302, 800/642-5389, 970/259-0370, e-mail: mtnguide@frontier.net, www.mtnguide.net, offer guided climbs up Cayambe, Cotopaxi, and Chimborazo for $1,895–2,595 pp, as well as a nine-day mountaineering school in Ecuador for $1,495 pp.

If you have it in you to tackle Fuya Fuya, Rumiñahui, Cotopaxi, and Chimborazo in two weeks, it will cost you $2,395 with **Camp 5 Expeditions,** 9 Exchange Place, Suite 900, Salt Lake City, UT 84111, 800/914-3834, fax 801/534-0515, e-mail: info@camp5.com, www.camp5.com. Rodrigo Mujica, an international guide with more than two decades' worth of experience, founded **Adventuras Patagonicas** in 1989. Their two-week expedition up Cayambe, Cotopaxi, and Chimborazo is $2,800 pp. Contact them at P.O. Box 11389, Jackson Hole, WY 83002, 888/203-9354, 307/734-5201, fax 307/732-0281, e-mail: climb@patagonicas .com, www.patagonicas.com.

Resources
Montañas del Sol, by Marcos Serrano, Iván Rojas, Freddy Landázuri, (Quito: Campo Abierto, 1994), is a small Spanish guide to Ecuador's major peaks with route descriptions and photos. Jorge Anhalzer's series of detailed individual mountain guides are available in Quito. Other books on climbing in Ecuador, including various historical accounts listed in the Resources section at the back of the book, are available from **Chessler Books,** P.O. Box 4359, 29723 Troutdale Scenic Drive, Evergreen, CO 80437, 800/654-8502, 303/670-0093, fax 303/670-9727, e-mail: chesslerbk@aol.com, www. chesslerbooks.com; and **The Mountaineers Books,** 1001 SW Klickitat Way, Suite 201, Seattle, WA 98134, 800/553-4453, fax 800/568-7604, mountaineersbooks.org. The most up-to-date information is available from the South American Explorers' Quito clubhouse, climbing clubs in Quito, or guides themselves.

HIKING AND CAMPING

With boots, backpack, tent, and sleeping bag, you're ready to explore just about any part of Ecuador's spectacular countryside. Even if all you brought is tough footwear, it's amazing how much lies within reach of a day hike, even from major cities. Longer trips can bring you to places accessible only by foot in the high Andes and remote jungle.

Parks and reserves are the most popular areas for camping, and the only ones with organized, maintained campsites. Park entrance fees range from $5–20 on the mainland (the Galápagos cost $100 to enter). Information is available from many branches of the Ecuadorian National Park agency.

Outside the reserves you'll have to find your own campsites, often on private property. This is usually no problem; just ask permission first. Camping near a house may discourage thieves. Avoid military zones, especially in the Oriente and along the coast. Keep your valuables in your sleeping bag with you, and don't leave anything

MOUNTAIN REFUGES

MOUNTAIN	COOKING FACILITIES	STORAGE	TOILETS	SLEEPING SPACES	RUNNING WATER	PRICE (PP)	CONTACT
Cayambe	Yes	Yes	Yes	25	Yes	US$10	Alta Montaña (Quito), tel. 2/254-798
Chimborazo	Yes	Yes	Yes	45	Yes	US$10	Alta Montaña (Riobamba), tel. 3/942-215
Cotopaxi	Yes	Yes	Yes	70	Yes	US$10	Alta Montaña (Quito) tel. 2/254-798
Guagua Pichincha	Yes	No	Yes	10	Yes	US$5	Defensa Civil in Quito
Ilinizas	Yes	No	No	13	Yes	US$7	Vladimir Gallo tel. 2/314-927
Tungurahua	Yes	No	Yes	15	Yes	US$7	n/a

behind if you go hiking during the day. You may be able to find shelter in a *tambo,* one of many small, thatched huts used by *campesinos* for emergency shelter in the Andes. Try and secure permission from the owner beforehand if you can.

Bring everything you think you may need from home; camping and hiking equipment in Ecuador tends toward high prices and low quality (although good hiking boots like Hi-Tec and Timberland are available at various shopping centers in Quito and Guayaquil). Water purification is essential, either through a filter or iodine tablets. Even day hikers should always carry 1–2 liters of water, snack food, warm and waterproof layers of clothing, a flashlight, at least a minimal first-aid kit, and either a map or compass (better yet, both). Never leave for a trip without telling someone where you're going, your approximate route, and when you expect to be back.

RAFTING AND KAYAKING

River running is just starting to take off in Ecuador, but you'd be hard-pressed to find a better country for it. Experienced paddlers describe the kayaking in Ecuador as some of the best they've seen anywhere, waxing rhapsodic about wide, brown rivers that wind through thick, green foliage and precipitous gorges before suddenly erupting into Class IV white water. The water is warm, the scenery is gorgeous, and the rivers are so easily accessible that it's a wonder this place isn't overrun yet with paddlers.

Guides in Quito and Tena can take you on day trips or weeklong expeditions. With some experience and your own equipment, you may be able to tackle many of the country's best runs on your own. The upper section of rivers in the Andes offer difficult, technical Class V runs best left to expert kayakers. As they flow downward and pick up volume, the flows become mellower but rapids can still be continuous, requiring sustained effort ("cardiovascular kayaking," as one paddler puts it) to manage the hours of Class III and IV white water. The eastern slope of the Andes is less polluted and more remote than the western slope.

Rivers

The **Río Blanco** is the most frequently run in Ecuador, in part because it's so close to the capital. Much of the 200 raftable km of white water in the Blanco valley can be seen in a day trip, which often starts in the Toachi. After navigating the technical Class III–IV run, including the notorious

El Sapo canyon, rafters enter the Upper Blanco for 47 km of sustained Class III–IV rapids in four hours—probably the most white water you'll ever hit in a day. Kayakers, if they're still hungry for more, can take on the Ríos Mindo (Class III–IV), Saloya (IV–V), Pilaton (IV–V), and the upper Toachi (IV–V), depending on the time of year and their ability.

Within a half hour's drive of the town of El Chaco, the "white water playground" of the **Río Quijos** offers everything from Class II white water near the Antisana Reserve to steep Class IV–V streams as it drops through narrow rock canyons. Rafters head for the main Quijos (Class III–V), and kayakers tackle the Papallacta (V), Cosanga (III–IV), and Oyacachi (IV) tributaries.

As it runs from Puerto Libre to Lumbaquí, the upper **Río Aguarico** has large Class II–III rapids within two hours of Lago Agrio. To the south the clear **Río Due** tributary flows off Volcán Reventador in Class III–IV rapids.

Near Tena, the **Río Napo** and its tributaries offer enough variety to let you paddle a different river every day for a week. The most popular trip in the area is the Class III Upper Napo, but the Class IV **Río Misahualli** is considered the prize. It's subject to sudden, extreme changes in water level but still draws paddlers with its jungle setting and the hairy portage around Casanova Falls.

Kayakers have a longer list of possibilities, including parts of the **Ríos Misahualli, Jondachi, Anzu,** and **Hollin,** which tend to stick around Class IV–V when there's enough water to ride. The **Río Patate** is run out of Baños, but pollution, the eruption of Volcán Tungurahua, and the death of four tourists here in the late 1990s have lessened its popularity. Some expert kayakers have called the **Río Ropo** (Class V) the best steep creek run in Ecuador, and they talk in hushed tones about the magnificent Namangosa Gorge of the **Río Upano** (Class IV) lined with primary rainforest and 100-meter waterfalls.

Choosing a Tour

Rafting and kayaking is a nascent sport in Ecuador, without any official safety or training regulations for guides and tour operators. When shopping around, look for experienced guides and new equipment in good condition. Ask about guides' rafting, rescue, and first-aid training, and make sure each trip has safety and first-aid equipment and repair kits. Safety kayakers and on-river emergency communications should also be mandatory.

The few reliable companies in the country are run by foreign or foreign-trained Ecuadorian guides. Steve Nomchong's Yacu Amu Rafting in Quito and Gynner Coronel's Ríos Ecuador in Tena are the best. Both offer day trips, longer excursions, and instruction courses to introduce newcomers to the thrills of white water.

When To Go

Most commercial companies run during the dry season from Oct.–Feb., when air temperatures are comfortable and water levels are reasonable but still challenging. The rainy season from Mar.–Sept. brings high flows and continuous white water that are more suited to expert kayakers.

Resources

River Odysseys West, Inc. (Remote Odysseys Worldwide), P.O. Box 579, Coeur d'Alene, ID 83816, 800/451-6034, 208/765-0841, fax 208/667-6506, e-mail: rowgorp@aol.com, www.gorp.com/row.htm, made the first commercial descent of the Río Upano in 1992. Eleven-day trips down the Upano are $2,195–2,495 pp. **Earth River,** 180 Towpath Rd., Accord, NY 12404, 800/643-2784, 914/626-2663, fax 914/626-4423, e-mail: earthriv@ulster.net, www.earthriver.com, also runs the Upano for $1,900 for a 12-day descent. (Prices do not include airfare to Ecuador.)

Small World Adventures, 1675 Larimer #735, Denver, CO 81233, 800/58-KAYAK (585-2925), e-mail: info@smallworldadventures.com, www.smallworldadventures.com, organize trips on the Ríos Quijos, Cosanga, Misahualli, Jatunyacu and Jondachi for around $1,500 pp per week. They also publish the small, but detailed *Kayaker's Guide to Ecuador,* which is available from them by mail order ($16.50) or in Quito at the Crossroads Cafe and Hostal.

SURFING

With 2,237 km of Pacific coastline, it's no surprise that plenty of tasty waves brush Ecuador's western fringe. Guayas province has the most well known breaks, especially the area from the tip of the Santa Elena Peninsula and north. Even though it lost a sizable chunk of its beach to the 1997–1998 El Niño, Montañita is still the biggest surfer hangout in the country. Manta and Bahía de Caráquez in Manabí province also see some action, whereas Esmeraldas province to the north is less explored. Quality tubes can even be found in the Galápagos.

The best months for large swells and little wind are Dec.–May. Warm shore currents mean wetsuits aren't necessary except in the Galápagos, but aqua sox are a good idea to protect your feet against lava rocks and spiny creatures. A few shops rent and sell boards, but bring your own if you have one. Some breaks in Guayas province are on military land; if you're polite and show your passport, you shouldn't have a problem.

The best resource for surfing in Ecuador is *The Surf Report,* published by Surfer Publications, P.O. Box 1028, Dana Point, CA 92629, 714/496-5922, fax 714/496-7849. Two reports have detailed information on Ecuadorian breaks: Vol. 15, no. 7 (July 1994) covers the mainland, and Vol. 10, no. 7 (July 1989) deals with the Galápagos. Each costs $6 and is updated periodically.

FISHING

Take some fishing tackle on your hikes into the high Sierra, and with minimal effort and luck you'll reel in some of the rainbow trout that have been introduced throughout the highlands (with an as-

yet unknown impact on native ecosystems). In the Oriente, a simple line and hook baited with meat is enough to catch the infamous piranha, a small bony fish with nasty chompers. It'll take a bit more to bring in a 90-kg *baigre* (catfish) from the muddy rivers, but the delicious meat makes it worth it. Deep-sea charters off the central coast yield black marlin, sailfish, tuna, and bonito.

WILDLIFE VIEWING

The Galápagos Islands are legendary for their unique, fearless species. Birds and animals on the mainland won't come up and nuzzle your leg, but with persistence, patience, and luck you may glimpse an example or two of Ecuador's stunning biological diversity.

Wildlife viewing is easier when you're not pinning all your hopes on what biologists call "charismatic megafauna" (i.e., big, pretty animals). These poster children of the natural world are rare and shy, especially in a country as full of people as Ecuador, so it's possible to be in the wild for months without meeting a spectacled bear, condor, or dwarf mountain deer. (Monkeys, on the other hand, are fairly common in the Oriente.) It's not impossible, but don't plunk down your money for a jungle trip expecting jaguars behind every tree; if that's what you're here for, you'll be disappointed. If you arrive willing to appreciate the bugs, birds, and buds that press on every side, though, your experience

parrot

JULIAN SMITH

will be incredibly rewarding. Think of the big ones as icing on the cake.

To maximize your chances of seeing anything—large or small—the best strategy is to sit still, be quiet, and wait. It's amazing what pokes its head or feelers out once you allow yourself to blend into the background after a few minutes or an hour. Most creatures try to avoid the heat of the day, making dawn and dusk especially good times for wildlife viewing. The jungle is like downtown Manhattan in terms of activity: the interesting characters really come out and play after dark. Many lodges offer guided nighttime hikes or canoe trips, with high-powered flashlights to catch the iridescent eyes of nocturnal creatures.

A small, tough pair of binoculars can be well worth the extra weight for backcountry ventures and are essential in the Galápagos.

Birding

Ecuador is one of the premier countries for birding in the world, hands down. With almost 1,600 recorded species of birds—twice as many as all of Europe—Ecuador has the highest avian diversity of any region its size on the continent. An incredible range of habitats shelter many endemic species (those found nowhere else).

It's almost futile to list the best regions in the country because they're all great. It's almost guaranteed you'll see new species every day anywhere in the Oriente. The western slope of the Andes is especially diverse, including the area around Mindo near Quito and the northern lowlands near the Hotel Tinalandia and the Río Palenque Biological Station. Southwest Ecuador, including Podocarpus National Park, is rich in endemic and endangered species.

Many parks and lodges offer checklists for nearby species. Guides to Ecuadorian birds are listed in "Books" in the Resources Section. Cornell University Press published Greenfield and Ridgely's two-volume *Birds of Ecuador* in 2001. Another good source for bird books and bird-call tapes on Ecuador and the Galápagos is the **Los Angeles Audubon Society Bookstore,** 7377 Santa Monica Blvd., West Hollywood, CA 90046-6694, 888/522-7428, 323/876-0685, fax 323/876-7609, e-mail: books@ laaudubon.org, www.laaudubon.org/ bookstore/bookstore.html.

Some of the tour companies listed in the Quito chapter have birding tours, particularly those that operate in the Mindo area. Several foreign tour companies focus on birds, led by **Victor Emanuel Nature Tours,** 800/328-VENT, fax 512/328-2919, e-mail: info@ventbird.com, www.ventbird.com, who offer half a dozen different birding tours throughout Ecuador. As an example, their 16-day Amazon and Andes tour runs $3,995 pp from Quito. They also do birding cruises of the Amazon and the Galápagos.

Wings, 1643 N. Alvernon, Ste. 105, Tucson, AZ 85712, 888/293-6443, 520/320-9868, 520/320-9373, e-mail: wings@wingsbirds.com, www.wingsbirds.com, have been leading international birding tours for almost 30 years. They have four tours to Ecuador, including a 14-day trip to southern Ecuador for $3,000 pp. **Field Guides Inc.,** 9433 Bee Cave Road, Bldg. 1, Ste. 150, Austin, TX 78733, 800/728-4953, 512/263-7295, fax 512/263-0117, e-mail: fieldguides@fieldguides.com, www.fieldguides.com, offer eight birding trips to Ecuador and the Galápagos, including a 10-day tour focusing on hummingbirds.

OTHER RECREATION

Ecuador's tortured topography makes **cycling** an arduous but rewarding way to experience the country. Various tour companies and private operators in major cities rent bikes and organize cycling trips in the Sierra. (See "By Bicycle" in the "Getting Around" section for more information on riding in Ecuador.) The vertical landscapes *are* conducive to **paragliding,** a sport that has recently taken off in the Sierra.

Before the introduction of cars and trains, everyone who could afford it got around on **horseback.** Today many people still do, and renting horses on your own or in a guided trip is a great way to see the countryside up close. Guided horseback tours cost approximately $25 for four hours.

The incredible sealife of the Galápagos makes the islands among the world's best spots for **scuba diving** and **snorkeling.** A few agencies in Puerto Ayora offer diving certification and rent snorkeling gear (an indispensable part of any island tour). Machalilla Park's Isla de la Plata is one of the few places to snorkel off the mainland.

SPORTS

Soccer *(fútbol)* is a Latin American passion and Ecuador's national game. Informal matches pop up on makeshift fields in the most improbable places: at the edge of a steep drop-off in the Sierra, or on a patch of cleared jungle with bamboo goalposts in the Amazon. Players on local teams compete fiercely for the chance to rise into the big leagues and play internationally.

Ecuavolley, the local version of volleyball, gathers larger afternoon crowds than just about any other sport in the country. (See the special topic, "Ecuavolley.")

Another sport particular to Ecuador is *pelota de guante* (glove ball), a strange-looking game played with a rubber ball and spiked paddles of heavy wood. Some authorities say the game has its roots in the Basque regions of Spain, whereas others say it has been played in Ecuador since well before the Spanish arrived.

Even small towns have pits for **cockfights** *(palea de gallos),* whose participants defend the sport by rationalizing that at least the losers end up in the cooking pot. Fiestas are the best times to catch **bullfights** *(corrida de toros),* which are held in *plazas de toro* (bullrings) throughout the high-lands. Be warned that inexperienced local matadors often lack the skill to make a clean kill. Other more pedestrian pastimes include **basketball** *(basquet),* **golf, polo,** and **billiards** *(billares).*

ECUAVOLLEY

It looks familiar—players grunt and dive to keep a ball airborne over a high net—but watching a few minutes will show you that Ecuador's take on volleyball is a unique sport in itself. Three players per side, instead of the usual six, makes defense all the more difficult and placement crucial; far-corner tips keep players running. A nine-foot net shifts the game's focus from flashy spikes to patient strategy, especially when you consider that most of the players are under 5' 8" tall. Palming the ball momentarily is legal, making split-second fake-outs and pinpoint redirections both important strategies.

The *principal* is the main offensive player, giving the team most of its points as well as its name. Lots of money can change hands over a single game, and as a result tempers flare over disputed calls and audience heckling. In poorer barrios, Ecuavolley can be played with as little as an old soccer ball and a rope tied over a patch of dirt.

Ecuadorian immigrants to the United States have brought their game with them; they've set up nets and leagues in larger cities. An Ecuadorian crowd has gathered in Riverside Park in New York City most warm weekends since 1973, coming from Queens and the Bronx to wager anywhere from tens to hundreds of dollars per player on matches. This is where you'll hear the well-worn story of the three cocky Americans who showed up one day, ready to wreak havoc on the shorter, dark-skinned regulars. Game after game the newcomers were crushed, unable to judge where the other team was going to send the ball.

ARTS AND ENTERTAINMENT

THE ARTS

Visual Arts

Early colonial sculptors and painters remained anonymous, remembered only by their gloomy but heartfelt images of the Virgin and saints in a Gothic style. Indigenous influences began to emerge with the push of the Renaissance and Baroque styles, allowing artists such as Gaspar Sangurima, Manuel Chili (a.k.a. Caspicara), and Miguel de Santiago more freedom for personal expression in their works.

The Quito School, spanning the 17th and 18th centuries, typified a new realism in Ecuadorian art. Only the extreme would convince the faithful: Jesus had to suffer more than average citizens in everyday life, and Mary had to be more radiant than anyone around. The 19th century brought "popular" art to the fore. Concerned with the secular as much as the holy, it consisted of intense colors and naturalistic images of landscapes and common people. This was followed in the 20th century by the reverberations of Impressionism and Cubism.

Powerful representations of the dignity and suffering of Ecuador's original inhabitants dominated the work of Ecuadorians Eduardo Kingman (1913–1999), Camilio Egas (1889–1962), Olga Fisch (1901–1990), and Manuel Rendón (1884–?). Before his death, Oswaldo Guayasamin (1919–1999) was probably Ecuador's most famous modern artist. His tortured, distorted figures, heavily influenced by Cubism, earned him the label "Americanista Picasso," while his landscapes of Quito and series of mother and child works are among the most beautiful in Quito's museums.

A school of "naïve" painting centered in the Tigua Valley in the central Andes began with images painted on ceremonial drums. Now the miniature paintings are made on animal skin stretched over a wood frame. Quality varies widely, but the better ones are true works of art—vibrantly detailed depictions of everyday life in the *campo*.

Music

The haunting melodies and wistful lyrics of the Ecuadorian Andes are played by groups throughout the highlands, from brass bands to guitar trios and lone crooners on street corners. Flutes were considered holy by the Inca, who provided the original set of instruments and tunes for modern-day Andean music. The *quena*, a vertical flute once made from condor leg bones, is used to play the melody, along with panpipes such as the *rondador* and *zampoña*. Bass drums made from hollow logs or clay are used to keep the beat, with the help of various rattles and bells.

The colonial Spanish tried their best to suppress indigenous music (to the point of an outright ban by the archbishop of Lima), but in the end only succeeded in adding a host of new instruments. Relatives of the guitar include the 10-stringed *charango*, originally from Bolivia and made from armadillo shells. The *charango* is strummed lustily next to *bandolinas* (15 strings) and familiar-looking *guitarras* with six nylon strings. Violins, clarinets, accordions, harmonicas, mandolins, and brass instruments were used to join in the fun along the way, and modern influence has added electric amplifiers, microphones, and the rhythms of salsa, merengue, and rock.

Along the coast you'll find some of the most African-influenced music on the continent. Rhythms such as marimba and the Caribbean-flavored *cumbia* from Colombia make it almost impossible not to move your hips while listening, especially to bands along the northernmost coast and up the valley of the Río Chota into the northern Sierra. Half the fun is the attitude: during the bottle dance, young women gyrate in front of male partners with an open bottle of liquor on their heads without spilling a drop.

Literature

Ecuadorian writers of the 20th century have focused on realistic social themes of injustice and race. Jorge Icaza's *Huasipungo* (The Villagers) (1934) is considered one of Ecuador's best novels, vividly portraying the hardships of everyday life in an indigenous village. *Cumandá* by Juan León Mera, written in the 19th century, is still popular with book-buyers as well.

Philosopher and essayist Juan Montalvo wrote *Los Siete Tratados* and *Capitulos Que Se Le Olviadaron a Cervantes* (Chapters Cervantes Forgot to Write), and José Joaquín de Olmedo eulogized the struggles for independence in *The Victory of Junín* and *Song of Bolívar*. Adalberto Ortiz's *Juyungo* (1942) deals with the lives of poor blacks in Esmeraldas. Jorge Carrera Andrade, from Cuenca, is one of the country's best-known poets for his *Place of Origin*.

FESTIVALS AND PUBLIC HOLIDAYS

Sometimes it seems like you could hop around Ecuador from fiesta to fiesta for an entire year. These celebrations come in many different flavors. Historical and political holidays commemorate famous generals, battles, and independence anniversaries, and can range from nationwide parties to special days for individual towns. Religious holidays combine the solemnity of Catholic processions and services with *chicha*-for-everyone indigenous festivals. After a day or two of this festivity, the streets are so filled with costumed revelers that no one's sure what exactly is being celebrated, just that *something* is and that's all that matters.

Many of the better festivals are worth scheduling a visit around (see "When To Go" in the "Other Practicalities" section). Most major holidays consist of a week of blowing off steam, getting looped, and generally celebrating life. Elaborate costumes show this merriment-making as probably the only acceptable occasion for cross-dressing in this hyper-masculine culture. Parades march to the beat of brass bands as entire towns dance in the street. Special food is cooked, fireworks lit, and beauty queens picked in between serious religious processions and private celebrations in homes. Hotels and restaurants often fill to overflowing and jack up their prices. During national holidays, it can be difficult to find space on a bus, or to find a bus period. Most businesses close on the public holidays, so make reservations and exchange money beforehand.

Catholic Spring Holidays

The Catholic Church's most festive season revolves around **Easter,** which technically occurs on the Sunday after the full moon of the vernal equinox. **Carnival** in February or March is the big blowout before the 40 days of fasting and penance known as **Lent,** which begins on **Ash Wednesday.**

Holy Week (Semana Santa) occurs just before Easter. **Palm Sunday** kicks things off, with parishioners bringing palm fronds to church (especially good in Cuenca). Four days later, **Holy Thursday,** similar to the Day of the Dead in November, precedes the solemn processions on **Good Friday** and elaborate nighttime masses on **Holy Saturday.** Businesses not closed already will close on Saturday. Easter morning Mass (Pascua) signifies the end of the deprivations of Lent and the holiday cycle.

Official Public Holidays

January 1: New Year's Day—Six days of post-holiday festivities include dancing and fireworks.
January 6: Epiphany
February 27: Patriotism Day—Speeches, parades, flag-waving.
May 1: Labor Day—Worker's parades.
May 24: Battle of Pichincha—Commemorates Battle of Tarquí over Spain in 1822.
May/June (ninth Thursday after Easter): Corpus Cristi—Honors the Eucharist. Heavy indigenous influence in the central Sierra.
July 24: Simón Bolívar's Birthday—Continent-wide celebration.
October 12: Columbus Day—Celebrates the "discovery" of the

CATHOLIC SPRING HOLIDAYS TO 2005

YEAR	ASH WEDNESDAY	PALM SUNDAY	EASTER
2001	February 28	April 7	April 14
2002	February 13	April 24	March 31
2003	March 5	April 13	April 20
2004	February 25	April 4	April 11
2005	February 9	March 20	March 27

New World—or in spite of it, under the name Día de la Raza (Day of the Race), celebrated by indigenous peoples.

November 1: All Saints' Day

November 2: All Souls' Day—also known as Day of the Dead. Indigenous families bring food, flowers, and offerings to the graves of loved ones.

December 24: Christmas Eve—Midnight Misa del Gallo (Rooster's Mass).

December 25: Christmas—Includes Pase del Niño (Children's Parade).

December 28: All Fool's Day—masquerades and clowns.

December 28–31: New Year's Eve—Life-sized effigies of prominent figures and the outgoing year called Años Viejos (Old Years) are ridiculed and burned at midnight.

NIGHTLIFE

Thanks to television and VCRs, **movie theaters** are losing popularity in Latin America.

Quito and Guayaquil have the country's most modern cinemas, showing North American films 6–12 months after their release. Grand old theaters in other cities hang by a thread. Pornographic movies are common and can make for some interesting double features, shown without a trace of irony (*Babe the Talking Pig* and *Burning Desires*?).

A new government law has decreed that **bars** and **discos** throughout the country have to close by 2 A.M. Until then enjoy your *cerveza* and new-found friends to the rhythms of Latin and North American dance music. Neon signs advertising Cocktails, Masaje, or showing an outline of a woman's leg usually indicate strip bars and/or brothels. Prostitution is illegal in Ecuador. *Peñas* host live folkloric music.

An enjoyable nightlife option is the traditional evening *paseo* (stroll). As the heat of the day fades, starry-eyed couples and entire families complete with infants stretch their legs and visit with friends in the central plaza of just about every town in the country.

SHOPPING

What economist Adam Smith called the "certain propensity in human nature . . . to truck, barter, and exchange one thing for another" has quite a few outlets in Ecuador. Even if you were planning to buy only one or two small souvenirs, the diversity, quality, and in most cases affordability of Ecuadorian crafts may have you shopping for another piece of luggage—to take a bit of everything home with you.

Textiles and Weaving

The legacy of Spanish colonial haciendas—often little more than weaving sweatshops—is evident in the wide variety of textiles made throughout the Sierra. Colorful wool sweaters, gloves, hats, socks, ponchos, and tapestries hang next to cotton shirts, blouses, and skirts in important markets such as Otavalo and Salasaca. The intricate embroidery of the Hacienda Zuleta and *ikat* weavings from the Cuenca area are also surprisingly inexpensive.

Canastas, baskets woven from cane or *tortora* reeds, are found in most markets. Hammocks are sold in the Oriente and on the coast, and shoulder sacks called *shigras* are used by men

and women throughout the country. Both can be woven from plant fiber or nylon.

Leather

Artisans in Cotacachi near Otavalo turn out most of the country's cowhide jackets, bags, and belts. Elsewhere you'll have to go to a *sastrería* (tailor shop) or *zapatería* (bootmaker's) for one of Latin America's greatest buys: custom leather clothes. Even the smallest towns have holdouts of this dying art, usually lone *sastreros* (tailors) who can make you custom-fit jackets, pants, or shoes for a fraction of what you'd pay back home. Repairs are also dirt cheap.

Wood

Sawdust and the sound of mallets on chisels fill the air in San Antonio de Ibarra, where a legion of carvers molds statues and wall hangings. In Cotopaxi province, garish festival masks come in the likenesses of dogs, apes, and menacing clowns. Balsa wood, common at lower altitudes on both sides of the Andes, is sculpted into tropical birds and animals, painted, and lacquered by

weaver with a backstrap loom, near Otavalo

JULAN SMITH

the Canelos Quechua on the eastern slope of the Andes. Artisans in Quito and Cuenca reproduce colonial crucifixes and antiques.

Ceramics
Reproductions of ancient pottery figurines and utensils are often passed off as genuine. Don't believe the hype (it's illegal to take antiquities out of the country anyway), but buying the fake ones at least supports the local economy and may well discourage *huaqueros* (grave robbers) from digging up originals to sell. Ceramics from the Amazon are the most beautiful, especially the bowls

and figures sculpted by the Lowland Quechua. Figurines of people and cartoonish overladen buses are made in small towns like Pujilí.

Amazon Souvenirs
Making blowpipes, seed necklaces, and bags woven from tough, flexible palm fibers keeps craftspeople busy throughout the Oriente (and will earn more expressions of gratitude back home than any other presents). Be aware that it's against Ecuadorian law to export products made from any kind of animal, endangered or not. This includes bird feathers and mounted butterflies.

BARGAINING

The art of making a deal takes practice, patience, some Spanish-language skill, and a little bit of chutzpah. Some travelers are uncomfortable arguing over what is usually just a few cents either way. It's true that the amounts involved are often trivial, but bargaining is expected in many situations—particularly in markets—and if you don't bargain, you risk leaving the impression that all gringos are rich suckers. It's important to keep things in perspective; no pittance is worth ruining anyone's day, but with the right attitude, bargaining can even be fun.

The trick is to get a feel for how much the price is being marked up—often more for tourists than for locals—and to conceal how much you're really interested in the item or service being offered. "I simply *must* have that shawl, at *any* price!" is not good bargaining language. When you're browsing wares at a market stall, try not to show which piece particularly catches your eye. Ask a few other prices, then, almost as an after-thought, add "OK, well, then how about . . . this?"

It usually works like this: when you ask how much something costs *("¿Cuanto es?")*, the vendor or hotel manager or truck driver will name a price higher than they expect to get (but will be happy to take). This can be anywhere from a fraction to more than twice as much as what they expect to get in the end. You counter with something like *"Es muy lindo, pero no puedo pagar tanto"* ("It's very nice, but I can't pay that much") or a plea for a *descuentito* (a small discount), and offer a price that's below what *you* expect to pay in the end. After a few rounds of back and forth, with maybe a *"Pués, gracias, pero talvéz la proxima vez"* ("Well, thanks, but maybe next time") thrown in for effect, you both settle on something in the middle, and everyone's happy.

Other Crafts

If you learn anything new from this book, most likely it will be that Panama hats do not come from Panama but from small weaving villages in the southern highlands and along the coast of Ecuador—Montecristi in particular. Detailed scenes of Andean life and landscapes grace tiny animal-hide canvases painted in the Tigua valley near Ambato. Tagua (Brazil) nuts are carved into figurines, buttons, and other doodads before hardening to an ivorylike consistency. Bread-dough figurines from Calderón and jewelry from craft towns such as Chordeleg near Cuenca are just two of many other local specialties.

ACCOMMODATIONS

HOTELS

The entire spectrum of accommodations is represented in Ecuador, from luxury international hotels to places where you'd hesitate to store your furniture. Reservations during festivals, holidays, and market days may be the only way to secure a room.

Prices vary depending on the season and whim of the owner, so bargaining is a possibility in cheaper hotels. Shared dormitory-style rooms are less expensive, and two people can share one *cama matrimonial* (marriage bed). Children under 12 often stay half price or free with their parents, and senior discounts may be available as well. A 20 percent tax is levied in more expensive hotels (it's added into prices when applicable in this book), along with a 10–20 percent surcharge for paying by credit card. All prices below are per person. You can often get a discount on more expensive hotels by asking if they have a promotional rate (tarifa promocionál) available.

Always look at the room before laying down your money, and don't be afraid to ask for a different one if it's too noisy, dirty, or otherwise unacceptable. Electric showers in less-expensive places can be dangerous if improperly wired; *don't* turn them on or off when soaking wet. Remember that "C" stands for "caliente" (hot—or at least warm) and "F" means "frio" (cold). The plumbing in Ecuador can't handle toilet paper, so be sure to throw it in the garbage instead of flushing it down the toilet.

Lock your valuables in the hotel safe, if possible, after getting a signed receipt with a list of the contents. Look out for possible security breaches when choosing a room, such as walls open at the top or a balcony outside your window. A small padlock comes in handy for double-locking doors in cheap hotels.

Less than $10

Budget accommodations go by many names: *hotel, pensión, hospedaje,* and *residencial. Hostal* is a loosely defined word in Ecuador; it doesn't always mean an accredited youth hostel but can also just mean a cheap hotel. **Motel**

Casa Mojanda in the Northern Sierra

JULIAN SMITH

rooms are often rented by the hour—wink wink, nudge nudge. Some budget accommodations are simply extra rooms in a house or store rented out to guests. Hot water isn't a given, and bathrooms are often shared. Caveats aside, some budget hotels will surprise you with their value and hospitality.

$10–25

A step up in price will usually get you hot water and a private bathroom, and occasionally breakfast included in the price. The quality difference between budget and inexpensive hotels can be minimal, but you'll often find good deals in this category.

$25–50

Moderately priced options, including *posadas* (guest homes similar to bed-and-breakfasts) and *cabañas* (cabins), usually offer the best value for the money. Breakfast and sport facilities like a pool *(piscina),* sauna *(sauna),* steamroom *(turco),* whirlpool *(hydromasaje),* or gymnasium *(gimnasio)* may be included in the price.

$50–75

Meals are sometimes included as part of a package in more expensive lodgings. Facilities are comparable to midpriced hotels in North America—clean, comfortable beds, regular maid service, and decent restaurants with fireplaces and/or reading rooms are all common.

$75–200

This large price range Includes a surprisingly small number of hotels. Country inns called *hosterías* and former country estate houses called *haciendas* (see following section) often fall in this category. Guests enjoy antique furnishings and activities such as horseback riding, tennis, and guided hikes.

More than $200

Luxury business hotels in larger cities cater to diplomats, international executives, and high-end tourists. You can have your clothes dry-cleaned and the morning paper delivered to your room if you so desire—just like in a Hilton back home.

Aparthotels and Private Homes

Small apartments with kitchenettes can be rented in larger cities by the week or month. Quality varies widely, from rooms in private houses to fully furnished suites.

HACIENDAS

Throughout the Sierra you'll find these relics of former huge estates, often dating to the 16th and 17th centuries when the King of Spain handed out parcels into the thousands of hectares. Recent land reforms have broken up most of the largest estates, which once served as social, political, and commercial centers for entire provinces. Nowadays flower farms, organic gardens, and computer technology have infiltrated the sprawling grounds, but legions of caretakers and housekeepers are still needed to keep everything running smoothly.

If you can afford it, staying in a hacienda is an experience not to be missed. The settings are invariably the most beautiful around, and accommodations and service are of the highest quality. Home-cooked meals by a roaring fire, thick white-washed walls hung with antique portraits and worn leather saddles, and lush flower gardens all create the feeling of stepping back in time. Hiking, horseback riding, and shopping for locally made crafts are among the many recreational opportunities.

Reservations can be made directly through the haciendas or through tourism agencies such as Safari Tours or Metropolitan Touring in Quito. Also check out EcuadorExplorer.com's hacienda listings (www.ecuadorexplorer.com/html/haciendas.html).

HOMESTAY ORGANIZATIONS

One of the best ways to get under the skin of a country is through an international homestay network that will put you in touch with hosts who feed and/or put you up for free. Remember that you're a guest representing your country; treat their home even better than you would your own. Show your appreciation with a small welcome gift from home, or through helpful chores like washing the dishes or walking the dog. Most organizations also give you the option of becoming a host for foreign travelers at home.

The largest and most experienced homestay network is **Servas,** 11 John St., Room 706, New York, NY 10038, 212/267-0252, fax 212/267-0292, e-mail: info@usservas.org, www.servas.org, which has 14,000 members in 130 countries. Travelers have to be 18 years old and pay a yearly membership fee. Once you're interviewed and accepted, you are loaned lists of hosts who have agreed to provide up to two nights' room and board with prior notice. Servas has members throughout South America, including three in Ecuador.

Hospex, e-mail: hospex@icm.edu.pl, hospex.icm.edu.pl, began in 1991 in Poland. Since then they've acquired members in 35 countries on six continents. There aren't any membership fees, and it's all done via computer. Fill out their online form to subscribe. **Hospitality Exchange,** P.O. Box 561, Lewistown, MT 59457, 406/538-8770, e-mail: hospitalityex@hotmail.com, www.goldray.com/hospitality, covers 20 countries. They publish a directory at least twice a year and charge members $20 per year. **Free-Stay.com** (www.free-stay.com) is another online homestay organization.

CAMPING

Official campsites in parks and reserves may have facilities such as running water and shelters, but don't count on it. A small fee is usually charged. It's possible to ask for permission to camp on private property—try to stay away from high-traffic routes but near houses for security. Keep your valuables in your sleeping bag at night, and don't leave anything unattended in your tent. For that matter, don't leave your tent unattended.

LAST RESORTS

If you find yourself stuck in the middle of nowhere without camping gear, you might be able to wrangle a spare room in a private house, school building, community center, or jail. Police officers *(policía),* the local mayor *(alcade),* the town headman *(jefe),* or the village priest *(cura)* are good people to ask.

FOOD AND DRINK

FOOD

Ecuador isn't known for gourmet food, but it does have a wide range of tasty and economical dining options. "Typical" Ecuadorian cuisine *(comida típica)* borrows from the country's indigenous and Spanish heritage, and often caters to a poor majority with two words: cheap and filling. For the most part *comida típica* isn't health food, so vegetarians and the health-conscious should consider preparing their own food occasionally or heading to one of the many vegetarian restaurants or *tiendas naturistas* (natural food stores) found throughout the country. More expensive restaurants serve just about every major world cuisine and often offer surprising quality and value.

Staples

Inexpensive, carbohydrate-rich foods such as rice, potatoes, plantains, yucca, and corn are staples for most of the country. Grains include wheat, barley, and native *quinua,* which was once sacred to the Inca and is now being discovered as an incredibly nutritious food with many of the same complete proteins as meat. Grains are popular in soups. Bread dishes such as empanadas are often filled with meat, cheese, or vegetables.

Maíz (corn) is eaten whole and fried into tortillas. Roasted *choclo* (corn on the cob) is often served with ketchup and mayonnaise, and small bowls of oily *mote* (boiled kernels, like half-popped popcorn) come with most meals. Sweet *humitas,* corn flour steamed in plantain leaves, are a popular afternoon snack with coffee.

Meats include *lomo* (beef, also called *res* or simply *carne,* "meat") and *chancho* (pork), served *a la parilla* (roasted) or *asada* (grilled). *Chorizo* is pork sausage, and *chuletas* are pork chops. Set meals often include a *seco,* literally a "dry" stew but often just a piece of meat served with rice and a side of vegetables. Choose between beef, *pollo* (chicken), *chivo* (goat), or *cordero* (lamb).

It's easy to remember the name of the hot

GRINGO'S GUIDE
TO SOUTH AMERICAN FRUIT

babaco: Resembles a skinnier green-yellow papaya and has pronounced ridges making a star in cross section. Soft, juicy flesh is lightly sweet with a citrus tang.

banana: Wide variety includes *guineos* (familiar, long, and yellow), *magueños* (red and stubby), and *oritas* (finger bananas).

chirimoya: Also known as custard apple or sweetsop, it's fist-sized with green dimpled skin, sweet flesh.

granadilla: Smooth, round crust 6–8 cm in diameter has yellow, red, or green colors and short stem. Crack it open to enjoy the delicious insides with the disgusting texture.

guanabana: Football-sized and vaguely pear-shaped, dark green outside with stubby spines. Spongy, white flesh has lunglike consistency, almost artificially sweet.

mango: Smooth, fist-sized, yellow, orange, green colors. Ripe when soft. Peel off the skin to uncover the stringy flesh around a large seed. Sweet, tart, a delicious mess: slice off sections of skin and eat from those.

maracuyá (passionfruit): Pale yellow baseball-sized rind is similar to granadilla, but crust is tougher and orange insides are more tangy.

naranjilla: Yellow-orange, bright and shiny, 5–7 cm in diameter, with stem. Tart citrus taste is best in juice. Only grown in Ecuador.

papaya: Dark greenish-orange skin, 20–30 cm in diameter, 20–100 cm long, heavy and slightly soft when ripe. Inside is smooth, pink-orange flesh great for *batidos*. Scoop out seeds and cut off skin to eat. Skin has peppery taste.

pepino: Yellowish oval about 10 cm long with dark stripes and/or spots. Sweet vegetable taste similar to cucumber. Just wash, crack open, and eat

plátanos: These green cooking plantains look like large bananas. Turn sweet when baked (served with cream), or crunchy when fried.

taxo: Elongated yellow-orange fruit 10 cm long with peachlike skin. Soft when ripe. Tightly packed flesh packets with orange seeds inside. Sweet and tangy, similar to maracuyá.

tomate del arbol: Tree tomato is sweet but still definitely a tomato. Good in juice.

tuna: Cactus fruit is 2–4 cm long and green, yellow, and red with spine stumps. Mildly sweet.

zapote: Solid and fist-sized with brown peach-fuzz skin and acornlike stem cap. Bright orange pulp surrounds four or five large seeds. Lightly sweet vegetable taste. Suck the stringy pulp off the seed, then go floss.

---

pepper sauce that sits on almost every table in the country: *ají* is also the sound you'll make when you put too much of it on your food. It comes in handy to flavor up bland dishes, leading to the saying, *"comida buena con ají es más plena; comida mala con ají resbala"* ("with *ají* good food is better; with *ají* bad food slips by").

When your plate is clean, treat yourself to a *pan dulce* (sweetbread), *helado* (ice cream), or *flan* (a sweet custard made with eggs). Toasted coconut sweets called *cocadas* and **bocadillos,** peanut nougat with honey, are also popular.

Specialties

Fanesca, a smorgasbord dish including everything from peanuts and fish to squash and onions, is eaten at Easter and is a leading contender for the Ecuadorian national dish. *Salchipapas* are the archetypal Ecuadorian snack: a plastic bag of half-cooked french fries topped with a chunk of hot dog and smothered with ketchup, mayonnaise, and mustard.

Dozens of varieties of potatoes have been grown in the Andes for centuries since they were first domesticated near Lake Titicaca between Perú and Bolivia. In some places they're cultivated as high as 4,000 meters. Potatoes figure prominently in piping hot soups: *caldos,* including *caldo de patas* (pig's foot soup) are thinner, whereas thick *locros* are made with potatoes, corn, and cheese. **Llapingachos** are fried potato cakes that originated in Perú.

Coastal delicacies start with fish but don't end there. Delicious *encocadas* are seafood dishes cooked with coconut milk. *Ceviches* consist of seafood (often raw), onions, and coriander marinated in lemon or lime juice, served with a dish of popcorn on the side. When shrimp is used in *ceviches,* it's cooked beforehand, but those made with raw *pescado* (fish) or *concha* (clams) may pose a cholera risk. *Patacones,* small pieces of plantain mashed flat and fried crispy, originally hail from Colombia.

Dishes made with *trucha* (trout), *pargo* (red snapper), *corvina* (white sea bass) or *atún* (tuna) are served *frito* (fried), *apanada* (breaded and fried), or *a la plancha* (filleted and baked, literally "on the board"). *Camarones al ajillo* (shrimp in garlic sauce) is popular countrywide, for good reason. Other shellfish include *cangrejo* (crab), *calamare* (squid), *ostione* (oyster), and *langosta* (lobster or jumbo shrimp).

In the Amazon you might be treated to piranha (more bones than meat), but you'll definitely sample a huge *bagre* (freshwater catfish), which often takes two or more people to drag from the muddy rivers. *Paca* is a large edible rodent similar to a capybara. The small heart of the *chonta* palm, called *palmito,* makes a tasty side dish, even though it kills the entire plant to harvest. Most are grown on farms.

Eating Out

A restaurant filled with locals usually means the food is good. These come in subcategories such as *parilladas* (steakhouses) and the ever-present *chifas* (Chinese food), where quality varies widely but there's always an excellent volume-to-price ratio. *Chaulafan* (fried rice) and *tallarines* (noodles) can be mixed with meat or vegetables at chifas, often for around $1. A set meal *(menú del día)* is the cheapest and most filling option for budget travelers in any restaurant.

Breakfast *(desayuno)* isn't big, often just enough to hold you over to lunch. For a dollar or so you can get a continental breakfast consisting of *tostada* (toast) or simply piping fresh *pan* (bread) with *mantequilla* (butter) and *mermelada* (jam), *cafe* (coffee), and a *jugo* (juice) to wash it down. It'll cost a little extra for a *desayuno Americano* (American breakfast), which adds *huevos* (eggs) served *fritos* (fried) or *revueltos* (scrambled). A bowl of fruit, yogurt, and granola is another popular breakfast option. Breakfast buffets in high-end hotel restaurants are a nice splurge—for $10 or so you might be able to cram down enough to

---

THE GUINEA PIG

In the Sierra you'll find Ecuador's most infamous dish, *cuy* (guinea pig). The Incas raised guinea pigs as food long before the animals found their way into the hearts and homes of North Americans. *El cuy* is still found on restaurant menus throughout the country today, even though the animals, usually killed 6–12 months after birth, seem to the uninitiated about as appetizing as a charboiled Easter bunny.

But hey, it's authentic as it gets here in Ecuador, so give it a try. And what a perfect conversation-starter back home.

---

last you all day.

At lunch *(almuerzo),* the largest meal of the day, everyone comes home from work or school to eat and relax during the hottest part of the early afternoon. Set lunches *(almuerzos)* include a *sopa* (soup), *segundo* (main dish, usually meat with rice), *verde* (small side salad), and *postre* (dessert). Dinner *(cena)* is eaten from 8 P.M. on. A set evening meal is called a *merienda.*

Do-It-Yourself Meals

Food from outdoor markets and supermarkets can be less expensive and better tasting, provided you have access to a kitchen or at least a knife and plate. Prepare fruits and vegetables by peeling and washing them in purified water or with a concentrated food bactericide like Vitalin, available in supermarkets. See the "Health" section that follows for more food safety guidelines. Ubiquitous *viveres* stores, found in every last town in the country, stock a little bit of everything from simple food and drinks to batteries and machetes.

DRINKS

Ecuador has more than its share of bottled-water mineral springs; bubbly Güitig near Machachi is the most common. Coca-Cola has worked its red-and-white tentacles into the farthest Andean village. Sprite (pronounced SPREE-tay) and Fanta are also popular—the latter is easier to get down when warm than other soft drinks—along with various maddeningly sweet local concoctions based loosely on different types of fruit. In one of the few instances of recycling in the country, glass bottles are always reused. If you need to take your soda with you, ask for it *para llevar* (to go); you'll be handed your drink in a plastic bag with a straw.

Juices

Delicious *jugos* can be made from just about any type of fruit available. They're often mixed with *agua* (water) or *azúcar* (sugar) but can be ordered *puro* (pure). *Batidos* are made with milk, juice, and often sugar.

Coffee

For a country that grows so much of it, the *cafe* in Ecuador is disappointing. "Here in the land where some of the world's best coffee grows," mourned Ludwig Bemelmans around World War II, "if you love coffee you must bring your own and a percolator besides." Instant varieties are the most common form of coffee served in restaurants (Nescafé is strong stuff—less than a teaspoon does a whole cup fine). *Cafe con leche* is mixed with milk instead of water, and a *tinto* is real brewed coffee.

Alcohol

Chilean **wines** yield the best value for the money because Ecuadorian vintages tend to be poor. Local **beers** such as Pilsener (large bottles) and Club (small bottles and cans) are watery but ubiquitous. U.S. and European imports of both wine and beer are available but much more expensive.

Chicha is a fermented Sierra home brew made with corn, yeast, and sugar. In the Oriente it's still made the old-fashioned way: women chew up yucca, spit it into water, and wait a day or so for the enzymes in the saliva to start fermentation. *¡Salud!*

Sugarcane liquor, alternately called *aguardiente, traigo de caña,* or simply *traigo,* is the rocket fuel of choice in most of rural Ecuador. Heated and mixed with cinnamon and sugar, the potent concoction is called *canelazo.* With honey and blackberry juice *(naranjilla),* it becomes a *hervida,* served hot at fiestas. In any form it can make a grown man cry. If you get too *borracho* (drunk) the night before, you may wake up *chuchaqui,* a Quechua word meaning "hangover" that proves even the Incas knew the perils of the morning after.

GETTING THERE

BY AIR

A wide range of airlines offer flights into Ecuador's two international airports, in Quito and Guayaquil. Tracking down the cheapest fare is more of a problem than finding a flight in the first place.

General Air Travel Suggestions

Make your reservations as early as possible, and *reconfirm your flight* more than once or make sure your travel agency does it for you. Otherwise you may find your seat mysteriously vanishing right before your eyes.

It may be less expensive to fly to other cities in South America than directly to Ecuador, depending on where you're coming from and how much time you have to complete the trip to Ecuador overland. Caracas, Venezuela is the cheapest city in South America to fly to from the

United States, and Lima, Perú is a travel hub for the northwestern section of the South America.

Published fares to Latin America can vary much more than flights within the United States—up to 30–40 percent from airline to airline. Comparing prices among various airlines can pay off in spades. Flights to Latin America don't get cheaper if you buy them ahead of time, but planes can be full for months in advance of the peak season during the North American summer and Dec.–Jan. Ask about "open jaw" flights, in which you can fly out of a different city than you flew in through, and don't consider one-way tickets unless you plan on staying more than a year.

It's usually much cheaper to book a round-trip ticket and change your return date if you need to instead of buying a ticket once you're in Latin America, where ticket prices are much higher. Tickets valid for 30 days, called bulk tickets, are almost always the cheapest. Stopovers are common among Latin American airlines, which tend to drastically overbook flights—always reconfirm flights two or three days before departure and arrive at the airport early to make sure you get your seat.

The website of eXito Latin American Travel Specialists (www.wonderlink.com/exito) has much more sound advice on flying to Latin America. Another good general resource for inexpensive globetrotting by plane is *The Worldwide Guide to Cheap Airfares* by Michael McColl (Insider Publications, 1998), as well as *The Practical Nomad: How to Travel Around the World* by Edward Hasbrouck (Avalon Travel Publishing, 2000).

Charters and Consolidators

Called bucket shops in the U.K., these legal discount ticket brokers often advertise in the classifieds and travel sections of major city newspapers. In exchange for a lower price, you may have to buy your ticket quickly before the particular fare is sold out, or put up with a narrow travel window.

eXito Latin American Travel Specialists, 5699 Miles Avenue, Oakland, CA 94618, 800/655-4053, fax 510/655-4566, e-mail: exito@wonderlink.com, live up to their name with great deals on airfare and tours throughout Latin America. Their website (www.wonderlink.com/exito) lists up-to-the-minute specials and has a handy FareFinder for Latin American airfare quotes online. They organize guided tours in Ecuador, Perú, and Bolivia, sell airpasses, and can set you up with language schools in many different countries. They're also a consolidator for American, Continental, United, Aerolineas Argentinas, Grupo Taca, COPA, Mexicana, and Lan Chile.

You can also find good deals on airfare and trips to Latin America with **Flight Coordinators,** 800/544-3644, fax 310/861-5620, e-mail: info@airfarekillers.com, www.flightcoordinators.com, and **Ticketplanet,** 800/799-8888, www.ticketplanet.com.

Student, Teacher, and Youth Fares

If you're under 26 and/or enrolled in some sort of school, you're eligible for a host of discounts. **Council Travel,** 800/2-COUNCIL, www.counciltravel.com, has a worldwide network of offices and affiliates geared to getting students and young

people where they want to go cheaply. They have dozens of offices in the United States (the listing is available on their website), and sell railpasses, airpasses, and organize tours and language programs. **STA Travel,** 800/777-0122, www.sta-travel.com, is another discount youth and student travel organization. They have more than 200 offices around the world, along with travel help "service locations" in 50 countries.

Both organizations issue the handy **International Student Identity Card** (ISIC) for $22, which can save you a great deal on airfare, lodging, and activities in Ecuador and other countries. It carries basic accident/sickness insurance coverage as well as access to a 24-hour traveler's assistance hotline offering legal and emergency medical services. Teachers can receive an **International Teacher Identity Card** (ITIC), and nonstudents under 26 are still eligible for an **International Youth Travel Card** (IYTC)—both offer similar discounts and insurance for the same price. The cards are also available directly from the **International Student Travel Confederation,** a worldwide network of organizations devoted to promoting travel, study, and work exchange opportunities for students, young people, and academics. Stop by their website (www.isic.org) or contact them by mail at Herengracht 479, 1017 BS Amsterdam, The Netherlands, tel. 31/20/421-28-00, fax 31/20/421-28-10.

Airpasses

While no one has yet come up with a magic all-Latin-America airpass yet, a few companies offer deals that can come in handy. **Avensa/Servivensa** (www.avensa.com.ve) has a round-trip pass from the United States to Caracas, priced according to the number of legs you fly within South America (at least two). You must complete your travels within 45 days to get this deal. **AeroContinente** (www.aerocontinente.com.pe) offers the Inca Airpass for travel within Perú. It costs about $83 per flight, and all travel must be completed within 30 days.

If you're interested in visiting several countries in Latin America, consider the **Mercosur Pass,** which is available from any travel agency or any of the participating airlines (i.e., Lan Chile, Aerolineas Argentinas, Varig, VASP, TransBrasil, Austral, Pluna, and LAPA). You can arrive from the United States on these or almost any carrier based in the United States. The pass is good for travel in Chile, Argentina, Brazil, Paraguay, and Uruguay, and is priced based on mileage. All travel has to be completed within 30 days.

Courier Flights
Anyone looking for inexpensive airfare from the United States, after checking with the various discounters and student travel agencies, should consider a courier flight. Usually the cheapest of all, these legal operations will give you a greatly discounted ticket in exchange for your baggage allotment in the belly of the plane. It's a trade-off: while tickets can go for as low as $200 round-trip, you can't take any baggage beyond what you can carry, and your stay is often limited to a few weeks (courier flights are always round-trip, and you're obligated to use the return ticket). Because most flights pass through Miami, plan on adding $20–30 in departure taxes to whatever taxes and/or membership fee the agency charges. Some courier flights also leave from New York, Los Angeles, or other major hubs. Excess personal luggage will cost extra, up to $80–100 and beyond.

Try **Air Facility,** 718/712-1769; **Line Haul Services,** 305/477-0651; **DTI,** 212/362-3636; **Now Voyager,** 212/431-1616; or **World Courier,** 718/978-9552. Two good resources for information on courier flights is the **International Association of Air Travel Couriers,** 220 South Dixie Highway #3, P.O. Box 1349, Lake Worth, FL 33460, 561/582-8320, fax 561/582-1581, e-mail: iaatc@courier.org, www.courier.org. They publish the monthly *Shoestring Traveler* newsletter. *Travel Unlimited* is another monthly courier travel newsletter. It costs $25 per year and is available from P.O. Box 1058, Allston, MA 02134, e-mail: SteveL2555@aol.com.

Baggage Restrictions
These restrictions vary by airline, usually hovering in the neighborhood of two checked bags per person of 20–30 kg each. Fees for more luggage add up quickly. A customs duty is sometimes charged when leaving Ecuador for any checked bags beyond the first two.

Leaving Ecuador
A $25 **exit tax** can be paid in either airport in sucres or dollars. The current **duty-free** allowance includes one liter of alcohol, 200 cigarettes or 50 cigars, and a "reasonable quantity" of perfume and gifts totaling no more than $200.

To/From the U.S.
American Airlines, 800/433-7300, has daily flights to Ecuador from most major U.S. cities via Miami. **Continental,** 800/231-0856, shuttles its planes through Houston, and some stop over in Panama. Ecuador's own **TAME,** 800/990-0600, passes through Miami from most major cities. All of these airlines offer top-quality service and can bring you down in either Quito or Guayaquil. Round-trip prices vary, but expect to pay $500–800 for a round-trip ticket.

To/From Canada
Most flights from the Great White North connect through gateway

TAME NATIONAL FLIGHTS

© AVALON TRAVEL PUBLISHING, INC.

cities in the United States. **Travel Cuts,** 171 College St., Toronto, Ontario M5T 1P7, 416/979-2406, fax 416/979-8167, www. travelcuts.com, is Canada's discount student travel agency, with more than 60 offices in Vancouver, Winnipeg, Calgary, Edmonton, Toronto, Quebec, Montreal, and Ottawa.

To/From Europe

Major European airlines, including British Airways, Air France, Iberia, KLM, and Lufthansa, service South America. You may have to stop off in Perú or Colombia before transferring to a connecting flight to Ecuador.

A cutthroat discount travel market in Great Britain keeps prices low. Good reports have come in on **South American Experience,** 47 Causton St., Pimlico, London SW1P 4AT, tel. 020/7976-5511, fax 020/7976-6908, e-mail: info@southamericanexperience.com, www.southamericanexperience.com, and **Journey Latin America,** 16 Devonshire Road, Chiswick, London W4 2HD, tel. 017/1747-3108.

To/From Latin America

Although major airlines connect Quito and Guayaquil with most other capitals in South America, it's usually cheapest (if far from convenient) to cross borders by bus because international flights are highly taxed. For prices and flight times, check in the various capitals for the national airline or a branch of an Ecuadorian airline in: **Argentina,** Aerolineas Argentinas; in **Bolivia,** Lloyd Aero Boliviano; in **Brazil,** VARIG; in **Chile,** LanChile, SAETA, and TAME; in **Colombia,** Avianca, SAETA (Bogotá), and TAME (Calí); in **Perú,** AeroPeru and SAETA; in **Venezuela,** VIASA and SAETA.

Airlines offering flights within Central America and the Caribbean include LACSA in **Costa Rica;** TAME in **Cuba;** COPA AND TAME in **Panama;** and TACA in the rest of Central America. The least expensive air route between Central and South America is via Colombia's tiny Caribbean island of San Andrés, connecting to Cartagena and beyond.

BY CAR OR MOTORCYCLE

Preparations

With the challenging road conditions that exist in much of South America, tougher cars create happier drivers. A 4WD vehicle is ideal, especially a diesel because diesel gas is the cheapest and most accessible. For driving in bad weather on the coast and in the Oriente, extra tire traction is essential. Two-wheel-drive automobiles should have high clearance.

When preparing your vehicle, think Mad Max. The more problems you're able to diagnose and fix yourself, the easier life on the road will be. Take every tool and spare part you can, and know how to use them. Spare tires should be full size, not the rubber donuts that come with most new cars. Security is equally important: lock up *everything,* down to wheel nuts and gas caps. Two antitheft devices, the more visible the better, are a good idea. If you plan on prolonged driving in the high Sierra, an altitude adjustment or even special carburetor jets may be necessary on older vehicles.

Crossing the Border

To drive a car into Ecuador, you'll need your passport, your license from your home state, and full registration papers in the driver's name. If someone else holds the title, bring a notarized letter from them authorizing you to use the vehicle. Most recently a *libreta de passage* or *carnet de passages en Douanes* was not required to enter, but double-check if possible because this situation changes from year to year. Hold onto all documents you are given so you can leave with a minimum of hassle.

Shipping

Until the Pan-American Highway penetrates the jungles of the Darién Gap between Panama and Colombia, driving from Central to South America will remain impossible. Shipping companies in Panama City will transport your vehicle around the gap by ferry, and some go all the way to Ecuador. Because it has the most incoming traffic, Venezuela (especially Puerto Cabello) is the easiest country to ship your vehicle to from Europe or the United States. You probably won't be able to travel on the same ship, so having your car secured in its own container is the best way to go. Customs can be a bureaucratic nightmare. A broker or agent—and some spare cash and patience—may make things easier.

Insurance

. If your own auto insurance won't cover you abroad (and most don't), international coverage is available through **Sanborn's Insurance** 2009 S. 10th Street, McAllen, TX 78503, 800/222-0158, 956/686-3601, fax 956/686-0732, e-mail: info@sanbornsinsurance.com, www. sanbornsinsurance.com.

BY SEA

One interesting way to get to Ecuador is on a **freighter.** Few people know that these floating warehouses usually carry passengers as well as cargo, and those who have taken freighters comment on the first-class service (amenities often include TV/VCR, swimming pool, and officer's-mess dining) and the chance to stop in different countries along the way. The biggest drawbacks are the itineraries, which can change at the last minute, and being cooped up on a ship for weeks at a time. As an example, the **Rickmeri Reederi** stops in Guayaquil on its 42-day journey from New York to Chile. Cabin prices range from $1,870 pp for a single cabin with an obstructed view to an owner's cabin for $3,780 s, $4,410 d. It can carry five passengers.

Resources

Ford's Freighter Travel Guide & Waterways of the World by Judith Howard, which is updated quarterly and is available from 19448 Londelius St., Northridge, CA 91324, 818/701-7414, lists freighter travel routes and pleasure cruises around the world. **Travltips Cruise & Freighter Association,** 163-07 Depot Rd., P.O. Box 580188, Flushing, NY 11358, 800/872-8584 or 718/939-2400, fax 718/939-2047, publishes the *Travltips* newsletter on worldwide freighter travel.

Freighter World Cruises, 180 South Lake Ave., Suite 335, Pasadena, CA 91101-2655, 800/531-7774, 626/449-3106, fax 626/449-9573, e-mail: freighters@freighterworld.com, www .freighterworld.com, is a freighter travel agency that publishes the *Freighter Space Advisory* newsletter for $29 per year. You can access the **Internet Guide to Freighter Travel** at www.maxho.com/~frman/mainmenu.html.

GETTING AROUND

BY CAR AND MOTORCYCLE

Driving in Ecuador

In 1993 the World Health Organization reported that Ecuador had 38 car related deaths per 10,000 people, which was higher than the United States (25), the U.K. (13), and Japan (15). Driving should not be taken lightly. The range of hazards includes potholes big enough to swim in, ice in the upper elevations, cows on the low roads, and a frightening lack of road signs and traffic lights.

On the whole, Latin Americans drive much more aggressively than most North Americans. Vehicles spend more time passing each other than in the driving (right-hand) lane, turn signals are unheard of, and red *pare* (stop) signs seem to elicit the same response as a matador's cape. It's even worse for pedestrians, as explained by Richard Poole in *The Inca Smiled*: "Crossings exist but they mean nothing, except that if you put your faith in one you are more likely to die there than anywhere else."

This offensive driving attitude is in part a product of *machismo,* as well as an understandable reaction to poor conditions and, ironically, other crazy drivers. I herefore, foreign drivers, with their unfamiliarity of the "rules" of the road, may actually be more dangerous than locals. In short: **Be careful.**

Roads

The Pan-American Highway (Panamericana, or usually just Pana) is the country's main artery, running through the Andes from Tulcán to Machala. Side branches lead east and west: the Oriente can be reached from Quito, Baños, or Loja, and roads run to the coast from Ibarra, Quito, Ambato, Riobamba, Cuenca, and Loja. Road numbers exist but are seldom used or even marked on the road. Most secondary roads are dirt tracks. Towns of any significant size will most likely have paved roads, smaller towns may have cobbled roads, and remote villages have only dirt roads.

Documents

Drivers should carry a driver's license from their home country, along with the title to the vehicle and a temporary import permit given at the border (if applicable). This should be enough to satisfy any official. Guard all of these documents like gold.

Safety and Security

In case of an accident, keep a level head. In one of Latin America's greatest ironies, pedestrians have absolutely no rights until someone is killed—then they can do no wrong. Drivers are usually assumed guilty until proven innocent and are often thrown in jail until everything is sorted out. (There may be some connection between this policy and the prevalence of hit-and-run situations.)

If you end up in one of these unfortunate situations, don't leave the scene or move anything or anyone, especially if they are damaged or hurt. Summon an ambulance or doctor if someone is hurt, and wait for the police to arrive. Gather any and all relevant information about the other car and witnesses, and get a copy of the *denuncia* (report) for insurance and possible legal tangles.

Put branches in the road 50 meters ahead and behind any stopped vehicle to warn other drivers (and try to remember to remove them before leaving, as few people seem to do). In case of a breakdown or flat, try to flag down help or a ride to the nearest repair shop *(taller de automoviles)*. Hundreds of *vulcanizadoras* (tire repair shops) line major roads, most no more than a wooden shack with an old tire hanging out front. It's fascinating to watch tires being repaired with brute force and the crudest of tools.

Try not to drive at night, if possible. Road hazards materialize out of the darkness, and thieves have been known to stop vehicles with roadblocks. Some local drivers keep their headlights off to save the batteries, igniting them only when other cars are dead ahead.

To discourage thieves, never leave anything of value in a parked car; take everything with you, and leave the glove compartment open and empty. Even so, one or more antitheft devices like The Club are necessary to ensure that your car will still be there in the morning. Some drivers go as far as lacing a heavy chain around the steering wheel, interior door handles, and/or foot pedals. A thick U-lock for a motorcycle is a good idea.

Street parking spaces often have a self-appointed guardian, often simply a scruffy child who will look after your vehicle for a dollar or two. While you might not have much choice in the matter, it's best to go along with this anyway.

Other Concerns

Police and military checkpoints, especially in the Oriente, are common. As a gringo in a rental or foreign car, you may just be waved through, but be prepared to stop and show your passport and documents. Gasoline ranges from unfiltered fuel siphoned out of drums in the Oriente to quality high-octane unleaded. With so many trucks hammering the highways, diesel is common.

Car Rental

You'll have to shell out as much or more than you would back home to enjoy the freedom of driving yourself around Ecuador. Drivers must be at least 25 years old and have a credit card. A hefty deposit is charged on the card to ensure that the car is returned in one piece. Prices vary widely, but don't expect to pay much less than you would back home. In the high tourist season, cars are more expensive and harder to come by without reservations.

Before driving your rental car off the lot, check the vehicle out carefully both inside and out, recording all dings and blemishes on the checkout form. Try to spot any missing parts such as a radio antenna or windshield wipers; once you leave the lot, the company can hold you responsible for any lost article not noted on the form. Make sure a jack and inflated spare tire are included, and check fluid and pressure levels.

Rental agency branches overseas often have nothing in common with their namesake agency back home besides the name, so have everything about the rental in writing, including prices, insurance, taxes, discounts, and where and when you're supposed to bring it back. Read the contract over carefully so you'll notice any charges that happen to materialize on the final bill. Be aware that rental cars are ripe plums for picking by thieves.

Taxis

Cabs in Ecuador are cheap by most standards, seldom charging more than $1–2 for crosstown trips. Taxi drivers are legally required to use a meter in the larger cities, although you'll often hear that *el métro está roto* (the meter is broken), or simply *no hay* (there isn't one). In this case, there are two schools of thought on how to proceed. You can get to your destination before negotiating a fare, since by already being there you'll have some automatic bargaining leverage, or you can agree on a fare before leaving to avoid any unpleasantries. In either case, it's a good idea to ask a store owner, hotel employee, or policeman for a ballpark figure to where you want to go (for example, *¿Cuanto debe a costar ir al teatro en un taxi?,* How much should it cost to go to the theater in a taxi?). Nights and week-

ends are always more expensive, and a small tip is appreciated.

This isn't to say that all taxi drivers are scam artists. I've gotten to the point where I'll give a driver a tip simply for *not* trying to overcharge me, and I've found that if you act like you know where you're going and how much it should cost, you'll end up doing this most of the time.

Longer trips of a half or entire day can be an economical and efficient alternative to renting a car, especially if the price is split between a group of people. You might even happen to get a driver who becomes a knowledgeable, friendly local guide.

Hitchhiking

I won't recommend it as a safe or reliable alternative to waiting for the bus, but in a pinch, hitching may be the only option. Even though sticking out your thumb (*ir al dedo,* thumbing it) means the same in Latin America as it does elsewhere, you'll have to wave down passing cars for them to stop. Truck drivers, often bored and lonely, are a good bet. But for this reason (among many others), women alone or even in a group should not consider hitchhiking. It's common to offer a token sum for the service: just ask *¿Le debo algo?* (Do I owe you anything?) when you're dropped off.

BY BICYCLE

Crossing Ecuador by bike will put you in intimate contact with the land, people, and weather. Along the way you'll experience well-paved highways, muddy tracks, and cobblestone roads populated by drivers whose idea of sharing the road is somewhat short of ideal.

Mountain bikes are the best for the terrain—the most important concern—even though they're heavier and the upright posture can become uncomfortable. Touring bikes are more delicate but more comfortable over long distances. Their higher speed can be a blessing until the first major pothole warps your wheel.

Toe clips, bar-ends, and a big granny gear make high-altitude grinds less of an ordeal. To carry your gear you'll have to invest in panniers (bags that attach to special frames on your bicycle) or a tow-behind trailer like the BOB Yak. Other extras you should include are two water

---

ADDRESSES

In Spanish the *planta baja* (ground floor) doesn't count as the 1st floor as it does in North America. This makes the 2nd floor up from the ground the *primer piso* (1st floor), and the 3rd floor from the ground the *segundo piso* (2nd floor), and so on.

In Ecuador, most street addresses have two numbers that make pinpointing the location easier, in theory. The first number refers to the block and the second to the house itself. Thus García Moreno 4-39 is on the odd-numbered side of the "4" block of García Moreno. *Cuadras* (blocks) are also referred to as multiples of *cien metros* (one hundred meters): i.e., *trescientos metros* (300 meters) will equal three blocks. A recently implemented system in Quito added letters to the first address number.

When asking directions, remember that "near" and "far" take on different meanings in a culture where some people have never been outside their province. In Latin American countries, people often prefer to give well-meant but erroneous directions rather than disappoint the asker and look ignorant themselves by admitting they have no idea.

bottle cages, a quality pump, an odometer, a rearview mirror, a U-lock, and a flashing red taillight or two. Also consider an ultrasonic dog zapper, fenders, a dust mask, and a tube or two of Slime to protect tubes against punctures. Don't bother with lights or a horn because riding at night is unadvised, and a shout works just as well.

Maintenance
It's best to be as prepared as possible without loading yourself down more than necessary. Carry as many lightweight tools and replacement parts as you think practical—the only things you can really depend on being available regularly in Ecuador are tubes, spokes, and cables. Although there are *talleres de bicicletas* (bike repair shops) in most moderate to large towns, mechanics may lack the experience to repair complicated modern mechanisms.

Safety and Security
Always yield to traffic, whether you have a choice or not. Paved shoulders are rare, so be ready for the unexpected, which could pop out in the road ahead of you at any moment: people, cars, animals, potholes, oil slicks, or debris. Buy a good, comfortable helmet and *wear it.*

Lock both tires and the frame to a solid object every time you park, and keep a photo of the bike, its serial number, and a photocopy of your bill of sale in a safe place in case of theft. Because panniers are the most visible and accessible target for thieves, lock them securely or take them with you. Always take bicycles inside at night.

Transporting Bicycles
Most airlines will accept bicycles as checked baggage. Bike stores will usually give you a box that new bicycles come in. Take off the wheels and pedals, deflate your tires to keep them from exploding, and pad your bike well before entrusting it to the baggage handlers.

Lock your bike to the roof rack on buses, and remove anything that can be taken or shaken off. Some buses may have room inside in the back for the entire bike, but this is rare.

Resources
Tour operators in various cities offer guided trips lasting from one to several days. The bikes sup-plied are often high-quality imports, and support vehicles and guides take some of the burden off novice riders. The Mountaineers publish two excellent books on cycling in Latin America: Walter Sienko's *Latin America by Bike* and *Two Wheels and a Taxi* by Virginia Urrutia.

BY BUS

The sight of a rattletrap old bus huffing its way uphill in a cloud of exhaust fumes inspires fond and not-so-fond nostalgia in anyone who's spent much time in Latin America. Ecuador's network of bus routes ties the country together like a spider's web, allowing the poorest *indígena* down the farthest dirt lane in the Sierra to reach the capital with relatively little expense and inconvenience. Bus travel is how most people get around here, and if you want to do any traveling on your own, you'll get to know Ecuador's buses well.

Most cities have a central *terminal terrestre* (bus terminal), or at the very least a park or intersection from which buses come and go. Many companies have their own office/terminal for arrivals and departures. With so many people to carry, long-distance schedules are strict and under fierce competition. Local schedules are looser, allowing drivers to leave early if their bus is full or circle around to gather up more people before they depart.

Comfort levels vary as widely as the buses themselves. Usually the longer the trip, the better the bus—all the way up to sleek, ultramodern vehicles with air-conditioning, toilets, reclining seats, and even hostess service. Some luxury routes depart in the evening and travel all night, saving you money on a hotel room but leaving your neck bent in strange angles by morning (an inflatable travel pillow makes life easier).

Shorter trips are handled by shoddier buses that might seem strangely familiar to North American riders (ever wonder where old school buses go to die?). Smaller *collectivos* and *busetas* make inner-city runs, and *camionetas* (pickups) and *rancheros* (wooden buses with open sides) ply rural areas. Drivers load buses to capacity, and then some: you may find yourself crammed among crates of chickens, sacks of *quinua,* and the obligatory motion-sick child. Riding on the roof is permitted and recom-

> *There was always at least one major breakdown somewhere between Riobamba and Guayaquil, and the general feeling was that the [bus] company liked to get it over with as soon as possible . . . so that the passengers could then sit back and enjoy the rest of the journey in peace.*
>
> —Richard Poole,
> The Inca Smiled

mended for the views and fresh air; just hold on tight and bring warm and waterproof layers for higher altitudes.

Baggage

If your luggage is small enough, it's best to keep it inside with you, either next to you, on your lap, or in an overhead rack. Don't let the bus company charge you for the extra seat your backpack may take up—it's their responsibility to find a place for bags, even if they have to put them on the roof. If it does wind up on the roof, get out the protective covering and lock everything up the roof rack to prevent the nightmare of arriving after a 12-hour journey to find all your belongings lost somewhere during the last 300 km.

Cost

On average, buses cost about 75 cents per hour. Prices climb slightly higher for longer luxury rides. It's possible to buy tickets a day or so ahead of time to reserve a seat, which never hurts. Watch for a "gringo tax," charged when buying your ticket on the bus itself—pay attention to how much everyone else is charged, or ask at the station for the correct price. Shop different companies in the terminal for the best prices and departure times. You should pay less if you're only going halfway—something you may need to remind the ticket collector. Don't forget to collect your *cambio* (change), even if you have to wait until the collector has gathered enough coins from everyone else.

Other Concerns

Ecuadorian bus drivers seem to have the same relationship to silence that vampires do to light. A pair of foam earplugs are worth their weight in gold to block out the constant, screeching music. Most buses have VCRs and TVs, but as far as the movie selection goes, let's just say that after a few long trips you'll be intimately familiar with the entire Jean-Claude Van Damme oeuvre. Long-distance buses stop for meals, and vendors climb aboard in most towns selling sodas, ice cream, and snacks, but you still might want to bring along something more substantial and/or healthy.

Weather is a major concern for bus travelers. Bad seasons like the 1997–1998 El Niño can block or wipe out roads completely with landslides in every part of the country. Occasionally you'll have to disembark to pass a landslide or washed-out bridge on foot to another bus waiting on the other side, especially during the rainy season. Keep an eye on your bus at military checkpoints, where you have to get off and register with the authorities in person, to make sure it doesn't leave without you. Be especially careful of thieves and pickpockets in terminals and on buses. Try to avoid the cramped back seats in older buses, whose rear suspensions are often shot. To get off along the way, yell *¡baja!* (getting off!), *¡esquina!* (at the corner!), or simply *¡gracias!* (thanks!).

International Buses

A few companies run buses as far as Lima or Bo-

bus and driver

JULIAN SMITH

JULIAN SMITH

gotá, but it's always easier and less expensive to take an Ecuadorian bus to the border, cross overland, and get on a Perúvian or Colombian bus on the other side.

BY TRAIN

Latin America is a gold mine of classic railroads, and Ecuador is—or at least was—a mother lode. Steam engines half a century old still puff along a network that includes one of the most impressive pieces of railway engineering in the hemisphere south of Alausí. Sadly, Ecuador's railways hang on by the barest of threads. The iron horse that cut two-week mule journeys to 12-hour jaunts has been swept aside by frequent landslides courtesy of El Niño, dwindling government subsidies and passenger demand, and an improving road system. Now their chief function is to ferry foreign tourists, for many times the normal price, through scenery that remains some of the best you'll ever see from the roof of a train—all the more reason to hop aboard quick, while there's still time.

The roof is the best seat, as long as you don't mind breathing some fumes and remember to duck for the tight tunnels. Vendors hop aboard at the frequent stops and roam inside the cars selling snacks and drinks.

Routes

The rail line that once connected Quito to Guayaquil has been reduced to a short ride from Riobamba through the short but hair-raising section downhill from Alausí. This section includes the Alausí Loops, built on a 5.6 percent grade, and the famous switchbacks at the foot of the Nariz del Diablo (Devil's Nose), which took nine years to build and actually forces the train to run backward for a moment. The weekly train from Quito to the edge of Cotopaxi National Park is as good a way to spend a clear Sunday as any.

Since it was replaced by a road, the *autoferro* (a bus body mounted on a train chassis) from Ibarra to San Lorenzo will now take you only a fraction of the way down to the coast, making it not worth the bother. Rumor has it that this line might be sold to a private company, but it will probably be years before the route is rehabilitated completely.

BY AIR

Flights within Ecuador, originating in Quito and Guayaquil, are relatively cheap and convenient; many travelers prefer them to long bus rides. Another option is to take buses on the way out, then fly back once you've gone as far as you want.

TAME offers domestic and internal flights, including the Galápagos. Booking seats can be a chore: flights are often overbooked and delays are common (though thankfully less so than outright cancellations). Reconfirmation is essential. On some flights, seats aren't even reserved, turning boarding into a first-come, first-served elbowfest.

Air prices have gone up in recent years. Tickets, payable up front, are nonrefundable, and cost more for foreigners than for Ecuadorians. Most flights within mainland Ecuador are still less than $50 pp one-way; Quito to Guayaquil, for example, is $46. It'll cost you $324–378 to get to Baltra in the Galápagos, depending on what time of year it is, but students under 26 can get discounts. A few smaller air companies such as Icaro Express have limited national flights. Flight schedules change often, so the information in this guide should be considered a rough indicator of flight availability, frequency, and cost.

Window seats are worth requesting for the views of the Andes.

VISAS AND OFFICIALDOM

Tourist Visas

Most travelers entering Ecuador are given a stamp in their passport and a stamped **tourist card** (also called a T-3) upon entry. The amount of time you're actually given is up to the guard on duty and therefore somewhat arbitrary—tuck in your shirt, smile, and ask for the full 90 days just in case. If you're given less time, you can easily extend it in Quito at the **Jefatura Provincial de Migración,** Isla Seymour 1152 and Río Coca, tel. 2/247-510, 450-573.

To enter Ecuador, U.S. citizens need to have a passport valid for more than six months, a return ticket, and "proof of economic means to support yourself during your stay," which is loosely defined and may just involve showing a wad of travelers' checks to the immigration authority. The latter two requirements are seldom invoked, and only then by a harried border official to someone really annoying. Hold onto your stamped visa card because you'll need to turn it in when you leave.

You will need to get a visa before arrival if you are a resident of Algeria, Bangladesh, Costa Rica, Cuba, El Salvador, Guatemala, India, Iran, Iraq, Jordan, Lebanon, Libya, Nicaragua, Nigeria, North Korea, Pakistan, Palestine Authority, Panama, the People's Republic of China, Sri Lanka, Syria, Tunisia, or Vietnam.

Tourist visas can be extended beyond the original 90 days, often a month at a time at the discretion of the customs official. The upper limit is typically 180 days. Extensions beyond 90 days are handled in Quito at the **Dirección Nacional de Migración,** Amazonas and República, Asesoria Jurídica, piso 2.

Longer Stays

Other types of visas include student visas, good for up to one year and renewable; professional or government visas, good for variable periods; religious or volunteer visas, good for two years; cultural exchange or teaching visas, good for one year; and business or tourism visas, good for 90–180 days. It's hard to get a visa in Ecuador, so you're much better off dealing with this at home.

To obtain a visa, call the Ecuadorian consulate nearest you to check on what you'll need (everything from bank statements to negative HIV tests have been required in the past) and follow their instructions. Start the process early because it may take awhile. For initial questions, check with the U.S. Passport and Information Service, 800/225-8472. If you're pressed for time, try an expeditor service such as **A Briggs Passport and Visa Expeditors,** 1422 K St. NW, Washington DC 20005, 800/218-6284, www. abriggs.com, with 14 local offices across the country. **Travisa,** 1731 21st St. NW, Washington, DC 20009, 202/463-6166, www.travisa.com, offers similar services, and has offices in San Francisco, Chicago, and New York.

If you're staying longer than six months, you'll need to get a *censo,* a temporary residence card that can save you lots of money entering Ecuador's national parks (the Galápagos are $25 with a *censo,* as opposed to $100 for foreigners).

> *I had been in Latin America long enough by now to know that there was a class stigma attached to the trains. Only the semi-destitute, the limpers, the barefoot ones, the Indians, and the half-cracked yokels took the train, or knew anything about them. For this reason, it was a good introduction to the social miseries and scenic splendors of the continent.*
>
> *—Paul Theroux,*
> The Old Patagonian Express

To get one, register your visa in Quito at the Dirección de Extranjería, Juan León Mera and Patria, Ed. Corporación Financiera, piso 6, then get your *censo* on the 1st floor of the Jefatura Provincial de Migración in Quito (see previous entry).

Because visa matters change often, including which office handles what, it's a good idea to check at the South American Explorers' Quito clubhouse for a recent update.

Leaving Ecuador

Tourists with 90-day visa cards simply turn them in at the border and get an exit stamp in their passport. Those with longer visas need to obtain a *salida* (official document of permission to leave the country), or else they may be denied exit. Present your *censo* at the ground floor of the Dirección Nacional de Migración in Quito (see previous entry) to get a *salida* good for one year and multiple exits.

Customs

It's prohibited to bring firearms, ammunitions, or illegal drugs into Ecuador. Importing plants or animals requires prior permission from the Ministerio de Agricultura y Ganadera (Ministry of Agriculture and Livestock). Exportation of any kind of plant or animal product or archaeological artifact is forbidden. Check with your country's customs office for details of what you can bring home legally. (U.S. Customs: 1301 Constitution Avenue, Washington, DC 20229, 202/566-8195)

Border Towns

The three major crossing points

ECUADORIAN CONSULATES IN THE U.S. AND CANADA

The **Ecuadorian Embassy** in the U.S. is located at 2535 15th St. NW, Washington, DC 20009, 202/234-7200 or 234-7166, fax 202/265-9325 or 667-3482, e-mail: mecuawaa@erols.com, conecuwa@erols.com, www.ecuador.org.

ECUADORIAN CONSULATES IN THE U.S.

800 Second Ave., Ste. 601, New York, NY 10017
212/808-0170 or 808-0171, fax 212/808-0188
e-mail: ecucon@mail.idt.net

30 Montgomery St., Ste. 1020, Jersey City, NJ 07302
201/985-1700 or 985-1300, fax 201/985-2959
e-mail: info@consuladoecuadornj.com

2925 Charles St., Baltimore, MD 21218
410/889-4435

B.I.V. Tower, 1101 Brickell Ave., Ste. M-102, Miami, FL 33131
305/539-8214 or 539-8215, fax 305/539-8313
e-mail: consecumia@aol.com

4200 Westheimer, Ste. 118, Houston, TX 77027
713/622-1787, fax 713/622-8105

World Trade Center, Ste. 1312, 2 Canal St., New Orleans, LA 70130
504/523-3229, fax 504/523-3229
e-mail: ccu@accesscom.net

500 North Michigan Ave., Ste. 1510, Chicago, IL 60611
312/329-0266, fax 312/329-0359
e-mail: chic@cscns.com

8484 Wilshire Blvd., Ste. 540, Beverly Hills, CA 90211
323/658-6020, fax 323/658-1934
e-mail: con1ec1lac@aol.com

455 Market St., Ste. 980, San Francisco, CA 94105
415/957-5921, fax 415/957-5923
e-mail: sfconsul@aol.com

3500 Paradise Road, Las Vegas, NV 89109
702/735-8193, fax 702/369-1773

Calle Recinto Sur 301, Of. 401A, Condominio Gallardo, Apdo. 9020078, San Juan, PR 00902-0078
787/723-6572, fax 787/724-2356

ECUADORIAN CONSULATES IN CANADA

1010 St. Catherine Quest, Ste. 440, P.O. Box H3B3R3, Montreal, Quebec H3B3R3
514/874-4071, fax 514/931-0252

151 Bloor St. West, Ste. 470, Toronto, Ontario M5S1S4 416/968-2077, fax 416/968-3348

into and out of Ecuador are at **Tulcán** on the Colombian border and **Huaquillas** and **Macará** on the Perúvian border. It is possible to cross at other points along the border, such as in the Oriente north of Lago Agrio, but this is more of a gamble, and you'll have to get your exit or entry stamp elsewhere. Now that the border with Perú has been decided once and for all, it's possible to cross into Perú to the east, although few travelers do this yet.

SPECIAL INTEREST TRAVEL

VISITING THE JUNGLE

Jungle trip—the words conjure up an image of explorers hacking through impenetrable undergrowth as dangerous animals and blowgun-toting natives lurk in the buzzing shadows. While this type of trip hasn't been on many people's itinerary since the 19th century, it's still possible to find yourself in a primeval world of overwhelming richness in the Ecuadorian Amazon for surprisingly little money and effort.

The key to getting the most out of your experience in the rainforest is to keep your expectations in perspective. Aside from monkeys, you probably won't see any large animals unless you're on a two-week pack trip through the farthest reaches of the forest. On the other hand, a good guide will have an incredible amount to teach you about everything else: medicinal plants, ants that taste like lemon, and a rainbow of bird species in every direction. So don't expect lost temples and anacondas in the trees, but make sure your affairs are in order before you go—this country is still wild.

Tour Options

As always, you get what you pay for: smaller operators and freelance guides are more flexible, cheaper, and may surprise you with their expertise, whereas larger, more expensive companies have the facilities, training, and staff to correct problems or to solve them before they occur. One thing holds true for all: a good guide, like a good schoolteacher, makes all the difference. There should be no more than 10 people per guide on your trip.

Freelance guides and small agencies can be found in most cities in or near the Oriente (especially Baños, Misahualli, Tena, Coca, and Lago Agrio). Guides cost anywhere from $25 pp per day and up, and you'll save time and money by being at the departure point already. Quality varies widely, so even highly recommended guides have the occasionally dissatisfied customer.

Check to see if guides are licensed and speak your language, or at least one you can understand. Companies often have their own lodges in the forest, but make sure you're not taken to zoos or other "prefab" sites during your stay—that's like paying for box seats at the ball game and then watching it on TV once you get to the stadium. Like in the Galápagos, it's a good idea to have all prices, itineraries, and services written up in a signed contract beforehand (available from the South American Explorers). A book of glowing comments by past participants may or may not be useful as an indicator of quality, but recommendations from friends or the SAE are usually objective and accurate.

Some indigenous communities are starting to arrange visits themselves, which provides much-needed income by employing locals as guides and support staff. If a visit to an indigenous community is on the itinerary of your tour company, make sure they have written permission (especially with the Huaorani), and that local people are being employed in some way. The best visits happen when villagers simply take a few minutes to chat with you about their lives and yours and show you around their homes.

Many tour operators have branches in Quito and Guayaquil. You may rest easier having things arranged before you hop on that bus or plane to the edge of nowhere, but you'll pay a little more ($50 pp per day and up). Check to see if transportation from Quito is included in the price, and remember that the days you spend getting to and from the site count as tour days.

Jungle lodges are the most comfortable and most expensive way to go. Guides at places such as Kapawi, La Selva, and the Flotel Orel-

FOREIGN TOUR COMPANIES

Cheeseman's Ecology Safaris: 20800 Kittredge Rd., Saratoga, CA 95070, 800/527-5330, 408/867-1371, fax 408/741-0358, e-mail: cheesemans@aol.com, www.cheesemans.com.
Smaller, more intimate trips led by husband and wife team of biology professor/wildlife photographer and birder. Two weeks in the Galápagos for $4,600 pp plus airfare.

Holbrook Travel, Inc.: 3540 N.W. 13th St., Gainesville, FL 32609, 800/451-7111, fax 904/371-3710, e-mail: advisor@holbrooktravel.com, www.holbrooktravel.com. Galápagos and custom tours starting at $1,795 pp.

Journey Latin America: 12 & 13 Healthfield Terr. Chiswick, London W4 4JE, tel. 44/020/8747-8315, fax 44/020/742-1312, e-mail: tours@journeylatinamerica.co.uk, www.journeylatinamerica.co.uk.
Trips all over Latin America, including many in the Ecuadorian Sierra, Amazon, and Galápagos.

Mountain Travel-Sobek: 6420 Fairmount Ave., El Cerrito, CA 94530, 800/227-2384, 800/282-8747, fax 510/525-7710, e-mail: info@mtsobek.com, www.mtsobek.com.
Moderately strenuous tours range from Galápagos cruises to hiking the haciendas in the Sierra.

Myths and Mountains: 976 Tee Ct., Incline Village, NV 89451, 800/670-6984, fax 775/832-4454, e-mail: travel@mythsandmountains.com, www.mythsandmountains.com.
Educational tourism combines classroom and hands-on study of religion, folk medicine, crafts, and natural history with fieldwork among indigenous communities in the Sierra and Oriente. Tours start at $1,895 pp.

Nature Expeditions International: 7860 Peters Rd., Ste. F-103, Plantation, FL 33324, 800/869-0639, 954/693-8852, fax 954/693-8854, e-mail: info@naturexp.com, www.naturexp.com.
Educational adventure travel for older active guests. Tours of the Galápagos and the Sierra starting at $2,300 pp.

Tread Lightly: 37 Juniper Meadow Rd., Washington Depot, CT 06794, 800/643-0060, e-mail: info@treadlightly.com, www.treadlightly.com.
Ecological tours with a strong conservation focus throughout Latin America. Ecuador choices include indigenous markets, volcano trekking, and river rafting.

Wilderness Travel: 1102 Ninth St., Berkeley, CA 94710, 800/328-2794, 510/558-2488, fax 510/558-2489, e-mail: info@wildernesstravel.com, www.wildernesstravel.com.
Tours of the Sierra, including haciendas and the Inca Trail, along with visits to the Galápagos and destinations in Perú, start at around $3,000 pp.

Wildland Adventures: 3516 N.E. 155th St., Seattle, WA 98155-7412, 800/345-4453, 206/365-0686, fax 206/363-6615, e-mail: info@wildland.com, www.wildland.com.
Honored in 1994 by *Condé Nast* as one of the 18 top ecotourism travel companies in the world. Visits to Kapawi, La Selva, the Galápagos, and highland haciendas can be customized for families and honeymooners starting at $1,260 pp.

---

lana are top-notch, and the amenities often approach those of luxury hotels back in "civilization." Packages start at $400 pp for 4 days/3 nights and climb from there.

Unfortunately, exploring the Amazon on your own isn't really an option. You won't run into a road or settlement eventually—get lost here and the next thing you know you're halfway to Brazil. Trails as such simply don't exist outside of short hikes near towns. River travel is the least risky way to venture into the Oriente wilds, either on your own raft or kayak or on a rented boat. Jungle permits may be necessary for the farther reaches, especially near the Perúvian border.

You'll need special permission and two week's paperwork-processing time to get the necessary permits and maps from the IGM (Military Geographical Institute) in Quito.

Where to Go

Naturally, the farther from human settlement you go, the more undisturbed the forest and its inhabitants are. The trade-off is how long it will take you to get there—a full day in some cases—and the expense of the luxury lodges, which are your only option that far out.

If you're limited on time, you might not be able to go farther than the parts of the upper Río Napo near Tena and Misahualli. This area has been the most disturbed by development, leaving little primary forest and few mammals. Similarly, the region near Lago Agrio and Coca suffers from settlement and oil exploration. But if these are your only options, don't let this dissuade you: even secondary jungle is a beautiful thing.

Farther down the Napo and into the Cuyabeno Wildlife Refuge, the environment has taken less of a beating. Far south into Yasuní and Pastaza province, east of the cities of Macas and Puyo, lie the largest areas of completely undisturbed rainforest.

What To Take

Leave your hiking boots at home—rubber boots (botas de cuero) are essential in the sodden rainforest. Rubber boots are available at hardware stores in larger cities and come in handy if your tour doesn't provide them or you need an usually large size (U.S. size 10 and up for men). It's also essential to bring insect repellent with as high a percentage of DEET (see "Diseases from Insects" in the Health Section) as possible. Careful, though—a high concentration of this stuff is potent enough to melt plastic. Even the U.S. Army has conceded to the insect-repelling properties of Avon Skin-So-Soft. Hanging mosquito screens for beds (mosquiteros) are available in most jungle cities. If you're planning on being out a long time, you can buy the insecticide permethrin to soak clothing and mosquito screens in.

Bring a photocopy of your passport for frequent military checkpoints, and make sure you have enough cash, since it's hard to find places in the Oriente to exchange travelers' checks and rates are bad. A cheap plastic rain poncho allows more air to circulate than waterproof jackets and pants. Plastic garbage and resealable Ziploc bags will protect your things from the insidious dampness. A hammock with a rain fly works as well as or even better than a tent.

When to Go

Although it rains just about every day in the Amazon, June–Aug. has the most precipitation, making many roads impassable. Less rain falls from Sept.–Dec. No matter when you go, don't make any important plans (especially connecting flights) the first day or two after you're due back, since the vagaries of climate and airplane mechanics can easily cause delays.

Activities

Every tour includes guided hikes along forest paths, ideally with an indigenous guide to spot and explain different species of plants and animals along the way. Often the sound of branches shaking overhead is your clue to troops of capuchin, squirrel, or saki monkeys moving through the treetops. (Don't let your guides hunt animals during the trip, even for food—this is illegal and hurts animal populations that have already been severely diminished.)

Canoe trips are another staple of rainforest tours. On large water stretches you may hear the huff of pink river dolphins surfacing to breathe, or spot the dark head of a river otter. Nocturnal hikes will show you how much more active and noisy the forest is after dark. Listen for the soft, quick fluttering of bats swerving to miss your flashlight beams. Along the shore, your light might catch the iridescent eyes of caimans or, if you're very lucky, a jaguar coming down to drink.

A visit to an indigenous village can easily be the high point of a tour. Some tours are based around cultural encounters—Safari's visits to the Huaorani are highly praised—but even if it's only for an afternoon, the chance to see how people eke out a living in the rainforest is not to be missed. Rest assured that they'll be as curious about you as you are about them; electronic cameras and blowguns can be equally fascinating depending on your upbringing. You may be invited to lend a hand in the manioc field, learn how to thread a bead necklace, or get your face painted and watch a traditional dance, complete with macaw feathers and gourd rattles.

It's up to you how large a grain of salt to take it all with. Sure, they probably wouldn't be dressing up and dancing if you weren't there, and the crafts are often made solely for the tourist trade. But if you consider yourself as much a cultural ambassador as the wide-eyed tribe members in front of you, you'll realize that exploitation can be a very relative term.

VISITING THE GALÁPAGOS

One of the world's outstanding natural treasures, the Galápagos Islands are a must-see for many travelers. Ecuador's National Park Service tightly controls visitor access to reduce the impact on the islands. For details on tour options, see the Galápagos chapter.

STUDYING, VOLUNTEERING, AND WORKING IN ECUADOR

Studying
Intensive Spanish instruction attracts students of all ages to Ecuador for anywhere from a week to a year. A host of schools, both foreign and national, offer language courses and programs in ecology, literature, and Latin American culture. Optional excursions to the Galápagos, Amazon, or out into the Andes are part of some curricula.

Ask beforehand if insurance and airfare are included in the price. Are there any prerequi-

STUDY ABROAD PROGRAMS

Several colleges, universities, and academic organizations in the United States offer study abroad programs in Ecuador. Many involve Spanish instruction and/or homestays with local families, and they can range in length from a few weeks over the summer to an entire academic year. Fees can range from $500 for two weeks to what you'd pay for a semester at a private college back home ($10,000–12,000) for longer programs.

In addition to the following programs, a few study abroad information websites are worth a peek. Try www.studyabroadlinks.com/search/Ecuador, www.studyabroad.com/simplehtml/ecuador.html, and dir.yahoo.com/Education/Programs/Study_Abroad.

Amerispan Unlimited: P.O. Box 40007, Philadelphia, PA 19106-0007, 800/879-6640, fax 215/715-1986, e-mail: info@amerispan.com, www.amerispan.com. Spanish language and volunteer/internship programs throughout Latin America.

Brethren Colleges Abroad: 605 E. College Avenue, North Manchester, IN 46962-1226, 219/982-5238, fax 219/982-7755, e-mail: inquiry@bcanet.org, www.bcanet.org. Spanish instruction in Quito, semester or full year.

Experiment in International Living: Hernando de la Cruz N31-120 and Mariana de Jesus, Quito, tel. 2/232-619 or 232-329, fax 2/232-327, e-mail: eilecua@access.net.ec, www.eilecuador.org. Homestay, Spanish instruction, and community service programs.

Kentucky Institute of International Studies, Murray State University, P.O. Box 9, Murray, KY 42071-0009, www.kiis.org. Month-long summer excursions to the Sierra, Oriente, and Galápagos.

National Registration Center for Study Abroad: P.O. Box 1393, Milwaukee, WI 53201, 414/278-0631, fax 414/271-8884, e-mail: inquire@nrcsa.com, www.nrcsa.com. One-on-one Spanish tutoring in Quito and Cuenca.

School for International Training: Kipling Rd., P.O. Box 676, Brattleboro, VT 05302-0676, 802/257-7751, fax 802/258-3248, email: info@sit.edu, www.sit.edu. Ecology, cultural, and language programs.

University of Michigan, Office of International Programs, 734/764-4311, e-mail: oip@umich.edu, www.umich.edu/~iinet/oip. Academic year at the Universidad Catolica in Quito.

University of South Carolina, Department of Spanish, Italian & Portuguese, Columbia, SC 29208, 803/777-4884, fax 803/777-7828, www.cla.sc.edu/sip/studyabroa.html. Summer study at the Universidád de Las Americas in Quito.

sites, such as a minimum grade point average or previous Spanish instruction? How large are the classes? What's the refund policy? Can you transfer credit to a college back home? Past participants are your best source for first-hand recommendations; most programs will supply you with a list.

Volunteering in Ecuador

Conservation and cultural organizations like Fun-

TEACHING ENGLISH IN QUITO

If you're interested in supporting yourself during an extended stay in Ecuador, teaching your native language is one of the surest ways to do it. Demand is high, so getting a position can be easier than you think. It's also possible to receive Spanish instruction in exchange for teaching English; check the bulletin boards at the South American Explorers' Quito clubhouse and the Catholic University language department in Quito.

Requirements vary from school to school. Teachers who can speak Spanish are usually preferred, and you may be asked to provide an English teaching certificate—Teaching English as a Foreign Language (TEFL) or Cambridge RSA—or sign an extended contract (and show up dependably). A curriculum vitae résumé listing any previous teaching experience is standard, as is a personal interview. Pay is enough to live on modestly, but since some teachers have reported problems getting paid, it's a good idea to go with a reliable, recommended institute like one of those listed as follows. Teacher training ranges from plenty to next to nothing, and contracts can be on a day-to-day basis or last six months or more. Private lessons offer higher wages and more flexible hours.

LANGUAGE INSTITUTES

British Council: Amazonas N26-146 and La Niña, tel. 2/540-255, 508-282, fax 2/508-283, mike.bailey@britishcouncil.org.ec. Require Cambridge RSA certificate and two years' experience.

Centro de Educación Continua of the Escuela Politecnica Nacional: Ladrón de Guevara opposite Coliseo Rumiñahui, Ed. de Ingeniería Civil de la EPN, tel. 2/229-163, e-mail: cec@mail.epn.edu.ec. Requires BA degree or equivalent, experience preferred.

Edinburgh Linguistic Center: Mariana de Jesus 910 and Amazonas, piso 2, tel. 2/549-188 or 259-500, e-mail: juliovel@uio.satnet.net. Two years' university education required.

The Experiment in International Living: Hernando de la Cruz N31-120 and Mariana de Jesus, tel. 2/551-937, fax 2/232-327, e-mail: eile-

cua@access.net.ec. Teaching English as a Foreign Language (TESL) degree preferred, but inexperienced conversation teachers OK.

Fulbright Commission: Almagro 961 and Colón, tel. 2/563-095, fax 2/508-149, e-mail: fulbrigh@fulbright.org.ec. Native speakers with TESL certification and experience preferred.

Harvard: 10 de Agosto and Riofrio, tel. 2/568-870, fax 2/503-302.

Mundi Lingua: Vicente Roca 176 and Tamayo, tel. 2/223-025.

Princeton International Language Institute: Colón 1133 and Amazonas, tel. 2/528-291, fax 2/547-944, e-mail: realitomartha@yahoo.com. Native speakers with TESL preferred.

Simón Bolívar: Plaza 690 and Roca, tel. 2/504-977, e-mail: khaugan@aol.com.

South American Spanish Institute: Amazonas 1549 and Santa Maria, tel. 2/544-715, fax 2/226-348, e-mail: sudameri@impsat.net.ec. Six-month or one-year contracts offered.

HIGH SCHOOLS

These international or bilingual schools offer extended contracts and may require teachers to instruct in other subjects besides languages.

Academia Cotopaxi: De las Higuerrillas and de las Alondras (Monteserrin), tel. 2/467-411, fax 2/445-195, e-mail: pris@cotopaxi.k12.ec. Teaching certificate, BA degree, and three years' international teaching experience required.

Colegio Albert Einstein: Diego de Contreras km 4.5, tel. 2/477-901, 470-144, e-mail: nvillacis@einstein.k12.ec. Sept.–July contract.

Colegio Americano de Quito: Manuel Benigo Cueva N80-190, Urb. Carcelén, tel. 2/472-974, fax 2/472-972, e-mail: dirgeneral@fcaq.k12.ec.

Colegio Menor de la Universidad de San Francisco: Camino Pillague, Cumbayá, tel. 2/893-391 or 893-392, e-mail: mcalderon@mail.cmsfq.edu.ec. BA and master's degrees required.

dación Golondrinas and Jatun Sacha accept volunteers for various lengths of time. Duties vary from the mundane to the fascinating—try to get a description of what you'll be doing before you show up. You may be asked to contribute something toward room and board. The SAE has information on volunteer programs in and out of Quito.

Volunteers for Peace, 1034 Tiffany Rd., Belmont, VT 05730-0202, 802/259-2759, fax 802/259-2922, e-mail: vfp@vfp.org, www.vfp.com, runs 1,800 different volunteer workcamps in 70 countries, including Ecuador. Most programs cost about $200 for 2–3 weeks. Their *International Workcamp Directory* is available online. **JustAct,** 333 Valencia Street, Suite 101, San Francisco, CA 94103, 415/431-4204, fax 415/431-5953, e-mail: info@justact.org, www.justact.org, formerly the Overseas Development Network, promotes global justice by linking students and youth in the United States to organizations and grassroots movements working for sustainable and self-reliant communities around the world. Their resource books, including *The Peace Corps and More: 175 Ways to Work, Study and Travel at Home and Abroad,* are good sources for people interested in international development.

Working in Ecuador

Teaching English is the most common job for foreigners. Regardless of your position, you'll need a working visa (see previous "Visas and Officialdom" section). Your employer should be able to arrange this, ideally before you enter the country. The *International Educator,* P.O. Box 513, Cummaquid, MA 02637, 508/362-1414, fax 508/362-1411, e-mail: tie@capecod.net, www.tieonline.com, lists teaching jobs worldwide. The paper is published five times a year for $35.

HEALTH

PREPARATION

The list of health risks and preventive measures for visiting tropical South America may seem overwhelming, but remember that, like official government traveler warnings, health information is often presented as a worst-case scenario somewhere between "forewarned is forearmed" and "better safe than sorry." You don't need to worry about everything listed here, but it's wise to be aware of what could happen if the stars are aligned against you.

This chicken-little mindset can even afflict doctors. Many North American physicians, unfamiliar with tropical medicine, will prescribe medicines against every virus or bacteria you just might happen to possibly come into contact with. You'll feel worse on getting your bill than you will when you get home. (Sometimes this can even be bad for your health—see the special topic "Lariam"). I'm not advocating second-guessing your doctor. Just take some of the decision making into your own hands. Read through the following information, consult the Centers for Disease Control and Prevention's (CDC) website, and get an idea of the risks particular to your type of trip and style of travel.

Major hospitals and those attached to universities in your home country usually have **traveler's clinics** or **occupational medicine clinics** that can recommend and administer pretravel shots. The *International Travel Health Guide* (see "Books" section) has a list of clinics in the United States. Also check with your local Department of Public Health for an **immunization clinic.** If you're sufficiently informed, you might just be able to walk in with a list of the shots and pills you want.

Vaccinations are recorded on a yellow **International Certificate of Vaccination,** which you should bring with you. You may be asked to show this document in Ecuador to prove your immunizations, especially in the case of a yellow fever outbreak. Take care of these vaccinations as soon as possible, since some shot series take a few months to take effect. Your doctor

FIRST-AID KIT

First-aid kits are available in prepackaged form (Adventure Medical Kits, available at camping stores, are good) or you can assemble one yourself. Check prescription drugs in old kits to make sure they haven't expired.

DEFINITES

Ace bandages

Adhesive bandages; also wound-closure strips (butterflies)

Adhesive tape

Alcohol swabs, prepackaged

Antibiotic ointment

Anti-itch medication/small bottle of Sting-Eze for insect bites

Insect repellent with a high percentage of DEET

Lip balm with sunscreen

Moleskin (for blisters)

Small scissors

Sunscreen with a minimum SPF 15, waterproof is best

Thermometers

Tweezers

Water purification tablets

GOOD IDEAS

Antifungal skin cream

Birth control pills, condoms, spermicidal ointment, other birth control devices

International Certificate of Vaccination

Packets of rehydration salts

Personal physician's address and phone number (clinic and home)

Personal medical record (for those with serious allergies, drug contraindications, or chronic medical problems)

Prescriptions

Syringes

Vitamin supplements

should know which ones not to mix with others (especially immune globulin) so as not to decrease their effectiveness.

Recommended Vaccinations

See your doctor at least 4–6 weeks before you leave to allow time for immunizations to take effect.

Malaria: Mefloquine (brand name Lariam) is the magic bullet of the day, even though it is reported to have serious side effects (see special topic "The Magic Bullet Ricochets"). One 250-mg tablet taken weekly, from one week before arrival through four weeks after you come home, is the standard dosage. A daily 100-mg dose of Doxycycline taken daily from one week before to four weeks after exposure is a less expensive option to Mefloquine, but as a tetracycline drug, it can affect your skin's sensitivity to light. Chloroquine (brand name Aralen), taken in 500-mg pills, and Hydroxychloroquine sulfate (brand name Plaquenil), taken in 400-mg pills, are alternatives.

Viral Hepatitis A: The new Havrix vaccine confers complete protection for 20 years after two shots spaced 6–12 months apart. Otherwise, immune globulin (IG) provides short-term protection.

Typhoid fever: Recommended if you plan on venturing into rural areas, this can be given as a live oral vaccine or through two injections taken at least four weeks apart.

Yellow fever: This is necessary when entering Ecuador from Perú or Colombia (both officially infected countries), but a good idea in any case.

Routine immunizations: Any trip is a good time to update the following: diptheria-tetanus, influenza, measles, mumps, poliomyelitis, and pneumococcus.

Other Concerns

Travelers who plan to spend extended periods in remote areas and come into frequent contact with local people and/or animals should also consider vaccines against **rabies** and **hepatitis B.** Although **cholera** is a problem, the vaccine against it isn't recommended because it's only partially effective, short-lived, and possibly as dangerous as the disease itself.

Try to get a **dental checkup** before you leave

on a long trip, stock up on any prescription medication you require (including oral contraceptives), and bring copies of prescriptions for eyewear and birth control pills (just in case).

WHILE ON THE ROAD

The best you can do while you're traveling, besides taking any prescriptions you brought, is to be aware of as many health risks as possible, be as careful as possible within reason, and pay attention to any unusual symptoms. In the end, nothing can take the place of qualified medical attention, both at home and in Ecuador.

Sunburn

It's easy to forget the amazing power of the equatorial sun when you're shivering in the Andes, but unexposed parts of your body can fry equally as badly whether you're wearing a sweater or a swimsuit. Sunscreen (SPF 30 and above), lip balm, and proper clothing—especially a wide-brimmed hat—will help protect you.

Diseases from Food and Water

If you're going to get sick while traveling, it will be through contaminated water and/or food. Minimize your chances by remembering this mantra: cook it, peel it, wash it, or forget it. Get in the habit of washing your hands at least two or three times a day, preferably before every meal. Be careful with salads—some restaurants wash their vegetables in purified or chemically treated water and will definitely advertise this. Otherwise, steer clear. Undercooked eggs and meats are a health risk; *ceviche* especially.

Fruit juices are occasionally mixed with unpurified water or unpasteurized milk, and ice cubes can be a risk as well (ask for drinks *sin hielo,* without ice). Even though it's handy and often tasty, eat food from a street vendor at your own risk. Purify water with a camping filter, boiling (a few minutes is sufficient), or chemical treatment. Iodine tablets like Potable Aqua or five drops of tincture of iodine per gallon will kill anything in 10 minutes.

No one is safe from **traveler's diarrhea,** although most cases are mild. Bloody stool or anything beyond mild diarrhea, gas, cramps, nausea, or fever may be cholera or dysentery, which requires medical attention. Treat a low-grade case of the runs with Imodium A-D or Pepto-Bismol, which can also be used as a preventive measure in modest doses (two tablets twice a day). Drink plenty of noncaffeinated fluids like fruit juice or ginger ale. More serious cases require antibiotics and an oral rehydration solution (one teaspoon salt and 2–3 tablespoons sugar or honey in a liter of water will work).

Cholera is an intestinal infection caused by bacteria. Luckily the risk is low and symptoms are often mild. About 5 percent of sufferers lose enough liquids through severe diarrhea and vomiting to require medical attention. Otherwise, a rehydration mixture does the trick.

Typhoid fever is also a bacterial infection courtesy of *Salmonella typhi*. Early symptoms resemble the flu: fever, chills, aches, and loss of appetite. Diarrhea, constipation, and rashes are less common. Seek medical attention, since 25 percent of cases can be fatal.

Hepatitis A attacks the liver and is transmitted by contaminated food or water or contact with an

THE MAGIC BULLET RICOCHETS

Malaria is a worldwide scourge that infects up to half a billion people per year and kills nearly 3 million of them. Approximately 30,000 U.S. and European travelers are infected each year. In the 1970s and 1980s, rates of infection skyrocketed as the parasite developed resistance to Chloroquine, the prophylaxis of choice since World War II. By the late 1980s, the U.S. Peace Corps even considered abandoning its African operations completely because half its volunteers were catching malaria.

So when malaria infection rates dropped almost overnight with the introduction of Mefloquine (commonly known under the brand name Lariam) in the late 1980s, the medical community hailed the medicine a blessing. Lariam is 95 percent effective against malaria, is currently the most prescribed malaria prophylaxis in the world, and remains the most effective by a wide margin.

Not everyone agrees with the conventional wisdom, however. Although most people would prefer the drug's minor side effects—nausea, dizziness, hypertension, and sleep disruption—to the disease itself, a growing number of users are reporting more serious conditions. Accounts of hallucinations, depressions, paranoia, nightmares, and outright psychotic episodes are being linked to Lariam, and the drug has been implicated in everything from aborted trips to suicide attempts. In the late 1990s, an ongoing storm of media coverage fueled lawsuits filed against the drug's manufacturer, Hoffman-La Roche, in the United States and Britain, and an investigation by the Canadian government into the military's use of Lariam in Somalia.

While popular opinion seems to be swinging against the drug, the medical community remains divided. Previous studies found the risk of severe psychotic reactions to be an "acceptable" 1 in 10,000, but a more recent British survey resulted in a much more disturbing 1 in 140. The drug's defenders note that at least 12 million people have taken Lariam, so the chance of a few of them having serious side effects is not insignificant—after all, even aspirin causes side effects in some people. But an evaluation of Lariam in the *British Medical Journal* in 1997 justified public concerns over the drug's safety and noted that "the absence of relevant research [made] it difficult for doctors to reassure or advise [patients] in an informed and convincing way." British doctors have noticed more and more travelers, perhaps frightened by sensational tabloid coverage of "Lariam poisoning," returning from visits to developing countries with malaria.

In the end, the question is simple: would you rather risk malaria or a small chance of Lariam's serious side effects? While most people can take Lariam without problems, it's worth evaluating the malarial threat in the country (or countries) you're traveling to and to consider alternate drugs—or even just sensible precautions against mosquitoes—if it looks like Lariam might not be warranted. (A promising malarial treatment combining pyrimethamine-sulphadoxine and a new compound called artesunate is currently being tested in Africa.) If you do take Lariam, start several weeks before you leave for your trip to test your own reaction, and be wary of any strange state of mind that springs up if you decide to continue. For more information, contact Lariam Action USA at 510/663-5168.

infected person. It's the most common type of hepatitis and definitely present in Ecuador's rural areas. Symptoms appear 2–6 weeks after exposure and include nausea, vomiting, aches, fatigue, fever, loss of appetite, dark urine, and jaundice (a yellowing of the whites of the eyes). Once you catch it, there's no treatment; the best medicine is rest and drinking a lot of fluids.

Diseases from Insects

You can triumph in the eternal fight against bug bites by taking a few simple precautions. Repellents include DEET (N-N-di-ethyl-methyl-toluamide), permethrin (sprayed on clothing), and pyrethrin (present in Raid and sprayed on surfaces). Higher percentages of the chemicals on a small area are more effective but also more caustic to humans. Camping store and mail-order catalogs carry mosquito netting to cover beds. These are also available in Ecuador at fabric stores.

Malaria gets its name from the Italian for "bad air," since it was once thought to be spread by infected winds. Now we know it's caused by the *Plasmodium* parasite spread by the bite of the *Anopheles* mosquito, but that doesn't keep the *P. falciparum* strain from killing three million people a year worldwide. Luckily for travelers to Ecuador, the nonlethal *P. vivax* strain is much more common—up to 95 percent in some areas— and 9 out of 10 cases occur in sub-Saharan Africa. Ecuador's Oriente and northern coast have the highest number of cases, which peaked in 1990 at almost 72,000. Symptoms don't necessarily appear right away but are unmistakable: dark urine and alternating cycles of chills and fever (which occur so regularly that one travel writer recalls telling his friends: "I have to go have malaria now, but why don't we have dinner at seven?"). A prophylactic drug regimen suppresses the symptoms, but nothing can kill the parasites but your own immune system.

Yellow fever is also spread by mosquitoes. Symptoms include jaundice, fever, headaches, chills, and vomiting. No treatment exists, but yellow fever is rarely fatal. Seek medical attention regardless.

Dengue fever, transmitted by the *Aedes* mosquito, is most common in coastal urban areas. Flu-like symptoms, such as nausea, bad headaches, joint pain, and sudden high fever, are often misdi-

agnosed as other tropical diseases. Severe cases leading to shock syndrome or hemorrhagic fever are rare. So far the only treatment is rest, fluids, and anti-fever medications. Medical attention is necessary, if only for diagnosis.

Chagas' disease is caused by the *Typanosoma cruzi* parasite in the bite of the nocturnal reduviid or "kissing" bug common to rural coastal regions. The insect usually bites near the mouth (hence the name) after dropping from the ceiling, leading to the nickname *vinchuca,* from the Quechua *huinchucum,* or "he who lets himself fall down." Only a small percentage of victims show symptoms beyond a hard swelling around the bite area. Even if you escape the fever, swollen lymph nodes, vomiting, diarrhea, and rash, you're not in the clear yet. Over decades the untreated disease attacks the heart, making it one of the leading causes of heart disease in Latin America. Apply insect repellent and use netting when camping along the coast, especially inside adobe buildings with thatched roofs. Seek medical attention if symptoms develop; a vaccine is in the works.

Leishmaniasis arrives aboard the tiny *Phlebotomus* sandfly. It's one of the world's most common parasitic diseases and occurs throughout Ecuador. Small, itching red bites develop into skin lesions that affect the mucous membranes. Death follows quickly once it spreads to the internal organs. Netting needs to be extra fine (more than 10 holes per square centimeter) to keep these buggers out. Keep an eye on any particularly annoying insect bites, and see a doctor if they don't heal.

Onchocerciasis, also known as "river blindness," occurs near rivers in Esmeraldas province. Tiny roundworms spread by the bite of a black fly cause itching, rash, and inflammation of the eye. Less than 10 percent of cases result in blindness, and no vaccine is available, but a simple complete blood count (CBC) test reveals the disease.

Other Diseases

Human immunodeficiency virus (HIV) is transmitted by direct contact with the bodily fluids of an infected person, most often through blood transfusions, intravenous injections, or sexual contact. It's a serious problem in Latin America but easy to prevent: do not have unprotected sex, share needles, or accept a transfusion that isn't 100 percent safe. To be extra careful, take and use your own syringes. There is as yet no cure for AIDS. Other types of **sexually transmitted diseases (STDs),** such as chlamydia, gonorrhea, syphilis, and herpes, reveal themselves through various types of genital pain, discharge, and sores. These are even more common than HIV—another reason to practice extra-safe sex. Some can be treated by antibiotics.

Hepatitis B, like its cousin A, is a viral infection of the liver, but it is spread through exchange of body fluids, such as the blood or semen of an infected person. Chances of complete recovery and subsequent lifetime immunity are excellent. Practice the same precautions as you would to prevent contracting HIV, and seek medical attention in cases of infection. Once commonly spread by body lice, **typhus** is on the way out worldwide. Symptoms include pounding headaches, a dark rash on the upper body, fever, and delirium. Medical facilities should have tetracycline drugs to cure it.

Animals
Any mammal bite leads to a risk of contracting **rabies,** which is fatal if left untreated. Immediately wash the wound with soap and hot water, disinfect it with alcohol or iodine, and try to capture or kill the animal—within reason. Treat any dog bite as a possible risk, and see a doctor in all cases.

The most dangerous creatures (to humans) frequent the water. Portuguese man-of-wars, sea wasps, and stingrays can each inflict a painful, even fatal, sting requiring quick medical attention. Male sea lions are the most dangerous animals in the Galápagos—don't approach them and back off if it looks like they want you to.

Ecuador's collection of potentially harmful **arthropods,** including scorpions, centipedes, black widows, and brown recluse spiders, ranges from one end of the country to the other. Pay attention to any bites to notice if unusual symptoms develop. **Poisonous snakes** are more frightened of you than you are of them. Even if you're bitten, there's a good chance that no venom was injected. If swelling, pain, numbness, or loss of consciousness occur, however, immobilize the bitten area and find a doctor. Try to bring the snake along for identification, if possible.

Mountain Health
High-altitude illnesses can be prevented by proper acclimatization. Spend a week in Quito before tackling any major peaks, eat a diet high in carbohydrates, drink plenty of fluids, and avoid caffeine and alcohol. Altitude sickness can strike even the prepared and experienced, however, so mountaineers should be able to recognize the symptoms.

About one in four climbers suffer some degree of **acute mountain sickness (AMS),** which feels like the world's worst hangover-headache, nausea, fatigue, insomnia, and loss of appetite. The drug acetazolamide (Diamox) can lessen the odds of getting it, and analgesics can handle some of the aches. Less common **pulmonary edema** occurs when fluids start accumulating in the lungs, causing shortness of breath and a rat-

---

ANDEAN GENETIC ADAPTATIONS

A 1991 research project in Perú by scientists from the University of British Columbia made some surprising findings among the highland Quechua. Not only do the high-altitude *indígenas* have larger lungs and hearts up to one-fifth bigger than normal—pumping two quarts more blood through their bodies than lowlanders—but their muscles also operate differently.

When you and I exercise our bodies to the point of anaerobic metabolism (relying on stored-up energy rather than oxygen from the outside air), our muscles produce lactic acid that eventually builds up and causes cramps. With such little oxygen at high altitude, you'd think that Quechua muscles would produce a lot of this, but instead they accumulate less lactate byproducts. It might have something to do with their preference for carbohydrates (i.e., grains) rather than fats as body fuel, but their muscles act the same when they're brought down to sea level, suggesting an actual genetic adaptation. Researchers hope to use this sort of information to help people survive the temporary lack of oxygen caused by strokes and heart attacks.

tling cough that eventually brings up blood. **Cerebral edema** is fluid in the brain, which is accompanied by severely impaired mental functioning and poor judgment. Each of these conditions is less common than the one before it, and all should be treated by immediate descent to a lower altitude. Edemas require medical attention.

Cavities can hurt like hell at high altitude because of a pressure difference between the inside of the tooth and the outside. **Hypothermia** occurs when your body loses more heat than it can produce. Wet clothing, wind, and an exposed head are the most common culprits. Always be prepared in the Andes, even on short hikes, with raingear and warm layers for the body, head, and hands. Watch your companions during climbs for signs of dropping body temperatures. Severe shivering reveals mild cases, where the body temperature doesn't drop below 33°C (90°F). Get the person warm and dry, and encourage him or her to move around to generate heat. Shivering actually ceases as body temperatures drop, followed by loss of coordination, impaired judgment, fatigue, and eventually death. One of the best ways to rewarm someone at this stage without doing it too fast is to climb naked into a sleeping bag together (thus, many cases of hypothermia are incorrectly diagnosed).

Pain in the extremities isn't necessarily the surest indicator of **frostbite,** when part of the body becomes frozen. Numbness is often the first symptom, followed by the area becoming hard and white, then black as it dies. Often the area has become wet or the person is exhausted. Keep extremities warm and moving, especially the toes, fingers, ears, nose, and cheeks. A little numbness is normal, but beyond half an hour you'll want to loosen tight clothing, stamp your feet, or warm your chilly parts against a friend's warm skin. Do not rub afflicted areas with snow. If frostbite has taken hold, special rapid rewarming techniques become necessary. There's no particular hurry to start this excruciating process, since frostbitten fingers and toes can, in effect, hibernate for days.

You'd be surprised the places sunlight bouncing off the snow can cause **sunburn** (inside your nose, for one). Spread high-SPF sunscreen, glacier cream, or zinc oxide everywhere you can reach. Reflected sunlight can also cause agonizing **snow blindness,** a temporary condition that only dark glacier goggles with side baffles can prevent. The goggles are a good investment if you plan to do several high-altitude snow climbs; you can buy them in Quito.

If Something Happens
Because many locals can't afford the services of a doctor, **pharmacists** *(farmacéuticos)* tend to be more proactive in Latin America. They can usually be trusted to recommend treatments and medicines for minor ailments. If you are hospitalized, try to talk to an English-speaking doctor before agreeing to any procedures. Be ready to pay up front, even if you have insurance coverage. Make sure to get a detailed, comprehensive receipt—in English, if possible—for insurance repayments.

Back at Home
If you're taking any medical regimens, such as malaria pills, make sure to continue taking them for as long as you're supposed to when you get back home. Pay close attention to your health for at least six months after returning home; many exotic diseases have an incubation period. Symptoms may resemble other illnesses such as the flu, causing doctors unfamiliar with tropical medicine to misdiagnose. If you have any mysterious symptoms, tell your doctor where you've been—fever especially should call for a malaria blood test. A post-travel checkup with blood and stool exams is a good idea in any case, as well as tests for STDs, particularly HIV, if you've had intercourse with unfamiliar partners during your travels.

RESOURCES

The **U.S. Centers for Disease Control and Prevention,** 1600 Clifton Rd., Atlanta, GA 30333, 800/311-3435, 404/639-3534, www.cdc.gov, has an extensive website with up-to-date information on health issues around the world. Their page on health information for travelers to tropical South America (www.cdc.gov/travel/tropsam.htm) is especially useful. The CDC also has a fax-back information service that offers the same information as the website for free. Dial 888/232-3299, and for the directory of all faxes available on traveler's health, request document number 000005.

The **Pan American Health Organization (PAHO),** 525 23rd St. NW, Washington, DC 20037, 202/974-3000, fax 202/974-3663, e-mail: postmaster@paho.org, www.paho.org, is the Americas branch of the World Health Organization. PAHO's website has country health profiles for travelers and information on many health topics.

The nonprofit **International Association for Medical Assistance to Travelers (IAMAT),** 417 Center St., Lewiston, NY 14092, 716/754-4883, www.sentex.net/~iamat, is one of the best general traveler's health resources. For free or a small donation, they'll send you tons of information on health risks abroad, including an immunization chart and a membership card that allows you access to their worldwide list of English-speaking doctors who operate for a fixed fee.

Emergency Services

The **Traveler's Emergency Network,** 5155 34th Street South, Box 146, St. Petersburg, FL 33711, 800/471-3695, www.tenweb. com, has membership programs ranging from $69–129 pp that offer worldwide medical assistance, 24-hour medical consultation, referral to English-speaking doctors, and emergency sickness or injury evacuation. **International SOS Assistance,** 8 Neshaminy Interplex, Suite 207, Trevose, PA 19053-6956, 800/523-8930, 215/244-1500, www.aeaintl.com, offers worldwide emergency medical and security services.

Specialized Health Resources

Travelers with chronic health problems or serious allergies can get a warning bracelet from the **Medic Alert Foundation International,** 2323 Colorado Ave., Turlock, CA 95381-1009, 800/736-3342. The **Undersea and Hyperbaric Medical Society,** 10531 Metropolitan Ave, Kensington, MD 20895, 301/942-2980, fax 301/942-7804, e-mail: uhms@uhms.org, www.uhms.org,

can point you toward divers' decompression facilities around the world. For $29 per year, the **Divers Alert Network,** Peter B. Bennett Center, 6 West Colony Place, Durham, NC 27705, 800/446-2671, 919/684-2948, fax 919/490-6630, e-mail: dan@diversalertnetwork.org, www.diversalertnetwork.org, offers members access to a 24-hour diving emergency hotline, emergency medical evacuation services, a medical information line, and dive accident insurance.

Travel Medicine, 351 Pleasant St., Ste. 312, Northampton, MA 01060, 800/872-8633, e-mail: travmed@travmed.com, www.travmed. com, and **Chinook Medical Gear,** P.O. Box 1736, Edwards, CO 81632, 800/766-1365, fax 970/926-9660, e-mail: chinook@vail.net, www.chinookmed.com, both sell medical supplies and books for travelers.

Books

The Hesperian Foundation, 1919 Addison Street, Suite 304, Berkeley, CA 94704, 510/845-1447, fax 510/845-9141, e-mail: hesperian@hesperian.org, www.hesperian.org, publishes the Peace Corps staples *Where There Is No Doctor* ($17), and *Where There Is No Dentist* ($9). They do take donations to provide their books to rural health care workers; send to the Hesperian Foundation Gratis Book Fund at the previous address.

Other excellent travel health books include Moon Publications/Avalon Travel Publishing's own *Staying Healthy in Asia, Africa, and Latin America,* by Dirk Schroeder, ScD, MPH; Stuart Rose's *International Travel Health Guide* (Chronimed Publications, 1998); *A Comprehensive Guide to Wilderness & Travel Medicine* by Eric A. Weiss, M.D. (Adventure Medical Kits, 1998); and *The Pocket Doctor* by Stephen Bezruchka (Seattle: The Mountaineers, 1999). The last three are available from Travel Medicine and Chinook Medical Gear.

SAFETY

"Violence is never far from the surface in Latin America," writes Tina Rosenberg in *Children of Cain,* her excellent study of the subject (Viking Penguin, 1992). "It is a culture of violence and has been ever since the Spaniards arrived, and, in some cases, well before." No exception to the rule, Ecuador does have crime problems, but it isn't nearly as dangerous as its neighbors. There's no more crime, on the whole, than in a large city back home. The same caveat applies here as it does in health matters (see previous section): remember that the list of potential problems illustrates a worst-case scenario. A few simple precautions and the right attitude will go a long way in keeping your trip trouble-free. In years of traveling in Latin America, I have yet to have any problems with crime whatsoever.

General Concerns

At the turn of the millennium, incidents of crime were increasing as the country's economic situation deteriorated. Muggings, burglaries, pursesnatchings, and encounters with pickpockets were on the rise, even in broad daylight, and armed gangs or rural protestors occasionally stopped buses. Most of these crimes are nonviolent—in many cases the victims didn't even know they were targeted until well after the crim-

inal had moved on—but the incidences of knives or guns being used were also increasing.

Kidnappings near the northern border showed that Colombia's problems were spilling over onto its southern neighbor. The U.S. Embassy (always the mother hen) advises against travel in certain parts of Carchi province and has restricted its personnel from visiting Sucumbios province after five U.S. citizens were kidnapped near the Colombian border in the late 1990s.

Now for the good news: As the switch to the U.S. dollar brings stability, chances are good that things will get better. As a traveler, you won't have to worry about many common types of crime, such as carjackings and home burglaries. Traffic accidents are still the primary hazard to foreigners (motorcycles kill more Peace Corps volunteers than anything else), followed by opportunistic crimes such as casual theft or pursesnatching. Armed muggings, assaults, and rapes do occur, though fortunately not often.

Staying Safe

The best defense, simple as it sounds, is to keep one eye open at all times and to look like you know what you're doing. Insecurity attracts criminals, and inattentiveness gives them a window of opportunity. You won't be able to prevent all

mask, Otavalo

JULIAN SMITH

crimes, but you can cut down the odds drastically. Pay attention to your gut instincts: if something tells you not to walk down that dim alley, don't. Lock the expensive items you bring (e.g., camera) in the lockbox *(caja fuerte* or *caja de seguridad)* available in most hotels, along with your passport, tickets, and money. Get a receipt for the exact contents.

Make copies of your passport, plane tickets, and traveler's checks. Keep one copy of these at home along with a list of expensive items you're bringing and their model and serial numbers, and take one copy with you separate from the originals. Find out if and what your insurance covers while abroad, and how to file a claim. Leave your valuables at home, especially jewelry.

Some travelers carry an emergency wad of money in their shoe or sewn into a piece of clothing. Velco strips sewn across pockets will slow down pickpockets. A small canister of mace and/or pepper spray may give you added confidence. Since it's considered a weapon, you can *not* travel with it. Once you've arrived, you should be able to buy canisters at any *ferreterias* (hardware stores), in major cities. Take a few practice squirts *(outside).*

Money

Don't carry your wallet in your back pocket. Most secure is a money pouch worn under or as part of your clothing, like a money belt or nylon leg or neck pouch. One trick is to wear a neck pouch with the string around the waist and the pouch down the front of the pants—nobody's going to search you there. It's a bad idea to carry all your money in one place. Leave most of it locked in a secure place, and keep a few handy dollars separate from the rest of the wad you carry.

Try to insist that all credit card imprints are made in front of you. Tear up any incomplete or void imprints yourself, and make sure you know the whereabouts of all carbons.

Luggage

Small locks for outside pockets and zip closures are available in most stores at home, or in Ecuador on the street and in hardware stores *(ferreterías).* Cable locks are useful to secure your bag to the roof of a bus or to something hefty in your room while you go out. These locks won't stop a determined thief but will at least slow one down long enough to prevent a casual theft. Discourage bag slashers and snatchers by carrying purses and day packs in front you, securely held in place with one arm. Keep hold of a strap when you put a bag down, and never leave anything hanging on the back of a chair behind you.

One of the best ways to secure your belongings is with a **Pacsafe** from Outpac Designs, PMB 218, 2701 California Avenue S.W., Seattle, WA 98116-2183, 888/837-1243, e-mail: custserv @pac-safe.com, www.pac-safe.com. These lightweight but sturdy steel-mesh sacks fit snugly over backpacks and duffel bags and lock closed, making it impossible to open your bag without a key. You can also use them to lock your bags to anything sturdy. Outpac also makes the Travel Safe, a small lockable nylon pouch reinforced with steel mesh. Pacsafes start at $50 and can more than pay for themselves in keeping your stuff secure.

Where and When to Be Careful

Airports and bus stations are favorite haunts of bag-snatchers. Pickpockets and bag slashers prefer city buses and jostling crowds, particularly in markets. Walk briskly and look like you know where you're going (or better yet, *know* where you're going), particularly at night and after coming out of a bank or exchange house. Everyone should be exceptionally vigilant after dark. For women, certain precautions can decrease your odds of assault—travel as much as possible by day, travel with men or in a group, and avoid situations where you could be cornered in an out-of-the-way spot.

Use your judgment if someone other than a good friend offers you food or drink; druggings are known to happen. If you decide not to accept it, the best strategy is to feign illness or allergy. Traveling in pairs allows one person to dig in and the other to decline.

Robberies, assaults, and rapes have occurred in the backcountry, especially on popular climbs like Pichincha and Tungurahua. Try to go in a group, and never leave gear unattended in mountain huts. (A Pacsafe is a good way to protect expensive climbing gear.) Everyone should avoid deserted beach areas after dark.

Scams

The most common scams involve one person distracting you momentarily while another cleans out your money or slashes your bag. Someone might "accidentally" spill or squirt something on you, or start an argument with you or someone else. There have even been reports of people being handed babies and cleaned out while they stand there stunned.

I've heard enough reports of strangle muggings, in which two or three people sneak up behind you and put you in a headlock until you pass out, to always be wary of running footsteps behind me.

Drugs

Even though Ecuador's drug situation is much better than that of Perú or Colombia, controlled substances still top the list of things you don't want to get mixed up in as a foreigner. Most of the foreigners in jail in Ecuador are there for drug offenses. Drug sales are often setups, and police can be in cahoots with informants. If you're caught, don't expect much support from your embassy or the Ecuadorian legal system. Jails are far from comfortable (think *Midnight Express*), the judicial process can take years, and penalties are steep. Steer clear.

Officialdom

Being stopped and asked to show your papers is often a new experience for foreigners, but it happens occasionally in Ecuador—just smile and comply. Police searches of cars and rooms can happen. Make sure you're present and request a *testigo* (witness). Because civil servants are paid next to nothing, corruption does occur among police.

Some are even outright criminals, or criminals posing as police or drug enforcement agents. Be wary of anyone posing as a plainclothes police officer. Insist on seeing his or her identification—for more than a brief flash—and don't go anywhere with him or her if none is produced (especially not into a vehicle). Even if everything seems on the level, insist on walking to the nearest police station in public.

If Something Happens

In the police station, you'll have to fill out a *denuncia* to report a crime. Get a receipt, for insurance purposes if nothing else, and ask for temporary identification papers if yours were stolen. Your embassy may be able to help arrange for emergency funds to be wired, or even (though loathe to admit it) a reimbursable loan in the interim. They can also help find a lawyer if you're thrown in jail.

In the unfortunate event of rape, Women's Health Clinics (*Clínicas de la Mujer*) in larger cities can provide specialized treatment and gather evidence for the police report. Don't expect too much from local police, but fill out a report as soon as possible in any case. A high dose of oral contraceptives (also known as the morning-after pill) lowers the odds of an unwanted pregnancy and is available at most *farmacías*. Every woman's emotional response to such a traumatic event will be different. For some, continuing their travels may be the best antidote, whereas others may prefer to end the trip early.

Travelers' checks and credit cards each have their own emergency number in case of loss or theft. Notify your travelers' insurance carrier, if applicable. In the case of a lost airline ticket, you'll probably have to buy a new one and wait until you get home to get reimbursed for the old one. Ask at the local airline branch for details. Your embassy will tell you what to do in case your passport goes missing.

Resources for U.S. Travelers

The **Bureau of Travel Affairs** of the U.S. Department of State, Washington, DC 20520, 202/647-5225, fax 202/261-8577, e-mail: secretary@state.gov, www.travel.state.gov, publishes *Travel Advisories* on individual countries available by mail, fax, or on the Internet at their website. Their list of publications, such as *A Safe Trip Abroad, Travel Warning on Drugs Abroad,* and *Tips for Travelers to Central & South America,* are available on the Internet at travel.state.gov/travel_pubs.html, or from the Superintendent of Documents, P.O. Box 371954, Pittsburgh, PA 15250-7954, 202/512-1800, fax 202/512-2250. They cost $1–1.50 each.

MONEY

CURRENCY

In September 2000, Ecuador officially laid the beleaguered old sucre to rest and replaced it with the **U.S. dollar.** The exchange rate was fixed at $1 to 25,000 of the old sucres. While the reasons for this switch were clear (see special topic, "The Big $witch"), the results remain to be seen. Naturally, the changeover is taking longer in the countryside, where as of late 2000 prices were still being quoted in sucre. It shouldn't be long, though, before Ecuador's old currency will be worth something only to collectors and Monopoly buffs.

Now more than ever, the U.S. dollar is the currency of choice to bring to Ecuador. Travelers carrying dollars from home, of course, will be happy they don't have to worry about exchanging money. The flip side of this convenience is that, for the near future at least, expect prices to change significantly from month to month. Guidebook prices are only approximate at best (a fact guidebook authors will explain until they're blue in the face), but in Ecuador in 2000 and beyond, everything is particularly up for grabs.

Outside of major cities, **cash** is the easiest—and often only—form of dollars to use. Ecuador has begun minting its own coins, equivalent to U.S. cents (100 to one dollar), nickels (5 cents), dimes (10 cents), quarters (25 cents), and half dollars (50 cents), but expect change *(cambio)* to be rare for a while. Even $5 bills are hard to change sometimes; it's best to bring small bills and hoard them. Keep an eye out for **counterfeit** bills, which can often be spotted by their smoothness (real bills are printed with faint impressions), limpness (real bills are crisp), and sloppy presidential portraits.

The bulk of your money should be in **travelers' checks,** which can be refunded if lost or stolen. Small denominations are again easiest to exchange and handiest when rates fluctuate. American Express and Visa travelers' checks are the most widely accepted, but Thomas Cook and Citibank can also pass. Always try to have some cash on you; the farther you get from Quito and Guayaquil, the harder it gets to change travelers' checks, especially on weekends. *Casas de cambio* (exchange houses) offer better services and lower commissions than banks—plus, their hours are better and the lines are shorter. (Banks often restrict hours during which you can exchange travelers' checks.) Commissions at *casas de cambio* are often between 1–2 percent, and sometimes depend on the amount charged.

Be sure to keep the serial numbers and the number to call if your checks are lost or stolen in a separate place from the physical checks. Exchange houses and some banks change travelers' checks to cash dollars, but only some businesses will let you pay with travelers checks—usually those near the high end. Some tellers can get picky with signatures, so if your chicken scratch doesn't match the one on the check, it may be rejected. If this happens with American Express checks, the office in Quito will issue you a new one immediately.

Credit cards are accepted in many higher-end shops, hotels, restaurants, and travel agencies. Although it's technically illegal, most businesses pass the 10 percent service charge for credit card transactions straight on to the customer. Some don't—most notably the Supermaxi supermarket chain and the South American Explorers—and others offer discounts for cash payments. It's generally best to pay with cash or travelers' checks whenever possible and save the credit cards for emergencies. MasterCard and Visa are the most widely accepted, and cardholders can draw cash advances. American Express, Diner's Club, and Discover are much harder to use.

Note that interest rates on **cash advances** are often compounded daily, and they may even carry a maintenance fee. These are available in Ecuador only at the credit card head offices listed in the Quito chapter. American Express members can buy AmEx travelers' checks at the office in Quito using a personal check from your account for a 1 percent fee (gold card members don't even need the personal check).

For any card, keep the customer service number in a separate place from the card in case your card is lost or stolen. Just because an establishment sports a credit card sticker, it doesn't necessarily take them. Always ask.

Automated teller machines (ATMs) are becoming more and more common in Ecuador. Some credit cards can now issue you a personal identification number (PIN) so you can use their cards to withdraw cash advances at ATMs. Machines accept ATM cards on the PLUS and Cirrus networks, as well as MasterCards and Visas that have been assigned a PIN—call your card issuer for information on setting this up. Most ATM machines have a daily withdrawal limit of $200 or less, which you can sometimes subvert by visiting multiple machines. Don't count on getting more than $400 in a single day. Look to the Internet for a list of ATM locations worldwide: www.mastercard.com/atm for MasterCard and Cirrus, and www.visa.com/pd/atm/main.html for Visa and Plus. Check with your bank about any transaction charge.

Money transfers are probably the least cost-effective way to get funds, but in a pinch they're often the only fast and sure way to get your hands on cash. Ask at your home bank about direct bank-to-bank transfers. Find out which banks in Ecuador, if any, your bank deals with and how long the transaction takes beforehand. **Western Union** has offices in Quito and Guayaquil.

THE BIG $WITCH

Ecuador's decision to join Panama as only the second country in Latin America to switch to the U.S. dollar was largely one of resignation. In abandoning the sucre, the Ecuadorian government was basically admitting that it and governments of the future could not be trusted with the nation's monetary policy. In the process, they linked their country's future to the economic decisions of policy makers a hemisphere away.

Politicians around the world like to spend money. The trick is to not spend more than you receive in taxes or can borrow from foreigners (as was the case in the United States in the 1980s and early 1990s), or else you end up in debt. Ecuador's governments have traditionally spent more than they received in taxes, and they chose to "create" more money by printing it instead of actually earning it in other ways.

The problem is, without the financial holdings to back it up, money can quickly become worth no more than the paper it's printed on—as the residents of Germany learned between the World Wars, when it took a wheelbarrow full of bills to buy a loaf of bread. Printing money unavoidably leads to unsustainable levels of price increases, or inflation. The economic costs of high inflation are devastating, particularly to the poor, who don't have the resources to adjust or the ability to convert cash into inflation-safe assets like gold or U.S. Treasury bonds.

By replacing the sucres with the U.S. dollar, the Ecuadorian government gave up the option of printing money and its subsequent inflationary effects. Ecuadorians no longer have to trust their government to exhibit political restraint—the government itself has thrown up its hands and entrusted its economy to the decisions of the policy makers in Washington, D.C. To spend more money, the Ecuadorian government must now either collect it in taxes or borrow it from abroad, case closed. Because it's unlikely that the U.S. Federal Reserve will engage in its own fit of reckless monetary policy, Ecuador's economy now rides on the credibility and stability of the U.S. dollar—as currencies go, a safe bet.

The main risk is that the U.S. Federal Reserve isn't obligated to take Ecuador's economy into account when it makes its economic decisions. When the U.S. Secretary of the Treasury sneezes, Ecuador's economy may catch cold. Interest rates are generally increased during economic boom times and lowered during economic busts. If the U.S. and Ecuador are on opposite sides of the economic cycle, Ecuador gets the wrong monetary medicine.

As of late 2000, though, things were looking good. Ecuador's monthly inflation plummeted from 14.3 percent in January to 1.4 percent in August. It remains to be seen whether this last-ditch measure will benefit everyone in Ecuador, or just a few at the top, as has traditionally been the case. Dollarization is no sure answer, but in a world where money hardly recognizes international boundaries and developing countries are desperate for access to that money, a sound currency is a must. The loss of policy flexibility may be worth it.

—Jeff Baker

OTHER MONEY MATTERS

Tipping

A *propina* (tip) isn't required or expected but usually doesn't take much out of your pocket and can make someone's day. Better restaurants often add 10 percent for *servicio* (service); if they don't, consider leaving it anyway. For cheaper restaurants, porters, hairdressers, taxi drivers, and guides, 5–10 percent will do. See "Life Onboard" in the "Visiting the Islands" section in the Galápagos Islands chapter for advice on tipping naturalist guides in the islands.

Taxes

Shops, hotels, and restaurants may charge up to 10 percent in *impuestos* (taxes), which should be noted separately on the *cuenta* (bill). More expensive restaurants and hotels add a 12 percent **value-added tax** *(IVA)* of 12 percent and another 10 percent for **service** *(servicio)* to their bills. Upon leaving the country, you'll be slapped with a $25 **airport departure tax.**

Budgeting

The flip side of Ecuador's recent economic woes is that it's one of the cheapest countries to visit in Latin America. Serious budget travelers can get by for under $10 pp per day by taking advantage of cheap buses, $3–5 hotel rooms, and $1–2 set meals. A more comfortable budget of $10–20 per day will leave you room for a movie, museum, and a *cerveza* or two when the day is done. While researching this book, my budget fell around $30 per day. Consider skimping on hotels rather than food: quality body fuel can affect your whole outlook, whereas almost all rooms are the same once you're asleep. Between $40–50 pp per day allows you to factor in quality hotels, national plane flights, and day tours, whereas $50 and up is the realm of luxury hotels and rental cars.

COMMUNICATIONS

MAIL

Sending

Ecuador's postal system is far from perfect, and international mail has the highest mortality rate. Don't send anything of value because theft from envelopes and packages is common. E-mail and faxes are quicker and surer alternatives to snail mail, and self-enclosed aerograms have better odds of reaching their destination. Have everything franked in front of you at the post office—steaming off unused stamps has been known to occur. The closer to the capital you mail something going out of the country, the lesser its chances of vanishing into the postal ether.

Rates have gone up considerably in recent years but are still among the cheapest on the continent. There are two categories: the Americas, and the rest of the world. Airmail postcards and letters to the Americas cost 68 cents if they're under 20 grams, and letters or packages between 21–100 grams are $1.52. First-class airmail for packages between 1–2 kg is $9.80, and every kg beyond that up to 10 kg is $4.92.

Rates to the rest of the world are significantly higher, particularly for packages. International certified mail *(con certificado)* is worth the extra charge. Private air courier services are more expensive but far more reliable.

Boxes to mail souvenirs or extra luggage home can be picked up for free at supermarkets or other businesses. Expensive stores can often arrange to mail home your purchases for you, although you'll pay for the service. Think twice before doing this at less expensive stores to lessen the odds of waiting for a package that never arrives.

Federal Express can send a 2-kg package to the United States for $42, to Canada for $65, and to Europe for $72 (5 kg costs $90, $131, and $144, respectively). Airlines are another option for mailing packages; KLM can send freight to London for $8.50 per kg up to 45.

Receiving

Receiving mail is as slow and chancy as sending it. Have the sender declare "no stated value" *(sin valor)* and mark packages "used clothing" *(ropa usada)* or "used books" *(libros usados)* in large letters to minimize import duties (often bogus) and the chance of theft. Don't send anything of value in any case (the U.S. Postal Service won't insure mailings to South America), and don't bank on receiving it any time soon.

To receive mail via general delivery *(poste restante)*, have items marked "your-first-name YOUR-LAST-NAME, Lista de Correos, Correo Central, Quito, Ecuador, South America." Pick it up at the post office at Espejo and Guayaquil, tel. 2/288-118. When asking the person at the post office if there's any *poste restante* mail for you *(¿Hay algo para mi en el poste restante?)*, have them check under both your first and last name. The South American Explorers' Quito clubhouse, American Express, and various Spanish schools can receive and hold mail for members.

TELECOMMUNICATIONS

The national telephone system, in comparison to the postal service, functions well under the auspices of the national phone company, which changes its name almost as often as Ecuador changes presidents. It's currently called Andinatel in the Andes and Pacifictel along the coast, although you'll still see old EMETEL signs in distant towns. Almost every town has its own office, but service varies; national calls are no problem, but international calls may be impossible. Some offices will charge you for calls if it rings more than eight times, even if no one answers. Connections to the Galápagos and some parts of the Oriente and the coast are tenuous at best.

National calls cost about 10 cents per minute. All calls cost up to 20 percent less on weekdays after 7 P.M. and from 7 A.M. Saturday to 7 A.M. Monday. Calls from hotels are always more expensive, and many businesses will let you use their phone for national calls for a small

charge. Hotel management will often try to charge you even if you're using a calling card or calling collect.

To make long-distance calls within Ecuador, dial a "0" followed by the regional prefix code and the six-digit phone number (see the special topic, "Telephone Prefixes," for a list of regional codes). Drop the "0" within the same region. Cellular phones are everywhere—it's estimated that up to half of all national calls are made on one—and their numbers begin with "09." For directory information, dial "104"; for help with national long distance, dial "105"; and for international long distance, dial "116" or "117."

Pay Phones
Recently, Ecuador has seen an outbreak of public cellular phones maintained by two competing companies, Bell South and Porto Alo. Bell South seems to have the most staying power, but each system takes its own type of calling card *(carta telefonica)*, which you can buy in various denominations just about anywhere. Phones display the amount left on your card; national calls cost about 12 cents per minute.

International Calls
Although it's possible to call other countries through the normal telephone network, the new Internet phone connections (see following section) are so much cheaper that it's almost not worth it. It will cost you about $2.50 per minute to talk on a normal connection through the national telephone system or one of the pay phone companies. Different countries have different codes to reach an international operator. All codes are preceded by 999. Codes for some countries follow: Canada, 175; Italy, 164/174; Spain, 176; UK, 178; Switzerland, 160; France, 180; U.S., 170 for MCI, 171 for Sprint/NYNEX, 119 for AT&T USA Direct.

TELEPHONE PREFIXES

PREFIX	PROVINCE(S)	MAJOR CITIES
2	Pichincha	Quito
3	Bolívar, Cotopaxi, Chimborazo, Pastaza, Tungurahua	Ambato, Puyo, Riobamba
4	Guayas	Guayaquil, Salinas
5	Los Ríos, Manabí, Galápagos	Manta, Portoviejo, Quevedo, Babahoyo
6	Carchi, Esmeraldas, Imbabura, Napo, Orellana, Sucumbíos	Esmeraldas, Tulcán, Ibarra, Latacunga, Tena, Coca, Lago Agrio
7	Azuay, Cañar, El Oro, Loja, Morona-Santiago, Zamora-Chinchipe	Cuenca, Machala, Loja, Zamora

To call Ecuador from the United States, dial the international access code (011), the country code for Ecuador (593), the province/cell phone code (02-07 or 09), and the six-digit local number—14 digits total. AT&T has a **Language Line,** 800/752-0093, ext. 196, e-mail: info@language line.com, www.languageline.com, with translators available around the clock ($2.50 plus $4.50 per minute).

Internet

After volcanoes erupting, governments mutating, and a whole new system of money, the most remarkable change in Ecuador in the late 1990s was the arrival of the Internet. Perhaps a dozen places in the country offered access in 1997; three years later, you could hit that many with a rock from some street corners in Quito. Instantaneous and inexpensive, e-mail *(correo electronico)* and the Internet makes it easy to keep in touch with friends back home.

Most Internet cafés are open daily 7 A.M.–10 P.M. and charge $1 or less per hour. There is even talk of companies starting to offer free access, which could lower café prices even further. Almost all cafés offer Internet phone services such as Net2phone (www.net2phone. com) that allow you to dial phone numbers worldwide and talk through the computer using a microphone and headset. This setup is much cheaper than normal long-distance calls (20–30 cents per minute from Ecuador to the United States), even if the quality isn't always as good and only one person can speak at a time. Most Internet cafés also have scanners, printers, fax services, and word processing programs. (Note: on Spanish-language keyboards, to type the "@" symbol for e-mail addresses, you often have to hold the "Alt Gr" key and hit "2.") If you plan to use the Internet to stay in touch, you can set up a free e-mail account through services like Hotmail (www.hotmail.com), Yahoo! Mail (mail.yahoo.com), or USA.net (www.usa.net/personal).

MEDIA

Newspapers and Magazines

Local publications include national Spanish-language newspapers such as *Diario Hoy, El Comercio,* and *El Universo.* International editions of *Time* and *Newsweek,* along with the foreign edition of the *Miami Herald,* are available in larger cities. It's often just as easy to keep up to date online at sites like CNN (www.cnn.com) or ABC News (abcnews.go.com).

Television and Radio

Television programming consists of three things more than anything else: soccer; slapstick comedy shows with adults dressed and acting like children; and *telenovelas,* the archetypal Latin soap operas in which poor Cinderellas from the *barrio* struggle for love against the wickedness of the rich.

Because they're inexpensive and not limited by mountainous terrain (as phone lines are), transistor radios are the only connection between much of the country and the outside world. They're the first thing plugged in when electricity is installed, and they are seldom turned off, or even down, afterward. Stations, mostly AM, broadcast music, news, and educational programming in Spanish and indigenous languages.

OTHER PRACTICALITIES

WHEN TO GO

The most important factors in deciding the timing of your trip are weather, tourist seasons, and events—namely festivals—that occur at specific times.

In terms of **weather**, there is really no "best" time to visit Ecuador. Climatic cycles in different parts of the country don't coincide, so knowing which area(s) you plan to visit is the key in figuring out when to go. See "Climate" under "The Land" section in the Introduction chapter for details on seasonal variations throughout the country.

Local **tourist seasons** occur near major holidays in late December and Feb.–March. South Americans often take their vacations, air ticket prices rise, and hotels are often full during these and other minor festivities. Many North American and European tourists come during the summer vacation months of Jun.–Aug. I prefer months like February, when there are enough visitors that you don't feel like you're the only foreigner in the country, but not so many that you feel as if you haven't left home.

Fans of local **festivals** might want to plan a trip to coincide with a few of the better ones, such as San Lorenzo's Santos Reyes and Santos Inno-

centes the first week in January or Cuenca's solemn Christmas processions. See "Festivals and Public Holidays" in the "Arts and Entertainment" section, as well as individual city descriptions, for festival dates and descriptions.

WHAT TO BRING

When packing for a trip, two old sayings hold true. First, lay out what you want to bring, then take half that and twice as much money. The second, an adage of international journalists and inveterate business travelers, warns to take only as much as you could carry at a dead run for half a kilometer.

In other words, pack light. It's amazing how much you think you might need, only to return home and find out that, not only did you not use the questionable items, but you also didn't unpack half of what you considered indispensable. Leave room for souvenirs. When you think you've packed all the right things, but before you hop on the plane, carry your bags around the block a few times and then reconsider what you *really* need.

Obviously, different types of traveling call for different styles of packing. Business and luxury

Otavalo

JULIAN SMITH

PACKING LIST

TOILETRIES

contact lens accessories
contraceptives (Don't trust the condoms in South America.)
dental floss
facecloth
first-aid kit
insect repellent (100% DEET is best)
moleskin for blisters
nail clippers or file
personal medicines with prescriptions for refills
Q-tips
soap in plastic case
shampoo and/or conditioner
toothbrush
toothpaste
tampons
towel

OTHER ESSENTIALS

books (Thick paperbacks are traveler's currency.)
cable lock to secure luggage
duct tape
extra batteries
film
iodine tablets or camping water filter (if you plan to go off the
     beaten track)
journal/address book
name tag securely attached to bag
photocopies of passport and plane tickets
replacement pair of glasses/contacts
rope or cord
sewing kit
small flashlight
small lock for luggage
small traveler's alarm clock or watch with alarm
soft foam earplugs
Spanish dictionary
spare flashlight bulb
sunglasses with retainers
Swiss army knife or multi-tool
water bottle
reseable Ziploc bags (Come in very handy.)

OTHER GOOD IDEAS

electrical adapter (There are very few grounded outlets in
     Ecuador.)
field guides, binoculars for wildlife viewing
flip-flop sandals for dirty shower stalls
mosquito netting (can buy there)
shortwave radio

travelers have more leeway than backpackers; leisure tourists fall somewhere in between. Do *not* bring jewelry or, for that matter, anything expensive and irreplaceable. Backpackers should avoid carrying everything in one bag to avoid losing it all at once; I've seen it happen. Split things up with a smaller daypack, and keep some emergency money in a pouch or in your shoe. It's easy and convenient to store belongings and purchases in Quito while you explore other parts of the country.

Luggage

Convertible **travel packs** have integral shoulder straps to carry like a backpack but can zip up snug like a suitcase for plane travel. These packs offer the best of both styles of luggage—you can pack and unpack it easily *and* sling it on your back—although they aren't as secure as a hard-shell suitcase and not as comfortable as a real backpack for long hauls. They often have special features like zip-off daypacks and lockable zipper pulls. I took the Continental Journey model made by **Eagle Creek,** 3055 Enterprise Court, Vista, CA 92083, 800/874-9925, www.eaglecreek.com, on my latest trip to Ecuador and, having never used a convertible pack before, was happily surprised with its performance. **TravelSmith,** 60 Leveroni Court, Novato, CA 94949, 800/950-1600, www.travelsmith.com, also makes travel luggage and clothing, and many backpack companies, such as Lowe, have started to turn out travel models.

Backpackers will find **internal-frame packs** the easiest to manage. External-frame packs get caught on everything and are more fragile. A waterproof pack cover and liner (garbage bags work well inside) will keep your things dry and protect the pack somewhat in transit.

If you don't plan to venture far afield, **suitcases** give your belongings the most protection, especially on airplanes. Whether you bring a large backpack or suitcase, a **daypack** is essential for short excursions.

Bedding

Sleeping bags are only really necessary for camping, but anyone who plans to sleep cheap should consider bringing a **sleeping sack,** for hygiene if nothing else. It's easy to make your own: just fold a sheet in half and sew across one narrow end (the bottom) and two-thirds of the way up the long side. While it's not surrounding a dirty hotel pillow, your own **pillowcase** can double as a dirty-clothes bag. Sleeping bags can be rented in Quito for backpacking trips.

TRAVEL INSURANCE

The best option for insurance abroad comes from your own insurance company, provided they cover you overseas. Check this before you leave, along with what exactly is covered and how to file a claim. Also check to see if your policy covers your belongings abroad. There's no sure answer on who needs travel insurance; if something goes wrong, you could wind up with hefty medical bills or something less serious, but still annoying, like lost luggage or canceled flights.

Travel insurance coverage options often include emergency medical evacuation, reimbursement for delayed flights and lost baggage, accidental death and dismemberment protection, and, in the worst-case scenario, repatriation of remains. Always take a copy of your insurance policy with you, and if you make two or more international trips a year, it's worth getting an annual policy instead of buying insurance on a trip-by-trip basis. You can compare travel insurance policies on the Internet at www.moneyextra-insurance.com.

Aside from specific travel insurance providers, a few other options exist. Major **credit cards** like MasterCard, Visa International, and American Express offer some form of travel insurance for their gold card or preferred cardholders if they pay for their tickets and/or hotels with the credit card. **ISIC** cardholders are covered for basic accidents and medical problems, and **AARP** (American Association of Retired Persons) members can secure supplemental coverage for foreign medical care.

Check your policy carefully and scratch any unnecessary riders—for example, trip cancellation insurance if you're not taking a group tour. Some companies have 24-hour emergency hotlines. Most operate on a reimbursement policy, in which you pay in full out of your own pocket at the time of treatment and are paid back once you return home and file the appropriate paperwork.

TRAVEL INSURANCE COMPANIES IN THE U.S.

Access America: 6600 W. Broad St., Richmond, VA 23230, 800/284-8300
e-mail: service@accessamerica.com,
www.accessamerica.com

TravelGuard.com: 1145 Clark St., Stevens Point, WI 54481, 877/216-4885,
e-mail: webmaster@noelgroup.com
website:www.travel-guard.com

Travel Insurance Services: 2950 Camino Diablo, Suite 300, P.O. Box 299, Walnut Creek, CA 94597-0299, 800/937-1387, 925/932-1387, fax 925/932-0442
e-mail: webinfo@travelinsure.com
www.travelinsure.com

TravelMed Assistance Group: 43 West 730 US Route 30, Suite 200, Sugar Grove, IL 60554, 877/307-7100, 630/466-7100
www.tmassist.com

TRAVEL INSURANCE COMPANIES IN THE U.K.

Navigators Travel Insurance: Consort Suite, Northern Assurance Buildings, Albert Square, Manchester, M2 4DN, tel. 0870/241-0576, fax 0161/973-6418
e-mail: inquiries@navigatortravel.net,
www.navigatortravel.co.uk (geared toward backpackers and independent travelers)

Medibroker: 17 Seatonville Road, Whitley Bay, Tyne & Wear, NE25 9DA, tel. 0191/297-2411, fax 0191/251-6424,
e-mail: medibroker@aol.com,
www.medibroker.com

Worldcover Direct: tel. 0800/365-121
e-mail: world.cover@gecapital.com,
www.worldcover.com

Clothing

Again, take less than you think you'll need. Veteran backpackers find one change of everything, with a few more socks and underwear, do nicely. Dark colors don't need to be washed as often, and a few months of hard traveling will leave your clothes a dull noncolor anyway, so leave Grandma's antique blouse at home. Light-to medium-weight clothing is the most versatile (nylon cloth dries more quickly than cotton). Try to avoid camouflage or army-style clothing and jungle boots, especially in the Oriente.

One or two long-sleeved shirts or blouses should be enough, along with two to three short-sleeve tops. One or two pairs of long pants and the same of shorts will do. Shorts that can double as swim trunks are ideal for the coast, Oriente, and Galápagos. Jeans are heavy and take forever to dry once they get wet, and long skirts are breezy but often impractical.

Three to five pairs each of socks and underwear should last you from one wash day to the next. Comfortable sports bras are easier to care for and can double as a top. Take thick socks and sock liners for heavy hiking.

A fleece pullover or thick sweater (available in Ecuador) will keep you warm during chilly Sierra nights, and it also makes a good pillow for long bus trips. Double the insulation with a wind and waterproof layer—either a poncho or, better yet, a light jacket. Five km into a muggy day hike, you'll be appreciating breathable waterproof fabrics like Gore-Tex or Helly-Tech. A pair of waterproof nylon pants that pack into a fist-sized ball come in handy for rainy hikes or walks through the rainforest. Some travel and outdoor clothing companies make convertible pants with legs than can zip off, transforming them into shorts.

Hiking boots are the most rugged (and, if already broken in, comfortable) footwear for exploring rough countryside. Give your feet a break with a lighter pair of sneakers or sport sandals. Nothing but nothing beats rubber boots for knee-deep Amazon mud. They're for sale all over the country ($5–10), and many lodges rent or loan them, but it can be difficult finding larger sizes (U.S. 10+). On the other hand, they're heavy and very bulky in luggage. Consider buying a pair in Quito to take on your jungle trip, and then resell them to another tourist before you leave, or donate them to your tour company.

Dressing up for a civilized evening out may make it worth bringing a light dinner jacket for men and a nice dress or skirt for women. A light, wide-brimmed straw or cotton hat is a good idea to keep the harsh sun off your face and neck.

PHOTOGRAPHY

In photogenic Ecuador, camera gear is expensive and the selection of film is limited at best, so bring everything you think you'll need.

Film

Slide film captures colors better, whereas prints are easier to pass around to friends and family. In either case, bring an assortment of speeds, from 100 ASA for bright Sierra sunlight to 400 ASA for the dim jungle. (Remember that faster film with higher ASA ratings is grainier.) Hand your film through airport X-ray machines just to be sure, and try to keep it cool before and after shooting. Unless you can't wait, don't develop your pictures in Ecuador; the quality isn't the greatest. On the other hand, it's not a good idea to carry exposed film around, so the best option would be to mail your rolls back or send them back with a friend in a prepaid developing mailer.

Cameras

The traditional 35-mm SLR cameras give you the widest latitude of control over your shots with their interchangeable lenses and the option of switching out half-shot rolls. Newer automatic cameras, though, are quickly catching up in terms of picture quality and ease of use. I like compact weatherproof models like the Olympus Stylus series; they do all your thinking for you and fit in your pocket. Better models run $300–400. Plastic resealable Ziploc bags protect camera and film from dust, and a UV filter for SLR models cuts through high-altitude Andean haze.

Shooting Advice

The best light falls within 1–2 hours of sunrise and sunset—some professional photographers hesitate to shoot outside these times. Here on the equator, the strong, vertical sunlight creates harsh shadows that develop as black holes. Around midday, a fill flash helps, as does shooting in the shade or on cloudy days. The strong light contrasts in the jungle can play havoc with light meters and are usually too much of a range for any film to capture. The trick is to shoot on cloudy days on a tripod for long (4–10 second) exposures. High-speed film and a flash can yield better results.

In the Galápagos, the trick isn't finding great shots—after a week you'll be sick of boobies and sea lions in your face—but to bring enough film and to take distinctive pictures. Film on the boats and in town is expensive. Sell any leftover to fellow travelers. Capture the animals' perspective by kneeling or lying down at their level. You don't have to shell out hundreds of dollars for a professional underwater camera to record the spectacular sea life; disposable underwater cameras can go down to four meters and cost about $15.

Always ask permission before taking a photo of locals (or use a long telephoto lens), and don't give money for photos or else it will become expected. A good alternative is to offer to take down the person's address and mail them a copy later. An instant camera can make you the most popular person in the village in two minutes flat. Latin Americans like to see photos of your family and where you come from—just be cautious with images of wealth like expensive cars.

WEIGHTS AND MEASURES

Ecuador uses the metric system. There is a U.S.-to-metric conversion chart in the back of this book.

ELECTRICITY

As in North America, electricity here is a 100 watt/60 cycle alternating current. Flat-prong outlets seldom have a third grounding hole. Plug in expensive electronic equipment, such as computers, using a three-to-two-prong adapter/surge protector available at U.S. hardware stores.

Power outages are common, even in major cities. Electricity is often shut off in rural areas after dark, and far-flung lodges usually operate on electric generators, limiting usage even further.

TIME

The mainland is five hours behind GMT, which is equal to U.S. Eastern Standard Time. The Galápagos are one hour behind the mainland (six hours behind GMT, equal to U.S. Central Time). Because days and nights on the equator last the same year-round, there's no need for daylight saving time.

BUSINESS HOURS

Hours of operation change with amazing rapidity, often at the whim of employees or owners. Many businesses are closed on Monday, adding a day to the traditional weekend. Long lunch breaks are the norm, and they last longer (up to two hours) in hotter areas such as the coast. A good strategy is to come 10–20 minutes before something reopens after the lunch break to ensure your spot at the front of the line.

Typical business hours are Mon.–Fri. 8 or 9 A.M. to 5 or 6 P.M., with a lunch break from 12:30–2 P.M. Saturdays are often half days ending at noon or 1 P.M. Banks operate weekdays 9 A.M.–1 P.M., occasionally in the afternoons and on Saturday. *Casas de cambio* stay open until 6 P.M. and are usually open on Saturday morning. Government offices and embassies often close by early afternoon. Restaurants tend to stay open later in typical Latin American fashion. Dinner usually starts at 9 or 10 P.M.

MAPS AND TOURIST INFORMATION

Maps
International Travel Maps, 530 West Broadway, Vancouver, BC V5Z 1E9 Canada, 604/879-3621, fax 604/879-4521, e-mail: itmb@itmb.com, www.itmb.com, have 150 of their own maps and distribute 23,000 more by other publishers. Their 1:1,000,000 Ecuador ($8.95) is without peer. In the United States, maps of Ecuador and South America are available from **Maplink,** 30 South La Patera Ln., Unit 5, Santa Barbara, CA 93117, 805/692-6777, fax 805/692-6787, e-mail: cust-

serv@maplink.com, www.maplink.com.

In Ecuador look for Nelson Gomez's foldout map/guides to Quito, Cuenca, Guayaquil, and all of Ecuador. They have blue covers and are written in Spanish. Topographical maps are available at the IGM in Quito, along with the detailed *Hojas de Rutas* (route guides) for Riobamba–Cuenca, Quito–Riobamba, and Quito–Esmeraldas.

Travel Resources

The *Latin America Travel Advisor,* run by Robert Kunstaetter out of Quito, is a free news bulletin with up-to-the-minute information on safety, health, politics, and travel. It's available at www.amerispan.com/lata (e-mail: LATA@pi.pro.ec). The **South American Explorers** have their headquarters in the United States (126 Indian Creek Rd., Ithaca, NY 14850, 607/277-0488, e-mail: explorer@samexplo.org, www.samexplo.org) and clubhouses in Quito and Lima. See "Information" in the Quito chapter for more information on this valuable travel clearinghouse.

Magellan's International Travel Corporation, 110 W. Sola St., Santa Barbara, CA 93101, 800/962-4943, fax 800/962-4940, e-mail: customerservice@magellans.com, www.magellans.com, has thousands of travel-related items in their catalog, including adaptor plugs, shortwave radios, airline pillows, and alarms. **Consumer Reports Online,** 101 Truman Ave., Yonkers, NY 10703, www.consumerreports.org, offers the highly recommended *Travel Buying Guide* and the *Consumer Reports Travel Letter* to members, and **Transitions Abroad Online,** P.O. Box 1300, Amherst, MA 01004-1300, 800/293-9373, fax 413/256-0373, e-mail: info@transabroad.com, www.transabroad.com, offer articles from their *Transitions Abroad* magazine at their website. They also publish the *Alternative Travel Directory: The Complete Guide to Work, Study, and Travel Overseas* and *Work Abroad: The Complete Guide to Finding a Job Overseas.*

Two good sources for guidebooks are the **Adventurous Traveler Bookstore,** 245 South Champlain, Burlington, VT 05401, 800/282-3963, fax 800/677-1821, e-mail: book@atbook.com, shop.gorp.com/atbook, and **Travel Books and Language Center,** 4437 Wisconsin Ave. NW, Washington, DC 20016, 800/220-2665, 202/237-1322, fax 202/237-6022, e-mail:

travelbks@aol.com, www.bookweb.org/book-store/travelbks.

LAUNDRY

Self-service laundry machines are few and far between. Many inexpensive hotels, though, have a *pila* (scrubbing board) and a clothesline out back. Water basins are often used for drinking water, so scoop water out instead of washing directly in the basin. Hotels generally frown on guests washing clothes in sinks. Packets of *detergente* are available at general stores.

Laundry services wash clothes by the piece or the kilogram. This can be expensive in high-end hotels and may take a day or two for everything to air dry. Laundromats can usually have your things back the same day or the next morning. You may be expected to wash out your own underwear in the shower. Dry cleaning *(lavaseco)* is available in larger cities.

SPECIAL NOTES

Women Travelers

Whistles, comments, honks, and catcalls are an ingrained part of Latin American culture. Thanks to pop culture stereotypes, foreign women—especially North Americans and *especially* blondes—get the most attention. Follow the lead of Ecuadorianas and simply ignore it. After all, a response is what they're after, and the more vehement the better.

LAUNDRY SPANISH

bleach	*blanquear*
dry	*secar*
fold	*doblar*
iron	*planchar*
laundromat	*lavandería*
starch	*almidonar*
wash	*lavar*
by the pound/ by the bag	*por libro/por bolsa*
in cold/warm/hot water	*en agua fria/tem perada/caliente*

Physical boundaries are a different story. Pinches and outright grabs should be dealt with immediately and unequivocally. Just make sure there are other people around. On that note, don't go anywhere alone at night. Even women in groups are hassled in some areas of the country.

All this doesn't mean that women can't travel alone; many do with no problem at all, despite repeated disbelief from Ecuadorians ("You're traveling *alone?*"). You just need to be extra careful in this sexist society. Women's hostels, such as Eva Luna in Quito, are good places to meet fellow *viajeras* (female travelers).

Gay Travelers

Technically illegal and condemned by traditional Catholic edicts, homosexuality exists far underground in Ecuador. Attitudes are starting to change—the August 1998 constitution recognizes "the equality of all before the law without discrimination against age, sex, ethnic origin, color, religion, political affiliation, economic position, sexual orientation, state of health, incapacity, or difference of any kind"—but on the whole Latin American society is anything but welcoming to the gay lifestyle. Gay travelers are advised to keep a low profile.

The only real way to join the community is to meet someone already inside. The few gay bars and discos in Quito and Guayaquil are often members-only. On the Internet, stop by the **Gay Guide to Quito** at gayquitoec.tripod.com for a listing of gay clubs and gay-friendly businesses in Quito and Guayaquil. *Conexión G&L,* a free bi-monthly publication of the gay and lesbian community in Ecuador, can be found at any of the gay-friendly businesses listed in the Gay Guide to Quito, or by calling 2/561-466, 9/849-201 (e-mail: glconexion@hotmail.com). Another local gay newspaper has a website (in Spanish) at www.geocities.com/geminis357.

Travelers with Disabilities

Travelers with disabilities shouldn't expect many concessions. Wheelchair ramps are rare on buildings and sidewalks, braille is nonexistent, and seeing-eye dogs need at least a rabies vaccine to enter the country. For more information, contact **Mobility International, USA,** P.O. Box 10767, Eugene, OR 97440, 514/343-1284 (TTY), fax 514/343-6812, e-mail: info@ miusa.org, www.miusa.org, and the online **Global Access Disabled Traveler Network** (www.geocities.com/Paris/1502).

Travelers with disabilities have a range of options for assistance planning trips: the **Information Center for Individuals with Disabilities,** P.O. Box 750119, Arlington Heights, MA 02475, fax 781/860-0673, e-mail: contact@disability.net, www.disability.net; the **Travel Industry and Disabled Exchange,** 5435 Donna Ave., Tarzana, CA 91356, 818/343-6339; and the **Access-Able Travel Source,** e-mail: access-able@home.com, www.access-able.com.

Health escorts can be arranged through **Travel Care Companions,** 6965 El Camino Real, Suite 105, Carlsbad, CA 92009, 800/555-2977, 858/481-9330, fax 858/481-9182, e-mail: info@travelcarecompanions.com, www.travelcarecompanions.com; or **MedEscort International,** 1730 Vultee St., Allentown, PA 18105, 800/255-7182, 215/791-3111, fax 610/791-3111.

Traveling with Children

Children are considered life's greatest reward in Latin America, so parents traveling with children will enjoy compliments and assistance throughout the continent. Child and baby products are available in department stores in larger cities.

Senior Travelers

Age is respected in Ecuador, but there aren't any senior associations or travel organizations in the country. Make sure you can handle the physical demands of tours and lodges (some of the Galápagos hikes are steep and strenuous), and bring along a printed medical history and enough prescription medications for the entire trip, plus some extra.

The **American Association of Retired Persons (AARP),** 601 E St. NW, Washington, DC 20049, 800/424-3410, e-mail: member@ aarp.org, www.aarp.org, offers a Purchase Privilege Program for discounts on airfares, car rentals, and hotels. **ElderHostel,** 75 Federal St., Boston, MA 02110-1941, 877/426-8056, 978/323-4141, fax 617/426-0701, e-mail: registration@elderhostel.org, www.elderhostel.org, Inc. is a not-for-profit organization that has offered educational adventures for adults over 55 for 25 years.

BOB RACE

QUITO
INTRODUCTION

Ecuador's capital is an odd mix that somehow works. Centuries-old colonial buildings huddle next to garish skyscrapers and fast-food outlets, business-suited and mini-skirted professionals pass beggars in rags on the sidewalk, and spanking new electric trolleys glide silently by ancient buses belching clouds of exhaust.

For all its contradictions, Quito is blessed with a near-perfect climate and one of the prettiest settings of any capital in the world. Even grouchy travel writer Paul Theroux admits, "of all the mountaintop cities in South America, Quito struck me as being the happiest." It's a city you can easily fall for despite yourself.

After La Paz in Bolivia, Quito is the second-highest capital in Latin America (2,850 meters). The Pichincha volcanoes tower to the west, trapping fleecy clouds that would otherwise drift by and creating the spectacular peach and robin's-egg-blue sunsets captured in the "Paisaje de Quito" paintings of Oswaldo Guayasamin. Much of the population of Ecuador's second-largest city lives in *barrios* (neighborhoods) or shanty-towns up the slopes of the mountains or spread north and south of the city center.

As the seat of Ecuador's government and enclave of traditional values, Quito displays a deeply rooted conservative streak. Some residents call it The Capital of *El ¿Que dirá?* ("What would they say?"), referring to a concern with appearances and surface politeness. On the other hand, a slew of schools, including the Central University, Catholic University, and the National Polytechnic School, and modern businesses inject a healthy dose of worldly, cosmopolitan attitudes.

HISTORY

According to a legend of the pre-Inca Quitu tribe, the city of Quito was founded by Qitumbe, son of the god Quitu, in honor of his father. It is known that the valley that would eventually cradle Ecuador's capital was originally occupied by the Quitu tribe, who united with the Cara from the north into the Shyris nation around A.D. 1300. In 1487 the Incas took over and turned the city into an important nexus of their northern empire, known as the Quitosuyo. Within a hundred years, the empire fell to infighting, leaving things wide open for the newly arrived Spanish to start almost from scratch.

The city of San Francisco de Quito was founded by Sebastian de Benalcázar on December 6, 1534, named in honor of fellow conquistador Francisco Pizarro. Benalcázar quickly set about

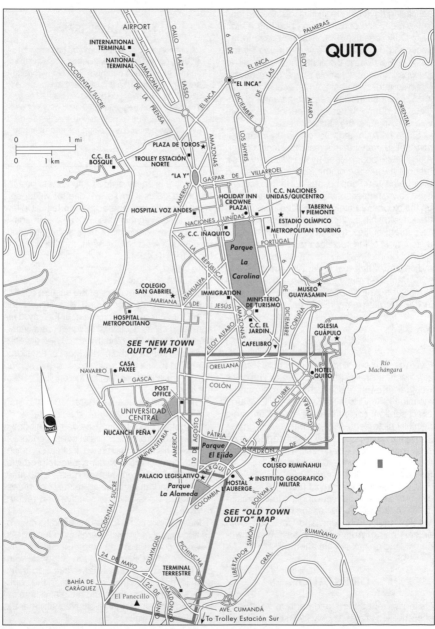

QUITO

AIRPORT

INTERNATIONAL TERMINAL ■
NATIONAL TERMINAL ■

"EL INCA" ●

PLAZA DE TOROS ★
TROLLEY ESTACIÓN NORTE ■
C.C. EL BOSQUE ■
"LA Y"

HOLIDAY INN CROWNE PLAZA ■
HOSPITAL VOZ ANDES ■
C.C. NACIONES UNIDAS/QUICENTRO
TABERNA PIEMONTE ▼
ESTADIO OLÍMPICO ■
METROPOLITAN TOURING ■

C.C. IÑAQUITO ■

Parque La Carolina

COLEGIO SAN GABRIEL ★
IMMIGRATION ■
MINISTERIO DE TURISMO ■
MUSEO GUAYASAMÍN ★

HOSPITAL METROPOLITANO ■
C.C. EL JARDÍN ■
CAFELIBRO ▼
IGLESIA GUÁPULO ★

SEE "NEW TOWN QUITO" MAP

CASA PAXEE ●
POST OFFICE ■
UNIVERSIDAD CENTRAL
HOTEL QUITO ●

Río Machángara

ÑUCANCHI PEÑA ▼

Parque El Ejido

COLISEO RUMIÑAHUI ★

PALACIO LEGISLATIVO ★
HOSTAL L'AUBERGE ★
INSTITUTO GEOGRÁFICO MILITAR ★
Parque La Alameda

SEE "OLD TOWN QUITO" MAP

RUMIÑAHUI

BAHÍA DE CARÁQUEZ
TERMINAL TERRESTRE ●
El Panecillo ▲
AVE. CUMANDÁ
↓ To Trolley Estación Sur

© AVALON TRAVEL PUBLISHING, INC.

0 — 1 mi
0 — 1 km

appointing government officials, distributing land to his men, and constructing churches. Originally Quito consisted only of the present-day section known as Old Town bounded by the Plaza de San Blas to the north, the Pichinchas to the west, and the Itchimbia ravine (currently La Marin square) to the east. An art school founded in 1535 helped the city become a center of religious art during the colonial period, complete with its own style, the Quito School.

Since its founding, Quito has been an administrative, rather than a manufacturing, center. A population boom, aided by the discovery of oil, brought thousands of immigrants who spread their homes and businesses north into today's New Town, farther south of Old Town, and west up the slopes of Pichincha. By the mid-1980s, these makeshift *suburbios* counted as much as 15 percent of the city's population and had acquired most of the services that the older areas took for granted. Today the city claims almost a million and a half residents. An earthquake in 1987 damaged many structures and left others in ruins, and the eruption of Guagun Pichinchu in 1999 terrified many residents.

CLIMATE

Quito reaps all the climatic benefits of its location in a mountain valley at 2,800 meters. The city's weather is often described as eternal spring, meaning balmy days between 8–21°C, warm, direct sunlight cooled by light, steady breezes, painfully picturesque clouds that usually gather for a short afternoon shower, all capped by a cool—but not cold—darkness. The saying that the city can experience all four seasons in a single day isn't far off the mark.

Dry season in the capital lasts June–Sept., with July and August receiving the least precipitation. A shortened dry season runs Dec.–Jan. More rain falls Feb.–Mar. and Oct.–Nov., with at least half of April seeing a torrential downpour taking up most of the afternoon.

ORIENTATION

Quito is about 30 km long north to south and about five km across. Luckily for first-time visitors,

NEW ADDRESSES

A new system of street numbers has been implemented in Quito, with letters prefixing the normal hyphenated numbers. The old numbers are often changed, so a business that was once at Coruña 5-43 might be at Coruña E34-22 now. The conversion began in 2000, and may not be universal yet, but it's definitely something to be aware of when you're looking for that all-night deli in the bad part of town.

the capital is easily divided into zones: one for historical sights (Old Town); one for visitor services, restaurants, and accommodations (New Town); and everything else. It's almost impossible to become disoriented: just look for the mountains to the west, or, at night, for the lights on top of them.

Old Town

Quito's historical heart sits at the eastern base of El Panecillo (Little Bread Loaf) hill, whose statue of the Virgin is visible from most of the city. This area, also called "Colonial" Quito, is roughly bordered by 24 de Mayo on the south and the Parque La Alameda to the north. Most of the sights are situated within a few blocks of the central Parque de la Independencia, the original core of the city.

Steep, narrow streets characterize this part of Quito, and cars barely fit in lanes designed for horse and foot traffic. Residents look down from wrought-iron balconies at street vendors—each with his own small crowd of skeptical but interested onlookers—hawking miracle products. Storefronts at ground level sell household wares, clothing, and an astounding number of shoes. Hotels are generally inexpensive and restaurants few.

Most visitors come for the outstanding churches and museums, which were key in having Old Town declared a World Heritage Site by UNESCO in 1978. Other visitors are content to wander the cobbled streets that evoke Ecuador's colonial past more than any others in the country—despite the handbills and red graffiti from the latest political uprising that occasionally mar the white-washed walls.

New Town

The split wedge formed by the Parques La Alameda and El Ejido point away from the commercial hub of the capital, enclosed by the Avenidas Pátria, Orellana, 10 de Agosto and 12 de Octubre. Tourists keep this part of Quito in business, supporting dozens of hotels and restaurants for every budget, along with enough souvenir shops, tour companies, and banks for two cities. Expensive apartments and embassies fill many blocks, especially Coruña on the eastern edge of the valley just before the initial drop-off toward the Amazon.

Other Neighborhoods

The section of Quito north of New Town sparkles with shiny highrises housing a large part of the city's businesses and is home to much of the capital's industry. Modern shopping centers and chic restaurants cater to the middle and upper classes who live in the area or in the fast-growing Valle Los Chillos to the east. The steep old neighborhood of Guapulo spills down below Avenida 12 de Octubre and the lofty Hotel Quito. More residential neighborhoods occupy the lower slopes of Pichincha west and north of New Town.

SAFETY

With one of the highest concentrations of bodies in the country, Quito naturally has its share of crime. It's nothing to cancel a trip over but definitely worth considering. By taking the standard precautions that you would in any major city, and avoiding a few problem spots, you should have little to worry about.

The diciest area in the city, and perhaps the country, is the Mariscal Sucre neighborhood of New Town. Robberies and muggings have gotten so bad in the blocks bordered by Vientimilla, Reina Victoria, Orellana, and 9 de Octubre that the U.S. Embassy has prohibited its employees from frequenting the area after dark. Definitely take a taxi if you're heading here at night, and reconsider walking alone even during the day. For that matter, with taxis so cheap, it's always a better idea to take a taxi at night around Quito instead of walking alone.

Watch for pickpockets and bag-slashers on the trolley, at the bus station, and in Old Town in general. Pay particular attention along La Ronda and when exiting tourist spots like churches while your eyes are still adjusting to daylight. Keep all bags and cameras in front of you, and don't leave your wallet in your back pocket. Don't go into any parks after dark.

El Panecillo, once off-limits to tourists even by taxi, has become safer since the local community started policing the streets. It's still recommended that you take a taxi here, though. As of late 2000, Guagua Pichincha was still considered too dangerous to climb—due to assaults and muggings, not eruptions—but check with the South American Explorers for the latest update.

SIGHTS

Quito's churches elicit more gasps and muted whistles than any of its other attractions. There certainly is enough opportunity; the city is said to have at least 86 of them, occupying up to one-quarter of the city's area. Most are accompanied by monasteries or convents. Large, blank exterior walls symbolize the division between the outer and inner world, where nuns from wealthy and poor backgrounds worship side by side. (Small details in the nuns' vestments traditionally revealed the owner's background.) Time away from prayer was often used to decorate walls and ceilings with elaborate paintings that praised the glories of heaven (especially in

the refectory of El Carmen) while hinting at the treasures of the present world just outside. Students, servants, and other secular residents still help tend indoor gardens and attend to daily tasks such as sewing, cooking, and cleaning.

Many churches closed for repairs after the earthquake of 1987, and it's anybody's guess when restorations will be complete. In some churches—notably El Carmen Bajo, La Compañia, and El Sagrario—the earthquake aggravated centuries-old weaknesses that threaten to bring the entire building down. Flash pictures are prohibited in most churches and historical museums to protect the fragile pigments of

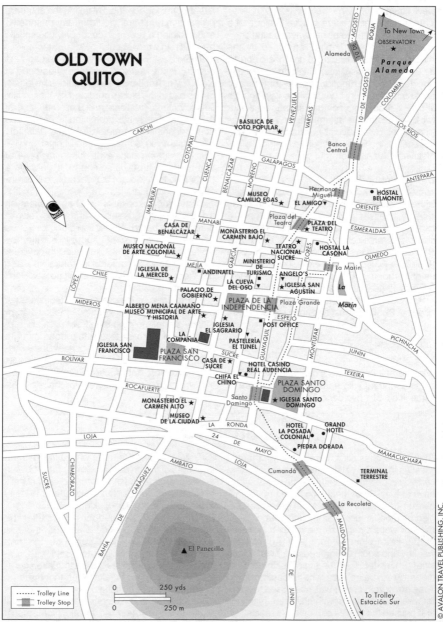

OLD TOWN QUITO

BASILICA DE VOTO POPULAR ★

CARCHI

VENEZUELA

VARGAS

10 DE AGOSTO

BORJA

To New Town

OBSERVATORY ★

Alameda

Parque Alameda

COLOMBIA

LOS RIOS

GALAPAGOS

Banco Central

ANTEPARA

COTOPAXI

BENALCAZAR

MORENO

CUENCA

MUSEO CAMILIO EGAS ■

Hermano Miguel

EL AMIGO ▼

ORIENTE

HOSTAL BELMONTE ●

ESMERALDAS

IMBABURA

MANABI

CASA DE BENALCÁZAR ★

MONASTERIO EL CARMEN BAJO ★

Plaza del Teatro

PLAZA DEL TEATRO ★

OLMEDO

MUSEO NACIONAL DE ARTE COLONIAL ★

GARCIA

TEATRO NACIONAL SUCRE

HOSTAL LA CASONA ●

FLORES

La Matin

CHILE

MEJIA

IGLESIA DE LA MERCED ★

ANDINATEL ■

MINISTERIO DE TURISMO

ANGELO'S ▼

La Marín

LÓPEZ

PALACIO DE GOBIERNO ★

LA CUEVA DEL OSO ▼

IGLESIA SAN AGUSTÍN ★

MIDEROS

ALBERTO MENA CAAMAÑO MUSEO MUNICIPAL DE ARTE Y HISTORIA ★

PLAZA DE LA INDEPENDENCIA

Plaza Grande

PICHINCHA

ESPEJO

POST OFFICE ●

IGLESIA EL SAGRARIO ★

MONTUFAR

JUNÍN

BOLIVAR

IGLESIA SAN FRANCISCO

LA COMPAÑIA ★

PLAZA SAN FRANCISCO

PASTELERÍA EL TÚNEL ▼

SUCRE

CASA DE SUCRE ★

HOTEL CASINO REAL AUDENCIA

TEXEIRA

ROCAFUERTE

CHIFA EL CHINO ▼

GUAYAQUIL

PLAZA SANTO DOMINGO

Santo Domingo

IGLESIA SANTO DOMINGO ★

MONASTERIO EL CARMEN ALTO ★

MUSEO DE LA CIUDAD ★

LA RONDA

HOTEL LA POSADA COLONIAL ●

GRAND HOTEL ●

MAMACUCHARA

LOJA

24 DE MAYO

PIEDRA DORADA ●

AMBATO

LOJA

Cumandá

TERMINAL TERRESTRE ■

SUCRE

CHIMBORAZO

CARAQUEZ

BAHÍA DE

La Recoleta

5 DE JUNIO

MALDONADO

To Trolley Estación Sur

▲ El Panecillo

- - - - Trolley Line
■ Trolley Stop

0 ——— 250 yds
0 ——— 250 m

© AVALON TRAVEL PUBLISHING, INC.

religious paintings and statues. Keep in mind that opening hours fluctuate almost daily; those given as follows are a rough guide at best.

OLD TOWN

The Municipality of Quito has put together an excellent map/guide to three historic walks through Old Town, written by Oscar Valenzuela-Morales and available throughout the city.

Plaza de La Independencia

The heart of colonial Quito features a winged statue to independence atop a high pillar. A park surrounding the base often echoes with the cries of evangelical preachers, who are ignored for the most part by the legion of old men out to feed the pigeons and enjoy the sun.

On the plaza's southwest side, the grimy **Catedral Metropolitana** is actually the third to stand on this site. José Antonio Sucre, the number-two man in South America's independence battles, is buried here. Behind the main altar is the smaller altar of Nuestra Señora de Los Dolores, where on August 6, 1875, president Gabriel García Moreno drew his last breath after being shot outside the presidential palace.

A long, arched walkway to the northwest lines the front of the **Palacio de Gobierno** (Government Palace). The balconies over the plaza, originally from the Palace of Les Tuilleries in Paris, were a gift from the French government just after the French Revolution. At the entrance to the main courtyard off the walkway stand two long-suffering guards in full uniform who must be the most-photographed people in the country. (It's probably for the best that guns aren't a part of the ceremonial outfit.) Inside the gate is a large painting depicting Francisco de Orellana's descent of the Amazon.

The former **Palacio Arzobispal** (Archbishop's Palace) on the northeast side now houses a series of small shops and boutiques. Cobbled courtyards, thick white-washed walls, and wooden balconies make it worth a peek. The plaza's colonial spell is broken only by the stark **City Hall** to the southeast, whose simple glass lines still manage to echo those of the Palacio de Gobierno opposite.

Plaza del Teatro

This plaza at Guayaquil and Sucre is home to the **Teatro Nacional Sucre,** one of Quito's finest theaters. The gorgeous building, erected in 1878, hosts frequent plays and concerts. The theater was closed as of late 2000 for extensive renovations, and from the looks of it there is still a long way to go.

Monasterio El Carmen Bajo

Enter this monastery on Venezuela between Olmedo and Manabí (there are three bells to ring—keep trying). White-washed stone pillars support a two-story courtyard inside surrounded by nun's quarters and schoolrooms.

El Panecillo as seen from Plaza San Francisco

TIM BEWER

Iglesia La Compañia

JULIAN SMITH

Iglesia El Sagrario

Formerly the main chapel of the Catedral Metropolitana, this separate church was begun in 1657 and completed half a century later. The walls and ceiling of the short nave are painted to simulate marble—even the bare stone is speckled black and white in a half-hearted granite imitation. Impressive paintings and stained glass windows decorate the center cupola. Bernardo de Legarda, the most outstanding Quiteño sculptor in the 18th century, carved and gilded the baroque *mampara* (partition) inside the main doorway.

Iglesia San Agustin

Ecuador's declaration of independence was signed at this church on Chile and Guayaquil on August 10, 1809. Many of the heroes who battled for independence are buried under the floor. No surface is left unpainted, including the likenesses of saints, which line the arches against a pastel background. A black Christ occupies a side altar.

The attached **Convento/Museo de San Agustin** on Chile and Flores features loads of colonial artwork on the walls and surrounds a palm-filled courtyard. Don't miss the incredible carved benches and altar of the Sala Capitular on the first floor.

Plaza San Francisco

This gently sloping, cobbled expanse can easily keep you occupied all afternoon. Head up the set of circular stairs to the front of the **Iglesia San Francisco,** where vendors of religious souvenirs keep visitors stocked with rosaries, candles, incense, icons, and amulets. This building, the largest and oldest colonial edifice in the city, was begun on the site of an Inca royal house within weeks of the city's founding in 1534. The first wheat grown in Ecuador sprouted in one of its courtyards, and Atahualpa's children learned to read, write, and add in its school. Much of the original construction has been lost to earthquakes, but some original work remains—look to the right of the main altar in the chapel of Señor Jesus de Gran Poder for an example.

Two white spires flank a glowering stone facade, which sets the perfect mood for the interior. Inside it's easy to imagine yourself in the 16th century, amid the musty odor drifting up from the creaking wooden floorboards. Bare lightbulbs are almost swallowed by the dusty gloom, with little help from the small, high windows. They didn't even bother to paint the walls here, choosing instead to gild first and ask questions later—thick encrustations cover almost every square inch. Seeing the carved roof alone is worth a visit. Notice how many of the design motifs come from the Inca, including the smiling/frowning faces of sun gods, repeated several times, and harvest symbols of flowers and fruit.

To the right of the main entrance, the **Franciscan Museum,** tel. 2/952-911, houses one of the finest collections of colonial art in Quito, dating from the 16th–19th centuries. (Open Mon.–Sat. 9 A.M.–6 P.M., Sun. 9 A.M.–noon, $1 pp.) On the other side, the **Capilla de Catuña** (Catuña Chapel) also has colonial art on display. As the story goes, this chapel was constructed by an indigenous man named Catuña who promised to have it completed in a certain length of time. When it became obvious that he wasn't going to come close to his deadline, he offered his soul to the Devil in exchange for help to get it done on time. Catuña finished and had a sudden change of heart, begging the Virgin Mary to save him from his hasty agreement. Sure enough, a foundation stone was discovered missing during the inauguration, negating his deal with the devil.

Plaza Santo Domingo

A statue of Sucre pointing to his victory site on the slopes of Pichincha decorates this plaza at the southern corner of Old Town. Crowds often surround performance artists in front of the **Iglesia Santo Domingo,** which was begun in 1581 and finished in 1650. Four clock faces and an off-center clock tower decorate the stone facade. Despite the stained glass behind the altar, the decorative elements inside somehow don't seem to work together; the baroque filigree of the Chapel of the Rosary to one side is especially jarring.

La Compañia

What is said to be the most beautiful church in the Americas is definitely among its most ornate. Seven tons of gold supposedly ended up on the ceiling, walls, and altars of "Quito's Sistene Chapel," which was built by the wealthy Jesuit order between 1605 and 1768. As of late 2000, the church was undergoing major restoration, primarily of the extensive damage done by the 1987 earthquake.

Even the outside is overwhelming, crammed with full-size statues, busts, sculpted hearts, and a garden's worth of leaves carved in stone. The interior has eight side chapels, one of which houses the guitar and remains of Santa Mariana de Jesus (see special topic). Some of the more expensive relics, including a painting of the Virgin framed with gold and precious stones, are locked away in a bank vault between festivals.

One of the more eye-catching objects in La Compañia is a painting depicting hell, which Paul Theroux described so glowingly in *The Old Patagonian Express:* "From a distance this mural seemed to me an accurate representation of a nighttime football game in El Salvador, but on closer inspection it was pure Bosch." Sinners with labels like *vanidad* (vanity) and *glotón* (gluttony) each receive an imaginative, excruciatingly appropriate punishment, a nightmarish panorama that is put to good use: "Schoolchildren from Quito are brought to the church and shown this mural so that, suitably terrified, they will stay on the straight and narrow."

Monasterio El Carmen Alto

This monastery at Rocafuerte and García Moreno was the home of Santa Mariana de Jesus from 1618–1645. Abandoned children were once passed through a small window in the patio to be raised by the nuns. The **Arco de La Reina** (Queen's Arch) over Rocafuerte marks the original southern entrance to Quito's center.

Iglesia de La Merced

One of Quito's newest churches (completed only in 1742) is entered on Chile just up from the corner with Cuenca. The 47-meter tower is the highest in the city and houses the largest bell in town. Pass the statue of Neptune out front to enter the high-vaulted nave decorated with white stucco on a pink background.

The church is dedicated to Our Lady of Mercy, whose statue inside is said to have saved the city from an eruption of Pichincha in 1575. To the left of the altar is the entrance to the **Monasterio de La Merced,** housing Quito's oldest clock, built in London in 1817.

SANTA MARIANA DE JESUS

Ecuador's first saint was so beautiful, they say, that she was forced to look at the world from beneath a dark veil her entire life. The one man who dared to look underneath was rewarded with the vision of a grinning skull. There were no more peeks.

A string of natural disasters and disease in the 17th century brought Quito to its knees. In 1645, at the age of 26, Mariana offered her life to God to spare the city's residents. Her blood was sprinkled in a garden, bringing forth a pure white lily, which has since been called the Lily of Quito.

Museo Nacional de Arte Colonial

Works by renowned artists Miguel de Santiago, Caspicara, and Bernardo de Legarda make up part of Quito's finest collection of colonial art in this museum at Cuenca and Mejía, tel. 2/212-297; the collection includes sculpture and furniture as well. The building itself began as the home of a wealthy Quiteño in the 17th century. It's open Tues.–Fri. 10 A.M.–6 P.M., Sat. and Sun. 10 A.M.–2 P.M., $1 pp.

Museo de la Ciudad

Quito's newest collection, tel. 2/283-882 or 283-883, traces the history of the city from pre-Hispanic times through the colonial era and the beginning of the 20th century. It's set in the old Hospital San Juan de Dios, founded by the order of King Philip in 1565. The collection, which is very well presented, includes Inca burials, photographs, clothing, and religious and scientific artifacts. Open Tues.–Sun. 9:30 A.M.–5:30 P.M., $4 pp. English- and French-speaking guides are available for $6 per group.

Alberto Mena Caamaño
Museo Municipal de Arte y Historia

The main draw to the Municipal Museum of Art and History, Espejo 1147 and Benalcázar, tel. 2/510-272, is a set of wax figures in the basement, depicting the death throes of patriots killed here in 1810 by royalist troops. The collection upstairs includes colonial and contemporary art. Hours are Tues.–Sat. 9 A.M.–5 P.M., free.

Casa de Sucre

The one-time home of Bolívar's southern counterpart has been preserved in its original, early-1800s state. Located at Venezuela 513 and Sucre, tel. 2/512-860, the home is open Tues.–Sat. 9 A.M.–noon, 1–4 P.M., $1 pp.

Casa de Benalcázar

Colonial art and furniture fills this house, Olmedo 962 and Benalcázar, tel. 2/215-838, which was constructed the year of Quito's refounding. Classical music performances are occasionally held here. It's open Mon.–Fri.; call for specific times.

La Cima de La Libertad

Follow the Avenida de Los Libertadores west into the foothills of Pichincha to reach this monument to Sucre's decisive victory over the royalist forces on May 24, 1822. An expansive mural by Eduardo Kingman competes with the view of the city below. The **Museo Temple de La Pátria,** tel. 2/952-860, open Tues.–Fri. 8 A.M.–4 P.M., Sat. and Sun. 10 A.M.–3 P.M. (50 cents pp), has a display of historical military tools and weapons.

El Panecillo

A huge statue of the Virgin of Quito punctuates this small hill at the southern end of Old Town. Mass is often held at the statue's base on Sunday, and the observation platform gives a great view of the city. Crime is still a problem when visiting El Panecillo; see the "Safety" section for details.

Basilica de Voto Popular

An alternative for a good view of the city is to head north up Venezuela to the Basilica, Quito's most impressive church from afar. Even though construction began in 1992, it's still not finished. Tours are given from 9 A.M.–5:30 P.M. ($1.50 pp), starting with the interior and moving on to the 115-meter Condor Tower, with views easily comparable to those from El Panecillo. (Notice the "gargoyles" are actually a menagerie of local animals, including armadillos.) You can buy a pass to the upper floors and, if you're feeling bold, even climb the bell tower. Although it's not part of the tour, if you have the chance, step up to the altar to see the Virgin of Quito atop El Panecillo framed in a heart-shaped glass window.

La Ronda

One of the best-preserved colonial streets in Old Town, also called Calle Juan de Díos Morales, La Ronda is nicknamed for the evening serenades (rondas) that once floated through its winding path. Old balconies almost touch over the narrow lane, lined with a few shops and budget hotels toward the end. It's reached most easily via Guayaquil, sloping down from the Plaza Santo Domingo.

BETWEEN OLD TOWN
AND NEW TOWN

Parque La Alameda

Ornamental lakes and a monument to Bolívar hold down opposite ends of this triangular park, which points at Old Town. In the center stands the oldest **astronomical observatory** in South America, inaugurated in 1864 by president García Moreno. The beautiful old building is filled with books, photos, and antique astronomical tools, including a gorgeous brass telescope that still works. Visitors can view the stars on clear nights Mon.–Sat. after 8 P.M. (five or more people), and there are nightly lectures on astronomical topics. For more information, get in touch at 2/570-765, fax 583-451, e-mail: observaq@uio.satnet.net, www.satnet.net/observatorio.

Palacio Legislativo
Drop by Gran Colombia and Montalvo when this arm of Ecuador's government is out to lunch and you may be let inside to see Guayasamin's infamous mural *Imagen de La Pátria*. The huge mural, depicting and protesting injustice in Latin America, caused a stir during its unveiling at a formal ceremony of ambassadors and dignitaries. An evil-looking face with a helmet labeled CIA caused the U.S. ambassador to storm out of the room. Copies of the mural are available in the Guayasamin museum.

Parque El Ejido
Avenidas Pátria, 6 de Diciembre, 10 de Agosto, and Tarquí form the wedge filled by Quito's most popular central park. Its origins as a botanical garden live on in a few trees that are more than a century old. Heated games of soccer fill the park most evenings and weekends, and a children's playground takes up the northeast corner. On weekends the area near the arch at Amazonas and Pátria becomes an outdoor crafts market; paintings line the sidewalk along Pátria, and Otavaleños and other artists sell textiles, antiques, and jewelry.

Casa de la Cultura Ecuatoriana
An unmistakable curve of mirrored glass surrounds the best collection of museums in one spot in the city (tel. 2/223-258). The **Museo Arqueológico/Etnología** of the Banco Central is a world in itself, with 1,500 pieces of pre-Inca pottery and other relics labeled in English and Spanish. A vault downstairs protects a dazzling collection of gold pieces. Upstairs the **Museo Colonial y de Arte** spans Ecuadorian

---

PRISON VISITS

If you're looking for something different to do in Quito and feel like spreading some cheer, consider visiting one of the three prisons in the city. Foreigners are being held in all of them (mostly on drug charges) and greatly appreciate the chance to speak their own language and meet new people. It's an easy way to brighten someone's day, and a safe way to get a glimpse into the dark side of traveling abroad. Inmates appreciate small gifts like toiletries, snacks, and books, but leave your valuables at home—pickpockets abound. Bring a photocopied ID to leave with the guards. The South American Explorers keeps a list of foreigners currently being held.

To reach the **Women's Prison** (Carcel de las Mujeres), head east three blocks from the El Inca roundabout and take a left onto Las Toronjas, then keep going another block and a half to the prison on your right. Visiting hours are Wed., Sat., and Sun. 10 A.M.–3 P.M., last entry 2:30 P.M. The **Penal García Moreno** at Rocafuerte and Chimborazo holds men. It's ten blocks uphill along Calle Rocafuerte from Plaza Santo Domingo in Old Town. Visiting hours Wed., Sat., and Sun. 9 A.M.–5 P.M., last entry 3 P.M. The **Carcel Municipal** is on García Moreno in Old Town, a block and a half south of 24 de Mayo on the left. Visiting hours are the same as the Penal García Moreno.

---

history from colonial furniture and paintings of the Quito School to modern works by Guayasamin and Kingman. Guided tours are available.

Head around the east side of the building to reach the museums of the Casa de la Cultura itself, along with the **Biblioteca Nacional** (National Library). A **Museo de Instrumentos Musicales** contains one of the better collections of musical instruments in the world, and the **Museo de Arte Moderno** and **Museo de Traje Indígena** (Museum of Indigenous Clothing) are also worth a visit. Plays and musical performances are often held in the **Teatro Promedio**. All museums open Tues.–Fri. 9 A.M.–5 P.M., Sat. and Sun. 10 A.M.–3 P.M.; admission $2 pp ($1 students).

Instituto Geográfico Militar

The hike up Paz y Miño is worth the commanding view of the city from the Military Geographical Institute, tel. 2/502-091. While you wait for the staff to process your map order (bring a book), consider a show at the **planetarium**, Mon.–Fri. 9 and 11 A.M. and 3 P.M., Sat. 9 and 11 A.M.; admission is 65 cents pp. The Institute is open Mon.–Fri. 8 A.M.–11 P.M., 2:30–4:30 P.M., Sat. 11:30 A.M.–2:30 P.M., and visitors must surrender their passports at the gate.

NEW TOWN

Avenida Amazonas

If you're going to bump into anyone you know in Quito, it'll be along New Town's wide commercial artery. Banks, shops, offices, travel agencies, and restaurants cluster like grapes on a vine, and the sidewalk cafés are the place to be seen with a cold beer and a pizza. Andean bands play occasionally in the plaza at Jorge Washington.

Museo Jacinto Jijón y Caamaño

The family of a prominent Ecuadorian archaeologist donated his private collection of colonial art and archaeological pieces to the Universidad Católica after his death. Now it's on display on the 3rd floor of the main library building (Libri Mundi), which can be entered off 12 de Octubre near Carrión—ask the guard to point you in the right direction. The museum, tel. 2/565-627, ext. 1242, is open Mon.–Fri. 9 A.M.–4 P.M., Sat. 10 A.M.–3 P.M., 40 cents pp.

Abya Yala

This small complex at 12 de Octubre 1430 and Wilson, tel. 2/562-622 or 506-247, contains a bookstore with the city's best selection of works on the indigenous groups of Ecuador. Shops downstairs sell snacks, crafts, and natural medicines. The 2nd floor is taken up by the excellent **Museo Amazonico** (formerly the Museo Shuar of the Salesian Mission). The obligatory guided tour will take you past stuffed jungle animals, stunning Cofán feather headdresses, and real Shuar *tsantsas* (shrunken heads). The pottery depicting Lowland Quechua gods, each with its accompanying myth, are particularly interesting, as are photos of oil exploration and its envi-

ronmental costs. Open Mon.–Fri. 9:30 A.M.–1 P.M. and 3–5:30 P.M., 60 cents pp.

Centro de Exposiciones y Ferías Artesanales (CEFA)

Even without explanations to accompany the pieces, the collection of this small artisan museum at 12 de Octubre 1738 and García merits a quick visit. Weavings, ceremonial costumes and masks, and musical instruments (including a marimba) are all original. It's open Mon.–Fri. 9 A.M.–5 P.M., free.

Vivarium/Serpentarium

Fans of creepy-crawlies will get their fill with more than 100 live reptiles and amphibians kept here on Reina Victoria 1576 and Santa Maria, tel. 2/230-998. The collection includes poisonous and constrictor snakes from the Oriente. Open Tues.–Sat. 9:30 A.M.–1 P.M. and 2:30–6 P.M., Sun. 11 A.M.–6 P.M., $1 pp.

Sinchi Sacha

This nonprofit foundation, Reina Victoria 17-80 and La Niña, tel. 2/230-609, fax 2/567-311, was set up to help support the peoples of the Oriente. It houses a small **Museum of Amazon Ethnic Art** (no labels, but the friendly staff will explain it all in English) and a shop selling indigenous crafts. Open Mon.–Fri. 9 A.M.–5 P.M.

Museo Arte Arqueologia

Although seldom visited, this collection of pre-Columbian ceramics is excellent and worth a stop. Hundreds of items on display include many rare works from the Oriente. Upstairs are changing art displays. It's at Veintimilla and 6 de Diciembre, tel. 2/222-506, open Mon.–Fri. 11 A.M.–5 P.M.

NORTH OF NEW TOWN

Parque La Carolina

Quito's largest park stretches from the intersection of Orellana and Eloy Alfaro almost one km east to Naciones Unidas. It's popular with early morning joggers, and the *laguna* has two-person paddle boats for rent for $2.35 for half an hour. An **orchidarium** is underway; botanists hope to fill it with as many of Ecuador's 3,500 orchid species as possible.

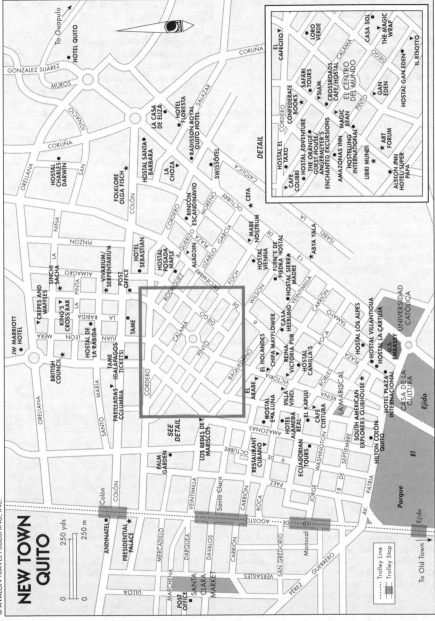

© AVALON TRAVEL PUBLISHING, INC.

NEW TOWN QUITO

Trolley Line
Trolley Stop

To Old Town

DETAIL

EL CAFECITO ▶
LORO VERDE ●
LORO VERDE
CASA SOL ●
THE MAGIC WRAP ●
CORDERO
DIEGO
EL CENTRO DEL MUNDO ●
IL RISOTTO ●
HOSTAL EL TAXO ●
CONFEDERATE BOOKS ●
SAFARI TOURS ★
★ SIAM
CROSSROADS CAFE/HOSTAL CALAMA ●
CALAMA
PINTO
GAN EDEN ●
HOSTAL GAN EDEN ●
CAFE COLIBRI ●
HOSTAL ADVENTURE ●
THE ORANGE GUEST HOUSE/ ENCHANTED EXCURSIONS ●
MAGIC BEAN ●
AMAZONAS INN ●
HOSTELLING INTERNATIONAL ★
ART FORUM ★
ALSTON INN ●
HOTEL/SUPER PAPA ●
LIBRI MUNDI ★

To Guapulo
HOTEL QUITO ●
GONZALEZ SUAREZ
MUROS
IGNACIO
CORUNA
LA CASA DE ELIZA ●
HOTEL FLORESTA ●
RADISSON ROYAL QUITO HOTEL ●
SALAZAR
SWISSOTEL ●
CATOLICA
ORELLANA
HOSTAL CHARLES DARWIN ●
SAN
HOSTAL SANTA BARBARA ●
LA CHOZA ★
CORUÑA
CEFA ★
OCTUBRE
MORENO
FOLKLORE OLGA FISCH ●
COLON
NINA
PINZON
RINCÓN ESCANDINAVIO ●
MARE NOSTRUM ★
DE LA ISABEL
SINCHI SACHA ★
ALMAGRO
PINTA
VIVARIUM/ SERPENTARIUM ★
POST OFFICE ■
HOTEL SEBASTIAN ●
HOSTAL POSADA MAPLE ●
ALADDIN ●
B. QUITO
PLAZA PABLO GARCIA
HOSTAL VIENNA ●
FUENTE DE PIEDRA ●
HOSTAL SIERRA MADRE ●
ABYA YALA ●
DE DICIEMBRE
CREPES AND WAFFLES ●
KING'S CROSS BAR ★
MERA
LA RABIDA
LEON
JUAN
HOSTAL DE LA RABIDA ●
TAME ■
TAME (GALAPAGOS TICKETS) ■
ROCAFUERTE
DIEGO
CALAMA
PINTO
FOCH
WILSON
HOSTAL-HOSTAL
EL HOLANDES ●
CHIFA MAYFLOWER ●
CASA HELBING ●
YENTIMILLA
CARRION
ROCA
HOSTAL LOS ALPES ●
JW MARRIOTT HOTEL ●
BRITISH COUNCIL ★
PATTILADAS COLUMBIA ●
ORELLANA
MARIA
SANTO
CORDERO
BAGUERIZO
REINA VICTORIA PUB ★
VICTORIA
HOSTAL CAMILLA'S ●
TAMAYO
ROBLES
PLAZA
HOSTAL VILLANTIGUA ●
HOSTAL LA CARTUJA ●
UNIVERSIDAD CATOLICA
SEE DETAIL
EL ARABE ●
HOSTAL EVA LUNA ●
VILLA VINCI ●
EL KAPULI ●
CAFE SUTURA ●
REINA
LA MARISCAL
SOUTH AMERICAN EXPLORERS CLUBHOUSE ★
HOTEL PLAZA INTERNACIONAL ●
U.S. EMBASSY ■
CASA DE LA CULTURA
Ejido
LOS REDES DE MARISCOS ●
PALM GARDEN ●
AMAZONAS
OCTUBRE
RESTAURANT CUBANO ●
ECUADORIAN TOURS ●
HOTEL ALAMEDA REAL ●
WASHINGTON
DE SEPTIEMBRE
HILTON COLON QUITO ●
9 DE
PAEZ
JORGE
18 DE
PATRIA
El
Parque Ejido

Colon
COLON
ANDINATEL ■
PRESIDENTIAL PALACE ★
MERCADILLO
DARQUEA
DAVALOS
CARRION
SANTA CLARA
VEINTIMILLA
CARRION
ROCA
SAN GREGORIO
MARISCAL
GUERRERO
PÉREZ
VERSAILLES
ULLOA
MARCHENA
POST OFFICE ■
SANTA CLARA MARKET
10 DE AGOSTO

0   250 yds
0   250 m

Natural history is the focus of the **Museo de las Ciencias Naturales,** Rumipamba 341 and Los Shyris, tel. 2/449-824 or 449-825, at the east end of the park. The Casa de la Cultura administers displays on zoology, botany, and geology. Open Mon.–Fri. 8:30 A.M.,–4:30 P.M., Sat. and Sun. 9 A.M.–12:30 P.M., $1.50 pp.

Museo y Taller Guayasamin

Ecuador's most famous artist once lived in this palatial spread, at Bosmediano 543 between Egas and Carbo in the Bellavista suburb. Pre-Columbian figurines and pottery fill the first building, while Guayasamin's paintings and an impressive collection of colonial art wait further on. The balcony outside the cafeteria offers a panoramic view of the southern mountains. In the gift shop, ask to see the many unique pieces of jewelry designed by the master himself.

To get there, take a bus bound for Bellavista (marked Batan–Colmena or Batan–San Diego). Some taxis can't even make it up Bosmediano, one of the steepest streets in Quito. Open Mon.–Fri. 9:30 A.M.–1 P.M. and 3–6:30 P.M., Sat. 9:30 A.M.–1 P.M., $1 pp.

Museo-Biblioteca Aureliano Polit

You'd have to be a real history buff to come all the way past the airport to this former Jesuit seminary at Nogales and Arcos in the barrio of Cotocollao, tel. 2/530-420, but if you do, a roomful of antique maps gives a fascinating glimpse into the development of the country and its vision of itself. You can view Quito's spread north from Old Town at the turn of the century into the megalopolis it is today, and notice how maps leave the Oriente area blank more often than not, or use terms such as *Pocos Conocidos* (Little-Known Areas) and *Naciones Bestiae Desconocidae* (Bestial Unknown Nations).

To reach the museum, take a bus down La Prensa from La Y at 10 de Agosto, past the airport, and almost to the neighborhood of Condado. It's open Tues., Wed., and Fri. 9 A.M.–noon and 3–5 P.M., $2 pp.

ACCOMMODATIONS

As any good capital should, Quito offers the entire spectrum of accommodations from by-the-hour rats' nests to luxury hotels rivaling any in the world. Most are found in New Town, with a handful scattered about Old Town (where you need to be careful after dark). A few crop up outside both areas.

Reservations are a good idea for busy times such as holidays, especially Christmas and Easter. Do this by phone or fax whenever possible. A tax of up to 20 percent may be added to bills in the more expensive hotels, and a separate charge may be tacked on for paying by credit card.

LESS THAN $10

With so many budget travelers passing through on a regular basis, Quito has adapted and grown a bumper crop of budget hotels. Most are concentrated in New Town, and many are excellent values. At last check, all those listed here passed the bug/brothel/bathroom test—no cockroaches, no rooms by the hour, and no crud in the showers—but things change, so take a glance for yourself before signing the register. All have hot water, and most offer luggage storage.

New Town

Remember that beach house you and 14 of your closest friends rented the summer before college? It's been relocated to Quito in the form of **El Centro del Mundo,** Lizardo García 569 and Reina Victoria, tel. 2/229-050, e-mail: centrodelmundo@hotmail.com, www.cenfei1.org/mundo.html. This archetypal "backpacker's" crash pad has dorm rooms with footlockers for your stuff for $2.50–5 pp, and private rooms for $7. Breakfast and 10 minutes of Internet access are included in the prices. The small rooftop patio features cooking facilities, and the cable TV is always on in the cushion-strewn common room.

More subtle is **El Cafecito,** Cordero 1124 and Reina Victoria, tel. 2/234-862, attached to one of Quito's best café/restaurants. Shared rooms in the cozy, artistic hostel are $6 pp, and the owners speak English. You'll find the headquarters of the Ecuadorian Hostal Association in the clean and modern **Hostelling International,** Pinto E6-12 and Reina Victoria, tel. 2/543-995. Cramped dorm rooms with shared baths are $5–10 pp (more expensive ones have private baths), including continental breakfast in the restaurant downstairs. IYH cardholders get a $1 discount. ISIC cards are issued in the Hostal office.

I wonder how many of the hungry hundreds who dine at **The Magic Bean,** Foch 681 and Juan León Mera, tel. 2/566-181, e-mail: magic@ecuadorexplorer.com, www.ecuadorexplorer.com/magic, know there are four comfortable (if dim) rooms upstairs for $8 pp with shared bath and $26 d with private bath, continental breakfast included. Across the street the **Crossroads Cafe and Hostal,** Foch 678 and Juan Leon Mera, tel. 2/234-735, crossrds @uio.satnet.net, occupies a restored colonial house that seems to go on forever. Dorm rooms in the orange building are $5–6 pp, and private rooms are $9–12, with plenty of hot water in the bathrooms and a VCR and cable TV downstairs. There's a café on the 1st floor that serves all meals, plus kitchen facilities for guests and Romeo, the coolest cat in Quito.

A stay at **La Casa de Eliza,** Isabel La Católica 1559 between Coruña and Pasaje Gangotena, tel. 2/226-602, e-mail: manteca@uio.satnet.net, is closer to living with a family than holing up in a hotel. Eliza Oñate of the Fundación Golondrinas rents rooms in their large house for $5 pp with shared bathroom. Breakfast is another $1, and a refrigerator and kitchen are open to guests—just do your dishes! An owner of Safari Tours runs the women-only **Hostal Eva Luna,** Pasaje Roca 630 between Amazonas and Juan León Mera, tel. 2/234-799, fax 2/220-426, e-mail: admin@ safari.com.ec. Dorm-style rooms are $5 pp, or $2 per night if you stay for 30 or more days.

Not to be confused with La Casona in Old Town, **La Casona de Mario,** Andalucia 213 and Galicia, tel. 2/230-129 or 544-036, is a comfortable house run by a friendly Argentine who offers a garden, kitchen, patio, and laundry facilities. Rooms run $6 pp. The quiet **Hostal Adventure** (formerly La Herradura), Pinto 570 and Amazonas, tel. 2/226-340, e-mail: rcedeno@ hoy.net, is conveniently near the center of things. Rooms go for $4 pp, and a few with private bath are $5 pp.

The modern and friendly **Hotel Vienna,** Tamayo 879 and Foch, tel. 2/235-418, also has a namesake in the Old Town and runs $5 pp with private bath and TV. Long-term stays are recommended at the hospitable **El Taxo,** Foch 909 and Cordero, tel. 2/225-593, where the sounds of English, French, German, and Italian fill the air. Dorm rooms are $3 pp, and rooms with private bath are $5, including use of the kitchen.

Right in the heart of New Town, the **Loro Verde,** Rodriguez 241 and Almagro, tel. 2/226-173, offers a safe and friendly haven for $7 pp including breakfast. The popular **Hostal Gan Eden,** Pinto 163 and 6 de Diciembre, tel. 2/223-480, e-mail: ganeden163@hotmail.com, is an Israeli stronghold in the center of Quito, down to the signs in Hebrew. Basic dorm rooms are $4, and private rooms are $6. There's cable TV in the lounge, laundry service, and luggage storage. The1st-floor restaurant offers a good breakfast, plus Middle Eastern food, of course. **El Kapuli,** Robles 625 and Amazonas, tel. 2/221-872, 9/552-069, is spare but spacious, offering rooms with private bath for $5 pp.

The **Casa Paxee,** Romulado Navarro 326 and La Gasca, tel. 2/500-441, is outside of the main tourist area on the lower slopes of the Pichinchas. Martha Ojeda, the friendly owner, rents out the upper floor of her house, which has a kitchen and a rooftop terrace with a view of the entire city and even Cotopaxi on a clear day. Rooms are $5 pp with shared bath or $10 with private bath.

Old Town

The bright yellow **Hostal Belmonte,** Antepara 413 near 10 de Agosto, tel. 2/956-235, is one of the funkier places to stay in Quito. The book exchange has a notoriously bad selection (*Vixens from Mars*?), and the pastel basement quarters are decorated like a teenager's bedroom circa 1965. On the other hand, it's a friendly, popular meeting place described as a "home away from home," with a terrace, phone, fax and Internet service, kitchen facilities, and luggage storage. Best of all, it costs only $2 pp with shared or private bath.

A three-story covered courtyard sets the colonial **Hostal La Casona,** Manabí 255 between Flores and Montúfar, tel. 2/514-764, fax

2/563-271, apart from most other hotels in this range. Rooms with color TV, private bath, and phone are a steal at $4 pp. The **Plaza del Teatro Internacional,** Guayaquil 1373 and Esmeraldas, tel. 2/959-462, 954-293, fax 2/519-462, is much nicer inside than it looks from the street. A popular restaurant and bar fill the 1st floor, and private parking is available for guests. Rooms cost $3.20 s, $6 d with TV and private bath.

Some of the dozens of cheap hotels near the bus terminal are quite good, whereas others are complete dives. The best of the bunch are **La Posada Colonial,** Paredes 188 and Rocafuerte, tel. 2/282-859; the **Grand Hotel,** Rocafuerte 1001 and Pontón, tel. 2/280-192, e-mail: grand-hotelquito1@hotmail.com; and the **Piedra Dorada,** Maldonado 3210, tel. 2/957-460. All have rooms with private bath for less than $5.

$10–25

Hotels in this category, although clean and comfortable, tend to lack the character of their cheaper counterparts. In some cases, that's good—in others, a slight shame. All have private bathrooms with hot water.

New Town
Warm colors and wood floors welcome visitors to the **Casa Sol,** Calama 127 and 6 de Diciembre, tel. 2/230-798, fax 2/223-383, e-mail: casasol@ecuadorexplorer.com, www.ecuadorexplorer.com/casasol/home, an inviting spot with a tiny courtyard and a big Golden retriever. Dorm rooms are $12 pp and private rooms are $26, including breakfast. The small and inviting **Hostal Posada del Maple,** Juan Rodriguez 148 and 6 de Diciembre, tel. 2/544-507, 237-375, e-mail: mgallego@pi.pro.ec, www.posadadelmaple.com, has a plant-filled porch and TV room. Shared rooms run $5 pp and private quarters are $12–16 s, $18–22 d with private bath; a tasty breakfast is included.

An outdoor patio graces the **Hostal Camila's,** 6 de Diciembre 1329 and Roca, tel. 2/225-412 or 527-387, which was undergoing complete remodeling in late 2000. Plans are to open a bar/Internet café and to put a BBQ pit in the patio. Rooms are $15 s, $25 d with TV and phone. Green trim highlights the yellow **Palm Garden,** 9 de Octubre 923 and Cordero, tel. 2/523-960, fax 2/568-944. A 2nd-floor deck and beautiful garden create a colonial haven in the heart of the city for $18 s, $22 d. The classy **Alston Inn Hotel,** Juan León Mera 741 and Baquedano, tel./fax 2/229-955, e-mail: alston@uio.satnet.net, www.angelfire.com/de/alston, runs $17 s, $24 d.

Old Town
Enjoy a sunset cocktail on the top-floor bar of the **Hotel Real Audencia,** Bolívar 220 and Guayaquil, tel. 2/952-711, 950-590, e-mail: realaudi@hoy.net, www.realaudencia.com. Rooms are spacious (ask for a quieter one in the back), and spotless, if a little overpriced, for $30 s, $40 d. The hotel also has a casino. The Swiss-owned **Hostal L'Auberge,** Gran Colombia 1138 and Yaguachi, tel./fax 2/569-886, is an inviting spot that features a kitchen, garden, pool table, sauna, and fireplace. Dorm rooms are $4 pp, and private rooms are $5 pp with shared bath and $8 s, $13 d with private bath. Yet another former colonial home now houses the **Hotel San Francisco de Quito,** Sucre 217 and Guayaquil, tel. 2/287-758, tel./fax 2/951-241, e-mail: jorge paredes@hotmail.com. A fountain and flowers fill the courtyard, and rooms with TV and private bath are a deal at $6 s, $11 d.

$25–50

A small rise in price brings you into the realm of charming old guesthouses, with all the amenities plus a healthy dose of character. Thick fur rugs in front of the fireplace and one of the more beautiful dogs I've seen in the city add to the old-world feel of **Hostal Los Alpes,** Tamayo 233 and Jorge Washington, tel. 2/561-128, e-mail: alpes@accesinter.net. Rooms, including breakfast, cost $40 s, $50 d, and the owners can organize tours around the country, including the Galápagos. Just around the corner stands the **Hostal Villantigua,** Jorge Washington 237 and Tamayo, tel. 2/227-018, 528-564, fax 2/545-663, e-mail: alariv@uio.satnet.net. The stately old colonial building was built in 1940, and the original blueprints hang behind the reception desk. Some of the rooms, which run $30–42 s, $42–57 d, have fireplaces and mini-refrigerators.

Angermeyer's Enchanted Excursions opened **The Orange Guest House,** Foch 726 and Amazonas, tel. 2/569-960, 221-305, fax 2/569-956, e-mail: angerme1@angermeyer.com.ec, behind their office in 1996. Very comfortable rooms with eye-catching outer walls are $24 s, $30 d, including a continental breakfast. Walk-in rates can be cheaper, depending on what's available. Opened in 1999, the bright yellow **Hostal La Cartuja,** Plaza 170 and 18 de Septiembre, tel. 2/523-577 or 523-721, fax 2/662-391, e-mail: cartuja@uio.satnet.net, ecuadorexplorer.com /lacartuja, occupies a converted mansion that once held the British Embassy. Twelve rooms ($33 s, $44 d, including continental breakfast) are arranged around a quiet courtyard, and English, French, and Italian are spoken.

The **Hostal Villa Nancy,** Muros 146 and González Suárez, tel. 2/550-839, fax 2/562-483, e-mail: nancita@pi.pro.ec, is a quiet, homey place with great views and friendly managers. Rooms with cable TV, phone, and refrigerators are $33 s, $44 d, and come with a pile of freebies such as a buffet breakfast, airport transfer, e-mail, and local calls. A recommended restaurant adds to the modern **Rincón Escandinavio,** Leonidas Plaza 1110 and Baquerizo Moreno, tel./fax 2/540-794, 225-965, where a well-apportioned room costs $20 s, $30 d.

The bright and clean **Hostal de La Rábida,** La Rábida 227 and Santa Maria, tel. 2/222-169, fax 2/221-720, has an Italian owner. Rates are $46 s, $58 d, with discounts for longer stays. The highly accommodating staff of the **Hotel Plaza Internacional,** Leonidas Plaza 150 and 18 de Septiembre, tel. 2/524-530, fax 2/505-075, e-mail: hplaza@uio.satnet.net, www.hostalplaza .com, speak English, French, and Portuguese. Look for the attractive building between the French and U.S. embassies; rooms cost $22 s, $33 d.

Opened in June 2000, the elegant **Villa Vinci,** Roca 518 and Reina Victoria, tel. 2/508-617 or 508-912, fax 2/509-547, e-mail: hmadison @waccom.net.ec, is in a converted yellow mansion with an intriguing domed roof. Double rooms in the back are nice enough for $35, but it's worth spending the extra $10 to stay in the main house, where the rooms have painted ceilings and balconies. The "special suite," with sunroom, whirlpool, and lounge, is a bargain at $75.

To round things out, there's a colorful bar/restaurant on the 1st floor with a fireplace.

The faux-colonial **Fuente de Piedra Hostal,** Wilson 211 and Tamayo, tel. 2/525-314, tel./fax 559-775, e-mail: ecuhotel@ecuahotel.com, has left a long list of pleased guests since it opened three years ago. Rooms are $35 s, $45 d, including TV, private bath, and breakfast. The adjoining restaurant gets good reviews for its fire-warmed atmosphere and economical *menú del día.*

$50-75

Setting the standard for midpriced hotels throughout Ecuador is the **Cafe Cultura,** Robles 513 and Reina Victoria, tel./fax 2/224-271, e-mail: info@cafecultura.com, www.cafecultura.com. Set in a beautifully restored colonial mansion—formerly the French cultural center—the hotel is full of dark wood and paintings, managing to be cheery and classy at the same time. The owners speak English, French, and German. There's a gourmet café downstairs, a small private garden out back, a library full of guidebooks, three stone fireplaces, and a grand staircase in the center of it all. The Cultura Reservation Center in the lobby, tel./fax 2/558-889, e-mail: info@ecuadortravel.com, www.ecuadortravel.com, is a great source of information, and its staff can make reservations just about anywhere in the country. Rates are $46 s, $58 d, with a few suites for $74-78.

Another restored colonial building houses the **Hostal Santa Barbara,** 12 de Octubre N26-15 and Coruña, tel./fax 2/564-382, tel. 2/225-121, e-mail: santabarbara@porta.net, just downhill from the Hotel Quito. Each of the 16 rooms have cable TV, and some have balconies. The Italian owner offers some of the best Italian food in the city in the hotel's restaurant. Rooms go for $42 s, $55 d. The venerable **Hotel Quito,** González Suárez 2500, tel. 2/544-600, fax 2/567-284, www.orotels.com, gazes over the city and the valley to the east on the eastern shoulder of New Town. New owners have made few changes other than to lower the price, but the view will always be one of the best in Quito, especially sunrise from the glass-walled restaurant. Rates are $48 per room, and there is a pool for guests.

$75–200

A nine-story skyscraper is home to the **Hotel Sebastian,** Almagro 822 and Cordero, tel. 2/222-300 or 222-400, fax 2/222-500, e-mail: hsebast1 @hsebastian.com.ec, which can be considered Quito's first "eco-hotel" (but doesn't promote itself as such because, after all, this is what everyone should be doing—right?). Only organically grown vegetables free of pesticides are served in its restaurant, and the building boasts one of the best water-purification systems in the country. Forty-nine rooms and seven suites start at $85 s, $96 d.

Smack in the middle of Amazonas sits the luxury oasis of **Hotel Alameda Real,** Roca 653 and Amazonas, tel. 2/562-345, fax 2/565-759, e-mail: apartec@uio.satnet.net. The 22 rooms run $82 s, $110 d, and 130 suites featuring kitchenette, minibar, and cable TV start at $145.

MORE THAN $200

A complete makeover in 1996–1997 transformed the Hotel Colón into the **Hilton Colón Quito,** Amazonas and Pátria, tel. 2/560-666, fax 2/563-903, e-mail: reserv@hiltoncolon.com. Towering over the Parque El Ejido, it's probably the most popular with tourists who have unlimited budgets. Facilities include a reading room, casino, shops, money exchange, car rental, pool, and 415 rooms and suites for $165 s, $400 d. Reservations can be made in the United States by calling 800/HILTONS.

Uphill to the east, the **Swissôtel,** 12 de Octubre 1820 and Cordero, tel. 2/567-600, fax 2/568-080, e-mail: concierge.quito@swissuio .com, www.swissotel.com, has 240 wheelchair-accessible rooms and a private health club, along with Japanese and Italian restaurants, a casino, and a gourmet deli. Rooms are $140 s, $155 d, and suites start at $170. Reservations can be made in the United States by phone at 800/63-SWISS.

Rates at the **Radisson Royal Quito Hotel,** Cordero 444 and 12 de Octubre, tel. 2/233-333, fax 2/235-777, start at $122 s or d, including breakfast, and suites are $125 each. Guests can expect the same service and amenities as any luxury hotel back home, including a business center, conference facilities, and a spa. For refueling, there's a bar, a café, and a restaurant. Farther north near Parque La Carolina is the **Holiday Inn Crowne Plaza,** Los Shyris 1757 and Naciones Unidas, tel. 2/445-305, fax 2/251-985, e-mail: admihote@accessinter.net. Rooms start at $145 s or d, and facilities include a casino, a sauna, and a spa.

The newest and perhaps largest luxury hotel in Ecuador is the **JW Marriott Hotel,** 1172 Orellana and Amazonas, tel. 2/972-000, fax 2/972-050. This glass palace contains 257 rooms ($120–135 each) and 16 suites ($175) with all the bells and whistles, along with a business center, business facilities, an outdoor heated pool, a health club, and a Mediterranean restaurant.

LONGER STAYS

Hotels
Most hotels will arrange a discount for stays of a few weeks or more. For example, the **Residencial Casa Oriente,** Yaguachi 824 and Llona, tel. 2/546-157, offers apartments with kitchen for $80 per month ($60 per month with shared kitchen), with a minimum stay of two weeks. Spanish lessons are available, and English, French, and German are spoken. You can also try the **Casa de Frederico,** Benalcázar 1235 and Oriente, tel. 2/289-661, where five three-room apartments with kitchen facilities go for $200 per week, including meals and four hours of Spanish lessons per day ($10 per day with meals).

At **Alberto's House,** Lizardo García 648 (E5-45) between Juan León Mera and Reina Victoria, tel. 2/224-603, e-mail: albertohouse@hotmail.com, a room in a nicely decorated house with shared bathrooms and kitchen is $35 per week or $100 per month. Facilities include a garden, hammocks, a TV/VCR, and a pool table.

The South American Explorers' Quito clubhouse is also a good source for information on apartments for rent, as are the notice wall at Super Papa (see "Food" section) and the classified ads in the local papers.

Family Stays
A homestay is a great way to practice your Spanish and get to know Ecuadorian culture from the

inside. Plus, it's often just as affordable as a budget hotel, as long as you're willing to make a longer commitment. Options change like the weather, so check at the South American Explorers' Quito clubhouse for the latest list.

One standby is **Ana Medina,** 10 de Agosto 1831 and Carrión, tel. 2/564-653, e-mail: ana_medina@latinamail.com, or cruzchristian@yahoo.com, who takes in boarders for $10 per day. That gets you a private room, your own bathroom, and all meals (lots of fruits and veg-etables). **Dr. Cecilia Rivera,** Salazar 327 and Mallorca, tel. 2/548-006, 569-961, has three double rooms for rent for $10 per day with two meals or $8 per day without. For $12.50 per day, **Jenny Chavez,** Selva Alegre 868 and Miguel y Solier, tel./fax 2/225-620, will provide three meals a day and laundry service to boot. In Old Town, the **Familia Gutierrez,** Montúfar 761 and Mejía, tel. 2/952-146, has two single rooms to rent for $10 per day with three meals or $3 per day without.

FOOD

Every major world cuisine is represented in Quito's culinary spectrum, with a healthy serving of cafés and fast-food joints tossed in for good measure. Like hotels, most restaurants are located in New Town, including almost all those serving foreign food. Old Town eateries are usually cheaper and more forgettable, and many close by 9 or 10 P.M. There's no pattern as to which are open or not on weekends and Monday; if you can't call ahead, have an alternate plan ready.

STARTERS

Breakfast

Crepes and Waffles, Orellana and Rabida, is one of the few places in Quito that is open on Sunday night. Ignore the gaze of the fat-faced Botero posters as you choose from a gigantic menu that includes crepes (sweet and savory), pita-pizzas, salads, and waffles for $1–3. Service is efficient, and there's even a nonsmoking section. You can find real bagels at **Mr. Bagel,** Portugal 948 and 6 de Diciembre; **Bagel Connection,** on the corner of Reina Victoria and Pinto; and **New York Bagel,** with two branches at Juan León Mera 535 and Roca and at Eloy Alfaro 2407 and Batán.

The award for best French toast in Quito—only $1—goes hands down to **Super Papa,** Juan León Mera 761 and Baquedano. Come back for lunch to try a scrumptious baked potato with your choice of vegetable or meat topping, hot or cold, either *guagua* (small) or *super,* starting at less than $2. It's also one of the best places in town to watch European sporting events. Breakfast is especially recommended at the **Cafe Col-ibrí,** Pinto 619 and Cordero—$2.50 will keep you going all day. They also have German food averaging $2 per plate, and serve German beers in the outdoor patio garden.

The $12 weekday morning buffet at the **Hotel Colón** is sumptuous, and it's hard to imagine, but it's even larger and better on Sundays.

Cafés

Attractive young couples seem to favor the **Gran de Cafe,** Baquedano 330 and Reina Victoria—maybe for its rosy-hued atmosphere, or its vegetarian options. The friendly owners offer a wide range of healthy dishes and safe-to-eat salads, including tempeh sandwiches, quiche, and veggie burgers. Soups, salads, and sandwiches are $1–3, with specials for $4 and desserts to die for.

Both the relaxed atmosphere and the pastas ($2) are excellent at the **Sun Cafe,** 1343 Reina Victoria. The 2nd-floor patio and classic juke-box with an eclectic collection of 45s are both nice touches. Owner John Papski is a font of knowledge about Quito and its environs, and he will enthusiastically share his favorite spots. He runs horseback-riding trips for $35 pp (minimum 4 people) and sells nice candles, too. **El Cafecito,** Cordero 1124 and Reina Victoria, serves a tasty, inexpensive *menú del día* for $3 in a warm pastel-colored dining room. Candles and crayons for coloring your placemat make things even cozier than the fireplace would alone.

Up the spiral stairs on Calama at Juan León Mera is the open-air **Cafe Sutra,** whose large menu spans the globe from Italy to the Middle East. Dishes average $2, and there's Internet service and a huge drinks lists. Peruse a selection of British magazines in the bright, cheerful **Gallery Cafe** of the British Council, Amazonas N26-146 and Orellana. The small menu has filling sandwiches and pizza for less than $1. **La Pajara Pinta,** 9 de Octubre 1540 and Orellana, is a women's coffeehouse, and **El Frutal,** Reina Victoria 328, has a rainbow of fresh fruit juices.

Coffee Shops

Head up the stairs at Juan León Mera 12-27 and Calama to reach **Books & Coffee,** a very comfy place with leather chairs by the fireplace, good tunes, and a book exchange. Enjoy a sandwich, salad, or coffee drink, exchange a book, or belly up to the bar. If you get beaten at the beautiful marble chess set, you still might be able to redeem yourself at the foosball table.

The **Cafe Galletti Espresso Bar,** Amazonas 1498 and Santa Maria, serves as good a cup of coffee as you'll find in Quito. For a quick pick-me-up, stop by the sidewalk window at the Magic Bean (see Vegetarian entry), and for a late-night fix you can hit the 24-hour **La Tertulia** coffee shop at the Hotel Alameda Real. The **Café Conquistador,** at Río Frio and Larrea between old and New Town, serves great *humitas* and coffee, a Latin American snack staple.

Pizza

North American residents of Quito gather to watch sitcoms and ESPN on cable at **Pizza Pizza,** Santa Maria 126 and Almagro. The pizza, available by the slice or the pie, gets good reviews. Just over a block past the only traffic light in the suburb of Tumbaco, the **Pizzeria La Gambugia** claims to have the best pizza and Italian food in Ecuador.

A plethora of options exist for ordering pizza to go. **Ch' Farina,** tel. 2/444-444, is the local champ, followed by **Roy's Pizza,** tel. 2/459-594, **El Hornero,** tel. 2/542-518, and **Don Diego,** tel. 2/260-320. You'll also find the foreign devils **Pizza Hut,** tel. 2/500-143, and **Domino's,** tel. 2/433-355.

Fast Food

For a quick grease fix, head to the south end of New Town, where the corner of Juan León Mera and Carrión is home to **Pizza Hut, Ch' Farina** pizza, and **Taco Bell. McDonald's** has staked out a spot at Patria and 6 de Diciembre, and a

Burger King occupies Orellana and Reina Victoria. **El Leñador Burguer,** a walk-up place on Carrión at Amazonas, always has lines of locals waiting to shell out 50 cents for a big, greasy burger.

Outlets of popular local chains such as **King Chicken, Gus,** and **Tropiburger** are scattered throughout the city. In Old Town, several fast-food joints, including Kentucky Fried Chicken and Tropiburger, are located on Guayaquil at Esmeraldas. Every mall has a good selection of fast food, especially the Mall El Jardin, with no less than 22 choices from the Hansel and Gretel Cookie Shop to Taco Bell.

Delicatessens

After browsing the selection at Libri Mundi, drift next door for a baguette and wine at **El Español Deli,** Juan León Mera and Wilson. A cappuccino bar serves sit-down customers, and a wide (if pricey) selection of cheeses and sandwiches are available to go. Another good source for a sub or fixings are **El Pavo Campestre,** Almagro and Calama.

La Iberica, Cordero 719 and Plaza, is a well-stocked deli that's been going since 1920. They also serve good ice cream. **Mozarella,** Alfaro 1732 and Los Shyris, is an Italian delicatessen with great pastas and desserts.

Bakeries and Sweets

With a great selection of French and whole-meal breads as well as pastries, **El Cyrano,** Portugal 860 and Los Shyris, is constantly lauded as the best bakery in town. **Corfu** next door is described as "ice cream heaven." Three bakeries closer to the center of action are **El Túnel,** 6 de Diciembre and Jorge Washington, **Sal & Pimienta,** outside the Hotel Colón, and **Pan del Río,** on Cordero just east of Amazonas.

The daughter of Rosalia Suárez (see the special topic "Helados de Paila" in the Northern Sierra chapter) runs **Helados Rosalia Suárez** at Los Shyris and Holanda, facing the bleachers In Parque La Carolina. Along with the authentic, hand-stirred *helados de paila,* this small place steams the best *humitas* in Quito. **Helado Chino Tse-Kao,** on Colón just west of Amazonas, has a large selection of flavors of ice cream and can turn out sundaes and banana splits like nobody's business.

MAIN COURSE

Ecuadorian Food

Restaurants that serve "local" fare conspicuously can be a strange thing. Dressed-up versions of everyday plates share the bill with traditional recipes that might otherwise be forgotten. **La Choza,** 12 de Octubre 1821 and Cordero, is a popular midpriced place. Appetizers such as *tortillas de maíz* run $1–3, with main dishes like the tasty *locro de papas* $3 and up. Tour groups often empty their buses here. For larger, less expensive portions, steer toward **Mama Clorinda,** Reina Victoria 1144 and Calama, where you can get *llapingachos* and a quarter chicken for $2.

Good for Lunch

The fun vibe at **La Boca del Lobo** on Foch in New Town extends from its blue exterior to the funky sheep-themed art on the warm walls within (The Wolf's Mouth—get it?). Pizzas, sandwiches, and other main dishes are $2–4. Not far away in another restored colonial building is **The Magic Wrap,** Foch 476 and Diego de Almagro, offering gourmet wraps (glorified burritos), Thai, Indian, and Mexican plates for around $2, along with desserts and drinks. (Open for lunch only.) Way up on the 3rd floor of the **Casa Tosi department store** in the Centro Commercial Iñaquito at Amazonas and Naciones Unidas is a small but fresh salad bar that gets repeat recommendations.

Seafood

Two restaurants stand out immediately in the *pescado* category. **Mare Nostrum,** Tamayo 172 and Foch, claims to have "70 ways of serving fish," and the few that I've tried have been outstanding. Boat models, suits of armor, and dark wood beams set the stage for delicious cream soups and *encocados* served in half a coconut shell. Dishes start at $2 but go much higher. The same owners run **Los Redes de Mariscos,** Amazonas 845 and Veintimilla, which has an extensive wine list. **La Jaiba,** Reina Victoria 1538 and Colón, has a good atmosphere and plates for $2–4.

On the other end of the price spectrum is **El Viejo Jose,** Veintimilla and Páez, which is not much to look at but cheap and delicious. Also recommended for seafood are **Su Cebiche,** Juan León Mera 1232 and Calama, and **Barlovento,** 12 de Octubre and Orellana.

Steak Houses

Burgers and grilled plates in the $3 range are the specialty of **The Texas Ranch,** Juan León Mera 1140 and Calama. The rustic-themed restaurant also doubles as an Argentinean grill. Three branches of the popular **Parilladas Columbia** serve decent-quality steaks for about $3. You'll find them at Colón 1262 and Amazonas, Tarquí 785 and 10 de Agosto, and 6 de Diciembre 4531 and Pasaje El Jardín. .

Prices and quality of the cuts rise quickly at places such as **La Casa de Mi Abuela,** Juan León Mera 1649 and La Niña; **Martin Fierro,** Avenida De La República 1428 and Inglaterra; and the **Shorton Grill Steak House,** Calama 216 and Almagro. A fireplace and penthouse view compliment the cuts at **Terraza del Tartaro,** Veintimilla 1106 and Amazonas.

Vegetarian

After all that meat, it's good to know that Quito also has a healthy range of vegetarian options. The overflowing Indonesian plate at **El Holandés,** Reina Victoria 660 and Carrión, has to be one of the best food values in the city. Other selections in the $1–2 range include Greek, Dutch, and Indian plates. Veggies at the cheery **El Maple,** Páez 485 and Roca, are washed in purified water, and you can surf the Internet while you wait for your $1.25 *menú del día.* The Hindu-run **El Marqués,** Calama 433 between Juan León Mera and Amazonas, is open daily for lunch. Everything is less than $2, from the faux burgers and chicken to the more traditional spaghetti, salads, and pancakes.

Although there are animals on the menu, **The Magic Bean,** Foch 681 and Juan León Mera, is still a vegetarian restaurant at heart. Salads, pizzas, and Colombian coffee—served inside or on the covered patio—have made this place one of the more popular gringo stopovers in New Town. At $3–5 per dish, it's not cheap, but the food is dependably good and comes in generous portions. They also have a long list of natural juices.

La Vid, Juan León Mera 1333, does a 100 percent vegetarian breakfast and lunch. Try the "bistek" for $1.25. **Manatial,** 9 de Octubre 1591 and Carrión, has the largest vegan menu in town, with nothing more than $1. Soy yogurt is the draw at the **Windmill,** Colón 2245 and Versailles.

Italian

As the city has spread north, several classy restaurants have followed the business lunch crowd up Eloy Alfaro. One of the best is the **Taberna Piemonte,** Tola 173 and Eloy Alfaro, with a great view of the city from the main dining room. Many local gourmands will name **La Viña,** Isabel La Católica and Cordero, as Quito's best restaurant. Delicious pastas and other Italian plates are around $4.

Il Risotto, Pinto 209 and Almagro, is another worthwhile splurge without being too pricey. Good service and generous portions make the prices ($3–4 per plate) more bearable, as does the heavenly tiramisú. **Le Arcate,** Baquedano 358 and Juan León Mera, has pastas and a bewildering array of tasty wood-oven pizzas (the "Russian" has vodka as an ingredient) for $2–3.

At **Il Pizzaiolo,** Juan León Mera 1012 and Foch, almost everyone orders pizza, and for good reason. The pastas, though, are also excellent for around $2.50. Don't be fooled by the exterior of the **Ristorante Roma Antica,** 618 Roc and Juan León Mera—inside you'll find excellent food in an atmosphere of quiet elegance. **La Briciola,** Toldeo 1255 and Cordero, has excellent dishes for less than $4 (try the ravioli classico), a good wine list, and a fire to ease the chill of a cold Quito evening. It's near the Radisson Royal and the Swissôtel.

Mexican and Tex-Mex

In an orange and blue colonial house at Reina Victoria 847 and Wilson, **Tex-Mex** serves south-of-the-border entrées ($1.50–4) and beer in a lively setting. At Carrión 619 and Amazonas, **La Guarida del Coyote** is good and inexpensive, with tasty dishes ($1–3) and a rustic atmosphere. A plate of fajitas at **Red Hot Chili Peppers** (no relation to the band), at Foch and Juan León Mera, will easily fill two people to bursting. It's a tiny place with a big TV and graffiti covering the walls, and it just may well serve the most authentic Mexican food in town. Dishes are $2–3.

La Cigarra Ranchera, Reina Victoria 228 and 18 de Septiembre, does great Tex-Mex. A massive vegetarian enchilada stuffed with black beans and rice is about $2.50, as are most other selections on the extensive menu. **Old El Paso,** Pinto and Reina Victoria, claims "genuine texas flavor," with similar prices as the Cigarra Ranchera for food that's almost as good.

Asian

Hundreds of inexpensive *chifas* fill the city, but some are better than others. The classy **Casa China,** Cordero 613 and Tamayo, offers the best value for your money, with the **Chifa China,** Carrión and Versailles, close behind. Also in the top 10 are the **Chifa Hong Kong,** Wilson between Tamayo and Plaza; the **Casa de Asia,** Amazonas 5416 and Isla Tortuga (near the bull ring); and **Mágico Oriental,** Páez 243 and Washington. The **Chifa Mayflower,** Carrion 442 and 6 de Diciembre, is one of seven in Quito, including ones in the El Bosque, El Jardín, Quicentro, and El Recreo malls. They all share the same fast-food plastic feel, bright but pleasant, with combinations around $2 with drinks and free rice. Home delivery is also an option.

Fifty-two different kinds of sushi start at less than $1 at the **Restaurante Japones Fuji,** Robles 538 between Juan León Mera and Reina Victoria. **Tanoshii** at the Swissôtel is also excellent. Japanese and Korean food are both on the menu at the **Restaurant Asia,** Eloy Alfaro 3027 (just down the hill from the Taberna Piemonte), for around $6 per plate.

Siam offers a delectably peanut-laden *phad thai* for $4.25 on a candlelit balcony over the gringoland at Calama and Juan León Mera. Many other dishes are approximately $2, and they have a large drink list. **Thai-an,** Eloy Alfaro N34-230 and Portugal, knocks the luxury factor up a notch with $4–5 entrées and excellent service in an elegant setting. Try the Goong Pu Kao Fai (shrimp in spicy bell pepper sauce), even if you can't pronounce it.

French

Gallic cuisine tends to be served in the most upscale of Quito's foreign restaurants, favored by natty executives and wealthy tourists. **Rincon de Francia,** Roca 779 and 9 de Octubre, and **Le Bistrot,** González Suárez 139, are among the best restaurants in the city. Make reservations and dress sharp. A French bakery occupies the ground floor of **Chantilly,** Roca 736 and Amazonas.

The small fondue bar at **Ile de France,** Reina Victoria 1747 and La Niña, is more intimate. **La Crêperie,** Calama 362 and JM, is one of the coziest restaurants in the city—except on Friday nights when it's packed for live jazz. Crêpes, of course, are the mainstay, but the cheese fondue ($4 for two people) is hard to beat.

Spanish

La Paella Valenciana, República and Almagro, specializes in large servings of seafood for $7–18 per plate. **La Vieja Castilla,** La Pinta 435 and Amazonas, is just as fancy and expensive, with dishes like *paella* ranging from $3–20.

On the budget end, the **Mesón Español,** Carrión 974 and Páez, offers a filling *almuerzo* in a pleasant setting across from the stuffed bull of El Toro Partido. Dishes are less than $2. Sit upstairs or on the patio at the **Puerto Español,** next door at 9 de Octubre and Carrión; breakfast and lunch are incredible bargains at $1 each.

Middle Eastern

One delectable specialty of Ecuador's Arab establishments—up there with hummus and grilled kebabs—are *shawarmas,* a serving of grilled meat in a warm pita with yogurt sauce and vegetables. **El Arabe,** Reina Victoria 627 and Carrión, serves a good version, either inside or to go on the sidewalk. Another newer branch on Coruña and Whimper is more expensive and comfortable; guests lounge on floor cushions in front of a fireplace, in a room decorated like a Bedouin tent. Call 2/549-414 for home delivery.

The patio at **Aladdin,** Almagro and Baquerizo Moreno, is always packed in the evenings. The water pipes and 16 kinds of flavored tobaccos probably have something to do with it, along with the $1 falafel and shawarma. **Gan Eden,** Pinto 163 and 6 de Diciembre, offers inexpensive Israeli fare. **Amizllala,** Reina Victoria at Pinto, is a popular Israeli hangout, with Middle Eastern dishes for around $2.

For Lebanese food, drop by **Hassan's Cafe,** Reina Victoria just south of Colón, a simple and friendly place with plates for $1.50. **Elefante,** Wilson and Reina Victoria, serves up true Indian tandoori cuisine. A set lunch is $1.50, while items from the extensive menu range from $1–7.

Cuban

The cuisine of this Caribbean island has become quite popular in Ecuador, although its cultural ebullience and beguiling music don't hurt either. The popular **Varadero Sandwiches Cubanos,** Reina Victoria and La Pinta, has a selection of—you guessed it—Cuban sandwiches for $3. Things heat up at night with live music by the bar. The **Rincon Cubano,** Amazonas 993 and Veintimilla, also serves Cuban food. Everything at the **Restaurant Cubano** is less than $2, including the *bistek al burro.* They're on Roca at Amazonas in the small La Villa Vieja mall. **La Bodeguita de Cuba,** Reina Victoria 1721 and La Pinta, is popular for its Cuban *bocaditos* (appetizers) for $2.50, as well as the live Cuban music on Thursday nights.

Other Ethnic Food

German würsts and steins of lager can be found at **Hansa Krug,** Salazar 934 between 12 de Octubre and Isabel La Católica, a fancy German eatery with plates averaging $5. For a tangy Swiss fondue, try **Los Monjes,** La Rábida 341 and La Pinta, or **Raclette,** Eloy Alfaro 1348 and Marín. The latter serves great fondue, if you have the money—few items are under $5, and the huge drink list can run a bill up fast. The **Chalet Swiss,** Calama and Reina Victoria, has entrées such as frogs' legs and cheese fondue with bread and wine starting at $4.

Doña Arepa is a tiny nook in the Centro Comercial El Obelisco at Amazonas and Colón that does Venezuelan food—all meals—for about $1. Afghan food is the specialty of **Ariana Restaurant,** Reina Victoria between Roca and Carrión, where full meals are $2 and photos on the menu come in handy when you can't pronounce the names of the dishes.

Old Town Eateries

At the top of colonial Quito's meager list of restaurants is **La Cueva del Oso,** Chile and Venezuela. Serenading *guitarristas* wander the tasteful dining room and bar area of the Cave of the Bear, with entrées in the $5 range. The attached **La Samba Teresa** coffee shop bakes excellent pastries daily, as does the **Pastelería El Tunel,** Venezuela between Sucre and Espejo.

For budget Ecuadorian dishes, you could do much worse than **Angelo's,** Mejía 265 and Guayaquil, or **El Criollo,** Flores 825. **El Amigo,** Guayaquil between Esmeraldas and Oriente, has also been recommended for typical meals and coffee.

The **Chifa El Chino,** on Bolívar just west of Plaza San Francisco, offers some variety from the usual Old Town eateries. **Sol Natura,** Sucre 209 and Guayaquil, is a vegetarian restaurant with a fairly large menu and an 80-cent *almuerzo*. Good bread and ice cream are on the menu of the **"Cafe-Restaurant"** at Chile 937 and Guayaquil.

Markets and Supermarkets

Gleaming aisles and air-conditioning make the larger Ecuadorian supermarkets almost indistinguishable from their North American or European equivalents. **Supermaxi** is the biggest, with a branch at La Niña and Yanes Pinzón, one block off 6 de Diciembre, as well as in the Centros Commerciales El Bosque, Iñaquito, Multicentro, America, El Jardin, and El Recreo, among others. It's open daily from 9 A.M.–8 P.M. (closes at 6 P.M. on Sundays). **Mi Comisariato,** with outlets in the Centro Commercial Quicentro, and at Rodrigo de Chávez and Galte, García Moreno and Mejía, and Nuñez de Vela and Ignacio San Maria, is open Mon.–Fri. 9 A.M.–7 P.M. and closes earlier on weekends.

A more economical food alternative is the **Santa Clara Market** at Ramirez Dávalos between Carrión and Antonio de Marchena, two blocks from 10 de Agosto. Open Mon.–Fri. 7 A.M.–3 P.M. and Sat. and Sun. mornings, this place has countless small food stands and meals-to-go, along with a few inexpensive markets.

ENTERTAINMENT AND EVENTS

Bars and Discos

Probably the most popular nighttime destinations for teenage and twenty-something Quiteños, bars and discos go in and out of popularity faster than the phases of the moon. Inquire locally for the latest list of what's hot. Many places with music have a small cover charge, a drink minimum, and a dress code (relaxed slightly for gringos). Unaccompanied males may have trouble getting in.

Santa Maria is the bar/disco street in New Town. **Papillon,** Almagro and Santa Maria, and **Tijuana,** one block west at Reina Victoria, are most popular with locals—and the loudest. On weekends they can get so crowded that you have no choice but to hang your coat on a rafter and dance to the Latin music on a table—or the bar.

With its college feel, **No Bar,** Calama and Juan León Mera, is also popular with locals and gringos. Somewhere in between the gyrating bodies is a pool table. On weekends the dancing starts in the afternoon at the dimly lit **X Bar,** just down the street. It also has a pool table somewhere inside. Look for the graffiti art at Juan León Mera and Calama to find the stairs up to **Arribar.** Heated games of pool and foosball and an interesting mix of music keep things interesting. The **Cafe Havana,** on Juan León Mera between Foch and Calama, is a warm, cozy nook offering drinks, taped music, and potent *mojitos*.

Some classier discos, such as **El Cerebro,** Shyris and 6 de Diciembre, have stricter standards of dress and steeper covers. These places include the many hotel nightclubs. At the **Zulu** dance club, Pinzon and Orellana, you'll hear everything from classic rock and funk to techno and trance. **Bloom's Bar,** Juan León Mera 1117 and Foch, plays rock, reggae, salsa, and merengue. **Gay bars** are harder to find—once again city residents are your best source of information. The online Quito Gay Guide (gayquitoec.tripod.com) has a listing of these and other gay-owned businesses.

Jazz and the occasional torch singer fill **Cafelibro,** Almagro 1550 and Pradera, to bursting. Photos of writers and well-stocked bookshelves decorate this literary place, which is open until midnight Tues.–Sat.; sometimes there's a cover. One of New Town's more intimate nooks, **El Pobre Diablo,** Santa Maria 338 and Mera, is a place to discuss philosophy or plot a poetic revolution, with its scarred wooden tables lit by candles and rotating art exhibits on the walls. For more jazz, try **Bangaló,** Carrión 185 and Tamayo, or the **Sambo Jazz Bar** at Lizardo García 1238.

Latin Dancing

Reservations are recommended for Thursday nights at **La Bodeguita de Cuba,** Reina Victoria 1721 and La Pinta, where Cuban rhythms will set your toes tapping and your hips swiveling. Claim the barside hammock for a drink, if you can, and be sure to leave your name on the wall; everyone else has. **Seseribó,** Veintimilla and 12 de Octubre, has been offering *pura salsa* for more than a decade. They occasionally have live music, too. Other popular *salsatecas* include **Mayo 68** at Lizardo García 662 and Juan León Mera and **Cali Salsateca** at 1699 Colón.

To brush up on your gyrating, spend a few hours (or days, if you're like me) at one of the **dancing schools** listed under "Other Fun Stuff."

Peñas

Live folk music happens after 9 P.M. Wed.–Sat. at **Ñucanchi Peña,** Universitario 496 and Armero. Things get going around the same time on Thursdays and Fridays at **Peña Dayumak,** Juan León Mera and Carrión.

Pubs

Quito's sizable population of British, German, and North American immigrants supports a handful of authentic taprooms. The **Reina Victoria Pub,** located in a 100-year-old house at Reina Victoria 530 and Roca, is one of the most well known. Chosen as one of the 22 best gathering places in the world by *Newsweek,* it's been open since 1973. Relax with a Guinness in front of the fireplace, or down a Newcastle between games of darts or pool. A small restaurant serves sandwiches and light fare.

King's Cross Bar, Reina Victoria and La Niña, features a good selection of ales, and **The Turtle's Head,** La Niña 626 and JLM, is a Scottish-owned pub that proudly promotes its wide selection of draught and bottled beer. They have pool, darts, and food. Don't miss the dirty British slang definitions on the wall by the foosball table (but keep Grandma's attention elsewhere). The **Bierkelle "La Casa del Cura"** at Muros and Gonzalez Suárez has pool tables and a selection of German beer.

Pool Halls and Other Games

In addition to the many bars with billiards, several places specialize in nothing else. Tables are

street performer

usually rented by the hour. Rack `em up at the **Bola Pool Bar,** on Colón just east of 9 de Octubre; **Pool Six,** Reina Victoria and Lizardo García; and **Pool.net,** which has pool tables and Internet service at Calama 233 and Almagro.

Run by the same owners as The Magic Bean, **La Cascada Magica,** Foch 476 and Diego de Almagro, offers pool, foosball, air hockey, and darts, along with jazz and blues on Thursday night. A Swiss chap runs **Ghoz,** La Niña 425 and Reina Victoria. Darts, pool, foosball, and pinball fill the large upstairs of this smoky cave. On the 1st floor, there's a wide selection of quality beers, board games, and a kitchen that whips up a good set meal—Swiss food, of course—for $2–4.

In addition to the Multicines movie theaters, the C.C. Iñaquito has an **ice skating rink.**

Casinos

Some of the more expensive hotels have a Vegas wing for guests who are interested in gambling. These gamerooms can be a fun—and surprisingly inexpensive, if you're careful and moderately lucky—way to spend an evening out. Dress codes may be enforced. Try the casinos at the **Hotel Colón,** the **Swissôtel,** or the **Hotel Reina Isabela** on Amazonas and Veintimilla. In Old Town, you can place your bets at the **Hotel Real Alameda.**

Movies

The sports section in *El Comercio* (section D) has a daily cinema schedule. Showings tend toward the violent and pornographic, but more respectable places can get mainstream releases about six months after they appear in the United States. Although most cinemas are dirt cheap, prices in the newer ones—especially in malls—have risen to $2–3 pp.

The ultra-modern **Cinemark,** Naciones Unidas and America, tel. 2/260-301, and **Multicines,** in the C.C. Iñaquito at Naciones Unidas and Amazonas, tel. 2/265-061 or 265-062, are both on the expensive side but comparable in quality to theaters in North America and Europe. Other good movie theaters in Quito include the **Cine Colón,** 10 de Agosto and Colón; the **Cine Republica,** Republica 476; and the **Cine 24 de Mayo,** Granaderos and 6 de Diciembre. For more artistic or non–North American films, look into the **Cine Universitario,** in the Universidad Central on América, and the theater in the **Casa de La Cultura.** One of the best ways to spend a rainy day in Quito is to set up shop at the **Cine Benalcazar,** 6 de Diciembre and Portugal, where you can bring your own food and enjoy movies all day for one price.

Theater and Concerts

El Comercio also runs information on theater performances and music concerts. When possible, purchasing advance tickets is a good idea. The **Teatro Politecnico,** Ladrón de Guevara and Queseras, hosts the National Symphony on Friday nights; tickets are a steal at less than $1. The colorful indigenous-themed **Jacchigua Ecuadorian Folklore Ballet** performs at the Teatro Aeropuerto, in front of the airport at Juan Pazminio and Avenida de la Prensa, on Wednesday and Friday at 7:30 P.M. Tickets are available from Metropolitan Touring (see "Tour Companies").

The **Teatro Malayerba,** Sodiro 345 and 6 de Diciembre next to the Iglesia El Belén, tel. 2/235-463, is one of the better places to see a play in the city. Smaller houses include the **Patio de Comedias,** 18 de Septiembre 457 and Ama-

zonas, tel. 2/561-902; **El Socavón de Guápulo,** Compte 424, tel. 2/220-449; the **Teatro Charles Chaplin,** 1204 Cordero, tel. 2/500-310; and the **Asociación Humboldt** at Polonia and Vancouver, tel. 2/236-910. The **student theater group** at the Universidad Central, tel. 2/521-500, is also very good.

Many concerts are held in the **Teatro Promedio** of the Casa de la Cultura, 6 de Diciembre between Tarquí and Pátria. The **Conservatorio Nacional de la Música,** Madrid 1159, is a good bet for inexpensive classical music. Rock concerts, including some international stars, pass through the **Coliseo Rumiñahui** and **Estadio Olimpico**—if they're coming, you'll know it.

MAJOR QUITO FESTIVALS

January 6: Día de los Inocentes

April: Good Friday—Thousands of residents fill the streets in solemn processions.

May 2: Festival of Las Cruces—General merriment in the neighborhood of Cruz Verde on Bolívar and Imbabura in Old Town.

May 31: Festival of La Cruz—Celebrated in the neighborhoods of Champicruz, Prensa, and Sumaco.

May 24: Anniversary of the Battle of Pichincha—Military parades down Los Shyris.

August 10: Independence of Quito—Military and school parades.

August: Mes de los Artes (Arts Month)—Artistic performances throughout the city. Information from the Casa de la Cultura.

September 23-24: Fiesta de la Virgen de las Mercedes—Festivities center around the Iglesia La Merced, including a midnight *Misa del gallo* (rooster's Mass).

last Sunday in October: Halloween—Costumed revelers march down Amazonas.

December 1-6: Founding of Quito—One of South America's largest fiestas. Among many other things, election of Queen of Quito, bullfights, and parades. 5 December is the main day.

December 28: Santos Innocentes (Holy Innocents)

December 31: New Year's Eve

SPORTS AND RECREATION

CLIMBING AND MOUNTAINEERING

A possibly life-threatening sport is the last place you want to skimp on quality, in either your tour company, gear, or guide. All mountaineering guides mentioned should be members of ASEGUIM, Ecuador's official mountain guide association. Not only are accredited guides the best of the best, but in case of a rescue requiring a search party, hikers accompanied by an ASEGUIM guide are responsible only for the food and transportation expenses of the rescuers—as opposed to a fee of $1,000 or more per day for search parties. Many tour companies offer discounts to SAE members.

Climbing Companies

A few of the many tour companies in Quito specialize in climbing and have the experience and professionalism to get you back down in one piece should anything go wrong. Founder and head guide Ramiro Donoso brings 17 years of experience climbing in South America and Europe to the **Ecuadorian Alpine Institute,** Ramirez Davalos 136 and Amazonas, Of. 102, tel. 2/565-465, 9/824-475, fax 2/568-949, e-mail: EAI@ecuadorexplorer.com, www.ecuador explorer.com/eai. Their climbs and treks are well-organized, professionally run, and span all experience levels—they even got me to the top of Cotopaxi in 2000.

The **Compania de Guías,** Jorge Washington and 6 de Diciembre, tel./fax 2/504-773, tel. 2/556-210, e-mail: guisamontania@accessinter .net, www.companiasdeguias.com, is a guide cooperative with members who speak English, German, French, and Italian. Hugo Torres operates **Pamir Adventure Travel,** Juan León Mera 721 and Veintimilla, tel. 2/542-605, 220-892, fax 2/547-576, e-mail: info@pamirtravels .com.ec, www.pamirtravels. com.ec. They run tours all over the country with a focus on mountaineering, and rent and buy used mountaineering equipment.

Javier Herrera is the head guide for **Safari Tours** (see "Tour Companies"), with highly recommended climbing trips to any peak in the country. **Sierra Nevada,** Pinto 637 and Amazonas, tel. 2/553-658, 224-717, fax 2/554-936, e-mail: snevada@accessinter.net, employs Freddy Ramirez as head guide. Rafting, climbing, the Galápagos, and Amazon trips are on the list, and the company rents and buys used mountaineering equipment.

SurTrek, Amazonas 877 and Wilson, tel. 2/561-129, fax 2/561-132, e-mail: surtrek@

JAVIER HERRERA

Cotopaxi

uio.telconet.net, www.surtrek.com, also has an office in Ambato, and has guides that speak German, English, and French. Good reports have also come in about **Agama Expeditions,** Venezuela 1163 and Manabi, tel. 2/518-191, fax 2/518-196; **Moggely Climbing,** Pinto E4-255 and Amazonas, tel./fax 2/554-984, e-mail: Moggely@hotmail.com, www. moggely.com; and **Ugsha,** Foch 747 and Amazonas, tel. 9/476-792, 495-428.

Climbing and Camping Equipment

Quito has by far the best selection of outdoor gear merchants in the country. Everything from plastic climbing boots and harnesses to tents, sleeping bags, and stoves are readily available, although not always of the highest quality or state of repair. Needless to say, check all zippers, laces, and fuel valves before you head off into the wilds. Large-size footgear (U.S. size 10 and up) may be hard to locate. Plenty of gear is available for sale as well, either imported (at a high markup) or made in Ecuador.

Tracking down gas for camp stoves can get your adventure started prematurely. White gas, also known as Coleman fuel or *gaz blanco,* can be hard to locate. Try Moggely Climbing (see above), the gas station on the corner of Amazonas and Colón, or one of the various hardware stores *(ferreterías)* in town: **Ace Hardware** has outlets in the C. C. Iñaquito at Naciones Unidas and Amazonas, tel. 3/252-041, and in the C. C. Cumbayá in the eastern valley, tel. 2/892-566; and **Kywi** hardware can be found at Luis Cordero 1641 and 10 de Agosto, tel. 2/501-713, or in the Centro

Commercial Olímpico, tel. 2/434-631.

Hardware stores and Moggely Climbing may have kerosene *(kerex),* and propane/butane canisters *(gaz para camping)* are available at most camping stores. Unleaded gasoline *(gasolina sin plomo)* is available at most gas stations. Check hardware stores or the **Farmacia Colón,** 10 de Agosto and Colón, tel. 2/226-534, for methylated spirits *(alcohol industrial)*—bring your own bottle to fill.

Andísimo, 9 de Octubre 479 and Roca, tel. 2/223-030, and **Agama Expediciones,** Venezuela 11-63 and Manabi, both have camping gear for rent. For climbing gear, try **Altamontana,** Jorge Washington 425 and 6 de Diciembre, tel./fax 2/504-773, e-mail: guiasmontania@access.inter.net, or **Antisana Sport** in the El Bosque Shopping Center, tel./fax 2/467-433, which is also good for large-sized hiking boots. **Campo Abierto,** Baquedano 355 and Juan Leon Mera, tel./fax 2/524-422, e-mail: sinlimite@ecuaword.com, also has climbing equipment for sale and rent.

Other places to buy camping gear include **Camping Cotopaxi,** Colón 942 and Reina Victoria, tel. 2/521-626; **The Explorer,** Reina Victoria 928 and Pinto, tel. 2/550-911; and **Los Alpes,** Reina Victoria 821 and Baquedano, tel./fax 2/232-326. **Equipos Cotopaxi,** 6 de Diciembre and Patria, tel. 2/517-626, make their own sleeping bags, backpacks, and tents for less than you'd pay for imported items. Fishing and hunting equipment are available at **Safari Sports,** 6 de Diciembre 2520 and Orellana, tel. 2/220-647, and the various **Marathon Sports** outlets in the Centros Commerciales El Bosque, El Jardin, Iñaquito, San Rafael, and Quicentro stock light-use sportswear at decent prices.

OTHER FUN STUFF

Mountain Biking

A neon-colored wire sculpture of a mountain bike marks the office of **Aventuras Flying Dutchman,** Foch 714 and Juan León Mera, tel. 2/542-806, fax 2/567-008, e-mail: dutchman@uio.satnet.net, www.ecuadorexplorer.com/dutchman. They run well-reviewed day trips to Cotopaxi and the Tandayapa-Mindo area for $45 pp, which includes bikes and safety gear, lunch, and van transport

---

DAY HIKES NEAR QUITO

Several mountains and hiking areas are within a day's travel of the capital. See the respective text sections for details on each of the following:

- Cerro Atacazo
- Cerro Corazón
- Guagua Pichincha
- Rucu Pichincha
- Cerro Ilaló
- Pasachoa Nature Reserve
- Papallacta lake district

up the steeper sections. The 30-km descent down Cotopaxi is guaranteed to raise your blood pressure. Their two-day trips ($100 pp) to Cotopaxi /Quilotoa and the upper Amazon include meals and overnight accommodations. For true pedaling fanatics, they also offer a five-day trip to Cotopaxi, Chimborazo, Baños, Baeza, Puyo, and Misahuallí that includes a rainforest canoe excursion ($360–460 pp).

Rafting and Kayaking

Steve Nomchong's **Yacu Amu Rafting,** Baquedano E5-27 and Juan León Mera, tel. 2/236-844, fax 2/226-038, e-mail: rafting@yacuamu .com, www.yacuamu.com, is the leader in whitewater trips out of Quito. Their year-round day trips down the Toachi and Blanco rivers offer more rapids per hour than anywhere else in Ecuador ($65 pp)—plus cold beers at the end of every trip. The Toachi/Blanco can be stretched to two days for $160, and they offer two-day trips down the Quijos ($180) and five- and eight-day trips on the Upano from Aug.–Feb. ($525 and $990, respectively). Customized itineraries are possible, and they rent kayaks and offer kayak courses.

ROW Expedicions, Foch 721 and J. L. Mera, tel./fax 2/239-224, does day trips on the Toachi and Blanco as well. Their parent company in the United States sends down guides from Idaho for weeklong expeditions down the Upano from Oct.–Feb.

Motorcycle Tours

Enduro Adventure Motorcycle Tours, tel. 2/372-092, 9/597-749, fax 2/374-280, e-mail: enduro@access.net.ec, specializes in off-road trips on large enduro-style bikes like Honda XR-600s and Suzuki DR-350s. Guide Thomas Fischer speaks English, German, and Spanish, and can take one to five people into the hinterlands for anywhere from one day to three weeks. Longer trips include 4WD backup for service and luggage transportation. Motorcycle experience and a license is required, although you don't necessarily have to have off-road experience. Prices range from $110–180 pp per day.

Horseback Riding

Kapok Expeditions, Pinto E4-255 and Amazonas, tel. 2/556-348, fax 2/504-713, e-mail: kapok@uio.satnet.net, run horseback-riding trips in the Valle de Amajuaña, one hour outside of Quito. Prices includes transportation, lunch, an English-speaking guide, and, of course, horses. **Equatorial Horse Trekking,** tel. 2/443-809, 9/462-798, has one-day riding near the capital for $50 pp per day, including a tasty lunch and transportation. Astrid Müller at the **Green Horse Ranch,** tel. 2/523-856, offers one- and two- day trips for $50 and $100 pp, respectively, to places like Pululahua Crater. This price includes food, accommodations, and transportation to and from Quito.

Ugsha, Foch 747 and Amazonas, tel. 2/447-024, 9/495-792, e-mail: egsha10@hotmail.com, also do mountain-biking trips around Cotopaxi, Pululahua, and the Laguna Mojanda. They specialize in "multi-adventures" that combine hiking, climbing, and biking to places like Chimborazo, the Pichinchas, and Papallacta. Prices start at $50–60 pp per day for mountain biking with at least two people. Stop by the Sun Cafe (see under "Cafés") to inquire about horseback-riding trips around the seldom-visited Ilaló volcano just east of Quito.

Bungee Jumping

Take the 80-meter plunge off a bridge over the Chiche River with **Andes Adrenaline Adventures,** Baron von Humboldt 279, tel. 2/454-049, 236-268, or **Sangay Tours,** Amazonas N24-196 and Cordero, tel. 2/550-176/180, e-mail: info@sangay.com, www.sangay.com. Jumps ($55 pp for two jumps) are held year-round on weekends and during the week with larger groups.

Paragliding

Tandem rides can be arranged through **Adventour,** Calama 339 between Reina Victoria and Mera, tel./fax 2/723-846, 520-647, e-mail: info @adventour.com, www.adventour.com. They offer paragliding tours of the Sierra and the coast for 4–10 days. Contact them for more information and prices on these and the long list of other adventure tours they offer.

Professional Sports

Soccer *(fútbol)* games fill the Estadio Olimpico on weekend afternoons, as well as the Estadio Liga, more commonly called the Casa Blanca. At the Reina Victoria Pub, they'll be happy to tell you about the Hashhouse Harriers **jogging**/drinking group that holds informal runs every other Sunday.

Dance Lessons

Sign up for Latin and Caribbean dance classes—including salsa, merengue, cumbia, and vallentano—at the **Ritmo Tropical Dance Academy,** 10 de Agosto 1792 and San Gregorio, Ed. Santa Rosa, Of. 108, tel. 2/277-051, e-mail: dancing@interactive.net.ec. The **Tropical Dancing School,** Carrión 768 and 9 de Octubre, tel. 2/466-855 or 466-854, also offers dance lessons, as do **Son Latino,** Reina Victoria 1225 and Lizardo García, tel. 2/507-315, e-mail: latinoson@yahoo.com, and **Rumba Zone,** Almagro 1170 and La Niña, tel. 2/222-809, 223-261. Prices at all of these schools are approximately $5 pp per hour for one-to-one or couple lessons.

Public Pools and Spas

The Concentración Deportiva de Pichincha maintains the indoor, heated **El Batán** pool at Cochapata and Manual Abascal, tel. 2/460-660. Swim caps are required, and lockers and keys are provided. Other heated indoor pools can be found at **Jipipjapa,** Río Coca and Isla Fernandina, tel. 2/265-752, and **Miraflores,** 10 de Agosto and Nicaragua. All of these facilities cost less than $1 pp per day and have daily public swimming hours.

Oasis, Ulloa 3315 and Republica, tel. 2/459-473 or 459-478, offers a sauna, steam room, hot tub, and pool open Mon.–Fri. 4–9 P.M. and Sat. and Sun. 10 A.M.–9 P.M. ($3 pp; women get in for half price on Mon. and Fri.). They also have a cafeteria, locker room, and massage therapy. Bring your own towel.

Everything Else

The **Academia Superior de Arte,** Jorge Washington 268 and Plaza, tel. 2/564-646, offers drawing and painting courses next to the Hotel Amaranta. Courses in tai chi and other martial arts are taught by **Sande and Jenny,** Felix Oralabal 337 between Joffrey and Zamora, tel. 2/432-497.

Bullfights are held year-round at the Plaza de Toros, on Amazonas and Juan de Azcaray just south of the airport (take the trolley to La Y). The festival of the founding of Quito during the first week of December is an especially popular time for bullfights.

TOUR COMPANIES

It seems that everyone and his brother now offers tours around Ecuador, which is all the more reason to heed positive reviews. Of the dozens of general tour operators working out of Quito, a few stand out for their quality, professionalism, and value. For more information on tour companies recommended for their eco-mindedness, contact the **Ecuadorian Ecotourism Association,** Coruña N26-207 and Orellana, tel. 2/564-448, 509-431, fax 2/565-261, e-mail: shamanistico@yahoo.com.

Angermeyer's Enchanted Excursions, Foch 769 and Amazonas, tel. 2/569-960, 221-305, fax 2/569-956, e-mail: angermeyer@accessinet.net, www.angermeyer.com.ec, covers the entire country with a focus on the Galápagos—boats such as the *Cachalote* and *Beluga* receive repeat praise. Their Quito staff is very helpful.

One of the largest tour operators in the country, **Metropolitan Touring** was the first to organize high-quality Galápagos trips in the 1960s. Since then they've branched out to include just about every tour in Ecuador, from the Flotel Orellana to hacienda stays, city and market tours, train trips, and mountain climbing. They have branch offices located throughout the country. In Quito, in addition to the main office at Republica de El Salvador N36-84, tel. 2/464-780, fax 2/464-702, they also have offices at Amazonas 239 and 18 de Septiembre, and in Old Town at Sucre and García Moreno in the C.C. Galerías Sucre. Information and bookings are available in the United States through Adventure Associates, 13150 Coit Rd., Ste. 110, Dallas, TX 75240, 800/527-2500, 972/907-0414, fax 972/783-1286, e-mail:info@ecuadorable.com, www.ecuadorable.com.

Nuevo Mundo Travel and Tours, Coruña N26-207, tel. 2/564-448, 553-826, fax 2/565-261, e-mail: nmundo@interactive.net.ec, www.nuevomundotravel.com was started in 1979 by a founder and former president of the Ecuadorian Ecotourism Association. Their tours and facilities, therefore, are as environmentally conscious as any in Ecuador—they don't even advertise a third of them to minimize impact on the destinations. Along with the usual Galápagos and Oriente tours, they offer several unique options, including a private solar museum at the original equator monument, 10-day shamanism programs, and one-month Spanish courses combined with environmental studies.

Safari Tours, Calama 380 and Juan León Mera, tel./fax 2/220-426, tel. 2/552-505, fax 2/223-381, e-mail: admin@safari.com.ec, www.safari.com.ec, is one of the most frequently recommended operators in the country. Owner Jean Brown knows the country intimately and can get you to just about anywhere in Ecuador with the company's trusty 4WDs to climb, hike, bird-watch, camp, or mountain bike. Female-only tours, including guides and drivers, are another option. They have a separate Galápagos office on Pasaje Roca in New Town, and they can be reached from the United States at 800/434-8182.

Tropic Ecological Adventures, República E7-320 and Almagro, Ed. Taurus, tel. 2/225-907, 234-594, fax 2/560-156, e-mail: zinfo@tropiceco.com, www.tropiceco.com, is run by Andy Drumm, a fellow of the Royal Geographic Society and the president of the Amazon Commission of the Ecuadorian Ecotourism Association. Their trips have won awards for socially responsible tourism and are especially strong in the Oriente, where a pilot program with the Huaorani permits guests to visit otherwise closed villages. Randy Borman leads Tropic trips to Cofán communities, and they can organize visits to the Cerro Golondrinas and Maquipicuna cloud forest reserves.

Green Planet, Juan León Mera 2384 and Wilson, tel. 2/520-570, fax 2/521-426, e-mail: greenpla@interactive.net.ec, operates out of a little shop under a tree across from Libri Mundi. Trips to Cuyabeno and Yasuni are both recommended for the guides and food. They also run many one-day tours to places like Otavalo and Cotopaxi.

Eco-Adventour, Calama 339 and Juan León Mera, tel./fax 2/223-720, e-mail: info@ecoadventour.com, www.ecoadventour.com, has a long list of adventurous outings, including mountain biking, rafting, horseback riding, Amazon tours, and ocean kayaking.

After the eruption of Tungurahua, **Rain Forestur,** Calama 127 and 6 de Diciembre, tel./fax 2/239-822, e-mail: rainfor@interactive.net.ec, moved from Baños to Quito. Their Cuyabeno trips have been applauded, but they have a full slate of other options, including a two-day skiing trip on Carihuayrazo ($80 pp with two people). **Emerald Forest Expeditions,** Amazonas 1023 and Pinto, tel./fax 2/541-543, e-mail: emerald@ecuanex.net.ec, www.ecuador-explorer.com/emerald, run five- to seven-day tours in the Oriente using local guides. They explore the Napo, Arajuno, and Juambuno rivers by dugout canoe and visit the Río Pañayaco and Laguna Pañacocha.

Native Life Tours, Foch E4-167 and Amazonas, tel. 2/550-836, 505-158, fax 2/229-077, e-mail: natlife1@natlife.com.ec, www.native-life.com, are most well known for their Cuyabeno trips of four to eight days. Also recommended in Quito are **Ecoventura,** Colón E9-58 and 6 de Diciembre, tel. 2/507-408, fax 2/507-509, e-mail: lmena@pi.pro.ec, www.ecoventura.com.ec/homei.htm; and **Etnotur,** Luís Cordero 1313 and Juan León Mera, tel. 2/230-552, 564-565, fax 2/502-682, e-mail: etnocru@uio.satnet.net.

SHOPPING

Crafts and Galleries

Once again, New Town is the place to spend your money; almost every block has some sort of crafts shop or sidewalk vendor's stand. Take your time, shop around, and compare quality. There are also a few standouts in Old Town.

Hungarian-born Olga Fitsch came to Ecuador to escape the ugliness brewing in Europe in 1939. After opening her first shop in 1943, she became a world-renowned expert on South American crafts and folklore; during her lifetime she was sought by the Smithsonian and collectors worldwide for her advice. **Folklore Olga Fitsch,** Colón 260, tel./fax 2/563-085, e-mail: folklore@olgafisch.com, was her house up until her death. The first floor is filled with gorgeous, pricey ceramics and textiles from all over the continent. A museum is planned upstairs. The house is open Mon.–Sat. 9 A.M.–7 P.M., with outlets in the Hotels Colón (tel. 2/526-667) and Swissôtel (tel. 2/569-003).

If you only have time to stop at one crafts store in Quito, make it **Tianguez,** tel. 2/230-609, e-mail: tianguez@uio.satnet.net, which is run by the Sinchi Sacha foundation underneath the Iglesia San Francisco. The store, which also has a small outdoor café on the Plaza de San Francisco, features an excellent selection of quality handicrafts from around the country for surprisingly low prices. Profits from the masks, ceramics, Tigua hide paintings, jewelry, and weavings go to fund their programs to benefit indigenous communities. Open daily 9 A.M.–6 P.M.

The **Tienda Comunitaria Artesanias y Alimentos "Maquita,"** Juan León Mera and Robles, tel./fax 2/552-308, provides a place for poor indigenous women from throughout Ecuador to sell their crafts. The store features a wide selection with good prices and quality. It's open Mon.–Fri. 10 A.M.–8 P.M., Sat. 10 A.M.–6 P.M. The **Centro de Exposiciones y Ferías Artesanales,** 12 de Octubre 1738 and Lizardo García, tel. 2/503-873, is a similar cooperative organization, which occasionally sponsors crafts fairs. The center is open Mon.–Fri. 9 A.M.–5 P.M.

Excedra, Carrión 243 and Tamayo, tel. 2/224-001, serves as a combination art gallery, folklore and antique outlet, and tea room. It's an offbeat little place with a good selection of crafts. Hours are Mon.–Fri. 9 A.M.–7 P.M., Sat. 9 A.M.–5 P.M. Beautiful, high-quality wool textiles for less money than you'd think are the specialty of **Hilana,** 6 de Diciembre 1921 and Baquerizo Moreno, tel. 2/501-693. **Rojas Nunez,** Buenos Aires 662 and America, sells guitars and *charangos,* and a streetside vendor on the corner of 9 de Octubre and Patria sells old coins and bills.

Professional browsers could spend a whole day on Juan León Mera and Veintimilla, where half a dozen highbrow crafts/antique stores and art galleries cluster within two blocks of Libri Mundi. Try **Artesanias Incario,** the **CDX Gallery, Art-forum,** or **El eKeKo. El Corozo,** Juan León Mera 453 and Juan León Mera, has a large selection of carved tagua nuts.

For Tigua hide paintings, check **Artesanias Folklore Los Pendoneros,** Juan León Mera 820 and Baquedano; or the **Galeria Folklore El Aborigen,** Jorge Washington 614, a large place that also stocks wooden festival masks. You can find more wood carvings at **La Bodega,** Juan León Mera 615 and Carrión, along with antiques and a little bit of everything else. **Amanos,** Veintimilla 564 between 6 de Diciembre and Plaza, stocks the famous Hacienda Zuleta embroidery in the form of shirts, napkins, and wall hangings. **Punto en Blanco** next door also has some nice work.

Otavaleño textiles are on display all along Amazonas, and along Juan León Mera in New Town.

Books

Without a doubt, **Libri Mundi,** Juan León Mera and Wilson, tel. 2/234-791, e-mail: librimu1@librimundi.com.ec, www.librimundi.com, is the best bookstore in Ecuador. Along with a wide range of titles in Spanish, they sell new and a few used foreign books (English, German, and French) at a markup. Fliers posted outside the door are a good way to find out about artistic and literary goings-on around Quito. Open Mon.–Fri. 8:30 A.M.–7 P.M., Sat. 9 A.M.–1:30 P.M. and 3:30–6:30 P.M., Libri Mundi also has a branch in the Centro

Comerical Quicentro at Naciones Unidas and Los Shyris.

For used paperbacks, head for the large used library of **Confederate Books,** Calama 410 and Juan León Mera. Owner Thomas Savage hails from Louisiana and proudly offers authentic New Orleans chicory coffee in the small outdoor café. (They no longer buy used books.) Open Mon.–Sat 10 A.M.–7 P.M. **Mr. Books** is a newer Barnes&Noble–style bookstore on the third floor of the Centro Comercial El Jardin.

Paperback trade-ins are taken at **Safari Tours,** Calama 380 and Juan León Mera; **Mr. Bagel,** Portugal 948 and Los Shyris; and **Papaya.net** at the corner of Juan León Mera and Calama.

The **South American Explorers' Quito clubhouse,** Jorge Washington 311 and Plaza, tel./fax 2/225-228, carries the best selection of guidebooks in town, along with maps, a trading shelf, and a lending library of more than 1,000 volumes that are open to members. The bookstore of **Ediciones Abya Yala,** 12 de Octubre 1430 and Wilson, tel. 2/506-247 or 562-633, specializes in books on Oriente cultures written in Spanish and has a library.

Magazines and Newspapers

A wide range of foreign magazines fills the shelves at **Libro Express,** Amazonas 816 and Veintimilla. Street vendors all along Amazonas also stock a few. Bookshops in expensive hotels sell foreign magazines and newspapers, but be sure they don't try to mark up the latter over the printed price.

Other Goodies

César Guacán, Chimborazo 108 and Bahía, tel. 2/583-475, makes and sells guitars starting at $100, and **Marcel G. Creaciones,** Roca 766 between Amazonas and 9 de Octubre, tel. 2/653-555, fax 2/552-672, carries a good selection of Panama hats. For exclusive jewelry designs, stop by the **Museo Guayasamin,** Bosmediano 543 between Egas and Carbo, or **Ag,** Juan León Mera 614 and Carrión, tel. 2/550-276, fax 2/502-301.

Many small leather-working shops in New Town can custom-make clothes, boots, bags, and other accessories for surprisingly reasonable prices. Try **Zapytal,** Pinto 538 and Amazonas, tel. 2/528-757.

If you're looking for a mask and snorkel (or even a wetsuit) for your Galápagos trip, you'll find them along with a whole storeful of modern sporting equipment at **KAO Sport,** Almagro and Colón, Ed. Ecuatoriana, tel. 2/550-005 or 522-266. Other KAO branches are located in many of the city's centros comerciales. **Saucisa,** with two locations on Amazonas (just north of Carrión and just north of Pinto), carries Andean instruments and music on CD and cassette.

Topographical maps of the entire country are sold at the **Instituto Geográfico Militar (IGM),** at Paz y Miño on top of a hill off Colombia. Leave your passport at the entrance and be ready for a textbook lesson in bureaucracy—order here, sign there, wait over here, pick up down there. Maps of some areas, including most of the Perúvian border and the south coast, can be bought only with special permission from the military and take two weeks to process. Open Mon.–Thurs. 8 A.M.–5 P.M., Fri. 8 A.M.–1 P.M.

Markets

In Old Town, the huge covered market at **24 de Mayo and Benalcázar** spills over onto the streets, including Cuenca and Loja. Clothing and crafts are plentiful, with the main markets open on Tuesday and Saturday. At the **Mercado Ipiales** centered on Imbabura between Chile and the Plaza de San Francisco, you'll find household odds and ends, stolen goods, and a few indigenous crafts. Watch your wallet or purse carefully at both locations.

On weekends, the north end of Parque El Ejido becomes an outdoor art gallery with a good selection of paintings, sculpture, and jewelry. The **La Mariscal** artisan market in New Town occupies half of the block south of Jorge Washington between Reina Victoria and Juan León Mera. Just about every indigenous craft in Ecuador makes an appearance daily from 9 A.M.–8 P.M.

Local produce is the main draw to New Town's **Mercado Santa Clara,** along Ulloa and Versailles just south of Colón (main Wednesday, also Sunday). Every Friday a fruit and vegetable market fills Galaviz between Toledo and Isabel La Católica, where children sell baskets of spices and wealthy shoppers hire elderly basket-carriers to tote the day's purchases.

Boutiques, supermarkets, and movie theaters find a home in Quito's many centros comerciales (malls), some of which would be right at home in downtown Beverly Hills. Major ones include **El Bosque,** Al Parque and Alonso de Torres; **Caracol,** Amazonas and Naciones Unidas; **El Espiral,** Amazonas and Jorge Washington; **El Jardín,** República and Amazonas; **Iñaquito,** Amazonas and Naciones Unidas; **Multicentro,** 6 de Diciembre and La Niña; **Naciones Unidas,** Naciones Unidas and Amazonas; **Quicentro,** 6 de Diciembre and Naciones Unidas; and **Plaza Aeropeurto,** Prensa and Salas.

SERVICES

POST

Quito's main **post office** is one block east of the Plaza Independencia in Old Town, on Espejo between Guayaquil and Venezuela. Hours are Mon.–Fri. 7:30 A.M.–7:30 P.M., Sat. 8 A.M.–2 P.M. All general delivery orders are sent here by default unless marked "Correo Central, Eloy Alfaro," in which case it will go to the branch at Eloy Alfaro 354 and 9 de Octubre. It's still a good idea to check both, though. There are other branches at the Torres de Almagro (Reina Victoria and Colón), on 12 de Octubre in front of the Casa de la Cultura, and at the airport and terminal terrestre. All have similar hours, can handle postcards and letters, and sell stamps.

Take packages larger than two kg to the **Correo Maritimo Aduana,** Ulloa 273 and Davalos. Here packages must be under 31 kg, with a combined length and girth of less than three meters and no one dimension over 1.5 meters. To mail packages between 10–100 kg, check with the cargo divisions of airlines at the airport. Continental and American fly to North America, and KLM, Luftansa, and Air France fly to Europe.

Packages larger than 100 kg are more of a hassle—not only to lift but also for the customs paperwork required. A few cargo companies will mail your package and handle the red tape: **Challenge Air Cargo,** Amazonas and Indanza; **Metropolitan Expreso,** Panamericana Norte, Km 3.5 and Los Cedros, tel. 2/475-731/732, fax 2/475-730; **Panatlantic,** Orellana 1791 and 10 de Agosto, piso 6, tel. 2/222-276 or 222-277; and **Transpack,** Amazonas 877 between Veintimilla and Wilson, piso 3, tel. 2/551-520, fax 2/503-829.

Several express couriers operate out of Quito, including **Express Mail Service (EMS),** Eloy Alfaro 354 and 9 de Octubre, tel. 2/543-468, 569-741; **Federal Express,** Amazonas 517 and Santa Maria, tel. 2/253-552 or 253-553; and **UPS,** Iñaquito N35-155, tel. 2/460-598 or 460-469. **DHL** has several offices throughout the city, including Eloy Alfaro and Av. de Los Juncos (tel. 2/485-100), Colón 1333 and Foch (tel. 2/556-118), and at the Hilton Colón and the airport.

TELECOMMUNICATIONS

Telephone

All of the **Andinatel** branches—Amazonas and Colón, Eloy Alfaro and Berlin, Benalcázar 769 and Mejía, the *terminal terrestre,* and the airport—are open daily 8 A.M.–9:30 P.M. and handle national and international calls and faxes. Almost every business in town, plus hundreds of impromptu sidewalk stands, will rent a phone for local calls, charging by the minute.

Computers and the Internet

The epicenter of Ecuador's Internet explosion, Quito is said by some to have more Internet cafés than any other city in the world. While this claim is up for debate, it's no question that there are plenty around town. Competition keeps prices down, and there is talk of free access (which is already in place in other Latin American countries) arriving in the near future. In the meantime, expect to pay $1 or less per hour and to have access at most cafés from 8 A.M.–9 P.M. daily, or at least Mon.–Sat. Although connection rates and computer quality vary widely, most cafés have fax service, scanners, printers, and Internet phone programs such as Net2Phone, allowing foreign visitors to call home for a fraction of the cost of a normal connection. The term "café" may be misleading, however, because many offer only water and snacks.

Listing Internet cafés in Quito may be an inherently futile gesture because they open and close faster than a fifth-grader's mouth at recess, but several are more convenient and offer better quality. In New Town, the block of Calama between Juan León Mera and Reina Victoria has no less than six Internet cafés, and there are three in the basement of the Ecuatoriana building at Almagro and Colón. Other locations worth checking out include the following:

British Council, Amazonas N26-146 and La Niña, tel. 2/508-225

CaféNet, Reina Victoria and Cordero, Ed. Torres de Almagro (downstairs), tel. 2/554-005

Café-Web, Amazonas 333 and Jorge Washington, tel. 2/553-725

Ciber-Net Café, Reina Victoria and Colón, tel. 2/226-148

Cybercafe Cultural, Juan Rodriguez 228 and Reina Victoria, tel. 2/231-656

Hipe-Mail, Foch 615 and Reina Victoria, tel. 2/569-767

Monkey On Line, Juan León Mera 21-10 and Jorge Washington, tel. 2/557-551

Mundo Net, Pinto E5-32 and Reina Victoria, tel. 2/230-411

net.Zone, Reina Victoria 100 and Patria, tel. 2/549-057

Plus.Net, Juan León Mera 741 and Veintimilla, tel. 2/521-587

Starnet Cafe, 12 de Octubre 1942 and Cordero, ed. World Trade Center, tel. 2/544-784

If you've brought your own laptop computer, you can dial 2/505-000 to access CompuServe and America Online through the **SCITOR** network for $10–12 per hour. (If you're having problems getting onto CompuServe, change to the SCI-

DAVE HURST

TOR connection in "session settings.") **Sercoin,** Foch and Reina Victoria, tel. 565-520/522, fax 2/565-521, rents Macintosh computers for $2 per hour and is the only official Apple computer servicer in Quito.

MONEY

Exchange Houses

Vaz Cambio at Amazonas and Roca below the Hotel Alameda Real is one of the most convenient *casas de cambio* in Quito. **Multicambio** has branches at Roca 720 and Amazonas, Amazonas and Santa María, Venezuela 689, and at the airport. **Produbanco** at Amazonas and Robles is also good.

Banks and ATMs

ATMs for most international systems (Plus, Cirrus, Visa, and MasterCard) can be found at major banks along Amazonas, including **Filanbanco** at Amazonas and Roca and the **Banco del Pacifico** at Amazonas and Veintimilla. **Citibank** is at Av. Rep. El Salvador and Naciones Unidas, and the **Banco de Guayaquil** can be found at Colón and Reina Victoria. Most of these banks will also exchange travelers' checks, but be warned of long lines and restricted hours. (BanRed is a local ATM network.)

Credit Card Branches

MasterCard, tel. 2/262-700, is at Naciones Unidas 825 and Los Shyris, open Mon.–Fri. 8:30 A.M.–5 P.M. and Sat. 9:30–1:30 P.M. The **Visa** office is located in the Banco de Guayaquil at Colón and Reina Victoria, open Mon.–Fri. 9 A.M.–4:30 P.M. and Sat. 9 A.M.–1 P.M. **American Express** has an office on the fifth floor of the Ed. Rocafuerte at Amazonas 339 and Jorge Washington, open Mon.–Fri. 8:30 A.M.–5 P.M. Card members can buy travelers' checks using personal checks against their accounts for a 1 percent fee.

Money Transfers

Western Union, República 433 and Diego de Almagro, tel. 2/502-194, 543-469, charges $50 plus 12 percent tax for a same-day transfer of $1,000. It'll cost you $25 to transfer any amount to and from the Americas ($35 to/from Europe) at the **Banco del Pacifico** at Amazonas and Jorge Washington. (You are expected to cover any costs in contacting your home bank.) If that much cash makes you itch, you can change it into American Express travelers' checks at the main branch of the Banco del Pacifico at República 433 and Almagro. This transaction costs $10 to change up to $1,000 and 1 percent from there on up.

Emergency Funds

U.S. citizens can have emergency funds transferred to them from abroad through the U.S. Department of State. Mail a cashier's check or money order for the desired amount plus a $20 processing fee, made payable to the Department of State, along with a letter with the sender's and recipient's names, addresses, and phone numbers to: Overseas Citizens Services CA/OCS, Room 4811, Department of State, 2201 C St. NW, Washington, DC 20520. (Money can also be sent through Western Union.) The funds will be available to the recipient on the next workday after receipt in the United States. For more information, call 202/647-5225, Mon.–Fri. 8 A.M.–10 P.M. and Sat. 9 A.M.–3 P.M.

HEALTH

General Concerns

Unless you're from some place like La Paz or Nepal, you'll feel Quito's **altitude** within the first few hours after arriving. Take it easy the first few days, drink lots of water, and get plenty of sleep. Save the jogging and the *cuba libres* for next week, if possible. Other than the altitude, the only health risks particular to the capital are the unforgiving **sun** and the **smog** from all the traffic. Busy streets seem to trap and hold the noxious gases, so smart pedestrians avoid them whenever possible.

Hospitals and Clinics

The American-run **Voz Andes,** Villalengua 267 and 10 de Agosto, tel. 2/262-142, receives the most business from Quito's foreign community. It's described as fast, competent, and inexpensive, with an emergency room and outpatient services. To get there, take any bus north along 10 de Agosto to just past Naciones Unidas. The **Hospital Metropolitano,** Mariana de Jesús and Occidental, tel. 2/261-520, is also recommended, although it's more expensive.

The **Clínica Pichincha,** Páez 738 and Veintimilla, tel. 2/562-296, has a laboratory that can perform analyses for intestinal parasites. Blood and stool tests are also performed at the **Laboratorio Clínica Patológico-Bacteriológico,** Cordero 410 and 6 de Diciembre, Ed. San Francisco, piso 4, tel. 2/226-990. Yellow fever shots are dispensed on Friday from 2–4 P.M. at the **Centro de Salud No. 1** near the Plaza Santo Domingo. Women's health problems should be referred to the 24-hour **Clínica de la Mujer,** Amazonas 4826 and Gaspar de Villarroel, tel. 2/458-000.

Private Doctors

Dr. John Rosenberg, Foch 476 and Almagro, tel. 2/521-104, e-mail: jrd@pi.pro.ec, is a highly recommended general practitioner who speaks English and German. He is the doctor for the U.S. Embassy and performs house calls. He has office hours weekdays after 3:30 P.M. and can administer hepatitis vaccines. **Steven Contag,** Mariana de Jesus and Occidental, tel. 2/267-972, beeper 555-000; and **Fernando Celi,** Veintimilla and 12 de Octubre, Ed. El Giron, Of. 601, tel. 2/567-634, 561-690, are both gynecologists who speak English. The latter is also a pediatrician.

Renato Leon, Amazonas and Orellana, Ed. Torrealba, piso 2, tel. 2/238-342, 552-080, is a tropical and infectious disease specialist who speaks English. Check with the various embassies for doctors who speak languages besides Spanish and English.

Dentists

Roberto Mena, Coruña E24865 and Isabel La Católica, tel. 2/569-752, 9/468-350, beeper 555-285, is a dentist who speaks English and German. **Sixto and Silvia Altamirano,** Amazonas 2689 and República, tel. 2/244-119, are also recommended for dental problems, as is **Dr. Fausto Vallejo,** Madrid 742 and Lugo, La Floresta, tel. 2/613-127, 9/803-213.

Other Specialists
Chiropractors **Patrick Bullock,** Atahualpa 315
and Ulloa, tel. 9/721-503, and **Reza Shapouri,** El
Día N37-189 and El Mercurio, tel. 2/245-115,
263-365, can get cracking on your aching back.
If that doesn't work, try a massage from **Annie
Verbik,** Sandoval 500 and Altar, tel. 2/253-581,
or an acupuncture treatment from **Francisco
Yang,** Felix Oralabal 337, tel. 2/432-497. **Albert
and Lissette Lagomarsini,** 10 A and Santiago, tel. 2/527-578, 546-921, are both optometrists
from the United States and welcome drop-ins.

SPANISH SCHOOLS

Ecuador is quickly becoming one of the best
places to learn Spanish in Latin America. Not only
do Ecuadorians speak slowly and clearly in comparison to their quick-talking, slang-tossing neighbors, but competition among dozens of schools
keeps prices low and quality up—and it's a great
place to travel.

Almost 60 Spanish schools in Quito offer intensive
Spanish instruction. With such intense competition,
it's worth your while to shop around for one that fits
your needs perfectly. Tuition usually includes four to
seven hours of instruction per day, either in groups or
one-on-one (some veterans say that four hours is
plenty). Costs are computed per hour, starting
around $4 and ending close to $10. An initial registration fee may be required, and discounts are often
possible for long-term commitments. Make sure to
get a receipt when you pay, and check to see if any
extras are not included in the hourly rate. SAE members often receive discounts of 5–15 percent.

Many schools draw business by offering extras such
as e-mail and fax service, sports facilities, and ex-
tracurricular activities. Some will even house you (for a
fee) or arrange for a homestay with a local family (typically $10–25 for full board, $9–12 for lodging only).
Don't sign any long-term arrangements until you're
sure of both the school and the family.

The following schools have received many positive reviews:

Academia de Español Equinoccial
Roca 533 and Juan León Mera
tel. 2/529-460, 525-690
e-mail: eee@eee.org.ec
www.equinoccial.edu.ec

Academia Latinoamericana
José Queri #2 and Eloy Alfaro
tel. 2/452-824, tel./fax 2/433-820
e-mail: delco@spanish.com.ec
www.ecua.net.ec/academia

Amazonas
Jorge Washington 718 and
Amazonas, Ed. Rocafuerte
tel./fax 2/504-654, tel. 2/527-509
e-mail: amazonas@pi.pro.ec
www.ecua.net.ec/amazonas

Beraca
García Moreno 858 between Sucre
and Espejo, Pje. Amador
tel. 2/288-092
e-mail: beraca@interactive.net.ec

Bipo and Toni's
Carrión E8-183 and Plaza
tel./fax 2/556-614
e-mail: bipo@pi.pro.ec
homepage.iprolink.ch/~bipo

British Council
Amazonas N26-146 and La Niña
tel. 2/540-225, 508-282, fax 508-283
e-mail: helpdesk@britishcouncil.org.ec

Cristóbal Colón Spanish School
Colón 2088 and Versalles
tel./fax 2/506-508
e-mail: ccolon@southtravel.com
www.southtravel.com

Instituto Superior de Español
Darquea Teran 1650
and 10 de Agosto
tel. 2/223-242, fax 221-628
e-mail: superior@ecnet.ec

La Lengua
Colón 1001 and Juan León Mera,
Ed. Ave Maria, piso 8
tel./fax 2/501-271, tel. 543-521
e-mail: lalengua@hoy.net

Pichincha Spanish School
Andres Xaura 182 and Foch
tel. 2/528-051, fax 2/601-689
e-mail: admin@pichinch.ecuanex.net.ec
www.qni.com/~mj-pich/pich.html

Simón Bolívar
Plaza 353 and Roca
tel./fax 2/504-977
e-mail: info@simon-bolivar.com
www.simon-bolivar.com

South American Spanish Institute
Amazonas N26-59 and Santa María
tel. 2/544-71,5, tel./fax 2/226-348
e-mail: sudameri@impsat.net.ec
www.southamerican.edu.ec

Recommended private teachers include **Ana Maria Reyes,** tel. 2/573-180, 581-346; **Emilia Castelo,** tel. 2/448-603; and **Mauricio Noboa,** tel. 2/624-880, e-mail: mauricionoboa@hotmail.com.

OTHER SERVICES

Laundry
Wash-and-dry places are common in New Town; three are on Pinto near Reina Victoria and the youth hostel, including two that will let you use the machines yourself. Laundry services are available in many hotels, and the receptionists in more expensive ones can point you toward a dry cleaner *(lavaseca).*

Bicycle Repair
For parts and service, try **Bicilandia,** Los Shyris 1080 (opposite the bandstand on the east side of La Carolina), or **Bici-Sport,** 6 de Diciembre 6327 and Berlanga, tel. 2/460-894 (also in the C.C. Quicentro, tel. 2/254-763).

Photography
You can buy slide film at **Fuji,** Amazonas and Carrión, and develop it at **Ecucolor** at Orellana

---

**QUITO EMERGENCY
TELEPHONE NUMBERS**

Police	101
Fire Department	102
Red Cross	131
Emergency	911

---

and Coruña. **Fotografos y Aficionados,** 6 de Diciembre 1944 and Cordero, is a good all-around custom photo lab, and **Di Foto,** Amazonas 893 and Wilson, will develop panoramic shots with excellent quality. If your camera isn't working, take it to Gustavo V. Gomes, a competent repairman at **Cemaf,** Asunción 130 and 10 de Agosto, Ed. Molina, Of. 1, tel. 2/230-855, beeper, 2/227-777.

Lawyers
Paz & Horowitz, Whymper 1105 and Diego de Almagro, tel. 2/222-057, 508-123, e-mail: bruceh@ph.com.ec, provide good legal services, as does **Marco Subia,** Foch 510 and Diego de Almagro, piso 5, tel. 2/508-198, 501-208, who speaks English. For visa problems, try **Carlos Zarates,** Pje. San Luis Recalde 104 and Santa Prisca, Of. 205, tel. 2/571-414 (Spanish only).

Delivery Services
La Cigüeña, tel. 2/228-227, will pick up and deliver anything (food, videos, etc.) from 11 A.M. to midnight.

INFORMATION

Libraries
Books in English can be borrowed from the **Fulbright Commission,** Diego de Almagro 961 and 6 de Diciembre, the **British Council** (see following section); and by members only from the **South American Exporers'** Quito clubhouse (see following section).

Visas
Tourist visa extensions up to 90 days are the main reason most travelers end up at the **Jefeatura Provincial de Migración,** Isla Seymour 1152 and Río Coca, tel. 2/247-510, 450-573. They're open Mon.–Fri. 8 A.M.–12:30 P.M. and 3–5 P.M., but go early and be ready to

wait. As horrendously inconvenient as it is, as of late 2000 you could only get an extension the day your tourist visa expires or the day before. Extensions between 90 and 180 days are handled at the **Dirección Nacional de Migración,** Av. Amazonas and República, Asesoria Jurídica, piso 2.

Visitors with nontourist visas need to register at the **Dirección de Extranjería,** Juan León Mera and Patria, Ed. Corporación Finaciera, piso 6, to be able to get a *censo* at the Dirección Nacional de Migración (piso 1), which is the same place you'll need to go to get your *salida* to leave the country. (See "Visas and Officialdom" in the On The Road chapter for more information.)

EMBASSIES AND CONSULATES IN QUITO

Argentina: Amazonas 477 between Robles and Roca, Ed. Banco de los Andes, piso 5, tel. 2/562-292, Mon.–Fri. 9 A.M.–1 P.M.

Australia: Whymper 1210 and Alpallana, Ed. Techniseguro, tel. 2/505-655 or 505-660

Austria: Veintimilla 878 and Amazonas, Ed. Hermanos, piso 4, tel. 2/524-811, Mon.–Fri. 10 A.M.–noon

Belgium: Juan León Mera 863 and Wilson, tel. 2/545-348 or 545-340, Mon. and Thurs. 9 A.M.–noon, Mon. and Wed. 2–5 P.M., Fri. by appointment

Bolivia: Bosmediano 526 and osé Carbo, tel. 2/446-450, 244-830 or 244-831, Mon.–Fri. 8 A.M.–2 P.M.

Brazil: Amazonas 1429 and Colón, Ed. España, piso 10, tel. 2/563-086, Mon.–Fri. 9:30 A.M.–12:30 P.M. and 2:30–5:30 P.M.

Canada: 6 de Diciembre 2816 and Paul Rivet, tel. 2/543-162, Mon.–Fri. 9 A.M.–noon, 2:30–5:30 P.M. by appointment

Chile: Sáenz 3617 and Amazonas, piso 4, tel. 2/249-403, Mon.–Fri. 8 A.M.–3 P.M.

China: Atahualpa 349 and Amazonas, tel. 2/433-407, Mon.–Thurs. 9 A.M.–noon and 3–4 P.M., Fri. 9 A.M.–noon

Colombia (Consulate): Atahualpa 955 and República, piso 3, tel. 2/458-012, Mon.–Fri. 8:30 A.M.–2:30 P.M.

Colombia (Embassy): Colón 1133 and Amazonas, Ed. Arist, piso 7, tel. 2/228-926, Mon.–Fri. 9 A.M.–1 P.M., 2–4 P.M.

Costa Rica: Rumipamba 692 and República, tel. 2/254-945 (embassy), 256-016 (consulate), Mon.–Fri. 8 A.M.–1:30 P.M.

Cuba: Mercurio 365 and El Vengador, tel. 2/260-981, Mon.–Fri. 9 A.M.–1 P.M.

Denmark: República de El Salvador 733 and Portugal, Ed. Gabriela 3, piso 3, tel. 2/437-163, Mon.–Fri. 9:30 A.M.–1 P.M. and 3–5 P.M.

Finland: 18 de Septiembre 368 and Amazonas, tel. 2/502-227

France (Consulate): Diego de Almagro 1550 and Pradera, tel. 2/543-101, Mon.–Fri. 9 A.M.–1 P.M. for visas, 9 A.M.–5:30 P.M. for other services

France (Embassy): Plaza 107 and Pátria, tel. 2/569-883, Mon.–Fri. 9 A.M.–1 P.M. and 2:30–5:30 P.M.

Germany: Patria and 9 de Octubre, Ed. Banco de GNB, piso 6, tel. 2/225-660, Mon.–Fri. 9 A.M.–noon

Guatemala: República 192 and Almagro, tel. 2/545-714, Mon.–Fri. 10 A.M.–1 P.M.

Ireland: Ulloa 2651 and Rumipamba, tel. 2/451-577, Mon.–Fri. 9 A.M.–1 P.M.

Israel: 12 de Octubre and Salazar, Ed. Plaza 2000, piso 9, tel. 2/237-474

Italy: La Isla 111 and Albornoz, tel. 2/561-077/074, Mon.–Fri. 10 A.M.–12:30 P.M.

Japan: Juan León Mera 130 and Patria, Ed. Corporación Financiera Nacional, piso 7, tel. 2/561-899, Mon.–Fri. 9:30 A.M.–noon and 2:30–5 P.M.

Mexico: 6 de Diciembre 4843 and Naciones Unidas, tel. 2/457-820, Mon.–Fri. 9 A.M.–1 P.M.

Netherlands: 12 de Octubre 1942 and Cordero, tel. 2/229-229, Mon.–Fri. 9 A.M.–1 P.M., 2–5 P.M. by appointment

Norway: Alonso Jerves 134 and Orellana, tel. 2/509-514 or 509-423, Mon.–Fri. 9 A.M.–noon

Paraguay: Gaspar de Villaroel 2013 and Amazonas, tel. 2/245-871, Mon.–Fri. 8:30 A.M.–1:30 P.M.

Peru: República de El Salvador 495, tel. 2/468-389 or 468-410, Mon.–Fri. 9:30 A.M.–12:30 P.M. and 3:30–5:30 P.M.

Russia: Reina Victoria 462 and Roca, tel. 2/505-098, Mon., Wed., Fri. 10 A.M.–1 P.M.

Spain: La Pinta 455 and Amazonas, tel. 2/564-373 or 564-377, Mon.–Fri. 9–11 A.M.

Sweden: Alonso Jerves 134 and Orellana, tel. 2/509-514 or 509-423, Mon.–Fri. 9 A.M.–noon

Switzerland: Juan Pable Sanz 120 and Amazonas, Ed. Xerox, piso 2, tel. 2/434-948, Mon.–Fri. 9 A.M.–noon

United Kingdom: Naciones Unidas and República de El Salvador, Ed. Citiplaza, piso 14, tel. 2/970-800 or 970-801, Mon.–Thurs. 8:30 A.M.–12:30 P.M. and 1:30–5 P.M., Fri. 8:30 A.M.–1:30 P.M.

United States: 12 de Octubre and Patria, tel. 2/562-890, Tues.–Fri. 8 A.M.–12:30 P.M. and 1:30–5 P.M.

Venezuela: Los Cabildos 115 and Hidalgo de Pint, tel. 2/268-635 or 268-636, Mon.–Fri. 9 A.M.–1 P.M. and 2–4 P.M.

Tourist Information

The main office of the **Ministerio de Turismo,** Eloy Alfaro 124 and Tobar (between República and Los Shyris), tel. 2/507-560 or 507-555, e-mail: ecuainfo@interactive.net.ec, is one of the most helpful in the country and can assist with hotel reservations. They have maps and some staff that speak English. Open Mon.–Fri. 8:30 A.M.–5 P.M. There are branches at the airport and Venezuela 976 near Chile.

Questions regarding Ecuador's protected areas should be directed to the **Ministerio del Ambiente,** Eloy Alfaro and Amazonas, Ed. MAG, piso 8, tel. 2/529-846, 563-423.

CULTURAL CENTERS

South American Explorers

The name may imply a smoky room full of wealthy expats in tweeds trading tales about running from the natives, but the SAE, Jorge Washington 311 and Plaza, tel./fax 2/225-228, e-mail: explorer@saec.org.ec, www. sameplo.org, is actually a houseful of bright-eyed, underpaid, and overworked vagabonds who know the country inside and out.

Although nonmembers are welcome to stop by the Quito clubhouse for a brief visit, the SAE puts most of its energy toward dues-paying members, making the annual fee ($50 pp, $80 per couple) a solid investment for those who plan to stay in Ecuador more than one month or to travel through many countries in South America.

With branches in Ithaca, New York, and Lima and Cuzco, Perú, the club stocks a wealth of information readily accessible to members by mail, e-mail, fax, or in person. Members can also store equipment, peruse the library, enjoy a cup of tea on the couch while listening to some mellow music, and ask the staff for advice on anything from bread recipes to river rafting. An SAE membership card entitles you to many discounts at hotels, tour agencies, and Spanish schools in Quito and around the country. Well-organized files of trip reports written by members give the latest scoop on destinations throughout the continent. The SAE has greatly expanded its volunteering database, making it the best place in the country to find information on volunteer positions. Open Mon.–Fri. 9:30 A.M.–5 P.M. (Thurs. to 8 P.M.)

British Council

Free English films every Wednesday are usually the reason most travelers first hear of this organization at Amazonas N26-146 and La Niña, tel. 2/540-255, 508-282, fax 2/508-283, e-mail: british@uio.satnet.net, helpdesk@britishcouncil.org.ec. Book and video libraries and Internet service are open to the public for nominal fees, and the Gallery Cafe stocks British magazines and newspapers to flip through over a cup of coffee and a croissant. It's open Mon.–Fri. 7 A.M.– 9 P.M., Sat. 9 A.M.–5 P.M.

Alliance Francaise

Classes and movies in French are only a few of the offerings of the French Alliance, Eloy Alfaro N32-468 and Suiza, tel. 2/246-589 or 246-590, fax 2/442-293, e-mail: alliancequito@eolnet.net. Open Tues. 2:30–6:30 P.M., Wed.–Fri. 8:30 A.M.–12:30 P.M., Sat. 8:30 A.M.–12:30 P.M.

TRANSPORTATION

BUS

Local

The easiest way to get around Quito by bus, rather than trying to decipher the city's web of local bus routes, is to travel between major intersections. Find an intersection near you and one near where you want to go, locate a bus connecting the two, and walk the few blocks at either end. Most major avenues, especially Amazonas and 10 de Agosto, have buses passing every few minutes in either direction.

Any of 10 de Agosto's major crossroads, including Pátria, Orellana, and Naciones Unidas, are a good place to find a bus heading south to Old Town or north as far as the Mitad del Mundo. "La Y," the meeting of 10 de Agosto with América and de la Prensa, and El Inca (technically Parque Huayna Capac) at the intersection of 6 de Diciembre and El Inca, are both major bus intersections.

National

An intercity bus ride begins southeast of Old Town at the **Terminal Terrestre** at the end of 24 de Mayo. It's by no means the safest or most inviting place in Quito, but it does have plenty of cheap restaurants, 24-hour luggage storage, a police station, an Andinatel office, an ATM, and even an information window on the 3rd floor.

Buses leave here for almost every town in the country or can drop you off at your destination on the way to somewhere else. Most of them stop momentarily at the intersection just outside the terminal, downhill and to the south, where they call out their destinations in an effort to cram on a few more bodies. Watch your things, and yourself, in ticket lines and waiting for departures.

The easiest way to get to the terminal is to take a taxi or the trolley (get off at the Cumandá stop, then descend the stairs from the bridge toward the station). Number 10 Terminal Terrestre buses head for the station, and Number 2 Colón-Camal or Aeropuerto buses leave from the Terminal Terrestre for the Amazonas area of New Town.

La Marín, a long, curving plaza along Pichincha near Chile, is the departure point for buses heading to destinations within Pichincha province, especially to the south. Ask here for buses to places such as Sangolquí, Alóag, and Machachi.

A few private companies have their own small departure terminals. **Panamericana Internacional,** Colón and Reina Victoria, tel. 2/551-839, travels to Guayaquil (8 hours, $6–7), Machala and Huaquillas (13 hours, $6.50–8.50), Tulcán (4.5 hours, $3), Loja (16 hours, $9), Cuenca (14 hours, $8), Manta (8 hours, $6), Portoviejo (9 hours, $6), and Esmeraldas (6 hours, $6); **Flota Imbabura,** Larrea 1211 and Portoviejo, tel. 2/236-940, heads to Cuenca ($6.75), Guayaquil ($5.50), and Manta ($5.50); **Ecuatoriana,** Jorge Washington and Juan León Mera, tel. 2/225-315, sends plush buses to Guayaquil ($5.50); **Pichincha,** at Seminario Mayor near Parque Italia, tel. 2/368-451, travels to Quinche (1.5 hours, 50 cents) and Guayllabamba (1 hour, 20 cents); and **Coop Cayambe/Flor del Valle,** Manuel Larrea and Asunción, tel. 2/527-495, goes to Mindo (2.5 hours, $1.25).

TAXI

One of the minor offshoots of the rivalry between Quito and Guayaquil is an apparent running competition between the Quiteño and Guayaquileño cab drivers to see who can rip off more tourists. Digital meters are required by law. When (not if) the driver tells you it is "out of order" ("no funciona"), negotiate the fare beforehand or offer to find another cab—this statement has a strange tendency to fix malfunctioning meters instantly. Prices increase at night, but not by more than double. Meters start at 20 cents, with a 50-cent minimum charge, and run except when the cab is stopped. Rides within Old and New Town shouldn't be more than $1 during the day.

Freelance yellow cabs prowl the streets, and various small taxi stands exist all over the city, especially in front of expensive hotels. These have a set price list for destinations and are usually more expensive than a metered ride.

Radio taxis can be called on a moment's notice or set up to pick you up the day before. Try the **Central de Radio Taxi,** tel. 2/500-600, 521-

QUITO TROLLEY ROUTE

NORTH TO SOUTH

ESTACIÓN NORTE

LA Y; 10 DE AGOSTO AND DIGUJA

LA Y; 10 DE AGOSTO AND PEREIRA

ESTADIO; 10 DE AGOSTO AND NACIÓNES UNIDAS

ESTADIO; 10 DE AGOSTO AND NACIÓNES UNIDAS

LA CAROLINA; 10 DE AGOSTO AND REPÚBLICA

LA CAROLINA; 10 DE AGOSTO AND REPÚBLICA

FLORON; 10 DE AGOSTO AND RUMIPAMBA

FLORON; 10 DE AGOSTO AND RUMIPAMBA

MARIANA DE JESUS; 10 DE AGOSTO AND MARIANA DE JESUS

MARIANA DE JESUS; 10 DE AGOSTO AND MARIANA DE JESUS

CUERO Y CAICEDO; 10 DE AGOSTO AND CUERO Y CAICEDO

CUERO Y CAICEDO; 10 DE AGOSTO AND CUERO Y CAICEDO

COLÓN; 10 DE AGOSTO AND COLÓN

COLÓN; 10 DE AGOSTO AND COLÓN

SANTA CLARA; 10 DE AGOSTO AND VEINTIMILLA

SANTA CLARA; 10 DE AGOSTO AND VEINTIMILLA

MARSICAL; 10 DE AGOSTO AND SAN GREGORIO

MARISCAL; 10 DE AGOSTO AND JORGE WASHINGTON

EJIDO; 10 DE AGOSTO AND BOGOTÁ

EJIDO; 10 DE AGOSTO AND BOGOTÁ

LA ALAMEDA; 10 DE AGOSTO AND ANTE

LA ALAMEDA; 10 DE AGOSTO AND ANTE

BANCO CENTRAL; 10 DE AGOSTO AND CALDOS

PLAZA DEL TEATRO; GUAYAQUIL AND MANABÍ

HERMANDO MIGUEL; MONTÚFAR AND LUIS BORJA

PLAZA GRANDE; GUAYAQUIL AND ESPEJO

MARIN; MEJÍA AND MONTÚFAR

SANTO DOMINGO; GUAYAQUIL AND RUCAFUERTE

SANTO DOMINGO; GUAYAQUIL AND BOLÍVAR

CUMANDA; MALDONADO AND 24 DE MAYO

CUMANDA; MALDONADO AND 24 DE MAYO

ESCOLETA; MALDONADO AND EXPOSICIÓN

RECOLETA; MALDONADO AND EXPOSICIÓN

MACHANGARA; CARDENAL DE LA TORRE AND MALDONADO

COLINA; MALDONADO AND UPANO

CARDENAL DE LA TORRE; CARDENAL DE LA TORRE AND PEDRO DE ALFARO

CHIMBACALLE; MALDONADO AND SINCHOLAGUA

VILLAFLORA; EMILIO TERÁN AND MALDONADO

VILLAFLORA; MALDONADO AND CERRO HERMOSA

SOUTH TO NORTH

ESTACIÓN SUR

© AVALON TRAVEL PUBLISHING, INC.

112, or **Taxi Amigo,** tel. 2/222-222 or 222-220. Both are reliable and available at any hour. The drivers at **Private Taxi,** tel. 9/583-551, speak English and offer comfortable and safe service. **Cooperativa Oro Verde,** tel. 2/221-646, 227-950, will do interprovincial trips (price set beforehand); and **Taxis Lagos de Ibarra,** Asuncion 381 and Versalles, tel. 2/565-992, sends five-person taxis to Ibarra for $3 pp round-trip. **Saloman Guerra,** tel. 9/736-981, is a friendly fellow with a Mazda station wagon that is available for rent by the day; and **Manuel Bucheli** of Transporte y Comercio, Cesar Chiriboga 451 and Inti, tel. 2/262-500, is a reliable, honest driver who speaks some English.

TROLLEY

From a commuter's point of view, Quito's electric trolley system seems almost too good to be true: it's clean, quiet, fast, and not much more expensive than its noisy, air-polluting competition. The line runs north to south between two endpoint stations, one (Estación Norte) north of New Town and the other (Estación Sur) south of Old Town. The main trolley thoroughfare, 10 de Agosto, reserves a pair of center lanes for the whirring plastic carriages. Detours down Guayaquil and Montúfar in Old Town rejoin on Montúfar south of El Panecillo. New bus routes connect both terminals with destinations even farther north and south.

One reason the trolley runs so smoothly is that, unlike buses, the cars don't have to stop to pick up or drop off passengers every 100 meters. Passengers pay 10 cents each upon entering the station and simply board the next car, which passes about every 5–10 minutes. No hassle, few lines, and everyone's happy—just watch you bags and wallets in the stations and in the cars. Trolleys run Mon.–Fri. 5 A.M.–midnight, Sat. and Sun. 6 A.M.–10 P.M.

CAR

Driving in Quito
With buses cheap and frequent and traffic often a nightmare, driving in Quito can be summed up in eight words: don't do it if you don't have to.

If you must drive, a few main thoroughfares are worth mentioning. Avenida 10 de Agosto briefly becomes Galo Plaza Lasso beyond the airport before turning into the Pana and curving northeast toward Calderón and beyond. The main artery east—sometimes called the Interoceánica—leaves from the intersection of 6 de Diciembre and Almagro (Plaza Pizarro), passing under González Suárez as it drops into the eastern valley toward the Oriente. Avenida Rumiñahui leads to Sangolquí from the Terminal Terrestre. To the south, Sucre and Maldonado eventually join to form the Pana on its way to Tambillo and Machachi.

Rental Services

Safari Tours, Calama 380 and Juan León Mera, tel. 2/552-505, e-mail: admin@safari.com.ec, have dependable 4WD vehicles and drivers available to head into the mountains, as do the **Ecuadorian Alpine Institute,** Ramirez Davalos 136 and Amazonas, tel. 2/565-465, e-mail: EAI@ecuadorexplorer.com, and **Moggely 4x4 Transport,** Pint E4-255 and Amazonas, tel./fax 2/554-984, e-mail: Moggely@hotmail.com.

Herman Bonilla, Pinto and Amazonas, tel. 2/565-028, can carry up to six people in his Chevy Blazer for $60 per day. **Manuel Hidalgo Transporte,** tel. 2/541-872, 552-991, has a 14-passenger van for trips; and **Hugo E. Abata,** tel. 2/596-530, has been recommended as a driver with 12- and 16-passenger vehicles. The folks at El Taxo Hostal, 909 Foch and Luis Cordero, tel. 2/225-593, rent a large *chiva* (motor home) christened "Mamá Rhumba." It sleeps 25 and has a kitchen, bathroom, and attached tent.

AIRLINE OFFICES IN QUITO

Air France: 12 de Octubre N24-562 and Cordero, Ed. World Trade Center, Of. 710, tel. 2/523-596, e-mail: A.FRANCE@uio.satnet.net

American Airlines: Amazonas 4545 and Pereira, tel. 2/260-900

Avianca: República de El Salvador 780, Ed. Twin Towers, tel. 2/264-392, e-mail: csw@pi.pro.ec

British Airways: Amazonas 1429 and Colón, Ed. España, tel. 2/540-000 or 540-902

Continental: 12 de Octubre and Cordero, Ed. World Trade Center, Of. 1108, tel. 2/557-170, 557-164, or 557-165

Copa: Veintimilla 910 and Juan León Mera, tel. 2/563-358

Cubana de Aviación: Los Shyris and 6 de Diciembre, Ed. Torre Nove, tel. 2/227-454 or 227-463

EL AL: Juan León Mera 453 and Roca, Of. 302, tel. 2/564-109

Iberia: Eloy Alfaro 939 and Amazonas, Ed. Finandes, tel. 2/566-009, e-mail: Iberia@pi.pro.ec

Icelandair: Diego de Almagro 1822 and Alpallana, tel. 2/561-820, e-mail: sales@icelandic.com.ec

Japan Airlines: Juan León Mera 453 and Roca, Of. 302, tel. 564-109, e-mail: repsemun@interactive.net.ec

KLM/Alitalia: 12 de Octubre and Lincoln, Ed. Torre 1492, tel. 2/986-828

Lacsa/Grupo Taca: República de El Salvador N34-67 and Portugal, tel. 2/923-170 or 923-169

Lan Chile: 18 de Diciembre E7-05 and Reina Victoria, tel. 2/541-300

Lufthansa: 19 de Septiembre 238 and Reina Victoria, tel. 2/508-396, e-mail: lhuiotcl@ecnet.ec

Mexicana de Aviación: Naciones Unidas and Amazonas, Ed. Banco La Previsora, Of. 410, tel. 2/253-042 or 253-123

TAME: Amazonas 13-54 and Colón, tel. 2/509-382 (information), 221-494 (reservations), 257-693 (airport), e-mail: tame1@tame.com, www.ecua.net.ec/tame

TAP-Air Portugal: Amazonas 477 and Roca, Ed. Río Amazonas, Of. 302, tel. 2/506-777

United Airlines: República de El Salvador 361 and Moscú, Ed. Aseguradora del Sur, tel. 2/269-753

Varig: Portugal 794 and República de El Salvador, Ed. Porto Lisboa, tel. 437-137

Several major car rental companies operate in Quito:

Avis, at the airport, tel. 2/440-270, 255-890.
Budget, Colón 1140 and Amazonas, tel. 2/221-814 or 221-815; at the airport, tel. 2/459-052, 240-763.
Ecuacar, Colón 1280 and Amazonas, tel. 2/523-673 or 2/529-781; at the airport, tel. 2/448-531.
Expo, América 1116 and Bolivia, Plaza Indoamérica, tel. 2/228-688; at the airport, tel. 2/433-127.
Premium, Orellana 1623 and 9 de Octubre, tel. 2/527-051/053.

TRAIN

Quito's **train station** is at Sincholagua and Maldonado a few kilometers south of Old Town. The trolley is the easiest way to reach it: heading south, get off at the Machangana stop and walk uphill along Maldonado, or exit at Cardinal de la Torra, pass over the hill and down Maldonado. The Chimbacalle stop on the northbound trolley is right at the station.

The train to **Riobamba,** which once ran on Saturdays, had been suspended in 2000 for lack of passengers (though how this will solve the problem is anyone's guess). Another train still runs to **Cotopaxi National Park** on Sundays at 7 A.M. ($20 pp round-trip) and is a gorgeous ride when the weather's clear. Passengers have about two hours to gaze and wander at the western fringe of the park before heading back to Quito around 2:30 P.M.

AIR

The **Mariscal Sucre International Airport,** tel. 2/440-080, sprawls north of New Town beyond the intersection of 10 de Agosto, Amazonas, and De la Prensa. Buses marked Aeropuerto head down 10 de Agosto, 12 de Octubre, and Amazonas. You can also take the trolley along 10 de Agosto and then transfer onto the Rumiñhaui connecting bus *(alimentador)* from the Estación Norte.

Upon arriving in Quito, hop a bus heading left (south) to reach both New and Old Town. A ride from the airport to New Town during the day should cost about $3, or $4 to Old Town if you hail a cab at the airport (subtract $1 if you walk out onto De la Prensa and find one yourself, and add $1 after dark).

Services at the airport include tourist information, a post office, money exchange, duty-free shops, Andinatel, and a few restaurants and cafeterias (the 2nd-floor restaurant makes a good cappuccino). A few men with a machine near the door will shrink-wrap your bag to protect it in-flight for $1.

TAME has flights from Quito to Baltra in the Galápagos ($324–378 pp round-trip), Coca ($20), Cuenca ($46), Esmeraldas ($24), Guayaquil ($46), Lago Agrio ($26), Loja ($37), Macas ($27), Machala ($52), Manta ($37), Portoviejo ($37), and Tulcán ($22). **Icaro Express,** Palora 124 and Amazonas, tel. 2/245-891, fax 2/439-867, has flights to Coca Mon.–Sat. ($55 one-way), to Cuenca Sun.–Fri. ($68), to Guayaquil Mon.–Fri. ($55), and to Loja Wed., Fri., and Sun. ($68). **Aerogal,** Amazonas 7797 and Juan Holgún, tel. 2/257-202, e-mail: aerogal@satnet.net, also goes to Coca. **Aerotaxis Ecuatorianos** (ATESA), tel. 9/447-299, 2/542-248, 503-242, fax 2/525-173, has Cessnas for rent to fly around the country.

VICINITY OF QUITO

NORTH OF QUITO

Calderón

Just outside Quito's northern suburbs, the Pana passes this tiny town—actually closer to Quito's Mariscal Sucre Airport than El Panecillo—where artisans craft figures out of a varnished dough called *marsapan*. This technique, unique to Ecuador, was begun in 1535 by a Flemish priest named Fray Jodoco Ricke. Ricke, who also introduced wooden plows to the area, taught the villagers how to craft shapes out of leftover corn flour and apply varnish to preserve them.

Today the town is filled with artisan shops and private houses that turn out the figurines by the hundreds. Tiny indigenous dolls called *cholas* stand in formation on tables and shelves next to brightly painted parrots, llamas, fish, and flowers. Each figure is molded by hand from flour paste, baked in the sun or an oven, painted, and varnished. The figures make unusual,

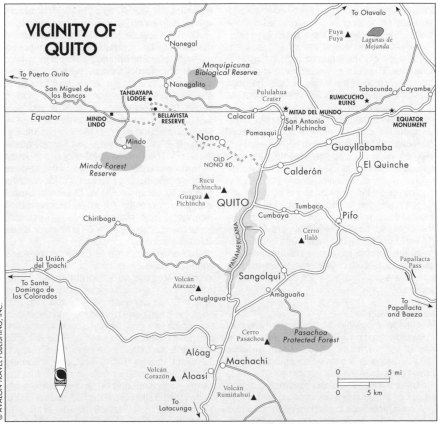

VICINITY OF QUITO

To Otavalo

Fuya Fuya ▲   Lagunas de Mojanda

Nanegal

Maquipicuna Biological Reserve

To Puerto Quito

San Miguel de los Bancos

Nanegalito

TANDAYAPA LODGE

Pululahua Crater

Tabacundo   Cayambe

RUMICUCHO RUINS

Equator

MINDO LINDO

BELLAVISTA RESERVE

MITAD DEL MUNDO

Calacalí

San Antonio del Pichincha

EQUATOR MONUMENT

Nono

Mindo

OLD NONO RD.

Pomasqui

Guayllabamba

Mindo Forest Reserve

Rucu Pichincha ▲

El Quinche

Guagua ▲ Pichincha

QUITO

Calderón

Chiriboga

Tumbaco

Cumbaya

Pifo

Cerro Ilaló ▲

La Unión del Toachi

To Santo Domingo de los Colorados

Volcán Atacazo ▲

Sangolquí

Papallacta Pass

Cutuglagua

Amaguaña

To Papallacta and Baeza

Cerro Pasachoa ▲

Pasachoa Protected Forest

Alóag

Machachi

Volcán Corazón ▲ Aloasí

0   5 mi

0   5 km

Volcán Rumiñahui ▲

To Latacunga

PANAMERICANA

© AVALON TRAVEL PUBLISHING, INC.

inexpensive gifts and are popular as Christmas ornaments. Models of crèches, Santa Claus figures, and decorated trees are sold everywhere. Shops line the main street, and buses for Calderón leave regularly from La Marín in Quito.

Guayllabamba

Winding its way down into a dry gorge, the Pana crosses the Guayllabamba River and ascends on the other side to the town of the same name. Head toward the main part of Guayllabamba, half a kilometer from the highway, and you'll notice piles of odd-looking fruit for sale. These are *chirimoyas,* which, along with small, dark avocados on the next table, grow well in the lush valley. They may look like relics from the Pleistocene Era, but *chirimoyas* (also known as custard apples or sweetsops) are actually quite tasty, once you get past the scaly-looking skin.

Six kilometers through the dry, eroded landscape south of Guayllabamba is the village of **El Quinche.** The town's ornate church and sanctuary dedicated to the Virgin of Quinche draw crowds of pilgrims from Quito in search of the Virgin's blessing year-round, and especially at processions honoring the Virgin held on 21 November. The shrine is thought to grant special protection to truck and taxi drivers. From here you can follow the road south to Pifo, then west into Quito's valley suburbs and up into the city.

Just north of Guayllabamba, you have a choice: follow the highway to the right through more dry, eroded landscape as it joins with the railroad tracks heading toward Cayambe, or take the left branch up into the hills toward Tabacundo and the Cochasquí ruins. This latter route passes a second, less-visited **equator monument** four km south of Cayambe, which is worth a stop if the crowds at the Mitad del Mundo aren't your speed.

Mitad del Mundo

The Middle of the World lies beyond the village of **Pomasqui,** past dry hills scarred by gravel quarries, at the gate of the village of **San Antonio del Pichincha.** Just before San Antonio, a long, paved pedestrian avenue slopes up to the left to the base of a massive monument resting *almost* smack on the equator (see following section).

A huge globe tops the square pedestal, which is bisected by a bright red line marking the planet's waistline. Here's your chance to shake hands or kiss from two different hemispheres, or pose with one foot on either side of the equator. An elevator inside the monument will take you to the top for a view of the encircling hills. You descend on foot through an excellent **ethnographic museum** on Ecuador's indigenous cultures. Museum hours are Mon.–Thurs. 9 A.M.–6 P.M., Fri. and Sat. 9 A.M.–7 P.M., 20 cents pp.

In the Disney-esque "tourist village" next to the monument, you'll find gift shops, an Andinatel office, a post office, a bank, a bullring, and a scale to find out if you really weigh less when you're this far from the center of the earth (since it bulges at the middle). Tourist agencies offer package tours to Pululahua and Rumicucho. **Calimatours,** tel. 2/394-796 or 394-797, has tours leaving daily for $5 pp, minimum four people.

Along the avenue, which is lined with busts of members of La Condamine's expedition, is a mediocre **planetarium** and a surprisingly neat **model of colonial Quito.** The three-square-meter model took almost seven years to build, at a scale of three blocks to one meter with labeled streets. Make sure to stay for "sunrise" and "sunset" (every 10–20 minutes), complete with tiny lights and sound effects. Models of Cuenca, Guayaquil, and the Galápagos Islands are in the works. The **Heroes del Cenepa** monument near the entrance is dedicated to the soldiers killed in border fighting with Perú in 1995, and the **French Museum** southeast of the monument traces the story of the ill-fated equator expedition (see special topic "Measuring the Earth" in the Introduction chapter). Admission is free with a ticket to the ethnographic museum.

Outside the complex—exit the complex and head left along the outside of the wall—is the excellent **Museuo de Sitio Inti-ñan,** tel. 2/395-122. Its name means "Museum of the Path of the Sun" in Quechua, and the family that owns and operates it has done a good job with the collection, which includes displays on local plants, indigenous cultures, and even a live Galápagos tortoise. Even better, the museum is actually at the exact equator (0°0' 0" latitude), according to the latest measurements. It seems that the earth's slight fluttering on its axis has already shifted the position of the original obelisk to 0°0' 12" latitude. Open daily 9:30 A.M.–6 P.M., 30 cents pp.

A fascinating **solar museum** sits exactly on the equator in the village of San Antonio de Pichincha. A unique solar chronometer, built in 1865, is the major attraction. It's accurate enough to set your watch by and tells the day, month, season, and year in both the northern and southern hemispheres. Visits must be arranged beforehand through Nuevo Mundo Expeditions in Quito.

Mitad del Mundo buses leave every five minutes from 5 A.M.–8 P.M. from the El Tejas bus stop north of Old Town near López and El Tejar, heading north along América and 10 de Agosto (10 cents pp). You can also catch them at the rotary at the intersection of America and Universitaria between Old and New Towns.

Pululahua Crater and Geobotanical Reserve
Where a volcano once burbled thousands of years ago, a steep-sided crater now yawns wide enough to support numerous farms on its flat, fertile bottom. This 3,200-hectare reserve, situated five km north of Mitad del Mundo, was declared in 1978 to protect the rich subtropical ecosystem within what is said to be the largest crater in South America.

Regular buses and taxis take the road from the base of Mitad del Mundo's pedestrian avenue toward the village of Calacalí. Along the way, a dirt lane turns off to the right to climb to the lip of the crater. You can also hike to Pululahua along a pair of well-marked trails that leave the road between San Antonio de Pichincha and Calacalí, eight km west. One trail starts at the Sangria Restaurant and passes the Ventanilla viewpoint; the other starts three km later and hits its own *mirador* (vantage point) called Moraspungo along the way. Both paths continue down into the crater. Admission to the reserve is $10 pp but is often not charged if you hike down in from the rim.

El Crater Restaurant, tel./fax 2/439-254, perches on the edge of the crater near the viewpoint. The panoramic view from the large windows easily outdoes the restaurant's small art gallery. Plates are $3–4, and it's open daily for lunch and dinner. There's also a smaller café that sells drinks and snacks.

A few hours' hike down the trail to the left will bring you to the bottom of the crater, where you can spend the night in a **hikers' refuge** that is included in admission to the reserve. Bring all your own food because there aren't any restaurants down here. Pass the village, turn left, and follow the dirt road up and over the rims to rejoin the paved road to Calacalí (10–15 km, three to four hours), where you can catch a bus back to the Mitad del Mundo. It's also possible to circle the crater rim on foot.

Horseback tours of the crater are available for about $50 pp per day from **Equatorial Horse Trekking,** tel. 2/443-809, 9/462-798, and the **Green Horse Ranch,** tel. 2/523-856.

Rumicucho Ruins
Usually tacked onto the end of tours of the area, these modest pre-Inca ruins consist of a series of rough, stone walls and terraces on a small hilltop with a commanding view of the dry, windswept surroundings. To get there, take 13 de Junio (the main drag) northeast out of San Antonio de Pichincha and turn right at the Rumicucho sign. The ruins are open daily 7:30 A.M.–5 P.M. and costs 20 cents pp. Guided tours in Spanish may be available, but are not guaranteed.

WEST OF QUITO

The Pichinchas
Quito's volcanic headboard is actually a pair of sibling mountains. Both are named Pichincha, which is thought to come from indigenous Colorado (Tsachila) words meaning "the weeper of good water." **Rucu** (Elder) is actually shorter (4,700 meters) and nearer to the city, whereas **Guagua** (Baby) stands 4,784 meters high and has always been the worse behaved of the two.

Guagua sat quiet from 1660, the year it last erupted (and was first climbed by friar Juan Romero), until October 1999, when it belched a mushroom cloud of ash that blotted out the sun over Quito for a day and covered the capital in ash. Although things seem to have calmed down, this activity prompted the Ecuadorian Geophysical Institute to close civilian access for the time being. Check in local papers or with the Instituto Geofisico online (server.epn. edu.ec/wig) for the latest update on volcanic activity and climbing—two things that should never coincide, if at all possible. Volcano World (volcano.und.nodak.edu/vwdocs/current_volcs

/ecuador/guagua_pichincha.html) is also a good source of up-to-date information.

Climbing Rucu isn't too difficult—it can be done in one long day with no special equipment—but has its own set of dangers. Frequent robberies and attacks along the route prompted the South American Explorers to warn against climbing the mountain at all in 1997. Even large groups have been victimized. Check with the SAE on the current situation, but regardless take only what you need, and try to go by car to one of the first lower peaks.

Your first target on Rucu is the top of **Cruz Loma** (3,945 meters), which is spiked with a radio antenna (not the major antenna cluster on the north side, however). Leaving the city proper can be the most confusing part of the whole climb. If you'd rather not just "follow your nose and keep Cruz Loma in sight," as one climber advises, take La Gasca all the way west from near the Santa Clara market. Make a left on Enrique Ritter just before Gasca crosses under Sucre, go three blocks to Chávez, then one more block to a dirt road passing under Sucre. Follow it through the tunnel, then keep heading straight up when it bears right toward the barrio of Armero. Cross a barbed-wire fence and climb up out of a gully to and through a eucalyptus grove. From there you can eyeball your way through pastures to the top.

At the top, a clear trail leaves to the right from the antennae. A graffiti-covered rock encountered after about half an hour offers some shelter beneath an overhang. Continue left up the scree to the peak of **Chuza Longo**. Near the peak of Rucu, about two hours from Cruz Loma, you'll have to cross and recross the ridge before scaling the last steep 10 meters.

Private transportation—preferably 4WD—is almost essential to reach Guagua, the farther peak. Here the real starting point is the pueblo of **Lloa**, almost due west of El Panecillo but reached by a roundabout route to the south of Quito (buy a map or ask directions locally). A tortuous dirt road leaves the main plaza up the valley between the Pichinchas, ending in a shelter maintained by the Civil Defense. Park here, but don't leave anything of value in the car. Sleeping space for 10 people costs $5 pp per night, including running water and cooking facilities.

Another hour will bring you from the shelter to the summit, which is actually around to the right, from where you'll initially look over the crater rim. The last 10 meters or so can be a moderately difficult rock scramble. The west-facing crater is pocked by smoking fumaroles, active domes, and collapsed craters. A rocky protrusion called the Cresta del Gallo (Rooster's Crest) separates the old, inactive side to the south from the newer, active area to the north. If you're considering descending the 700 meters to the bottom, think again—it has been declared off-limits since the latest eruption. And besides, seven of the 10 highest peaks in the country are visible from the rim already.

It's also possible to traverse between the peaks of Rucu and Guagua along a clearly marked path, turning either day trip into an overnight venture.

Hostería San Jorge

Four km up the road from Cotocollao to Nono—as close to Quito's airport as New Town—is an 80-hectare mountain ranch run by the friendly and enthusiastic George Cruz. The traditional country house is surrounded by gardens, a lake, and a spring-fed swimming pool. Warm rooms with fireplaces are $55 d, suites are $60–70, and shared eight-person cabins are $20 pp, including breakfast and access to the sauna, steam room, and hot tub. Guests can choose from a list of highland excursions, from cloud forest treks to mountain biking and rafting. Contact their office in Quito at Carvajal 969 and Las Casas, tel./fax 2/565-964, e-mail: sanjorge @impsat.net.ec, www.hostsanjorge.com.ec.

Maquipucuna Biological Reserve

More than 5,000 rugged hectares, purchased by The Nature Conservancy in 1988, protect one of the last remaining chunks of cloud forest in northwestern Ecuador. Most of this reserve is undisturbed primary forest, ranging from a low-altitude (1,200 meters) subtropical zone to cloud forest at the base of 2,800-meter Cerro Montecristi. Amazingly, it's located less than three hours from Quito.

Temperatures vary between 14–24°C, allowing thousands of plant species to thrive in a wide range of climates. More than 330 species of birds include the cock-of-the-rock and the empress brilliant. The reserve is also the first place where spectacled bears have been reintroduced into the wild. Wander afield and chances are you'll stumble across a burial mound or a *culunco*—half-trail, half-tunnel between the Andes and the Oriente—left by the pre-Inca Yumbos tribe.

Accommodations and guided tours center around the Thomas Davis Ecotourism Center at 1,200 meters. Separate research stations keep visiting scientists busy between field trips, and nearby rivers and waterfalls are perfect for a quick dip (the water is *cold* up here). Five more rooms are available in the **Maquipucuna Biological Reserve Lodge,** with a kitchen and top-floor balcony. Admission is $5 pp, and you can secure a bed and three meals for $45 pp per night. Guides are $10 per group. Try to give the reserve notice before you arrive, even if you're visiting only for the day. For more information, contact the Fundación Maquipucuna, Baquerizo Moreno E9-153 and Tamayo in Quito, tel. 2/507-200, fax 2/507-201, e-mail: root@maqui. ecuanex.net.ec, arodas@maqui.ecuanex.net.ec, www.arches.uga.edu/~maqui.

The road past Mitad del Mundo, Pululahua, and Calacalí eventually passes **Nanegalito** to reach **Nanegal,** the nearest village to Maquipucuna. Two companies send buses in that direction: Transportes Alóag leaves the terminal in Quito daily at 1 P.M., and the San José de Minas line at the Plaza San Blas departs daily at 1 P.M. and 4 P.M., plus Fri. at 10 A.M.

From Nanegal you'll have to hire a truck or taxi to take you to Marianitas, which is four km from the reserve entrance. You can also get off the bus at a big green house with yellow trim known as La Delicia (bus drivers know where it is) and walk two km to Marianitas and another four km to the reserve.

Mindo and Vicinity

This small, tranquil village has been receiving more and more visitors as its reputation as a birding hotspot has spread. Set in a quiet, lovely valley dotted with flowers and surrounded by forested mountains, Mindo is smack in the middle of one of the best—if not *the* best—birding regions in South America. Part of the Chocó Bioregion, the area counts hundreds of species of birds, from flycatchers and hummingbirds galore to woodcreepers, manakins, and cotingas. Nineteen endemic bird species share the Tandayapa Valley with pumas, spectacled bears,

ocelots, and 80 species of orchids.

Mindo is still a low-key place—there's only one phone in town, at the Andinatel office on the plaza—but word is starting to get out. Lots of development is underway, and Mindo rings with the sounds of hammer and saws. In part because it's so close to Quito, the surrounding forest is starting to be affected by an influx of settlers and tourists. Most worrisome is an oil pipeline from Quito to Esmeraldas that the Ecuadorian government is trying to build right through the middle of the area. With the help of foreign tourism operators and business owners, locals are fighting to stop the pipeline and link the Mindo Protected Forest and the Maquipicuna Reserve into one big Tandayapa Corridor.

Accommodations and Food: The cheapest place to stay in Mindo is the **Hostal Arco Iris** on the main plaza. Plain shared rooms are $1.75 pp, and there's a restaurant downstairs. Next to the soccer field and sports complex one block from the main plaza, the **Hostal Gypsy** offers shared rooms with balconies and mosquito nets for $3 pp. It's a backpacker kind of place run by an Ecuadorian-English couple, with hammocks and a café/bar downstairs. Another rustic place adjoining the soccer field is the **Hostal Armonia,** which is packed full of orchids and has shared rooms with hot water for $4 pp. They run river tubing and other outdoor tours for $4 pp.

Head half a kilometer up the road from the southwest corner of the plaza to reach the **Hacienda San Vicente,** otherwise known as La Casa Amarilla (The Yellow House). The canary-colored farmhouse and adjoining organic farm is owned by the gracious Garzón family, who have a guesthouse down by the river with hot showers for $20 s, $30 d, including breakfast and dinner. They'll be glad to show you around the grounds, point out nearby hiking trails, or introduce you to their two German shepherds (whose barks are worse than their bites). Reservations can be made in Quito by calling 2/235-276.

Near the Mindo Gardens Lodge, the **El Monte Sustainable Lodge,** e-mail: elmonte @ecuadorexplorer.com, www.ecuadorexplorer/elmonte.com, is run by American Tom Quesenberry and his Ecuadorian wife Mariela Tenorio. They offer three wood cabins at the edge of the Río Mindo with hot water, private baths, and thatched roofs. The cabins are $45 pp per night, including lodging, all meals, and birding guides for the hiking trails nearby. You have to cross the river on a small cable car to reach the hotel, but once you do, you can take your pick from white-water tubing, nature walks, or a snooze in a hammock. They have an office in Mindo at the Cafe El Monte, two blocks from the plaza past the school, and you can book through the Cafe Cultura reservation desk in Quito.

Mindo's eating options outside of the various hotels are limited. A few inexpensive restaurant and cafés in town include the **Cafe Mindo,** the **Restaurant de la Señora Niiquito,** and the **Restaurant Francisco,** which all serve inexpensive set meals.

Birding: Almost 21,000 hectares of forest, from tropical jungle to *páramo,* fall within the **Mindo-Nambillo Protected Forest** that wraps around the town to the east and south. Drained by the Ríos Mindo, Nambillo, and Cinto, the area is home to almost 400 species of birds, including the Andean cock-of-the-rock, toucans, barbets, and golden-headed quetzals. It's run by the **Amigos de la Naturaleza,** e-mail: amigosmindo @hotmail.com, a local conservation group that has an office two blocks from Mindo's plaza. Visits can be arranged in town or in Quito through the Eurovip Travel Agency, Cordero 1119 and Foch, tel. 2/562-178 or 562-182. The Amigos de la Naturaleza maintain a two-story open shelter and a cabaña in the forest, which cost around $20 pp, including all meals and a local guide. Camping is also possible.

A German-Ecuadorian couple own a section of land uphill from Mindo called **Mindo Lindo,** which offers easier access to the cloud forest than other properties in town. They charge $2 pp to use the trails and were planning to build a guest cabin in 2000. A few freelance **birding guides** operate out of Mindo and can guide visitors on day trips out of Quito. Vinicio Pérez, tel. 2/451-035, charges around $50 for a morning's guiding. You can contact two other guides through the Tandayapa Lodge (see following entry): Rafael Furniss, e-mail: tours@tandayapa.com, and Iain Campbell, iainc@tandayapa.com.

Transportation: The old cobbled road to Mindo passing through Nono on its way northwest from Quito has been overtaken by a new paved road west from the Mitad del Mundo. It joins the old road just north of Mindo and con-

tinues west to Puerto Quito. An eight-km dirt road connects Mindo to the pavement. Direct buses from Quito with the Cooperative Flor del Valle (still occasionally called by its old name Cayambe) leaves from Manuel Larrea and Asunción, just west of Parque El Ejido, Mon.–Thurs. 3:30 P.M. and Fri.–Sun. 8:30 A.M. and 3:30 P.M. One daily bus leaves Mindo for Quito at 6:30 A.M., joined by another at 2 P.M. on Fri.–Sun. It's also possible to catch a bus bound for Santo Domingo, get off at the intersection with the road from Alóag (called "La Y"), and catch a passing bus to Quito from there.

Yanacocha

The old Nono-Mindo road, rough as it is, offers great birding along almost its entire length. One particularly good spot is in the Pichincha foothills. Take a turnoff to the left (south) 18 km from Quito and drive up to the gate. Explain to the caretaker, if he's there, that you're there to watch birds ("para observar las aves"), and he should let you in for free. Twenty-two species of hummingbirds have been spotted in the vicinity, including the black-breasted puffleg, the rarest hummingbird in the world.

Tandayapa Lodge

Iain Campbell, a geology expert turned birding guide, runs this luxury birder lodge along the old Mindo-Nono road. Eight double rooms are $67 s, $104 d, including all meals, and two dormitories are open to budget travelers for $36 pp. The fireplace, bar, library, and trail network are open to all. They've seen 18 species of hummingbirds from the balcony feeders alone, and 320 species of birds in all on their trails. Many species are "staked out," meaning the guides know where they are on a regular basis.

Tandayapa is also one of the few places in the country that accepts volunteers for free instead of making them pay a fee, although they must have some biological experience. The lodge has already planted 11,000 trees in the immediate area. One-day birding packages from Quito are $56 pp, including transportation, lunch, and two guided walks ($37 pp without transportation), and two- and three-day stays cost $120 and $195 pp, respectively.

To reach Tandayapa, either head up the old Nono-Mindo road or take the new road and get off the bus at the old turnoff, 32 km past the bridge west of the Mitad del Mundo. It's another six km to the lodge from there (11 km from Nanegalito); you can walk, hitch, or hire a taxi in Nanegalito ($4). Tandayapa has an office in Quito above the Flying Dutchman at Foch 714 and Juan León Mera, tel. 2/543-045, 529-589, 9/735-536, e-mail: tandayapa@tandayapa.com, www.tandayapa.com. It's open as a birding and natural history resource center, with books and advice readily available.

Bellavista Reserve

British ecologist and teacher Richard Parsons purchased 100 hectares of prime cloud forest near the town of Tandayapa, where he built a three-story lodge looking out over the moss-covered treetops. The 1st floor of the thatched-roof dome—one of most distinctive and comfortable accommodations for birding in Ecuador—encloses the living and dining rooms, while guest rooms upstairs have private baths, hot water, and balconies with hummingbird feeders. Birders can search through the pre-montaine cloud forest (1,400–2,600 meters) for the tanager finch, giant antpitta, and white-capped dippers who frequent nearby streams.

Private rooms cost $115 d, including all meals ($66 pp without), and accommodations in the shared quarters downstairs are $39 pp with meals ($17 pp without). Campsites are available for $5 per night. Packages including transportation from Quito run $110–128 for two people for two days, or $152–183 for two people

for three days. Day trips, including transportation, breakfast, lunch, and a guided hike, are $61 pp for two or more people ($96 for one). Visits can be arranged through the reserve's office in Quito at Jorge Washington E7-23 and 6 de Diciembre, tel./fax 2/232-313, 224-469, cell 9/720-190 or 905-338 (at the lodge 9/490-891), e-mail: bellavista@ecuadorexplorer.com, www.ecuadorexplorer.com/bellavista/home.html.

Transportation can be arranged from Quito, or you can take a public bus to Nanegalito from the Terminal Terrestre. (Any bus to Pacto, Puerto Quito, San Miguel de los Bancos, or Mindo passes Nanegalito.) Ask in Nanegalito about renting a pickup truck to take you the last 15 km to the reserve. If you're driving yourself, head for the Mitad del Mundo and Calacalí on the new road to Esmeraldas and turn left at km 32 after a bridge. Follow this road to the village of Tandayapa and uphill 6 km further to the reserve. You can also take the road to Esmeraldas through the town of Nanegalito to km 42 on, then turn left and follow signs along the ridge 12 km to Bellavista.

SOUTH OF QUITO

Sangolquí

Corn is king in this town southeast of Quito. A 10-meter statue of a cob called "El Choclo" greets visitors in a traffic circle at the entrance, and in late June festivities mark the end of the harvest. During the fourth and final day, bullfights become

JULIAN SMITH

Iglesia de Guápulo

arenas for raging displays of *machismo,* as alcohol-benumbed locals goaded by "friends" try to get as close to the bull as possible without getting killed, although someone usually does. The town hosts an excellent indigenous market on Sunday and a smaller one on Thursday. To get there, take a Vingala bus from Colón and 12 de Octubre.

Pasachoa Protected Forest

This long, sloping valley preserves the original lush, wooded state of the area surrounding Quito. Fundación Natura administers the reserve, which ranges from 2,700–4,200 meters. Primary and secondary forest topped by *páramo* support a wide diversity of birds, from the sword-billed hummingbird—whose upturned bill is longer than its body—to a family of condors living atop Cerro Pasachoa (4,200 meters).

A series of loop paths of varying lengths and difficulty lead higher and higher into the hills, ranging from 2–8 hours in length. It's also possible to climb to the lip of Cerro Pasachoa's blasted volcanic crater in 5–6 hours. Campsites and a few dorm rooms with showers and cooking facilities are available near the bottom, along with a small souvenir store. Free guided tours are sometimes available. The reserve is open daily; admission for foreigners is $7 pp.

To get there from Quito, take a bus from the south end of the Plaza La Marín in Old Town to the village of Amaguaña (20 cents, 30–40 minutes). Hire a pickup ($2–3) from the plaza of Amaguaña to the turnoff for the reserve, which is marked by a green sign facing south one km toward Machachi on the Pana. From there a dirt road leads seven km up a rough, cobbled road to the reserve. Drivers may agree to come back for you, or you could catch a ride down with the reserve personnel in the evening.

Volcán Atacazo

A moderate training climb up this extinct volcano (4,457 meters) can be done in a day if you have your own transportation. If not, count on spending the night along the way. It's not the prettiest climb in the country—a forest of antennas cluster around the summit—but if you've exhausted other options, it's still a decent challenge.

One route begins in the Quito suburb of Chillo-gallo, north of the mountain. Proceed through the villages of La Libertád and San Juan, then bear south 10–12 km toward the antennas. A 4WD vehicle can take you within an hour's hike of the summit. Atacazo can also be climbed from the east via the town of Cutuglagua. The IGM 1:50,000 *Amaguaña* map covers the area.

EAST OF QUITO

Guápulo

Take the precipitous Camino de Orellana down the hill behind the Hotel Quito—or else the footpath from the park and playground—to reach this hillside neighborhood. Narrow, cobbled streets are lined with shops, cafés, and homes, including lavish walled-in residences favored by ambassadors. (On the way down, keep an eye out for Guápulo's notoriously nasty feral dogs.) At the center is the 17th-century plaza fronting the beautiful **Iglesia de Guápulo,** which was built between 1644 and 1693 on the site of an even older convent. The sparkling church is in view from far above and houses a collection of colonial art, including crucifixes and a pulpit carved by Juan Bautista Menacho in the early 18th century.

One block up from the plaza is the **Hostal La Casa de Guápulo,** Leonidas Plaza 257, tel./fax 2/220-473, e-mail: gualupo@mailexcite.com, www.ecuador-yellow-page.com-lacasa deguapulo.htm. A charming place that is more vertical than horizontal, the hostal shares its neighborhood's Mediterranean feel and boasts a weimaraner, a bar, a garden, and many terraces and balconies. Rooms with cable TV are $8 pp with shared bath, $10 pp private, including breakfast. The owners speak French, English, and Italian and offer guests free transportation from the airport or bus station. Just uphill from the hostal, a small, unnamed **family restaurant** offers heaping, inexpensive seafood portions on an open terrace.

Farther East

Head down Avenida Rumiñahui as it turns into the Autopista de Los Chillos, turn left at the Triangulo traffic light in San Rafael, and continue four km to **El Tingo,** where a set of thermal pools hide on the southwest flank of **Cerro Ilaló** (3,185 meters). Seven km past El Tingo is La Merced, and it's another four km to the village of **Ilaló.** A road leads from here to the top of the mountain on the west-southwest side.

BOB RACE

NORTHERN SIERRA
INTRODUCTION

Ecuador's northern highlands, stretching from Quito to the Colombian border, enclose everything that makes the Sierra special: incredible scenery, picturesque towns with bustling indigenous markets, unspoiled parks, and ice-capped volcanoes. Even better, almost everything is within a day trip of Quito. It's no surprise, then, that the northern Sierra is one of the country's most popular regions for tourists. What may surprise you is how easily you can leave the beaten path and find yourself in rural areas and villages you'd swear no traveler has ever seen before.

Otavalo's textile market, one of the most spectacular in South America, is the biggest draw in the northern highlands. Many of the smaller villages around Otavalo specialize in particular crafts; the city and its environs demand at least a few days' exploring. Farther north, the quiet colonial "White City" of Ibarra is larger and quieter. Unless you have some urgent, unresolved, unpleasant business with the border police, there's no excuse not to stop by the famous Tulcán topiary cemetery at the Colombian border.

Large and small ecological reserves offer hiking, camping, and mountaineering to rival any in Ecuador. The Cotacachi-Cayapas and Cayambe-Coca Ecological Reserves—so big

that each needs two names—spill from the highlands into the coastal lowlands and the Oriente, respectively. Many smaller reserves, such as El Angel, Intag, and Los Cedros, are tucked into the corners of the larger ones, offering a more personal glimpse of virgin cloud forest or *páramo*. After a long hike to a remote *laguna* or a slog up a volcano that turned out to be higher than it looked, soak your aches away in one of the many hot springs bubbling up from the hillsides.

> *. . . the Andean spirit is, indeed, a special one. From* **páramo** *to* **puna** *it speaks to you of silence, space and peace, in limitless measure, shaped by the easy arcs of the cruising condor. Its essence is of solitude, and such transcendence as it inspires can rarely be shared with anyone.*
>
> —*Richard Poole,*
> The Inca Smiled

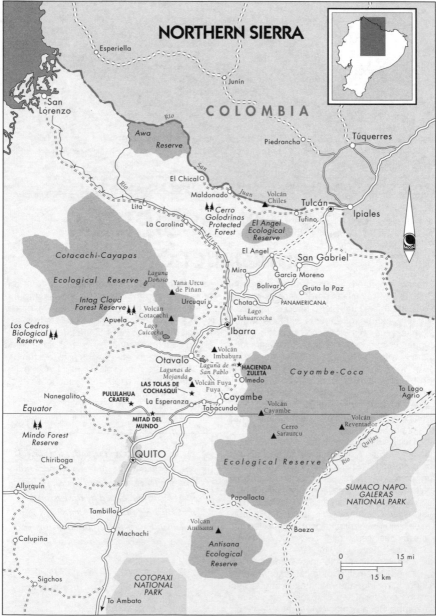

NORTHERN SIERRA

COLOMBIA

Esperiella

Junín

San Lorenzo

Awa Reserve

Rio

Piedrancha

Túquerres

El Chical

San

Maldonado

Juan

Volcán Chiles

Tulcán

Ipiales

Lita

Cerro Golodrinas Protected Forest

La Carolina

Mira

El Angel Ecological Reserve

Tufino

Cotacachi-Cayapas

El Angel

San Gabriel

Ecological Reserve

Laguna Donoso

Mira

Garcia Moreno

Yana Urcu de Piñan

Bolívar

Gruta la Paz

Intag Cloud Forest Reserve

Volcán Cotacachi

Urcuquí

Chota

PANAMERICANA

Apuela

Lago Cuicocha

Lago Yahuarcocha

Los Cedros Biological Reserve

Ibarra

Otavalo

Volcán Imbabura

Lagunas de San Pablo

Laguna de San Pablo

HACIENDA ZULETA

Cayambe-Coca

Nanegalito

LAS TOLAS DE COCHASQUÍ

Lagunas de Mojanda

Olmedo

PULULAHUA CRATER

Volcán Fuya Fuya

Cayambe

Equator

La Esperanza

Tabacundo

Volcán Cayambe

To Lago Agrio

MITAD DEL MUNDO

Mindo Forest Reserve

Cerro Saraurcu

Volcán Reventador

Chiriboga

QUITO

Rio Quijas

Allurquin

Ecological Reserve

SUMACO NAPO-GALERAS NATIONAL PARK

Tambillo

Papallacta

Calupiña

Machachi

Volcán Antisana

Baeza

Sigchos

Antisana Ecological Reserve

COTOPAXI NATIONAL PARK

0   15 mi

0   15 km

To Ambato

© AVALON TRAVEL PUBLISHING, INC.

THE *INDÍGENAS* OF OTAVALO

Otavalans are a special case among indigenous groups. Their unusual financial success and cultural stability has allowed them to travel and educate their children abroad while still keeping a firm hold on their traditions at home. In many countries in Europe and the Americas, it's almost commonplace to see Otavaleños selling textiles or playing Andean music. Although most of Otavalo's residents are white or mestizo, more than 40,000 full-blooded Otavalo *indígenas* live in town and in the surrounding villages.

Typical dress and their unmistakable carriage makes Otavaleños easily recognizable. "They walk, sit, and stand with exquisite grace," wrote Ludwig Bemelmans in the early 20th century. "The men have historic, decided faces, and the women look like the patronesses at a very elegant ball." The women's dress is said to be the closest to the Inca costume of any outfit still worn in the Andes. They traditionally wear an elaborately embroidered white blouse over double-layered wool skirts, white underneath and black on top. Shawls ward off the sun, keep them warm at night, or carry a baby. Dozens of necklaces of gold metal or red beads (once *Spondylus* coral, now usually colored glass or plastic) are worn around the neck, and their long, black hair is tied back in a single braid and wrapped in a *faja*. Men also wear their long, black hair braided in a *shimba,* often to the waist. (This long hair is such an important symbol of ethnic identity that Otavaleños aren't required to cut it off when they enter the army.) Blue wool ponchos are worn in all types of weather over white calf-length pants and rope sandals. A straight-brimmed felt fedora tops it off. Otavaleños are often exceptionally beautiful, with dark eyes, bronze skin, lustrous hair, and fine features.

The history of their famous weavings starts before the arrival of the Incas, when the backstrap loom, which is still around today, was already in use for centuries to make textiles. The Incas, appreciating the fine work, collected the weavings as tribute. Specially chosen women dedicated their lives to weaving fine textiles, some of which were burned in ritual offerings to the sun. Upon their arrival, the Spanish forced the Otavalans to labor in *obrajes*. As terrible as conditions in these sweatshops were, the Otavalo *indígenas* did become familiar with new weaving technology and learned how to produce textiles in mass quantities.

In the early 20th century, Otavalan weavers caught the world's attention with a popular and inexpensive copy of British tweed called *casimir*. The 1964 Law of Agrarian Reform, which outlawed debt peonage and granted workers title to their own land, turned weaving into a true cottage industry as locals began to weave in their own homes. Today the clack and rattle of electric looms turning out fabric by the roll can be heard in the smallest towns. Most private homes have at least an antique, treadle-operated Singer sewing machine or two, along with a free-standing manual loom. Many weavers, though, still go through the entire wool process by hand—cutting, washing, carding, dying, and weaving it over a period of days. A few backstrap looms are still in use; weaving a blanket on one can take up to 240 hours. Men traditionally operate the looms, either full time or after finishing the day's work in the field, while women perform the embroidery. Up to 85 percent of the area residents weave part or full time, from young to old: a child of 12 can easily weave up to 20 shawls a day. Families start training children to weave as young as three.

Most important, and unusual, Otavaleño weavers have been able to organize themselves efficiently, enabling them to hold onto their historical roots while keeping their business feet firmly in the present. Otavalo *indígenas* own most of the businesses in Otavalo, as well as many stores throughout Ecuador and in other countries in South America. They travel extensively abroad to sell their products or simply visit around North and South America and Europe. Otavalan weavings can be seen on store shelves as far away as Japan. The election of Otavalo's first indigenous mayor in 2000 shows how strong the native presence is in the Valley of Sunrise, and gives hope to other more downtrodden groups.

This success and visibility attracts both admiration and envy. One question often heard is whether the *indígenas* of Otavalo are exploiting their culture for the sake of profit. Spend some time here, however, and you'll see that this isn't the case. Otavalans are very good at marketing a certain part of their culture, but it isn't a part created simply to be sold, as is often the case. They've learned to straddle the fine line between making a profit and selling out, and they seem to have come out ahead for their efforts.

Otavalan family

JULIAN SMITH

The Land

The inter-Andean plateau proceeds majestically northeast into Colombia, broken only by the small valley of the Río Guayllabamba outside Quito, and the larger, dryer gorge of the Río Chota north of Ibarra, plunging northwest toward the coast.

Hemming in the plateau are the Cordillera de Taisán to the west and the Cordillera de Pimampiro to the east, which is lined with the usual stunning peaks. Cotacachi and Cayambe are the largest, attended by smaller mountains like Fuya Fuya, Imbabura, and Chiles. Cold alpine lakes dot the land in between, from the well-known Lagunas San Pablo and Cuicocha to the Lagunas de Piñan, farther afield. Near the border, highland valleys climb into damp, moody *páramo* straight out of a Scottish historical epic. Earthquakes occasionally rattle the region, explaining mountaineer Edward Whymper's description of the irregularity of the countryside as "not very unlike that of a biscuit which has been smashed by a blow of the fist."

The People

Otavalo's weavers have become one of the most famous and prosperous indigenous groups in the Americas. The neighboring department of Carchi, in contrast, has very few indigenous residents. The Río Chota valley has a higher concentration of blacks, who've migrated up from the coast, than almost any other area of the Sierra, resulting in a distinctive blend of African and Andean traditions. Far to the north in their preserve near the border, the Awa tribe has been recently helped by a joint Ecuadorian–Colombian program to protect them from extinction.

Getting Around

The Pan-American Highway, or Pana, fillets the northern Sierra all the way to the border. After slicing through Cayambe, Otavalo, and Ibarra, the road splits into an older northern section and a newer southern section. More of an adventure, the older route passes through high-altitude country with spine-compacting stretches that are almost bad enough to keep you from noticing the gorgeous scenery. The train tracks that connect Ibarra to Quito and San Lorenzo are no longer in service, but regular flights still connect Tulcán and Quito.

The Pana can be rough in spots, but a few even more arduous options exist for leaving the northern Sierra. A dry waterfall of a road leads through the Cayambe-Coca Reserve via Olmedo to El Chaco in the Oriente. Alternately, leave Otavalo to the west by way of García Moreno, and once there you'll have to choose from many options for rejoining the highway to Esmeraldas—by foot, of course. The faint trail along the border southeast of Tulcán, down to the highway to Lago Agrio, is only for the truly determined.

NORTHEAST FROM QUITO

Hiking and Climbing

In the mountains to the east await numerous possibilities for stepping into the wilds. The **Cerros Las Puntas** (4,462 meters), which can be climbed in 4–6 hours from El Quinche, Checa, or Yaruquí, are recommended. You might also try **Coturcu** (3,575 meters), a few kilometers east of Pifo, or **Pambamarca** (4,075 meters). This last mountain is approached by way of Cangahua up a rough road that heads south from El Tingo near the equator monument. Adventurous hikers could continue south toward the gorgeous lake region north of the Papallacta pass, or even make a complete traverse of the southern section of the Cayambe-Coca Ecological Reserve via Oyacachi to El Chaco in the eastern lowlands. Just don't try either trip without stocking up on maps, food, and water; both routes are longer than they look.

LAS TOLAS DE COCHASQUÍ

Fifteen pre-Inca pyramids, built by the Caranqui in A.D. 700, gaze out from the foothills of Fuya Fuya. By A.D. 1200, the eight-hectare site had reached its peak, with an estimated local population of 70,000. It was abandoned by the time the Spanish wrested control from the Inca and was rediscovered only in 1932. Three decades passed before excavations began into the earth-covered hills. Shamans still come here to absorb the site's "special energy," and festivals are held at the solstices (22 June and 22 December) and equinoxes (21 March and 23 September).

The ruins are no Chichén Itzá, but the setting itself is worth the trip. The view from 3,000 meters is spectacular—on a clear day you might spot Cotopaxi, the Ilinizas, Antisana, and even El Panecillo in downtown Quito. The purpose of the site is still unclear, but an astronomical-observatory theory is supported by a solar calendar atop pyramid 14. Here two circular platforms represent the sun and moon, and the shadows thrown by upright stones are thought to have marked the best times to plant and harvest.

A nearby mound, found by a German excavation team in 1932, contained 400 Inca and Caranqui skeletons, probably the victims of a skirmish. Smaller mounds are thought to be more mass graves or the houses of nobles. Each pyramid has a flat top originally occupied by a wooden ceremonial structure, and most have long, sloping access ramps pointing downhill to the south. The relatively soft volcanic blocks of up to 200 kg, brought from five km to the north, have been protected from the elements by the gradual accumulation of earth and grass.

Even if you're not an archaeology buff, Cochasquí is great for a picnic lunch in the sun. Visitors must be accompanied by a guide. Free tours leave hourly, and the guided tours (mandatory) are definitely worth a tip. An outdoor scale model of the site makes it easier to visualize, and two small museums display artifacts found nearby. The site is open Tues.–Sun. 9:30 A.M.–3:30 P.M.

Getting There

Take a bus from Quito to Otavalo that goes by way of Tabacundo (make sure of this ahead of time) and have the driver drop you off 10 km past Guayllabamba, just south of Tabacundo at the cement sign for the ruins (Pirámides de Cochasquí). From here it's eight km up a cobbled road to the site. If you plan on walking, there are a few soda stands along the way, but bring water anyway—it can be a hot two hours uphill. Time it right and you might be able to hitch a ride with the employee either up to the site in the morning or down to the Pana for a bus back to Quito in the afternoon. You can also rent a taxi from Tabacundo. Campsites are available uphill of the ruins, and hiking up and over to the Lagunas de Mojanda makes a gorgeous six-hour trip.

CAYAMBE

Nestled in a wide, shining valley, the quiet burg of Cayambe (pop. 17,000) is surrounded by the heavily cultivated pastures of old haciendas. This rich agricultural region is known for its cheeses, and many of the surrounding acres

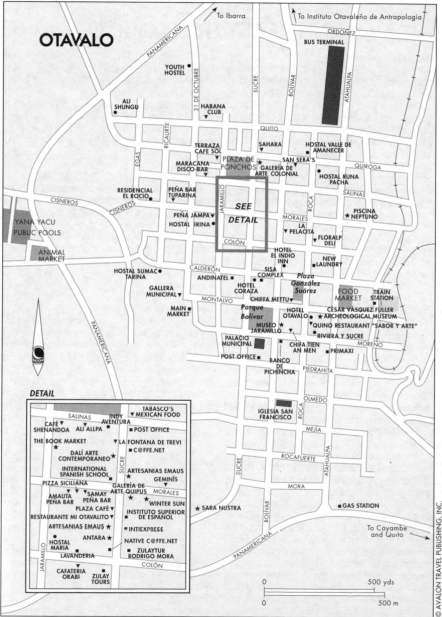

OTAVALO

To Ibarra

To Instituto Otavaleño de Antropología

ORDONEZ

BUS TERMINAL

PANAMERICANA

YOUTH HOSTEL

31 DE OCTUBRE

SUCRE

BOLIVAR

ATAHUALPA

ALI SHUNGU

HABANA CLUB

RICAURTE

QUITO

EGAS

TERRAZA CAFÉ SOL

SAHARA

HOSTAL VALLE DE AMANECER

QUIROGA

MARACANA DISCO-BAR

PLAZA DE PONCHOS

SAN SEBA'S

GALERÍA DE ARTE COLONIAL

HOSTAL RUNA PACHA

RESIDENCIAL EL ROCIO

PEÑA BAR TUPARINA

JARAMILLO

SALINAS

CISNEROS

CISNEROS

SEE DETAIL

ROCA

PISCINA NEPTUNO

YANA YACU PUBLIC POOLS

PEÑA JAMPA
HOSTAL IRINA

MORALES

LA PELACITA

ANIMAL MARKET

COLÓN

FLORALP DELI

HOTEL EL INDIO INN

NEW LAUNDRY

CALDERÓN

SISA COMPLEX

HOSTAL SUMAC TARINA

ANDINATEL

Plaza González Suárez

FOOD MARKET

TRAIN STATION

GALLERA MUNICIPAL

HOTEL CORAZA

CHIFFA METTU

MONTALVO

Parque Bolivar

HOTEL OTAVALO

CÉSAR VÁSQUEZ FULLER
ARCHEOLOGICAL MUSEUM

MAIN MARKET

QUINO RESTAURANT "SABOR Y ARTE"

MUSEO JARAMILLO

RIVIERA Y SUCRE

PANAMERICANA

PALACIO MUNICIPAL

CHIFA TIEN AN MEN

PRIMAXI

MORENO

POST OFFICE

BANCO DE PICHINCHA

PIEDRAHITA

OLMEDO

ROCA

IGLESIA SAN FRANCISCO

MEJIA

ROCAFUERTE

SUCRE

MORA

BOLIVAR

GAS STATION

ATAHUALPA

To Cayambe and Quito

DETAIL

SALINAS

TABASCO'S MEXICAN FOOD

CAFÉ SHENANDOA

INDY AVENTURA

ALI ALLPA

POST OFFICE

THE BOOK MARKET

LA FONTANA DE TREVI
C@FFE.NET

DALÍ ARTE CONTEMPORANEO

SUCRE

INTERNATIONAL SPANISH SCHOOL

ARTESANIAS EMAUS

PIZZA SICILIANA

GEMINIS

GALERÍA DE ARTE QUIPUS

MORALES

AMAUTA PEÑA BAR

SAMAY PEÑA BAR

WINTER SUN

PLAZA CAFÉ

INSTITUTO SUPERIOR DE ESPAÑOL

RESTAURANTE MI OTAVALITO

ARTESANIAS EMAUS

INTIEXPRESS

SARA NUSTRA

ANTARA

NATIVE C@FFE.NET

HOSTAL MARIA

JARAMILLO

LAVANDERIA

ZULAYTUR RODRIGO MORA

COLÓN

CAFATERIA ORABI

ZULAY TOURS

0   500 yds

0   500 m

have been planted with ornamental flowers (see special topic, "Flower Exports: To Russia with Love"). Over it all looms Volcán Cayambe, whose snow-covered dome is blinding in the sunlight and seems to glow even at night. The city is a good jumping-off point for climbing Cayambe or Saraurcu to the east or for visiting the ruins at Cochasquí to the west.

The **Fiesta de San Pedro y Pablo** (Saints Peter and Paul) on 28 and 29 June is one of the most elaborate because San Pedro is the patron saint of the district. During the festival, the streets are filled with indigenous groups representing their communities. You might see more roosters, in cages and suspended from poles, than you would expect. This is for the *entrega de gallo* (delivering of the rooster), a reminder of a colonial tradition in which hacienda workers gave the *patrón* (owner) a ceremonial gift of a rooster every year. Inti Raymi in late June is also an important festival.

Accommodations

The flashy **Hotel La Gran Colombia,** tel. 6/361-238, was opened in 1996 on Avenida Natalia Jarrín about half a kilometer south of the city center. For $10 d, guests enjoy TV, a private bathroom, and a children's playground out back. Their restaurant is popular with locals. Half a kilometer farther is the **Hostería Mitad del Mundo,** Ave. Natalia Jarrín 208, tel. 6/361-607, 9/846-734. Along with the usual bar and restaurant, it boasts a covered pool, sauna, and steam room. Clean rooms with private bath, hot water, and TV are $5 pp.

The clean, friendly **Hostal Cayambe,** Bolívar 23 and Ascazubi, tel. 6/361-007, has rooms for a few dollars and can store luggage. Five km north of town, the **Moulin Rouge** restaurant serves French cuisine and real espresso in a restored windmill. Cyclists can camp here for free.

Five kilometers south of Cayambe sits the **Hacienda Guachala,** a 400-year-old estate straddling the equator. The hacienda dates from 1580, when the land was bought by a Spanish colonist whose grandson eventually acquired the title for 300 ounces of silver. La Condamine's globe-measurers lodged here in

FLOWER EXPORTS: TO RUSSIA WITH LOVE

You've probably already noticed the long, plastic-sided greenhouses that line the landscape throughout the Sierra. In the last few decades, the ornamental flowers grown in these greenhouses have become the Sierra's most economically important export. Between 1990 and 1995, Ecuadorian flower exports blossomed from US$9 million to US$45 million, with roses and tulips leading the bunch. Cut flowers were Ecuador's fourth-largest export in 1997, trailing only petroleum, bananas, and shrimp. All of this success is the result of Ecuador's climate, which is ideal for flower growing. The dependable 12 hours of daily sunlight year-round, rich soil, and particular combination of altitude and humidity produce what some florists call the highest-quality roses in the world.

Many old haciendas have been converted into flower farms to take advantage of the rise in demand. The greenhouses are run with scientific precision: bulbs that can take a year and a half to mature before they're ready for export receive water by the drop, regulated by computer-monitored humidity readings. The Impresa Plantador plantation in Tabuela, between Pifo and Yaruquí, leads Latin America in rose production and is fourth in the world. Ecuadorian floriculturists can now buy bulbs directly from the Plantador that they once had to import from France and Israel. Ecuadorian tulips are even said to be sold in Holland.

The next time you're buying roses in Moscow, take a second look—more than half the flowers sold in Russia today come from Ecuador, 15,000 km away. One third of Ecuador's 130 flower farms grow plants exclusively for the Russian market, shipping US$10 million worth of flowers in 1995. With the recent turmoil in the former Soviet Union, flower prices have more than doubled since 1994, and even though Russian flowers are cheaper, imported blossoms are in great demand. The only limiting element, in fact, is the number of daily flights from Ecuador to Russia, which are down sharply since 1995 when Aeroflot cancelled its Quito–Moscow flights because of a lack of passengers. This explains why your flight home to Paris or Amsterdam might be particularly fragrant—most Ecuadorian flowers are now shipped across the Atlantic on KLM and Air France passenger flights.

1743, and two centuries later it was inherited by Neptali Bonifaz Ascazubi, who was elected president of Ecuador but disqualified for being of Perúvian nationality. It was opened as a hotel in 1993.

Old saddles line the entrance hallway, giving the place the smell of old leather. All the buildings were built with terra-cotta tile roofs in the rammed-earth style except the church, which was constructed of brick in 1938. An underground spring feeds the sun-heated pool, surrounded by vibrant flowers. Browse through hundreds of pictures from the early 20th century in the photographic museum. The 21 rooms ($25 s, $35 d) are simple and comfortable, and horses and bicycles ($5 per hour) are available to explore the countryside as far as a set of Inca ruins on a windy hilltop.

There's a sign ("Hostería 800 meters") near a small green shack on the Pana five km south of Cayambe. Follow a tree-lined dirt road past the FLORESMA flower plantation gate to the entrance of the hacienda, tel. 2/363-042, tel./fax 2/362-426, e-mail: guachala@ecuadorexplorer.com, www.ecuadorexplorer.com/guachala/.

Getting There

The Pana passes almost directly through Cayambe, briefly becoming Avenida Natalia Jarrín before heading north to Otavalo and Ibarra. All buses between Quito and Otavalo, Ibarra, and Tulcán pass through here before heading through picture-book scenery of rolling hills, streams, and far-off mountains to the north. Just beyond Cayambe, the road forks again, heading to the right toward Olmedo, Zuleta, and eventually Ibarra. The main branch to the left peaks at a police checkpoint before descending toward Lago San Pablo and Otavalo.

CAYAMBE-COCA ECOLOGICAL RESERVE

The second-largest Andean reserve in Ecuador spills from the snowy heights of Cayambe down the eastern face of the Cordillera Oriental. The reserve's 404,685 hectares stretch across four provinces and range in altitude from 800 to 5,790 meters. Three major peaks and more than 80 lakes dot the incredibly varied landscape, which includes everything from alpine tundra in the west to tropical forest in the eastern lowlands along the Baeza-Lago Agrio road. In 1987 Cayambe-Coca shared the benefits of a $1 million debt-for-nature swap by the World Wildlife Fund with the Cotacachi-Cayapas Ecological Reserve.

Artifacts found in Cayambe-Coca give evidence of a prehistoric migration from the Amazon to the Andes. Typical village ruins consist of houses around a central plaza, which contains a communal ceremonial house. These ruins, along with shards of thin-walled ceramics, have been unearthed in a zone extending from Papallacta to the valleys of the Oyacachi and Quijos rivers. Today about 600 Cofán *indígenas* live in a handful of communities near the northeastern corner. Descendants of the Caranqui tribe inhabit the more southern, tropical part as high as Oyacachi, where their ancestors fled after the massacre at the hands of the Inca at Lago Yahuarcocha.

Getting There

The reserve can be entered from a few different directions. From the west, the route used to climb the Volcán Cayambe, via Juan Montalvo and the Piemonte guardpost, is the most direct. Alternately, a recently improved road leads from the town of Cayambe through Olmedo and east to the Guaybambilla guardpost and the Laguna San Marcos. Here at 3,400 meters, you'll find an interpretation center, paths, and campsites. You can also follow the road from Chota in the north through Pimampiro and Sigsipamba to hike to the Lago Puruanta. This beautiful lake high in the *páramo* is one of the unspoiled jewels of the Ecuadorian Andes (see "Southern Route" under "Ibarra to Tulcán").

From the east, the La Virgen guardpost lies a few kilometers before Papallacta on the road from Quito to Baeza. From here the Laguna Sucos is a 45-minute hike. Between Baeza and Lago Agrio, the El Chaco and Aguarico guardposts provide access to the more difficult and less explored eastern section of the reserve. The Volcán Reventador and the San Rafael Falls (see the Oriente chapter) are both found along this stretch of road. The entrance fee to the reserve is $5 pp for foreigners.

SANDRA FORRESTER

Volcán Cayambe

Volcán Cayambe

Drag yourself atop Cayambe, and you've reached a spot as unique as it is beautiful. The top of Ecuador's third-highest peak (5,790 meters) is not only the only place in the world where the temperature and latitude reach zero simultaneously, but it's also the highest point in the world on the equator.

The name for this wide, white mountain means "water of life" in Quechua. Edward Whymper and the Carrels were the first to summit the volcano's northeast peak in 1880, but their route wasn't repeated until 1974 by Quito's San Gabriel Climbing Club. Cayambe has the reputation of being a dangerous climb, especially since three famous Ecuadorian climbers were killed by an avalanche in 1974 on the mountain's slopes.

The main obstacle is the ever-changing network of crevasses. Climbers also face unusually high winds, strong snowstorms, and the occasional avalanche; thus, Cayambe is recommended only for advanced climbers. If you have experience with crevasses, glaciers, and avalanche safety, though, you should be fine. Be careful to flag your route because fog is a constant reminder of the Amazon basin looming just below. Try to get the most up-to-date information possible on the crevasse pattern at the summit, and leave early for a summit attempt (11 P.M. or midnight is suggested) in order to be off the snow before it starts to soften in the morning sun.

Cayambe is becoming increasingly popular as a destination for high-altitude glacier training because the refuge is rarely full and the Hermoso Glacier offers lots of space for various mountaineering techniques. Safari Tours in Quito offer a three-day glacier school.

A cobbled road leaves the city of Cayambe east through the town of Juan Montalvo. Six and a half km later is the Hacienda Piemonte Bajo, known locally as "El Hato." Traffic is sparse, so hitchhiking is difficult. Walk or drive up to the Hacienda Piemonte Alto and the entrance to the reserve (trucks can make it to just below the stream above this hacienda), then bear left at the "T" in the road toward the Cayambe peak. The Bergé-Oleas-Ruales refuge (4,600 m), named after the three climbers, is 10 km from the Hacienda Piemonte Alto. The services of a permanent guardian, cooking stove, and running water are yours for $10 pp per night. It's owned by the San Gabriel Climbing Club, which built it in 1984, and is administered by Alta Montaña in Quito (tel. 2/254-798). Food, water, soda, and beer are for sale.

Leaving by midnight, scramble over the rocky hill to the north of the hut. Head toward the rock points called the Puntas Jarrín, looking for cairns along the way. From there a ramp leads around huge crevasses to the upper headwall. The southeast summit is almost completely surrounded by a large crevasse, which is occasionally spanned by snow bridges. The IGM 1:50,000 *Cayambe* and *Nevado Cayambe* maps cover the mountain, and Jorge Anhalzer's pocket guide (#4), available in Quito, is recommended.

Cerro Saraurcu

One of the few nonvolcanic peaks in Ecuador, Cayambe's smaller sister (4,676 meters) isn't climbed nearly as often as Cayambe. The "Corn Mountain" (from the Quechua *sara,* meaning "corn") is also known, more ominously, as Devil Mountain in both Quechua (Supaiurcu) or Spanish (Cerro del Diablo). It's pretty in any case, and a straightforward climb.

The approach is the killer—kilometers of trudging through boggy *pantano,* the evil cousin of the high-altitude *páramo.* Follow the route to Cayambe until the road forks near the reserve entrance gate. Head right to the southeast to the Farinango family house. The family members know the route and can locate mules and guides, which is a good thing because from here it's at least a day's slog to the base of the mountain. Along the way, you'll pass down the Dormida de Mayorazo valley, across rivers and a lava flow known as El Paso del Diablo (Devil's Pass).

From here the route is clear up the southwest ridge. Near the summit you may find small ice walls or glaciers, and the top may be snow-capped. Definitely consider hiring mules for the approach, and pack rubber boots regardless. A machete might be useful to clear a path through the tall, tough grass. The IGM 1:50,000 *Cangahua* and *Cerro Saraurcu* maps cover the area.

Cayambe to the Oriente

It's possible to cross the entire southern part of the reserve from Cayambe town, by way of Cangahua and Oyacachi to El Chaco in the Oriente. The partly cobbled trail, dating back to pre-Inca times, is one of the country's best hikes, but it's only passable Nov.–Mar.

Trucks and buses leave hourly from Cayambe for Cangahua, from where it's a full day's hike to Oyacachi. Alternately, you can hire a taxi in Cayambe to take you as far as Oyacachi (1.5 hours) for $20–25. The small town sits at 3,200 meters on the river of the same name. Archaeologists have determined that the ruins, which lie about 40 minutes past Oyacachi, were built using traditional stone methods. Visitors much register

and pay the entrance fee at the new guardpost below the pass.

In Oyacachi you might be able to stay at the house beside the carpenter's place on the main square (ask for David Pareon), or camp near the hot springs across the river. Horses are available for rent as far as Cedro Grande (1–2 days) for about $5 per day, and guides can be hired for $10 per day plus food. After that you'll have to pack it yourself because the going gets rough and the rivers widen. Forests nearby hide red-crested cotingas, black-billed mountain toucans, and the onomatopoeic shining sunbeam hummingbird.

The trail east to El Chaco follows the left side of the Río Oyacachi. You'll have to cross a few rivers along the way. Often a single cable is all that's left of the bridge—locals use loops of barbed wire to slide across, but a climbing harness and pulley will work. Wading is possible in places. You'll have to ford the Ríos Cariaco, Chaupi, and Santa Maria during the descent to El Chaco (horses can go only as far as the Río Cedro). The IGM 1:50,000 *Oyacachi/Santa Rosa de Quijos* map covers most of the hike.

HACIENDA ZULETA

This venerable estate was owned by former Ecuadorian President Galo Plaza Lasso in the 1940s. The original farmhouse, nine km north of Olmedo on the road from Cayambe, dates to 1691. It was later augmented with workshops and a chapel when the Spanish Crown deeded the entire region to the Jesuits.

Zuleta is best known for the signature embroidery turned out in its handicraft shops. Inspired by crafts in Italy and Spain, Lasso's wife set up the original workshop to put the local women's embroidery talents to work. The Peace Corps helped get things going in the 1960s, and today the hacienda and its environs are famous for the "Zuleteño" style, in which intricate, colorful designs are sewn onto white cloth shirts, napkins, and wall hangings.

Andean peaks loom beyond the grass fields and eucalyptus forests that fill the 1,800-hectare spread. Tree-lined lanes and a cobbled central plaza set the stage for home-cooked meals of organic vegetables, fresh trout, and dairy products straight from the cow. Guided tours on horseback, mountain bike, and foot can take you to indigenous villages and some of the more than 140 mounds left by the pre-Inca Caranqui tribe. Three- to seven-day horseback-riding programs are available, and the hacienda's Galo Plaza Lasso Foundation oversees a condor re-

habilitation project and the women's community embroidery project.

Advanced reservations are necessary for the nine guest rooms, and a minimum stay of two nights is required. For information and prices, contact the hacienda at e-mail: hacienda@zuleta.com, www.zuleta.com.

OTAVALO AND VICINITY

Despite its modest size, Otavalo is probably the best-known city in Ecuador outside of the capital. Every Saturday, thousands gather in the Plaza de Ponchos to buy, sell, bargain in, or simply watch the granddaddy of all Andean markets. Otavalan textiles and indigenous music are carried around the world by the distinctive Otavalo *indígenas* (see special topic), making the city a must-see for most travelers to Ecuador. Add to

this the beautiful surrounding countryside dotted with crafts villages and Otavalo's proximity to Quito, and you have one bustling—yet somehow still authentic—market town.

Nestled in the lovely Valle del Amanecer (Valley of Sunrise) at 2,530 meters, Otavalo (pop. 30,000) is said to be the second-oldest town in Imbabura province. It was a market town before the Incas arrived, surviving as a trading center for

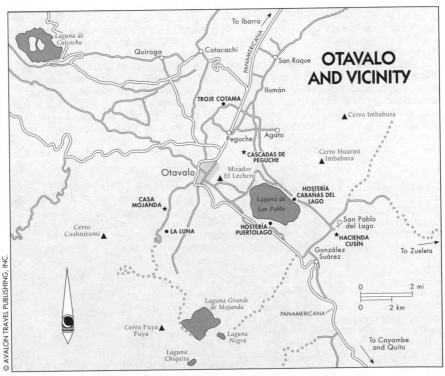

produce and animals brought up from the low-lands. Since then textiles have become the product of choice, earning the Otavalo *indígenas* worldwide fame and a quality of life worlds apart from most other indigenous groups in South America. It's easy to see there's money here, with shiny new 4WD vehicles blasting contemporary music in the streets. But as the drivers flip their long braids and adjust their woven blouses, you'll notice that both the town and its inhabitants seem to have kept in solid touch with their heritage.

Sadly, the high numbers of tourists have led to occasional robberies and assaults. Never leave your hotel room unlocked, and be careful of bag-slashers and pickpockets in the crowded markets. Also, try to explore the area's trails and more remote locations in groups because lone hikers have sometimes been robbed. On the whole, however, the streets of Otavalo are safe at night.

SIGHTS

Textile Market

The reason most tourists come to town (and the reason you probably can't find a hotel room on Friday night) is the Saturday textile market. Vendors from town and surrounding villages set up shop well before dawn. Coffee steam mingles with clouds of breath as vendors chat, gobble a quick breakfast, and set up scaffolding to display their wares. By 9 A.M., the plaza is packed with a brightly colored, murmuring throng of vendors and tourists haggling over every imaginable type of textile and craft. The market has become so successful that there are now smaller ones every day of the week, with a slightly larger market on Wednesday. The Saturday market is the biggie, though, and it's worth experiencing even if you don't intend to buy anything. Just getting up early and watching the market slowly come to life as the sun rises over Volcán Imbabura is a wonderful experience.

If it can be made out of wool, cotton, or synthetic yarn, you'll find it here. Wall hangings are popular, woven with abstract patterns or M.C. Escher–inspired motifs of intermeshed birds and lizards. Thick wool and alpaca sweaters come in interesting color combinations, and carpets and blankets of the same materials are often covered in llama designs. Cloud-soft alpaca teddy bears are for sale in white or brown. The best (and most expensive) ponchos, worn by the Otavalans themselves, are made of thick wool dyed blue with agave juice, with a collar and gray or plaid fabric on the inside. Ponchos are also made of synthetic materials like orlon, which is less expensive but more garish. Piles of hats made of felt or wool teeter next to mounds of surprisingly inexpensive wool mittens, socks, and handbags.

Long cloth strips called *fajas,* used by *indígenas* in the Sierra to tie back long hair, hang next to their wider cousins *cintas.* Also known as *calluas,* many of these belts are woven in La Compañía on the other side of Lago San Pablo.

tapestries at Otavalo's
Saturday market

JULIAN SMITH

A single belt woven on the traditional backstrap loom (stretched between a post and the waist of the seated weaver) can take as long as four days to complete. Jewelry similar to that worn by indigenous women is spread out on tables: necklaces of black or red beads, interspersed with earrings of turquoise and lapis lazuli. Other treasures include raw fleece, yarn, and dyes, textiles from Perú and Bolivia, painted balsawood birds, and piles of assorted junk hiding the occasional valuable antique.

For the Saturday market, it's best to spend Friday night in town; arrive early to secure a hotel room. Get up early Saturday morning for the best selection and prices because vendors often give their first customer the best price of the day for good luck. Bargaining is expected, even in many stores in town, and proficient hagglers can talk prices down significantly. (See special topic "Bargaining" in the On the Road chapter.) Prices peak when the tour buses from Quito are in town, usually from 9 A.M. to noon, so arrive early or linger late for the best deals. Finally, consider making your main purchases midweek when things are less hectic, leaving you free to observe on Saturday with your shopping already done.

MAILING TEXTILES FROM OTAVALO

"Hey, wait a minute," you think after an hour in the Plaza de Ponchos. "All these cheap sweaters . . . worth ten times that back home. . . ." After some quick math, suddenly you're sipping daiquiris in your new hot tub.

There is money to be made in reselling textiles—just look at the export businesses all over town—but there are a few angles to consider. First you have to buy the goods in bulk. If you're going to the bother of buying the goods, sending them home, and then somehow selling them, ask yourself how much profit would make it worth the effort. Twenty pairs of mittens probably aren't worth it; 100, maybe; 500, probably. Most shipping companies in Otavalo also have a minimum weight for handling—usually 50 to 100 kg.

Then there's the paperwork, which is where the shipping companies come in very handy. For a price, they'll take care of everything, including customs forms and various taxes such as the *tramite* (transit) for the goods to leave the country. These shipping services are the safest and most reliable but also the most expensive. If you're shipping a smaller amount, consider doing it yourself. Take the goods to the Santa Clara post office in Quito, packed but unsealed (for customs inspection) on an afternoon when you have nothing else planned. If you're stuffing everything in your bag, or one you've bought for the occasion, be aware of your country's import policies.

Finally, unless you want to give everyone you know a pair of wool socks every Christmas for the rest of your life, you have to consider how you're going to get rid of the darn things. Selling techniques range from spread-a-blanket-on-the-sidewalk to dealing directly with stores who'll buy everything from you and resell it all to the public for even more. In the latter case, it would obviously be best to have the deal arranged before you lay your money down. Ideally, you would have an example to show to set up the deal ahead of time, but this would require more than one trip or a friend who just returned from Ecuador, so the most you'll probably be able to do is spark some interest beforehand. Consider your market: wool hats and sweaters will sell better in colder climates, whereas tapestries and *fajas* are more suited to warmer places.

Good luck!

Other Saturday Markets

Get up early and follow the squeals, honks, snorts, and moos to the **animal market,** which is held on Saturday mornings starting at sunrise. Enough farm animals to film a Disney movie, from cows to guinea pigs, are for sale here in the Viejo Colegio Agricultural (Old Agricultural College). To get there, head west on Morales and cross the bridge, passing the stadium. The market is straight ahead across the Pana. The **produce market** overflows with food, housewares, and clothes in and around the Plaza 24 de Mayo all day. More food is sold at the **Mercado Copacabana** on Atahualpa between Montalvo and Calderón.

Museums and Galleries

The singular **César Vásquez Fuller Archaeological Museum** occupies a dusty room above the Pensión Los Andes, on Montalvo between Roca and Atahualpa. Ancient owner César has

TIM BEWER

Otavalan woman selling beans and corn in the market

TOURS

Tour companies have sprouted up all over Otavalo to accommodate visitors who wish to watch the actual production of crafts and textiles, or who just want to get out into the countryside and see how the artisans themselves live. Competition keeps prices low, and seeing the work and skill that go into the crafts is fascinating. Most agencies offer a spectrum of options, including hiking, driving, biking, and horseback trips of varying lengths and itineraries. All agencies offer tours in English.

Kitty-corner from each other at Colón and Sucre are two operations with similar names but little love lost between them. **Zulay Tours,** tel./fax 6/921-217, bills itself as the "original," and stresses the fact that it's owned by *indígenas.* The staff runs excellent all-day tours to weaving villages, Cotacachi, and Lago Cuicocha for $16 pp, and does trekking and horseback-riding tours as well.

Opposite Zulay Tours is **Zulaytour Rodgrigo Mora,** tel. 6/921-176, fax 6/921-188 or 921-176, on the 2nd floor above a telephone/fax/money exchange business. Tours are offered in French and German. **Intiexpress,** Sucre 11-10 and Colón, tel. 6/921-436, fax 6/922-969, offers similarly priced village tours, horseback riding, and treks to Lagos Cuicocha and Mojanda.

You can do tours of the area yourself almost as easily by hiking or renting a mountain bike or taxi. The rolling countryside around Otavalo is spiderwebbed with country lanes, and you could easily spend days wandering aimlessly from one village to the next. If you're in the mood for a moderate climb, head east on Morales, up past the large cross to the **Mirador El Lechero** for a great view of Otavalo and the Lago San Pablo.

something to say about almost every one of the 8,500 pieces in his collection, from clay models of astronomical observatories to distorted skulls and bone flutes. Other artifacts made of gold, silver, copper, and ceramic crowd the display cases, and thousands of stone ax heads are enough to equip a small army. The museum is open whenever César's available—usually in the afternoon (40 cents pp).

The **Instituto Otavaleño de Antropología,** on the north end of town off the Pana, also houses an impressive collection. Walk up Sucre and turn left at the Banco Internacional. Open Tues.–Sat. 8 A.M.–12 P.M. and 12:30–6:30 P.M., but closed irregularly. In the center of town, the **SISA** complex, Calderón 409 between Bolívar and Sucre, tel. 6/920-154, packs a handicraft shop, bookstore, art gallery, bar, and restaurant into two floors. The name is an acronym for Sala de Imágen, Sonido y Arte (Image, Sound, and Art Space), and also means flower in Quechua. They offer live music at night from Fri.–Sun.

ACCOMMODATIONS

Otavalo certainly has no shortage of hotels, especially in the budget category (three dozen at last count, with more popping up all the time), but rooms can still be scarce on Friday night. At some hotels, water is heated only during certain hours.

Less than $10

I've never gone wrong with the colorful **Riviera Sucre,** Moreno 380 and Roca, tel./fax 6/920-241, with its open courtyard and large, cozy rooms for $3.50 pp (private) and $2.25 (shared). The managers are friendly, the showers are hot, and breakfast at the downstairs cafeteria is a good way to start the day. The **Hostal Valle del Amanecer,** Roca and Quiroga, tel. 6/920-990, fax 6/921-159, goes with the *Gilligan's Island* theme in its cobbled, plant-packed courtyard and outdoor fireplace. Rates run $2 pp with shared bath, $3 pp private. They have a restaurant and offer motorcycles and bicycles for rent ($30 and $4 per day, respectively).

One of the best budget deals can be found at the immaculate **Hostal Maria,** Jaramillo and Colón, tel. 6/920-672. For only $1.50 pp, you can have a private room with 24-hour hot water and TV.

The **Hostal Sumac Pacarina,** Colón 6-10 and 31 de Octubre, is a little cave of a place (watch your head) but homey in a well-worn way. Rooms cost $2 pp, and you can get a good breakfast. The hot showers are especially good at the friendly **Hostal Irina,** Jaramillo 5-69 and Morales, tel./fax 6/920-684, e-mail: hostirin@uio.satnet.net. Rates are $1.50 pp with shared bath, $2 pp with private bath. Try to get a room on one of the upper floors because the ground floor can be a bit noisy. A French restaurant is said to be on the way. The **Hostal Samac Tarina,** Calderón 7-13 and 31 de Octubre, tel. 6/920-182, and the **Residencial El Rocio,** Morales between Ricaurte and Egas, tel. 6/920-584, are both clean and friendly and in the same price range.

At the **Jatún Pacha Youth Hostel,** 31 de Octubre and Quito, tel. 6/922-223 (also called the Chalet Sol), they bake their own bread on Thursday, and you can rent mountain bikes. Guests eat Saturday morning breakfast on the Terraza el Sol overlooking the market. Your bed ($10 with private bath, or $8 with ISIC card) or floor space ($5) includes a full breakfast. It's hard to miss the plant- and flag-draped balconies of the **Hostal Runa Pacha,** Roca and Quiroga, tel. 6/921-730, fax 6/921-734. They offer a rooftop terrace, restaurant, and clean rooms for $3 pp with private bath.

$10–25

The venerable **Hotel Otavalo,** Casilla 11, Roca 504 and Juan Montalvo, tel. 6/920-416, e-mail: hotavalo@im.pro.ec, www.hotelotavalo.com.ec, offers the best midprice value. Its 30 large, simple rooms cost $10 s, $16 d, and they should be getting cable TV and phones soon. The owners speak English, and there's homemade ice cream at the coffee shop and pizza in the restaurant near a wonderful two-story, plant-filled interior courtyard. The **Hotel El Indio Inn,** Bolívar 904, tel 6/922-922, 920-325, has in-room TVs, private parking, and a restaurant. Rooms cost $20 s, $24 d. Rooms at the **Hotel Coraza,** Calderón and Sucre, tel/fax. 6/921-225, are especially comfortable, equipped with TV, and go for $12 pp.

More than $25

Otavalo's most distinctive hotel is the **Ali Shungu,** Quito and Quiroga, tel. 6/920-750, e-mail: alishungu@uio.telconet.net, at the northwest corner of town. American owners Frank Keifer and Margaret Goodhart are hospitable and friendly. (Ali Shungu means "good heart" in Quechua, from Margaret's last name.) They employ a bevy of local women in traditional clothing who perform a myriad of tasks—from ordering you a taxi to stoking the fire in the sitting room on chilly nights. Every wall is lined with colorful masks, dolls, and weavings by José Cotacachi of Peguche, and leafy plants fill all the corners. Out back is a patio overlooking the flower garden and exclusive gift shop. The restaurant offers vegetarian and meat entrées for $5 (try the oriental vegetable stir-fry and the New York–style cheesecake), along with hefty sandwiches. Breakfast is served from 7:30 A.M., and live Andean music entertains guests and diners on Friday night. Guests can rent bicycles, and a private bus shuttle service is available to and from Quito for $15 pp each way. Rooms are $30 s, $43 d, and two apartment suites are available for two-night minimum stays—$85 d, $98 t.

FOOD

The **Quino Restaurant "Sabor y Arte"** is an intimate little place with art on the walls and a yellow plastic ceiling that gives it an underwater, otherworldly glow. The seafood, for about $1.50, is recommended. The best of the many *chifas* is the **Chifa Tien an Men,** which is popular with locals for its generous portions (around $1). On Friday and Saturday nights, Andean music drifts from the open courtyard of the **Cafetería Oraibi,** which serves vegetarian food in the $1 range next to Zulay Tours.

With all these tourists around, it's no surprise that pizza is one of the most popular dishes in town. A small book exchange and big-screen TV grace **La Fontana de Trevi,** an American-owned restaurant on the 2nd floor that features pizza and pasta from $1.50. **Pizza Siciliana** also serves Italian food, starting at $1.50 for a small pizza. They have music most nights. The **Rincon de Italia,** Sucre and Calderon, is an interesting little hole in the wall with art ranging from nudes to portraits of John Lennon. Cannelloni, lasagna, spaghetti, and pizzas are $1.50–4. **Pizza Siciliana,** on Morales one block south of the plaza, sells tasty pies for $1.50–4.50.

On the south side of the Plaza de Ponchos, the **Café Shanandoa** has been serving homemade pies (the fruity kind) and sandwiches for years. Next door, **Ali Allpa** offers meat and vegetarian options for $1–2. No longer on the plaza, the **Plaza Cafe,** tel. 6/921-729, still offers board games, mellow tunes, and funky decorations a few blocks south on Sucre, along with coffee and vegetarian dishes like stir-frys for around $2. Low tables, straw mats, and candles hint at the falafel, hummus, and shawarmas to come at **Sahara,** on Quiroga east of the plaza. A limited range of dishes are $1–2, but plenty of drinks are available, and water pipes are $2.

Tabasco's Mexican Food has a good view of the Plaza de Ponchos from its second-story patio, and does Mexican dishes, pizza, and pastas for $2–4. The award for Best Market View, though, has to go to the **Terraza Cafe Sol,** overlooking the plaza from a rooftop to the west. Breakfast, vegetarian food, coffee, and snacks are on the menu. **San Seba's,** one block farther east, is a bakery that does a good breakfast for under $1, with real espresso.

One of the best dishes in town is the pepper steak at **Geminis,** a funky little place on Salinas between Sucre and Bolívar. Generous vegetarian and meat dishes are $1–3, and they have a wide range of drink choices made with purified water. Try the Trucha Otavalito (trout in

a seafood sauce) for $2 in the sunny open patio of the **Restaurant Mi Otavalito,** Sucre and Morales. Although it's not Chinese-run, the **Chifa Metta** on Montalvo and Roca is probably the best *chifa* in Otavalo. Both the *chaulafanes* and *tallarines* are good ($1).

If you're shopping for food to make your own meal, try **Floralp,** a gourmet deli with organic fruits and vegetables, bread, honey, and cheeses, on Colón one block from the La Pelacita ice cream shop on Bolívar. The best panaderia in Otavalo is on Jaramillo under the Hostal Maria.

If you're looking for something special to splurge on, try lunch at a nearby hacienda. Both **La Mirage Garden Hotel and Spa** and the **Hacienda Cusín** offer exceptional set lunches and weekend brunches. They're not cheap, but the beautiful surroundings and first-class service are included. Reservations may be required, so it's best to call ahead. For details on La Mirage, see "Accommodations and Food" under "Cotachi" in the "Northwest of Otavalo" section; information on Hacienda Cusín can be found under "Laguna de San Pablo."

ENTERTAINMENT AND EVENTS

Fiestas

The Inca festival of the summer solstice, known as Inti Raymi, has been absorbed into the Catholic **Festival of San Juan** held from 24–29 June. Boats of every description dot the Lago de San Pablo, and people cheer local favorites (of both species) in bullfights. In the San Juan barrio northwest of Otavalo, a ritual rock-throwing called *tinku* claims victims every year. Until things were calmed down in the 1960s, some people were killed during the mock battles.

The festival everyone looks forward to, though, is **Yamor,** traditionally begun near the first of September. In this case, the Inca festival of Colla-Raymi, a harvest celebration of the earth-'s fertility, was conveniently combined with the festival of San Luis Obispo, patron saint of the harvest. El Yamor, as it is known today, is a two-week blowout of the largest order. Parades, marching bands, bullfights, outrageous costumes, and dances are all fueled by a special Yamor *chicha* made of seven different grains and drunk only during the festivities. Be warned—all that alcohol can occasionally bring out the less hospitable side of revelers.

In the *entrada de ramos* (entrance of the branches), food and animals—from bread and fruit to live guinea pigs—are displayed, re-creating a ritual presentation of food to the landowner dating to colonial times. A highlight is the appearance of the *coraza,* often a patron of the festivities, who wears an elaborate costume with a three-cornered hat and silver tinsel covering the face. The *coraza* is the only participant on horseback and is greeted with respect worthy of his or her position.

Nightlife

Good Andean music is easy to find in Otavalo's *peñas* (nightclubs). Ask around to find out when and where to go, since live bands aren't always on the ticket. If you're lucky, you might find the music interspersed with poetry readings, dramatic monologues, and indigenous dance performances. Grab a high-octane pitcher of *canelazo* (hot cinnamon tea with *aguardiente*), sit back, and enjoy.

Your best bets are the **Amauta Peña Bar,** on Morales between Jaramillo and Sucre, the **Peña Bar Tuparina** two blocks west, and the **Peña Jampa** at Jaramillo and Morales. The **Samay Peña Bar** is on the same block as the Amauta and has taped music as often as live bands. Young locals crowd the **Habana Club** discotheque and the **Maracana Disco-Bar** on weekends.

For a bit of bloodsport, try a Saturday night **cockfight** at the Gallera Municipal near the food market.

Public Pools

After a long, hot ramble through the country, take a dip in the **Yana Yacu** public pools, west of town across the Pana. They're open daily 8 A.M.–5 P.M., 10 cents pp, with changing rooms available. The **Piscina Neptuno** is another clean public pool at the east end of Morales, and **Sara Nustra,** on Sucre at the south end of town, has a water slide, pool, and sauna.

SHOPPING AND SERVICES

One thing about Otavalo: if you can't spend it here, you can't spend it anywhere. In addition to the markets, stores throughout town carry huge selections of woven goods. **Antara,** a store on Sucre near Colon, sells handmade Andean musical instruments. For more by local artists, try the **Galería de Arte Quipus** at Sucre and Morales, which specializes in oils and watercolors. **Dalí Arte Contemporaneo,** at the same intersection, is more exclusive, with high-quality works by artists from Otavalo and elsewhere in Ecuador. **Artesanias Emaus** has two locations on Sucre near Morales. You can buy, sell, or trade books at **The Book Market,** Jaramillo 6-28 and Morales, which has a good selection of works in several languages.

Spanish Lessons

The **Instituto Superior de Español,** Sucre 11-10 and Morales, tel. 6/922-414, fax 6/922-415, e-mail: institut@superior.ecuanex.net.ec, gets repeated recommendations for having the best Spanish classes in Otavalo. One-on-one instruction ($5.50 per hour) is offered for speakers of English, German, and French, and they can arrange homestays and tours for students. Another option is the **Mundo Andino Spanish School,** Salinas 404 and Bolívar, tel./fax 6/921-864, e-mail: espanol@interactive.net.ec, www .geocities.com/mundo_andino, which offers 4–7 hours of classes per day ($4.50 per hour) and homestays with local families. Martha Vaca Flores relocated her **International Spanish School** from Banos to Otavalo. It's at Morales and Sucre, tel. 9/928-967, e-mail: martaiss@hotmail.com, and she charges $4 for one-on-one lessons.

Services and Information

The **Banco del Pichincha,** Bolívar and García Moreno, changes travelers' checks at a slightly worse rate than in Quito. You can also try **VAZ money exchange** on the west side of the Plaza de Ponchos, which handles many foreign currencies, travelers' checks, and Western Union money transfers. Some tour agencies change cash and travelers' checks as well. The **post office** is on the corner of Sucre and Salinas and is open Mon.–Fri. 8 A.M.–7 P.M. and Sat. 8 A.M.–1 P.M. You'll find the **Andinatel** office on Calderón east of Jaramillo.

Most hotels do laundry, or you can try the **New Laundry** at 9-42 Roca or the *lavanderia* at 5-14 Colón. Internet cafés, of course, have started to spring up in Otavalo. Two of the best are on Sucre south of the Plaza de Ponchos: **C@ffé.net** and **Native c@ffé.net,** both of which charge around $1.50 per hour and offer food and Internet phone calls as well.

Run by Patricio and Ruben Buitron, the **Centro Medico El Jordan,** tel./fax 9/921-159, is the best in town. It's on Quiroga next to the Valle de Amanecer hostal. Two good general information websites on Otavalo are www.otavalo.com and www.otavalo-net.com.

TRANSPORTATION

Otavalo's **bus terminal** is on the northeast corner of town at Atahualpa and Ordoñez. Here you can catch buses to Quito ($1.25, 2–3 hours) and Ibarra (20 cents, 30 minutes), as well as nearby villages such as Iluman, Carabuela, Peguche, and Agato. Otherwise, you can take any bus heading north along the Pana and ask the driver to let you off at the appropriate village turnoff, then walk from there. Coming back is even easier; just flag down any bus heading south toward Otavalo.

Taxis, which congregate at the plazas and parks, charge about $3 per hour around town and $5 per hour for more out-of-the-way locations like the Laguna Mojanda. Try **Taxi 31 de Octubre,** tel. 6/920-485. **Mountain bikes** are another possibility for extended excursions. The best ones for rent are at **Primaxi,** Atahualpa and Moreno, and **Indy Aventura,** on Salinas across from the Plaza de Ponchos. Both charge $8 per day.

Sadly, the **train** from Otavalo to Ibarra is no longer running.

LAGUNA DE SAN PABLO

You'd think that at an altitude of 3,900 feet,
Any successful lake would come out some form of pink.
You, however, are dark, and, to top that, shallow.
Mount Imbabura has crushed you under her.
She dominates you, and makes you servile.
Oh! Eel-colored lake!

—Henri Michaux,
Ecuador, A Travel Journal

Regardless of its color and depth, the crater lake at the foot of Volcán Imbabura presents a beautiful sight, circled by pastoral hamlets and women washing clothes among tall reeds. Legend has it that a giant living in the lake reached out and grabbed Imbabura long ago, giving it its characteristic indentations (look for the heart-shaped dark patch on the southern end).

A dirt road surrounds the lake, perfect for a full day's walk. The bus from Otavalo marked Araque follows this road (catch it in front of the market on Atahualpa). A swimming race is held every September as part of Otavalo's Yamor festivities—the current record across the frigid waters stands at around 45 minutes. The festivals of Corazas (19 August) and Los Pendoneros (15 October) are celebrated in the tiny shoreline villages, which specialize in crafts as varied as fireworks and woven reed mats. The walk south from Otavalo to the lake takes about one hour.

At the northwest corner of the lake is the Club de Caza y Pesca (Hunting and Fishing Club), the defunct Hotel Chicapan, and a green building with a dock where you can rent rowboats for $1 per hour.

Climbing Imbabura from the West

The volcano can be climbed from this side with a little more effort than from the northeast via La Esperanza. Turn off the Pana at González Suárez (where taxis often wait for passengers) to reach the town of San Pablo del Lago. The trail leads uphill from the right of the church, passing a eucalyptus plantation after about one hour. Take the left fork straight uphill following an underground water pipe (water is available in spots) until you leave the *páramo.* You'll want to follow the ridge, but there is no path, so be ready to sweat. Just below the summit, a trail leads horizontally to the left to a break in the steep summit rocks. Count on at least six hours up and four down, and take warm clothes, food, and water. Another, easier option is the **Cerro Huarmi Imbabura,** a 3,845-meter foothill between Imbabura and the lake.

Hacienda Cusín

Outside of San Pablo del Lago is the oldest and one of the most famous and luxurious country inns in South America. Built in 1602, the Hacienda Cusín is named after a young local warrior who fought bravely against the Inca. English owner Nick Millhouse had it fully remodeled into a country inn in 1990. Situated in a wide, scenic valley just south of Imbabura at 2,400 meters, the hacienda is a relaxing, Old World type of place where llamas and sheep graze in the shadows of avocado trees. Old stone walls topped with moss encircle two acres of gardens, which bloom continuously in the mild climate. Hummingbirds can't seem to believe their luck in the forests of bougainvillea, belladonna, orchids, and foxgloves.

Twenty-five rooms are spread over seven guest houses, all with private bathrooms and garden views. Some have bathtubs and fireplaces. Fifteen garden cottages echo the white walls and terracotta tile roof of the main building. This ancient edifice, decorated with colonial antiques and tapestries, houses the game room, conference room, and library graced by French windows. The outstanding restaurant seats 40 under its leather ceiling. Food is served on carved wooden plates in front of a log fire. An excellent set lunch is $17 pp. Horses are available to rent, and many kilometers of trails wind into the hills and fields. Guests can be met at the airport in Quito. Rates are $86 s, $120 d, including breakfast.

Contact the hacienda at 6/918-013 or 918-316, fax 6/918-003, e-mail: hacienda@cusin .com.ec, www.haciendacusin.com; in the U.S., 800/683-8148, fax 617/924-2158; in the U.K., tel. 020/8788-7542.

More Accommodations and Food
A billboard along the Pana points down a dirt road to the **Hostería Puertolago,** tel. 6/920-900 or 920-920, fax 6/920-901, e-mail: efernand @uio.satnet.net, on the southern shore of Lago de San Pablo. Meticulously landscaped grounds surround a main building housing a nautical-motif bar, a restaurant, and an atrium with a wide window over the lake. Posh rooms with TV and fireplace cost $55 s, $62 d. Rowboats and kayaks are available by the hour or the day, as are motorboats and paddleboats. Lake tours are $5 pp by day or night.

The comfortable **Hostería Cabañas del Lago,** tel. 6/918-001, around on the eastern lakeshore, has two restaurants specializing in trout—El Cazador (the hunter) and El Pescador (the fish-

erman)—as well as El Refugio bar. Foot-powered paddleboats and motorboats are available for rent. Two-person cabañas with fireplaces and private baths run $39, including breakfast and dinner, or $51 pp with all three meals. For reservations, contact Unicentro Amazonas, Local 18, Amazonas 3814 and Japón, Quito, tel. 2/435-936, fax 2/461-316.

LAGUNAS DE MOJANDA

Half an hour from Otavalo by car lie three moody, beautiful lagoons in the shadow of jagged mountains. The Lagunas Grande (also known as Caricocha), Negra (Huarmicocha), and Chiquita (Yanacocha) are clustered 18 kms up a steep, cobbled road through the *páramo,* 1,200 meters below Otavalo. Clouds play across the dark surfaces of the lakes and wrap themselves around Fuya Fuya (4,263 meters) to the west.

Campsites are available along the south and west sides among the ruins of old shelters. Be careful with fires—notice the burn scars that mar the dry surrounding hillsides. A clear trail leads up Fuya Fuya, which can be climbed in a long day with no special equipment.

A series of violent crimes have been reported at the Lagunas through 2000. Local residents have banded together to patrol the area, but it's still recommended that you visit only in a group, and don't spend the night. Check with the South American Explorers in Quito or the Casa Mojanda (see following entry) for safety updates.

A taxi from Otavalo costs $3–5 depending on whether you're going to one of the hotels or the lakes themselves.

Casa Mojanda
For the price, it doesn't get much better than this: an ecologically and socially minded hotel with some of the best views from any rooms in Ecuador. A Brooklyn (NY) –Ecuadorian couple opened the Casa Mojanda in 1995, five km south of Otavalo at 9,800 feet on the road to the Lagunas de Mojanda. The hotel clings to the edge of a valley facing Cotacachi and the Cerro Cushnirumi, one of the few undisturbed tracts of Andean cloud forest in Ecuador. All of the buildings were constructed in the *tapial* (rammed-earth) process in a tasteful, simple

style of white-washed walls, wood, terraces, and hammocks.

The airy main building houses the dining and living rooms, and outside are a separate library building and a small amphitheater facing the valley. The owners provide plenty to keep their guests busy: hiking trails, mountain bikes, gentle riding horses, videos, and a two-seater kayak, for starters. They also oversee the nonprofit Mojanda Foundation, working for the environmental protection and social welfare of the surrounding communities. Donations and requests for more information can be directed to the hotel.

Eight guest cottages cost $45 pp d, including breakfast and dinner, and housing in the two 10-person hostels is $35 pp for groups of four or more. Student, child, and senior discounts are available. Contact Casa Mojanda at tel./fax 9/731-737, 720-880, e-mail: mojanda@uio.satnet.net, www.casamojanda.com.

La Luna

Just up the road to the Laguna from the Casa Mojanda is this budget *hostería,* tel. 9/737-415, 816-145, with private rooms ($6–8 pp), dorm rooms ($3 pp), and campsites ($1.50). The main building has a small restaurant and bar, and you can rent videos, take a 4WD tour, or just enjoy the setting and resident dogs. To get there, take the first left past the Casa Mojanda and head downhill a few hundred yards and over the bridge. They can pick you up in Otavalo for free until 6 P.M.

CARABUELA

This tiny village lies to the left of the Pana a few kilometers north of Otavalo. Trudge uphill to find the house of **José Carlos de la Torre,** labeled "Artesania, Tejido de Poncho," where Sr. de la Torre weaves fine wool scarves called *bufandas* on a backstrap loom. Each scarf takes up to three days to make and costs only $4. It's fascinating to watch the entire process—which Sr. de la Torre is glad to demonstrate—from nappy, knotted wool through carding and weaving to the final scarf. He also weaves and sells authentic blue wool ponchos.

Accommodations

Troje Cotama, tel./fax 6/946-119, e-mail: trojecotama@otavalo-web.com, sits in the middle of nowhere in the Otavalan countryside four kms north of Otavalo. Cotacachi and Imbabura tower in either direction, and at night the only sounds and lights come from the hotel itself. The main house, a converted grain barn, was rebuilt with all natural materials by an Ecuadorian–Dutch couple. On the 2nd floor above the kitchen and dining room is a living room with TV and VCR, a loom for weaving demonstrations, and a great view from the wide window.

Accommodations in 10 double rooms are cozy and simple, with wood, adobe, and indigenous crafts giving a tasteful country chic atmosphere. Beehive-oven fireplaces, muslin sheets, and

creating one of Ecuador's famous embroidery pieces

JULIAN SMITH

thick comforters ward off the nighttime chill. Mountain bikes are for rent, and resident llamas provide company for those who'd rather just sit and relax. Troje Cotama's three hectares of pasture and cornfields are just the beginning of what could easily turn into a week or more of exploring the countryside and enjoying the solitude of evening walks down a country lane as the stars come out.

Owner Helena van Maanen speaks English, Dutch, German, and Spanish. Meals are available for $3–4 and often include homegrown ingredients. Rates are $20 s, $24 d. Taxis from Otavalo (20 minutes) cost $1.25.

PEGUCHE

One of the most financially successful indigneous villages near Otavalo, Peguche is a rapidly growing village of about 4,000. It's home to a few *tiendas* (shops) and restaurants (more every year), as well as artisans who turn out all kinds of textiles and musical instruments. Through open windows drift the clack of mechanical looms and the first halting notes of newly made *flautas* (reed flutes) and *rondadores* (Andean panpipes). Primaxi, just off the Pana, has mountain bikes for rent.

Various homes and workshops around town specialize in rugs, blankets, tapestries, and scarves. If you're looking for fine tapestries, stop by the home/workshop of either **Antonio Qinatoa** or **José Cotacachi** (ask around for directions). José's work hangs in the Ali Shungu hotel in Otavalo and is some of the best in the Otavalo area. His tapestries come in many different sizes and designs, some with tassels of loops for hanging.

Cascadas de Peguche

This small park's waterfall is perfect for cooling your feet after a day's hike or a spray of mist on the face on a hot day. From Otavalo, the 45-minute walk begins by following the railroad tracks north out of town. Follow the road when it leaves the tracks up to the right and look for the Ministerio del Ambiente (INEFAN) sign at the park entrance. A dirt road leads straight from the Pana through Peguche, passing under two white arches and the remains of an old *obraje* (colonial weaving workshop) to the sign and park entrance.

Small stands sometimes sell food at the entrance, where a new indigenous hotel/restaurant should be finished by late 2001. The wooded valley has relatively clean picnic areas in eucalyptus-scented clearings. A clear path leads under tall trees toward the falls, but the footing at the base can be tricky, especially crossing the damp logs. A narrow log-lined path leads up to the left to the top of the falls, where a perpetual mini-rainbow glistens in the sunlight. Some robberies have been reported at the falls, so don't go alone or at night. Part of the 25-cent entrance fee is supposed to go toward paying guards, but they aren't always there.

Accommodations

Peguche offers a few options for those who want to stay outside of but still near Otavalo. Just off the Pana into town, turn left and you can't miss the round main building of the **Peguche Tío Hostería**, tel./fax 6/922-619, which calls to mind a big wooden spaceport. Inside is a dance floor, restaurant, and music, video, and book libraries specializing in local indigneous cultures. The 12 rooms outside near the gardens each have hot water, fireplaces, and private bathrooms ($8 pp). Entrées in the restaurant are around $3, and there are occasional music and dance performances. Peguche Tío was opened by seven local brothers of the Vega family, who between them speak Spanish, Quechua, English, French, and Dutch. Classes are offered in Quechua and Spanish as well as indigenous dance and weaving, often by local artists themselves.

Straddling the railroad tracks farther into town is the **Hostal Aya Huma**, tel. 6/922-663, fax 6/922-664, e-mail: ayahuma@uio.telconet.net, www.otavalo.com.ec/ayahuma. This beautiful place was opened in 1995, and it's as comfortable as they come: fireplaces, hammocks, book exchange, Spanish classes, vegetarian restaurant, live Andean music on Saturday night, and a garden to die for. Hot water runs 24 hours a day, and fax and laundry services are available in the main building. Entrées in the restaurant (serving all meals) are around $3. Follow the signs through town, or ask directions. Rates run $14 s, $20 d with private bath and $8 s, $12 d with shared bath.

AGATO

About four kms northeast of Otavalo is another weaving village, a few kilometers east of the Pana up the base of Imbabura above Peguche. Artisans here are known for their traditional-style weaving and fine embroidery, and nowhere is better to see them in progress than the workshop of master weaver **Miguel Andrango** and family (tel. 6/923-682). Here you can watch the artists weaving wool on backstrap looms, while others create fine, intricate embroidery on the finished cloth. Even locals are impressed by the quality of Miguel's work. Many of their high-quality textiles are for sale. Practically anyone in town can give you directions to the workshop, and many area tours stop by there as well. Look for a sign on the right of the Pana just past Peguche, or ask in Peguche for the correct road toward Agato.

ILUMÁN

A little farther up the Pana from Peguche, across from the turnoff to Cotacachi, lies this small town noted for its felt hats and weavings. Follow the cobbled road uphill straight toward Imbabura, and turn right when it levels out to reach the center of town and the plaza. South of the plaza on Bolívar is a sign for Carlos Conteron's **Artesanías Inti Chumbi** workshop, tel. 6/946-387, operated with his wife Roselena and daughter Breenan. The couple presents backstrap loom weaving demonstrations and sells textiles and beautiful indigenous dolls. Throughout Ilumán are *talleres* (crafts workshops) specializing in the colorful felt fedoras worn by the area's *indígenas*. Buses from Otavalo go straight to the town center.

HACIENDA PINSAQUÍ

An equestrian theme pervades this hacienda just north of Otavalo, on land that has been in the family of owner Pedro Freile for centuries. It began in 1790 as a textile workshop that supported as many as 1,000 workers at one time. Simón Bolívar was a repeat guest on his way

ILUMÁN'S FAITH HEALERS

A long with its crafts, Ilumán is known for its *curanderos* (faith healers), who can be hired to cure or curse. Residents have been passing down knowledge on natural remedies and spiritual cures here for centuries, treating everything from respiratory and back problems to heart disease and cancer. In 1988 there were 85 registered faith healers in Ilumán (eight of them women), but according to locals only a small percentage were genuine. Dozens of locals come to Ilumán daily to be cured or to hire black magic, and even a few foreigners seek the wisdom of the healers every year.

Curing rituals are a blend of ancient wisdom, folklore, and modern faith. Invocations in Quechua to Mama Cotacachi and Taita Imbabura, the old gods of the volcanoes, are sent up alongside prayers in Spanish to the Christian God and Jesus. *Curanderos* spit water or blow cigarette smoke on the patient, or rub him or her with special stones. A candle is passed over the patient's body, then lit to learn about the patient by studying the flickering flame. Cures can take the form of prayers or medicinal herbs like eucalyptus, poppies, and lemon, either rubbed on the patient's body or drunk as a tea.

Less public are the *brujos,* practitioners of the black arts. Traditionally working only at night, these wizards will cast malignant spells for jilted lovers or failing businessmen—for the right price, of course. Rumor has it that their powers extend even to murder.

between Ecuador and Colombia during the struggles for independence.

Horse racing and hunting trophies grace the bar area next to pictures of fine horses above the stone fireplace. Rooms feature canopied beds, fireplaces, and tiled floors, and some suites contain hot tubs. Across the railing from the main hall and its fountain is a 60-seat restaurant. Tours on horseback venture up the lower slopes of Imbabura. Rates are $74 s, $96 d, including breakfast. For reservations, contact tel./fax 6/946-116 or 946-117, e-mail: info@pinsaqui.com, www.pinsaqui.com.

NORTHWEST OF OTAVALO

COTACACHI

Across the Río Ambi gorge from the Pana, Cotocachi is said to have been created during an earthquake when Volcánes Imbabura and Cotacachi made love. The town is a smaller, quieter version of Otavalo, with leather goods instead of wool. Shops line the main streets, selling the bags, saddles, jackets, boots, vests, and purses for which the city is known—so many you can smell the cowhide from a block away. Just about anything that can be made out of suede or leather is available here or can be made to order. Duffel bags that zip down to purse size make good, inexpensive gifts. Quality is generally high, although it does fluctuate, and prices are reasonable (some bargaining is possible on larger purchases). The main market day is Saturday.

Sights
The **Museo de las Culturas,** tel. 6/915-945, is a small but well-done museum one block off the main square on García Moreno. Set in a lovely colonial building, it houses displays on local music, festivals, arts, and more, with descriptions in English and guided tours available. Admission is $1 pp. The area around Abdón Calderón Plaza has several other restored colonial buildings worth a look.

A **crafts market** in the Parque San Francisco at 10 de Agosto and Rocafuerte, two blocks south of Bolívar, is tiny during the week but blooms to a respectable size on Saturday and Sunday.

Accommodations and Food
For the budget-minded, the friendly folks at the **Hostal Plaza Bolívar,** Bolívar 12-26 and 10 de Agosto, tel. 6/915-327, offer the best deal in the area. The hotel and its restaurant are on the 2nd floor (enter on Bolívar), and there's private parking below. Breakfast is available, and you can use the kitchen when you want. Rooms (some with balconies) are $2.25 pp with private bath. Around the corner on Bolívar is the **Inti Huasi** restaurant, which specializes in trout and

serves a tasty, economical *menú del día* for $1.25. The **Restaurant Wipala,** one block from the bus station at 11-06 Sucre, caters to locals instead of tourists like most of the other places in town. A *plato del día* is only 50 cents.

Next to the museum sits the **Hostería El Mesón de las Flores,** tel. 6/915-264 or 915-009, fax 6/915-828. Inside the spacious colonial building, you'll find a bright, three-story courtyard with sky blue balustrades. Flowers spill over the edges, and old musical instruments grace the walls. Notice the murals in the Imbabura coffee shop, and don't miss the cozy Pisabo bar, with its leather chairs and fireplace. All rooms have private baths and phones, and some have TVs. Rates run $20 s, $24 d.

Just outside of Cotacachi on 10 de Agosto is **La Mirage Garden Hotel and Spa,** tel. 6/915-237, 915-077, 915-561, fax 6/915-065, a hotel designed in the style of an old hacienda. Carloads of Quiteños and diplomats converge here every week to stay the night or simply enjoy a meal while watching the tame peacocks wander across the grounds. Opened in 1985 by Ecuadorian designer Jorge Espinosa and his Danish partner Michel Duer, La Mirage sets the standard for luxury country hotels in Ecuador.

Two hectares of spectacular gardens, brimming with bougainvillea and six species of hummingbirds, are maintained by eight full-time gardeners. Oriental rugs and tiled floors decorate the white-washed buildings. As you wander the grounds, you'll come across a gym, an exclusive gift shop, and a small private chapel used occasionally for weddings and baptisms. Each of the 23 palatial rooms features a high canopied bed, an antique writing desk, a fireplace, and a TV. The hiking, horseback riding, and birding in the surrounding countryside beneath Volcán Cotacachi is outstanding. The spa has hot tubs, a steam room, a solar-heated indoor pool, and staff trained in massage, aromatherapy, facials, and reflexology.

After a long wait, La Mirage's restaurant gained acceptance into the Relais & Chateaux international gourmet restaurant association, making it the only member in Ecuador and only one of 13 in South America. If you've made reservations, you'll know your table by the small flag of your home country in the center. Entrées are universally excellent, and the wine selection (displayed on a converted church confessional) includes varieties from Chile, Argentina, France, and the hotel's own Perafan vineyard, the highest vineyard in the world. The restaurant overlooks the gently sloping front yard where flags flutter in the breeze, and the glass-walled breakfast pavilion stands nearly buried by radiant flowers.

Single rooms start at $180 and doubles at $200, including breakfast. Hotel staff will meet guests at the airport or at their hotel in Quito. Weekend lunches are popular, so call ahead. In the United States, make reservations through the Latin American Reservation Center, Inc., 800/327-3573, fax 863/439-2659, e-mail: larc1@att.net, www.larc1.com. They also offer all-inclusive package tours of four days/three nights ($1,800 d) and eight days/seven nights ($3,500 d). Photos of the whole spread are available at www.larc1. com/ecuador/lamirage /lamirage.html.

Soon after the turnoff for the Hostería La Mirage, you'll reach the **Hostería La Banda,** tel./fax 6/915-176 or 915-507, or in Quito tel. 2/541-387, e-mail la.banda@ecuador.com, where private rooms set around a grassy courtyard and fountain are $18. A restaurant, bar, and cafetería fill the main building. Horse rides and tours of the area are available.

Fiestas

Thousands of people pack the streets of Cotacachi for the **Fiesta de San Juan** (24 June), during which local men dance and drink at night in the main plaza until their wives drag them home. On the last day, though, it's the ladies' turn to carouse while their patient husbands watch over them. The fiestas of **Jora** (6–14 Sept.) and **San Pedro y Pablo** (28–29 June) arc also popular.

Transportation and Practicalities

Frequent buses run to Otavalo and Ibarra from the bus station at Sucre and 10 de Agosto, returning just as often. Trucks to Laguna Cuicocha (see following section) cost $3, and you can arrange to have them pick you up later. **An-** dinatel is at 14-27 Sucre and Peñaherra, one block from the Parque de la Matriz; the **post office** is on Peñaherra and Bolívar.

COTACACHI-CAYAPAS ECOLOGICAL RESERVE

This huge reserve northwest of Cotacachi stretches from the chill Andean *páramo* over the western edge of the Andes and well into the tropical western lowlands. In 1979 its 206,000 hectares were defined as reaching north from the Laguna Cuicocha to the old Ibarra-San Lorenzo rail line and west over the Cordillera de Taisán to the headwaters of rivers flowing into the Pacific.

Cotacachi-Cayapas is defined by water. The Ríos Bravo Grande, Agua Clara, San Miguel, and Santiago all drain the reserve's lower regions, and waterfalls like the Salto del Bravo and the Cascada de San Miguel await a few hours upstream by boat from the San Miguel

Cotacachi from Casa Mojanda

Laguna Cuicocha

guardpost. In the Andes, the reserve is dotted with trout-stocked lakes, including the Lagos Yanacocha, Sucapillo, and Burrococha at the feet of Yana Urcu de Piñan (4,535 meters).

Harboring a range of rich habitat, the reserve is a naturalist's dream. It includes the southern part of the Chocó biological zone, which encompasses the region between the Andes and the coast from southwest Colombia to northwest Ecuador. With its abundance of rainfall (the reserve's rainforest can get up to five meters of precipitation a year), the Chocó is one of the most biologically diverse zones on earth. Research has shown that Cotacachi-Cayapas has one of the highest rates of endemism (species found nowhere else) in the world. All four species of monkey that live in western Andean tropical forests swing through the trees here, including black howlers, and *nutria* (river otter) tracks often turn up on the banks of the muddy rivers. One of Ecuador's three species of tapir hides in the underbrush, along with the occasional jaguar and ocelot. The rare Andean spectacled bear inhabits the Cordillera de Taisán and the Andean forests on the flanks of Cotacachi.

Access

From Cotacachi, a road leads west through the town of Quiroga to a park entrance gate near Laguna Cuicocha. A guardpost near Lita, halfway along the route between Ibarra and San Lorenzo, offers entrance into the reserve's lower-altitude cloud forests. Boats are available from Borbón, near San Lorenzo, to travel upriver to the San Miguel guardpost, where the Río San Miguel joins the Río Cayapas. From here you can rent motorized canoes to enter the reserve's lowest regions. The entrance fee to the reserve is $5 pp for foreigners.

Laguna Cuicocha

The "Lake of the Guinea Pigs" (from *cuy*, Quechua for guinea pig, plus *cocha*, meaning lake) is one of the most visited locations in Ecuador's protected areas thanks to its beauty and easy access. At the foot of Volcán Cotacachi, 3,070 meters up in the Andean *páramo*, this icy crater lake is full of azure water so clear you can see the caldera's steep sides plunge almost straight down into the depths. No outlet for the lake's water has ever been found. The two islands that huddle in the center, Teodoro Wolf and Yerovi, are separated by a narrow channel known as the Canal del Ensueño (Canal of Dreams).

A new **visitors center** overlooks the water, with exhibits on the ecology, geology, and human history of the lake, open Tues.–Wed. 11 A.M.–3 P.M., Thurs.–Sat. 9 A.M.–5 P.M. Just down the hill, the **Muelle Restaurant** on the lakeshore offers a large selection of entrées for around $2. Boat rides are available from the restaurant's dock for 50 cents pp.

A few hundred meters almost straight uphill behind the Muelle is the **Restaurant El Mirador**, tel. 9/908-757, with better views and food for

$1–2, including a *plato típico* for $1.50 and a *cuy* (guinea pig) special for $3.50. From behind the restaurant, you might glimpse the Volcánes Cayambe, Imbabura, and Fuya Fuya off in the hazy distance. Ernesto the owner is a recommended guide for climbing and backcountry exploration in the area, and he rents basic rooms next to the restaurant for $3 pp with hot water.

From here a gorgeous trail winds all the way around the lake with views of Cotacachi and the islands. The hike takes between four and six hours, so bring water, sunscreen, and sturdy boots. Robberies of lone hikers and small groups have been reported, so try to find at least a few friends to go along. Tour groups often come to El Mirador, and it's a good place to meet people to hike around the lake with or share a truck back to Cotacachi. Driving from Cotacachi, take a left at the park entrance gate and follow the road uphill.

Buses run regularly from Otavalo to Cotacachi and Quiroga. From Cotacachi, take a left at the last traffic light in town on 31 de Octubre, and follow the road west through the town of Quiroga to the park entrance gate near the Laguna Cuicocha. From Quiroga, you can also hire a private truck from the main plaza for about $1.50, or tackle the two-hour uphill hike on foot. The scenery on the way to the lake is spectacular. If you have time, there's a great shortcut footpath through the countryside back to Quiroga that leaves the road about one km from the gate. Local drivers know where it is.

Volcán Cotacachi

According to local folklore, Mama Cotacachi (a.k.a. "Mother Ti-Ti") wears a cap of snow after a visit by her lover Taita Imbabura during the night. The 4,939-meter climb, first done in 1880 by Edward Whymper and the Carrels, is fairly straightforward and nontechnical, and the lower part is worth hiking even if you don't intend on summiting. The top can be tricky (some climbing experience and a helmet are a good idea because of the loose rock), so climb with a partner or be sure you know what you're doing. If you're leaving from Otavalo, you need to get going by 5 or 6 A.M.

Begin the climb by taking the road to the right from the park entrance gate 13 km to the north toward the radio antennae. The five-hour walk follows cairns up a grassy ridge by the antennae, then climbs to the west across the mountain's southern slope. There are a few campsites on the ridge above the radio tower, and water is available from pools a few minutes away. The trail continues across and down to the base of Cotacachi to the west, but you'll want to head north to arrive at a large amphitheater beneath the summit. Follow a series of cairns up to the left onto an area of yellowish rock scree—keep an eye out for falling rock. From here you'll have to negotiate a short chimney of loose rock, pass over a col, and scale a final rock wall to reach the summit.

Yana Urcu de Piñan

This mountain is climbed much less often because the access can take up to three days. It rises from the *páramo* in a less-visited region of the reserve near the Gualaví guardpost north of the Volcán Cotacachi. One route leaves south from the Juncal bridge, where the Pana passes over the Río Chota north of Ibarra. It can also be approached from the south near the Hacienda El Hospital. Reserve personnel at the entrance may be able to help you plan a route. The ascent itself, up the southeast ridge, is relatively simple; it should take 5–6 hours. The hike northwest from Irunguichu (four km west of Urcuqui) to the **Piñan Lakes** at the base of the mountain is a beautiful way to spend three or more days. For more information on hiking in this area, see "West of Ibarra."

LOS CEDROS BIOLOGICAL RESERVE

The largest privately owned reserve in Ecuador is tucked up against the southwestern corner of Cotacachi-Cayapas, whose southern flank and watershed it helps protect from human intrusion. The Centro de Investigaciónes de los Bosques Tropicales (Tropical Forest Research Center) runs this remote reserve 70 km from Otavalo. Founded in 1991 and named for the cedar trees once found in abundance, Los Cedros is a small chunk of what a good one-third of Ecuador used to be like: humid rainforest and cloud forest covering rough mountains and deep valleys like a damp green blanket, woven by tumbling, crystalline rivers. Three river systems tie together three mountain ridges within the reserve, drenched by up to 3.5 meters of rain per year.

Kilometers of trails wander through the reserve's 6,390 dripping hectares, passing waterfalls, swimming holes, and a ridge-top camping spot with a stupendous view of the forest. Mules are available for longer forays into the 6,000 hectares of primary forest. Along the way you'll quickly realize what a rich ecosystem you're lucky enough to be experiencing. Preliminary studies have found 160 species of birds in the reserve, including the Andean cock-of-the-rock and the spectacular golden-headed queztal. Gangly troops of brown-headed spider monkeys, endemic to the region, share the branches with white-throated capuchins and howler monkeys. Botanists will appreciate the 200 known species of orchids found amid ferns and palms galore. At night, huge, silent moths of every color and pattern crowd light bulbs like rush-hour commuters at subway turnstiles.

A 100-meter canopy walkway and lodge have been completed. The food has been described as jungle gourmet, and the water comes fresh from mountain streams. As many local residents are employed as possible. The driest months, and thus the best for visiting, are July and September. The reserve is set up for researchers and volunteers only.

Research opportunities are wide open, including nature tourism and various programs on environmental and health education being developed with local communities. Contact the center for more information. Rates are $30 per day, including all meals. Volunteers are expected to contribute $250 per month. Bring waterproof clothing, rubber boots if you have them, and insect repellent for the deerflies (it's too cold here for malarial mosquitos).

Reaching Los Cedros is half the adventure. Buses run from Quito to Sanguanal (6 hours), where you can spend the night at Don Pepe's ($3 pp) or tackle the six-hour hike to the reserve straight away. Mules can be arranged to haul baggage. For reservations and more information, contact the reserve in Quito at 2/540-346, Alemania and Eloy Alfaro, on the fourth floor, or get in touch with the Centro de Investigacion de los Bosques Tropicales (CIBT) at Casilla 17/7-8726 in Quito. Visits can also be arranged through **Ecolé-Adventures International,** P.O. Box 2453, Redway, CA 95560, 800/447-1483, fax 707/923-3001, e-mail: staff@ecole-adventures.com, www.ecole-adventures.com.

INTAG CLOUD FOREST RESERVE

The Cotacachi-Cayapas reserve bends around the town of Apuela, leaving a large oxbow of land outside the border. Luckily, the Intag Cloud Forest Reserve takes up the slack. This 505-hectare private reserve is owned and operated by Carlos Zorilla and his wife Sandy and, like Los Cedros, has been opened to the public to help defray operating costs. Similarly, Intag's mission is not only the preservation of the area's ecosystem, but also to bring local communities directly into the conservation picture through educational programs and projects. The reserve ranges in altitude from 1,850 to 2,800 meters—70 percent of the acreage is primary or secondary cloud forest. Some parts receive up to 2.5 meters of rain per year during the Oct.–May rainy season.

The bird-watching, naturally, is outstanding, offering the occasional glimpse of the plate-billed mountain toucan or the highly endangered yellow-eared parrot and more than 20 species of hummingbirds. When he's available, Carlos serves as an interpretive guide. Hiking trails from 1–5 hours in length lead into primary and secondary forests; for less adventurous types, there's a waterfall less than 10 minutes from the cabins.

Facilities at Intag include a main building, where Carlos and his wife live, with an attached dining area and library nearby. Simple but comfortable guest cabins feature sun-heated showers and solar lights. Much of the organic, vegetarian food is grown nearby in the 30 percent of the reserve that is dedicated to sustainable agriculture, and the coffee is roasted on the farm. The atmosphere is strictly informal, and guests are encouraged to help with doing the dishes, milking the cows, and feeding the chickens.

To help fight the destruction of the surrounding forests, the Zorillas founded the Organization for the Defense and Conservation of the Ecology of Intag (DECOIN) in 1995. Through the group, they've successfully organized resistance to government-funded mining projects that would have destroyed even more of the cloud forest and have organized a local organic coffee growers' association as well as a province-wide environmental congress. If you'd like more information on their work or would like to make a donation, contact them at Casilla 144, Otavalo, tel./fax 6/648-593, e-mail: decoin@hoy.net, www.decoin.org.

Staying at the reserve costs $40 pp per day. Because the amount of visitors is strictly controlled, advance reservations are a must. Minimum group size is eight people, and a two-night minimum stay is required. No walk-ins, please—remember, this is also their home. To set up a visit, contact the reserve ahead of time by mail at Casilla 18, Otavalo.

Junín

In 1997 this small community near Intag, with help from DECOIN, banded together to force Mitsubishi and the Ecuadorian government to abandon plans for an open-pit copper mine that would have caused the displacement of the entire town. Since then they have started building a cabin for guests who come to enjoy the isolation and gorgeous scenery of small farms, steep cloud forest, and pristine rivers. When it opens, the cabin will cost around $30 pp per day, including all meals and Spanish-speaking guides, but not transportation. With room for 16 guests, the cabin will feature four rooms and large verandas.

At 1,200 meters elevation, Junín receives as much rain per year as Intag. Most of it falls from Dec.–May, effectively closing the dirt road from García Moreno. This means the only way to get there during those months is by horse or foot—a four-hour journey either way. With DECOIN's help, profits from the cabin will help the people of Junín keep mining out of their community in the future and start their own protected reserve (400 hectares have already been bought as of 2000). For information on visiting Junín, contact Carlos Zorrilla at Intag (see previous entry).

APUELA

This isolated village, at 2,000 meters on the western edge of the Cordillera Occidental, serves as a good jumping-off point for even more remote destinations northwest of Otavalo. The bus ride there, through the cloud forests of the western Andes, is spectacular in itself. The road to Apuela leaves to the left of the Cotacachi-Cayapas entrance gate near Laguna Cuicocha, heading up and over into the Río Intag valley. Accommodations are available in town at the inexpensive **Residencial Don Luís**, a few blocks from the main plaza (50 cents pp). **La Forastera** restaurant is recommended for inexpensive, tasty local dishes.

The area around Apuela is just begging to be explored by foot. The clean, quiet hot springs of the **Piscinas Nangulví** are about seven kms from the town center. Accommodations are available next to the baths at the pretty **Cabañas Río Grande**, tel. 6/920-548, 534-196, for $1 pp with private baths. Flowers surround each cabin's porch, and the restaurant is good and inexpensive. Advance reservations are recommended, especially on weekends. Buses from Otavalo may take you all the way to the baths—ask first—or you can catch one from Apuela bound for García Moreno.

If you'd prefer to walk, take the main road out of Apuela to the crossroads after the second bridge. Head left to the *piscinas* (1 hour) or right to the **Gualimán** archaeological site (2 hours). Here you'll find pre-Inca burial mounds, a run-down pyramid, and a small museum, with breathtaking views all around. The elderly Pereira couple that takes care of the site can feed and house you for $4 pp per day if you call ahead (tel. 6/648-588, or call their daughter in Quito at 2/501-867). Another good hike is the downhill road from Santa Rosa, on the road to Otavalo, to Apuela.

Five or so buses leave from Otavalo to Apuela daily (3 hours). Buy your ticket at least one hour before departure. Eight buses per day head back to Otavalo.

IBARRA AND VICINITY

The sign at the entrance to Ibarra (pop. 120,000) calls it "The city you always come back to," and a few hours in town will show you why. The wide, clean streets are lined with the white-washed colonial buildings, most no more than two stories tall, that give Ibarra the nickname La Ciudad Blanca (The White City). Ibarra enjoys a slow, dignified pace of life more suited to a small town than a provincial capital.

Wander the outer residential streets by day, dodging horse-drawn carts and peeking into garden courtyards of old houses, and it seems as if you have the whole city to yourself. At night, though, the Parque Pedro Moncayo is alive with families chatting and children playing in front of the cathedral and municipal government building. Even the climate here at 2,225 meters is pleasant and mild. The Monumento a la Madre, a large statue of a woman breast-feeding a baby, welcomes visitors coming in on the Pana.

Ibarra was founded in 1606 under the full title Villa de San Miguel de Ibarra. It served early on as the administrative center for the textile *obrajes* of the Otavalo region. In August 1868, an earthquake tore through the quiet streets, laying the city to ruin and most of its 6,000 inhabitants to rest. Passing through a decade later, Edward Whymper found most of the city, save the fragile but resilient homes of the *indígenas,* still in rubble. Today Ibarra (pop. 90,000) is home to a mixture of highland *indígenas,* especially Otavaleños, and blacks from the western lowlands and Río Chota valley. There's a lot to see in the area, making Ibarra a good home base for a week of hiking, climbing, or just daydreaming. The streets in the city center are safe to walk at night, but take care farther downtown.

SIGHTS

In such a placid city, it's not surprising that most of the sights are churches. The **Iglesia La Merced** stands on the west side of the park of the same name. Inside is a small religious museum and a famous image of the Virgin of La Merced, which is worshipped by pilgrims from throughout the province. Opposite is the castle-like **Ministerio de Agricultura y Ganadería.** The **cathedral,** which underwent a major restoration in 2000, shares the north side of the leafy Parque Pedro Moncayo with the **Iglesia El Sagraro,** while to the west stands the stately **Palacio Municipal.**

On the north end of town, the drab, modern **Iglesia Santo Domingo** backs the small Plazoleta Boyacá, decorated with a monument celebrating Simón Bolívar's victory at the battle of Ibarra in nearby Caranqui. This church also houses a small museum of religious art and some rather gaudy paintings of Jesus in action; it's open daily 8 A.M.–noon and 2–6 P.M., 20 cents pp (the art section is open only Sun. 2–6 P.M.). Across town is the **Basílica La Dolorosa** at the corner of Sucre and Mosquera. Built in 1928, this church suffered a collapsed dome during the 1987 earthquake but was reopened in 1992. A huge, ornate wooden altar fills the otherwise plain interior.

The **Museo Regional Banco Central del Ecuador,** Sucre and Oviedo, opened its excellent collection of ancient artifacts from the northern highlands in a restored colonial building in 1999. Descriptions are in English, and the museum is open Mon.–Sat. 8:30 A.M.–1:30 P.M. and 2:30–4:30 P.M.

ACCOMMODATIONS

Hotels in Ibarra

The popular **Hotel Imbabura,** Oviedo 933 and Narváez, tel. 6/950-155, is a good bet with roomy, spartan quarters, great showers, and friendly owners. Little caged birds in the courtyard fluff themselves up at night against the cold and sing in the morning as you eat breakfast ($2 pp with shared bath). They have Internet access and lots of information on the area. A few blocks away, the **Residencial Madrid,** Olmedo 857 and Oviedo, tel. 6/951-760, is clean and friendly at $2 pp with private bath, hot water, and TV, as is the **Residencial Imperio,** Olmedo 8-62, tel. 6/952-929, across the street. The Imperio also features a disco and costs $1 pp with private

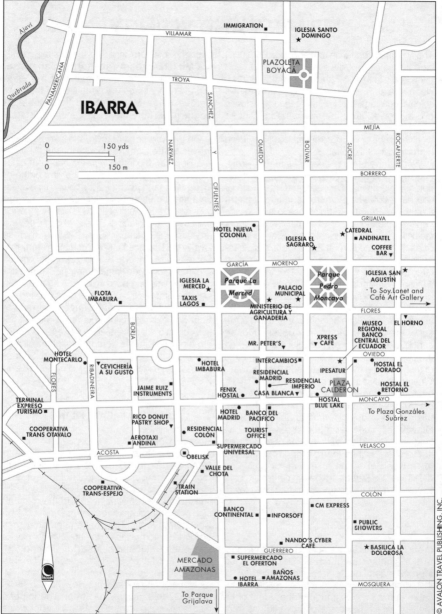

IBARRA

bath and TV, and hot water in the morning and evening. Near the train station and obelisk is the **Residencial Colón,** Narváez 862 and Velasco, tel. 6/950-093, with laundry service and the Iceberg disco next door. Simple rooms around the flower-filled courtyard are $1.75 pp with private bath.

You can enjoy the view from the terrace of the pleasant **Hostal El Retorno,** Pedro Moncayo 4-32 and Sucre, tel. 6/957-722, for $2 pp with TV and private bath. It's at the mouth of the alley

SANDRA FORRESTER

between Sucre and Rocafuerte. The pink and yellow **Fenix Hostal,** Pedro Moncayo 7-44, tel. 6/959-729, is a good deal with a covered parking garage, cable TV, and restaurant for $3 pp. Facing it is the comparable **Hotel Madrid,** Pedro Moncayo 7-14 and Olmedo, tel. 6/956-177. Rates are also $3 pp with private bath, cable TV, Internet service, and covered parking.

The **Hotel Ibarra,** Mosquera 6-158 and Sánchez y Cifuentes, tel. 6/955-091, is handy to the Mercado Amazonas and charges $3 pp with private bath. The **Hotel Nueva Colonia,** Olmedo 5-19, tel. 6/955-543, takes up a whole corner of the block north of the Parque La Merced. It has seen better days but has a pleasant restaurant in the interior courtyard. Rooms go for $3 pp with private bath and cable TV.

Probably the nicest place in Ibarra for the money is the **Hotel Montecarlo,** Rivadeneira 5-61 and Oviedo, tel. 6/958-266, fax 6/958-182. Their small pool, hot tub, sauna, and steam room are open to the public Tues.–Fri. 3–9 P.M., Sat. and Sun. 11 A.M.–9 P.M. for $1 pp. A stay at the Montecarlo runs $7 s, $12 d and includes cable TV and phone. A few hundred meters down the Pana is the **Hotel Ajavi,** Mariano Acosta 16-38, tel. 6/955-555, fax 6/955-640. Luxurious amenities include a pool, a sauna, a gym, and private parking. Rates are $24 s, $30 d.

Hotels Outside Ibarra

Several high-quality hotels can be found among the estates and flower farms just south of Ibarra

along the Pana. The **Hostería San Agustín,** Apdo. 46, Ibarra, tel./fax 6/955-888, at Km 2.5 offers the best views of Imbabura looming to the south. The hostería was renovated after a change of ownership in 1995, adding a pool to its list of amenities, which includes cable TV and basketball and volleyball courts. The sumptuous main building is filled with antiques, where you can while away the hours with a game of chess in the lounge until dinner is served. Private cabins and family suites are available. Turn east at the sign on the Pana and follow the cobbled road one km to the hotel. Rates are $10 s, $15 d.

The magnificent **Hostería Chorlaví,** tel. 6/932-222, 955-777, fax 6/932-224, e-mail: chorlavi@uio.satnet.net, lies 1.5 kms farther south. It's been run by the Tobar family for 150 years, since the days when the *hostería* commanded farmlands stretching to the slopes of Imbabura, and was opened to tourists in 1972. The name supposedly translates as "nest of love lulled by the waters of the yellow river," but with a pool, sauna, tennis and squash courts, cockfighting ring, and a soccer field to keep you busy, you might not have time left for anything else. The occasional scrub tanager has been known to make a birder's day. On weekends, services are held in the tiny church, and folkloric music and dance performances are offered on Saturday and Sunday afternoons. Antique art and furniture adorn the 52 rooms, some of which sport fireplaces. An excellent restaurant serves organic vegetables grown in the gardens smack in the middle of the grounds. Evening cocktails are served next door at the **Taberna Los Monjes** (Monks Tavern), open Thurs.–Sat. 6 P.M.–midnight. Rooms at the hostería are a steal at $15 s, $17 d.

Down the same cobbled road west of the Pana is the **Rancho Carolina**, tel. 6/955-215, e-mail: rancho-c@uio.satnet.net. They seem to be going for the Hacienda Minimalist style here, with dark wood railings contrasting the thick white-washed walls. The dining room surrounds a pretty covered courtyard with fountain. All food, including the rabbits, is grown on the premises. Seventeen rooms decorated with plants and antiques surround the pool and whirlpool. Rates are $25 s, $30 d.

Finally, six km south of Ibarra near the town of Bellavista lies the **Hostería Natabuela**, Apdo. 10-01-683, tel./fax 6/932-482, tel. 6/932-032, which is more a classy hotel than an antique hacienda. Neatly trimmed hedges and flowers line the brick paths between the 19 rooms, pool, sauna, steam room, and gym. Take time to venture down country lanes (ask directions to the Paso de los Incas, a nearby fragment of Inca highway), but leave time to enjoy the folklore music on Sunday afternoon. Rooms are $20 and come with TV, phone, private bath, and fireplace.

FOOD

Ibarra definitely has a sweet tooth. Besides its *helados de paila,* Ibarra is known for its *arrope de mora,* a blackberry sweet, and *nogadas* (nougat candies). Numerous shops selling these and other sweets crowd the southeast corner of the Parque la Merced. Several *chifas* and small restaurants line Olmedo south of the park, enough to dine at a different one every night for a week. For the best **cuyes** in the area, though, you'll have to go five km west to the town of San José de Chaltura, where a whole little squeaker costs $3, cooked to order. (You can also find one at the Amazonas market.)

For starters, the **Rico Donut Pastry Shop** has great fresh doughnuts and cakes. You'll recognize the **Coffee Bar** by its sign with the word coffee written in a dozen languages. **El Horno,** Rocafuerte 6-38, makes a good pizza; and the

2nd-floor **Cafetería Barbudo,** one floor below the Residencial Rosenkrantz, has a decent *menú del día* with a view over the street. **Mr. Peter's** is popular with locals and tourists for its $1 chicken tacos—sorry, no pizzas. At the **Cevichería A Su Gusto,** they'll whip up a shrimp, clam, or oyster *ceviche* to your taste for $1.50 a bowl. The **Casa Blanca Restaurant,** on Bolí and Moncayo, serves a good *menú del día* ($1) in the open courtyard of an old colonial house. It's a good place for breakfast, too.

To buy your own food, head to the covered **Mercado Amazonas** near the railway station, or the **Supermercado Universal** within a few blocks. A large plaza about 10 blocks out the road to Otavalo has a **Supermaxi** and a **Kentucky Fried Chicken.**

CAFÉS, BARS, AND NIGHTLIFE

Ibarra is a sleepy city, but it does have a few options for after-hours entertainment. On the sleepy eastern edge of town is a real find: the **Café Art Gallery,** Salinas 543 and Oviedo, tel. 6/950-806, a contemporary art gallery/café opened by local painter Olmedo Moncaya in

---

HELADOS DE PAILA

Ibarra's most delicious product is the famous *helados de paila* of Rosalía Suárez. Actually a type of sherbet (*helado* means ice cream), these treats are made by hand in a *paila,* which looks like a large copper wok. Ice, sugar, and fruit—the only ingredients—are mixed by hand with a large wooden paddle. Salt sprinkled on the ice under the *paila* keeps the mixture from freezing solid. The result is a delectable treat, as close to pure frozen fruit as you can get.

The process was begun by Rosalía in her kitchen in 1896, and has been carried on virtually unchanged by her descendants since her death at age 105. The *heladería* (ice cream shop) on the south side of Olmedo at Oviedo is run by Rosalía's daughter, and one run by her grandson is across the street. Now *"helados de paila"* are sold everywhere, but only Rosalía's are the real thing.

1996. Browse exhibits of paintings and sculpture by local and national artists over a cappuccino or burrito, and maybe even stay for a music recital, poetry reading, or theater performance on a weekend evening. It's open daily from 4 P.M.

El Encuentro, Olmedo 9-59, has been described as the "best little bar in northern Ecuador," with saddles instead of bar stools. **Baraka,** Rocafuerte between Rosales and Mospuera, has a pool table and dancing on weekends. You'll have to stop by in person to see if the **Cine Grand Columbia,** Moreno between Sucre and Rocafuerte, is showing something enriching or depraved.

ACTIVITIES

Do you have the strange urge to see Ibarra and a big chunk of the northern Sierra from above? If so, ring up the **Condor Escuela de Parapente,** Velasco 780 and Olmedo, tel. 6/953-297, 951-293, fax 6/957-332, e-mail: flyecuador @ yahoo.com, www.vr-site.com/flyecuador, for a tandem paraglider ride from the slopes of Imbabura ($20). They also rent and sell equipment and have an office in Otavalo at Jaramillo 8-35 and Quiroga, tel./fax 6/922-893.

Blanca Vaca Rosero, tel. 6/641-408, has been repeatedly recommended for excellent Spanish lessons ($3 per hour). She can be contacted through the Hotel Imbabura.

EVENTS

Neighboring Laguna Yahuarcocha (see following entry) is the focus of the **Fiesta de los Lagos,** which is celebrated the last weekend of September with car races around the water and an agricultural/industrial fair. The **Fiesta del Virgen del Carmen** is held on 16 July.

SHOPPING

Musicians will love the handmade guitars, mandolins, and *requintos* (small guitars) of Marco Carrillo at **Guitarras Carillo,** Mariano Acosta 13-32 and Galindo. Instruments start at $68. **Jaime Ruiz** also makes instruments, including *charrangos* and *tiples,* in his shop around the corner from the Hotel Imbabura. His guitars start at $72, *charrangos* at $40.

SERVICES AND INFORMATION

The folks at the **tourist information office,** Olmedo 9-56, tel. 6/958-547, are friendly but limited in information. Open Mon.–Fri. 8:30 A.M.–1 P.M. and 2–5 P.M. There's also a helpful **municipal tourist office** in the Plaza Calderon, tel. 6/955-051, open 9 A.M.–noon and 3–6 P.M. Mon.–Fri. and 9 A.M.–noon Sat. The **post office** sits way to the east on Salinas, one block from the Iglesia San Francisco and the Plaza González Suárez. **Andinatel** has a branch located half a block north of the Parque Moncayo. Keep trudging north for **immigration,** on Villamar next to the Iglesia Santo Domingo.

A set of public showers called the **Baños Amazonas** on Sucre is open daily 6 A.M.–6 P.M. (40 cents pp), but for a real treat try the facilities of the Hotel Montecarlo (see "Accommodations"), which are open to the public. **Nando's Cyber Café,** 6-50 Guerrero, has Internet access for $1 per hour, as does **Inforsoft,** Olmedo and Guerrero; **CM Express,** Bolí 10-24 and Colón (open until midnight on weekends); and **Soy.Ianet,** 3-32 Flores.

To change travelers' checks, try the **IPESATUR** travel agency, Bolí 7-54 and Oviedo, 6/958-857 or 958-858. They also handle currencies other than the U.S. dollar. The **Banco del Pacífico** around the corner also changes travelers' checks. You can have money wired to you via **Western Union** at their office in the Banco Continental, 11-67 Olmedo.

TRANSPORTATION

Buses

Midway between Quito and the border, Ibarra is a travel hub of the northern Sierra. Most bus companies have offices and bus yards within a few yards of the obelisk. **Cooperativa Trans Espejo** runs buses to El Angel every hour at half past the hour ($1, one hour); and **Cooperativa Cotacachi** sends buses to—you guessed it—Cotacachi every 15 minutes from morning to night

(20 cents, 30 minutes). Buses to San Antonio de Ibarra leave regularly from the obelisk for the 15-minute journey. **Cooperativa Trans Otavalo,** where the railroad tracks meet Acosta, runs regular buses to Otavalo every five minutes from early morning to night (20 cents, 30 minutes).

From the Terminal Expreso Turismo on Moncayo, **Cooperativa Urcuquí** and **Transportes Oriental** go to Urcuquí (20 cents, 30 minutes). The latter also runs to Pimampiro ($1, one hour). **Aerotaxi Andina** drives to Quito four times per hour ($1.50, 2–4 hours), Esmeraldas, Guayaquil, and Santo Domingo, while buses leave from the **Flota Imbabura** yard on Flores and Rodriguez for Tulcán ($2.50, three hours), Quito, Guayaquil, and Cuenca. **Cooperativa Espejo** and **Valle del Chota,** both near the train station, run to San Lorenzo ($2–3, six hours).

Trains

The singular train ride from Ibarra to San Lorenzo on the coast has been suspended indefinitely because of the expense of maintaining the tracks and the completion of a road down the same route, but *autoferros* may still be leaving as far as San Juan de Luchas. From there you can walk from the Mira river bridge to the main road (15 minutes) and catch a bus the rest of the way to San Lorenzo. Check with the tourist office in Ibarra for the latest report.

Getting Around

A taxi is one of the best ways to see the area and costs about $4 per hour or $25 per day. **Taxis Lagos de Ibarra,** Flores 9-24 and Cifuentes, tel. 6/955-150, can be hired for local tours and trips all the way to Otavalo and Quito. A ride to the capital will cost you $3 and takes a fraction as long as the bus.

SOUTH OF IBARRA

San Antonio de Ibarra

On an early morning walk through this town, known for its wood-carvers, you'll hear wood mallets striking chisels, smell fresh cedar shavings, and glimpse bands of sunlight slanting through clouds of sawdust. The back streets and main plaza are lined with workshops, which are often just the artist's empty living room, where they hew, plane, and sand blocks of cedar and naranjillo wood.

Pieces range from artistic (copies of Michelangelo's David and the Venus de Milo) to religious (saints, crucifixes, angels) to frivolous (cute animals and busty nudes). Beggars and *campesinos* are popular subjects. The abstract works are often the most attractive—smooth, idealized mother-and-child pieces or Mayan and Aztec-based designs. Some of the sculptures of people, especially saints destined for religious processions, have ingeniously articulated limbs. Many pieces are painted or varnished; carved furniture, frames, and utensils round out the selection. Prices range from $1 into the hundreds.

The main plaza has the largest stores, including one with interesting abstract stone sculptures. The gallery of **Luis Potosí,** tel. 6/932-056, is the most famous, with a selection of beautiful and expensive carvings.

Buses to San Antonio de Ibarra leave from the obelisk in Ibarra (5 cents, 15 minutes). If your bus lets you out on the Pana, follow the street uphill to the east to the town's main plaza.

Caranqui

The birthplace of Atahualpa, two kms southeast of Ibarra, boasts the remains of a pre-Inca stone temple to the sun and the archaeological **Museo Atahualpa,** tel. 9/813-056, open Wed.–Sun. 9 A.M.–12:30 P.M. and 3–6 P.M. (20 cents). Outside of town is the Hacienda La Victoria, where Simón Bolívar led his troops to victory over the royalists in the Battle of Ibarra on July 17, 1823.

LA ESPERANZA

Many Ibarrans relocated to this pretty town (technically La Esperanza de Ibarra) nine km south of Ibarra after the 1868 quake. In hopes of avoiding future catastrophes, La Esperanza's new residents dedicated it to Santa Marianita, the patron saint of earthquakes. At 2,505 meters, La Esperanza sits at the foot of Volcan Imbabura, making it a good departure point for climbs. The local embroidery is famous. Cooperativa La Esperanza buses run from the Parque Germán Grijalva in Ibarra, five blocks south of the obelisk on Sánchez y Cifuentes (10 cents, 30 minutes). Taxis to La Esperanza cost $1.50.

Imbabura

JULIAN SMITH

Climbing

La Esperanza is the best starting point for climbing either Imbabura or Cubilche. The initial approach is the same for both: take your first right at the panadería 100 meters past the Casa Aida. Known locally as "el camino para Imbabura" (the road to Imbabura), this cobbled road climbs gently through beautiful farmland worked by colorfully dressed *indígenas,* good for a stroll even to nonhikers. You can hire a taxi to come up here if you're in a hurry, or catch the 5:30 A.M. bus to Cherihuasi to save more than one hour of climbing. Aida at the Casa Aida can also arrange transportation for you up this first part if you ask the night before.

To climb **Cubilche** (3,802 meters), the smaller mountain to your left, simply head left and up through the fields and past houses until you enter the *páramo* near the peak. On top you'll find a few small lakes and great views of Lago San Pablo, Ibarra, and Imbabura (this gently sloping hill began as a pressure vent for the larger volcano). The climb takes about four hours from La Esperanza, and you can descend the other side to Lago San Pablo in another three hours or retrace your steps. Watch the deep, matted grass in the valley between Cubilche and Imbabura on the way down; it can be a hassle to wade through.

Imbabura (4,609 meters) is a bit more of an undertaking, but it's still possible to reach the summit and get back in one long day with no special equipment. Don't underestimate the climb: plan on leaving at or before dawn and taking a solid 8–10 hours round-trip from La Esperanza. "Taita" (Father) Imbabura is still a very real figure to the local *indígenas,* who ask his blessing for an abundant harvest from the crops planted on his flanks (when's it's raining on the valley, it's said to be Imbabura relieving himself). No one is sure when the first ascent was made, but local *indígenas* used to climb the mountain to collect ice to sell in Ibarra. The route follows the cobbled road uphill, cutting off a few switchbacks with paths through the increasingly steep fields.

Skirt the left (north) side of the large ravine to a cement water tank (the third one you pass) at its upper end, which is your last chance to refill water bottles. From here stay to the right-hand (south) side of the large basin in the upper reaches of the mountain that has been visible since La Esperanza. Be ready for moderate rock scrambling, which can be tricky in wet weather. Many people stop at the edge of the rim (sadly marred by graffiti), but to reach the true summit you'll have to continue another one km across loose rock. The entire trip can be done in a day with an early start (count on 8–10 hours round-trip). The IGM 1:50,000 *San Pablo del Lago* map covers the mountain, although it's not crucial for the climb.

A day hike around the base of Imbabura is another option that is best done clockwise starting from La Esperanza. Along the way you'll pass cows grazing and children waving from fields of grass, all in the mountain's shadow until Lago San Pablo comes into view around the corner. You can choose to follow the road south to Zuleta, then head cross-country southwest to San Pablo del Lago, or keep to the fields the whole way. This hike has turned into an unofficial local speed contest (the current record stands at under seven hours). To fully enjoy it, though, plan on a full day with an early start, and bring food and water.

Accommodations

Señora Aida Buitrón has run the rustic, tranquil **Casa Aida,** tel. 6/642-020, for the last 15 years. She'll reminisce about visits from Bob Dylan and Joan Baez in the '70s, when the famous musicians used to search for magic mushrooms in the fields after rains. Hot bread and *huevos criollos* starts the day, and tasty vegetarian meals are $1.25. The guesthouse is on the main (really, only) road in town and costs $2 per bed with hot showers, a garden, and plenty of pets. Spanish lessons can be arranged with local residents; Blanca is recommended.

LAGUNA YAHUARCOCHA

Northeast of Ibarra, Yahuarcocha takes its name (blood lake) from the legend that its waters turned red when the Incas slaughtered thousands of local chieftains in the 15th century for daring to side with the Spanish invaders. Despite its gruesome title, Yahuarcocha is quite pretty, surrounded by mountains and lined by *tortora* reeds, which are woven into *estreras* (mats) and Titicaca-style canoes. The wide road encircling the lake is used for annual car races and by local teens learning to drive (usually not simultaneously). On weekends it's lined with vendors selling small lake trout, and at a few places near the entrance from the Pana you can rent rowboats for $1.25 an hour. The Laguna Golf Course is on the far side of the lake from the entrance. Birders should keep an eye out for silvery grebes near the shore.

To get there, head north from Ibarra along the Pana to the large sign announcing the lake turnoff to the right. Alternately, you can turn right slightly earlier onto a dirt road leading up to a hilltop with a beautiful view of Ibarra and the lake. Pass the small disco and bar, and descend the other side to the lakeside pueblo of **San Miguel de Yahuarcocha,** which is known locally for its *curanderos* (faith healers) and *brujos* (witches). This route would make a great half-day hike up and over, allowing about two hours from Ibarra to the lake. Buses run to Yahuarcocha every few minutes from the market in Ibarra at Guerrero and Sanchez y Cifuentes—buses marked "Aduana" pass the entrance.

Accommodations and Food

Overlooking Yahuarcocha is the **Hotel El Conquistador,** tel. 6/953-985, fax 6/640-780, with a large restaurant and expensive discotheque. Rooms with TV and private bath are cheap at $5 s, $11 d. Next door is the newer, slightly nicer **Hotel Club Del Sol,** tel. 6/959-794 or 959-795, fax 6/959-796, with similar rooms and facilities. Rates are $12.25 s, $14.50 d. Across the street on the lakeshore is the **Estudio 54 Discoteque,** popular with Ibarreños on weekends. You'll pass the **Hostería El Prado,** tel./fax 6/959-570, 643-460, on the Pana just before arriving at the entrance to the lake. It's a pleasant country hotel with an indoor pool, sauna, steam room, minizoo, and restaurant. Ten huge rooms have phones, color TVs, and private baths, and laundry service is available. Rates run $8 s, $12 d, including continental breakfast.

WEST OF IBARRA

Piñan Lakes Hike

Ibarra is a good jumping-off point for the southeastern portion of the Cotacachi-Cayapas Reserve. Transportes Urcuqui buses from the Terminal Expreso Turismo in Ibarra head west every half hour via **Urcuquí** (one basic hotel) to **Irunguicho** ("Irubincho" on the 1:250,000 *Ibarra* map), four kms away. Irunguicho is the departure point for the lovely loop hike to the numerous **Lagunas de Piñan** at the base of Yana Urcu de Piñan. (The Laguna Doñoso, farther to the west near the hamlet of Piñan, actually has a more official claim to the title of Laguna Piñan, but for clarity I'll refer to it as Doñoso and the lakes around Yana Urcu as the Lagunas de Piñan.)

A clear, steep path leaves from Irunguicho to the north-northwest. Cerro Churuloma is one hour away, where you'll find campsites and the last available water until the lakes. Heading west you'll pass Cerro Hugo (4,010 meters), with beautiful views of Cayambe, Cotopaxi, and Cotacachi, followed by Cerro Albuqui (4,062 meters). Five to six hours from Irunguicho lies Lago Yanacocha, the first of this cluster of tiny *páramo* jewels.

Lago Yanacocha is just east of Yana Urcu and is mirrored by Lago Sucapillo to the west. To the south is the larger Lago Burrococha, with a good campsite to the south. To reach it from Yanacocha, climb the ridge to the south, then head west-southwest past some small ponds until you hit a trail heading west. Many other small lakes and ponds dot the landscape. It's possible to continue from here another 12 km west to the larger and more remote **Laguna Doñoso.**

The hike out winds south then east, joining with a dirt road. The last two hours of the six-hour walk is on a cobbled road, leading to **Otavalillo** and the Hacienda El Hospital. From there it's one more hour uphill to Irunguicho, three km north, where you can catch a ride back to Urcuquí or Ibarra. The IGM 1:50,000 *Imantag* map is sufficient, but the 1:25,000 *Cerro Yana Urcu* provides more detail. Take a compass regardless.

Chachimbiro Hot Springs

These mineral-water pools, 42 kms northwest of Ibarra, are run by a local foundation dedicated to encouraging sustainable development and environmental education in the area. Surrounded by trails and organic gardens, the pools range from cool to scalding and are used by locals to treat a range of illnesses. There's also a steam bath and sauna.

A daily bus leaves from the Expreso Turismo terminal on Flores in Ibarra at 7 A.M. and takes two hours to reach the pools. You can also hire a taxi for $6 each way from Ibarra (one hour), but be warned that the road deteriorates seriously for its last third, so your driver must (and, granted, probably will) have nerves of steel. Taxi drivers will often wait to take you home. Entrance is 25 cents pp, and you can spend the night at the **Hostal Chachimbiro** near the springs or the **Hosteria San Francisco** about three kms away. The place is often packed on weekends, when the good restaurant at the springs is open.

Bospas Forest Farm

Belgian Piet Sabbe, formerly of the Golondrinas Foundation, manages a tropical farm near Limonal in the Mira Valley 1.5 hours northwest of Ibarra. The Bospas Farm is an ongoing experiment in sustainable, organic farming, and its staff is constantly experimenting with crop diversification, agroforestry, and permaculture techniques. Traditional crops such as beans, yucca, and corn are grown among fruit trees that provide shade, timber, water conservation, and soil anchoring, aided by vetiver grass planted in contour lines on the slopes.

The farm accepts volunteers who are interested in learning about sustainable farming practices. Volunteers are expected to stay for at least a few months and to pay $150 per month. Two private rooms are also available for travelers for $8 pp per night, including breakfast. Hiking and horseback rides in the surrounding mountains can be arranged. For more information, contact Piet via e-mail at bospas@hotmail.com.

IBARRA TO TULCÁN

North of Ibarra, the Pana takes a sharp right-hand turn east to follow the Río Chota upstream. The road soon splits in the village of **Macarilla,** giving you a choice of routes to reach Tulcán. The older, rougher road heads north through Mira and up into the wilds of El Angel. The newer, southern route is the way most traffic passes (including countless cargo trucks) through Chota, Bolívar, and San Gabriel. Either way you go is a wild stretch of road once you leave the hot, dry Río Chota valley, winding through cloud forest–covered mountains sparkling with lakes, waterfalls, and rivers. It's a great area to get out and explore if you don't mind the occasional cold and dampness. The farther north you go, though, the harder it is to get hold of good topographical maps because of border sensitivities.

THE LANGUAGE OF THE INCAS

More people speak Quechua today than did when the last Inca died in the 16th century. Also known as *runasimi* (the language of the people), Quechua is pronounced much as Spanish is, with the addition of glottal stops popped in the back of the throat and indicated by apostrophes (as in "hayk'aq," meaning when). The consonant "q" is exaggerated until it sounds almost like the "g" in "guitar," and "th" is aspirated toward the sound of "t" alone. The accent is always on the next-to-last syllable.

Ama sua, ama llulla,	
ama quella.	Don't steal, don't lie, don't be lazy.
	traditional Inca greeting
Quampas hinallantaq.	To you likewise.
	traditional response
Napaykullayki	Greetings
Allin p'unchaw.	Good morning
Wenas tardis.	Good afternoon from the Spanish "buenas tardes"
Allin tuta.	Good evening
Allichu	Please
Yusulpayki	Thank you
Imamanta.	You're welcome
Tayta/Mama	Sir/Madam
Wayqi	Brother, friend spoken to another man of the same age
Allinllanchu?	How are you?
Allinmi	Fine
Ima-tam sutiyki?	What is your name?
[Bill]mi sutiy.	My name is [Bill]
Maymantan kanki?	Where are you from?
[Chicago]-mi-manta kani.	I am from [Chicago]
Allinllaña	Goodbye
Ratukama.	See you later

THE OLD ROAD TO EL ANGEL

After turning left at Macarilla, the old road to Tulcán crosses a bridge and passes a police checkpoint before beginning to climb out of the Río Chota valley into Carchi province. The lower hills are almost totally dry and denuded but become greener the higher the road climbs. Eventually, stretches of cloud forest begin to appear on each side.

Mira

The "Balcony of the Andes" (pop. 6,000) perches on the edge of the Río Chota valley, with one of the best views in the northern Sierra. Shaggy burros carry loads of firewood through the breezy, sunny town surrounded by fields of eucalyptus and evergreens. Mira is known for its high-quality sheep-wool textiles, sold in Otavalo and at the *cooperativa* across from the bus station and up the hill.

One block off the main plaza is the **Residencial Mira,** which is run by friendly, helpful owners who can point you to weaving workshops. They have rooms for $1 pp with shared bath and hot water. Mira also has a few unexceptional restaurants and an **Andinatel** office on the main street just past the gas station. Don't wander near any steep drop-offs after you try a Tardón Mireño, a well-known drink made with orange juice and the local firewater.

Mira is a very *tranquilo* place that sees few tourists outside of the two main festivals: the **Virgin of Charity,** celebrated on 2 February throughout Carchi province, and Mira's own **Fiestas del Cantón** on 18 August. Buses run past Mira hourly between Ibarra and El Angel.

EL ANGEL

By the time your bus finally chugs all the way up to El Angel (pop. 6,000), the town's motto— Paradise Closer to the Sky—doesn't seem so far from the truth. It definitely feels like you're up on top of something here at 3,000 meters. The clouds are closer, the air a bit thinner. There's even a street called Río Frío (cold river). Most travelers come here to visit the Reserva El Angel to the north, even higher in the bright, cold *páramo.*

Sights
The rough topiary works in the Parque Libertad were begun by José Franco, the father of Tulcán's famous topiary cemetery. A small collection of pottery is displayed in the **Museo Arquelogico Municipal** in the municipal building.

Accommodations and Food
The **Hostería El Angel,** tel./fax 6/977-584, in Quito tel. 2/221-489, fax 2/221-480, e-mail: rsommer@uio.satnet.net, right at the turnoff, is easily the nicest accommodation in town. Eight rooms are surrounded by flowers, and facilities include a living room with fireplace, a cafetería, laundry service, and, bless them, hot water. Private rooms go for $15 s, $30 d with private bath, and shared rooms are $12 pp (all prices include breakfast). The owners offer tours of the *páramo* by foot, mountain bike, horse, or car.

Otherwise you might try the well-worn **Residencial Viña del Mar** up in town on the Parque Libertad. Basic rooms cost $2 per bed with shared bath, which is outside.

The best of the handful of restaurants in town is the **Asadero Los Faroles** on the Parque Libertad, which serves a full meal of chicken, french fries, and soda for less than $1. For cheap meals and grocery shopping, the **Mercado Central** is on Salinas 9-74 next to the Ministerio del Ambiente (INEFAN) office. The Monday market fills the surrounding streets.

Services and Information
For information on the El Angel reserve, stop by the office on Salinas 9-32, inside the small courtyard and on the 2nd floor, tel. 6/977-597. **Andinatel** has an office on the Parque 10 de Agosto.

Getting There
Cooperative Trans Espejo, tel. 6/977-216, has an office on the Parque Libertad to the left of the Residencial Viña del Mar. They run buses to and from Quito ($2, four hours), Ibarra ($1, 75 minutes), and Tulcán ($1, two hours). If you miss the last bus of the day, hitch a ride or hire a taxi to take you down to the Pana at Bolívar, where it's easy to flag down a bus passing in either direction. Shared taxis often run down Espejo, the main road into town, to Bolívar and Mira.

La Calera
Three kms south of El Angel is the turnoff for the steep, cobbled road that leads seven kms downhill to a pair of thermal pools set in a beautiful valley. On weekends the pools can be crowded, and trucks leave from El Angel when full (50 cents pp). Weekdays the place is yours, but from El Angel you'll either have to hike the whole way, find a ride (not so easy this far out), or hire a taxi for $5 round-trip.

EL ANGEL ECOLOGICAL RESERVE

High above the town of the same name is Ecuador's premiere *páramo* reserve. Created in 1992, the El Angel reserve ranges from 3,650–4,770 meters across some of the most pristine high-altitude country in Ecuador. Throughout the reserve's 15,700 hectares you'll see the spiky heads of the giant *frailejón* plant for which El Angel is famous. Locals use it for various curative purposes, including relief of rheumatism—crush a piece of leaf to release the medicinal-turpentine smell. Sharing the plant's fuzzy green leaves, but without the tall stem, is the *orejas de conejo* (rabbit ears). Andean and torrent ducks swim in the streams flowing between lakes stocked with rainbow trout. Hawks and the occasional condor soar on the thermals over the heads of grazing deer.

It is possible (and highly recommended) to camp out here, but be prepared for serious weather. Temperatures in El Angel can drop below freezing, and 1.5 meters of rain per year is not uncommon. Wherever in the reserve you go, take care with the fragile vegetation—a footprint can last for months. The best season to visit is during the (relatively) dry season May–Oct., when high winds and intense daylight sun alternate with clouds, drizzle, and nightly chill. The Nov.–Apr. wet season is marked by mud and more precipitation, including snow. Admission is $10 pp.

Getting There

From the town of El Angel, hire a taxi or jeep or hike north through La Libertad into the reserve. This dirt road leads to the crystalline Laguna Crespo near the Cerro El Pelado (4,149 meters) and continues all the way through the reserve to Tufiño. To the west is the Colorado guardpost, the Cerro Negro (3,674 meters), and the Laguna Negra.

An alternate entrance route is along the old road to Tulcán, past the guardpost at La Esperanza. Look for a parking area 16 km from El Angel. A 45-minute trail leads from here to the striking Lagunas Voladero and Potrerillos. The former was named after a legendary Carchi chief who is said to have flown to these lagoons pursued by the Spanish (hence the name, meaning "flyer") and lost himself in the waters rather than surrender. The road from Tufiño to Maldonado traverses the northern part of the reserve, skirting the Volcán Chiles and the Lagunas Verdes.

For more information on the reserve and how to get there, stop by the office in El Angel. Gerardo Miguel Quelal has been recommended as a guide, and Fenando Calderón, tel. 6/977-274, as a jeep driver.

SOUTHERN ROUTE

Chota

This dusty town, also know as Ambuquí, sits on the bank of a muddy tributary of the Río Chota 40 minutes north of Ibarra. Almost all of Chota's residents are *morenos,* black descendants of slaves brought to Ecuador in the 17th century to work the sugar plantations of the coastal lowlands. The *morenos* eventually made their way up the valley of the Ríos Chota and Mira high into the Sierra. A unique culture has evolved in the high valley over the centuries, a blend of African and Andean spiritualism best seen in local dance and music performances. There's not much to do here besides chat with the friendly residents and watch women wash clothes in the river. The municipal tourist office in Ibarra has information on local festivals.

Bolívar

After a steep climb up out of the Río Chota valley, the Pana reaches Bolívar, an attractive young town with many black residents from the nearby valley. If you're looking for a quiet spot well away from other tourists, this is your town. The **Residencia Santa Elena,** tel. 6/289-212, on Julio Andreada just off the main plaza, has rooms with hot water at night for $1. The **Restaurant Los Sauces,** on the Pana where buses drop you off, is the best of a few eateries. The brightly painted church with its crumbling ceiling is worth a look, and there's a market on Friday mornings northwest of it.

The patron of Bolívar's **Santuario del Señor de la Buena Esperanza** is celebrated in a festival of the same name on the first Sunday in May, and the town's own fiesta occurs on 12 November. From Bolívar, good roads lead northwest to El Angel and northeast to San Gabriel and Tulcán.

Gruta la Paz

One of the most famous icons of Ecuador's northern Sierra sits in a natural cave just north of Bolívar. The Gruta la Paz (Peace Grotto), also called Rumichaca, containing a chapel dedicated to the Virgen de Nuestra Señora de la Paz, is dwarfed by a huge natural stone overhang. Stalactites and stalagmites lend the site a gothic atmosphere, which is amplified by the fluttering bats and dark waters of the Río Apaquí. Besides the subterranean chapel, there is a set of thermal baths just outside the cave (baths open Wed.–Sun.) and an inexpensive guest house for pilgrims. Pilgrims fill the cave on weekends and holidays, especially Christmas, Holy Week, and the **Fiesta del Virgen de la Paz** on 8 July. At other times, you can have the bat-filled grotto almost completely to yourself. Private buses can be hired from Bolívar or San Gabriel, and trucks carrying groups leave from San Gabriel and Tulcán on weekends.

San Gabriel

About 20 km north of Bolívar, this district capital earned the status of Centro Historico of Carchi province for its early buildings in the center of town. San Gabriel is an important trading center for legumes and grains grown in the surrounding region, which is also famous for its milk products, especially cheeses. The nude statue of Bolívar in the city center has startled many a stodgy historian. Of the handful of cheap *pensiones* in town, the **Residencial Montúfar,** with its quiet courtyard, is probably the best ($1 with private bath and hot water). Buses between Ibarra and Quito pass through town on the Pana, and trucks to Tulcán leave from the main plaza when full for 50 cents. To walk to the 60-meter **Paluz Waterfall,** take Bolívar north and turn right after the bridge. Taxis will take you the four kms and wait for you for $2, but the road is horrible.

CERRO GOLONDRINAS

Even farther into the northern wilds hides this small cloud forest reserve managed by the **Fundación Golondrinas.** Northwest of Ibarra and El Angel, it protects a wide range of habitats, from *páramo* at 4,000 meters to premontaine forest below 1,500 meters. Birders stand a good chance of adding to life lists here; 210 species of birds have been recorded near Cerro Golondrinas peak (3,120 meters), along with condors in the mountains and toucans and parrots at lower elevations. Sloths, monkeys, and coatimundis hide in the

lower forests, and foxes and deer inhabit the *páramo.*

You can enter the reserve from the bottom via the village of Guallupe, which is near La Carolina on the road to San Lorenzo, or from the top by way of the town of El Angel. One of the best ways to see the reserve is to go on the four-day trek organized by the foundation. This moderately strenuous journey takes you by foot and horse from the *páramo* in El Angel down to the cloud forest and Guallupe ($210 pp, $185 in groups of 5–8).

It's possible to do the trek on your own. Independent travelers can stay in the foundation's **El Tolondro** hostel in Guallupe, tel. 6/648-679, which costs $12 pp per night, including all meals. To get there, ask to be let off the Ibarra-San Lorenzo bus in Guallupe (48 kms from Ibarra), then walk 10 minutes uphill, following the signs. During the trek you can also stay at the foundation's **El Corazon Cloudforest Lodge** at 2,200 meters in the heart of the reserve. It takes four hours to get there (local guides and horses can be arranged at the foundation's office in Guallupe), and it's a bit spartan, with only four bunkbeds, an outhouse, and a fire for cooking, but for $5 pp per night ($15 with all meals), the incredible views from the ridgetop are a steal.

Also along the trek route, the inhabitants of the village of **Moran** on the edge of the *páramo* run the **Cabana de Moran** for $10 pp with all meals, plus the $2 pp entrance fee. For reservations, contact Fernando Calderon, the driver of the local milk truck, at 6/977-274. Requests for information and lodging reservations should be directed to the Casa de Eliza hostal in Quito, preferably via e-mail. The trek is also run by Tropic Ecological Adventures in Quito (see "Tour Operators" in the Quito chapter, or www.tropiceco.com/html/golondrinas.html). If you're pressed for time, the foundation also offers two-day visits to the lower reaches of the reserve from Guallupe for $120 pp.

In addition to managing the reserve, the foundation is deeply involved in local conservation and education issues. Its main goal is to protect the forest from lumber interests and encroachment by settlers. They administer conservation, environmental education, and agroforestry programs in local communities, along with demonstration farms. The foundation accepts visiting scientists as well as short- and long-term **volunteers.** The latter need some experience in horticulture or permaculture techniques and should have a solid grasp of Spanish. Contributions of $240 pp per month are requested for

stays of at least one month, in exchange for room and board.

You can contact the foundation through the Casa Eliza hostel in Quito (Isabel La Católica N24-679, tel. 2/526-926, 226-602, e-mail: manteca@uio.satnet.net, www.ecuadorexplorer .com/golondrinas).

TULCÁN AND THE COLOMBIAN BORDER

Tulcán, the highest provincial capital in the country (3,000 meters), seems like an old shopping mall someone stuck up on a chilly shelf and forgot about. A wintry cold descends at night and lingers well into the morning, making it feel a lot farther than 125 km from the springtime mildness of Ibarra. Tulcán (pop. 45,000) isn't the prettiest of cities, but the amazing topiary gardens in the municipal cemetery can easily occupy an afternoon. Throughout the city, no hedge is left unshaped, in both parks and military bases. For visitors with more time, the high *páramo* road west through Tufiño and Maldonado is unique in Ecuador.

Approximately six kms from Colombia, Tulcán bustles as only a border town can. You can buy anything here, from shoes, leather jackets, and Otavalan weavings to toasters, VCRs, and chainsaws. It's also shifty as only a border town can be; without something to buy or sell you might feel somewhat out of place, and you

should take care walking around at night. The city used to thrive on smuggling, but since the 1992 free-trade agreement with Ecuador's northern neighbor, Tulcán's main source of commercial revenue is the busloads of Colombians crossing the border to take advantage of Ecuador's lower prices.

SIGHTS

Local resident José Franco started the famous topiary works in Tulcán's **municipal cemetery** decades ago. Today Franco is buried amid the splendor of his creations in what is called the Escultura en Verde del Campo Santo (Sculpture in Green of the Holy Field), under an epitaph that calls his creation "a cemetery so beautiful it invites one to die." Monumental cypresses have been trained and trimmed into figures out of Roman, Greek, Inca, and Aztec mythology, interspersed with

topiary in the municipal cemetery

TIM BEWER

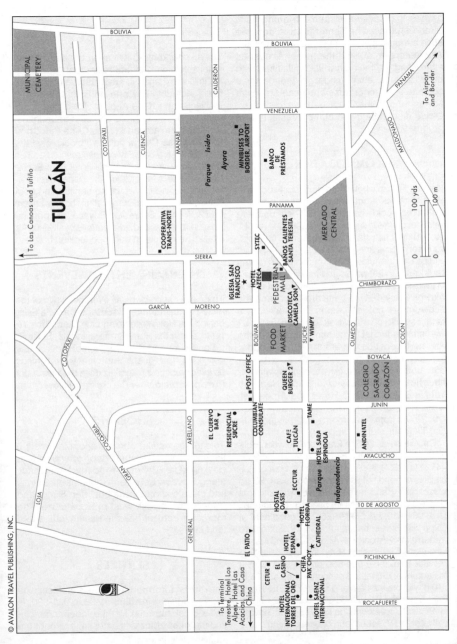

© AVALON TRAVEL PUBLISHING, INC.

TULCÁN

To Las Canoas and Tufiño

To Airport and Border

MUNICIPAL CEMETERY

BOLIVIA
BOLIVIA
CALDERÓN
VENEZUELA
PANAMA
MANABI
CUENCA
COTOPAXI

Parque Isidro Ayora

MINIBUSES TO BORDER, AIRPORT

BANCO DE PRÉSTAMOS

COOPERATIVA TRANS-NORTE

SIERRA

SYTEC

BAÑOS CALIENTES SANTA TERESIA

MERCADO CENTRAL

IGLESIA SAN FRANCISCO

HOTEL AZTECA

PEDESTRIAN MALL

DISCOTECA CAMELA SON

CHIMBORAZO

MORENO

GARCÍA

FOOD MARKET

WIMPY

BOLÍVAR

SUCRE

OLMEDO

COLÓN

BOYACÁ

POST OFFICE

QUEEN BURGER 2

COLEGIO SAGRADO CORAZÓN

ARELLANO

EL CUERVO BAR

RESIDENCIAL SUCRE

COLUMBIAN CONSULATE

CAFÉ TULCÁN

TAME

JUNÍN

ANDINATEL

GENERAL

ECCTUR

HOTEL SARA ESPINDOLA

AYACUCHO

HOSTAL OASIS

Parque Independencia

HOTEL FLORIDA

10 DE AGOSTO

EL PATIO

HOTEL ESPAÑA

CATHEDRAL

PICHINCHA

CETUR

EL CASINO

CHIFA PAK CHOY

To Terminal Terrestre, Hotel Los Alpes, Hotel Las Acacias, and Casa China

HOTEL INTERNACIONAL TORRES DEL ORO

HOTEL SAENZ INTERNACIONAL

ROCAFUERTE

COTOPAXI
COLOMBIA
GRAN COLOMBIA
LOJA

100 yds
100 m
0
0

arches, passageways, and intriguing geometric shapes. The cemetery has become such a tourist attraction that vendors sell film and ice cream outside the gates. Almost as interesting are the high white walls filled with burial spaces, each just large enough for a coffin to enter lengthwise and decorated with flowers and mementos. Needless to say, exercise discretion if a burial procession is in progress.

ACCOMMODATIONS

None of Tulcán's hotels are particularly notable. Double-check if hot water is available and at what time—cold showers at 10°C are up there with root canals in my book. On weekend nights, most hotels fill with shoppers from Colombia, so reservations are a good idea.

The **Residencial Sucre** on Junín has rooms for $1 pp with hot water, and funky red couches in the sitting area. The thin-walled **Hostal Oasis** may be noisy, but the beds are comfy and the showers are hot (at least in the morning); a room costs $2 pp with private bath and TV, or $1 with shared bath. On the same block near the Parque Independencia are the **Hotel Florida,** tel. 6/983-849, and the **Hotel España,** tel. 6/983-860, both with decent private rooms with 24-hour hot water for less than $3 pp. Near the Terminal Terrestre, the **Hotel Los Alpes,** tel. 6/982-235, and the **Hotel Las Acacias,** tel. 6/982-501, both have rooms with private bath and TV for less than $3 pp.

Down the Pasaje San Francisco between Bolívar and Atahualpa, the **Hotel Azteca,** tel. 6/981-447 or 981-899, fax 6/980-481, is the best of Tulcán's lower-end hotels. The 52 rooms are $3 pp with cable TV, and there's a disco downstairs (light sleepers beware). The **Hotel Saenz Internacional,** tel. 6/981-916, fax 6/983-925, is a good deal at $5 pp with private bath and cable TV. Suites are available for $8, along with a bar, disco, and restaurant. Across Sucre is the **Hotel Internacional Torres del Oro,** tel. 6/984-660 or 984-670, with a restaurant and guarded parking. Rates are $6 s, $10 d with private bath and cable TV. The **Hotel Sara Espindola,** tel. 6/985-925, 6/986-209, is entered off Sucre. Rooms go for $7 pp with private bath, cable TV, sauna, and private parking.

FOOD

Tulcán's food picks are even thinner than its hotel selection. Several restaurants specializing in Colombian food are scattered throughout town, including **El Patio** on Bolívar between Pichincha and 10 de Agosto, with a tiled courtyard decorated with old photos and antiques. Set meals are around $1. The **Chifa Pak Choy** and the **Casa China,** both two blocks past the terminal, serve up tasty *chaulafans* for $1. The **Cafe Tulcán** across from the Hotel Sara Espindola is perfect for reading the paper over coffee and ice cream, while the service and trout dinner at the **Queen Burger 2** are both excellent for $2. **Wimpy,** Sucre and Boyacá, is a popular place for burgers and grilled meats of all kinds for $1–2. They also turn out good-looking pizzas.

ENTERTAINMENT AND EVENTS

There are dance clubs all over town; two of the more popular are the **Discoteca Camela Son,** behind the Hotel Azteca, and the **Discoteca Titanic,** under the Hotel Sara Espindola. **El Casino** on Sucre and Pichincha is open every day until 3 A.M. The **Fiesta Municipal** warms things up every year on 11 April, as does the **Fiesta del Provincilización del Carchi** on 19 November.

SHOPPING

Tulcán seems like one big shopping mall; it seems that every other door opens onto a clothing store. The main **food market** spreads along Boyacá between Bolívar and Sucre, and there's another one between Sucre and Olmedo two blocks west of Rocafuerte. The **mercado central** has the usual clothes and food stalls.

SERVICES

The **tourist information office** is on Pichincha on the 2nd floor. **Andinatel,** tel. 6/981-300, is half a block from the Parque Independencia, and the **post office** sits across the street from the food market on Bolívar. A host of exchange houses and sidewalk money changers along Ayacucho are happy to transform your dollars into pesos. Rates are better in Tulcán proper than at the border or in Colombia. The **Banco de Pichincha,** Sucre and 10 de Agosto, and the **Banco de Préstamos** on Parque Ayora change travelers' checks. If your hotel doesn't have them, hot showers are available at the public **Baños Calientes Santa Teresita** for 20 cents pp. You can hop on the Internet at **C@fenet,** one block south of the terminal, for $1 per hour, or at **Sytec,** Atahualpa 6-099 and Bolí, 4th floor.

TRANSPORTATION

Buses

The **Terminal Terrestre** is at the annoyingly far southern end of Tulcán—either a 50-cent taxi ride or a 30-minute walk from the main plaza. It's surrounded by restaurants and has an Andinatel branch inside. Being the only northern border town, Tulcán has buses leaving for just about every major city in the country, including Quito ($2.50, 5–6 hours), Ibarra ($1.25, 2–3 hours), and even an *ejecutivo* to Huaquillas ($10, 18 hours).

In town, **Cooperativa Trans-Norte** buses depart hourly to Tufiño (20 cents, one hour) in the morning and when full in the afternoon. They also send buses to Chical ($1.50, five hours) daily at noon, and at 1 P.M. on Mon.–Thurs. and Sun., and 11 A.M. on Thurs. *Collectivos* run to the border and the airport from the Parque Isidro Ayora when full.

Air

The **TAME** office next to the Hotel Sara Espindola sells tickets to Quito (Mon.–Fri., $12 one-way), Guayaquil (Mon.–Fri., $20 one-way), and Calí, Colombia ($70 one-way). The airport is two km north on the road to the border; a taxi costs $1 each way.

COLOMBIAN BORDER

Seven km north of Tulcán, a bridge over the Río Carchi marks the border with Colombia. It's open around the clock and crawls with moneychangers. Keep your eyes open if you decide to change money on either side of the border; official Ecuadorian changers should have photo IDs. Try to know the rate beforehand, and rates for groups or for larger amounts may be better. There's an ATM on the Colombian side and an Andinatel office back on the other side, open Mon.–Fri. 8 A.M.–6 P.M.

Exit formalities from Ecuador are relatively straightforward, if less orderly, than in Colombia. Direct any questions to the **Ecuadorian immigration office,** tel. 6/980-704 (open 24 hours), or alternately, the **Ministerio de Turismo** office, tel. 6/983-892, in the CENAF buildings at the bridge, open Mon.–Fri. 8:30 A.M.–1 P.M. and 1:30–5 P.M.

Taxis from Tulcán to the border cost $2 one-way, and microbuses leave from the Parque Isidro Ayora when full for 40 cents. On the Colombian side, it's 13 km to Ipiales, and *collectivos* make the trip regularly for 600 pesos. Buses run from Ipiales to Pasto, 90 km farther (500 pesos, two hours).

WEST OF TULCÁN

The road west from Tulcán follows the Río San Juan (called the Mayasquer in Colombia), which serves as the international border much of the way to the ocean. This unspoiled area has been described as even more beautiful than the El Angel Reserve because it's even more remote. Condors circle over kilometers of untouched *páramo* and cloud forest all the way to El Chical, where the driveable road ends. Because there aren't too many hotels out this way, consider camping out near Volcán Chiles or the Lagunas Verdes. Exposure is a very real danger, so be sure to pack a tent, waterproof clothing, and *warm* sleeping bags.

After passing the Tres Chorros swimming pool one km west of Tulcán, the bone-rattling road passes through a hilly landscape dominated by agriculture. Farther down the road is a spot called **Las Canoas,** near an island in the gently meandering Río Bobo, lined with pines and wildflowers. Alfonso Castillo hires boats starting at 20 cents pp for 30 minutes. When the bus drops you off, follow the dirt track, and when the path forks, take the upper route. Bring a picnic lunch—a combination of this and a visit to the cemetery make a relaxing day. There is a military checkpoint just before Tufiño.

Tufiño

Thermal baths bubbling up from the smoldering core of Volcán Chiles are the main attraction of this town, 18 km from Tulcán. There aren't any places to stay in Tufiño, but you can get a meal in the market or at one of several small *viveres* shops. A restaurant/discoteca is open on weekends. Bring your passport to cross the border to the pools.

The **Balnearios Aguas Termales** are actually in Colombia, but crossing for the day should be no problem. The three-km walk there isn't difficult, but asking for directions couldn't hurt. Cross the border and look for the large green sign, where you head left. Admission to the warm pools is free.

To get to the **Aguas Hediondas** ("stinking waters") pools—the hottest and most scenic—head west from Tufiño on a dirt road for three kms, then turn to the right at the old sign and go another eight kms into a beautiful, remote valley. Several buses a day connect Tulcán with Tufiño, but only the noon one goes up this dirt road to the turnoff. A direct bus to the pools leaves from in front of Tulcán's cathedral on Sunday at 8 A.M. A truck there will cost you $2, and the driver will wait for you.

Past Tufiño, the road enters the El Angel Reserve and climbs the lower reaches of Volcán Chiles, approaching on the right. The higher the road winds, the more windswept and impressive the *páramo* becomes. You'll pass at least five waterfalls on the way to the town of **Maldonado,** some within a short walk of the road. Untouched cloud forest and pre-Inca ruins can be found near the Río La Plata before Maldonado, on the left-hand side of the road. The town has at least one basic hotel.

Volcán Chiles

Climb this summit (4,768 meters) and you can stand with one foot each in Colombia and Ecuador because Chiles' peak pokes right through the border. The scenery is unusual, even for Ecuador: rough and strange and studded with alien-looking *frailejón* plants. The weather is the main concern in the otherwise straightforward ascent. Dress for rain and snow and get ready to be clouded in most mornings. Guides can occasionally be found in Tufiño.

The trailhead is about 20 km and 30 minutes past Tufiño, where the road crosses a saddle near a small concrete shed on the left with a "22" painted on it. A private truck to the trailhead from Tufiño costs 20 cents, or you can hop off a bus to Maldonado or El Chical. From the trailhead, a faint trail leads north, topping a low ridge in the direction of the summit. After about 20 minutes, you'll reach a small lake in a flat, boggy section with a good camping spot on the side nearest the summit. This is a good place to spend the night before or after the climb.

The faint trail continues across the boggy flat and up a shallow gully toward the mountain and near a stream, eventually following small but frequent cairns. Head slightly left along a gently sloping ridge leading uphill to the right. Follow this to a sulfur-green lake about one hour up, pass the lake to the right, and climb up a well-defined ridge. The rocks become steep and loose—a short rope might be helpful here, and it's definitely treacherous when wet or snowy. The climb from the road to the peak and back takes about six hours. The IGM 1:50,000 map *Tufiño and Volcán Chiles* is helpful, but it may be hard to buy because of border restrictions.

BOB RACE

CENTRAL SIERRA
INTRODUCTION

Quito and Cuenca are the bookends enclosing the Avenue of the Volcanoes—that perpetually impressive stretch of real estate that makes up the bulk of Ecuador's mountainous spine. Strung along the Panamerican Highway like beads on a string, large colonial cities rest beneath soaring peaks. Each city is tucked into its own basin valley, and farmland fills in most of the level space in between. The more remote and spectacular areas, fully stocked with volcanoes, lakes, and rivers, have been set aside as parks or reserves.

Whether you're seeing how far that dirt road goes past the next village or hiking a well-worn trail around the base of a volcano, you can't beat the scenery, air, and just plain open space that permeates this part of the Sierra. Cotopaxi park sees the most traffic in the Ecuadorian Andes, while it's likely no one has seen some parts of sprawling Sangay park in centuries. If climbing 5,000-meter peaks isn't your thing, give a thought to the popular Inca trail to Ingapirca, Ecuador's only major Inca ruin, or the legendary lost gold of the difficult Llanganati range.

More sedate diversions also beckon. Several fine old haciendas offer luxury accommodations with a colonial twist, such as the famous La Ciénega near Cotopaxi park. Indigenous markets range from the authentic bustle of Saquisilí and Zumbahua to anything-goes spreads in Ambato and Riobamba. A stop in the resort town of Baños is compulsory for most travelers.

The Land

The Avenue of the Volcanoes, Alexander von Humboldt's 19th-century nickname for this part of Ecuador, stuck for good reason. You can't go 10 minutes in the central Sierra without finding your gaze drawn upward to a snowy slope along the intermountain avenue, from wide, confident Chimborazo to wrinkled Rumiñahui, lurking in the shadow of Cotopaxi. The Pana climbs and descends the spurs separating each valley from its neighbors to the north and south. Rivers tumble and join to drain the Andean snows into either the Amazon or the Gulf of Guayaquil, and glacier lakes sparkle in the farther reaches.

The People

Home to roughly half of Ecuador's total population, the central Sierra is farmed on almost every available acre. Large plantations hearken back to the days when forced labor supported farms stretching beyond the horizon. Small communities in the mountains plant crops as high as 4,000 meters, supplementing their income through shepherding and crafts.

The central Sierra has always been the most dyed-in-the-wool indigenous region of Ecuador. During their reign, the Incas established outposts all along the road to Quito to keep the local populations in line. Today, three-quarters of Chimborazo province considers itself of native descent. Dozens of different groups inhabit the highlands, often each in its own town. Clothes and customs are the most distinguishing characteristics, from the white and black garments of the Salasacas to the white-fringed red ponchos of the Quisapinchas.

Getting Around

Once again, the Pana ties everything together, stretching from Quito to Cuenca with barely a turn east or west. Side roads spill down from the hills in both directions; toward Santo Domingo and Quevedo to the west and Puyo to the east. The train route from Quito to Riobamba has fallen into disuse, but the famous rail spur west of Alausí, including the hair-raising switchbacks of the Devil's Nose, is still running, if barely, and well worth a detour.

MACHACHI AND VICINITY

After the ugly urban sprawl immediately south of Quito, this quiet, pretty little city is an oasis. The small valley it occupies is surrounded by peaks in almost every direction; face north toward the Volcán Atacazo and rotate to the right to see Pasochoa to the northeast, Sincholagua to the east, Rumiñahui to the south, the Ilinizas to the southwest, and Corazón to the west. Machachi is a good base for climbing any of these volcanoes.

Machachi's central plaza is surrounded by an ornate painted church, the Teatro Municipal, and a handful of mediocre restaurants. A few scattered leather shops sell clothes and shoes, and the main market day is Sunday.

Sights

Machachi's main tourist attraction is the **Güitig factory** four km out of town to the east. Mineral-water pools take on a slightly different meaning here—this is the same stuff, more or less, that comes in those chipped glass bottles all over Ecuador. The three crystal-clear pools (two cold, one lukewarm) just past the bottling plant are set among gorgeous flower gardens, picnic areas, and sports facilities, and tours of the plant itself are available on weekdays (ask the guards at the entrance). Taxis to the plant cost 80 cents one-way, or you can just walk east on Pareja out of town, following it as it turns into Ricardo Salvador about halfway to the factory, which is open daily 7 A.M.–4 P.M., 20 cents pp.

Accommodations

The only passable place in town to spend the night is the **Hotel La Estancia Real,** Cordero and Panzaleo, tel. 3/315-760 or 315-393. It was opened in 1999 on the south end of town—head two blocks south of Plaza on Colón, then west a few more blocks on Barriaga and look for the sign. Rooms with private bath, TV, and hot water are only $5, with Rumiñahui right out the window, almost close enough to touch.

Transportation

Any bus running south along the Pana can drop you off at one of the two entrances to Machachi, leaving you with a two-km walk into town. Buses from Quito run from the Terminal Terrestre, and more often from the trolley's southern station (30 cents, one hour). Buses back to Quito leave from Amazonas, one block west of the plaza (if you want to go to the Terminal Terrestre, make sure to ask if your bus is going all the way there). Taxis can be hired to take you up the rough roads to the bases of nearby mountains; one-way to Cotopaxi runs about $20.

ILINIZA ECOLOGICAL RESERVE

Set aside none too soon in 1996, this 149,000-hectare reserve consists of three separate parts enclosing its twin namesake peaks, Cerro Corazón, Laguna Quilotoa, and a significant chunk of cloud forest. No infrastructure, publicity, or true protection has yet been implemented, however, making one wonder where exactly the $5 pp entrance fee goes.

For information on the laguna and the western part of the reserve near Chugchilán and Zumbahua, see the "Latacunga Loop" section.

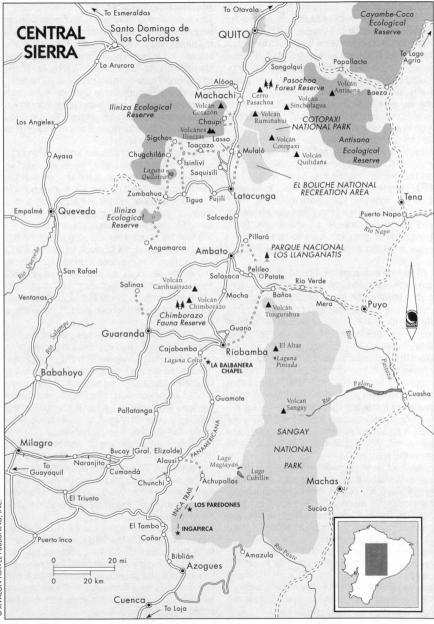

CENTRAL SIERRA

Volcán Corazón

A short distance west of Machachi across the Pana sits this extinct volcano, first climbed in 1738 by Charles-Marie de La Condamine on a break from measuring the planet. At 4,788 meters, Corazón is a challenging day climb, consisting mostly of easy uphill hiking through grassy fields, with some moderate rock scrambling at the top. With a 4WD vehicle you can drive to within two hours of the top. You'll need permission to enter the park with a vehicle.

The road toward the peak leaves the Pana through the town of Aloasí. Follow the cobbled road west, zigging right at the railway station and hotel following the train tracks for 100 meters. Turn left and cross the tracks onto a dirt road that winds up toward the mountain. You'll pass through a tree farm (the tallest trees on this side of Corazón) to a T in the road. From here continue straight ahead on foot through a break in the fence, or to the right up the dirt track if you're driving.

The foot trail continues uphill, crossing the dirt track every so often as it cuts wide switchbacks toward the peak. Following the road eventually becomes easier than wading through the grass. The road ends at the base of the rocky nipple forming Corazón's peak. Hike through the spongy *páramo* up to the right toward the saddle between the main peak and a smaller one to the right, reaching a sandy gully topped by large boulders. From here all that stands between you and the peak is about 500 meters of moderate rock climbing—not for the faint of heart because a few meters to your right is an almost sheer drop-off. Be careful of loose rock. A few faint arrows and rock cairns mark the way.

An hour or so of climbing brings you to the highest, southern peak, a flat area marked by graffiti with a 360-degree view of the surrounding mountains. Count on about 5–6 hours of hiking from the Pana. If you descend at sunset, you can watch Corazón's shadow climb through the fiery light bathing the peaks to the east. A taxi from Machachi can drop you off partway up the road (usually near the tree farm) for about $5, cutting the ascent time by 1–2 hours. Corazón can also be approached from the north, a longer trip beginning three km west of Alóag along the road to Santo Domingo.

Approaching the Ilinizas

The sister peaks are remnants of what used to be one volcano. *Iliniza* means male mountain in Quechua and refers more to Iliniza Sur, the larger of the two. By this logic, Iliniza Norte should technically be called *Tioniza,* or female mountain. The adjoining peaks are like night and day for climbers. Iliniza Sur's ice walls, glacier, and crevasses are a world apart from Iliniza Norte's rocky scrambles. Iliniza Sur is a good introduction to Ecuador's more difficult peaks higher than 5,000 meters.

The approach to both leads from the Pana to a hut on the saddle separating the two peaks. Ten km south of Machachi, look for a bridge over the Jambelí creek. The turnoff is 100 meters north of the bridge and leads seven km southwest across the train tracks to the village of El Chaupi. Buses run to El Chaupi from Machachi as well.

Three km beyond the village, you'll hit the **Hacienda San José del Chaupi,** tel. 9/713-986, a working farm that provides a good base to climb any of the peaks in the area. Rooms with hot water, kitchen, and fireplace cost $10 pp, with continental breakfast included. Horses are available for rent for $5 per hour and $25 for an entire day.

From El Chaupi, a dirt road passes the Hacienda El Refugio and leads to the parking area at the shrine of La Virgen, 16 km from the Pana. (Please leave your vehicle here if you're driving yourself because driving beyond this point has caused severe erosion in the fragile *páramo* and polylepis forest above.) A trail leads uphill to the southeast from La Virgen to the Nuevos Horizontes hut at 4,700 meters, only about 500 meters below either peak and one of the oldest mountaineering huts in Ecuador. It can accommodate about 24 people and features bunk beds, stoves, and cooking and eating utensils. One of the 13 beds will cost you $7 pp per night (beware of overcharging), and water is available from a nearby stream.

It's a good idea to check at the Nuevos Horizontes club office in Machachi, across the street from the buses to El Chaupi, about paying the fee and seeing if you might need the key to unlock the hut. Vladimir Gallo, tel. 2/314-927, can be contacted for information and reservations as well. La Ensillada, the saddle between the peaks, is above the hut.

Iliniza Sur

The higher and more difficult of the two, Iliniza Sur (5,265 meters) is the sixth-highest peak in Ecuador. Besides El Altar, Iliniza Sur was the only mountain in Ecuador that Edward Whymper couldn't climb, although he tried twice. The trusty Carrel brothers, though, kept the 1880 expedition a success by reaching the summit on their own. The first Ecuadorian climber reached the top in 1950.

Even experienced mountaineers will find Iliniza Sur challenging. Ice-climbing experience and equipment is mandatory, with front-pointing necessary on some pitches. The ascent is easiest after a recent snowfall because a dry spell can make the slopes even steeper and icier. The route from La Ensillada heads left across moraines to a glacier. After crossing a flat section known as La Terraza (the terrace), the route follows a wide couloir. It can be slippery, necessitating ice-screw protection. If the couloir is too icy, an alternate ascent via the slope to the right is possible. The peak is 3–4 hours from the refuge.

Many alternate routes are possible from the east and the south, including the rocky Celso Zuquillo route on the east ridge and the difficult South Ridge route, first climbed in 1973.

Iliniza Norte

Ecuador's eighth-highest peak (5,126 meters) was one of the few in the country to be first climbed by Ecuadorians—in this case, by Nicolás Martínez and Alexandro Villavicencio, accompanied by an Australian climber in 1912. In the dry season, technical equipment and experience is not necessary, making Iliniza Norte accessible part of the year to hardy hikers undaunted by some minor rock climbing. Some small snowfields may be found along the way (usually Nov.–June), but the largest obstacle is the thin air—one night in the hut is still not enough acclimatization for some. The relentless uphill route from La Ensillada follows a ridge to a vertical rock wall. Skirt the wall to the right for access to the summit, 2–3 hours from the hut.

MACHACHI TO LATACUNGA

VOLCÁN SINCHOLAGUA

Twenty-five km directly east of Machachi as the condor flies, Sincholagua can be reached from Cotopaxi park or from the north. From the park, pass Lago Limpiopungo and the turnoff for the Cotopaxi refuges, crossing a small bridge straight ahead on the park road north of Cerro Pamba (4,065 meters). After five km, a trail leads back to the left (northwest), crossing the Río Pita and the northern park boundary. Look for a trail up the ridge heading northeast toward the base of Sincholagua's rocky peak. It's about a three-hour hike across the *páramo* from the park boundary to the base. Four-wheel-drive vehicles can continue as high as a parking area at 4,200 meters.

Reaching Sincholagua from the north requires braving a maze of trails, roads, and tracks south of Sangolquí. From Quito, turn off the road to Pifo 6–7 km east of Sangolquí, heading south through the villages of Pintag (five km) and Rafael Delgado (12–13 km). The road continues southeast, more toward Antisana than Sincholagua,

so you'll want to leave the road near the Lagunas Quingray, Tipa Pugru, and Secas and continue southwest toward Sincholagua. Access is also possible through the village of Rumipamba, south of Sangolquí. From there a few tracks lead to salt and rock mines at over 4,000 meters on Sincholagua's northern flank. (A new access road through the Antisana Ecological Reserve to the north may offer a clearer access.)

Sincholagua's north peak is highest (4,919 meters) and was first climbed by Whymper and the Carrels in 1880. The climb is mainly a scramble, with loose, rotten rock at the summit making a helmet a good idea. Descend by downclimbing or rappelling. The south peak (4,780 meters) remained unconquered until 1974. The 12-hour ascent begins in a small valley on the east face of the southern peak and requires aid climbing and a bivouac.

Hiking from Sincholagua east to Volcán Antisana, via the Laguna de Mica, then north to El Tango near Papallacta is a good two- to three-day expedition, part of the longer Trek del Condor (see special topic). Get permission from Sr.

Delgado to cross the Hacienda Pimantura along the way (see "Antisana Ecological Reserve" under "Quito to Baeza" in the Oriente chapter). The IGM 1:100,000 *Pintag* map covers Volcánes Sincholagua, Antisana, and Papallacta.

COTOPAXI NATIONAL PARK

Ecuador's premier Andean park, within a few hours of Quito, covers the intersection of Pichincha, Cotopaxi, and Napo provinces. Cotopaxi is the most popular national park on the Ecuadorian mainland, second only to the Galápagos in total number of visitors annually. Inside the 33,400 stunning hectares, you'll find the park's namesake volcano, one of the most beautiful in the Americas, along with two other peaks higher than 4,700 meters. Wild horses gallop between the mountains over grassy *páramo* dotted with wildflowers.

Flora and Fauna

Wet montane forests fill Cotopaxi's lowest altitudes, which are characterized by short trees and bushes. There's not much of this zone left, but what does remain ranges from 3,400 to about 4,000 meters. Subalpine *páramo* covers everything between 4,000 and 4,500 meters, which is where you'll find most of the park's animals: puma, dwarf deer, *páramo* rabbits, and the endemic marsupial mouse. Even casual birders will probably spot carunculated caracaras, shrike-and ground-tyrants, great thrushes, rufous-naped brush finches, Andean gulls, and brown-backed chattyrants (related to flycatchers). American coots, speckled teals, and pintail ducks flock around the park's lakes, while Andean lapwings claim the shoreline. Above it all soars the occasional condor.

Many of the plant species in the *páramo* grasslands have relatives in North America because Ecuador's high altitudes simulate the northern hemisphere's higher latitudes. Shrubby blueberries and lupines bloom next to Indian paintbrushes and members of the daisy family, while the occasional terrestrial bromeliad is probably pollinated by hummingbirds. You might spot the *urcu rosa,* a small blue mountain rose, hidden among the tough *tortora* grass used by locals to weave mats. Above 4,500 meters to the snow-

line at 4,700 meters, plunging temperatures keep the mossy tussocks of the alpine tundra relatively empty.

Access

A badly rutted road runs southeast from Machachi to enter the park from the north, but to reach the main entrances to Cotopaxi, head farther down the Pana. There are two turnoffs. The first, 16 km south of Machachi, is also the entrance to El Boliche National Recreation Area. It passes the CLIRSEN satellite tracking station before forking three ways. Take the right-hand fork, then follow the train tracks for 500 meters. From here it's six km downhill through a forest to a campsite with fireplaces and minimal shelters. One km farther is the Raúl Daule campsite, with water available from a nearby river.

The second turnoff to the main entrance from the Pana is nine km farther south and is marked by a cement billboard. This is the best of all the entrances and sees the most traffic, making it easier to hitch a ride into the park (although it does wash out occasionally in the rainy season). It joins with the other Pana access road at the park boundary, where you pay the entrance fee ($10 pp from July–Sept., $7 pp otherwise) at the gate, which is open daily.

The road through the park curves in a semicircle north around Volcán Cotopaxi. As it heads northeast, it passes the administrative center at Campamiento Mariscal Sucre, 10 km from the gate (5–6 hours by foot from the Raúl Daule campsite). A small museum has exhibits on the geology, history, and flora and fauna of the park. Shortly beyond the museum, you'll reach the Llanura de Limpiopungo, a wide plain at 3,800 meters between Cotopaxi and Rumiñahui. The birding along the shore of **Lago Limpiopungo** is excellent.

On a small hill 15 km beyond the lake are the ruins of **El Salitre,** formerly an Inca *pucara* (fortress). A large oval perimeter wall encloses the small dwellings of guards and officials who once manned the outpost. Competition for this scenic assignment was probably fierce, but the spectacular views of Cotopaxi, Rumiñahui, Sincholagua, and Pasochoa weren't enough to make up for Cotopaxi's constant eruptions—El Salitre was all but abandoned by the arrival of the Spanish.

A trail leads around the lake to the northwest for access to Rumiñahui. Shortly beyond that trail, another jeep track heads south nine km to the Cotopaxi refuge. After joining the road from Machachi, the park road eventually crosses the eastern park boundary, passing north of Cerro Chuguilasín Chico. Ten km outside the boundary, the road meets the Río Tambo and a hacienda of the same name near the base of Quilindaña. The IGM 1:50,000 *Cotopaxi, Mulaló, Machachi* and *Sincholagua* maps cover the park.

Volcán Cotopaxi

Cotopaxi's shape is the most beautiful and regular of all the colossal peaks in the high Andes. It is a perfect cone covered by a thick blanket of snow which shines so brilliantly at sunset it seems detached from the azure of the sky.

—Alexander von Humboldt

Tack another 2,000 meters onto the perfect conical point of Japan's Mount Fuji and stick it in the middle of the Andes, and you'll have a good picture of Volcán Cotopaxi (5,897 meters). There's some debate as to whether this famous mountain is the highest active volcano in the world, but it's definitely in the top three. The name means "neck of the moon" in Quechua.

It's hard to believe this beautiful peak is also one of Ecuador's most historically destructive volcanoes. The first recorded eruption disrupted a battle between the Spanish and the Inca in 1534, and eruptions in 1742 and 1768 flattened Latacunga, killing hundreds of people. A deceptively quiet century followed before the volcano began to belch again in 1853. The latter half of the 19th century saw many eruptions, including one in 1877 that sent a *lahar* (landslide of earth and melted ice) all the way to the Pacific, leveling Latacunga again for good measure. The 20th century was relatively quiet, with only about two dozen minor murmurings.

A German and Colombian climbing team first set foot on Cotopaxi's glacier-covered peak in 1872, followed 10 years later by Edward Whymper, who opened the northern route still in use today. The climb is not difficult, as the many climbers who scale the ice-covered slopes regularly will attest. Crevasses are usually large and obvious, making the climb mostly an uphill slog; however, it's not for the inexperienced—technical equipment is necessary (ice axes, crampons, ropes, and marker wands), along with the services of a guide or experienced climber who is fully up to date on the changing glacier conditions.

Although Cotopaxi can be climbed year-round—it sees more clear days than almost any other peak in the Ecuadorian Andes—the best months are December and January. August and September are also good but windy. Feb.–Apr. can be clear and dry as well, whereas Aug.–Dec. is usually windy and cloudy. Acclimatization is essential, either by spending a week or two in Quito or by climbing a shorter peak or two beforehand.

The road to the refuges heads south from the main park road for nine km to the parking area at 4,600 meters. A half-hour hike up a steep, sandy trail brings you to the José Ribas refuge, which was built in 1971 by the San Gabriel Climbing Club, stands at 4,800 meters, and is adminis-

climbing Cotopaxi

JULIAN SMITH

tered by Alta Montaña in Quito (tel. 2/254-798). The two-story shelter is fully equipped with 70 bunk beds, cooking facilities, running water, snacks and water for sale, and lockable storage space for gear. A night's stay is $10 pp.

The country's most popular refuge, strangely, was built in a gully prone to avalanches. A surprise slide on Easter Sunday in 1996 buried dozens of day trippers in the uphill courtyard, killing 11 people. Safety measures have been suggested to reduce the possibility of future disasters, but so far nothing has been done.

The only major obstacle in the standard north-face route is a towering rock wall below the summit known as Yanasacha (large black rock). Most climbers bypass this wall to the right and continue up left to the peak. The open crater peak, anywhere from 6–10 hours' climb from the refuge, contains smoking fumaroles reeking of sulfur. Leave the refuge between midnight and 2 A.M., and plan on 3–6 hours for the descent. An alternate route scales Cotopaxi's south side near Morurcu. Regardless, try to be off the snow by 10 A.M.

A hike completely around Cotopaxi's 20-km base is an ambitious undertaking. Follow the park road clockwise to the eastern border, then follow the Río Tambo upstream to the southwest after crossing the park boundary. From there head west, passing north of Quilindaña to eventually reach the Pana. The full circuit can take up to one week.

Volcán Rumiñahui

This homely mass 13 km northwest of Cotopaxi was named after Atahualpa's stoic general (who in turn takes his name from the Quechua "rumi," meaning stone, plus "ñawi," for eye). The straightforward climb is a mixture of uphill hike and scramble, but because the quality of rock can be poor, a rope and climbing protection is recommended for the more exposed stretches. Rumiñahui has three peaks: the northern, highest peak (4,712 meters), a southern peak (erroneously labeled Rumiñahui Central on the IGM map), and a central peak.

The east side of Rumiñahui is reached through Cotopaxi park along tracks that skirt Lago Limpiopungo to the north or south. A path toward the central peak is clearly visible along a well-defined ridge. From the lake to the base is about a two-hour hike, and camping along the way is possible. The route to the central peak follows a sandy stretch up to the east known as the "W" for its peculiar shape. It can be snowy or wet and slippery on occasion. The south peak involves some moderate technical rock climbing (class 5.5). Traverse south-southeast to a ridge joining the central and southern peaks, then head south to gain the peak. The northern peak is reached by following the central-southern connecting ridge to the north. The IGM 1:50,000 Machachi and Sincholagua maps cover this area.

Volcán Morurcu

This smaller cousin to Cotopaxi sprouts out of its larger neighbor's southern flank, true to its name (seed hill). First climbed in 1972, Morurcu (4,881 meters) is also known as Picacho or Cabeza de Inca (Inca Head). The ascent involves some moderate rock pitches, so climbers should take a helmet, rope, and climbing gear.

Morurcu is approached from the south by a route that can also be used to set up an attempt on Cotopaxi's southern slopes. Turn off the Pana 85 km south of Quito toward Mulaló south of the Hacienda La Ciénega. Head east on a dirt road, taking a left at the first junction and a right at the second, 200 meters beyond. At the town of San Ramón, you'll pass a soccer field on the right as you follow a dry river bed. Turn left at the next junction, pass the church, and take a sharp right through low gates.

You'll pass a water treatment plant before reaching Rancho María, about one hour's drive from the highway. You may be able to leave your car here if you get the owners' permission. Four-wheel-drive vehicles and hikers can continue on a dirt track that leads up the valley. Halfway up is the last spot to get water, a small dammed spring. The valley opens onto plains, with Cotopaxi to the left and Morurcu to the right. You'll notice a large, distinctive rock on a small ridge between the two. To climb Cotopaxi, pass the rock on the left and continue down the other side into a deep valley, where you can camp at about 4,400 meters. The route gains the ridge to the right of the campsite and isn't too technical if the weather cooperates.

To climb Morurcu, aim directly for the rock, continuing over and down the ridge to the south. The ascent itself leads up a 20-meter, class 5 wall that tops out to a wide terrace. A series of small channels descend from the peak to the south-southeast. The peak consists of third- or fourth-grade rock surrounded by a sandy area, which is surmounted from the north. From the bottom to the peak takes about five hours.

Volcán Quilindaña

At the mouth of the Valle Vicioso (Vicious Valley), Quilindaña carries an air of mystery. The name means "it is cold there" in a pre-Inca language, and climactic conditions keep it almost perpetually shrouded in clouds. Consequently, Quilindaña was first climbed only in 1956, and infrequently since then. Nonetheless it's one of the more challenging rock routes in the country. A helmet, rope, and crampons are vital.

Quilindaña sits just outside the Cotopaxi park boundary to the southeast and is reached by following the park road north and around Volcán Cotopaxi to the park border. Even with a car, this is at least a two-day trip. The Hacienda El Tambo sits along the Río Tambo outside the southeastern corner of the park. It's about five hours from the Hacienda El Tambo southeast to the foot of the mountain, where you'll want to set up camp.

The Northern (Bermeo) Route follows the northwest ridge up old moraines and erratic rocks, with some mild stretches of technical rock climbing. The ridge flattens near the peak. From base camp to the peak is about five hours, with a descent of three hours. The Direct Route, which is similar but more difficult, was opened in 1972, and an easier Southern Spur Route ascends the mountain from the southeast (more easily accessed via the road from the Pana).

EL BOLICHE
NATIONAL RECREATION AREA

Ecuador's smallest nationally protected area (1,077 hectares) hugs the southwestern side of Cotopaxi park. Boliche is perfect for visitors who are more interested in weekend family picnics and mild hikes than mountaineering—offering cabins, camping spots, sports fields, and self-guided trails. The habitat here at 3,500 meters is similar to Cotopaxi's *páramo* and Andean forest, but with less of the original flora and fauna.

Half the area is covered with pine trees planted in an early-20th-century reforestation program. Visitors may catch sight of deer, rabbits, and the occasional wolf. Llamas and guarizos (offspring of llamas and alpacas) are raised near the headquarters. The entrance to El Boliche is the same as the northern turnoff for Cotopaxi off the Pana—16 km past Machachi, past the CLIRSEN tracking station, and across the train tracks. Admission to the area is $5 pp.

ACCOMMODATIONS
NEAR COTOPAXI

Hacienda San Agustín de Callo

San Agustín de Callo, tel./fax 3/719-160 (2/242-508 in Quito), e-mail: info@incahacienda.com, www.incahacienda.com, owes as much of its history to the Inca as to the colonial Spanish. It was originally built as an Augustinian convent on the site of a ruined Inca outpost. The chapel and dining room both incorporate massive Inca stonework, and Inca remains have been unearthed during restorations. The nearby Cerro de Callo is a perfectly round hill thought to be an Inca burial mound.

Lodging, including breakfast and dinner, starts at $150 s, $190 d, and lunch is $20. The hacienda sits along the road that parallels the Pana north of Mulaló. Take the southern turnoff to Cotopaxi park and turn right (south) toward Mulaló instead of continuing straight into the park. You'll pass the Hacienda Los Nevados before reaching the San Agustín turnoff to the west, opposite a white rock.

Hacienda La Ciénega

Your first glimpse of the Hacienda La Ciénega is also the most impressive. It lies at the end of a long dirt lane lined with towering eucalyptus trees worthy of an English country manor. One of Ecuador's oldest haciendas, La Ciénega now operates as a hotel and restaurant. The setting is straight out of the 17th century, when the estate belonged to the Marquis of Maenza and stretched from Quito to Ambato. La Condamine, von Humboldt, Juan José Flores, and Velasco Ibarra all found shelter here over the centuries.

The main building has been aptly described as a "living museum," with meter-thick white-washed walls, wrought-iron banisters, and bare stone steps worn down by centuries of traffic. The square building surrounds a flower-filled courtyard with a fountain, where a set of ornately carved wooden doors open into the small private chapel. Horses graze near flower greenhouses to the rear of the courtyard.

Of the 28 rooms, those in the original main building are more authentic and comfortable (more rooms have been added in a separate building). Room eight, the only one on the 3rd floor, is the honeymoon suite, with excellent views of the estate. A sign on the west side of the Pana opposite Lasso points down a dirt road,

SAQUISILÍ'S THURSDAY MORNING MARKET

Cotopaxi gleams in the early morning sun as vendors labor to set up one of the most economically important and authentic markets in the country. This one isn't oriented to tourists: the atmosphere here is strictly business, and almost everything for sale serves some utilitarian purpose, from cratefuls of chickens to homemade shotguns, and shoes to leeks.

Buses from Latacunga drop shoppers in the Plaza Condordia, where racks of tools and mountains of neon-colored yarn line the square. Grab a 20-cent *pan dulce* (cornbread, Andean-style) and head in just about any direction. The entire city, in effect, becomes one big market. Although most of the major buying and selling takes place in one of eight plazas, every street seems to have its own particular offering—some of which earn a double take. On one street, you can find car radios dangling wires; head down one block and over for the fried pig heads. While chickens are confined to the food market along with the roosters, rabbits, and guinea pigs, pullets (young hens) are sold on a different street altogether. Tinny loudspeakers trumpet miracle herbal cures for everything from diarrhea to gonorrhea, as ragged old men shuffle by with crates of goods secured on their backs by rough lines around the shoulders.

Past the food market, with its haggling crowds and pots stewing over smoking coal fires, you'll eventually reach the large metal roof shading the textile market. Otavalan weavers display sweaters and tapestries, and garish wooden festival masks from Cotopaxi province glare off racks in the form of dogs, monkeys, and clowns. To one side sits an elderly row of tailors, each pumping the treadle of an antique Singer sewing machine. More than a few tables are covered with the intricate, colorful paintings from the Tigua valley to the southeast.

The real treat, though, waits about one km out of town. Follow the pig squeals down a dusty lane to the animal market, where creatures of every description are bought, sold, and bartered. This market is also divided into sections. Placid, dreadlocked llamas cluster with cloud-fleeced alpacas near the entrance, whereas cows, sheep, and horses congregate toward the back.

Some women resemble strange parodies of New York City dog-walkers, with dozens of piglets on strings milling around their ankles. Occasionally someone screams, but no one turns to look—it's just a huge hog being loaded into the back of a truck by a group of sweating, swearing farmers. Aside from the few tourists with cameras, this scene in the blowing dust and harsh equatorial sun seems plucked out of time.

Accommodations in Saquisilí can be found at the **San Carlos Hotel,** tel. 3/72-057, for $2 d with private bath and hot water.

JULIAN SMITH

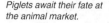

Piglets await their fate at the animal market.

where the hacienda gate opens on the left after one km.

Rates are $30 s, $40 d, and six suites are $50–70. Breakfast is $5 pp, and lunch and dinner are $10 pp. Tours, including accommodations at the hacienda and visits to Cotopaxi, Laguna Quilotoa, or indigenous villages (or all of the above), start at $180 for two people for a two-day tour. For reservations, phone 2/541-337, 549-126, fax 2/228-820, e-mail: hcienega@uio .satnet.net, www.lacienega.com.

Hostería San Mateo

Numerous recommendations have come in about this new lodge, which is located in Lasso about 10 minutes by car south of the main park entrance, tel. 3/719-015, fax 3/719-471, e-mail: san_mateo@yahoo.com. Five beautiful rooms with private bath and cabins for up to four people are decorated in Ecuadorian country style. The proper service at the restaurant, where the outstanding *menu del día* is $6 (breakfast $2.50–4.50), and the general air of classiness about the hostería make it a steal for $14.50 s, $19 d (cabins $21 pp). There's a swimming pool and bar for those who don't take advantage of the horseback riding and hiking. Owner Juan Bernardo Baca's family has a four-century history in Ecuador, and he maintains interests in cattle and dairy ranching as well as organic vegetable farming.

Volcano Land

The northern entrance road to Cotopaxi park passes this new lodge shortly before it hits the park boundary. The trio of Ecuadorian owners offer tours on foot, mountain bike, and horse-back into the nearby hills and can organize climbs of Rumiñahui or Cotopaxi. Straw mats on the roof and walls and fireplaces in the dining room and living rooms give the hostería a comfortable air. Enjoy homemade food from the farm or a board game in the game room/bar above the dining room. The view of Sincholagua and Cotopaxi from the large patio, complete with beehive bread oven (a type of outdoor oven), are spectacular. Rates for rooms, food, activities, and transportation from Quito are $55–65 pp with two people, depending on how long you stay. You can also get just a bed and breakfast for $15 pp, with lunch or dinner an additional $8 each pp. For more information, contact their office in Quito at Wilson 470 and Diego de Almagro, tel. 2/225-208, e-mail: info@volcanoland.com, www.volcanoland.com.

Hacienda Yanahurco

Opened in 1995, this luxury retreat is near Volcano Land on the northern entrance road to Cotopaxi park. They offer the same sort of outdoor activities as their neighbors—guided hiking, fishing, bird-watching, and horseback-riding excursions over 26,000 private hectares. All-inclusive packages, including activities, food, and accommodations in the expansive main hacienda, are $179–458 pp for 2–5 days (transport from Quito is extra). They have a private, locked entrance road that is reached by turning east from the main park entrance road at the Laguna Limpiopungo. For the key, maps, and reservations, contact their office in Quito at Mariana de Jesus 1607 y Jorge Juan, tel. 2/545-472, 226-360, e-mail: yanahurc@impsat.net.ec, www.yanahurco.com.ec.

LATACUNGA AND VICINITY

Before returning to his capital of Cuzco, Tupac Inca Yupanqui left his regional chiefs to oversee his newly conquered northern domains with the words *"Llagtata-cunuai"* ("I leave this land in your care"). From this edict comes the name Latacunga, claimed today by a midsized colonial city (pop. 50,000). Less than 30 km from Cotopaxi, Latacunga has been repeatedly de-

stroyed by Cotopaxi over the years, but something keeps drawing its inhabitants back to the banks of the Río Cutuchi.

The first volcanic stones were laid for Latacunga in the late 1500s. Early on, the city prospered from textile sweatshops and the spoils from a nearby Inca gold mine. Cotopaxi always loomed to the northeast, and it made good on its

silent threat on December 21, 1742 in an eruption that obliterated most of the city. Survivors described birds falling from the sky, asphyxiated by sulfur fumes. The city was rebuilt, only to be partially destroyed again in 1768. Stubborn residents dug themselves out and repaired the city yet again. More than a century of peace followed until 1877, when a third massive eruption brought Latacunga III to an end.

The inevitable emigrations between eruptions left the city as a sort of time capsule, halting further growth while preserving what Cotopaxi hadn't yet ruined. Today its modest but pretty colonial heart—across the Río Cutuchi from the ugly stretch of the town along the Pana—is a network of bumpy streets cobbled with volcanic blocks and lined by narrow sidewalks. Courtyards open off just about every block, and the only constructions over two stories are churches and municipal buildings. Residents are friendly and proud of their home—don't be surprised if children come up to you on the street and ask you how you like their city. Mountain-guiding services and a strange preponderance of beauty salons complete the picture.

SIGHTS

The central **Parque Vicente León** features a few topiary works in a garden setting that's locked tight at night. South of the park sits the plain white **cathedral,** a solemn building with ornate carved wooden doors and a small picturesque gallery behind. To the east, the **town hall** also borders the west side of **Parque Bolívar,** while across Ordóñez is the **Iglesia de San Francisco.** A few blocks southwest, the **Parque La Filantrópica** is guarded by the grand old **Hospital General,** a historic landmark to the south.

Markets
Plaza Chile near the bridges hosts Latacunga's **market,** which spills down almost to the river on Tuesday and Sunday. Huge colorful bundles of yarn and felt hats (for small heads) predominate, while the cilantro-scented fruit section features impressive pumpkins, melons, and watermelons. To the east the less spectacular daily **municipal market** borders the **Iglesia de la Mercéd** between Valencia and Echeverría.

TIGUA HIDE PAINTINGS

The brightly colored paintings by the artists of the Tigua valley are some of Ecuador's most distinctive (and portable) souvenirs. The style began as a way to decorate small drums used in traditional festivals, until the early '70s when local artist Julio Toctaquiza began to paint Andean scenes on small canvases of sheep hide stretched over a wooden frame. Julio taught his family the skill and watched the craft acquire a life of its own. Today more than 200 artists turn out the paintings in a handful of communities nestled in the Andes west of Latacunga. The Toctaquiza family painters are still the best. The family consists of Julio; his children Alfonso, Gustavo, Alfredo, and Tarjelia (one of the few women painters); Alfredo's wife María; and cousins Fausto and Bernardo. Orlando Quindigalle in Pujilí is also renowned.

The original bright enamel paints have been supplanted to an extent by more durable oils and acrylics. Many of the larger frames are works of art in themselves, covered with intricate patterns. The frame can often determine the overall quality of the work—look for even, straight frames with taut hides. Typical scenes include *campesinos* tilling their fields as llamas look on, with condors flying over a snow-covered volcano in the background.

Tigua paintings can be found all over Ecuador, but the best selection and prices are at the source. There's an Artists' Cooperativa in the small community of Tigua-Chimbacucho, 52 km west of Latacunga on the road to Quevedo, as well as a few artists in Quilotoa and Pujilí. In Quito, the Tianguez shop run by the Fundación Sinchi Sacha below the Iglesia de San Francisco has a good selection. Safari Tours runs trips to the villages.

Museums
Built on the site of an old castle along the river, the **Molinas de Monserrat** contains part of the old castle as well as an impressive ethnographic collection of ceramics, paintings, dolls in indigenous festival costumes, and colonial artifacts. It's open Tues.–Sat. 8 A.M.–noon, 2–6 P.M.; admission is 50 cents pp. A bridge over a rushing stream leads to the **Casa de la Cultura** next door.

The lovely flower-filled courtyard of the hodgepodge **Casa de los Marqueses** is more interesting than the rusty tools, stamps, paintings, and antique furniture that fill it. Open Mon.–Fri. 8 A.M.–noon and 2–6 P.M., free.

Guides and Tours

Latacunga's location between volcanoes, while occasionally dangerous, does make it a good climbing and excursion base. Two tour companies recently relocated from Baños: **Expediciones Amazonicas,** Quito 16-67 between Guayaquil and Salcedo, tel. 3/800-375, and **Selvanieve Expediciones,** Quito and Guayaquil, tel. 9/906-045/836-891. Both offer guided mountain climbs, hikes in the Andes, jungle tours, and trips to indigenous markets. **Estambul Tours,** Quevedo 6-46 and Salcedo, tel. 3/800-354, 9/713-230, sends tours daily to Zumbahua, Quilotoa, and Cotopaxi.

ACCOMMODATIONS

Although Latacunga has a few decent hotels, nothing in town even enters the midrange (i.e., more than $10 pp) category. Those in search of luxury should head to one of the **haciendas** a short drive north or south on the Pana.

Latacunga's best hotels are within a block or two of the Parque Vicente León. The **Hotel Tipulo Suite,** tel. 3/810-611, run by the amiable Lucilla Molina, opened in 1996. The cheery cafeteria serves a good breakfast, and rooms are $3 pp with private bath and TV. Half a block south, the quiet **Hotel Estanbul,** tel. 3/801-293, is a perennial budget traveler's favorite, run for 50 years by a gaggle of elderly *dueñas* (proprietresses). Good views of the mountains await from the rooftop balcony, and luggage storage and parking facilities are available. Rooms have desks and—hey!—garbage cans! Rooms go for $3 pp with shared bath, $4 pp private.

The best rooms in the musty **Hotel Cotopaxi,** tel. 3/801-310, overlook the plaza; rates are $3 pp with private bath. The **Hotel Rodelu,** tel. 3/800-956, fax 3/812-341, e-mail: rodelu@uio .telconet.net, has Latacunga's most expensive rooms at $5.50 s, $10 d, with private bath, TV, and in-room telephone. Facilities are clean, and the 1st-floor restaurant is one of the best in town.

On the Plaza Chile, the **Residencial Amazonas,** tel. 3/812-673, and **Residencial El Salto,** tel. 3/803-578, all have passably clean quarters in run-down buildings for less than $2 pp with private bathrooms and hot water (in theory, at least). The good, clean rooms at the **Residencial Santiago,** 2 de Mayo and Guayaquil, tel. 3/802-164, 800-899, all have TVs for $3 pp with private bath ($2 without).

FOOD

Local specialties include *chugchucara*—a singular fried dish including pork skins, bananas, and corn—and *allullas* (ah-YU-yahs), doughy cookies made with cheese and pork fat.

The cozy, rustic **Parilladas Los Copihues** south of Parque León serves a spicy *lomo a la diablo* (devil's steak) for $2, and the **Restaurant La Borgoña** near the municipal market is good for cheap traditional dishes. Watching a soap opera may take precedence over taking your order with the staff at the **Pizzeria Rodelu,** but the pies, which are topped with enough cheese to induce a heart attack and start at about $1.25, are worth waiting for. Pizzas at the **Pizzerias Los Sabores de Italia** are similarly priced, whereas a heaping helping of rigatone al forno is just $2.50. They also have a wide range of salad choices.

Step into the **Burger Zone** on the Salcedo pedestrian mall for your basic American fast food under 50 cents. At the hole in the wall known as the **Cevicheria Viña del Mar,** they're justifiably proud of their *ceviche de concha.* You can find tasty desserts at **Helados de Paila,** half a block north of Parque Vicente León, and guess what you'll find at **Las Ensaladas de Frutas,** across from the market? That's right—salad and fruit. Finally, the usual smattering of Chinese restaurants includes the **Chifa Hong Kong** and the **Chifa China.**

ENTERTAINMENT AND EVENTS

Festivals

Latacunga's Fiesta de la Santissima Virgen de la Merced (22–24 Sept.), known familiarly as the **Mama Negra,** is one of the more colorful and outstanding events in Ecuador. It centers around a small black icon of the Virgin, which residents half-facetiously identify as the Virgin Mary's cook. The incongruous image was carved by an indigenous artisan in the 17th century, and it was dedicated in 1744 (in vain, as it turned out) as Latacunga's patron saint to protect against Cotopaxi.

During the Mama Negra festivities, the streets are filled with a colorful cast of characters. Versetellers—more or less public jesters—tell poems and recite bawdy *loas* (limericks) filled with nuggets of ironic truth. Whip-wielding *camosonas* share the stage with *huacos,* dressed in dazzling masks and white costumes decorated with an intriguing assortment of trinkets, buttons, religious images, and random scraps of glass and plastic. *Huacos* wander the street in pairs brandishing painted sticks and animal skulls, looking for patients (or victims) on whom to work their ceremonial healing powers. The *ángel de la Estrella* (Angel of the Star), played by a young boy in plaster wings, asks the Virgin on behalf of the entire city for her protection against future natural disasters.

Latacunga's **Independence Celebration** is held on 11 November.

Nightlife
Sadly, my favorite place to boogie 'til dawn—**Yulian's Discoteque**—has closed. Luckily, the **Paradise Discotec,** Maldonado and Amazonas, is there to fill the void. Beyond that, a quiet evening stroll down one of the city's pedestrian streets such as Salcedo (perhaps with a stop at **Iglü Ice Cream**) is the extent of Latacunga's nightlife.

SERVICES

On the Parque Vicente León, the **Banco del Pichincha** exchanges travelers' checks, and the **Banco de Guayaquil** is located just off the park. The Banco del Pichincha also handles some foreign currencies. The **post office** and **Andinatel** sit next to each other on Quevedo.

You can hop online at **AJ Cybercafe** on Maldonado between Quito and Quevedo, at **Cafe-Net** on Quevedo near Guayaquil, or at the creatively named **Internet** on the Salcedo pedestrian mall, all for around $1 per hour.

TRANSPORTATION

Buses passing north and south along the Pana usually stop long enough to pick up and drop off passengers on their way to Quito (75 cents, two hours) or Ambato (60 cents, one hour). Buses to **Saquisilí** (20 cents, 20 minutes) leave regularly from Benavides, one block north of Valencia. Transportes Cotopaxi leaves from near the Hotel Los Nevados on the Pana for **Quevedo** ($2.25, five hours) via **Zumbahua,** and Transportes Pujilí heads to—you guessed right—**Pujilí** (20 cents, 15 minutes). For more information on buses going west, see "Transportation" under "Latacunga Loop." Transportes Primavera buses leave often from along the river for **Salcedo** (20 cents, 20 minutes). A new terminal terrestre is in the planning stages on the Pana and may be open by late 2001.

Taxis are available in Latacunga for day trips to Zumbahua and/or Quilotoa and Cotopaxi park (about $25).

LATACUNGA LOOP

The loop road west of Latacunga offers independent travelers one of the easiest ways to get into the remote reaches of the Sierra. Along the way are dusty, antiquated market towns and a striking lake in a volcanic caldera, while in every direction roll the windswept earthen waves of the high Andes.

Plan at least 2–3 days to appreciate the circle at a bearable pace, even with your own transportation. Less than half of the 200 km is paved, leaving the outer section between Toacazo and Latacunga merely a rough dirt track.

Transportation
Along the Latacunga Loop, getting there is half the fun and most of the effort. This is not a day trip—plan on taking at least 2–3 days to do the entire loop at a reasonable pace, and more like a week to really explore the region. The rough road is not for the faint of heart—buses getting stuck in the mud or stopped by landslides are the norm rather than the exception in the rainy season—but if you're willing to hop aboard (or better yet, on top) and focus on the scenery rather than

church and sheep
above Chugchilán

JULIAN SMITH

the comfort or lack thereof, this can be one of the most enjoyable parts of your trip.

Two regular buses make the loop on any given day, one in either direction. One, "La Iliniza," heads counterclockwise around the loop from Latacunga to Chugchilán, leaving from Calle Melchor de Benavides at 11:30 A.M. on its way through Saquisilí and Sigchos. (On Thursdays, this bus leaves half a block from the crafts market in Saquisilí at 11:15 A.M.) In Chugchilán it meets the second bus, also called "La Iliniza," which leaves daily at noon from the west side of the Pana in Latacunga, heading clockwise around the loop via Zumbahua ($1, 3.5 hours). Both buses spend the night in the plaza at Chugchilán, bidding farewell before dawn the next morning as they head in opposite directions back to Latacunga. The ride on top of either of these buses is one of the most spectacularly scenic in the country. Be ready for any kind of weather, low power lines overhead, and plenty of dust to chew on. Regular buses leave Latacunga every half hour for Zumbahua (50 cents, two hours) on their way to La Mana and Quevedo, heading back just as often until 9 P.M. daily.

Renting a private truck can make the farther reaches of the loop easier to navigate. Pickups to Quilotoa ($5–10) and Chugchilán (about $20) can be hired in Zumbahua (expect to pay more for them to wait for you). On Saturday mornings, many vehicles are making the trip already, but by the afternoon they're all off taking people home to villages in the hills. Many of the winding backroads are recommended for scenic (if long) walks, especially the one between Pujilí and Zumbahua, and a spiderweb of paths wander off in all directions.

Sangay Tours in Quito, Amazonas N24-196 and Cordero, tel. 2/550-176 or 550-180, e-mail: info@sangay.com, www.sangay.com, can take you to Chugchilán in a private jeep for $70–80 one-way. Taxis to Chugchilán start at $40 from Latacunga. Before you leave, it's a good idea to check with the Black Sheep Inn (see entry under "Chugchilán") for an updated bus schedule in case anything has changed.

Isinliví

Jean Brown of Safari Tours (see "Tour Companies" in the Quito chapter) opened the **Llu Llu Llama Hostal** in this tiny town in 2000. It's set in a renovated old country house with five private rooms ($8 pp), four loft rooms ($6 pp), and a dormitory ($5 pp). The name, which is pronounced "Zhu Zhu Zhama," means "new flame" or "baby llama" in Quechua. Breakfast and dinner are available, as are box lunches on request. Horses can be rented with local guides.

There are many excellent hiking and mountain-biking routes in the area, including trails to Quilotoa (seven hours by foot), Chugchilán (three hours), and the colorful Monday market in Guantulo (one hour). Jean is trying to promote permaculture techniques in the local community, and an Italian-run cooperative in the village does superb woodworking.

Sigchos

Unfiltered sunlight warms this high, bright town, which is stuck abruptly in a lovely valley as if it fell out of the sky. A Sunday market and a few basic *residenciales* await visitors who decide to stay for more than a few minutes as their buses pass on to Chugchilán or Latacunga.

Chugchilán

A poor, remote mountain village north of the Laguna Quilotoa is home to about 15 families and the **Black Sheep Inn,** Apdo. 05-01-240, tel. 3/814-587, e-mail: info@blacksheepinn.com, www.blacksheepinn.com, run by Michelle Kirby and Andy Hammerman from the United States. Over the years, they've turned the place into a model of ecological sustainability and self-sufficiency. Composting toilets (illustrated instructions provided), organic gardens, a greenhouse, and a full recycling program are already in place, and a sauna is planned by 2001. In the main lodge, guests can play a board game, snuggle up to the wood stove, or check their e-mail on the Internet computer. Llamas, ducks, dogs, chickens, and—sure enough—a few black sheep, wander the grounds, spilling down a hillside above the town proper.

Six beds are $15 pp, and six private rooms with two or three beds are $18 d, as is the two-bed private cabin. Prices include hot showers, tea and coffee, breakfast (or a box lunch), and vegetarian dinner, where bright orange nasturtium flowers may add their peppery flavor to a garden-fresh spinach salad. Meals are for guests only, and snacks and other drinks are extra.

The inn is a great base to explore the area; photocopied maps are available to point the way to Laguna Quilotoa, the local cheese factory, and pre-Inca ruins on the edge of the cloud forest. Horseback tours are $10 for four hours, and they organize 4WD and mountain-biking tours as well.

In Chugchilán itself, the **Hostal Mama Hilda** offers comfortable, basic accommodations for $7 pp including vegetarian breakfast and dinner. Mama Hilda herself is a dear, and she can arrange horseback riding in the area. The nearby **Hostal Cloud Forest** is not nearly as pleasant for $4 pp ($5 including meals). There aren't any restaurants in Chugchilán, but you can buy provisions at stalls in the **Sunday market** or at a few small shops in town. There's an **Andinatel** office on the plaza, where phone calls can be made Tues.–Sun. It's the only public line in town, so residents listen for the speaker announcements to see who incoming calls are for.

It's possible to hike from Chugchilán to the Laguna Quilotoa or back in a long day. Time your trip to catch a bus back or spend the night at the lake. The six- to seven-hour hike starts downhill from the main square. Cross the Río Toachi and climb a switchback trail up and out of the steep canyon. Pass through the tiny community of Huayama (why-AM-ah), where you can buy a soda or fresh bread roll for the final push up the edge of the crater. Follow the parallel rows of pine trees and proceed around to the right (counterclockwise) to join the road between Chugchilán and Zumbahua. In the opposite direction, the route is more downhill (see under "Laguna Quilotoa").

Laguna Quilotoa

Bright turquoise water, caused by dissolved minerals, makes this deep crater lake a startling mirage amid the breezy surrounding hills. Now part of the Iliniza Ecological Reserve (see previous section), the laguna charges a 50-cent entrance fee. Accommodations can be found along the turnoff from the main road, where a few Tigua artists run humble shelters with fireplaces, wool blankets, and not much else. Humberto Latacunga's **Cabanas Quilotoa,** tel. 3/814-625, has rooms with fireplaces for $3 pp and was being augmented in 2000 by an incongruous three-story addition. It includes a small *tienda* (shop) and a dirt-floored restaurant, where Humberto's beautiful paintings and carved wooden masks are for sale. Next door is the bare-bones **Hostal Quilotoa** ($1 pp).

The precipitous hike around the rim takes 4–5 hours, and the steep plunge down to the lake itself can be done in a three-hour round-trip. Horses are available for rent at the rim for the ascent. The water is said to contain too many minerals to be purifiable. A walk of five hours takes you back to Chugchilán. The tricky part is finding where to drop over the rim to head north: pick out the third sandy patch visible from the rim nearest the hotels—it's the lowest and largest one, about one-third of the way around to the left (between 12 and one o'clock, looking down on the rim from above). Hike to it in about one hour (passing a great campsite on the rim just beyond the second sandy spot), then cross over a desertlike area of dunes and down the rows of parallel trees pointing north. In the center of the village of Guayama, where you can buy sodas and snacks at a small *tienda,* zig left then quickly right on the second trail past the cemetery. Descend into the precipitous Río Toachi gorge, then make the final uphill push to Chugchilán. Maps are available at the Black Sheep Inn in Chugchilán and at the Cabanas Quilotoa. Buses run from Chugchilán to the *laguna* in the early morning, passing as high as 3,914 meters along the way.

Zumbahua

This far up into the mountains can feel as much like the Himalayas as the Andes. The rocky knobs along the road from Latacunga have become spires, and the wind carries a distinctive hint of grit and loneliness particular to mountain towns near the snow line. Zumbahua itself is a bleak, dusty place surrounded by steep hillsides and inhabited by foul-tempered dogs, children asking for handouts, and, oddly enough, cacti.

Zumbahua's **Saturday market** brings the place to life from 6 A.M. onward. A sea of felt fedoras and bright shawls swirls around piles of onions and potatoes. Llamas led by a rope through a hole in the ear don't seem to notice the tinny sales patter blaring out of loudspeakers in Spanish and Quechua.

A few basic hotels cluster around the main plaza. The **Hostal Condor Matzi,** tel. 3/814-610, is the best for $1.25 pp with shared bath and hot water. Their restaurant is open only on Saturday, but other meals can be arranged. The **Hostal Richard** and **Hotel Oro Verde** have also been recommended for budget lodgings. It can be hard to find a room on market day, so try to arrive early to give yourself a chance to catch a bus back if none are available.

Pujilí

West of Latacunga, the road winds up into the hills, where patches of evergreen dot a landscape that becomes more and more barren. Soon you're into that moody Andean landscape that is so hard to capture on film: cloud shadows racing over undulating fields as the wind sends waves through an ocean of grass. Indigenous ponchos provide the occasional flash of color, as shepherds follow ragged white and brown sheep, shaggy burros, and placid llamas.

In Pujilí itself, the markets on Sunday (main) and Wednesday draw *indígenas* from even tinier settlements. Gustavo Quindigalle sells excellent Tigua-style paintings from his house in the *ciudadela* Vicente León (ask locally for directions). The festivals of Carnival and Corpus Cristi are especially colorful.

AMBATO AND VICINITY

Only slightly behind Riobamba in size, the capital of Tungurahua province (pop. 140,000) serves as the commercial hub for the section of the Sierra between Quito and Cuenca. Richard Poole, in *The Inca Smiled,* tells of a rivalry between the neighboring provincial capitals: ". . . to an Ambateño the inhabitant of Riobamba is a *chagra,* a yokel . . . whereas for the Riobambeño, the inhabitant of Ambato is something of a city slicker."

Although lacking much character, Ambato does have a few things to offer. The city's markets are among the most important in the Sierra. A reassuring number of bookstores is scattered throughout town, while *indígenas* in red ponchos and colorful felt hats—white bowlers and green and brown fedoras—conduct their business. The setting, although geologically volatile, is pretty, with steep hillsides to the southeast sandwiching the city against the river to the northwest. For a pleasant afternoon stroll, head west along Bolívar as it turns into Miraflores and follows the banks of the river. Out here you'll find a few of the city's better hotels, along with the country houses of famous local sons Juan Montalvo and Juan León Mera.

History

Ambato's interesting past has left it, ironically, a rather dull city. The immediate area was inhabited for millennia before the Inca arrived. The Cara conquered the original inhabitants, the

To Quinta de Mera

RESTAURANTE
VEGETARIANO ▼   ● HOTEL SAN FRANCISCO

HORIZONTE
TURISMO
ECOLÓGICO

COLEGIO NACIONAL BOLIVAR/
MUSEO DE CIENCIAS NACIONALES

OASIS HELADOS
DE PAILA ▼

MERCADO
MODELO

CHIFA NUEVA
HONG KONG ▼   KARAOKE

● IGLÚ ICE CREAM

COMISARIATO
SUPER ALAMO

CINE
SUCRE ▼

BANCO DEL
PICHINCHA

CASA DE
MONTALVO ★

■ CAMBIATO

*Parque
Cevallos*

BANCO DEL
PACIFICO

ANDINATEL ■

SWEET
KISS

CASA DE LA
CULTURA

CATHEDRAL ■

ARCADE

LA BUENA
MESA ▼

*Parque
Montalvo*

HOTEL
AMBATO ●

PARILLADAS
EL GAUCHO ▼

POST
OFFICE

RESTAURANTE
GRAN ALAMO

MERCADO
CENTRAL

● EL SABOR

CETUR ■

▼ BAR
HOLLYWOOD

HOTEL CEVALLOS ●

HOTEL
DEL SOL ■

OK TACO ▼

LA FORNACE ▼

*Parque 12
de
Noviembre*

COYOTE
CAFE-BAR

EL ALAMO CHALET ▼

CONFECCIONES EN
PIEL MAYORGA ★

LA CASCADA DISCOTEC/
▼ BABALU 2000

RESIDENCIAL 9 DE OCTUBRE ■

HOTEL GUAYAQUIL ●

■ ARCADE

★ KANGAROO'S
BAR

JORGE FLORES
HIDALGO ★

■ EL PORTAL

▼ MACARÁ POOL HALL

RESIDENCIAL SAN ANDRES ●

To Hotel Villa Hilda,
Hotel Miraflores, and
Quinta de Montalro

CARLOS
BARONA ★

MARKET

AMBATO

0   200 yds

0   200 m

Cashapamba, before being overrun themselves by the Inca. The invaders from Cuzco soon established a waystation here along the Inca highway to Quito. The city of Ambato was founded in 1535 on the bank of the Río Ambato by Sebastián de Benalcázar, founder of Quito.

Then the fun started. In a pattern that had become common in the Sierra, the inhabitants of Ambato found themselves shaken, stirred, and occasionally buried by the restless earth. The fledgling city was first destroyed by an earth-

quake in 1698, leading the surviving residents to rebuild a few kilometers south of the razed site. The most recent quake to cause severe damage occurred in 1949. As a result, Ambato has seen most of its colonial character reduced to rubble, leaving it a relatively faceless city compared to many in Ecuador. Much of what hasn't been rebuilt within the last four decades is run down.

Still, Ambato managed to become an intellectual gathering place in the 19th century, drawing writers and intellectuals from Quito and

Guayaquil. The authors Juan Montalvo and Juan León Mera owned homes in Ambato in the 1800s, both of which are preserved today as museums. The city also hosted political essayist Juan Benigo Vela (1843–1920), as well as Pedro Fermín Cevallos and Luís Martinez, all well-known intellectuals in their time who are immortalized in countless Ecuadorian street names to this day.

For some reason, Ambato has two street-numbering systems in operation. The ones used here are found on the white signs, not the blue ones.

SIGHTS

The **Parque Montalvo,** graced by a statue of Juan Montalvo, is backed by Ambato's drab modern **cathedral,** which was rebuilt after that last earthquake. On the corner of Montalvo and Bolívar is the **Casa de Montalvo,** tel. 3/824-248, where author Juan was born and laid to rest. Tours of the house and lavish mausoleum are available Mon.–Fri. 9 A.M.–noon and 2–6 P.M., Sat. 10 A.M.–1 P.M.; admission is $1 pp. The complete Montalvo Experience is achieved with a visit to the writer's summer home, known as the **Quinta de Montalvo.** It's open to the public Mon.–Fri. 9 A.M.–5 P.M. (free) in the suburb of Fioca, west on Miraflores and across the river onto Ave. Los Guacamayos.

The home of the other Juan (groan—sorry) is also along the Río Ambato. Juan León Mera sought solace at the **Quinta de Mera** between penning his country's national anthem and *Cumandá,* a novel depicting indigenous life in 19th-century Ecuador. The old mansion rests amid well-maintained gardens in the suburb of Atocha, north of the city center. To get there, walk north on Montalvo to a bridge over the river. From here you can take a bus labeled Atocha or walk, taking a right on Capulíes. The walk should take about one hour. Open Tues.–Sat. 8:30 A.M.–noon and 2–5 P.M., 20 cents pp.

For some reason, almost every stuffed monkey in every museum in Ecuador is posed with its claws out and teeth bared. The **Museo de Ciencias Nacionales,** in the Colegio Nacional Bolívar on the Parque Cevallos, is no exception. Menacing herbivores notwithstanding, the museum's collection is quite good. Highlights include beautiful stuffed birds, especially the condors, and a display of historical photographs taken around the turn of the 19th century by famous Ecuadorian mountaineer Nicolás Martínez. In the back you'll find incredibly ornate Píllaro festival costumes down the hall from a menagerie of barnyard freaks. Open Mon.–Fri. 8:30 A.M.–noon and 12:30–6 P.M., 40 cents pp.

ACCOMMODATIONS

Less than $10
Most of Ambato's budget accommodations are clustered around the Parque 12 de Noviembre—no fewer than seven within one block. The **Residencial 9 de Octubre,** tel. 3/820-018, and the **Residencial San Andres,** tel. 3/821-604, both have rooms with shared bath and hot water for around $1. The **Hotel Guayaquil,** tel. 3/823-886, and the **Hotel Del Sol,** tel. 3/825-258, are both a step up, with rooms with private bath and TV for $2.50 pp.

The **Hotel San Francisco,** Egüez 2-14 and Bolívar, tel. 3/840-148, is a further step up for $2.50 pp with private bath and color TV. It's just north of the Parque Cevallos. The **Hotel Cevallos,** Cevallos and Montalvo, tel. 3/847-457, fax 3/820-570, is even nicer still, for $3.25 s, $5.50 d with private bath and TV.

$10 and Higher
The most swank accommodations in Ambato are at the **Hotel Ambato,** Guayaquil and Rocafuerte, tel. 3/412-005 or 412-006, fax 3/412-003, e-mail: hambato@hotmail.com. Overlooking the Río Ambato, the hotel has all the amenities: pool, gift shop, casino, laundry facilities, and room service. The Restaurante Ricoa is one of the best in the city, and carriage tours of Ambato are offered to guests. Rates are $21 s, $28 d, with private bath, phone, radio, cable TV, and breakfast.

Head out of town on Miraflores and you'll soon pass the **Hotel Villa Hilda,** Miraflores 600, tel. 3/845-014 or 845-571, a German-run hotel with a pool surrounded by gardens. Rooms with private bath and TV cost $18 s, $26 d with breakfast. A little farther on your left is the **Hotel Miraflores,** Miraflores 2-27, tel. 3/843-224 or 848-

971, with a similar lawn/garden setup. Rates run $19 s, $27 d with private bath and TV, including continental breakfast.

FOOD

For typical Ecuadorian food, the Swiss-run **Restaurant Gran Alamo**, Montalvo 5-20, is the local choice. Typical Ecuadorian fare and spaghetti are on the menu. The Gran Alamo is so good that it's spawned a few spin-offs, including the similar **Gran Alamo Chalet**, Cevallos 6-12, and the cafeteria-style **Gran Alamo** on Sucre. Dishes at all three places are around $1.50, and all boast pleasant settings with art-covered walls. **Parilladas El Gaucho**, at Bolívar and Quito, is also recommended for typical food for around $2.25 a plate.

Francophiles should look for **La Buena Mesa**, Quito 9-24, tel. 3/822-330, where a two-person fondue runs $7 (other dishes are much more and less expensive). Wood-oven pizzas at **La Fornace** average $1.50, with service so good you might momentarily forget you're in Ecuador. The folks at **OK Taco**, Bolívar and Guayaquil, will sing the praises of their eponymous entrée, but they also offer a few other Mexican favorites for 50 cents to $1.

If you're after a snack, try **El Sabor**, serving sandwiches, frozen yogurt, and fresh-baked breads and cakes. Ice cream can be found at the **Oasis Helados de Paila** and **Iglü Ice Cream**, both near the Parque Cevallos. The **Restaurant Vegetariano** near the Hotel San Francisco offers a small vegetarian menu. The set lunch is a good deal for 50 cents, or try a veggie burger for a quarter. On that note, it shares a building with **El Palacio de la Hamburguesa** without a trace of irony.

ENTERTAINMENT AND ACTIVITIES

The **Cine Sucre** offers double features, but check the rating—*The Little Mermaid* and *Pink Midnights* are meant for different audiences entirely. For purely mindless entertainment, try the **arcade** near the cine, with its selection of modern video games, or croon to Sinatra tunes at the **karaoke bar** on the same block.

Climbing
SurTrek, Luis Cordero 2-10 and Espinoza, tel. 3/844-448, fax 3/844-512, offers tours up most major mountains in the Sierra. Guides speak English and German, and South American Explorers' members receive a 10 percent discount. It's run out of a private house, so call ahead before stopping by. Fredrico Gonzales of **Horizonte Turismo Ecologico**, tel./fax 3/411-958, e-mail: horizonte@hotmail.com, offers climbing and jungle tours for $35 pp per day. His office is in a funky little passageway across from the cathedral.

Festivals
The end of February brings two large fiestas to town. Ambato's **Carnival** is famous for what it lacks: the traditional water-throwing, which was officially outlawed by the city government. The concurrent **Fiesta de las Frutas y las Flores** (Fruit and Flower Festival) is one of Ecuador's most lavish annual affairs. Activities range from the usual bullfights, parades, and midnight dancing in the streets to a book fair and painting and theater exhibitions. Hotels are often full during this time, so book ahead if you plan to spend the night.

Nightlife
Those in search of an evening's entertainment could do worse than a round of snooker at the **Macará Pool Hall**. For your own Boogie Nights, try **La Cascada Discoteque**, which plays Colombian music, or **Babalu 2000** next door. The area south and east of Parque 12 de Noviembre is hopping at night, but a bit seedy, so take a cab. For meeting Ambateños, the **Bar Hollywood**, **Coyote Café-Bar**, and the **Casa de la Cultura** are all on Bolívar. You can also buy the house a round of tequila and tacos at **Kangaroo's Bar**—don't worry, it's a small place.

SHOPPING

Although there might not be much to see in Ambato, there's certainly no lack of things to buy. In addition to the city's huge markets (see following section), Ambato is the leather center of the Central Sierra. Almost every block has its own upscale boutique selling suede and leather clothes, luggage, shoes, and accessories; *chompas* (jackets) are popular. Almost everything is high quality, so expect to pay accordingly.

Clothes can also be custom-made by several private *sastreros* (tailors). Fausto Mayorga, of **Confecciónes en Piel Mayorga,** Mera 07-30 and Vela, tel. 3/821-622, can make you a beautiful leather *chaqueta* (jacket) in a few days for about $70, or a pair of Jim Morrison–style leather pants for slightly more. You can let him take your measurements or just bring him a pair that fits you well and he'll copy them.

A pair of Ambato artisans make instruments. **Carlos Barona,** Castillo 8-30, makes guitars, drums, *requintas, charrangos,* and wooden flutes, while **Jorge Flores Hidalgo,** Vela 4-79 and Castillo, builds electric and acoustic guitars from scratch.

Markets

Ambato is famous for having some of the largest markets in the country. The **Mercado Central,** east of the Parque 12 de Noviembre, has hosted a main market on Monday and smaller ones on Wednesday and Friday since 1861. (Markets are held daily, but those three days are the largest.) One of the main attractions here are the flowers, which are grown in farms throughout the central Sierra and sold in gaudy, fragrant bunches along a whole row of stalls. There's also the **Mercado Modelo** a few blocks northeast of the Mercado Central. More than half a dozen smaller markets throughout the city specialize in everything from vegetables and fruit to shoes, animals, and tourist goods. For supermarket goods, try the **Comisariato Super Alamo** on Mera between Bolívar and Rocafuerte.

SERVICES AND INFORMATION

Cambiato, Bolívar 17-07, exchanges travelers' checks and a good selection of foreign currencies with surprising efficiency and very low commission. Both the **Banco del Pichincha** and the **Banco del Pacifico** around the Parque Cevalloe handle travelers' checks as well. The **tourist information office,** tel. 3/821-800, has a helpful branch next to the Hotel Ambato, open Mon.–Fri. 8:30 A.M.–noon and 2–5 P.M. The **post**

office holds down the southwest side of the Parque Montalvo, and **Andinatel** is one block northwest along Castillo.

You can enjoy an ice cream cone or milkshake while you surf the net at **Sweet Kiss,** or get online at **El Portal** or the **Casa de la Cultura.** All are open daily and charge around $1 per hour.

TRANSPORTATION

Ambato's **bus station,** two km north of town, can be reached by taxi (60 cents one-way) or local buses from the Parque Cevallos. Quito is three hours north by bus ($1.50), Latacunga one hour (60 cents). Riobamba is one hour south (80 cents), and Baños is 45 minutes southeast (40 cents). Buses heading to Riobamba and other southern cities crawl through town picking up additional passengers, so you can save yourself some time by telling a taxi driver where you are going and having him drop you off on the south side of where the buses pass. The only downside is that you can't guarantee a window seat for the views of Chimborazo—or a seat at all, for that matter.

Frequent departures also leave for Guaranda ($1, two hours), and buses for **Píllaro** leave regularly from the corner of Colon and Nacional, north of the city center (30 cents, 40 minutes). Taxi prices around town are fixed, so ask someone what the fare should be beforehand to avoid being overcharged. Minimum fare is 50 cents.

PÍLLARO

A little less than 20 km northeast of Ambato, San Antonio de Píllaro sits at 2,800 meters amid rich farmland planted with grains, papayas, and oranges. Píllaro is the gateway to the forbidding Cordillera de los Llanganatis, with their tales of Inca treasure. Local *indígenas* wear blue ponchos and make the wide, smooth-brimmed hats that are worn by the inhabitants of Chibuela and Salasaca.

The town's fiestas are outstanding. Examples of traditional, ornate **Corpus Christi** costumes still worn in Píllaro during the June festival are on display in the Ambato Natural History Museum.

During the festival of **San Lorenzo** on 10 August, a Pamplona-style bull run thunders through Píllaro's narrow streets. Bullfights are also a part of the **Celebration of Apostle Santiago the Elder** (St. James) on 25 July. Budget lodging is available at the **Pensión Acapulco**, tel. 3/876-292, half a block south of the main plaza on Bolívar. Tiny, basic rooms with shared bath and hot water are $1.25 pp. For $2 pp, you can get your own bathroom as well as a bed at the **Hostal Pillareñita**, tel. 3/873-220, on the northwest corner of the plaza.

The bus ride to Píllaro is lovely (once you get past the quarry and garbage dump), through a deep, snaking valley. Head south of town for great views of Tungurahua, whether it happens to be erupting or not. Signs around town warn you what to do in case of an eruption.

PARQUE NACIONAL LOS LLANGANATIS

Part of the Eastern Cordillera, the Llanganatis are Ecuador's version of Mexico's Sierra Madre: forbidding, inhospitable, and filled with legendary riches. The range stretches from the Río Patate valley north almost to Volcán Quilindaña, with the highest point at Cerro Hermoso (4,571 meters), also known as Yurac Llanganti. Cerro del Topo (4,257 meters) is one of the supposed hiding places of Atahualpa's gold, which was spirited away after his death (see the special topic, "The Inca's Ransom"). It's a wild, untouched place where trout fill the streams and hillsides choke with dripping greenery. Lakes such as the Lagunas Aucacocha, El Cable, and Tambo abound.

Traveling in the Llanganatis
Venturing into these mountains is not for the faint of heart or inexperienced. Almost perpetual rain, cold temperatures (3–12°C), and even snow make any serious penetration of the Llanganatis more of an expedition than a trip. Freezing rain and fog for weeks on end are just the beginning. Wet rock walls plunge almost vertically into raging rivers, while over everything lies a coarse tangle of vegetation described by one who survived it as like "a million claws of weasels."

Check travel agencies in Ambato or Baños for guides. Groups must be completely self-sufficient and prepared for extreme conditions, with sharp machetes and in excellent physical shape and stamina. A compass and good navigational skills are essential (and an altimeter recommended) because clouds often obscure landmarks. Traveling here for less than one week isn't really worth the trouble because guides and porters or mules are essential. Entrance to the newly created national park is $5 pp, but as of 2000, developed facilities were nonexistent.

From Píllaro, an old route heads east into the hills past the Pisayambo dam and San José de Poalo to the end of the road. From there it's *pura montañas* (pure mountains). You can hire a truck from Píllaro to take you this far; ask in the municipal offices in that town for more information. The higher reaches of the park can also be accessed through El Triunfo, north of Baños via Patate or Ulba. Safari Tours in Quito organizes trips into the region, and the IGM 1:50,000 *San José de Poalo, Sucre* and *Mulatos* maps cover most of the area—at least the part that has been mapped. Jan.–Mar. is the least miserable time to visit.

SALASACA

Fourteen km southeast of Ambato, Salasaca is home to an indigenous group of the same name, one of the most distinctive in the Ecuadorian highlands. The ancestors of the Salasaca *indígenas* were relocated to Ecuador from Bolivia by the Inca, under a policy intended to minimize local uprisings among conquered tribes by sticking them in unfamiliar surroundings.

Happily, the Salasaca prospered in their new home. Today they're known by their distinctive dress, most of all the long black ponchos (the color supposedly represents perpetual mourning for the fate of the Inca Atahualpa). Men wear *calzónes* (wide, white pants), and both sexes wear white hats of bleached and pressed wool.

For food, the cheap basic meals at the **Samarina Restaurant/Peña** one block north of the market is the only game in town.

Crafts
Most of the Salasaca *indígenas* make their living working the land, spending their spare time

THE INCA'S RANSOM

Placed in the town of Píllaro, ask for the farm of Moya, and sleep (the first night) a good distance above it; and ask there for the mountain of Guapa . . .

Thus begins the guide to Atahualpa's ransom, one of the richest and most plausible treasure legends in South America.

The story begins in 1537, with Atahualpa in the hands of the Spanish. Pizarro has just declared that the Inca will be killed unless he can buy his freedom by filling a room with gold and silver. Soon llama trains from all over the Inca empire are creaking toward Cajabamba, laden with riches. When the news arrives that Atahualpa has been strangled, his general Rumiñahui quickly hides the ransom, estimated at 15,000 kg of gold and silver, including an 82-kg throne of solid gold. Every ingot is spirited away almost overnight on the shoulders of porters who are later killed, directed by nobles who take their own lives. Soon no one is left alive who could lead the Spanish to the treasure, despite a frantic campaign of searching, torture, and killing. As they are burned alive, Inca nobles taunt the invaders that the treasure will never be found.

Over the years, accounts of the treasure's size, location, and even existence have drifted like clouds over the Andes, alternately condensing into certainty or dissipating into myth. In the mid-18th century, a poor farmer named Sanchez Orinjana came across a cache of gold earrings, noseplugs, and ingots in the Quinara Valley near Vilcabamba. Orinjana promptly took his treasure to Quito and bought himself the title of Marquis of Solana, and the modern quest for Atahualpa's gold began in earnest.

The first organized expedition set out for the Quinara Valley under orders from the King of Spain, headed by the magistrates of Latacunga and Ambato, Don Antonio Pástor, and Marín de Segura. Three days later, the group emerged from the forest, treasure-free and minus a friar who disappeared mysteriously one night. Despite the expedition's apparent failure, the story continues to circulate that the group actually did find the treasure and spirited it away to Europe—a rumor substantiated by the 1803 departure of the ship *El Pensamiento* from the port of Lambayeque in northern Perú, laden with US$1 billion in gold, silver, and jewels later deposited in the Royal Bank of Scotland.

The Llanganatis eventually emerged as the most probable location of the lost riches. Historians pointed out that if Rumiñahui wanted the ransom hidden forever, he could hardly have found a more inhospitable, forbidding spot in the entire Inca empire. Gold nuggets, fishhooks, and nails found among the sheer hills and icy rivers kept the legend alive.

Then, in a story to make Hollywood proud, the map and guide to the treasure turned up. It seems a poor Spanish soldier under Pizarro named Valverde had married an indigenous girl in Latacunga. He must have made quite an impression on the in-laws because his wife's father—chief of Píllaro, the closest town to the Llanganatis—told him about the ransom and directed him to it. Whether or not Valverde profited himself isn't certain, but on his deathbed in Spain he dictated his famous *Derrotero* (Path) for the King of Spain.

weaving the famous Salasaca *tapices* (narrow tapestries). Unique in Ecuador, these cloth decorations usually feature fine weaving and intricate designs of animals, birds, and plants. You can even have one custom-made with pictures or words of your choice in about one month. Weaving is the domain of men, and boys first sit at the looms as early as age 10.

Shopping

You can buy Salasaca weavings in the Plaza Central daily, but choices are particularly good on weekends. Weaver **Alonso Pilla** welcomes visitors to his home/workshop, where he weaves *fajas,* the traditional Andean belt. His house sits about 600 meters north of the evangelical church, where a dirt road meets the main road—look for the sign. Alonso is very friendly and offers customized tours to surrounding villages for an incredible $2 per hour. Enough visitors have enjoyed his hospitality that he's opening a hotel, which should be in operation by 2001. It will be located away from the highway so guests can fall asleep to the sounds of rushing water instead of passing cars. Inquire about his tours or the hotel at tel. 9/840-125.

The original *Derrotero* remains in the Archivo General de los Indies in Seville, but numerous copies of the guide to the treasure's resting place are circulating. The British botanist Richard Spruce came across a copy in the Latacunga city archives while traveling in Ecuador for the British government in the mid-19th century. He also uncovered a map drawn by one Anastasio Guzman, a Spanish botanist and farmer who had lived in Píllaro. Drawing on the knowledge of many trips into the Llanganatis, Guzman drew up a map in 1800 that roughly corresponded with Valverde's guide. Seven years later, he walked off a cliff in his sleep. The account of the treasure, along with a copy of the *Derrotero*, appeared as the final chapter in Spruce's *Notes of a Botanist on the Amazon and Andes*, published in 1908.

The route is simple and detailed, yet maddeningly vague in crucial passages. One pencilled squiggle directs seekers around a mountain, after leading them through "quaking-bogs," "great black lakes," tunnels, ravines, and streams running with gold grains. The lake where the treasure supposedly lies, described as man-made, is said to lie between three peaks that form a triangle.

A tale of lost gold grabs the imagination like few others, and Atahualpa's riches have inspired countless treasure-hunters—usually foreigners—and authors to spend years unravelling the mystery. Commander George Miller Dyott, famous for his quest for Colonel Fawcett in Brazil's Matto Grosso, was among the first explorers to mount a serious expedition. The first half of the 20th century saw three books that detailed the legend: *Llanganati*, by Luciano Andreade Marin (1937, reprinted in Spanish in 1970); *Fever Famine and Gold*, by Erskine Loch (1938); and *Buried Gold and Anacondas* by Rolf

Blomberg (1954). German adventurer Eugene Brunner spent decades in the 20th century compiling information and maps and venturing into the Llanganatis, and died convinced that he had pinpointed the treasure lake itself. Peter Lourie tells Brunner's tale in his own book of treasure fever, *Sweat of the Sun, Tears of the Moon.*

The sheer impossibility of the terrain and its weather have kept the story a legend. During one trip, Brunner said he saw the sun three times in 127 days, and only had five days in which the weather was good enough to travel. Marin writes off the Llanganatis as "a region which without doubt should be marked on the maps, as few others in the world, with the words FOREVER UNINHABITABLE . . ." Some say the mountains are cursed, sending compasses spinning and clouding the minds of anyone foolish enough to venture in. There's even a legend that a lost indigenous tribe inhabits the deepest valleys, standing over two meters tall in their bare feet.

Airplane pilots consider the Llanganatis similar to the Bermuda Triangle: probably an old wives' tale, but best to avoid the area all the same, just in case. Planes crash regularly in the mountains—or at least are reported to because wreckage and bodies are seldom recovered. Some veteran travelers in Ecuador even reroute their flights between Quito and Cuenca through Guayaquil to avoid flying over the cursed peaks.

But the legend continues to draw seekers, and the *Derrotero* lures them into the hills. After a final ambiguous landmark, it ends:

. . . and in this manner thou canst by no means miss the way.

Find more crafts at the **Cooperative Salasaca** and **Raymi Tuta Handicrafts,** both near the plaza as well. About a dozen shops along the highway sell *tapices* and other goods you've probably already seen in Otavalo. A **Sunday market** expands your choices considerably, but bargaining here is anything but easy.

Festivals
During the festival of **Corpus Christi** in June, residents dress up in elaborate masks and costumes and dance, accompanied by marching bands, from here to Pelileo. **Santo Vintio** on 15

June is also significant, and during the **Day of the Dead** festivities on 2–3 November, Salasaca hosts the "Tzawar Mishki" festival of Andean music and dance.

PELILEO

Pelileo sits just beyond Salasaca on the road from Ambato to Baños. Actually, it used to sit a bit farther down the road, but continual earthquakes convinced the town's residents to migrate. After its founding in 1570, Pelileo was pounded by quakes in 1698, 1797, 1840, and 1859. A final roller-coaster on August 5, 1949 left the town in shambles: 2,500 of the total 6,000 dead lived in Pelileo. Pelileo Nuevo (today's Pelileo) was soon built two km to the west. The old town (Pelileo Viejo) still stands in its original unlucky location, a ghost of its former self with a mere handful of people, a church, and a school.

The new Pelileo is known as the blue jeans capital of Ecuador, as well as for its Saturday market that brings together vendors and buyers from a handful of nearby villages such as Salasaca and Patate. Bullfights and dances take place during the **Canonization Celebration** on July 22, while the **Festival of the Dead** on November 2 finds residents in cemeteries, visiting with departed loved ones.

The road continues from Pelileo down toward Baños, a spectacular descent. The light-colored Río Patate and darker Río Chambo crash in slow motion along the way, forming the Río Pastaza, which eventually passes Baños and drains into the Oriente. Topping the lush river gorge is snow-capped Volcán Tungurahua to the south.

BAÑOS AND VICINITY

Ecuador's premier resort town counts hiking trails, hot springs, and one of the most beautiful settings in the country as part of its almost irresistible draw. Add an important religious shrine and dozens of tour operators vying for business, and you have a destination popular with both Ecuadorian and foreign tourists. If you can stand the crowds and party-'til-dawn mentality this kind of place can draw, you may well find yourself spending weeks where you meant to spend days—that is, if it all isn't buried by lava first.

Perched on a shelf at 1,815 meters between the base of the Tungurahua volcano and the Río Pastaza gorge, Baños enjoys a mild subtropical climate year-round. Water flows on every side: the Cascada Cabellera de la Virgen (Virgin's Hair Waterfall), visible from anywhere in town, tumbles down the steep hillside, and Bascún Creek to the west joins the brown Pastaza to rush downhill into the Oriente. Hot springs bubble up from the depths of Tungurahua, which towers to the south and is often wreathed in clouds. Flowers of every color dot the dripping green backdrop and burst over house walls in eruptions of purple, red, orange, and yellow. Frogs chirp among the fruit trees at night.

Ecuadorian tourists are drawn not just to the town's beauty but also to the Church of Our Lady of the Holy Water, one of the more important pilgrimage sites in the central Sierra. Foreign travelers, on the other hand, come by the busload to relax in the hot pools, enjoy fresh fruit-topped pancakes for breakfast, and hike and ride horses through the hills above town.

All this traffic has taken an inexorable toll. It seems as if almost every establishment in the town's 30-odd square blocks is either a trinket shop, bar, tour agency, restaurant, or hotel. Weekends can be hectic, with the wide pedestrian stretch of Ambato between Halflants and 16 de Diciembre jammed with tourists strolling and shopping to the slap of toffee stretchers in store doorways.

Although this influx of jostling bodies hasn't yet destroyed Baños' undeniable charm, the active volcano towering overhead is another matter entirely. A limited eruption in September 1999 prompted the Ecuadorian government to evacuate the city. Residents protested the loss of business but were forcibly removed by the army. Four months later, about half the city's inhabitants returned to retake the city, finding it still in one piece but many of their homes and businesses burglarized.

The orange alert, which presumed a major eruption within weeks, was held until August 2000, by which time many businesses had closed for good or relocated to the Sierra. Although Baños has yet to regain its former glory, most of its inhabitants have returned, and once again it's hard to walk one block without being offered a bike or horse for rent. Tungurahua remained at yellow alert as of September 2000, adding a significant risk to any activity on its slopes, especially the higher you go. It remains to be seen whether the volcano will be kind to Baños as the city tries to recover.

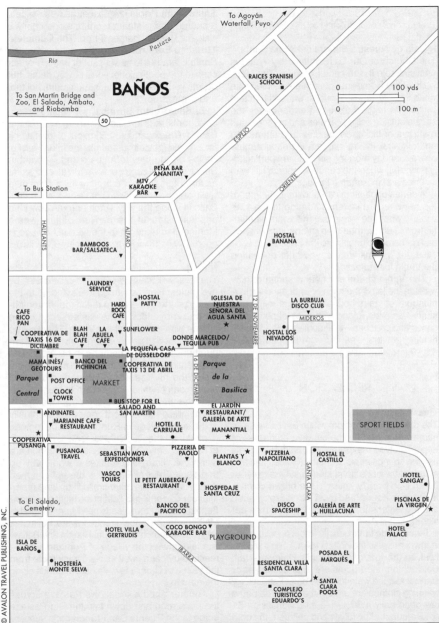

BAÑOS

To Agoyán
Waterfall, Puyo

Rio Pastaza

RAICES SPANISH
SCHOOL

0 _____ 100 yds
0 _____ 100 m

To San Martín Bridge and
Zoo, El Salado, Ambato,
and Riobamba

50

To Bus Station

PEÑA BAR
ANANITAY

MTV
KARAOKE
BAR

ESPEJO

ORIENTE

HALFLANTS

ALFARO

BAMBOOS
BAR/SALSATECA

HOSTAL
BANANA

LAUNDRY
SERVICE

HOSTAL
PATTY

HARD
ROCK
CAFE

IGLESIA DE
NUESTRA
SEÑORA DEL
AGUA SANTA

LA BURBUJA
DISCO CLUB

MIDEROS

CAFE
RICO
PAN

COOPERATIVA DE
TAXIS 16 DE
DICIEMBRE

BLAH
BLAH
CAFE

LA
ABUELA
CAFE

SUNFLOWER

LA PEQUEÑA CASA
DE DÜSSELDORF

DONDE MARCELDO/
TEQUILA PUB

12 DE NOVIEMBRE

HOSTAL LOS
NEVADOS

MAMA INÉS/
GEOTOURS

Parque

Central

BANCO DEL
PICHINCHA

POST OFFICE

CLOCK
TOWER

MARKET

COOPERATIVA DE
TAXIS 13 DE ABRIL

16 DE DICIEMBRE

Parque
de la
Basilica

ANDINATEL

MARIANNE CAFE-
RESTAURANT

BUS STOP FOR EL
SALADO AND
SAN MARTÍN

HOTEL EL
CARRUAJE

EL JARDÍN
RESTAURANT/
GALERÍA DE ARTE

MANANTIAL

SPORT FIELDS

COOPERATIVA
PUSANGA

PUSANGA
TRAVEL

SEBASTIAN MOYA
EXPEDICIONES

VASCO
TOURS

LE PETIT AUBERGE/
RESTAURANT

PIZZERIA DE
PAOLO

PLANTAS Y
BLANCO

HOSPEDAJE
SANTA CRUZ

PIZZERIA
NAPOLITANO

HOSTAL EL
CASTILLO

SANTA CLARA

HOTEL
SANGAY

To El Salado,
Cemetery

BANCO DEL
PACIFICO

DISCO
SPACESHIP

GALERÍA DE ARTE
HUILLACUNA

PISCINAS DE
LA VIRGEN

ISLA DE
BAÑOS

HOSTERÍA
MONTE SELVA

HOTEL VILLA
GERTRUDIS

COCO BONGO
KARAOKE BAR

PLAYGROUND

IBARRA

RESIDENCIAL VILLA
SANTA CLARA

POSADA EL
MARQUÉS

HOTEL
PALACE

SANTA
CLARA
POOLS

COMPLEJO
TURISTICO
EDUARDO'S

© AVALON TRAVEL PUBLISHING, INC.

SIGHTS

Iglesia de Nuestra Señora del Agua Santa

The Church of Our Lady of the Holy Water is unmistakable in the center of town. The black walls of the Dominican church are painted with white lines to simulate bricks, with red trim and twin white-topped towers. Vendors pack the streets outside selling candles and rosaries, and the trays of flickering candles and ornate red and gilt altar inside evoke a Baroque atmosphere. Sunday morning services are particularly powerful, when the candle-lit church fills with incense and murmuring throngs.

A series of paintings around the perimeter of the nave record instances dating to the 17th century when the Virgin began saving the faithful from Tungurahua's eruptions, car wrecks, and numerous plunges into the Pastaza. In each case, the victims were saved after entreating the Virgin for protection.

The Virgin statue sits near a spring of holy water to the left of the main body of the church. A museum upstairs houses religious relics and stuffed animals, along with piles of discarded canes and crutches—testimonials to the Virgin's healing powers. The museum is open daily 7 A.M.–4 P.M.; admission is 25 cents pp.

RECREATION

Thermal Baths

The thermal springs from which Baños takes its name are touted for the curative properties of their dissolved minerals. Because many locals use the springs as actual baths (clothes and all), it's probably not a good idea to submerge your head. Don't worry, though, the brown color is from the minerals, and most baths are cleaned and the water changed at least a few times per week.

Piscinas de la Virgen, the most popular baths in town, are also the hottest (50°C) and the prettiest, at the foot of the Virgin's Hair waterfall. Cold, chlorinated pools are also available, or stand under the waterfall if you dare. Facilities for washing clothes are around the side. The baths are open daily 4:30 A.M.–5 P.M.; admission $1 pp. Frequented by locals and children, the cold

Santa Clara Pools (24°C) feature water slides, a sauna, and a steam room. It's open daily 9 A.M.–6 P.M. and charges $1 pp. The **Complejo Turistico Eduardo's** on Ibarra across from the Santa Clara is the newest set of baths. For access to the pools alone, you'll pay 50 cents, but $2 lets you use the sauna, steam room, hot tub, and gymnasium.

El Salado Hot Springs, with both hot and cold pools, sits on the far (east) side of the Bascún Creek canyon, 1.5 km out of town. Look for a paved footpath just across the bridge east of Baños on the way to Ambato and Riobamba. Buses from the center of town run at least as far as this intersection. From here it's a 40-minute walk or 10-minute drive, passing the Chalets Bascún along the way. Another route down the opposite side of the canyon begins where Martínez leaves town to the west. El Salado is open daily 4:30 A.M.–5 P.M. and costs 50 cents pp.

Hiking

The steep hillside west of town can be scaled by two routes. Head south on Mera and go to the right past the cemetery to reach the **Virgen Mirador,** an overlook at the eastern edge of the hillside with a statue of the Virgin. The walk up takes about half an hour, and the views of Tungurahua around the corner can be great. The path continues above the statue all the way to the top of the hillside and Runtún, or a downhill branch can be taken back down to Mera (to ascend this way, head left initially from Mera).

The hillside flattens out somewhat eventually at the small village of **Runtún** at 2,600 meters, named from the Quechua for fortress. Needless to say, the views of Baños and Tungurahua are worth the climb, which takes a whole day up and back. East of Runtún is the aptly named **Bellavista,** with its huge cross lit up lime-green after dark, seeming to float in the night sky above Baños. Another route leads uphill from the end of Maldonado in Baños directly toward Bellavista with a side branch to Runtún. Runtún and Bellavista, along with the village of **Puntzan,** can be reached by car as well as via a back route from the village of **Ulba,** a few km east of Baños along the road to Puyo.

Another good hike follows Pastaza across the main road and down into the Río Pastaza gorge to the **Puente San Francisco,** a suspen-

STEVE NOMCHONG

river-running near Baños

sion bridge over the river. A network of trails crisscrosses the hillside facing Baños. The village of **Illuchi,** about a two-hour hike from the river, is a good turning-around point with views of Baños, Tungurahua, and the river.

The **Puente San Martín** crosses the Pastaza just to the west of town. To reach it, cross the bridge out of Baños, pass the turnoff to El Salado, and turn right near a religious shrine and police checkpoint. Near the bridge is the **Cascada Inés María,** a small waterfall, and the **San Martín Zoo,** opened in 1994 as a refuge for sick and injured animals from the Amazon. The collection of birds and mammals was evacuated to Quito during Tungurahua's activity, but most have been returned. Across the Puente San Martín is the village of **Lligua,** a three- to four-hour hike to where the Río Lligua enters the Río Pastaza. Farther up is the crest of Chontilla hill (2,700 meters), followed by a radio antenna on the hilltop. A loop up this hillside is a good option for a day hike, crossing at one bridge and re-crossing at the other.

Mountain Biking and Horseback Riding

Baños couldn't be in a better setting to explore by wheel or hoof, and it shows. Almost every agency in town offers rentals and guide services, competing with the many individuals operating out of their homes. Most trips are four hours, with some time spent driving to or from your destination. One of the more popular bike excursions is down the road to Puyo to the Agoyán Waterfall near the mouth of the first tunnel. The ride east is all downhill, leaving it up to you to ride back up or catch a ride from a bus. The road can be very muddy during the rainy season.

Horses are the most popular way to get into the hills. Reports of ill or mistreated horses have been on the rise in the last few years, to the point that an association was being organized to fix fair prices and ensure proper veterinary treatment of the animals. (An office is to be opened at Montalvo and Halflants with lists of tour operators who have joined the voluntary association.) Look for healthy, well-treated horses and try out the saddle for fit before you leave. Don't accept blankets instead of saddles; they cut festering sores into the animals' sides. Expect to pay about $16 for a three-hour ride, and be wary of operators willing to be bargained down to less than $10.

Baños' most acclaimed horse trips are with **Caballos con Christían** from the Isla de Baños hotel. Christían Albers offers 10 years of experience and robust horses.

Rafting and Kayaking

Rio Loco, Maldonado and Martínez, offers rafting trips, including transportation, guide, and lunch. Rates are $60 pp for a whole day of shooting rapids and $30 pp for half-days (10 percent SAE discount). Experienced rafters and kayakers with their own equipment should consider the Río Patate between Patate and Baños (also known as the "crazy river"), the Río Pastaza farther downstream closer to Puyo (the stretch below Shell is recommended), and the Río Toro, which empties into the Río Pastaza in the direction of Puyo.

Tours

So many tour agencies operate in Baños that it's tough to keep the trustworthy separate from the fly-by-night rip-off artists. The following agencies have been repeatedly recommended, but it's a good idea to also check with the South American Explorers' clubhouse in Quito for a current list. Almost all agencies offer hiking and mountain-biking tours, climbing trips, and rainforest expeditions. Many agencies that offer climbing trips buy, rent, and sell new and used mountaineering equipment. Rates for overnight trips should be $40–50 pp per day, all inclusive.

Geotours, Ambato and Halflants, tel./fax 3/741-344, www.ecuadorexplorer. com/geotours, run biking, horseback-riding, rafting, and trekking tours. They also handle reservations for Río Loco rafting trips. **Cordova Tours,** Maldonado and Espejo, tel. 3/740-92, 9/838-631, e-mail: ojosvolcan@hotmail.com, does general tours and rents 4WD vehicles. **Willie Navarette,** who can be contacted through the Cafe Higueron, tel. 3/740-910, is the only recommended climbing guide in town.

A few agencies specialize in tours of the Amazon. **Sebastian Moya Expediciones,** Alfaro and Martínez, tel. 3/740-690, e-mail: moyatours@gmx.de, is owned by the Shuar guide Sebastián Moya. It's run under the auspices of the Yawa Jee Shuar Indigenous Foundation, a private, nonprofit organization dedicated to sustainable, low-impact tourism to benefit Shuar communities. Along with highly recommended jungle tours, **Tsantsa** offers work and study opportunities at research stations in the Oriente. They have an information center on the Parque Central. **Expediciones Amazonicas,** Ambato between Alfaro and Halflants, tel. 3/740-506, has gotten a few positive reports.

Most comments on **Rainforestur,** Ambato and Maldonado, tel. 3/740-743, fax 3/740-743, have been positive. They speak English, French, and German, and offer tours of the Galápagos in addition to the surrounding area. Cuyabeno trips of 4–5 days cost $45 pp per day, including all meals. **Vasco Tours,** Martínez and Eloy Alfaro, tel. 3/740-017, is run by Flor Vasco and Juan Medina in Quito. People returning from Vasco jungle trips rave about the guides' knowledge, professionalism, and relationship with the Huaorani tribes the tours visit.

ACCOMMODATIONS

Less than $10

The **Hostal Plantas y Blanco,** Martínez and 12 de Noviembre, tel. 3/740-044, is well known among repeat visitors for its rooftop terrace, guest services, and value. The hotel's fresh-fruit double pancakes are one of Baños' best breakfasts, served first thing in the morning from a dining room overlooking the city. Board games, music, and honor-system beer and sodas are available to guests until the patio closes at night. A special therapeutic steam bath is open to anyone in the morning, and movies on the VCR, luggage storage, and laundry service are available downstairs. Guests can make and receive phone calls and faxes at the front desk. Rooms are comfortable, cleaned daily, and have wonderful hot showers—all this for only $4–8 pp. A friendly Salasacan *indígena* named José but better known as "Zaracay" sells his wares through the hostel.

Plantas y Blanco's owner has opened the **Hospedaje Santa Cruz,** 16 de Diciembre and Martínez, tel. 3/740-648, with two ground-floor patios with fireplaces, games, magazines, self-service bar, and similar prices. Off Montalvo near the waterfall is the **Posada El Marqués,** tel. 3/740-053, a homey, family-run crash pad with room for 38 people in the large main house. Rooms are large, clean, and quiet, with private baths and hot water for $5 pp. Laundry service is available ($1 per kilo), as are *quena* flute lessons.

The **Isla de Baños,** Montalvo 131, tel./fax 3/740-609, a few blocks west on Montalvo, is run by Christían Albers of Caballos con Christían (see "Mountain Biking and Horseback Riding" under "Recreation"). The glass-walled atrium on the 1st floor looks out into a well-tended flower garden—the perfect place for one of the hotel's famous breakfasts. A book exchange, security boxes, and baggage storage are all included in the price—$4–8 pp with private bath with hot water, including continental breakfast.

The cozy **Hostal Banana,** tel. 3/740-309, fax 3/740-126, is a blue place marked with the Swedish flag one block north of the church on 12 de Noviembre. Up to 11 guests can enjoy an evening fire in the dining room decorated with stained glass (note the sax player). The smell of a homemade breakfast draws you out of bed in the morning. Kitchen, laundry, and phone and fax services are available to guests. Rooms go for $5 pp with shared bath. Also within one block of the church is the friendly **Hostal Los Nevados,** Ambato and El Rosario, tel. 3/740-673 or 740-827. Clean rooms feature private baths and hot water for $4 pp.

One block west of the church, the family-run **Hostal Patty,** Alfaro 556, tel. 3/740-202, offers decent budget accommodations with laundry and kitchen facilities. It's a bit run-down, but at $1 pp it's the cheapest place in Baños next to the rooms at the Cafe Hood (see following entry). Around the corner at Alfaro 4-24 and Ambato is the **Casa Matilde,** tel. 3/740-495, new in 2000 with rooms for $4 and laundry service available. The **Hostal El Castillo,** Martínez and Santa Clara, tel. 3/740-285, is painted black with white lines like the Iglesia de Nuestra Señora del Agua Santa. They exchange travelers' checks, rent bikes and horses, and run a small book exchange with Internet service in the cafeteria. For $2 pp you get a private bath and hot water.

At the southern end of 12 de Noviembre, the **Residencial Villa Santa Clara,** tel. 3/740-349, has rooms in the main house with shared bath for $2 pp. Private cabins in the back with their own bathrooms are $5 pp. Lodging at the **Hotel El Carruaje,** Martínez and 16 de Diciembre, tel. 3/740-913, costs $6 pp with private bath and hot water. The place is named after the horse-drawn carriage they have available for city tours.

A long and sordid tale of betrayal and imitation led the original **Cafe Hood** to change its location to Maldonado and Rocafuerte on the Parque Central. Rooms are available upstairs for $1, and there's a book exchange, message board, and videos available to customers.

$10–25

Probably the prettiest hotel within Baños proper, the **Hostería Monte Selva,** tel. 3/740-566 or 820-068, fax 3/854-685, consists of a collection of cabañas at the foot of the hillside at the south end of Halflants. Papasan chairs and a bamboo bar remind you that above all else this is a place to relax. The beautiful pool, sauna, and steam room are open to the public for $10 pp ($5 for children). Rates for the *hostería* are $12 s, $18 d. Family cabins go for $5–7 pp, and all prices include breakfast and the use of the ample facilities.

Near the pools at the southeast end of town, the musty **Hotel Palace,** tel. 3/740-470, fax 3/940-291, features a small historical museum and spa facilities open to the public (Tues.–Fri. 4–8 P.M., Sat. and Sun. 9 A.M.–8 P.M., $1.50 pp). Rooms are available in three classes: economy ($11 s, $16 d), standard ($17 s, $23 d), and premium ($23 s, $30 d).

Head west down Montalvo to reach the **Hotel Villa Gertrudis,** Montalvo 20-75, tel. 3/740-441, fax 3/740-442, a villa-style old home surrounded by beautiful gardens. The owner used to swim competitively in Argentina, which explains the hotel's Olympic-size covered pool across the street; the pool is open to the public daily 7 A.M.–1 P.M. and 2–6 P.M. for $1 pp. Rates at the hotel run $7 s, $14 d, including breakfast and use of the pool.

$25–50

The big peach-colored building at the base of the waterfall is the **Hotel Sangay,** tel. 3/740-917, fax 3/740-056. Guests can choose between rooms in the main hotel and cabañas out back and can work up a sweat with tennis or squash before crossing the street to the baths. The hotel's restaurant is highly recommended. Rooms are $12 d, and cabins are $20 s, $30 d. Prices include breakfast and use of the considerable facilities, and there's even aromatherapy treatment available for $10.

Near Baños

On the crest of the hill overlooking Baños sits the **Luna Runtún Resort,** Cacería Runtún km 6, tel. 3/740-882, fax 3/740-376, e-mail: info @lunaruntun.com, perhaps the area's most luxurious lodging. A hacienda feel is enhanced by flower gardens, fountains, and tiled roofs. Eucalyptus beams, handmade bricks, and hand-cut windows adorn the comfortable accommodations. The rooms with the best views are closest to the edge of the hill. Luna Runtún's Swiss owners speak Spanish, English, French, Swedish, and German and offer Spanish courses and tours of the area. A taxi to the hotel from Baños costs about $7 one-way, and a private shuttle is available. Rates run $125–160 d (10 percent SAE discount).

Two more hotels are found on the road to El Salado springs. The **Casa Nahuazo Bed & Breakfast,** tel. 3/740-315, fills a beautiful colonial house close to the springs. Rooms are $5 with private bath and breakfast. One km from the springs across the Bascún Creek canyon are the **Chalets Bascún,** tel. 3/740-334, fax 3/740-740. The hotel has a restaurant, steam room, sauna, and pool. Rooms cost $14 s, $18 d.

FOOD

The two main options for eating in Baños are continental and healthy. It seems like just about every country in Europe has a representative restaurant in town, whereas countless others offer pizzas, salads, and other meat-free fare. Most restaurants close by 10 P.M.

Le Petit Restaurant, 16 de Diciembre and Montalvo, tel. 3/740-936, is part of the Le Petit Auberge hotel, serving excellent (albeit pricey) French food. Their fondues are especially good. For dishes from the south of France, try the **Marianne Cafe-Restaurant** on Halflants between Martínez and Rocafuerte, a neat little place serving all meals. The bright and cheery **Sunflower,** Eloy Alfaro and Ambato, is owned by a pair of Venezuelan siblings of German descent. They serve up tasty European fare in the form of a set lunch and dinner menu with different rotating options for the main course.

Regine's **Cafe Alemán** once served à la carte dishes in a small flower garden at Montalvo and 16 de Diciembre. It was closed in late 2000 but was planning to reopen soon. In the meantime, try **La Casa Vieja de Düsseldorf,** with a long and varied menu that should actually have a few German dishes by late 2001.

Pasta in all its variations can be found at the popular **Mama Inés** on the corner of the Parque Central. Pizza or spaghetti dishes are around $2 at **La Bella Italia** on 16 de Diciembre between Montalvo and Martínez, where it's sandwiched between Le Petit and the competing (and good) **Pizzeria de Paolo.** The **Pizzeria Napolitano,** across the street from Plantas y Blanco, cooks up 11 different kinds of pizza along with meat and seafood dishes. If you haven't satisfied your pizza craving by now, try

Manantial, 16 de Diciembre and Martínez, whose gimmick seems to be offering the most famous national dish of as many countries as possible.

Ambato between Halflants and Alfaro hosts an overwhelming array of bars and cafés. The tiny **Blah Blah Cafe** serves breakfast and sandwiches, and **La Abuela Cafe** offers pasta, salads, soups, and vegetarian dishes in a cozy atmosphere of *buenas vibraciónes* (good vibrations). One block west, the **Cafe Rico Pan** is popular for its breakfasts, pizza, and homemade breads.

For more vegetarian options, **El Jardín Restaurant/Galería de Arte,** Rocafuerte and 16 de Diciembre, offers a good selection. Breakfast is inexpensive, and the outdoor garden/patio is perfect for afternoon cakes and coffee. The **Cafe Hood,** always a Baños mainstay for healthy food among travelers, has relocated to Maldonado and Rocafuerte. Funky art and comic books will keep you busy until your tasty food arrives, accompanied by fresh juice, pastry, or herb tea. They have a bookstore, and a large message board advertises tours, rooms for rent, and jobs in town.

SHOPPING

Baños' most plentiful souvenirs—along with the usual postcards, T-shirts, and hats—are woven straw bags, baskets, hand-stretched toffee, and heart-shaped cakes of *guanabana* (a sweet guava paste). Browse through the handful of antique stores and you might come across something interesting, from kitschy paintings of Ché Guevara to old tools and pre-Columbian-style artifacts.

Albert Guzñay Saenz of **El Cade** has been carving tagua nuts for almost four decades and offers one of the best selections of carvings in Ecuador. The nearby area of Maldonado between Espejo and Oriente is full of crafts shops and taffy pullers, as is Calle Ambato.

The **Galería de Arte Huillacuna,** tel. 3/740-187, at Santa Clara and Montalvo, displays sculptures, paintings, and drawings by local artists. A second studio/gallery is around the corner. Both are open daily 8 A.M.–7:30 P.M. The award for most eclectic selection goes to the **Cooperativa Pusanga,** Halflants and Martínez, a cooperative of female artisans from the Oriente. Walls and shelves are stocked with ceramics and pottery, palm-fiber *shigra* bags, seed jewelry, blowpipes, and hammocks.

ENTERTAINMENT AND EVENTS

Nightlife
The **Donde Marceldo Bar/Restaurant,** popular with gringos for its food and atmosphere, is on Ambato near 16 de Diciembre. Upstairs lies the **Tequila Pub,** where darts, pool, and music videos draw the crowds, along with two-for-one *cuba libres* from 8–9:30 P.M. (There's another smaller bar also named Donde Marceldo on Alfaro near Ambato, with stools on the sidewalk.) Graffiti art marks the outside of the **Hard Rock Cafe** on Alfaro between Ambato and Oriente. **Bamboos Bar/Salsateca,** Alfaro and Oriente, packs 'em in the tiny upstairs dance floor. If it's too crowded, there's a pool table at the base of the stairs. Entrance is $1 pp.

The **Peña Bar Ananitay** has folklore music from 9:30 P.M. on weekends, and the **La Burbuja Disco Club** on Mideros around the corner from Hostal Los Nevados plays standard disco fare Thur.–Sat. 8 P.M.–12:30 A.M. Entry is free on Thursday, and on Friday and Saturday you're greeted with a free welcome drink. Two karaoke bars—**Congo Bongo** at Montalvo and 16 de Diciembre and **MTV Karaoke Bar** at Espejo and Alfaro—offer a novel way to practice your Spanish in front of a barful of new friends.

One can only imagine how much fun the unmistakable **disco spaceship** building was in its heyday.

Festivals
Baños' **Canonization Festival** is celebrated 15–16 December with bands and processions, and the festival of **Nuestra Señora del Agua Santa** draws great crowds of pilgrims in October.

Other Fun
Quena flute lessons are available for $5 per hour at the Posada El Marqués. The hotel also sells the Andean reed flutes. **Movies** are shown on the VCR at the Cafe Hood.

SERVICES AND INFORMATION

Money Exchange
Both the **Banco del Pichincha** and the **Centro Commercial Dom Pedro** change travelers' checks. The latter charges a 4 percent commission. The **Banco del Pacífico** on the corner of Montalvo and Alfaro has an ATM.

Laundry
Laundry services are available at most hotels. If your hotel is lacking, try the **Lavandería Alexander** next to Bicicletas Alexander on Oriente and Alfaro, or **Victor's Laundry** at Maldonado 6-97 and Espejo. At the public wash area near the El Virgen baths, you can wash your own clothes for free or have them done for you.

Internet Access
Not even a volcanic eruption could keep Baños from joining the online revolution. There are close to 10 **Internet cafés** in town, all charging around the same price ($2 per hour). There's no local service provider, so calls to Quito tend to make connections slow. Try the **Café.com** of the Hostal Banana, where you get a free hour with dinner, the **Cyber Cafe Internet** on Ambato between Eloy Alfaro and 16 de Diciembre, **Baños.net** at Alfaro and Ambato, **Link-Net** at 16 de Diciembre and Montalvo, or **Planet.Net** on Maldonado and Ambato.

Spanish Schools
Outside of Quito and Cuenca, Baños is probably the most popular place in Ecuador to stay and study Spanish. Most schools offer individual and group instruction. At the northeast end of town, the **Raices Spanish School,** tel./fax 3/740-090, occupies the yellow house of J. Silva Romo. They feature flexible schedules with instruction for $4.50 per hour, as well as laundry and fax services.

José María Pepe Eras runs the 16 de Diciembre Spanish School, tel. 3/370-232, 740-453, marked by a big sign reading "Spanish School." He has been teaching for 15 years and employs four other teachers. Dr. Martha Vaca Flores is director of the **International Spanish School for Foreigners,** 16 de Diciembre and Espejo, tel. 3/742-612, e-mail: martaiss@hotmail.com, where instruction is $4.50 per hour.

The **Baños Spanish Center,** tel./fax 3/740-632, e-mail: elizabethschool@yahoo.com, is run by Elizabeth Barrionuevo, who speaks Spanish, English, and German. She has been recommended as an excellent teacher and offers dancing and cooking lessons in addition to language instruction.

Other Services
Mochilas Varoxi, Maldonado 651 and Oriente, makes backpacks, daypacks, jackets, and custom waterproof backpack covers. They can also repair most packs, luggage, and covers. A small sewing shop on Martínez between Maldonado and Halflants will repair clothes for a modest fee. An attractive **map** of the Baños area, painted by resident José Urquizo, is for sale in most stores for $1.

Andean scenery

TRANSPORTATION

The central **bus station** is bordered by Reyes and Maldonado along the main road at the north end of Baños. Buses run to most cities in the Sierra as well as to the Oriente: Quito ($3, four hours), Ambato (50 cents, one hour), Riobamba (75 cents, one hour), and Puyo ($1.50, two hours). (As of late 2000, the road from Baños to Riobamba was not only closed but basically gone, with washed-out canyons up to 10 meters deep.) Local buses to **El Salado** and **San Martín** leave regularly from the bus stop at Alfaro and Rocafuerte.

Taxis can be found at the **Cooperativa de Taxis,** 16 de Diciembre at Ambato and Halflants, and the **Cooperativa de Taxis 13 de Abril** at Ambato y Alfaro. You can also find lots of taxis at the bus station.

VOLCÁN TUNGURAHUA

A narrow appendage of Sangay National Park reaches north to enclose Tungurahua, only 10 km south of Baños. The young volcano has one of the more lengthy rap sheets in the Ecuadorian Andes. A look at the paintings in Baños' church would lead you to believe that during the 18th and 19th centuries the volcano was erupting every day and twice on Sundays. Especially destructive eruptions came in 1711 and 1877, and the two Germans who first climbed the peak in 1873 must have been crushed to hear that subsequent eruptions changed the mountain's appearance so drastically that, in effect, a new unclimbed summit was created.

Tungurahua II was first climbed in 1900 by Ecuadorian mountaineer Nicolás Martínez. The eruptive sequence that began in October 1999 soon forced the evacuation of Baños, blocking access roads (including the one between Baños and Riobamba) with slides of mud and ice. The crater has more than doubled in size.

Tungurahua has been called the easiest snow climb in Ecuador—one of the few in the country where you start out sweating in a T-shirt amid tropical vegetation and finish with your eyelashes freezing shut at 5,000 meters. Until the eruption alert is lifted, however,

TREK DEL CONDOR

Snow-capped volcanoes, challenging *páramo* hiking, and the chance to see the endangered Andean condor make this four- to five-day trek one of the best in the country. Weather-wise, Nov.–Mar. is the prime season, but bring raingear and rubber boots at any time and be ready to use them. Along the way you'll follow muddy cattle trails through completely unspoiled countryside with great views of the Antisana, Sincholagua, and Cotopaxi if the weather is on your side. The IGM 1:50,000 *Papallacta, Laguna Micacocha, Sincholagua,* and *Cotopaxi* maps cover the hike.

The route starts about eight km west of Papallacta, at a place called El Tambo marked by a group of buildings near a bridge at a sharp bend in the road from Quito. Follow the Río Tambo southwest toward Cerro El Tambo (4,134 m), then turn southeast to camp on the western side of the Laguna Volcán (a.k.a. Laguna Tumiguina) on the Río Tumiguina. This should take about 3–4 hours from the road.

From here the trail leads generally south through cloud forest, passing over the western flank of Antisana toward the Laguna Santa Lucía to its northwest, 5–7 hours from the Laguna Volcán. The camping here is great, if the weather cooperates; otherwise it's somewhat exposed. A trail heads from the west side of the Laguna toward the southwest, passing the stone building of the Hacienda Antisana before connecting with the road to Píntag. It may be necessary to pay to cross the hacienda's land—check with José Delgado in Quito, tel. 2/435-828.

You can head back to civilization on the road to Píntag, or keep going cross-country to the southwest to complete the full trek. Cross a few streams on your way across spongy tussocks of vegetation called *almohadones* that make walking a chore. If the track fades, just keep heading toward Sincholagua. You can camp 6–8 hours from the second campsite. The next day, find the Quebrada Huallanta in a U-shaped valley where condors are often seen. Follow it southwest to climb and pass over the eastern flank of Sincholagua. There's another good campsite near the pass between Sincholagua and smaller peaks to the southeast, 5–7 hours from last night's spot.

From the pass, descend toward Cotopaxi and Rumiñahui to a bridge over the Río Pita. It's another half-day hike to the Laguna Limpiopungo or the Cotopaxi refuge from here, or you can hike or hitch back to the Pana along the park road.

climbing is highly discouraged. Although some agencies in Baños offer up-close volcano observation tours, many of the more reputable and safety-conscious agencies are not going near the mountain for the time being. Check with the SAE or in local papers for the latest update. You can also try the websites of the Instituto Geofisico (server.epn.edu.ec/wig) or Volcano World (volcano.und.nodak.edu/vwdocs/volc_images/south_america/ecuador/tungurahua.html), both of which are updated regularly.

Palictagua Hot Springs

For those put off by the crowds in Baños, a second set of springs can be found on the west side of Tungurahua on the way to Riobamba. Look for an arrow and the word "Puela" painted on a rock on the left about 15 km west of the intersection with the road to Ambato, near where the Río Puela joins the Río Chambo. Take the turnoff and cross through the town of Puela. Just before the village of Palictagua, you'll cross a bridge; take a track to the left to another bridge. Cross this (you'll have to park somewhere around here if you're driving because the road ends) and follow a footpath to the right across the field to the trees, where you'll head to the left up the valley. Soon you should be able to see a hut and waterfall higher up. The pools are near the hut, reached by a steep climb. The higher pool is hotter and yellow from mineral deposits, whereas the lower pool is cooler and clearer. The hike takes about 1.5–2 hours from Palictagua.

EAST TO PUYO

The road downhill from Baños to Puyo clings to the edge of the verdant Río Pastaza gorge, diving into tunnels and emerging to wispy waterfalls spilling down the green hillsides. Badly needed road repairs are constantly holding up traffic.

The first stop after leaving Baños to the east is the village of **Ulba,** from which a road leads uphill to the south to Runtún. Soon after Ulba, you'll see the Agoyán dam and hydroelectric project on the left, which has reduced the Río Pastaza to a mere whimper of its former self while providing electricity for much of the region. Near the mouth of the tunnel, about five km from Baños, is the brown **Agoyán water-fall**—imagine what this must have been like before the river was dammed. A small restaurant serves passersby waiting to get through the tunnel.

About seven km on the other side of the tunnel, the Río Verde spills into the Pastaza from the north. Here you'll see a sign indicating a path down to the river to a suspension bridge. From the middle of the bridge is the best view of **El Pailón del Diablo** (Devil's Cauldron), a waterfall tumbling into a deep depression. Puyo is another 50 km downhill.

WEST OF AMBATO

One of the most spectacular detours in the country leaves Ambato to the west, moves up and over the flank of Volcán Chimborazo, down to Guaranda, and onward to Babahoyo and the coastal lowlands. The road was once one of the main thoroughfares between Quito and Guayaquil. Today traffic crosses the Cordillera Occidental elsewhere, but the 100-km route—the highest paved road in Ecuador—has retained all its beauty.

Cultivated fields cover every square meter of countryside along the initial stretch west of Ambato. Soon you'll be climbing into the misty, moorish *páramo,* where chunks of the rich, dark-brown hillside have crumbled onto the road as it cuts between pine forests. Suddenly, right there less than 10 km away, squats ancient, massive Volcán Chimborazo, the highest mountain in Ecuador. Volcán Carihuairazo sulks deferentially to one side.

Hardly any vegetation is left this high up, and wind across the bleak base of the mountains whips grit into the air. Somewhere in this rocky, sandy moonscape the road peaks at higher than 4,000 meters. Soon you begin the descent into the Tolkien valley where Guaranda awaits, but Chimborazo always lingers in the distance, its snowy cap shining brilliantly in the sun.

The journey takes about two hours by bus. Because the road from Guaranda to Riobamba is almost as thrilling, the ride out and back is a highly recommended detour if you're heading north or south on the Pana, even if Guaranda isn't on your list. Just sit back, trust your driver, and enjoy the views.

CHIMBORAZO FAUNA RESERVE

The provinces of Cotopaxi, Tungurahua, and Bolívar intersect within this 58,560-hectare reserve enclosing Chimborazo and Carihuairazo. The four Holdridge life zones within the reserve are all basically *páramo* by another name, ranging from the low, dry mountain steppe to the more humid mountain and subalpine forests. Much of the original vegetation, sadly, has been cut down. A **camelidae** reintroduction program oversees the breeding and care of llama, vicuña, and alpaca herds with the direct participation of local indigenous communities.

The reserve can be entered from either Pogyos on the road between Ambato and Guaranda or from Mocha on the Pana south of Ambato. Admission is $10 pp, and the IGM 1:50,000 *Quero* and *Chimborazo* maps cover the area.

Volcán Chimborazo
Ecuador's highest peak (6,310 meters) caps the southern tip of the Cordillera Occidental, a final upward thrust before the mountain chain fades off to the south. Chimborazo, whose name comes from the Quechua for "snowy place to be crossed," actually consists of two peaks with five separate summits between them. The climb is straighforward and memorable.

Chimborazo used to be thought of as the highest mountain in the world, a fact that perhaps eased the sting when both La Condamine and Humboldt failed to achieve the summit (the latter repeatedly). Whymper and the Carrels, in what was probably the sweetest moment in their travels in Ecuador, were the first to stand atop Chimborazo in 1880 via what is known today as the Whymper Route. Although Mount Everest has since been deemed higher, Chimborazo has one thing over Everest: even if it is shorter when measured from sea level, Chimborazo's peak is actually farther from the center of the earth than Everest's because of the earth's equatorial bulge.

Looking back on his achievement, Whymper wrote that "it was clear that an ascent was not to be affected without labour." This sentiment holds true today: while the route isn't technically difficult, it still demands a minimum of knowledge, experience, and above all acclimatization. The upper slopes are prone to avalanches—a bad one in 1993 killed 10 climbers—so a guide and a certain amount of discretion are indispensible. The melting of the mountain's glaciers have led to recent changes in the route. Although Chimborazo can be climbed year-round, the best months are December and January. April brings heavy snowfall, and by June you can expect high winds but a clear sky and good snow.

On the road from Ambato to Guaranda, look for a solitary abandoned white house on the left where the road reaches its highest point a little west of Pogyos. A dirt road leads southeast, forking southwest of Chimborazo after 10 km. Head right to go to Riobamba, or turn left to reach the Whymper hut at 5,000 meters at the foot of Thielmann Glacier, 10 km uphill. Accommodations in this refuge, which is operated by the Alta Montaña agency in Riobamba (tel. 3/942-215), include cooking facilities and bedding. Taxis from Riobamba, Ambato, or Guaranda may go as high as the lower hut.

Leave the refuge at midnight. The original Whymper Route ascended the ridge to the right of the hut, but deglaciation has made this way unstable and often deadly. Instead follow the new Direct Route, heading for the ridge to the left facing the peak. Before reaching the very top of the ridge (protected by a rock wall), cross toward the beginning of the glacier farther up under the same rock wall.

The steep glacier is crossed by crevasses near the bottom, but these gradually disappear farther up. The Whymper Route joins from the right after a dangerous, icy traverse under a serac looming above. The Veintimilla summit (6,260 meters) is farthest west, and a little less than one km east is the Whymper summit (6,310 meters). The snow between the peaks can be soft after mid-morning, making it a royal pain to wade through without snow shoes.

Setting foot on the top of the highest volcano in Ecuador will make you want to celebrate, if you have the breath left. "We arrived upon the summit of Chimborazo standing upright like men," wrote Whymper, "instead of grovelling, as we had been doing for the previous five hours." Allow at least 8–10 hours for the ascent from the Whymper hut and half as much for the descent. Continuing in a straight line west from the Veintimilla and Whymper peaks are the Politécanica summit (5,820 meters), first climbed in 1971, and the Nicolás Martínez summit (5,570 meters), the mountain's most difficult.

An old, little-used, but easier route leads from Pogyos southeast to the ruined Zurita hut at 4,900 meters on Chimborazo's northwest side. From here the route goes straight for the top, intersecting the Direct Route between the Veintimilla and Whymper summits. The new Integral or Sun Ridge Route, opened in 1980, ascends the mountain from the east, leaving the Pana from the village of Urbina. It reaches the Whymper summit by way of Nicolás Martínez and Politécanica in 4–6 days (the current record is two).

Volcán Carihuairazo

Sharing the Abraspungo Valley with its big brother Chimborazo, Carihuairazo (ka-ree-why-RAH-zo) takes its name from the Quechua for "strong, cold wind." Both the Maxim (5,020 meters) and Mocha (height disputed) peaks are covered with snow and ice, making technique and experience necessary for the ascent. Both summits are part of a large caldera almost two km in diameter, open to the north. Whymper and the Carrels first climbed the Mocha peak in 1880, while Maxim remained unconquered until a Colombian, German, and French expedition reached the summit in 1951.

Mocha is accessed most easily from the town of Mocha, midway between Ambato and Riobamba on the Pana. A dirt road leads northwest from Mocha and is partially accessible by 4WD vehicle (trails also lead west from Mochapata and 12 de Octubre, smaller villages a few km south of Mocha). The trail passes a ruined hut at 4,300 meters near Cerro Piedra Negra peak (4,500 meters). To ascend the Maxim peak, head directly east from Pogyos. Camping along the way will probably be necessary; a spot near the Laguna Negra is recommended.

Either route can be used as a starting point for the beautiful, challenging hike between Chimborazo and Carihuairazo. The four- to five-day trip starts at Mocha, on the road between Ambato and Riobamba. The route heads west, skirting the southeastern flank of Carihuairazo and passing between the volcano's two main peaks and two smaller side hills (Cerro Piedra Negra to the south and Loma Piedra Negra to the southeast). It ends near Pogyos on the Ambato-Guaranda road, where it's possible to hitchhike in either direction.

SALINAS

If few travelers experience the road to Guaranda, even fewer make it another 33 km up to Salinas, a little isolated town at the foot of interesting cliff formations. Salinas' cooperatives turn out several quality products, including some of Ecuador's best European-style cheese, fine sweaters, sausages, and mushrooms. An artisan store sells crafts of wood, tagua, ceramic, and porcelain, and the **Quesera de la Cooperative Salinas** (Salinas cooperative cheese factory) offers explanatory tours; it's open daily from about 8 A.M. to 4 P.M. You can arrange tours through the **oficina de turismo** (tourism office) on the main plaza. Guides, bikes, and horses can also be arranged through

the office. Look to the map on the main plaza for information on walking routes in the area. You can buy cheese and other food staples in a **shop** on the 2nd floor of the west side of the plaza.

Mineral-water springs and old salt mines are a two-hour walk past the stadium. Snug accommodations are available in the nearby **Hotel Refugio,** tel. 3/981-253, tel./fax 3/981-266. Rooms with all meals are $13 pp, which is a

SALINAS: A SUCCESS STORY

The first known inhabitants of the region around Salinas (technically Salinas de Guaranda so as not to be confused with the city of the same name on the coast) were a pre-Inca indigenous group known as the Tomavelas. They began mining mineral deposits left by natural saltwater springs, a practice continued until the late 1960s, when new techniques made salt extraction from seawater more economical. Hacienda owners closed the mines, and Salinas began to shut down as well. Male residents went to the coast to find work on banana plantations, and houses once ringing with the voices of entire families stood empty. By the 1970s, barely the shell of a town remained.

In 1971, a young Italian priest was summoned in hope of injecting some life into the dying village. Father Antonio Polo's first attempt at an economic cooperative, the 15-partner Cooperativa Salinas, never made it. Other attempts to organize residents over the next few years, including cheese and textile cooperatives, also floundered, but Polo continued to try. When a group of European volunteers arrived in 1976 to teach the inhabitants of Salinas the Swiss art of cheese-making, things finally began to turn around.

Today Salinas thrives. Twenty-four of 28 parish communities are arranged into cooperatives under the umbrella organization FUNORSAL. Salinas cheese is in demand as far away as Quito, and new projects are springing up continually—mushrooms sprouting in the shadows of pine trees planted in a reforestation project led to a successful mushroom-growing business. The cheese cooperative alone earned close to $30 million in 1993.

Cooperative members enjoy social security, low-interest loans, job training, and health benefits. Profits are reinvested in the cooperative and the community for buying new equipment and maintaining the local infrastructure. Infant mortality and illiteracy rates have dropped and nutrition levels have risen, prompting more and more young residents to stay and work rather than leave. Some say that the cooperatives have served their purpose by now—that they are in fact hampering further development by stifling individual creativity and initiative—and that the next step to privatization is overdue. Regardless, Salinas remains an economic model for towns throughout Ecuador.

good thing because there isn't anywhere else to eat in town. They can fix trout and sometimes *cuy* (guinea pig) in the evenings. Carnival brings the **Fiesta de la Lana** (Wool Festival), celebrated with food and music. Three daily **buses** leave from Guaranda, or you can rent a pickup or catch a bus to "quatro esquinas" (four corners), the intersection with the road to Salinas, and hitch the 20 km from there to Salinas.

GUARANDA AND VICINITY

Guaranda's nickname, "The Rome of Ecuador," seems to make about as much sense as "The Quito of Italy," but a glance at the city's setting explains it. The capital of Bolívar province is built on, around, and in between a set of rolling hills— seven, to be exact, just like ancient Rome. Guaranda's setting is made even more superb by the snowy bulk of Volcán Chimborazo over the hills to the northeast. Cobbled streets climb through this bright, breezy town (so breezy, in fact, that power outages from blown-down lines are not uncommon).

Like Latacunga, Guaranda (pop. 16,000) is a provincial capital with a small-town feel. After an evening *paseo* around the Parque Bolívar, you'll hear your footsteps echo alone down the steep side streets, while elsewhere children play soccer and roller-skate in the narrow, sloping Plaza Rojo along Calle Enriquez. No longer part of the main land route between Quito and Guayaquil, Guaranda has kept its hilly charm intact.

Sights
The city's castlelike **cathedral** sits on the edge of the Parque Bolívar, solidly built of large stone blocks. Overlooking the town is **La India Guaranga,** a five-meter statue of a heavily muscled *indígena.* The views from the small plaza surrounding the statue are worth the hike if you decide to walk. Follow the same road to the La Colina complex and keep going a few kilometers past it, or hire a taxi.

Accommodations
Guaranda's poshest digs perch above the city from a nearby hillside. The 19-room **Complejo Turístico La Colina,** 117 Guayaquil, tel./fax 3/980-666, 981-954, has a bar and restaurant,

along with a pool and sauna open to the public ($2.50 pp, 8 A.M.–6:30 P.M.). Tours can be arranged to nearby villages and sights. To reach the hotel, head east on Moreno and take a left uphill on Guayaquil. Rates are $15 s, $17 d.

Next to the municipal building in the city center is the **Hotel Cochabamba,** García Moreno and 7 de Mayo, tel. 3/981-958, 982-124, fax 3/982-125. The hotel's restaurant is probably the best in town, with entrées for $2–3 and a set lunch for $2. The owners also organize local tours. Rates run $6 s, $8.50 d with private bath, $2.50 s, $5 d with shared bath. There's also a six-person room for $18.

My favorite part of the pleasant **Hotel Bolívar** is the 10-meter cactus in the plant-filled inner courtyard. Rooms have rugs, TVs, and hot water. Rates are $2 pp shared, $3 pp private. Pastel wall stripes reminiscent of the 1960s decorate the **Hotel Santa Fe,** 804 10 de Agosto and 9 de Abril, tel. 3/981-526, with a restaurant and electric showers. Rooms go for $1.75 pp shared, $2.75 pp private.

Food
Guaranda is seriously lacking in the food department (no Roman feast here). Along with the restaurant at the Hotel Cochabamba, the best possibilities for a decent meal in the city are the **Restaurant El Rincon del Sabor** and the **Restaurant Rumipamba.** Coffee and snacks are on the menu at both locations of the **Kofy Bar.**

Entertainment and Events
Carnival in Guaranda is rated as one of the most festive and traditional in the highlands—expect plenty of drunken street dancing, water balloons, and sprayed foam. If you can't wait to party, try **Los Balcones de la Pila** at García Moreno and Pichincha, and the **Cafetacuba** downstairs from the Corte Superior de la Justicia on the Parque Central.

Shopping
There are a few small **supermarkets** around the city, or try one of the city's two **markets,** held on Saturday and Wednesday in the Plaza 15 de Mayo and the concrete Mercado 10 de Noviembre. A few cobblers around the city can custom-make you a pair of cowboy boots or walking shoes for surprisingly little.

Services and Transportation

The **Banco del Pichincha** will change travelers' checks at a rate of less than 1 percent. Guaranda's **bus station** is a 20-minute walk from the city center east on Moreno. At the **Flota Bolívar** ticket window at Enriquez and Azuay you can book passage to Ambato, Guayaquil, Quito, Santo Domingo, and Babahoyo.

Toward Riobamba

The narrow road east from Guaranda is as exciting for its knuckle-biting danger as its scenery.

Clinging desperately to the side of green velvet hills, the dirt road is barely wide enough for one lane of traffic. Don't look down around the curves or you might see the bus tires skirting the edge of a sheer hundred-meter drop-off. The surrounding hills are so steep that houses are built on shelves dug out of the hillsides, and field workers can till the ground in front of them standing up straight. Above a tiny trickle of river, the reforested slopes sport tiny, evenly planted saplings. Workers enveloped in clouds of sawdust saw larger pine trees along the road.

RIOBAMBA AND VICINITY

There were moments in Riobamba . . . times, usually in the early morning and evening, when I felt myself so transfixed by the gentleness of the light, the softness of the breeze and the scented stirrings of the eucalyptus, that I had no desire to move from where I was ever again.

—*Richard Poole,*
The Inca Smiled

The history of the capital of Chimborazo province begins in prehistoric times. Puruhá *indígenas* were the first to settle here at the south end of the Avenue of the Volcanoes, among the low, rolling hills within sight of Chimborazo, Tungurahua, and El Altar. Next came the Inca, followed in 1534 by the Spanish, who founded their first capital near the present-day city of Cajabamba. An earthquake in 1797 destroyed most of Riobamba, prompting the surviving residents to rebuild in the city's present location. Ecuador's first constitution was written and signed here, an event commemorated in the name of the city's main thoroughfare, Primera Constituyente.

Riobamba's nickname, "Sultan of the Andes," fits it perfectly. The city has an elderly, settled feel, as if nothing has changed in a long while and that's just fine. Cobbled streets and well-maintained antique cars add to the air of comfortable complacency. Colonial buildings in every shade of pastel imaginable line the city's short blocks. Turquoise, peach, lime, and lavender

facades stand behind elderly women selling ducklings out of cardboard boxes on streetcorners. It's no surprise that long lunch hours (noon–3 P.M.) are the norm.

As a trading center for the south-central Sierra, Riobamba (pop. 140,000) sees more indigenous traffic than most cities its size. Cattle being led down the street are a common sight, and even the city's name reflects its mixed heritage—a combination of the Spanish word for river plus the Quechua word for valley. Riobamba is also known for the chill winds that blow through its streets, sent down from the slopes of Chimborazo and El Altar.

SIGHTS

Museums and Galleries

One of South America's foremost religious art museums is housed in the former **Convento de la Concepción,** at Argentinos and Larrea in the church of the same name. The 16th-century convent was donated to the city when the convent life began to fall out of vogue among aspiring young women. Today the former nuns' cells hold priceless works of colonial religious art. Paintings, sculptures, and crucifixes abound. Don't miss the incredibly inlaid *barguesos* (chests of drawers) or the museum's priceless monstrance—a gold- and jewel-encrusted vessel in which the consecrated Host was displayed to the faithful during Mass. A spartan reconstructed nun's room, complete with wire scourges, gives an idea of convent life during the colonial period.

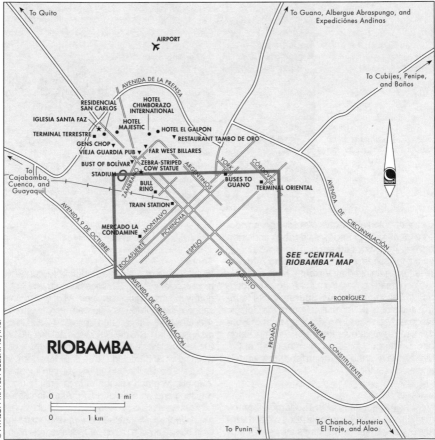

RIOBAMBA

To Quito

To Guano, Albergue Abraspungo, and Expediciónes Andinas

To Cubijes, Penipe, and Baños

AIRPORT

AVENIDA DE LA PRENSA

RESIDENCIAL SAN CARLOS

HOTEL CHIMBORAZO INTERNATIONAL

IGLESIA SANTA FAZ

HOTEL MAJESTIC

TERMINAL TERRESTRE

HOTEL EL GALPON

RESTAURANT TAMBO DE ORO

GENS CHOP

VIEJA GUARDIA PUB

FAR WEST BILLARES

BUST OF BOLÍVAR

ZEBRA-STRIPED COW STATUE

STADIUM

To Cajabamba, Cuenca, and Guayaquil

BULL RING

BUSES TO GUANO

TERMINAL ORIENTAL

TRAIN STATION

MERCADO LA CONDAMINE

ZAMBRANO

AVENIDA 9 DE OCTUBRE

ROCAFUERTE

MONTALVO

PICHINCHA

ARGENTINOS

YORK

CÓRDOVEZ

ESPEJO

10 DE AGOSTO

AVENIDA DE CIRCUNVALACIÓN

SEE "CENTRAL RIOBAMBA" MAP

RODRÍGUEZ

PROAÑO

PRIMERA CONSTITUYENTE

AVENIDA DE CIRCUNVALACIÓN

0   1 mi
0   1 km

To Punín

To Chambo, Hosteria El Troje, and Alao

© AVALON TRAVEL PUBLISHING, INC.

Free guided tours are available, with a tip expected and deserved. The convent is open Tues.–Sat. 9 A.M.–noon and 3–6 P.M., Sun. and holidays 9 A.M.–12:30 P.M.; admission is $1 pp.

A small historical collection can also be found in the **Cordoba-Román Family Museum,** Velasco 24-25 and Veloz, tel. 3/961-503, open Mon.–Fri. 8 A.M.–5 P.M., $1 pp.

Parks, Churches, and Monuments

Named after the date on which Riobamba was founded, the **Parque 21 de Abril** occupies a small hill called La Loma de Quito at Argentinos and León. It offers a great view of the city and mist-shrouded volcanoes on the horizon, along with a mural depicting the history of Ecuador with special emphasis on Riobamba. Climbers take note: one of the park's outer walls is perfect for rock-climbing practice. On the north side of the park sits the small **Iglesia San Antonio de Padua** with an impressive wood altar. Crypt visits (bring a date!) are held Sat.–Sun. 3–6 P.M.

The **Basilica** next to the **Parque La Libertad** is famous for being the only round church in the country. Riobambeños are particularly proud of this one because local talent was responsible for most of its design and construction during the late 19th century. A few blocks west, the

Tungurahua erupting behind the Church of San Antonio de Padua in Riobamba

TIM BEWER

pleasant colonial **Parque Maldonado** encloses a monument to Pedro Maldonado under the gaze of the city's **cathedral.** Two blocks north sprout the spires of the **Convento San Alfonso,** resembling an old gray Victorian house.

Keep heading west from the Parque Maldonado to reach the **Parque Sucre** with its fountain and statue of Neptune in front of the Colegio Nacional Maldonado. An imposing **bust of Bolívar** keeps watch over the intersection of Borja and Zambrano, while on the other end of the dignity scale is the **zebra-striped cow statue** one block south.

Markets

Most of the goods sold in Riobamba's many markets are of the household, tool, or food variety, but a few offer tourist items as well. Of particular note are the baskets and mats woven by nearby *indígenas* out of reeds from the Laguna Colta. Saturday is the main market day, with Thursday close behind. Crafts and indigenous clothing are sold in the **Parque de la Concepción** at Orosco and Larrea, south of the convent. The produce market in the **Plaza Simón Bolívar** also carries pottery and baskets. Also significant are the **Mercado Borja,** across Espejo from the Iglesia La Merced, the **Mercado La Condamine,** five blocks south of the train station, and the **Mercado San Francisco,** between 10 de Agosto, Primera Constituyente, Velasco, and Benalcázar. **Su Comisariato** supermarket occupies a corner of Parque Sucre.

RECREATION

Tours

Within range of a sizable handful of Ecuador's most popular peaks, Riobamba hosts several high-quality mountain guide services. All of the organizations and individuals listed are fully licensed. **Alta Montaña,** Daniel León Borja 35-17 and Ibarra, Apdo. 06-01-523, tel. 3/963-694, tel./fax 3/942-215, e-mail: aventura@laserinter.net, is the most well known and trusted. They offer trips for just about any destination and activity you can imagine, from climbing and hiking the Inca Trail to bird-watching and horseback riding. Alta Montaña's services are more expensive than most, but they really have their act together. A four-person trip up Chimborazo costs $170 pp, all inclusive. Alta Montaña trips can be booked in the United States through High Road Adventures, 1091 Industrial Rd., Ste. 160, San Carlos, CA 94070, 415/592-2444 or 800/589-4229. Alta Montaña is open Mon.–Sat. 9 A.M.–7 P.M. and Sun 9 A.M.–1 P.M.

Marcelo Puruncajas directs **Andes Trek,** Colón 22-25 and 10 de Agosto, tel./fax 3/940-964. He has climbed since 1958 and speaks English. Andes Trek rents equipment, runs mountain-biking trips and Amazon tours, and has a 4WD service available. Chimborazo for four (side of glaciers, hold the scree) costs $130 pp. The office is open daily 9 A.M.–7 P.M.

Marcelo Cruz operates **Expediciónes Andinas,** tel. 3/964-915, e-mail: marcocruz@laserinter.net, three kms toward Guano across the street from the Albergue Abraspungu (see "Accommodations"). Climbing is their specialty, but llama treks and mountain-biking tours are on the bill. A four-day, four-person trip up Chimborazo costs $300 pp, including use of the high-quality equipment that they also rent.

The **Julio Verne** travel agency relocated here from Baños after the eruption of Tungurahua. They receive regular recommendations for their climbing, trekking, and jungle trips, and the staff speaks German, Dutch, English, and a little French. Climbing Cotopaxi or Chimborazo is $120 for two people, with one guide for every pair of climbers. They're at 5 de Junio 21-46 and 10 de Agosto, tel. 3/963-436, 9/712-766, e-mail: julver@interactive.net.ec.

Galo J. Brito of **Pro-Bici,** Primera Consti-tuyente 23-51 and Larrea, tel. 3/942-468 or 941-734, guides mountain-biking excursions per-sonalized to each group's ability, from extreme descents of Chimborazo to quiet village tours. Galo offers high-quality Cannondale aluminum frame bikes and a support vehicle and speaks English and a smattering of French and German. Day trips are about $30 for one person, $55 for two, and $25 pp for three or more. He also rents bikes and equipment.

The Hostal Montecarlo (see "Accommodations") offers evening tours of Riobamba for $30 pp and can take people to see Tungurahua. **Majestour-ing,** Carabobo 22-09 and 10 de Agosto, tel. 3/946-624, tel./fax 3/944-673, has city tours from $6 pp.

ACCOMMODATIONS

In Town

Many of the budget hotels clustered around the train station redefine the word "basic," offering lit-tle more than a mattress and a door to shut. The **Hotel Imperial,** Rocafuerte 22-15 and 10 de Agosto, tel. 3/960-429, has laundry, luggage storage, and mail service for $2 pp with private bath. The friendly owner runs tours to Chimbo-razo and Tungurahua and has a small book ex-change. The Imperial is better looking than the **Hotel Bolívar,** tel. 3/968-294, on Caraboro fac-ing the platform, which still isn't bad for $1.20 with shared bath and hot water.

The friendly and clean **Hotel Los Shyris,** 10 de Agosto and Rocafuerte, tel. 3/960-323, is an-

other good deal for $3 pp with private bath and hot water. Adjacent to the Terminal Terrestre, the **Residencial San Carlos,** tel. 3/968-017, is cheap and basic with rooms for $1.50 pp with hot water. The **Hotel Tren Dorado,** Carabobo 22-35 and 10 de Agosto, tel. 3/964-890, has a restau-rant, TV and VCR room, and rooftop balcony. Nicely decorated rooms are a good value at $5 pp with private bath and hot water. They also run tours of the area. One block south of the terminal on Borja is the **Hotel Majestic,** tel. 3/968-708, where rooms with private bath and hot water are $4 s, $7 d.

Four blocks west of the train station, the friend-ly **Hotel Humboldt,** Borja 35-48 and Uruguay, tel. 3/961-788 or 940-814, has a bar, restaurant, private parking, and a lounge with a TV and VCR. Rooms ($4.50 s, $7.25 d) include TV and phone. Of all of these options, the small **Hostal Montecarlo,** 10 de Agosto 25-41, tel. 3/960-557, has the most character, with a covered courtyard and marble floors. The 17 small rooms all have TV and private bath for $5 pp, and the Cafe Real Montecarlo is next door. Although a bit timeworn, the **Hotel Whymper,** Leon 23-10, tel. 3/964-575, fax 3/968-137, is still clean and friend-ly. Rooms are only a bit overpriced at $4 pp with private bath and hot water in the mornings and evenings. Their tours in the surrounding area have been recommended.

Two of Riobamba's fancier hotels command a view of the city from a hill on the elbow of Zam-brano and Argentinos in the suburb of La Giral-da. Both show their age a bit, but they're still good deals. Up the steps at the end of Argenti-nos is the unmistakable pink edifice of the **Hotel Chimborazo International,** Argentinos and No-gales, tel. 3/963-474 or 963-475, fax 3/963-473. Each of the 36 rooms features color TV, phone, and private bath, and guests can enjoy the pool, sauna, and whirlpool on the 1st floor. Rooms here cost $5.50 s, $9.25 d. The **Hotel El Galpon,** tel. 3/960-981 or 960-982, fax 3/960-983, has a disco, indoor pool, private parking, and up-scale restaurant for $8 s, $11 d.

Out of Town

Begun in 1555, the Hacienda Chuquipoggio of Don Hernando de la Parra oversaw 151,700 hectares of land at its peak, spread across four provinces. Simón Bolívar himself once

HOTEL SPANISH

(shared/private) bathroom	*baño (compartido/privado)*
(two-person) bed	*cama (matrimonial)*
chair	*silla*
checkout time	*hora de salida*
clean	*limpio (-a) (adj.)*
dirty	*sucio*
door	*puerto*
double	*cuarto para dos, doble*
key	*llave*
to lock, lock (n)	*cerrar, cerradura*
maid	*criada*
(in the) morning	*(por la) mañana*
(for a) night	*(por una) noche*
noisy	*ruidoso (-a) (adj.)*
to pay	*pagar*
pillow	*almojada*
pillowcase	*funda de almojada*
quiet	*quieto, tranquilo (-a) (adj.)*
room	*cuarto*
sheet	*sábana*
shower	*ducha*
single	*cuarto para uno, sencillo*
table	*mesa*
toilet	*inódoro*
toilet paper	*papel higiénico*
(hot/cold) water	*agua (fría/caliente)*
window	*ventana*

graced Chuquipoggio—conveniently located between Quito and Cuenca—with his liberating presence. The hacienda's main buildings were recently converted after five years of restoration into the **Hostería Andaluza,** Apdo. 913, tel. 3/904-223 or 904-248, fax 3/904-234, e-mail: andaluza@uio.telconet.net, a fine country hotel located 16 km north of Riobamba along the Pana, within shouting distance of Chimborazo.

The hotel boasts 45 rooms, including four suites, and a pair of restaurants located in the former stable area that are capable of holding 150 people. Iron stoves steam beneath deer- and bull-head trophies inside, near old horse saddles gleaming in the firelight. Elsewhere on the manicured grounds are a gym, sauna, steam room, game room, and playground. Tiled roofs and fountains lead back to the workshops, where the *hostería's* famous An-

daluza hams are slowly cured in sea salt as they have been for centuries. Rooms ($30 s, $36 d), include private bath and satellite TV.

Set in the Las Abras suburb three km north of Riobamba on the way to Guano, the **Albergue Abraspungu,** tel. 3/940-820 or 940-821, fax 3/940-819, e-mail: valisa@laserinter.net, www.hosteria-abraspungu.com, began its career as a pre- and post-climbing lodge before metamorphosing into a country inn in 1994. Everything here rings of mountaineering, from the hotel's name (after the valley between Chimborazo and Carihuairazo) to the black-and-white photos of climbers and mountains on every wall, taken by Marco Cruz of Expediciones Andinas across the lane. Four-wheel-drive vehicles fill the parking lot, and antique climbing gear hangs from the walls. Each of the 20 rooms is named after a different Ecuadorian mountain, and they're all connected by white-washed hallways trimmed with rough wood beams and decorated with indigenous hats, masks, and old farming tools. Rates are $18 s, $24 d; breakfast costs $3, lunch and dinner $7.50 each.

Head four km in the other direction, southeast on Primera Constituyente toward Chambo, and you'll hit the **Hosteria El Troje,** tel./fax 3/960-826, 964-572, e-mail: info@eltroje.com, www.eltroje.com, another country inn with 40 fully equipped suites, resturant, and bar. Facilities include an indoor pool, steam room, sauna, hot tub, and mini gym. Rates are $40 s, $55 d, and meals are $12.

FOOD

At night an entire colony of food kiosks lines Carabobo near the train station, making it a popular place among locals to have dinner. Most Riobamba restaurants close by 10 P.M.

Simón Bolívar once owned the building where you'll find the **Cafe Concert El Delirio,** a snug, classy restaurant surrounding a small courtyard garden. The ambience inside is pure Old World Spain, with movie posters, paintings, and a fireplace to ward off the chill. Backpackers, here's a place worth splurging: a glass of wine with their $5 filet mignon or $2 hamburger will balance the karma of a dozen terrible *almuerzos.* Rounding out the classy category are the **Restaurant Tambo de Oro,** Carlos Zambrano 27-20 and Junin, serving Ecuadorian and international food, seafood, and a Sunday brunch; and the **Cabaña Montecarlo,** García Moreno 21-40, offering decent Ecuadorian fare and pasta in a chalet atmosphere for less than $3.

For more typical food at reasonable prices, try **Che Carlitos Parillada,** grilling up steaks for less than $2 at Colón and Primera Constituyente. **Charlie's Pizzería,** 10 de Agosto and Moreno, has vegetarian pizzas and lasagna. A small pie will feed two people for $4. Next door the **Chifa Pak Hao** has good, inexpensive food, as does the **Chifa Joy Sing** by the train station. **El Sabor Costeño Donde Lukas** by Parque Maldonado serves coastal dishes like *arroz con menestra* and *sopa marinera.* Watch that ají—it's potent.

On Guayaquil and Pichincha, the **Fuente de Soda Cafe Paola** serves breakfast and fruit salads and is a quiet place for a snack and a cup of coffee in the evening. For another good breakfast option, head to **Johnny Cafe,** a funky little place decorated with old photos of Riobamba just off the Parque Maldonado on Espejo. The **San Valentine Club** almost feels like a '60s soda fountain, except they serve pizzas, Mexican food, and—well, why not—Mexican pizzas. Small pies are less than $2 and a vegetarian burrito is just 65 cents. It's only open in the evenings. Vegetarians will be thankful for **Café Ashoka** half a block east of the train station on Carabobo, even though the service is soporific. Veggie lasagna is $1.20.

My favorite eatery in all of Riobamba is still **El Hongo,** a mushroom-shaped snack stand that adds a touch of Smurf to the solemn streetcorner of the Iglesia La Merced. Two small **supermarkets** share the same corner of the Parque Sucre.

ENTERTAINMENT AND EVENTS

Lectures and videos are sometimes held at the **Casa de la Cultura,** past the Aztec mural behind the mellow Bambario Cafe/Bar, and at the **Colegio Nacional Maldonado** on the Parque Sucre. The latter is home to the tiny **National Science Museum,** which is even better than the one in Ambato; the museum is open Mon.–Fri. 8 A.M.–noon, 20 cents pp. The **bullring** next to the train station features the occasional taurine nightmare.

Festivals

The **Founding of Riobamba,** celebrated on 19–21 April, coincides with an **agricultural, livestock, and crafts fair** to produce the city's largest annual festival. Other occasions to tie one on and dance all night include the **Independence of Riobamba** on 11 November.

Shopping

Several shops on Borja sell tagua nut carvings. **Ricardo Tagua,** Borja and Leon, is one of the best, as is the **The Tagua Shop,** which shares the office of Alta Montaña (see "Tours"). You can watch the carvings being made at the latter, which stocks other crafts as well.

Nightlife

Shoot a game or two at **Far West Billares,** a pool hall at Zambrano and Veloz. The **Vieja Guardia** (Old Guard) pub, popular for drinking and dancing, sits at Flor and Zambrano by the bust of Bolívar, and the **Peña Portón Dorado** has music every night. Between the train station and the bus station is **Gens Chop,** with plenty of neon and dancing at night. On the way to the Oriente bus terminal you'll pass the **Discothek Underground** and **Club Tropical Billas Bar,** both at the corner of Espejo and Cordero. The Club Tropical has pool, foosball, and ping-pong. Of the many discotecs within a few blocks of the main bus terminal, the two most popular are **Mix** and **Grin Livs** (pronounced like the things you find on deciduous trees). The latter attracts an older crowd.

SERVICES AND INFORMATION

If you can manage to find it open, the **tourist information office** on the corner of 10 de Agosto and 5 de Junio (tel. 3/941-213) can recommend mountain guides and equipment sources in the city. The **Ministero del Ambiente** has a small green-roofed office to the left of the larger Ministerio de Agricultura y Ganadera building on 9 de Octubre, tel. 3/963-779. This is the headquarters for Sangay National Park, and therefore the place to go for any information on the park or climbing Volcánes Sangay or El Altar. The guardposts at Candelaria and Alao can be contacted from here by radio to check on trail conditions. The office is open Mon.–Fri. 8 A.M.–1 P.M. and 2–5 P.M.

Viajes Qualitas, 10 de Agosto 22-44 and Colón, Apdo. 558, tel. 3/960-081, has a fax service and sells tickets for most national airlines. The **post office** is one block north under the fish-scale clock dome, and **Andinatel** sits on Tarquí between Veloz and Primera Constituyente. Internet cafés are scattered around the train station. Both **Café Ashoka** and the Hotel Los Shyris have good connections and are open daily ($1 per hour).

Money Exchange

The exchange houses **MM Jaramillo Arteaga** at 10 de Agosto and Pichincha and **Chimborazo** one block down both exchange travelers' checks efficiently and at good rates and handle a reasonable selection of other currencies.

TRANSPORTATION

Bus and Taxi

Riobamba's main **Terminal Terrestre** is on the east end of town, near the Iglesia Santa Faz at the intersection of La Prensa and Borja. Buses come and go between here and Quito ($2.25, 3.5 hours), Ambato (50 cents, one hour), and Cuenca ($4, 5.5 hours). To reach Baños ($1, one hour) and cities in the Oriente like Tena ($3.25, seven hours), though, you'll have to get to the **Terminal Oriente,** 12 blocks north of Primera Constituyente along Espejo. Buses to Guano

a native woman in Riobamba

leave from Pichincha and York, nine blocks north of Primera Constituyente. The road to Baños was completely washed out as of late 2000, and it's expected to be impassable for at least a year.

A private taxi to the refuge on Chimborazo costs about $10 and can hold up to five people.

Train

The status of the train heading toward the coast from Riobamba is constantly changing, so it's a good idea to check with the South American Explorers or the train office in Riobamba for the latest update. As of 2000, the train was running to just below the Nariz del Diablo (Devil's Nose), the spectacular set of switchbacks below Alausí, and then returning uphill to Riobamba the same day. Trains leave Wed., Fri., and Sun. at 7 A.M. for $15 pp one-way (foreigners), and return in the late afternoon. It's hoped that service to Quito and Durán (Guayaquil) will be restored in the future, but don't bet your nest egg on it.

Metropolitan Touring in Quito runs a **private**

ferrocarril (a bus chassis set on train wheels) on Wed., Thurs., Fri., and Sun. for $30. This is less likely to break down than the public train, but it only goes with a minimum of 10 people. (If you can get together that many, they might go on other days as well). Their office is on Borja 37-64, tel./fax 3/969-600 or 969-601.

VICINITY OF RIOBAMBA

The small colonial town of **Cajabamba** occupies Riobamba's original location 17 km west of the city, beneath a huge scar on a hillside from the devastating earthquake of 1797. A few km south at the intersection with the road to Bucay and Guayaquil is **La Balbanera Chapel,** the oldest church in Ecuador. When the Spanish first arrived in Ecuador in 1534, one of the first things they built, true to form, was this church on the shore of the reedy **Laguna Colta.** Since then it's undergone a complete renovation, by man and earthquake, but stepping inside the meter-thick stone walls still comes close to taking you back centuries (except for the steel grill in front of the altar). The touristy **Restaurant Balbanera** sits to one side.

Eight km north of Riobamba, artisans in the craft village of **Guano** turn out distinctive wool rugs and wall hangings. Abstract and pre-Colombian motifs predominate in the weavings, which are much thicker and more durable than the usual thin tapestries. Carlos Orozco's store and home workshop sells quality textiles, along with a craft shop on the main plaza. Ancient ruins stand watch on a nearby hillside. Saturday is market day. From Guano it's a 20-minute walk to the tepid **Santa Teresita thermal baths,** which at least have great views of the volcanoes to the east. Camping is permitted and there's a small cafeteria.

Chambo, on the road to Alao, is the home of the Festival of the Virgin of Carmen on 16 July. *Indígenas* come from all over Chimborazo province in traditional dress to pray to the town's miraculous shrine, dedicated to the Virgin de la Fuente del Carmen de Catequilla. Human remains dating to 8000 B.C. have been unearthed in **Punín,** nine km directly south of Riobamba. A small museum is open daily.

SANGAY NATIONAL PARK

The largest park in Ecuador's central Sierra connects Chimborazo, Tungurahua, and Morona-Santiago provinces. The park contains three of Ecuador's best climbs—to the tops of Volcánes Tungurahua, El Altar, and Sangay. At its creation in 1979, the park protected 270,000 hectares of such biological richness that UNESCO declared it a World Heritage Site four years later. In 1992 the Ecuadorian government added a large chunk to the southern end, more than doubling the size of the park to 517,725 hectares.

One year after that, Sangay was placed on UNESCO's World Heritage in Danger list primarily because of problems caused by the construction of a road bisecting the park from Guamote to Macas. No environmental impact studies were ever ordered to predict the consequences of this road on Sangay's delicate ecosystems. Heavy machinery and explosives used in the construction triggered landslides and polluted waterways, and the road opened Sangay's mountainous center to colonization and deforestation. Most of Sangay's backcountry, though, is still pristine and hard to reach.

Flora and Fauna
The park's 4,400-meter altitude range encloses 10 different life zones, from lowland rainforest to alpine tundra, and not surprisingly is home to a staggering diversity of flora and fauna. Most of the larger animals are concentrated in the park's lower, southern side, including anteaters, jaguars, monkeys, and most of Sangay's estimated 500 species of birds. The higher regions protect one of the last sizable refuges of the Andean tapir near Volcán Sangay. The highly endangered Pudu deer can also be found in Sangay park, but you'll have to look carefully—the nocturnal deer is one of the world's smallest, weighing in at 10 kg and standing 40 cm at the shoulder. The Pudu's stubby horns have earned it the nickname "Mephistopheles" from scientists.

Indigenous Cultures
Two groups currently live in Sangay park: the Canelos (lowland) Quechua to the north and the Shuar near Macas. Artifacts in the valley of the Río Chiguaza (a tributary of the Pastaza) have

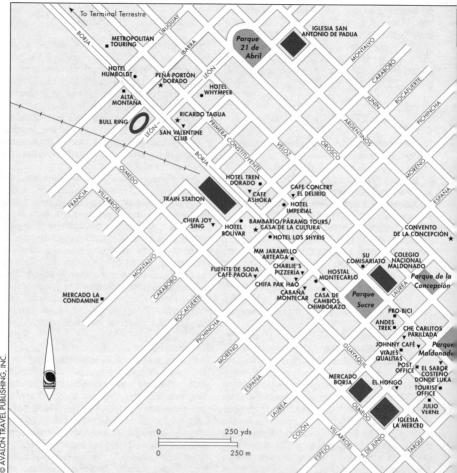

been dated as far back as 500 B.C., and a ceremonial center uncovered 30 km north of Macas is considered perhaps the most important archaeological site in the Ecuadorian Amazon. The Río Upano area around Macas was the home of the Río Upano culture during the Formative Period (4000–500 B.C.).

Access

The main gateway to Sangay from the west is through Alao, southeast of Riobamba, via Chambo, Guayllabamba, Pungala, and Licto. Hiring a private truck or taxi is the most certain way to make the journey. Trucks also leave from the Parque Libertad in Riobamba to Alao on Monday, Wednesday, Saturday, and Sunday at 1 P.M. Buses run from Riobamba at least as far as Licto. For the return, a milk truck leaves Alao for Riobamba early every morning.

There aren't any restaurants or hotels in Alao, but you might be able to sleep in the park office if it's open. If not, break out the tent. Admission to

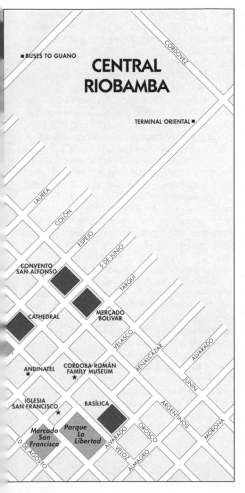

CENTRAL RIOBAMBA

- BUSES TO GUANO
- CORDOVEZ
- TERMINAL ORIENTAL ■
- LAUREA
- COLÓN
- ESPEJO
- 5 DE JUNIO
- CONVENTO SAN ALFONSO
- TARQUI
- CATHEDRAL
- MERCADO BOLIVAR
- VELASCO
- ANDINATEL ■
- CORDOBA-ROMÁN FAMILY MUSEUM ★
- BENALCAZAR
- ALVARADO
- JUNÍN
- IGLESIA SAN FRANCISCO ★
- BASÍLICA
- ARGENTINOS
- MORONA
- Mercado San Francisco
- Parque La Libertad
- OROSCO
- 10 DE AGOSTO
- ALVARADO
- VELOZ
- ALMAGRO
- ALEGRO

all the way down to Macas, 130 km from Guamote—an adventurous crossing not yet traversed by buses. Climbers can reach El Altar from Penipe between Riobamba and Baños, via a track southeast past the Candelaria guardpost.

Local Guides

The **Asociación de Guías Indígenas de Guargualá** (AGIG) is a confederation of indigenous mountain guides from Guargualla, one valley south of Alao. They offer four-day horseback excursions to the foot of Sangay, as well as guided climbing and hiking trips. All profits from their activities go directly to help the marginalized communities of Chimborazo province. None of the guides speak English, so having someone in your group who speaks Spanish (or just has plenty of patience) will help. You can contact them in Riobamba through the office of the Movimiento Indígena de Chimborazo (MICH), 1430 Casa Indígena, Guayaquil and Juan de Velasco, tel. 3/941-728, or through the Hotel Canadá, Borja and La Prensa, tel. 3/946-677.

Volcán Sangay

Climbing Ecuador's most active volcano adds rockfall, tremors, and enough sulfur to turn your ice-axe yellow to the normal mountaineering dangers of avalanches, crevasses, and plain old falling. Towering above the jungle on the edge of the Cordillera Oriental, smoky Sangay (5,230 meters) is a mountain few ever see, let alone scale. But if its name (from the Quechua *samkay,* meaning "frighten") and reputation don't scare you off—and if the cosmic dice governing volcanic eruptions roll in your favor—you just might be able to say you've completed one of the most difficult, dangerous, and thrilling climbs in South America.

Sangay's recorded history of activity dates back to 1628, and the mountain hasn't let up since: a French expedition in 1849 counted more than 250 explosions in one hour. The first successful ascent was made in 1929, followed by the first national ascent in 1962. But Sangay didn't go quietly: an eruption killed two members of a British expedition in 1976 (a story recounted in Richard Snailham's book *Sangay Survived*).

The mountain's continual activity quickly

the park is $10 pp. The road continues into the park between El Altar and the Volcán Sangay to the abandoned settlements of La Esperanza and Huamboya along the Río Palora, with a southern spur to the base of the Volcán Sangay. Near the end of the route is a site called El Placer, 25 km from Alao, where a small refuge has been built near a set of hot springs.

From Guamote, a road leads 48 km southeast to the Atillo guardpost near the Lagunas Ozogoche. From there it keeps pushing west

makes any detailed route description obsolete because the contours of the peak are being continually reformed. You should definitely hire a guide and pack animals for the long, difficult hike to the base of the mountain. Members of the guide co-op in Aloa will be up to date on the mountain's activity and the safest current routes. Vinecio Caz in Alao has been recommended.

Take rubber boots and wear a helmet because the hike to the base can be muddy and lava rock bombs are harder than your head. Protect your gear in plastic bags. Ice axes and crampons are helpful for the smooth, compacted snow near the top. Finally, leave for the peak attempt early in the morning and ascend and descend quickly to minimize your time on the slopes. Most guides won't even make the ascent themselves, instead choosing to point out the way and wait for you at the bottom. Sangay is, in the end, a mountain best admired from afar.

The best months to make the climb are Oct.–Feb., the driest time in the area. July and August are sodden, making the hike to the base more of a two-day slog. Several maps from the IGM will make your life easier: 1:50,000 *Sangay* and *Lagu Tinguichaca,* and the 1:25,000 *N IV-F3c Río Culbreillas* and *NV-B1.*

Enter Sangay park via Alao as described previously. From Alao, two routes head southeast to the base-camp site, known as La Playa. Both take between two and four days and would make a beautiful, challenging hiking trip even for nonclimbers. The first follows the Río Alao west from Alao, then bears south to the junction of the Ríos Ilapo and Culebrillas about 10 hours from Alao. Camp here, and the next morning follow the Río Culebrillas southeast for six hours until it joins the Río Yanayacu to form the Río Sangay. There's no real trail, so be prepared to cross streams, crash through vegetation, and get muddy. Near this intersection is the Yanayacu campsite. It's about six more hours hiking southeast to La Playa.

The southern route leaves from the Hacienda Etén a little more than five km south of Alao. Bear south along the Quebrada Azashuycu, then southeast after crossing the upper Río Ilapo. You'll also have to cross the Quebrada Plazabamba and Río Yanayacu before reaching La Playa, so expect to wade at the very least. Pack animals are very helpful.

La Playa is a flat lava platform at the base of Sangay. It's an amazing, humbling site, like Hell seen from the high bleachers: lava rocks rain down (pitch tents close to the mountainside to avoid them) and explosions ring out overhead every few minutes. The route climbs the smooth southeast face, an unremarkable snow slope that can get steep (35 degrees) in places. Falling rocks are your biggest worry. Three perfect craters await on top—the largest central crater, flanked by smaller ones to the west and northeast. Fog usually moves in by mid-morning, making a compass handy on the way down. Allow about six hours for the ascent and four for the descent.

THE SARAGUROS

Indigenous Saraguros, whose name means "corn worm" in Quechua, thrive in Saraguro and nearby mountain villages of Oñacapa, Lagunas, Qiusuginchir, and Tuncarta. Numbering about 30,000 in 1986, the Saraguros have held onto their cultural identity particularly well ever since being moved here from Perú by the Inca.

Both sexes wear white hats with wide, flat brims, and the predominance of black in their wardrobe is thought to reflect perpetual mourning for their betrayed Inca, Atahualpa. Men wear a sleeveless shirt called a *cushma,* along with a poncho and knee-length black or blue wool pants held up by a leather belt decorated with silver. A double shoulder bag called an *alforja* is hung over one shoulder, and long hair is worn braided. Special occasions call for white wool chaps called *zamarros.* Women wear black wool shawls, embroidered blouses, and pleated black skirts called *anacus.* Glass bead necklaces and silver earrings provide some sparkle, and silver shawl pins called *tupus* are often family heirlooms.

The financially successful Saraguros began as craftsmakers, but they've since moved on to herding cattle as far as the Amazonian province of Zamora-Chinchipe in search of grazing land. Women still weave wool by hand on a pair of ever-present palm sticks called *huangus.*

El Altar

The jagged remains of El Altar's crater bear witness to what must have been an incredible cataclysm, as one of the highest mountains in the world blew apart in an ancient explosion, leaving a C-shaped crater larger than three km in diameter open to the west. Also know as Capac Urcu (Grand Mountain), El Altar is merely a shell of its former self, but it's still the fifth-highest mountain in Ecuador and probably the most technical climb.

Nine separate summits echo El Altar's religious name. Counterclockwise from south to north they are: Obispo, "the bishop," El Altar's highest (5,315 meters); Monjas Grande (5,160 meters) and Chico (5,080 meters), "the big and little nuns"; Tabernáculo, "the tabernacle," actually three peaks of which Sur (5,100 meters) is the highest; Los Frailes, "the friars," a quartet topped by Grande (5,180 meters); and finally Canónigo (5,260 meters), "the canon." None of these peaks were climbed before 1963, when an Italian team led by Marino Tremonti first stood atop El Obispo. All have been climbed since then, but many new routes remain open.

Even with one of the longest approaches in the country—or perhaps because of it—El Altar is thought by many to be Ecuador's finest climb. It's not something you can toss off in a weekend, so you have no choice but to enjoy the valley, lakes, and views along the way. Climbers should check with outfitters in Quito or Riobamba on the condition of the track to the base and to see if the guardpost near Candelaria is open. A recommended equipment list includes snow picks, ice screws, runners, two ropes, helmets, and a small rock rack. Hikers can enjoy the trek to the base, one of the most impressive mountain spectacles in Ecuador, with jagged snowy peaks cupping a volcanic lake. The IGM 1:25,000 *Cerros Negros* and *Laguna Pintada* cover the area.

Two routes to El Altar leave from the road between Riobamba and Baños. A trail to the Collanes plain at the foot of El Altar begins in Penipe, just across the Río Pastaza 22 km northeast of Riobamba, reached by any bus toward Baños. From Penipe, make your way southeast to Candelaria. Buses leave from the market plaza on Sunday; otherwise, rent a pickup or hike the 12 km. Cargo trucks leave the Terminal Oriente in Riobamba for Candelaria on Wednesday, Friday, and Saturday. A small telephone office in the Candelaria's center can call a truck from Penipe for the return trip, if there isn't one waiting already ($8 one-way). A milk truck also runs back downhill a few times per week.

Two km past the center of Candelaria (don't blink) is the left-hand turnoff for the ranger station, where you register and pay the park entrance fee. About one km up the track is the Capac Huasi hostal at the Hacienda El Reliche (tel. 3/847-160 in Candelaria, 3/964-133 or 960-848 in Riobamba). Surprisingly comfortable accommodations with shared hot-water showers, kitchen facilities, and a great fireplace for drying sodden clothes are $4 pp, and horses can be rented (a good idea for the trek to the base).

The first part of the track beyond the hacienda is a confusing maze of cow paths, so try to get directions at the ranger station if it's open. Two small arrow signs mark important turns—the first left and the second right, just after cresting the ridge (one hour). From there it's 3–4 hours of moderate uphill hiking on a clear trail up the left-hand side of a river valley. After rounding a bend near a large boulder, the plain and El Altar itself come into view. The owner of the Hacienda El Reliche hostal has built a set of inexpensive bunkhouses at the far end of the Collanes plain ($4 pp). Each has bunks and kitchen facilities, and booking in advance is recommended.

An alternate route to El Altar leaves from Cubijes, a few km northeast of Riobamba. From Cubijes, head east to Quimiag, then on to the Hacienda Puelazo on the Río Blanco. From here a track continues east along the Río Salí to the Vaquería de Inguisay (Inguisay Dairy), about five km past Puelazo. The road is better than the trail via Candelaria—good enough for even non-4WD vehicles to negotiate as far as the Vaquería (if a bridge en route that washed out in 1996 has been repaired, that is). A truck from Cubijes to the Vaquería costs about $25 and takes 2.5–3 hours. You can camp at the Vaquería and hire horses or mules the next day to take you to the Campamiento Italiano (see following entry). José Colcha Mandsands is a recommended guide.

The Collanes plain is a welcome sight, crisscrossed by rivers to the west of El Altar. During rainy periods it becomes a sodden bog, but in clear weather the view competes for Best in the

Country. Those muted rumblings aren't planes crossing overhead, but rather ice sliding into the laguna from steep glaciers inside the crater. You'll have to climb the 350-meter rocky ridge to the east to reach the crater. Stay to the path up the left-hand ridge because the right-hand route is dangerous. The crater shelters the gray-green Laguna Amarilla in the shadow of El Altar's pious peaks.

The mountain is usually climbed from the outer face (the crumbly inner face wasn't scaled until 1984). To ascend Obispo or any of its southern neighbors, you'll want to first head south to the Campamiento Italiano (Italian campsite), a set of tent platforms between the Lagunas Azul and Mandur just south of Obispo. It's a six-hour walk from the Collanes plain and four hours by horse from the Vaquería. For the northern peaks (clockwise from Canónigo), a trail leaves northeast from the Collanes plain.

ALAUSÍ

Just less than 100 km south of Riobamba, this train town rests on a ledge overlooking the Andes' steep western plunge. A few kilometers below, the Quito-Guayaquil train line tackles the Nariz del Diablo (Devil's Nose), one of the more impressive feats of rail engineering in the Americas. Most tourists come the night before to take the ride, either to Bucay, where the tracks flatten, or all the way to Durán and Guayaquil. There's nothing else special about Alausí, but you could do much worse than this pretty, quiet town for a night's stopover.

Accommodations and Food
Almost everything is along the main street, 5 de Junio, which ends at the train station. Buses stop in front of the **Hotel Panamericano**, tel. 3/930-278, with a restaurant downstairs and decent rooms with private bath and hot water for $3 pp. The narrow, plant-filled **Hotel Tequendama**, tel. 3/930-123, makes a good rest for budget travelers with shared-bath rooms for $2.25 pp and breakfast for $1.50. One block from 5 de Junio at García Moreno 159 and Chile, the **Hotel Europa**, tel. 3/930-089, offers rooms for $1 with shared bath and hot water. Your best bet for food in Alausí is one of the various hotel restaurants; try the one at the Hotel Gampala on 5 de Junio.

Services and Information
You can exchange travelers' checks at the **Banco de Guayaquil**, at 5 de Junio and Ricaurte, in the ground floor of the municipal building near the train station. The **post office** is at García Moreno and 9 de Octubre, one block uphill from 5 de Junio past the Hotel Panamericano. **Andinatel** hides behind the fire station—go around it to the left down the pedestrian lane. A covered **market** spreads along García Moreno between Pedro Loza and Chile, uphill from 5 de Junio.

Transportation
Alausí's **train station**, the goal of most visitors, sits behind the small plaza at the north end of 5 de Junio. The train through the famous *Naríz del Diablo* (Devil's Nose) now runs only on Wednesday, Friday, and Sunday—and be happy for that. It starts in Riobamba at 7 A.M., stops off in Alausí near 11 A.M. for about half an hour, and then descends through the famous switchbacks, so tight that the entire train has to back up momentarily to fit through. (Sit on the right-hand side of the roof for the best views on the way down.) Just below the switchbacks, the train stops near Sibambe, turns around, and climbs back through the entire route. The whole trip from Riobamba to Sibambe and back up costs $30 pp and takes all day, but you can buy a ticket in Alausí through the Nariz itself and back up for less. Be at the window at 10 A.M. at the latest to make sure of a seat. Buses wait in Alausí in the early afternoon to pick up passengers when the train stops on the way back up and takes them to Riobamba, Quito, or Cuenca.

Buses head to Ambato (75 cents, three hours), Cuenca ($1, 4.5 hours), Guayaquil ($2, five hours), Quito ($2, 5.5 hours), and Riobamba (50 cents, two hours) from the corner of 9 de Octubre and 5 de Julio.

BOB RACE

THE ORIENTE
INTRODUCTION

"El Oriente," muses Henri Michaux in his *Travel Journal*, "an Ecuadorian says this word as if it were Paris: both dangerous, hard to reach, and presumably awe-inspiring." Though Ecuador's eastern half isn't as dangerous as it once was—the Shuar *indígenas* no longer perform their famous head-shrinking ritual, at least not on humans—it remains the wildest part of the country, with thousands of square kilometers only accessible by motorized canoe or airplane. And it still has the ability, in its fiery sunsets, endless coiling rivers, and sheer explosion of life, to leave you in speechless wonder that a place like this still exists on earth.

Images of Ecuador's frontier are strange but familiar, with a rugged tropical twist. Shotguns and rubber boots, machetes, and hard liquor are as practical as they are common in stores, bars, and homes. Head-high dust in the dry season is replaced by knee-deep mud when the rains come.

Some roads consist of smooth river stones, whereas others are simply a car-wide gap in the vegetation heading into the trees. Ragged children wave down from crumbling riverbanks, and entire families pole upriver in dugout canoes on their way to town. Around it all the rainforest buzzes, shrieks, breathes, and waits, a living backdrop that inspires humility at its vastness, outrage at its seething disorder, or some strange combination of the two.

The Land
The Oriente comprises everything east of the Ecuadorian Andes,which by most definitions approaches 50 percent of Ecuador.Seven of 21 provinces fall within this flat expanse—Napo, Pastaza, Morona-Santiago, Sucumbíos, Zamra-Chinchipe, and Orellana, split off from Napo in 1998— but only a scant 5 percent of the country's people live there.

Although the Pacific defines the coast and the mountains comprise the Sierra,the Oriente finds its heart in the rivers that tie it to the Amzon

---

SPEAKING ACHUAR

Wiña jai . . .Good morning/afternoon/evening
Ja ai . . . . . .Yes
Atsa . . . . . .No
Yaitiam . . .What is your name?
Wiyait jai . . .My name is . . .
Maketai . . .Thank you
Wea jai . . . .Goodbye

FRANCISCO DE ORELLANA

One of the most remarkable journeys in the history of the Americas almost ended before it began. In 1539, Francisco de Orellana, former governor of Guayaquil and relative of the Pizarros, was assisting Gonzalo Pizarro in leading a few hundred Spanish soldiers, thousands of natives tribesmen, and an ark's worth of dogs, horses, and food animals in an exploration of the upper Amazon. Half the party, including 2,000 *indígenas,* perished during the grueling journey over the Eastern Cordillera without ever seeing the jungle. The rest survived by eating their horses, then their saddles.

When the group finally stumbled across the Río Napo, Pizarro ordered Orellana to build a boat to carry the weakest members and explore downriver in search of food. Two months' labor produced a large raft, which was pushed from the muddy shore on 1 January 1542. Within minutes, the strong brown current had swept the raft and its crew of 57 Spaniards and several hundred *indígenas* out of sight. Foremost on every Spanish mind was the Andes faded into the mist was the legendary golden city of El Dorado, along with a fabled land of spices, peopled by the Canelos, or People of Cinnamon.

The first part of the river, through what would become Ecuador, passed quietly. Native villages received the explorers with peaceful offers of food, and the Spanish planted crude crosses to claim the land for the King. Within one month, the party had reached the Napo's confluence with the Río Aguarico.

A strange encounter followed when the group had stopped in a native village to build a larger boat. Gaspar de Carvajal, a Dominican friar who served as the journey's chronicler, wrote how one day four tall, light-skinned men dressed in gold stepped out of the trees. This account began a long series of rumors about a wealthy tribe of "white Indians." The rumors persisted throughout the New World for centuries, despite a complete lack of concrete evidence.

Aboard the new raft, Orellana's group began to fight for their lives as they entered a region of increasingly hostile natives. By 3 June, the exhausted survivors were amazed to reach the great joining of waters (today near Manaus in Brazil), where the coffee-black Río Negro (named by Orellana) joins the lighter Río Marañon and the two flow side by side for kilometers without mixing. An attack shortly after the meeting of the rivers sparked another legend. The Spanish soldiers described being set upon by a

---

zon basin and, eventually, the Atlantic Ocean. The speed and strength of these flows never ceases to amaze. Often the only way to tell a flow is by the small wakes behind protruding twigs, yet the silent, inexorable waters can undercut a huge clay bank or snip a bend overnight, stranding an oxbow kilometers long.

The muddy Río Napo, more than one km wide in spots, drains the Ríos Coca and Aguarico and heads off into Perú. Colombia's Amazon lies across the Río Putumayo to the north. Farther south the Río Pastaza flows from Sangay National Park, while the Río Curaray empties everything in between.

Most of the Oriente lies below 600 meters, which explains why the rivers take their time. The Andes, though, make two appearances in the Oriente before giving up completely. The Volcánes Sumaco (3,732 meters) and Reventador (3,562 meters) poke far above the surrounding green at the western edge of the rainforest.

Human History

The earliest residents of Ecuador's Amazon moved down from the Andes 5,000–10,000 years ago. Slash-and-burn agriculture was the only way to raise crops like sweet potatoes and manioc in the poor topsoil, resulting in a nomadic existence that left few archaeological traces in the hot, wet climate.

The Quijos region east of Coca was well known to the Incas, who ventured downhill to meet lowland tribes in peace and battle. It was also the first area east of the Andes to be penetrated by the Spanish. Diego de Pineda, exploring the upper Río Payamino in 1538, gave the region its nickname, "Country of Cinnamon," shortly before Francisco de Orellana pushed off for the Pacific (see special topic, "Francisco de Orellana"). The anniversary of the European discovery of the Amazon River (12 February) is still celebrated in jungle cities with markets and fairs.

Fleeing deeper into the forest couldn't protect native groups from foreign diseases, and

native group that included tall, light-skinned women armed with bows and arrows. The defenders dubbed the fierce females "Amazones," after the mythical women warriors of Greek legend. Just as the story stuck in the collective imagination for centuries, the name stuck to the river as well.

On 26 August, the waters suddenly spread to the horizon and a tang of salt drifted in on the breeze. The straggling band had finally reached the Atlantic Ocean, becoming the first Europeans, and most likely the first human beings, to travel the entire length of the world's longest river—a trip that was not repeated for more than a century.

After skirting the coast north of the Margarita Islands off what would become Venezuela, Orellana rested and dispersed his group before leaving in May 1543 for Spain. King Charles I was delighted with Orellana's tale, making him governor of the territories he had discovered and authorizing (though not financing) him to lead a follow-up colonization expedition. In 1545 Orellana left Spain with a ragtag force, paid for out of his own pocket and consisting of 300 men on four small ships. By the time the expedition reached the mouth of the Amazon six months later, one boat had been lost and half the men had died or deserted. Some of the crew managed to reach Venezuela, but Francisco de Orellana died of fever in November 1546, somewhere in the lower delta of the river that made him famous.

ORELLANA'S JOURNEY 1542–1543

© AVALON TRAVEL PUBLISHING, INC.

within a few centuries after European contact most of the region's tens of thousands of inhabitants had fallen victim to smallpox and cholera. The remaining cultures, splintered and scattered, were safe—for the moment.

The discovery of oil in the 1960s brought this once-stagnant backwater into the national consciousness. Ecuador's supposed economic salvation has also been described by one tour company owner as "the worst curse ever placed on Ecuador." In the north, the oil pipeline serves as a constant reminder of the vast reserves that make Ecuador the third-largest oil exporter in Latin America, while simultaneously wielding the power to obliterate entire cultures and ecosystems within decades.

Indigenous Groups
Throughout the Oriente, Quechua names for lakes ("cocha") and rivers ("yacu") show the influence of the Lowland Quechua, who inhabit the foothills and forests in western Napo and northern Pastaza provinces. Also in the north are pockets of Siona/Secoya and Cofán. The Huaorani have their own reserve in central Napo and spill over into Yasuní National Park. To the south, the Shuar and Achuar saw their ancestral lands divided and torn by the decades-old border dispute with Perú, which ended in 1998.

Regions
The northern Oriente, most of which is within a (long) day's bus trip of Quito, sees the most traffic. Oil's influence predominates here, creating roads that open the region to nonindigenous settlers and tourists. Lodges along the lower Río Napo offer access to some of the most unspoiled rainforests in Ecuador, and popular tourist destinations like Pañacocha and Cuyabeno have seen lots of recent development. Farther up the Napo, the central region around Tena and Misahualli is almost as popular with travelers, many of whom visit Quechua villages with indigenous-run tour operators.

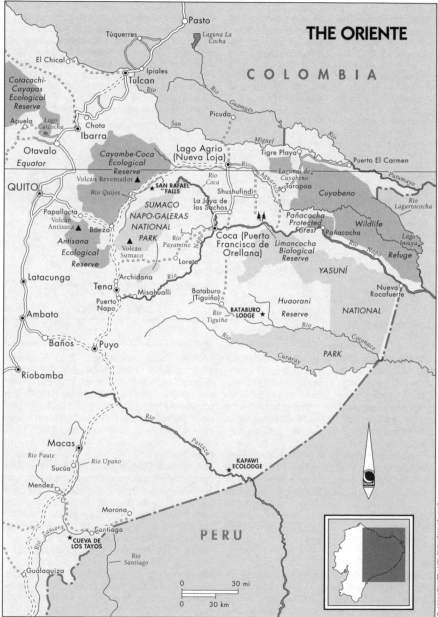

THE ORIENTE

COLOMBIA

Pasto
Túquerres
Laguna La Cocha
El Chical
Ipiales
Tulcán
Río
Picudo
Río Guamués
Cotacachi-Cayapas Ecological Reserve
Apuela
Lago Cuicocha
Chota
Ibarra
San
Río
Miguel
Tigre Playa
Puerto El Carmen
Lago Agrio (Nueva Loja)
Río
Putumayo
Otavalo
Equator
Cayambe-Coca Ecological Reserve
Volcán Reventador
Río Quijos
★ SAN RAFAEL FALLS
Río Coca
Shushufindi
Aguarico
Lagunas de Cuyabeno
Tarapoa
Cuyabeno
Río Lagartococha
QUITO
Papallacta
Volcán Antisana
Baeza
SUMACO NAPO-GALERAS NATIONAL PARK
La Joya de los Sachos
Pañacocha Protected Forest
Pañacocha
Wildlife
Lago Imuya
Antisana Ecological Reserve
Volcán Sumaco
Río Payamino
Coca (Puerto Francisco de Orellana)
Limoncocha Biological Reserve
Refuge
Latacunga
Archidona
Loreto
Río Napo
YASUNÍ
Nueva Rocafuerte
Tena
Misahualli
Bataburo (Tiguiño)
Ambato
Puerto Napo
BATABURO LODGE ★
Huaorani Reserve
NATIONAL
Baños
Puyo
Río Tiguiño
Río
Coconaco
Riobamba
Río Curaray
PARK
Río
Macas
Río Paute
Río Upano
Río Pastaza
KAPAWI ECOLODGE
Sucúa
Mendez
Morona
PERU
Santiago
★ CUEVA DE LOS TAYOS
Río Zamora
Río Santiago
Gualaquiza

0   30 mi
0   30 km

MOON

© AVALON TRAVEL PUBLISHING, INC.

Perhaps the least-visited area of Ecuador lies around the Río Pastaza, where the province of the same name extends virtually devoid of people all the way to Perú. This emptiness is mostly because the oil industry hasn't arrived in force yet, although it has already made inroads. In the meantime, the southern Oriente offers a glimpse of how the entire Amazon basin used to be, for better and worse. Access roads via Loja and Puyo are often washed out by rain and/or landslides.

QUITO TO BAEZA

Of the handful of roads that connect the Oriente to the rest of Ecuador, the one to Baeza is used the most. Finished in 1972, it was built to provide access to the oil towns of Lago Agrio and Coca and to provide access to the all-important oil pipeline. Countless oil tankers, supply trucks, and buses follow the pipeline as it snakes up out of the jungle carrying the black gold toward the coast. The winding road is narrow but in good condition for most of the way to Lago Agrio. During the dry season, each vehicle travels in its own private dust storm.

The gradual but relentless climb out of Quito up the Eastern Cordillera slows buses to a crawl. This pace gives you more time to enjoy the rugged scenery, though, as the air grows cold and the landscape looms rocky and barren. Just as most vehicles are ready to gasp and die, the Papallacta pass opens a window onto the entire Amazon basin. An entrance to the Cayambe-Coca Ecological Reserve is across from a statue of the Virgin, with trails leading off into the *páramo* (see under "Papallacta" for hiking details). Look for a stupendous view of the Volcán Antisana to the south if the weather's clear. From here it's all downhill, with the roadside vegetation turning almost instantly to cloud forest fed by the Amazon mists from below.

Despite the heavy traffic, the excellent **birding** makes the road to Baeza from Quito worth a jaunt for birders who don't have the time or inclination to plunge all the way into the jungle. Pull off on a side road and you might glimpse buff-winged starfrontlets, viridian metaltails, a buff-breasted mountain tanager, or one of a few types of quetzals native to the area.

ANTISANA ECOLOGICAL RESERVE

Since 1993 this reserve has protected a large chunk of the Ecuadorian Andes between the provinces of Pichincha and Napo, presided over by Volcán Antisana. An altitude range of more than 4,500 meters encloses two distinct ecosystems. Temperatures in the lower, humid cloud forest (1,200–3,800 meters) can reach 25°C, while nights in the high *páramo* (3,800–4,700 meters) often drop well below freezing.

The reserve's upper reaches are home to more than 50 bird species. The most significant population of condors in the country (about 10 of an estimated 70) soar through the high, thin air. Other rare species, such as the caruncalated caracara, giant antpitta, and black-faced ibis, stick closer to the ground. Tapirs, spectacled bears, pumas, and dwarf Pudu deer hide in the lower forests. Such species richness is partly because of the proximity of the Cayambe-Coca Ecological Reserve and the Sumaco-Napo Galeras National Park: animals can migrate between Antisana's 325,000 acres and the other reserves relatively easily, and conservation efforts often carry over the boundaries.

The Antisana Reserve protects one of the most important watersheds in the country, providing 75 percent of the capital's potable water. The glaciers of Antisana Volcano feed the Río Quijos to the west and trout-filled Laguna Micacocha in the direction of Sincholagua. Hunting, overgrazing, and encroachment by settlers fill out the usual list of threats, which also includes timber extraction in the eastern reaches. Further damage has been done by EMAP (the Quito Water Authority) in constructing an access road and dam across the Micacocha to provide water to the capital. The condor population has suffered particularly badly.

Visiting the Reserve
Before leaving for Antisana, contact Jose Delgado, the owner of the Hacienda Pimantura (tel. 2/462-013 in Quito) for permission to use the access road from Pintag that crosses his farm (a

situation of dubious legality, but the situation nonetheless). He charges about $10 pp. Admission to the reserve itself is $5 pp.

Volcán Antisana

Ecuador's fourth-highest peak (5,704 meters) looms southeast of Quito in a remote, cloudy area seldom seen even from afar. Four peaks surround an ice-filled crater that was active into the 18th century. Whymper and the Carrels first climbed the highest peak in 1880, leaving the other three (all within a hair of 5,500 meters) for later adventurers. Its remote location, bad weather, and lack of huts make Antisana a difficult climb.

One route begins 6–7 km east of Sangolquí on the road to Pifo, passing through the villages of Pintag (five km) and the Hacienda Pimantura of Sr. Delgado (12–13 km) as it heads southeast toward the mountain. Antisana can also be approached from the north as described in the following section, through the Hacienda El Hato of the Delgado family to the southwest of the volcano. A graded dirt road curves south and then east, deteriorating as it finally heads north toward the volcano, where base camp is set up near the snowline. The area between Antisana and Sincholagua, crisscrossed by rough trails and spotted with lagoons, is well worth exploring. The IGM 1:100,000 *Pintag* map covers the area.

PAPALLACTA

Lake District

Shortly after the road to Baeza crests the Eastern Cordillera, about 60 km from Quito, the Papallacta Lake District approaches to the north (left). This gorgeous stretch of country, filling the southern tip of the Cayambe-Coca Ecological Reserve, offers plenty of hiking possibilities among moody glacial lakes and crumbling hills that evoke the craggy countryside of Scotland. It's only a few hours from Quito, and any bus heading toward Tena or Lago Agrio can drop you off along the way. Be ready for wet, boggy conditions during the rainy season. The IGM 1:50,000 *Papallacta, Laguna de Mica,* and *Sincholagua* maps cover the area.

At the crest of Papallacta Pass (4,064 meters), a statue of the Virgin on the right (south)

side of the road marks the start of a great day hike among the lakes. Head up the dirt road oposite the Virgin (to the north) toward the antenna-topped hill, which has a sweeping view of the surrounding *páramo*. From here hike downhill to the northeast toward the southern end of Laguna Parcacha, then southeast from there toward the park guard station south of Laguna Loreta. (It may be necessary to secure prior permission to enter the reserve in Quito— or you can always plead ignorance.) A dirt road heads south to the Papallacta hot springs, where you can soak your aching tootsies in the steaming water and catch a bus back to Quito (every hour on the hour until evening) in time for bed.

The rest of the Lake District spreads north from Papallacta, with multiday hikes connecting bordering towns like Pifo and Oyacachi. Laguna Papallacta, the largest in the area, lies to the south of hot springs on the Río Papallacta. An old lava flow has stuck a tongue into its eastern side.

The Trek of the Condor (see special topic in the Central Sierra chapter) begins at El Tambo, a sharp bend in the road about four kms west of Papallacta where the Río Tambo meets the Río Papallacta.

Papallacta Hot Springs

A sign on the left-hand side of the road to Baeza, a few kilometers past the Laguna Papallacta, points you up a dirt track to the finest set of developed hot springs in Ecuador. Nestled in a steep alpine valley at 3,225 meters, the springs attract crowds of Quiteños on weekends. It's hard to beat the combination of steaming water and dripping cloud forest, especially after a hike among the lakes.

It's 1.5 km up to the **Termas de Papallacta** and **Jambiyacu** pools. Along the way you'll pass the **Hosteria de Papallacta,** tel. 2/572-369, 433-024, with bunk beds in simple rooms for $2.50 pp with private bath. Shortly beyond that there's a fish hatchery on the left, built with the help of the Japanese government, and three restaurants serving the trout (*trucha*) that have been introduced into many of Ecuador's mountain streams.

The *Jambiyacu* pools, the first ones past the "Termas de Papallacta" gate, are 75 cents pp and offer camping on the premises. At the top of the road you'll reach the **Termas de Papallacta** proper, the nicest and most expensive pool. Ranging from kiddie-wader to swimming-pool size and from river-cold to boiled-lobster (36–42°C) in temperature, the pools are pleasantly landscaped and surrounded by newly redone facilities that include changing rooms, bag storage, towel and locker rental, a pricey café/restaurant, and a small store. Horse trips leave the ticket window on weekends. Open daily 6 A.M.–10 P.M., $2 pp.

If you just can't tear yourself away, reserve one of the 14 rooms or 6 cabins at the **Hotels Termas de Papallacta** right next to the baths. Family cabins are $75, and rooms with private bath are $33 s ($16 with shared bath) and $44 d, including access to the hotel's private baths. The Termas have an office in Quito at Foch E6-12 and Reina Victoria, Of. 4A, tel./fax 2/557-850, tel. 9/701-621, e-mail: papallac@ecnet.ec, www4.ecua.net.ec/papallacta. They also operate a 250-hectare ranch on the Papallacta River for birding and hiking excursions into the cloud forest.

The Fundación Terra operates an information center on the hill to the right of the baths called the **Exploratorio,** which introduces visitors to the ecology of the section of the Papallacta River canyon between the baths and the border of the Cayambe-Coca Reserve. Three short walking trails have been developed; you can traverse the one-km trail on your own, but the two- and four-km trails require a guide. The entrance fee (40 cents to $2 pp) depends on which trail you take.

Cheaper options for accommodations and food, including campsites, are available next to the springs, and the budget **Hotel Quito** is recommended in the town of Papallacta. Also in town, the **Coturpas** pools are not nearly as nice as the Termas uphill but cost only 50 cents pp (open Mon.–Fri. 7 A.M.–5 P.M., Sat. and Sun. 6 A.M.–6 P.M.).

BAEZA

After the mostly unpaved ride down from Papallacta, this pretty little mountain town is a good place to break up the long bus journey to the Oriente from Quito. It was founded in the 16th century as a mission settlement on the eastern slope of the Andes, and since then it hasn't progressed much beyond wide-spot-in-the-road status. Horses carry riders down the main street past well-kept wooden houses lined with potted plants, and frogs chirp in the roadside grass at night. The beginnings of the Amazon spreads out endlessly to the east.

The road from Quito splits just west of town. The left fork follows the oil pipeline and the Río Quijos northeast toward Lago Agrio and Coca—fill up with gas here if you're driving this direction because the next station isn't for quite a distance. The right fork heads through the middle of Baeza to Tena. A gas station and the Bar-Restaurant Don Gonzales at the crossroads are usually the last stop for buses bound from the jungle to Quito. The old section of Baeza comes first, consisting of a few streets sloping up steeply toward the church. A newer section of town sits a bit farther along across the Río Machángara.

Activities
A few great hiking trails take full advantage of Baeza's lofty views. To follow the **Camino de la Antena** (Antenna Trail), head up through the old part of town to the right of the church. You'll pass a cemetery on your way to a fork in the trail just across the Río Machángara. The right-hand fork continues along the river for quite a ways, whereas the left fork climbs up to a set of antennas overlooking the area. A farther branch continues along the mountaintop over town, with great views of the entire Quijos Valley on clear days. Expect to take 3–4 hours to reach the antennas, and more if the trail is muddy from recent rain. Whichever path you pick, the **birding** in the pastures and cloud forest is bound to be great: dusky pitas, gross-green tanagers, Andean guans, or cloak-billed mountain toucans all might make an appearance.

Accommodations and Food
At the edge of town toward Tena, the **Hostal San Rafael,** tel. 6/225-120 or 523-224, is a good value at $3 pp for rooms with private bath and TV. A small restaurant and store operate out of the same building, and you can choose from hundreds of movies in the video room. The hotel's operators organize tours of the area, including rafting in the Río Quijos, San Rafael

AYAHUASCA™

In the mid-1980s in the United States, California resident Loren Miller applied for a patent on a cultivated variety of hallucinogenic vine he had learned about in the Ecuadorian Amazon from the Secoya *indígenas*. According to the patent, Miller, as the sole employee of his home-based International Plant Medicine Corporation, intended to study the plant's possible uses in psychotherapy and as a treatment for cancer. Unfortunately for Miller, that particular variety of vine, known more commonly by its indigenous name *ayahuasca*, has been used for millennia in ceremonies by the rainforest residents—and they are taking the issue to heart.

Translated as "vine of death" in Quechua, Ayahuasca is well known to almost all Amazon tribes. The Shuar and Achuar call it *natema,* the Cofan *yajé,* the Colorados *nepe,* the Huaorani *mii,* and the Cayapas *pindé,* but they're all talking about *Banisteriopsis caapi,* a vine that grows up to eight cm in diameter and sprouts white, yellow, or red flowers. Its hallucinogenic properties come from an orchestra of alkaloids that give Ayahuasca its intense yellow-brown color when cut. In carefully controlled ceremonies, tribe members use the vine to talk with dead ancestors, discover the causes of sickness, and communicate with the forest itself.

Once they found out about the patent application—10 years later—outraged *indígena* leaders likened Miller's act to patenting the Catholic Eucharist, and in 1999 went to court to challenge the patent. Miller, described in Quito newspapers as a "bio-pirate," was banned from the Ecuadorian Amazon as a coalition of indigenous leaders warned they could not be responsible for "the physical security of Mr. Miller and the officials of his company if they enter[ed] . . . the Amazon Basin." (Considering the declaration a death threat, the U.S. government rescinded $1 million in aid it had been providing to Secoya communities.) Some countries banned biological researchers altogether and forced others to return collected plant samples. Indigenous tribes began to back out of contracts with other "bioprospectors" throughout the Amazon.

At issue is the accountability of pharmaceutical companies who learn of plants with potential value—medicinal and commercial—from indigenous groups. According to detractors, they then take the product home to reap the benefits without giving anything back to local communities. Ayahuasca is a perfect example: even though Miller eventually declared that there was almost no promise for drug development from his variety, named Da Vino, other entrepreneurs (including many in Ecuador) still sell it over the Internet and market "shamanic tours" in which visitors take it under the guidance of a medicine man—whose presence, say the defendants, shows that local tribes are happy to participate.

The U.S. Supreme Court has ruled that, under certain circumstances, living organisms such as genes and new strains of plant life can be patented. Indigenous peoples are stunned that plants and animals they have used for generations can suddenly be claimed by foreigners. They point out that the United States is the only major world power that has refused to sign the Convention on Biological Diversity, drafted in 1992 and signed by 171 countries.

At the same time, local governments worry that an accord protecting the intellectual property rights of local tribes from foreign exploitation could scare off potential investors, particularly pharmaceutical companies with their eyes on the rainforest. Indigenous groups say they're fighting to keep their ancestral knowledge theirs, and for the right to profit fairly on any breakthrough discoveries.

One proposed solution is a countrywide system of registering native plants, which might have prevented the original controversial patent in the first place. Another law in progress would guarantee shamans the rights to their vast body of medicinal plant lore, and would require community leaders to give foreign companies authorization for any floral prospecting and receive a portion of any benefits in return. Everyone involved would profit from such an agreement; although two-thirds of all cancer drugs and half of all major pharmaceuticals have their roots in the plant kingdom, less than 1 percent of the estimated 250,000 flowering plants on Earth have been investigated for their medicinal properties. Mistrust and recrimination makes sure this potential remains untapped.

As the argument over money continues, the sad fact remains that most of the rainforest's biological riches may be destroyed before anyone profits.

falls, and the Cavernas de Jumandí. If you're heading to Lago Agrio, they'll even drive you to the intersection where Lago-bound buses pass.

The **Hotel Samay,** tel. 6/320-170, in the new section is clean, friendly, and simple, if a bit overpriced, for $4 pp. Some hot water is available on the first floor. Just off the highway in the old part of town, the **Hotel El Nogal de Jumandí,** tel. 6/320-208, has a great view north from the balconies off rustic rooms; rates are $1 pp with shared bath and hot water, pinups included. The building is in disrepair, with clutter piled high in the office/lounge, but the result is charming in a strange sort of way.

The most promising of Baeza's scant selection of eateries is in the old section of town: where the **Bar-Restaurant Gina** serves one of the best fried chicken plates east of Quito for $1.50. They even have a couple of vegetarian options. Head uphill into the new part of town and take your first left to find the **Cevichería-Cafetería El Viejo,** which comes recommended as well. The

Restaurant Guayas is another good choice. It's on the main road at the west end of town near El Viejo, as is the restaurant at the Hostal San Rafael.

Services and Information

The local **Andinatel** office is on the west end of town; as always, look for the big satellite dish. There's a **disco and karaoke bar** near the Hostal San Rafael, and a tiny **police** station sits in the old section of town, along with a small military base.

Transportation

Any bus between Quito and cities in the northern Oriente passes through Baeza, making it easy to hop on or off in town. Buses to and from Coca and Lago Agrio pass by "La Y" (pronounced "La Yay"), the highway intersection just west of town, whereas those to Tena and spots south head right through town. Buses to Quito ($1.50, three hours) stop below the Hotel El Nogal de Jumandí.

NORTHERN ORIENTE

The road northeast from Baeza descends into the wide, flat valley of the Río Quijos, where the jungle becomes more and more dense as the altitude drops. It's a beautiful and surprisingly unspoiled landscape for most of the way. Trees take over completely as the dirt road leaves the slate-green Quijos to join the Río Aguarico flowing west.

SAN RAFAEL FALLS

The highest waterfall in Ecuador roars over a rock shelf in the Río Quijos, 66 km and 1.5 hours from Baeza. A small bus stop on the right marks the turnoff, flanked by a small sign reading Entrada Al Campamiento San Rafael y La Cascada. Follow the dirt road downhill, over the small Río Reventador and past a guardpost (deserted as often as not), where foreigners are supposed to pay 40 cents.

The two-km trail to the falls starts between two of the yellow bunkhouses. Painted green arrows mark the way at first. Continue down the hill beyond the campsite, ignoring a blocked-off

branch to the right after 500 meters. The trail is clear but can get muddy as it crosses streams and winds though a series of wooden gates. Bromeliads and cecropia trees decorate the forest alongside giant ferns with fronds as big as horses. Birders, keep your eyes peeled: the Amazonian umbrella bird and the cock-of-the-rock are both found in the area. After about 45 minutes, you'll arrive at a small clearing overlooking the falls as they fill a leafy gorge with mist. Be careful near the edge: the small cross is in memory of a Canadian photographer who fell to his death. The best view of the brown torrent is from a little farther down. The path continues to the base of the falls, a three-hour round-trip of steep and slippery scrambling.

The **San Rafael Lodge** at the falls has rooms for $52 s, $79 d, dorm rooms for $5, and camping spots, with discounts for students. They can arrange ornithologist guides who speak English, French, German, and Spanish, as well as trekking and rafting on the Quijos River. Contact them through Via Natura at the Hotel Quito, tel. 2/236-879, fax 2/567-284, e-mail: hoquito@ibm.net, www.altesa.net/srfalls.htm.

VOLCÁN REVENTADOR

True to its name ("exploder" in Spanish), Reventador is one of the most active volcanoes in Ecuador. It sits surrounded by cloud forest on the eastern edge of Cayambe-Coca Ecological Reserve. Lava rocks on the way up are warm to the touch, reminding nervous climbers of the ancient explosion that chopped down one of the highest mountains in the country (judging from the size of its caldera) to a mere 3,562 meters. Recorded activity began in 1541 and continued into the 1970s. It's thought that the devastating Amazon earthquake in March 1987 that ruptured the oil pipeline and killed hundreds may have reawakened the volcano.

Since its first ascent by a scientific expedition in 1931, Reventador hasn't been climbed often because of its muddy approach and constant, if low-level, activity. If possible, check with locals before starting out to determine recent activity. The best months to climb are Sept.–Dec., with June and July the wettest. Because the three- to five-day trek to the top crosses everything from pastures to lava-covered wasteland, hiring a guide is a good idea; ask for Luis "Lucho" Viteri in Baeza or Edgar Ortíz in the town of El Reventador just up the road. Because the approach is so wet—it's practically under water and the peak is often clouded over—any climber should bring a machete, rubber boots, a waterproof tent and rope, a compass, and maps. The IGM 1:50,000 *Volcán El Reventador* map covers the area, and *The Ecotourist's Guide to the Ecuadorian Amazon* by Rolf Wesche includes a small topographical map.

Route

The trail begins shortly past the entrance to San Rafael Falls. The road to Lago Agrio crosses the Río Reventador, makes a sharp left and right, and passes under the oil pipeline. Look for a small metal shelter on the left.

Head west and uphill, crossing the pipeline, until you spot a faint trail (it gets better). You'll know you're on the right track if you cross several small streams within the first few minutes.

The track becomes clearer as it passes from grass to forest. Be ready to wade through mud and scramble over and under fallen trees. If no one has been this way recently, you might have to hack your way through the undergrowth. Cross a small stream, head left at a fork shortly thereafter, and descend to the Río Reventador. After two ridges and ravines, you'll reach your first lava flow, which you should follow to the northwest. Try to keep from breaking your ankles on the treacherous boulders for the next hour, then ascend to a plateau to the left and head southwest to the refuge, which sits at 2,300 meters near the junction of two small rivers. Here you'll find eight bunk beds and a fire pit, along with what may be the last water before the summit depending on the season. In theory, it should take you 4–5 hours to reach the refuge from the road.

Beyond the refuge, the trail continues west between the two rivers. There are many side branches, so make sure you enter the steep forest soon after the refuge. One hour of trees brings you to a landscape of loose, treacherous lava rocks, which by skirting to the southwest you'll exchange for solid, dependable lava. From here you have two choices on where to camp. Option one is a base camp halfway up at a small flat area known as La Playa (The Beach), at 3,100 meters about four hours from the sum-

JULIAN SMITH

mit. If you push it, you could make it to the old crater rim the first day (option two), 5–6 hours of toil from the road, for a great morning view of the jungle.

It's also possible to make it to the summit and back to the refuge in one long day, but be warned that finding your way over lava in the dark is difficult. It takes 7–8 hours to reach the summit from the refuge, and another five or so to descend. On the other hand, there are no water sources at either of the campsites, so you'll have to bring at least two days' worth if you decide to spend the night.

The peak shows you just how big this mountain used to be. The entire south rim of the old three-km crater is missing, opening a view of a new, smaller volcanic cone in the middle surrounded by sulfur-encrusted rocks.

LAGO AGRIO

The capital of Sucumbíos province, Lago Agrio (pop. 25,000) is barely older than its province, which was declared in 1984. American oil giant Texaco carved the city from the jungle in 1972 as a field headquarters for its explorations in the Oriente. Although it's officially named Nueva Loja, the city is better known by the Spanish translation of Sour Lake, Texas, where Texaco got its start at the turn of the 20th century.

"Lago" is an oil town pure and simple—a scruffy frontier outpost that's hot, remote, and full of rough-knuckled oil workers and prostitutes. Its lawless feel has risen with the recent influx of drug trafficking and guerrilla activity from Colombia, only 15 km north.

Accommodations

Most hotels in town don't bother with hot water, but in this heat you won't miss it. The well-run **Hotel Oro Negro,** Quito 164, tel. 6/830-174, has basic but clean budget rooms for $2 pp with fan and shared bath. The **Residencial Marcella** isn't the friendliest place in town, but it's clean and a good value, with the most plants of any hotel in town. Rooms run $2 pp with private bath, or $1.60 pp with shared bath.

Just north of Quito on Colombia, the **Hotel Machala No. 2,** tel. 6/830-073, has yellow and green tables outside its ground-floor restaurant, a color theme that continues inside. Rooms with color TV, private bath, and hot water are $3.50 pp. Next door the **Hotel Lago Imperial,** tel. 6/830-453, fax 6/830-460, is comparable and slightly nicer, with a purified-water cooler and balcony over the street. For a room with a fan, cable TV, and private bath you'll pay $4 pp, or $2.75 pp with shared bath. At the popular **Hotel D'Mario,** tel. 3/830-172, fax 3/830-456, rooms with TV, air-conditioning, and private bath are $6 s, $8 d; add hot water, telephone, and a refrigerator for $13 s, $15 d.

The poshest place in town is the **Hotel El Cofán,** tel. 3/832-409, fax 6/830-526/527, on 12 de Febrero between Quito and Añasco. The small, expensive restaurant is good, and rooms with private bath, cable TV, mini-bar, and air-conditioning cost $14 s, $19 d.

Food

Several restaurants along Quito spill out onto the sidewalk and cater to tourists. **Restaurant D'Mario** does an okay pizza for $2.60 and is often packed with gringos after hours. They also have good ice cream. A few doors down, the **Restaurant Machala** is a friendly alternative, although it's also relatively expensive.

For typical fare, the **Restaurant La Chola Cuencana** on Añasco has a large selection—make your choice from the paintings of dishes on the wall (dishes average $1.50), or ask for the English menu.

At the corner of Amazonas and Quito, the **Asadero El Capitan** is a good spot to watch street life go by over a plate of grilled meat, and the **Chifa Estrella China** on Quito is available for those who need a **tallarin** fix.

The **Panadería/Cafetería Jackeline** across the street from El Capitan serves juices, fruit salads, and ice cream, while the **Heladería Milwaukee** just south of the plaza offers a range of fast food and, of course, ice cream.

Shopping

Lago Agrio's main **market** takes up the triangular corner of Quito and Amazonas. Cofán *indígenas* still come into town for the main market day on Sunday, although they seldom wear traditional dress like they once did.

A small fruit and vegetable market is set up along Sucre west of Orellana, and vendors and food stands line the busy section of Quito. For

Amazon souvenirs, try **Artesanía Amazonicas** on Quito, with a selection of painted balsa birds and woven Cofán bags and necklaces. They even have functional blowguns. **Arte Galería** also has lots of balsa birds, along with some more artistic sculptures.

Entertainment

Finding a bar for a drink in Lago Agrio is no problem—after all, this is a frontier town. Then again, it's a frontier town, so after dark you should probably limit yourself to the few busy blocks of Quito, where most gringos spend the evening in one of the many sidewalk cafés. Join the locals on the sidewalk in front of the Vaquero Bar for a Pilsener day or night.

The most exciting thing to do in Lago is probably the TAME flight into the city, which scrapes the rooftops on its initial buzz of the center before landing.

Tours

Adonis Muñoz is the main naturalist guide for **Caiman Safaris,** Quito 414, tel. 6/830-177. Trips led by English-speaking guides to Secoya communities along the Ríos Aguarico and Coca, or to Cuyabeno or Lagartococha, cost about $50 pp per day depending on the number of people. They also have more economical trips to Cofán villages. They can be contacted in Quito through Expediciones Ecuatorianos, tel. 2/559-389.

Galo Sevilla Lara of **Cuyabeno Tours,** tel. 6/831-737, 9/492-210, e-mail: cuyabeno@imp-sat.net.ec, was born and raised in the Amazon and worked for other companies for years before starting his own business in 1996. He works out of a room in the former Hotel Río Amazonas, but more often than not you'll find him sitting out front in one of the restaurants nearby. With two people, tours of 4–5 days to Cuyabeno are $35 pp per day, and camping trips are $40 pp per day for eight days. They have an office in Quito at Juan León Mera 345 and Jorge Washington, tel./fax 2/522-768.

Services and Information

You can change travelers' checks at the Hotel El Cofán. You'll have no problem changing Colombian pesos because almost every block has at least one place that changes them. If you're planning on crossing into Colombia north of Lago at La Punta, you'll need to visit **immigration** on 18 de Noviembre and Colombia, and the Colombian Consulate in Quito.

The **post office** is on Rocafuerte a few blocks west of the market, and **Andinatel** sits near the plaza on Orellana and 18 de Noviembre. The **Ministerio del Ambiente** has an unsigned office on Eloy Alfaro near Colombia, and you can get tourist advice at the **Casa de la Cultura** on Manabí around the corner from the **police station** at Manabí and Quito. There weren't any Internet cafés in town in 2000, but considering some of the one-horse towns that have them already, it probably won't be long.

Transportation

There is a *terminal terrestre* north of town, but almost everyone goes directly to the bus company offices instead. **Transportes Baños** has the most daily departures to Quito ($6, eight hours) and has a 7 P.M. overnight bus to Guayaquil ($8.75, 14 hours). **Transportes Loja** goes to all kinds of unlikely places, including Loja ($12, 24 hours,

1 P.M.), Cuenca ($10, 18 hours, 9 P.M.), Ambato ($6, 10 hours, 9 P.M.), and Machala ($11, 18 hours, 1 P.M.). **Transportes Putumayo,** at the southwest corner of the market, drives to Quito and Coca ($1.25, three hours) as well as Tarapoa ($1), and *rancheros* to Coca and Shushufindi ($1.50, three hours) leave often from Amazonas. Rattling rancheros and buses line up on Quito to pick up passengers to villages in the surrounding jungle; ask around for destinations.

TAME, with an office on Orellana at 18 de Noviembre, flies to Quito every day of the week except Sunday for $50 one-way. Book a few days in advance if you can. Local buses run to the airport, or you can go to the TAME office and try to find fellow passengers to share a cab.

LIFTING THE EARTH

This song is traditionally sung by Shuar women during manioc planting to invoke the goddess Nungui and her husband Shakaema to bless and watch over the crop.

Shingi wairu tu tahei
Lifting the earth with the *shingi** we have done the work,

Tu aweiru shindyantamryá
Thus we have dug in the earth to awaken you.

Tu tahei, tu tahei.
Thus we have done, thus we have done.

Nungui noachi assana,
Daughters of Nungui, the woman,

Hui tu tahei, tu tahei.
Thus here we have done.

Mamankutu untsuaheitá,
May you multiply our manioc crop,

Shindyantamryá, shindyantamryá.
Wake up, wake up!

Aishirú kutú, tsukahei vaityá,
Dear husband, I am hungry,

Aishirú kutú, tsukamá huahuá.
My husband, my child is also hungry.

Shindyantamryá, shindyantamryá,
Wake up, wake up,

Wari kureitkurá.
Quickly appear!

*ceremonial stick planted in ground to
 symbolize steadily growing manioc

Quichua guide demonstrating how to make face paint

TIM BEWER

SOUTH TO COCA

The route from Lago Agrio to Coca serves as a sad study in the effect of unregulated development on tropical rainforest. After crossing the Río Aguarico, you pass a stretch of houses, farms, and oil refineries lit by bright, hissing spouts of flame that bathe what trees are left with a hellish nighttime glow. The 93-km road is paved most of the way to endure the constant onslaught of tanker trucks, but it's still rough enough that the trip takes three hours in a bus. (Two military checkpoints slow things further.)

The road follows the oil pipeline to La Joya de los Sachas and has made it that much easier for colonists to move in and set about clearing the jungle to cultivate fields that will have a lifespan of no more than a few years. Notice how many signs read *se vende* (for sale). Branches of the oil pipeline head north into Colombia and south well into Pastaza province; others follow the route to Shushufindi and reach east into the Cuyabeno Wildlife Refuge.

Sitting on top of the bus, gritty and windy as it may be, is a good opportunity to see a slice of frontier life. People play volleyball and soccer in fields backed by towering, vine-laden trees, and lines of bright-colored clothes, freshly washed, stretch from house to tree to house. At the intersection of the road east to Shushufindi, buses are swarmed with kids hawking sodas in plastic bags and kebabs topped with chunks of plantain. After a detour west that leaves the pipeline behind, the road crosses the Río Coca then follows it south 16 km to the town of Coca.

COCA

If the Oriente is Ecuador's Wild West, Coca is its Dodge City. Here on the banks of the Río Napo, the taxis are pickup trucks, and helicopters and puddle-jumper planes roar overhead. Oil workers and colonists keep the dozens of bars and pool halls in business, while residents watch Perúvian TV shows in front of slowly spinning fans.

Officially named Puerto Francisco de Orellana, Coca (pop. 16,000) was declared the capital of the newly made province of Orellana and split off from Napo in 1998. Development dollars are starting to pour in, but Coca still exudes the feeling that anything would be for sale—if only they could get it out here. It's the closest sizable city to undisturbed rainforest in Ecuador—the Cuyabeno Wildlife Refuge is just downstream—so Coca has more than its fair share of tour operators, which makes it a good place to join a group.

Some roads are paved, but most are still dirt or mud, depending on how recently the rain last fell. The tree-lined Malecón along the Río Napo has potential, but at the moment it's just a dirt track with a few thatched huts serving food and drinks.

Sights

The **Casa Parocial** next to the Iglesia Nuestra Señora del Carmen contains a tiny **museum** with indigenous crafts and weapons. More interesting is the photo album that includes pictures of the body and funeral of Monsignor Alejandro, who was killed by the Huaorani in 1986 while doing missionary work. Open Mon.–Fri. 9–11:30 A.M. and occasionally in the afternoon, free.

Accommodations

Only a few of the many budget hotels are passable, and most of them don't have hot water. The **Hotel Florida,** tel. 6/800-177, costs $1.50 pp for a basic room with shared bath. Near the river

on Antigua Misión, the **Hotel Oasis,** tel./fax 6/880-206, is far from the best hotel in town, but it's much nicer than you would expect from your first look. Rooms are $2.75 pp with fan and private bath.

In the center of town, the **Hotel El Auca,** tel. 6/800-127, tel./fax 2/460-417, e-mail: aucacoca @ i n t e r a c t i v e . n e t . e c , www.interactive.net.ec/hotel-auca, is a popular meeting place for tour groups. Wooden cabins fill an inner courtyard filled with hammocks, flowers, and jungle birds. Cabins are $5 pp with private bath, fan, TV, and hot water. The hotel features a restaurant with a patio overlooking the

street. The **Amazonas Hostería,** on the far west end of town, tel. 6/880-444, 2/441-533, has rooms with hot water, cable TV, and fans for $6 pp, along with a restaurant. If all of these places are full, the run-down **Hotel Cotopaxi,** tel. 6/880-875, offers clean rooms with private bath for $2.50 ($1.25 shared).

Oil-company managers and other bigwigs stay at the **Hotel La Misión,** tel. 6/880-544 or 880-260, fax 6/880-263, where rooms with private bath, hot water, TV, and air-conditioning cost $10 s, $14 d. A restaurant and disco sit next to the balcony overlooking the muddy Río Napo, next to the bar and a pool with a waterslide. Nearly tame toucans, parrots, and parakeets perch on the white railings and chairs. For reservations in Quito, contact Ed. Alamo, piso 2, Of. 204, tel. 2/553-674, fax 2/564-675.

For reasons of safety and cleanliness (or lack thereof), hotels around the bus station should be avoided, as should the Residencial Rossita by the bridge.

Food

The **Bar/Restaurant Ocaso** on Moreno is a local favorite, serving solid food at reasonable prices. Breakfast is about $1, while lunch or dinner will set you back $2–3.

For seafood all the way from the coast, stop by the neon-lit *Restaurant Marisqueria,* where a set meal is just $1.25. Entrées off the menu go for $2–7. The **Chifa Dragon Dorado,** on Bolívar at Napo, gets points for food (plates average $1.50), service, cable TV, and air-conditioning, and a full, heart-stopping *parillada* costs $6 at the **Parilladas Argentina** on the wood-covered second floor along Cuenca.

Some of the restaurants in the nicer hotels are worth a visit, including La Misión. The restaurant at the Hotel El Auca is easily the most popular dining option with gringos, and not just because they're staying in the hotel. A large and varied menu includes *camaroncc al ajillo* (shrimp in garlic sauce) and *chuleta Hawaiana* (Hawaiian pork chops), as well as a few vegetarian options. Entrées range from $2–3.

Coma pan, across from the Hotel El Auca, is a good bakery. Coca's main **market,** the Mercado Municipal Virgen del Cisne, occupies a series of green and blue buildings at the north end

of Napo. Plenty of *comedores* inside serve those looking for the cheapest set meal in town or interested in shopping for do-it-yourself meals. A second, open market sits along Eloy Alfaro and Moreno between Amazonas and Napo, and there's also a small **supermercado** next door to the Hotel El Auca.

Shopping and Entertainment

Amazonia, around the corner from the Hotel Auco on Rocafuerte, has a variety of souvenirs, including Cofán weaving and accessories.

For an evening's diversion that doesn't necessarily involve firearms or fistfights (those frontiersmen can be a rough bunch), check out **La Jungla Discotec** at the Hotel El Auca, or **El Bunker** at the Hotel Misión. A good place for a drink at night is under the thatched roof of Pappa John's down by the river. Coca really lets loose on 30 July, when everyone celebrates the **city's founding.**

Tours

Coca serves as the getaway to Ecuador's upper Amazon, offering relatively easy access to the rainforest down the lower Napo River. There are plenty of operators, so it's worth taking your time to shop around. Because most destinations are far down the Río Napo, tours of less than three days—and those that don't leave the Río Napo itself—are seldom worth the effort. At least five days are needed to visit the Yasuní National Park or the Huaorani Reserve (make sure your guide has written permission to visit this tribe—only a few do).

Jungle trips from Coca start at around $30 pp per day. Julio Jarrin of **Expediciones Jarrin,** tel. 6/880-860, e-mail: exjarrin@impsat. net.ec (in Quito, Reina Victoria and Veintimilla, tel./fax 2/525-096), has been leading tour groups to visit the Huaorani for years. He runs the company with his family and employs some female and English-speaking guides on trips of 4–10 days. He also visits Yasuní and a lodge in Pañacocha.

A small, thatched hut near the riverfront houses **Etnoturismo Anasanga Supay,** tel. 6/886-997, a Quechua-run company that offers tours to Pañacocha, Tiputini, and Yasuní for $35 pp per day (minimum four people). If you have some time to kill, they can take you up the Río Napo and send you back down on an inner tube. Their guides speak only Spanish.

Wimper Torres of **Expediciones Torres,** tel. 6/880-336 (or contact Maddy Duarte in Quito, tel. 2/659-311), runs tours for $30 pp per day down the Río Napo and other rivers for $40 pp per day. (Only a little English spoken.)

Pedro Orozco of **Jungle Excursions,** Napo at Espejo, tel. 6/880-771, runs trips into the rarely visited Nuevo Rocafuete area starting at $55 pp per day. **Paushi Tours,** tel. 6/880-219, 881-555, operate out of the Hotel El Auca. Their three- to nine-day tours in Sumaco-Galeras are recommended for $35 pp per day. They have an office in Quito at Calama 3-54 and Juan León Mera, tel. 2/554-560.

River Dolphin Expeditions, tel. 6/881-563, 880-489, e-mail: panacocha@hotmail.com, www.aamazon-green-magician.com, specializes in wildlife-watching trips, including bird-watching and plant identifications. This highly respected outfit is run by Randy Smith, a Canadian who has worked closely with the Huaorani for nearly a decade, and Ramiro Viteri, a local Quechua. Visits to the Huaorani Reserve cost $50 pp per day with at least six people. They also do paddle trips and treks and have guides that speak English, French, and some German.

The Yarina and Yuturi Lodges both have offices at the Hotel Oasis.

Services and Information

Cambiaria near the Hotel El Auca changes travelers' checks, and Coca's **police station** is on Rocafuerte between Amazonas and Napo.The tourist information office on the riverfront is no longer operating, so your best bet for general tourist information is at the Hotel El Auca, Expediciones Jarrin, or one of the other tour operators in town.

Coca's **post office** is on 9 de Octubre and Espejo, and **Andinatel** is one block away at 6 de Diciembre and Alfaro. For information on Cuyabeno, the **Ministerio del Ambiente** has an office on Amazonas north of Cuenca. The Hotel El Auca has a slow and unreliable **Internet** connection that is open to the public.

Transportation

Coca's **terminal terrestre** is about one km north of the river. A recently opened road connects Coca to the road between Baeza and Tena, heading through Loreto and south of Sumaco-Napo Galeras National Park. Make sure your bus to Quito goes via this route instead of through Lago Agrio, which is a much longer ride. *Rancheros* to Lago Agrio ($1.50, three hours) line up just north of the bridge and leave frequently.

Three companies share the route to Tena ($4, six hours) and send buses roughly every hour from 5 A.M.–10 P.M. **Transportes Baños** sends the most comfortable buses to Tena at 4:15 and 8 P.M. from their office in town. They also offer six buses a day to Quito ($7, 10 hours) leaving in the morning and evening, along with service to Ambato ($6, 10 hours) and Guayaquil ($10, 22 hours). **Transportes Esmeraldas** has comfortable coaches to the capital each night at 8:30 P.M., and **Transportes Zaracay** goes to Guayaquil at 3 P.M. **Transportes Loja** goes to Quito at 8 P.M. and to Machala ($12, 20 hours) and Loja ($14, 27 hours) at 6:30 P.M.

If you need a **taxi,** you'll find the Coca version—white pickups—on Eloy Alfaro and Via Coca-Lago Agrio. Trips within Coca are under $1, including going out to the terminal terrestre.

Among them, **TAME, Aerogal,** and **Icaro Express** fly to Quito every day of the week except Sundays for about $55 one-way. Buy your tickets at the airport as far in advance as possible. If commercial flights are booked, you might be able to wrangle a seat on one of the regular oil company or Air Force flights to Quito, but don't bet on it.

Boats down the Río Napo leave at 8 A.M. on Mondays, heading as far as Nuevo Rocafuerte on the Perúvian border for $15 pp (11 hours), with a possible stop at Pañacocha. Ferries to Misahualli have been rendered nearly obsolete by the new road over the same route, but ask at the **Capitanía del Puerto** just north of the dock for information on occasional unscheduled departures.

To hire a canoe for trips downriver, ask at the dock or stop by the **Cooperativa Transportes Fluvial** on Chimborazo. Expect to pay around $40 per day pp.

LOWER RÍO NAPO

Ecuador's largest river is a great, flowing highway into the lowland wilderness that stretches all the way to Brazil. Even though the main channel has lost most of its original wildness, watery backroads and sidestreams reach into virgin rainforest where the 20th century—or any century, for that matter—has yet to make an appearance. Several lodges take advantage of the wide river's easy access, from wooden shacks to luxury bungalows.

DOWNRIVER TO THE BORDER

Yarina Lodge
Opened in 1998 on 400 hectares of primary forest by the same owners as Yuturi Lodge (see following section), Yarina is run as professionally as its elder sibling. Despite being just one hour downriver from Coca, the wildlife viewing here is quite good—caimans are particularly common. Top-notch native guides take visitors to visit local homes, pan for gold, and climb the 40-meter tall observation tower. During night floats on the nearby lagoon, luminous insects resting on aquatic plants give you the feeling you're paddling through the sky. Because of its proximity to Coca, you can leave and return on any day of the week and stay as many days as you wish. One recommended option is to arrange to be dropped off here after visiting Yuturi Lodge. A night in one of the 20 double cabins, meals (including tasty vegetarian options), guided trips, and a translator costs $40 pp per day (20 percent SAE discount). For reservations, contact Yuturi Jungle Adventure, Amazonas 1324 and Colón, tel./fax, 2/504-037, 503-225, e-mail: yuturi1@yuturi.com.ec, or ask at the Hotel Oasis in Coca.

Limoncocha and Vicinity
The **Limoncocha Biological Reserve** was created in 1985 to protect some 28,000 hectares of rainforest surrounding the lake of the same name and a five-km stretch of the Río Napo. Once considered one of the premier birding spots in the country, Limoncocha boasted more than 400 species sighted within 12 square km of the lake.

Seventeen species of hummingbirds, hoatzins, and the rare agami heron were all common along the shore.

The area has seen its share of turmoil, however. For decades, oil companies have blasted and drilled almost directly on the shores of the lake. In 1991, six years after the creation of the reserve, Metropolitan Touring decided that the local habitats were impacted too much by oil drilling and moved their main tourism area to the eastern end of Cuyabeno Wildlife Reserve. In 1982 the Ecuadorian government ordered the Summer Institute of Linguistics (SIL), the largest missionary/linguistic organization in the world, out of its Ecuadorian headquarters in Limoncocha. Because the SIL provided many services

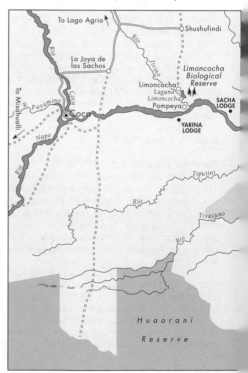

that otherwise would have gone lacking, the group's abrupt departure left the fate of the small town in jeopardy.

Things have recovered somewhat since local communities lobbied the oil companies to build a road bypassing the village and to alter their blasting methods. Bird populations have begun to rebound, and now the lake echoes with screeches and caws more often than with the roar of dynamite.

Besides its birds, the oxbow lake is known for an important ceramics find nearby. Pieces from the Napo Phase (c. A.D. 1190–1480) reflect a great aesthetic jump in indigenous pottery. Archaeologists have deduced from paintings decorating the works that the ancient inhabitants practiced secondary burial, a practice in which bodies were buried, then exhumed after a few months and reinterred in large ceramic containers sculpted especially for the ritual.

The three cabins called **Cabañas Limoncocha** were graciously left by Metropolitan Touring to the local indigenous community. Today they are among the least expensive accommodations on the river. For prices and reservations, contact the Asociación Indígena de Limoncocha (AIL), c/o CONFENIAE, Av. 6 de Diciembre 159 y Pazmino, of. 408, Apdo. 17-01-4180, tel. 2/543-973, fax 2/220-325, e-mail: confeniae@applicom.com, www.applicom.com/confeniae. Entrance to the reserve is $5 pp.

Also on the lake is the Quechua village of **Limoncocha,** where locals have formed an ecotourism cooperative that provides Quechua lessons, guided tours, and accommodations to visitors. It's possible to stay in town and explore the area for about $30 pp per day, including lodging in cabañas, food, and guides. Two small shops sell supplies, and canoes can be rented. To get there from Coca, take one of the frequent

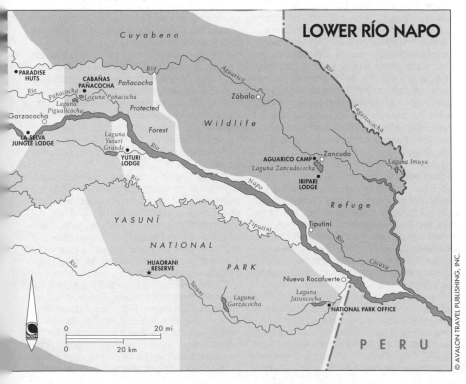

LOWER RÍO NAPO

SPEAKING COFÁN

Meenga'kay . . . . How are you?
Hayo . . . . Yes
May'en . . . . No
Chietzafpopoem . . . . Thank you
Chieegaychu . . . . Goodbye
Vatoova . . . . Caiman
Cornsipeendo . . . . Harpy Eagle
Taysy . . . . Jaguar
Na'en . . . . River
Coovy . . . . Tapir
Tsa'coer . . . . Water

buses or rancheros to Shushufindi ($1.25, two hours), then catch another bus to Limoncocha—one leaves in the early morning, another near noon, and a third late in the afternoon ($1.25, 90 minutes). The Hotel El Auca in Coca is a good source of information about Limoncocha because one of their guides is from the area.

A short ride downriver is the Capuchin mission and archaeological museum at **Pompeya,** on a small island near the north bank of the Napo. Keep going to the **Isla de los Monos** (Monkey Island), where a few different species of primates roam wild—with a good guide, sightings are nearly guaranteed. Both of these sites are often combined with a visit to Limoncocha and can easily be visited independently from the town.

Sacha Lodge

This Swiss-owned lodge offers first-class accommodations and service only 2.5 hours downstream from Coca. The lodge owns 2,000 of the more than 7,000 hectares of mostly primary rainforest that surround the small complex on the shore of Laguna El Pilche. Ten cabins with private bath and gas-heated hot water are connected by thatched walkways to the dining hall, where gourmet meals are the norm

A 43-meter viewing tower built around a kapok tree affords guests the occasional view of snowy Volcán Sumaco to the west, along with at least some of the 200 bird species that have been spotted from the tower. Birders will love the 270-meter canopy walkway and the salt lick just downriver near Añangu, where squawk-

ing flocks of parrots, parakeets, and macaws squabble over the mineral-rich soil exposed by the river.

All nature-viewing excursions from the lodge are accompanied by two guides (one local and one English-speaking biologist) for every 4–7 people. A five-day visit costs $720 pp, not including airfare from Quito (10 percent SAE discount), and a four-day trip is $577 pp, leaving Mon.–Fri. For reservations, contact the lodge in Quito, tel. 2/566-090, 509-504/115, fax 2/236-521, e-mail: sachalod@pi.pro.ec, www.sachalodge.com.

La Selva Jungle Lodge

Ever since it won the main ecotourism award from the World Congress on Ecotourism and the Environment in 1992, La Selva Jungle Lodge has been considered the Hilton of the Ecuadorian Amazon. It's also the (relative) granddaddy, having offered a combination of luxury accommodations and outstanding jungle experience since 1985. Many people come to Ecuador *just* to stay at La Selva.

The main lodge and 16 cabins overlook the Laguna Garzacocha. The menu features a combination of French, North American, and Ecuadorian cuisine, along with a dash of the rainforest, including local river fish and a special Amazon Pizza. Residents of two local indigenous communities are employed at the lodge, whose list of services include the Slothful Laundry, where clothes are "washed and often dried" but "never ironed."

Guests can go birding with native experts, climb the 30-meter canopy tower, or venture out by night to spot black caimans in the lake shadows. For an adventurous and wealthy few, the lodge offers the Amazon Light Brigade, a six-day safari with all the luxury of British Africa—two staff members per guest, gin and tonics in the evening, gourmet food, the works, for $1,324 pp plus airfare to Coca.

Those who stay near the lodge can visit the **butterfly farm** in the nearby village of Garzacocha. Here, in the first professional operation of its type in South America, 30,000–35,000 pupae from 24 species are reared from eggs to be exported abroad. If you meet an intent-looking person along a trail peering into the canopy or measuring a root diameter, chances are they're from the **Neotropical Field Biology Institute,** a field station begun by the lodge in 1992.

Four- and five-day packages cost $547 and $684 pp, respectively, not including airfare to and from Coca. Guests arriving from other countries can be met at the airport and escorted to the lodge. Make reservations in Quito at 6 de Diciembre 2816 and Paul Rivet, ed. Josueth Gonzalez, tel. 2/550-995, 554-686, fax 2/567-297, e-mail: laselva@uio.satnet.net, www.laselva-junglelodge.com.

Pañacocha

A Protected Forest encloses a town and lagoon of the same name, connected to the Río Napo by the blackwater Río Pañacocha. It's probably the most popular site on the lower Napo for tours organized in Coca and Misahualli, and it has seen lots of development in the late 1990s. More than a dozen guides have built cabañas on the shore of the lake, but as of yet most of the wildlife hasn't decided to relocate.

Twenty-six guests can occupy the six cabins, and trails connect the Lagunas Pañacocha and Pigualicocha to a flooded forest and an observation tower. Packages of five days/four nights cost $260 pp, including meals, guides, and transportation from Coca. Four-day packages are $210 pp. For reservations, contact **Emerald Forest Expeditions,** Amazonas 1023 and Pinto, tel. 2/541-278, tel./fax 2/541-278, e-mail: emerald@ecuanex.net.ec,www.ecuadorexplorer.com/emerald.

Yuturi Lodge

One of the upper Napo's more remote lodges sits on a hill overlooking the Río Yuturi five hours from Coca. More than one million hectares of flooded primary forest encompass countless lagoons, streams, and marshes fed by the blackwater river. All of it is leased from the Quechua community of Samona, whose Spanish-speaking residents serve as knowledgeable guides (English translation is available). Twenty cabins built in the traditional style—except for the electricity and private baths—are comfortable and the meals are excellent; even vegetarians will find themselves well cared for.

With more than 500 species of birds in the surrounding forest, including crested eagles, orange-cheeked parrots, black-crowned tityras,

collared puffbirds, and paradise tanagers, birdwatchers can almost be guaranteed to add to their life lists during a visit. The list of excursions includes hikes deep into the forest, visiting Quechua families, and visiting Monkey Island near Limoncocha. Between trips, you can gaze over the canopy from the 30-meter observation tower or watch the mob of hoatzins that perches next to the lodge. Tours cost $70 pp per day, including meals and lodging (20 percent SAE discount). Make reservations with **Yuturi Jungle Adventure,** Amazonas 1324 and Colón, tel./fax, 2/504-037, 503-225, e-mail: yuturi1@yuturi.com.ec, or through the Hotel Oasis in Coca.

Nuevo Rocafuerte

The weekly boat from Coca chugs into the last real "town" on the Ecuadorian section of the Río Napo every Monday. Rooms can be found to rent, although you'll have to rely on your own supplies or private citizens for food. Guides are available in Coca to take you from here into Yasuní National Park. It's supposedly possible to find guides here as well, but I don't recommend coming all this way to find out it's not true. You can continue from Nuevo Rocafuerte to Iquitos, Perú on a ferry, but check with immigration in Coca beforehand. The boat back to Coca leaves at 8 A.M. on Thursdays.

CUYABENO WILDLIFE REFUGE

Most of the eastern half of Sucumbíos province falls within this gigantic reserve created in 1979, including some parts that are so unspoiled that researchers have dubbed it the Pleistocene Refuge. Persistent oil activity and settlement in the western part of the reserve throughout the 1980s prompted the government to more than double the reserve's size in an effort to compensate indigenous peoples and to protect even more of the Río Cuyabeno's watershed from colonization.

Today Cuyabeno covers four million hectares, including most of the Río Aguarico all the way to the Perúvian border. More difficult access promises to keep much of the park pristine for the foreseeable future (a day-long motorboat ride is the only way to reach the new eastern section). Most important, Cuyabeno serves as an example of how a combination of profitable ecotourism and politically active indigenous populations can keep "progress" in check. After a visit to the reserve in 1993, former president Duran Ballén pledged to keep the park free from development.

Things look good so far, at least in the east. Western Cuyabeno still suffers from the ravages of the oil industry, along with the added pressure of colonization. A 1992 resettlement plan proposed by the provincial government of Sucumbíos would award thousands of settlers with land in the original section of the reserve in exchange for clearing and planting it—a region where, according to the Ecuadorian environmental organization Fundación Natura, 1,000 families have already destroyed 185,000 hectares of rainforest. The occasional bit of trash that floats as far as the border is a sad reminder of the situation upriver.

The only real way to experience the reserve is by staying at a lodge. Access is via the road southeast from Lago Agrio, where groups board motorboats at Dureno or Chiritza to be whisked downriver to their lodges. The road continues to the oil outpost of Tarapoa, with a park administrative center and guardpost, before continuing north across the reserve toward Colombia.

A $20 fee is charged to enter the reserve from July–Sept. ($15 during the rest of the year).

Habitats, Flora, and Fauna

Cuyabeno encompasses three types of rainforest that generally become wetter to the east. In the west, the terra firma forests stay dry most of the year, whereas seasonally flooded areas of low-water marshes border permanently flooded forests to the east. An average annual temperature of 25°C makes the Apr.–Aug. rainy season more bearable, and just over three meters of rain in a year is not unusual.

The Río Aguarico is Cuyabeno's main outlet, emptying into the Río Lagartococha that forms the Perúvian border as it flows south into the Napo. Pink freshwater dolphins and endangered giant river otters inhabit the Lagartococha's upper reaches. Fourteen major lagoons, such as Zancudococha, Lake Imuya, and the Laguna Grande de Cuyabeno to the north, are interspersed with countless seasonal marshes and lagoons.

More than 200 species of trees per hectare have been recorded in Cuyabeno's forests, including many species of palm, guavas, and native trees like the *zapote silvestre* (forest apple), *uva de arbol* (tree grape), and *cerezo de tierra* (ground cherry). Birders, of course, won't be disappointed because Cuyabeno contains at least one-third of all the bird species in the entire Amazon basin. Raucous blue and yellow macaws fly overhead, and the ringed kingfisher, the largest of five species in the reserve, is often startled from its riverside perch by passing canoes. Mammal species include the capybara (at up to 40 kg, the largest rodent in the world); the fisher bat, which snatches fish from lakes and rivers; and saki monkeys with long, furry tails.

Indigenous Peoples

The Siona-Secoya inhabit the upper reaches of the Río Aguarico near the Río Cuyabeno. Groups of Lowland Quechua are occasionally encountered downstream, along with a small enclave of Cofán at Zábalo. Two Shuar communities have recently moved into the far eastern part of the reserve.

Metropolitan Touring Lodges

Ecuadorian tourism giant Metropolitan Touring has a pair of lodges in the far eastern corner of the reserve and provides a first-class glimpse into a virgin corner of the Amazon. Nearly a full day's travel from Lago Agrio brings you to the **Aguarico Lodge** situated on a bluff over the river near the community of Zancudo. This comfortable cam, set near the Sacha Pacha Research Station and a small military outpost, can accommodate 40 guests in 20 twin rooms. From the canopy tower upriver you might be lucky enough to see a scarlet-crowned barbet or the many-banded aracari—small toucans that usually travel in pairs.

A short canoe ride from the Aguarico takes you up the meandering Yanayacu Creek, a blackwater backroad where you never know what's going to peek, fly, or crash out of the vegetation pressing in on both sides. Soon you emerge onto **Zancudococha** (mosquito lake), the largest permanent body of water in the

Ecuadorian Amazon. Deep enough to remain year-round, Zancudococha is an important breeding spot for freshwater fish, including two-meter *bagres* (catfish).

On the far bank of Zancudococha, you'll spot the thatched roofs of the **Iripari Lodge.** Iripari was built in 1991 using native materials and methods and incorporates environmentally sound systems such as solar power and biodigestors for human waste. Twenty guests can stay in 10 double rooms with shared baths, next to a combination dining room/lounge overlooking the mirror of the lake where clouds, storms, and stars are reflected with equal perfection. Paddling canoes around the lake (motors are forbidden to keep from scaring the wildlife), your group will see hoatzins galore sharing the foliage with white-necked and tiger herons. Listen for the space-age sounds of the dark blue greater ani, with a call like an avian R2-D2.

Among the many trips departing from either lodge is a three-hour ride down the Aguarico to the Perúvian border. After a cursory stop at the Ecuadorian border post, you'll head up the Río Lagartococha to the **Laguna Imuya,** one of the most unspoiled spots accessible in the Ecuadorian Amazon. Part of a large system of blackwater lakes, Imuya is home to endangered freshwater manatees, dolphins, and four species of caimans. Floating islands, trees and all, occasionally drift across the surface.

Excursions include a swim with pink river dolphins in a nearby *laguna*—an experience almost beyond words—as well as walks and floats through the rainforest. Keep an eye out for the rufescent tiger heron, the wattled jacana—whose long, spindly feet allow it to walk delicately across lily pads—and the laughing falcon, a yellow bird that dines on snakes.

Metropolitan Touring's lodges cost $650 pp for four days in the high season ($520 in the low season) and $735 for five nights ($590). For more adventurous travelers, they have started to offer the **Aguarico Trekking** program in conjunction with the Cofán community of Zabalo. Participants trek into unspoiled rainforest, learning how to spot and track wildlife and identify medicinal plants along the way from Cofán guides. Lodging is provided in rustic camps with open-sided sleeping houses built in traditional Cofán design, equipped with mattresses and mosquito nets. Visitors must carry their own personal supplies during each day's hike (3–6 hours per day), and English-speaking naturalist guides accompany each group. Rates are $1,384 pp.

All prices are double occupancy and do not include airfare. For reservations, contact Metropolitan Touring in Quito, Republica del Salvador N 36-84, tel. 2/464-780, fax 2/464-702, e-mail: info@metropolitan.com.ec,www.ecuadorable .com. You can also make reservations in the United States through Adventure Associates, 13150 Coit Rd., Ste. 110, Dallas, TX 75240, 800/527-2500, 792/907-0414, fax 972/783-1286, e-mail: info@adventure-associates.com.

Flotel Orellana

One of the most unusual, comfortable, and overall enjoyable ways to experience the rainforest is aboard Metropolitan Touring's 42-meter floating luxury hotel built in 1975. Picture a Mississippi steamboat, minus the coal stacks and paddle wheel, stuck in the middle of the jungle—something out of a Warner Hertzog film, perhaps, but here it's become reality. On the river-level deck you'll find a small boutique, the dining area, kitchen, and engine room. Up the steep stairs are 20 twin and four-berth cabins, snug but plush with private bath, hot water, bunk beds, and bottled drinking water. Behind the pilot-house on the top floor extends a covered lounge area with TV and VCR, bar, and a small reference library. An open solarium with deck chairs takes up the rear.

Visiting the Amazon aboard the Flotel is an experience very much like a first-class Galápagos Islands cruise. Two site visits per day are interspersed with gourmet meals, briefings, and quiet time to read, nap, or scan the riverbanks. A full-time doctor lives on board, and the experienced naturalist guides are always available to answer questions or tell stories. Guests are free to join in on hikes, canoe trips, or nighttime excursions, or simply to stay on board and relax. Wildlife viewing from the deck can be as rewarding, on occasion, as from the trails: three-toed sloths dangle in treetops like forgotten teddy bears, and the occasional peccary parts the muddy water as it swims across the river.

Four days on the Flotel cost $545 pp in the high season ($435 pp in the low season), and visits of five days are $650/$520 pp. All prices are double occupancy and do not include airfare. For reservations, contact Metropolitan Touring (see previous listing).

Cuyabeno Lodge
Set near the refuge's Lagunas Grandes, this luxury lodge offers comfortable bungalows built in indigenous style with natural materials and private baths. Some of Ecuador's finest naturalist guides lead hikes and canoe trips into the forest. Four- and five-day expeditions cost $395 and $495 pp, respectively, not including transport from Quito and the reserve entrance fee. For reservations, contact Neotropic Turis in Quito at Amazonas N24-03 and Wilson, tel. 2/521-212, fax 2/554-902, e-mail: neotropic@ecuadorexplorer.com, www.ecuadorexplorer.com/neotropic/index.htm.

Paradise Huts
You'll come across this small set of bungalows 1.5 hours downstream from Chiritza, at the confluence of the Ríos Shushufindi and Aguarico. Six simple huts, built in 1992, each include a large porch and three double bedrooms with private bathrooms. Water and 110-volt electricity are provided. At $220 pp for five days, including meals and a bilingual guide, Paradise Huts' programs are less expensive than Cuyabeno's other lodges. For reservations, contact OrientGal in Quito at Amazonas 8-16 and Veintimilla, tel. 2/561-104, 501-418, fax 2/501-419, e-mail: orientgal@punto.net.ec.

YASUNÍ NATIONAL PARK

Ecuador's other showpiece Amazon reserve was named a Biosphere Reserve and World Heritage Site by UNESCO in 1979, the same year it was created. At almost one million hectares, Ecuador's largest protected area is nearly the size of Yellowstone Park in the United States and one of the most truly "protected" in the country. With its difficult and carefully monitored access, Yasuní truly shelters its plant, beast, and human residents more than it opens them up to tourism.

Close to 1,500 Huaorani *indígenas* live within the park's boundaries and in a special reserve set aside for them to the west. This tribe, along with the park's long list of native species (including an estimated 5,000 species of flowering plants, harpy eagles, anacondas, and a unique type of manatee), have been threatened by colonization and by oil company exploration into the park's eastern regions. In years past, only four guards have been expected to oversee the entire park.

local lodging

JULIAN SMITH

Visiting the Park

The dry season (late Dec.–Mar.) is the best time to come. Aside from short excursions from lodges along the lower Río Napo, such as La Selva and Sacha Lodge, the only other option to enter Yasuní is by boat via Nuevo Rocafuerte. From there head up the Río Yasuní to the Laguna Jatuncocha, where the main park guardpost sits on the south bank near the entrance. Five campsites are open to visitors who might sight the lake's manatees drifting in the still waters. Three more hours upriver brings you to Laguna Garzacocha.

At the moment, a few Huaorani communities can be visited through tour groups, and more would like to become involved. "Tolls" are imposed on visitors for passage through lakes and rivers and for visiting villages, an erratically enforced practice that is considered a necessary evil by tour operators. Oil companies seeking entrance to Huaorani lands have encouraged and abused this system, while the proceeds from tour groups, in theory, go toward bettering life in the community.

Both **Safari Tours** and **Neotropic Turis** (see "Tour Companies" in the Quito chapter) run tours to visit the Huaorani. The entrance fee is $10 pp.

BATABORO LODGE

One of the more culturally sensitive ways to visit the Huaorani is to stay at this new lodge built in 1997. Not only do the Huaorani serve as guides (Spanish-, English-, French-, or German-speaking translators accompany groups), but Bataburo also will be handed over to the Huaorani organization ONHAE after 15 years of operation. The traditionally built cabins—each with electricity, private bathroom, and mosquito nets—plus a 132-foot observation tower are located in remote and pristine forest on the Río Tiguiño three hours south of Coca by road and four hours down the Río Tiguiño by boat.

More adventurous visitors can take advantage of camping trips from 6–15 days, spending the first and last nights at the lodge. Four- and five-day packages are $235 and $275 pp, respectively, including transportation from Coca but not the $20 fee to enter the reserve. Longer trips are available, and an eight-day camping trip runs $460 pp. Reservations can be made through Kem Pery Tours, Pinto 539 and Amazonas, tel. 2/226-583 or 226-715, fax 2/226-715, e-mail: kempery@ecuadorexplorer.com.

SOUTH TO TENA AND BEYOND

BAEZA TO TENA

SierrAzul

Word is just starting to get out about this small private lodge and reserve tucked on the eastern doorstep of Antisana Reserve, protecting one of the most unspoiled and beautiful tracts of cloud forest in the country. Decades ago, a North American engineer stumbled on this remote area on the eastern slope of the Andes. According to Ecuadorian law, a quick survey of the land made it his. Also according to law, though, the land had to be "improved" for human use. He cut a minimum amount of trees to start a small dairy farm, leaving most of the land untouched.

Today that same engineer heads Azul, a company that supplies services and materials to oil interests working in the Amazon. Plans are to develop SierrAzul enough so that it will pay for itself through tourism, while leaving enough cloud forest intact to make biologists drool. It seems to be working: the 7,000 private hectares are still so pristine you can drink right out of the icy streams.

More than 150 species of birds have been recorded so far, but ornithologists estimate that up to 300 species pass through here. The list includes one special member: the giant antpitta, *Grallaria gigantea.* It was thought to be extinct, but the rare bird's call was recorded for the first time anywhere in SierrAzul. The mountain tapir and endangered spectacled bear *(Tremarctos ornatus)* are sighted in the nearby woods, along with 50-cm earthworms as fat as a cigar. Part of SierrAzul's conservation mission is to support ongoing research on the cloud forest. Everyone from the Smithsonian Institute to The Nature Conservancy has funded projects here, and the University of Wisconsin is currently studying hummingbird feeding.

The accommodations are simple and comfortable, with rooms big enough for four people sharing bathrooms with hot showers. Up to 18 people can enjoy the home-cooked fare. It's hard to decide which is better, the fresh clay-oven bread or the dairy products straight from the cow. Don't forget that SierrAzul is also a working farm. Horses, cows, and alpacas graze in partially cleared fields (many acres are being allowed to return to their natural state), and it's hoped that the organic gardens will eventually provide enough to feed the entire camp.

Hiking is the most popular activity. Just follow your bilingual guide as he or she leads you through the cloud forest, which presses on every side like a living curtain before parting suddenly to reveal a beautiful valley view or thundering waterfall. Along the trails, your guide will point out medicinal plants such as *cichona,* or quinine, the Ecuadorian national plant, and Sangre de Drago (Dragon's Blood, *Croton* sp.), which is good for skin irritations and stomach problems. Twenty-five km of trails are lined with boards and topped with gravel.

Up here at 2,200–2,600 meters it can get downright freezing at night (3°C), with Jun.–Sept. the coldest months. Consider visiting outside the Apr.–Aug. wet season if rain isn't your thing (though if it isn't, the cloud forest probably isn't the place for you in the first place). A doctor is permanently stationed at the camp.

SierrAzul is 155 km from Quito, reached via a side road from the Baeza-Tena highway just north of Cosanga. Getting to SierrAzul originally involved a long, rough drive followed by a mule ride the last few kilometers to the camp, fording rivers and winding through the underbrush. Since then a five-km road to the camp has been completed, cutting the trip from Quito to three hours.

The daily cost per person is $55, including lodging, meals, and the services of bilingual naturalist guides. Transportation from Quito is another $22. A program has been set up through the Academia Latinoamericana de Español in Quito where students can study Spanish at SierrAzul. For reservations, contact the reserve's office in Quito at Floreana E8-129 and Los Shyris, Ed. El Sol, tel. 2/264-484, fax 2/449-464, e-mail: sierrazul@access.net.ec.

Cabañas San Isidro

Out the same access road as SierrAzul, the Cabañas San Isidro is an ecotourism lodge combined with a working farm. Señora Carmen Bustamente and her family have welcomed visitors to their ecofriendly cattle farm in the Cosanga Valley since the 1970s. One-quarter of the income from ecotourism goes toward buying more land for conservation.

Eleven cabins with private bath and hot showers surround a main farmhouse enclosing the dining area, bar, and sitting room. An observation tower overlooks the surrounding cloud forest, where numerous trails lead off to archaeological sites, streams, and waterfalls.

San Isidro sits a few kilometers on the road toward SierrAzul on the left. Advance reservations are essential. A double room is $159 per night and a single $91.50, including all meals. (Naturalist guides are extra.) For reservations, contact their office in Quito at Carrión N21-01 and Juan León Mera, tel. 2/547-403, tel./fax 2/228-902, e-mail: sanisidro@ecuadorexplorer.com, www.ecuadorexplorer.com/sanisidro/.

Sumaco-Napo Galeras National Park

Volcán Sumaco juts from the rainforest east of Baeza, anchoring one of Ecuador's newest national parks. Created in 1994, Sumaco-Napo Galeras covers more than 200,000 hectares of lowland and high-altitude rainforest where countless tributaries of the Ríos Napo and Coca begin. A small island section of the park encloses the Cordillera Galeras, south of the road between Narupa and Coca.

Cloud forests on the slopes of the volcano are special, completely isolated from other cloud forests by the intervening lowland rainforest farther down. Many unique species have evolved as a result, including 28 species of bats and 13 types of rodents. Pumas, jaguars, and tigrillos leave their prints in the mud, and river otters occasionally doze on riverbanks. Up to four meters of rain per year is the norm, and temperatures can vary between 10–25°C. The dry season runs Nov.–Feb. The entrance fee is $5 pp.

East of the Cordillera Galeras, the Olalla Torres family runs a small lodge on their farm. It's a great base for climbing Sumaco or just getting away—*far* away—from it all. The turnoff for Cotapino, the closest village to the farm, is about 50 km out the road to Coca near the town of Venticuatro (24) de Mayo, west of San José de Dahuano and Avila. A rolling dirt trail leads south

to the farm. Arrangements to visit can be made in Venticuatro de Mayo, or just show up (prices are negotiable).

Volcán Sumaco

Most of the few people who venture into Sumaco-Napo Galeras are intent on scaling the park's namesake volcano. The 3,900-meter volcano was first climbed in 1865. It's a long, difficult approach requiring 5–6 days of hiking and hacking before the final steep ascent.

Sumaco is called "potentially active" because, although there aren't any recent records of eruptions, its conical shape indicates activity within the last few centuries. Odds are low that it will erupt when you're on it, but smart money says it isn't dead yet. Oct.–Dec. offers the driest conditions and clearest views from the summit. For maps of the ascent, look for the IGM 1:50,000 *Volcán Sumaco* map or the detailed topo included in the *Ecotourist's Guide to the Ecuadorian Amazon*.

Take the road east from Narupa to Coca to begin the ascent. Even though it's the shortest route to Coca from Quito or Tena, not much traffic passes this way because there aren't any facilities or even real towns the entire 135 km and it's only paved part of the way. Ask for guides in the Quechua settlement of Guamaní: at least one is essential, and two are recommended for three or more climbers to help carry supplies, clear the trail, and ready campsites. Guides costs around $10 pp per day, and a small monetary contribution to the community ($25) is expected as well.

The 27-km trail leaves from the village of Sumaco, five km east of Guamaní. It winds north through primary and secondary forest, well-maintained at least the first six km to the community of Pacto Sumaco. Beyond here the trail worsens and the vegetation closes in, making you glad you brought your machete (you did, didn't you?), along with food, water, a waterproof tent, and maps. You'll pass two lagoons on the way to the final 500 meters of *páramo* before the summit.

Jumandy Caves and Tourist Complex

Four km north of Archidona, on the Baeza to Tena road, sits an eight-hectare ecological park centered around the largest of many caves in the reopening in the hillside, filling a pool that is equipped with waterslides and surrounded by playgrounds, sports fields, a restaurant, and a bar.

The main cave itself is named after a warrior chief who fought against the Spanish and was rediscovered in the late 1960s by a priest chasing an ocelot that disappeared into the cave's hidden mouth. The beginning section is heavily trafficked, illuminated, and riddled with graffiti, but the entire complex extends for kilometers underground. Three hundred meters in, you have to swim across a small lake, and that's just the beginning. Guides are available for aspiring spelunkers. The complex is open daily 9 A.M.–5 P.M., costs $5 pp, and has a hotel with private rooms with hot water for $3 pp.

More Caves and Petroglyphs

The stretch between Baeza and Tena features dozens of caverns and rock carvings, most of which are accessible to travelers with a minimum of effort. The *Ecotourist's Guide to the Ecuadorian Amazon,* with its detailed descriptions and topographical maps, is the best source for visiting caves and viewing carvings.

Archaeologists are unsure exactly why or when the petroglyphs (pictures carved into exposed rocks) were made. They're usually found near running water or on the tops of hills, suggesting either a ceremonial purpose or simply decorative doodling on the way downriver to trade. Often the *piedras escritas* (written stones) are obscured with earth and vegetation, making a quick clearing and/or chalk retracing necessary (it washes off in the rain).

Running water quickly forms caves in the soft Napo limestone underlying the surrounding forest. Visiting these is a more serious matter. Never enter a cave without an experienced guide and proper equipment (including at least three light sources, a first-aid kit, a rope, and warm clothes), and be ready to wade, swim, and crawl through mud and water once underground. Secure permission for caves on private property, and be careful with the delicate mineral formations, which can take centuries to form.

Archidona

About 10 km north of Tena, this small town has a striking church in its main plaza that is said to be a replica of one in Sienna, Italy. Quijos *indígenas* come to town on Sunday to attend mass and the market. The **Residencial Regina,** tel. 6/889-144, has rooms on Rocafuerte across from the clinic for $2 with private bath.

One km north of Archidona, the **Hostería Orchids Paradise** is a comfortable jungle-style lodge opened in 1997 on the bank of the Río Archidona. Six-person bamboo cabañas with glass windows (really!), hot water, refrigerators, and satellite TV are available in three- and five-day packages for $30 pp per day, including meals and tours into the surrounding jungle ($20 pp for accommodations and breakfast only). You can contact them at tel./fax 6/889-232, or through their office in Quito at Pinto 426 between Juan León Mera and Amazonas, tel./fax 2/526-223, 9/699-095, e-mail: paraizoo@orchids_paradise.com, orchids_paradise.com.

TENA

The steady descent from Baeza, across rattling metal bridges over muddy streams, eventually reaches Tena (pop. 20,000), the capital of Napo province. Ecuador's self-proclaimed "cinnamon capital," at the confluence of the Ríos Tena and Puno, began in the 16th century as a missionary and trading outpost—about as far into the forest as the Spanish were willing to settle.

Tena is not at all what you might expect from a midsized jungle town —it's peaceful, orderly, and clean, in a beautiful setting surrounded by forested hills and the edge of the Andes just visible to the west. It's also more geared toward tourists than many of its counterparts, making it a better choice for more than an overnight stay than, say, Lago Agrio or Coca. Many inexpensive hotels, tourist agencies, and restaurants serving vegetarian food cater to backpackers who use the town as a jumping-off point for trips into the rainforest. Red macaws croak from housetops over Sunday-afternoon volleyball games near the bus terminal.

Two bridges connect the two halves of the town across the Río Tena downriver from where the Río Puno enters—notice the different colors of the waters. A one-lane vehicle bridge crosses to the north, and a small footbridge to the south leads to a great little park on the west

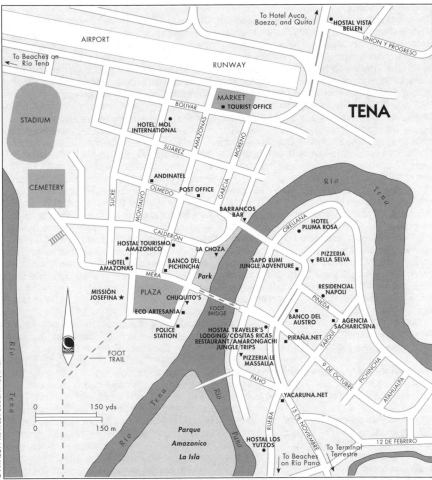

bank; it's lit at night and features interesting canoe sculptures and a bar overlooking the river.

Sights

To kill a free day in town, you could do worse than the **Parque Amazonico La Isla,** a well-done jungle-style park occupying the wedge-shaped piece of land between the two rivers. Gravel paths wander through 22 forested hectares, past spacious cages with native animals and reptiles. (A word of warning: don't get to close to the monkey who lives near the animal cages—he likes to steal cameras.) Highlights include the 10-meter diving boards into the Río Pano, the canopy view from the Mirador 2, and an ornamental and medicinal plant garden. Precocious kids wait at the covered bridge to act as guides. The park is open daily 8:30 A.M.–6 P.M.; admission is $1 pp, plus another 40 cents for a brochure and map.

Accommodations

The friendly Rivadeneyra family runs the **Hostal Vista Bellen,** tel./fax 6/886-228, tel. 2/492-852, at the north edge of town, with a small open cafeteria under a thatched roof. The 18 rooms all have fans, private baths, cable TV, and hot water for $4, and breakfast is $1.50. The clean, modern **Hostal Traveller's Lodging,** tel. 6/886-372, offers good beds, luggage storage, and a strongbox. Dorm rooms are $2, and private rooms with cable TV, hot water, and private bath start at $4 s, $5 d. The Costitas Ricas Restaurant and Amarongachi Jungle Trips operate out of the same building, near the eastern end of the footbridge.

The **Hotel Amazonas,** tel. 6/886-439, at the northwestern corner of the main plaza, is a tightly run ship with second- and third-floor balconies over the street. One-dollar rooms are a mixed bag, with thin mattresses and no fans, but the quiet location and friendly owners make it worth considering. Nicer and pricier with the same good location is the **Hostal Turismo Amazonico,** tel. 6/886-487 or 886-508. Spotless rooms with private bath, TV, fan, phone, and refrigerators are just $2.50 pp

Only $1.50 pp gets you a room at the clean **Residencial Napoli,** tel. 6/886-194, a small, quiet place above the Servi Bar/Restaurant on Pineda. Farther down 15 de Noviembre on Via del Chofer (turn right past the bus terminal) is the **Hostal Camba Huasi,** tel. 6/887-429, where decent rooms with private bath but no fans ($2 pp) are often full of tour groups. Rooms at the new **Hotel Puma Rosa,** tel. 6/886-320, 2/443-023, on Orellana north of the bridge, are centered around a plant-filled courtyard. Here $7.50 s, $13.50 d gets you a private bath with hot water and cable TV.

The closest thing to luxury accommodations in town is found at the **Hostal Los Yutzos,** tel./fax 6/886-717 or 886-769, on Rueda along the Río Pano. Rooms with private bath, cable TV, hot water, fans, and refrigerators are $15 s, $20 d or $22 s, $25 d with air-conditioning. Rooms at the **Hotel Mol International,** Sucre 432 and Suárez, tel. 6/886-215, have private bath, cable TV, air-conditioning, and phones for $16 s, $27 d, but since the pool has been permanently retired, it's even less of a deal. Breakfast in the restaurant is another $1.

Food

Chuquitos, a local favorite near the police station, has a great riverside location. The portions are immense, and few items on the huge menu, which ranges from seafood to Chinese, are more than $2, except the frog's legs for around $4.

The **Costitas Ricas Restaurant** in the Hostal Traveller's Lodging serves generous portions of breakfast, vegetarian plates, muesli, and yogurt, and like the hotel is always packed with gringos. Most meals, including pizza, vegetarian spaghetti, and fried chicken are about $2 (breakfast is $1). The thatched-roof **Pizzeria Le Massilia** is applauded for its pies, which start at $1.50. The **Pizzeria Bella Selva** also tosses a good pizza for about the same price under a thatched roof.

A **market** backs the tourist office on Bolívar near the airport, and scattered vendors sell fruit and vegetables on the street near the bus terminal. The **Heladeria Iglu** on the east end of the footbridge is a welcome sight on sunny days, and the **Panadería Espgal,** a few doors down from the Hostal Travellers Lodging, has tasty breads and sweets.

Tours

With all this water all around, it's only natural that Tena has one of the best rafting companies in Ecuador. Gynner Coronel's **Ríos Ecuador,** tel. 6/886-727, 2/569-252, e-mail: info@riosecuador.com, www.riosecuador.com, has an office on 15 de Noviembre across from the Hostal Traveller's Lodging, and another on the second floor of the Hostal Camba Huasi. His trips are described as professional, well-organized, and "absolutely fabulous." Whether you're a white-water novice or a seasoned paddler, English-speaking guides will lead you down Class III and IV rapids on rivers like the upper Napo and Misahualli from Oct.–Mar. One day's rafting costs $50–65 pp, including a tasty lunch. They also have kayaks for rent, vehicles for shuttles, and offer weeklong kayak lessons.

Operating out of the Hostal Traveller's Lodging, **Amarongachi Jungle Trips,** tel./fax 6/886-372, e-mail: pattyco64@hotmail.com, offer well-reviewed tours within a relatively short distance of town. A four-day trip visiting lowland Quechua communities and viewing wildlife from the Cabañas Shangri-La atop a 150-meter riverside cliff costs $120 pp.

The **Cerda family**—Olmedo, Oswaldo, Fausto, and Blanca—are all repeatedly described as excellent private guides for the upper Río Napo. Tours of 2–8 days focus on indigenous cultures and the native flora and fauna, and can be based out of cabins or tents for $30–35 pp per day. They also offer rafting and motorized canoe tours. (Some English and German spoken.) Contact them through their Agencia Sacharicsina, Tarquí 256, tel. 6/886-962.

Another branch of the Cerda family runs **Sapo Rumi Jungle Adventure,** tel. 6/887-896, fax 6/886-608, e-mail: cerdafamily@hotmail.com. They have an office on 15 de Noviembre near the bridge and have gotten good reviews for their four-day "difficult" trips, starting at $30 pp per day, and their three-day "easy" trips from $25 pp per day. None of the guides speaks English.

Eco-Adventour, e-mail: info@adventour. com.ec, www.adventour.com.ec, an established agency in Quito, recently opened an office in Tena across from the Hostal Traveller's Lodging. They run kayaking and rafting trips on a variety of Class II–Class IV rivers in the area. One-day trips range from $45–50 pp. They also have a four-day kayak school for $245 pp and jungle treks with camping every night from $35 pp per day.

Tours to the Cabañas Pimpilala, set on 30 undeveloped hectares 45 minutes by car from Tena, consist of two- to four-day visits with Quechua families for $35 per day. These tours can be arranged though **Delfín Pauchi** in Tena, tel. 6/886-088 or 886-434, or in Quito through the Naturgal travel agency at Reina Victoria and Foch. Delfín speaks Spanish and Quechua and is incredibly knowledgeable about medicinal plants and local indigenous culture. With advance warning, he can meet you at the bus terminal in Tena.

RICANCIE, an established ecotourism network of 10 Quechua communities along the upper Río Napo, offers hiking, canoeing, and explanations of traditional lifestyles and medicine during their well-run three- to seven-day programs (four people minimum) for $45 pp per day. Some of the guides speak a little English, but you'll get more out of the experience if you or someone in your group knows some Spanish. Contact them at 15 de Noviembre 772, a few blocks toward the terminal terrestre, tel./fax 6/887-072, tel. 6/776-953, e-mail: ricancie@ ecuanex.net.ec, RICANCIE. nativeweb.org.

If all of those options aren't enough, two of the best guides in Misahualli also have offices in Tena: **Douglas Clarke** is on 15 de Noviembre on the way to the bus station, and **Ecoselva** is on the east side of the car bridge. See under "Misahualli" for details on their services. If you'd like to take an **ultralight ride** over Tena—with room for the pilot and one passenger—ask at Ríos Ecuador or Amarongachi Jungle Trips, who both work with the same pilot.

Recreation and Nightlife

On weekends it seems as if everyone in Tena under 21 (and quite a few over) is wearing a bathing suit and carrying an inner tube. They're heading for one of the riverbank **beaches** near town, on foot and packed in trucks. The "playa del sol" (Sun Beach) and "isla del amor" (Island of Love) are west of town on the Río Tena (keep going past the end of the airport runway), and there are a few more beaches south of the main plaza (reached by a foot trail from the Misión Josefina) and on the Parque Amazonico La Isla.

The **Gallera Bar** at the Hotel Ruma Rosa is a good spot to shoot some pool or play ping-pong. It's also one of the city's most popular and largest discotecs. On the other end of the size scale, the **Boli "Bar" Pub,** before the bus terminal on 15 de Noviembre, is tiny but has a great music selection (take note that in such close quarters, darts may not be such a good idea). The best spot for an evening beer in Tena has to be **La Choza,** a bar in a raised wooden hut overlooking the river. **Barrancos Bar** on the other side of the bridge is similar, except that it has a discotec above it. The bar below Chuquitos is another good riverside watering hole.

Tena celebrates its **founding** on 15 November.

Shopping

You'll find Tena's best selection of souvenirs, particularly woven bags and jewelry, at **Eco Artesania** on the main plaza.

Services and Information

The folks at Tena's **tourist office** on Bolívar near the market are friendly and helpful. They offer a free map and city brochure and take their job of overseeing tour companies seriously (stop by with any complaints). Open Mon.–Fri. 8:30 A.M.–12:30 P.M. and 1–4:30 P.M.

Travelers can **change money** at the Banco del Pichincha on the north side of the plaza, and at the Banco del Austro on 15 de Noviembre between the bridges (better rate, longer wait). On the southeast corner of the plaza is the local **police station,** and **Andinatel** and the **post office** are on Olmedo near Amazonas.

Visitors will be glad to find Internet access at **Yacuruna.net** and **Piraña.net**—the latter has a book exchange and espresso drinks.

Transportation

The **terminal terrestre** sits about one km south of the foot bridge on 15 de Noviembre (the Selva Virgen *comedor* has good fruit juices and *batidos*). Local buses labeled "Terminal" run down 15 de Noviembre.

The ride to Quito takes six hours ($3.50) and is slightly longer and more expensive by way of Ambato. Other buses run to Baeza ($1.50, three hours), Puyo ($1.50, three hours), Baños ($2.50, four hours), and Coca ($4, six hours). Buses to Misahualli (50 cents, one hour) pass the bus stop on 15 de Noviembre in front of the terminal more or less hourly. Buses to Archidona and the Jumandy Caves leave often from the corner of Bolívar and Amazonas. (Buses to Coca and Quito via Baeza also pass here.)

Tena's **airport** is not currently in use, although there is talk of TAME starting flights to Quito at some point in the future.

MISAHUALLI

Seven km south of Tena is Puerto Napo, which was once the main port on the upper Río Napo. Two roads lead east from here along the river—one on the south side across the bridge and one on the north to the town of Misahualli.

The upper Río Napo's new Paraíso Turístico (according to the sign at the entrance), set on a rocky spit where the Río Misahualli empties into the lazy Río Napo, is the main departure point for tours in the upper Río Napo area. Misahualli is still only a speck of a town—one central telephone number (6/584-965) serves most of

it—with a few streets around the weedy plaza full of cheap hotels, restaurants, tour agencies, and stores stocked with jungle supplies. In a living lesson of the dangers of feeding wildlife, the monkeys who frequent the main plaza and the beach one block away have developed a kleptomaniacal taste for Coca-Cola.

Accommodations and Food in Town

The least expensive hotels and restaurants crowd the plaza. **La Posada Residencial/ Restaurant** serves good food on its open corner porch that monkeys wander into from time to time. Rooms are clean with private bath, hot water, and fans for $5 pp.

Just off the plaza, jungle guide Douglas Clark's **Hotel Marena International** rents rooms with private bath and small refrigerators for $4 pp. The **Hotel Shaw,** part of Ecoselva, has rooms on the plaza for $2 pp with shared bath and fan.

Accommodations and Food Outside of Town

Half a kilometer down the road toward Puerto Napo, you'll pass the **Albergue Español,** tel./fax 2/584-912, offering the most luxury and best food in the area. Rooms with fans, 24-hour hot water, and private bath cost $5 pp with views of the Río Napo. The hotel owns the Jaguar Lodge (see "Upper Río Napo") and organizes day trips for guests.

Shortly beyond on the other side of the street is **Napo Gardens,** e-mail: napogradens @ yahoo.com, a lodge recently purchased by an American and an Ecuadorian with big plans to build cabañas and a bar/restaurant with music, a pool table, and Tex-Mex food. They say they intend to keep prices low.

Keep going and take a right at the fork in the road (left to Puerto Napo), and just over two km farther you'll reach **El Jardin Alemán,** Tomás Bermur 22 and Urrutia, tel. 2/247-878, fax 2/462-213, e-mail: jarnatra@pi.pro.ec. A main lodge with satellite TV, restaurant, bar, and laundry facilities sits on 264 acres of primary rainforest on the west bank of the Río Misahualli. Accommodations include five suites and eight comfortable double rooms with fan, terrace, private bath, and hot water. While you're here, you can choose between hikes, jeep trips, or horseback rides into the forest, rafting on the river, or panning for gold. Rates start around $45 pp per day, depending on

TIM BEWER

wild monkey sitting on bench in main plaza, Misahualli

the length of stay and tour options chosen. (English guides and transportation included bump prices up to about $150 pp per day.)

The **Misahualli Jungle Lodge,** Ramiro Dávalos 251, tel. 2/520-043, 2/fax 504-872, e-mail: miltour@accessinter.net,website:www.miltour.com/paginas/pginmisa.htm, occupies a tranquil clearing in a 145-hectare preserve across the Río Misahualli from town. Fifteen cabins with fans, private baths, and hot water can hold 50 guests who are free to wander along well-marked trails into the forest or chat, read, and relax in front of the satellite TV in the central building. Rates are $30 s, $48 d, and transportation can be arranged from as far as Quito. Drop-ins are welcome, and it's worth an afternoon visit from Misahualli. Regular canoe service runs until 9 P.M. for 25 cents.

River Hike
One of the best excursions from Misahualli starts seven km west of town on the road to Puerto Napo, where a bridge crosses the Río Latas. There are two small signs—one indicating the *cascadas* (falls) and another advertising the Cabañas Gran Eden. Climb the stairs to the snack bar, pay the small entrance fee, and keep going another half hour or so down a slippery, muddy path past smaller falls to the big one with a swimming hole at the base.

There are also a few caves up this way: stalactites decorate one cave located about one hour north of the village of Umbini on the west bank, and two more caves wait across the river just north of Ponce Loma. Ask in either village for directions.

Tours and Guides
Dozens of guides operate out of Misahualli—some reputable, many barely adequate, a few irresponsible to the point of being dangerous. What follows are a few of the best, but shop around—carefully. Remember, the agency is responsible for the trip organization, but in the end the guide makes or breaks a trip. Fewer tourists are coming to Misahualli as once were, making it harder to put a group together. It would be easier to join a group in Tena, and some tours arranged in Tena start in Misahualli.

Expediciones Douglas Clark, tel. 6/887-584, has been run by its Ecuadorian namesake for more than two decades and is considered one of the best. Operating out of an office on the plaza and at his Hotel Mavena Internacional, Douglas runs tours to his Cabañas Sinchi Runa, south of Misahualli at the confluence of the Ríos Arajuno and Puni, as well as to Pañacocha and the Río Yasuní. Some profits are used for conservation efforts such as purchasing land and helping reintroduce native species. For reservations, call in Misahualli or stop by his office in Tena.

Ecoselva, e-mail: ecoselva@yahoo.ec, run by the friendly and highly regarded Pepe Tapia Gonzalez, is another excellent agency. Tours from 1–10 days are possible for as low as $25 pp per day, depending on the destination. Pepe speaks English (as does his brother Lenyn) and teaches biology at the Universidad Ecologica in Tena. His office is on the plaza, and he also has an office in Tena.

Hector Fiallos is a highly recommended guide who runs **Sacha Tour,** tel. 6/886-679 or 886-563, from the Hostal Sacha down on the beach. Trips range as far as Yasuní and Cuyabeno in up to 10 days, and some of his guides know a little English (Hector speaks some French). He also uses the name Fluvial River Tours because other guides have copied the Sacha name. It's best to ask for Hector by name. Tours in the Misahualli area are $35 pp per day, and he has an office in Quito at the Hotel La Posada, tel. 2/282-859, fax 2/505-240.

Two women-run agencies on the plaza also get good marks. **Viajes y Aventuras Amazonicas,** tel. 6/881-444 in Tena, is based at the Hotel La Posada and run by the amiable Carmen Santander. Tours in the Misahualli area are $25 pp per for three or four days. The **Billy Clarke Travel Agency,** tel. 2/572-399 in Quito, charges $30 per day and can arrange English-speaking guides with advance notice. Billy's son Thomas is helpful and often in the office. **Marcos Estrada,** who has an office on the plaza, has also been recommended.

Services and Information

A few **handicraft stores** are located on the plaza, along with some small shacks with pool tables. **Andinatel** has an office just off the northeast corner of the plaza, and the **police station** is just off the northwest corner. More phone lines were scheduled to be installed as of late 2000.

Transportation

Buses from Tena circle the plaza before heading back out of town roughly every hour. The rocky sandbar at the confluence of the Ríos Napo and Misahualli is usually occupied by **motor canoes** waiting to depart to lodges and villages downriver. Boat prices are fixed, but ask in town beforehand to avoid overcharging. River service to Coca leaves daily between 10 and 11 A.M., or whenever eight passengers have been gathered. (Ask around by the boats to find out how many others are waiting.) Foreigners pay $15 for the trip, which takes six hours downriver and 10–14 hours back.

UPPER RÍO NAPO

From Puerto Napo to Coca, the river is the main artery of life, bringing water and nutrients to the forest, supplies to the colonists, and tourists to the lodges. This stretch is narrower and more wild than the river below Coca, twisting around islands as it rises and falls abruptly in response to rainfall and drought.

Oil prospecting brought the first wave of settlers to the area decades ago, when towns like Misahualli were barely a crossroads and a general store. Recent roads east from Puerto Napo have opened the region even more to colonization, agriculture, and cattle ranching.

Today almost all of the rainforest along the first 50 or so kilometers of the river has been disturbed in some way, except for small protected areas around the lodges and Jatun Sacha. The jungle becomes more pristine farther down-

---

JEENCHAM (THE BAT)

Once, long ago, the animals of the forest were about to go to war with the birds. The animals called on the bat to fight with them, but he refused. "No, I am not an animal," he said. "I am a bird—see, I have wings like a bird." Soon the birds, looking for allies, also asked the bat to join on their side. The bat answered, "No, see that I have teeth and fur. I am not a bird, I am an animal."

The fight began. The bat, seeing that the animals seemed to be winning, went to their side. But the animals spurned his help. As the tide of the battle shifted, the bat ran to the birds and offered its help. The birds also turned him away.

In time, the animals won. As was the custom, the victors held a celebration for everyone involved, animals and birds alike. The bat tried to sneak into the festivities but was discovered. Soon everyone was chasing after the bat, hitting him and shouting at him. And thus the animals and birds together cursed the bat, saying that he would always be a coward who lived in caves and only emerged at night for fear that he would be caught and killed.

-Shuar myth

river and away from the banks of the upper stretch.

Butterfly Garden

Roughly five minutes downstream from Misahualli is a new butterfly garden opened by Pepe Tapi Gonzales of Ecoselva. The large mesh enclosure had 20 species of *mariposa* in 2000, with more on the way as appropriate food and cocoon plants are added. To visit the gardens, stop by Ecoselva's office on the plaza in Misahualli to pick up the key and pay your $1 entry fee, then take a boat from the beach (all the drivers know it) for $1.50 one-way. You can pay the driver to wait for you, or have him return at a set time. Another option is a planned trail from the garden back to the junction of the Napo and Misahualli rivers, where you can yell for a boat to take you across (25 cents). Some tours include a stop here.

Caipirona

This small Quechua community south of Misahualli welcomes visitors interested in experiencing indigenous life and traditions in a realistic and rustic setting. Tours begin with a three-hour hike to the village from Misahualli and can include hiking, camping, and visits to nearby caves. You can pick the minds of local experts about medicinal plants and forest life, visit with a shaman, learn to make pottery or play traditional music, or participate in a *minga* (communal work event).

Four-day tours cost $180 pp, and longer visits are possible. There are no telephones in Caipirona itself, so to arrange a visit, contact the RICANCIE under "Tours" in Tena.

Jatun Sacha Biological Station

Ecuador's premiere tropical field research station was begun in 1986 by an Ecuadorian and two North Americans, who gained title to 140 hectares of forest along the upper Río Napo. With the help of various foreign organizations and charities (including the former music group The Grateful Dead), the nonprofit Fundación Jatun Sacha was created in 1989 to manage the field station and promote conservation of and education about the rainforest to Ecuadorians and foreigners alike.

Now Jatun Sacha is one of the most prestigious tropical research stations in South America, welcoming scientists, school groups, and natural history tours to their 2,000 hectares of protected rainforest. The name means "big forest" in Quechua, and it rings true: 70 percent of Jatun Sacha's holdings are primary, undisturbed jungle, forming a transitional zone between the lower slopes of the Andes and the true Amazon lowlands farther east.

Jatun Sacha isn't a resort lodge, but independent visitors can spend the night for $25 pp—advance booking is necessary. Facilities for visiting scientists and students consist of bunk beds in raised wooden cabins, along with a main building with a dining hall, kitchen, bathrooms, electricity, and a modest library. Well-maintained trails lead to the river and a canopy observation tower. Group reservations should be made at least one week in advance, and prices run $30 pp per day, including lodging and three meals. For information, contact the Fundación Jatun Sacha, Pasaje Eugenio de Santillán N34-28 and Maurián, Urb. Rumipamba, Casilla 17-12-867, tel./fax 2/432-240, 432-173, 432-246, e-mail: jatsacha@ecuanex.net.ec, www.jatunsacha.org.

Volunteer positions are available at Jatun Sacha in education, station maintenance, and conservation, including the station's new Amazon Plant Conservation Center, an experimental medicinal garden completed in 1993. A fee of $225 per month, payable in advance, covers meals and lodging. To apply, send a curriculum vitae, cover letter, recent health certificate, a police record stating recent offenses (if any), two passport photographs, and $30 to Jatun Sacha, Programa de Voluntarios, Box 5721, Dept 2301-148, Miami, FL 33102-5721. The Fundación also arranges volunteer positions at its Bilsa and Guandera Biological Stations, on the northwest coast and in the northern Sierra, respectively.

If you don't think you'll be able to make it to Jatun Sacha but would still like to help support its efforts, money is always needed for station upkeep, new equipment, and research. Donations can be sent to Save the Rainforest, Inc., 604 Jaime St., Dodgeville, WI 53533.

Jatun Sacha is 22 km east of the bridge over the river at Puerto Napo; it's marked by a sign on the right-hand side of the road. Buses from Tena headed for the villages of Campococha or

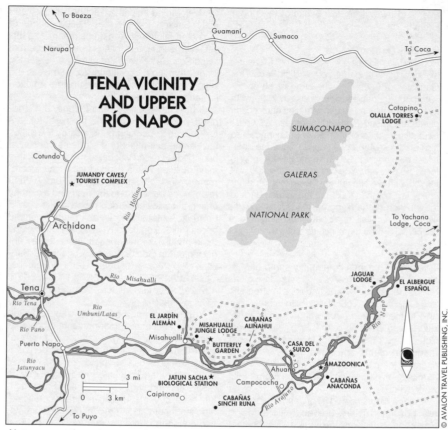

TENA VICINITY AND UPPER RÍO NAPO

Ahuano pass the entrance to the station (look for the Centinela de Tena bus in Tena's main terminal).

Cabañas Aliñahui

Since it was bought by Jatun Sacha and the U.S. Health and Habitat Foundation in 1994, this former cattle ranch has evolved into one of the most ecologically minded lodges on the upper Río Napo. Eight cabins, comfortably appointed with hammocks and private bath, can fit a total of 45 people. Three lookout towers provide jaw-dropping views of the surrounding forest and ice-capped volcanoes on the horizon. Rainwater fills the toilets and sinks, solar power provides the electricity, and septic tanks

take care of waste. The food is simple and wholesome, and an evening drink at the bar goes well with the muted roar of the forest.

A wide range of activities starts with visits to Jatun Sacha, a few hours by foot on the other side of the river. Along the way, the vista of the river and the Andes in the distance show why the cabins were named for the Quechua word meaning "beautiful view." Aliñahui's other name, the Butterfly Lodge, probably has something to do with the 750 species of butterflies spangling the trees along self-guided trails that wind through the forest. More than 100 species of orchids have been found nearby. Excursions to native communities, caves, or the AmaZOOnica can be arranged by canoe or on horseback.

Tours of 3–6 days start at $142 pp for three days, rising to $351 pp for six days (SAE discount). Special eight-day native culture tours are possible for $437 pp (minimum four people), and you can visit Aliñahui on your own for $51 pp per day, meals included. Profits from Aliñahui help support the biological station and its work. Reservations and information are handled through an office in Quito at Los Shyris 760 and El Salvador, Ed. Tapia, Of. 204, tel. 2/253-267, fax 2/253-266, e-mail: alinahui@interative.net.ec, www.ecuadorexplorer.com/alinahui.

To reach the cabañas, take the road east from Puerto Napo along the south bank of the Río Napo. After 25 km, a turnoff heads north 1.5 km to the bridge over the river. Five or so buses per day leave Puerto Napo in this direction, and public canoes from Misahualli take half an hour and cost $2.

Casa del Suizo

If luxury and service are most important, the Casa del Suizo should do nicely. Owned by an Ecuadorian–Swiss partnership, the elegant lodge offers 20 rooms, 30 cabins, and a pool on the Río Napo's north bank near Ahuano. Views from the rooms and the *mirador* (balcony) topping the three-floor main building are superb, as is the buffet-style food (a level of quality reflected in the price—those on a restricted budget will want to eat in Ahuano). For relaxing, there's a pool and a bar.

The immediate area isn't great for wildlife viewing, so the Casa del Suizo has more of a cultural focus. Visits to a local Quechua village are just one of a list of possible activities, as are rainforest hikes. The lodge is also relatively easy to reach, making it the perfect place for those who want to see the forest without much effort or discomfort. Rooms are $70 per night, and four-day packages are $298 pp, including everything plus transport from Quito with a stop in Papallacta along the way. Make reservations through their office in Quito at Julio Zaldumbide 375 and Toledo, tel. 2/509-504, 509-115, fax 2/508-872, e-mail: suizho@ecnet.ec, www.casadelsuizo.com.

Cabañas Anaconda

You'll find this small complex at the eastern tip of Anaconda Island, where the Río Arajuno empties into the Río Napo. The rest of the island is home to a handful of Quechua families, many of whom work for the cabañas as guides or maintenance staff.

Three basic bungalows have space for almost 50 guests, who will have to get used to cold showers and no electricity (the hearty food will help). Like many jungle lodges, Anaconda has its own zoo of forest birds and animals, with an endearing assortment of monkeys roaming free over the island. Canoe and hiking trips are led by guides who know the forest like their own backyard—which, after all, it is—providing fascinating explanations of the flora, fauna, and local uses of medicinal plants. Guides speak Quechua and Spanish, and other languages are available by advance request.

Prices vary depending on whether visits begin in Quito or Misahualli. If you can get to Misahualli on your own, prices are just $42 s and $72 d for three- to five-day trips, including all meals and guided excursions. The canoe trip from Misahualli takes one hour. Reservations are required and can be made through Napotur in Quito, Foch 635 and Reina Victoria, tel. 2/557-841, fax 2/224-913, e-mail: hectorba@uio.sat-net.net.

AmaZOOnica

A Swiss biologist runs this small animal shelter on the south bank opposite Anaconda Island. Its official name—Centro de Rescate para Animales Víctimas de Tráfico (Rescue Center for Animal Victims of Smuggling)—tells AmaZOOnica's true mission: to rehabilitate animals, reptiles, and birds seized from smugglers by Ecuadorian customs officials for eventual re-release into the wild. A tour of the facilities is somehow depressing and uplifting at the same time, and donations and volunteers (particularly those with veterinary skills) are greatly appreciated.

Jaguar Lodge

One and a half hours downriver from Misahualli sits one of the oldest lodges in the Ecuadorian Amazon. Set on 1,000 hectares of primary forest, this historic place has been in business since 1969 and is now owned (and was recently renovated) by the same owners as El Albergue Español in Misahualli. Ten cabins blend wooden beams and clean white walls. Each has a private bath with hot water. Vegetarians will find themselves well looked after at the restaurant, which has a great view over the river.

In the other direction, thanks to the hotel's relative isolation, stretches primary forest begging to be explored by foot and canoe. Jungle treks and visits to Quechua villages with local guides are all included in the surprisingly reasonable prices. Visits run $105 pp for three days and $170 pp for five days. Transportation isn't included, so factor in another $20 for the trip by private canoe. The contact for reservations is the same as for El Albergue Español.

El Albergue Español

Another 15 minutes downstream on the opposite shore sit six new cabins designed in traditional thatched-roof style and owned by the same company that owns the Jaguar Lodge. Although more rustic, they are still comfortable, and like the Jaguar Lodge get their electricity and hot water from solar panels. Up to 50 guests can enjoy canoe rides, forest hikes, kayak excursions, and a vivarium full of reptiles. Prices range from $105 pp for three days, up to $170 pp for five days. Contact their office in Quito at Eloy Alfaro 3147 and Arosemena, tel. 2/453-703, 466-925, fax 2/466-911, or in Guayaquil at García Aviles 606, piso 7, tel. 9/431-236, e-mail: alb-esp@uio.satnet.net.

Yachana Lodge

FUNEDESIN, a foundation that fosters long-term community development in the Ecuadorian Amazon, operates this complex that is located two hours by motorized canoe from Misahuallí. It's aimed at educating visitors while providing a source of funds for local community development. Perched near the village of Mondaña, the lodge oversees 280 hectares of land stretching for 30 km in either direction, including primary and secondary forest and agricultural land.

Yachana bills itself as "a place for learning," giving guests the opportunity to become a bee-keeper for a day (bee suit included) or to enjoy a cup of coffee made from beans you picked yourself and roasted over an open fire. Canoe excursions and 15 km of trails allow you to enjoy the rainforest on your own or under the direction of local guides, before returning to the rustic but comfortable accommodations for the night.

Packages, including transport from Quito, are $320 pp for four days and $400 for five days (students and SAE members receive discounts). Regular canoe service runs to Yachana on Tuesday and Friday. Make reservations at Marin 188 and Almagro, Casilla 17-17-92, tel. 2/237-278 or 237-133, fax 2/220-362, e-mail: info@yachana.com, www.yachana.com.

SOUTHERN ORIENTE

PUYO

Puyo is a drab little town whose military air base and isolation from popular Amazon destinations have kept it from becoming a major tourist center. Instead it's a working-class jungle town (pop. 22,000) where stores buy *oro en polvo* (gold dust) and almost every street bears the date of a famous event that happened far away and long ago.

When (not if) the southern Oriente starts opening up to tourism, however, Puyo is poised to take advantage of its direct link to the highlands in one direction and pure forest in the other. The climate here reminds you that you're in the rainforest: the town's name means "cloudy" in a local indigenous lan-

guage, and hot and wet weather is the norm. "Everywhere and everything seemed to be permanently saturated," wrote Richard Poole in *The Inca Smiled,* so that "in the brief moments that the sun shone, Puyo became one huge steam-bath."

Accommodations

The best hotel in town for the money is the **Hotel Araucano,** tel. 3/833-834, 885-686, fax 3/885-227, where rooms with private bath and hot water are $1.50 pp. Add a TV for $2 more, and breakfast for another 75 cents. The friendly staff are knowledgeable about the area. Rooms with private bath are $2 pp at the **Hotel Chasi,** tel. 3/883-059, and shared-bath rooms are only $1. Please hold the Eagles jokes if you stay at the **Hotel California,** tel. 6/885-189, where $1.50

gets you a cramped but clean and colorful room with private bath. Guests can watch videos in the lobby.

A sparkling new building houses the **Hotel Cristian's,** tel. 6/883-081, 885-588, where rooms come with private bath, hot water, cable TV, and fan for $5 s, $8 d. The **Hostería Turingia,** tel. 3/885-180/384, features alpine-style cabins surrounded by flowers, a pool, a bar, a patio, and "Sneaky" the boa constrictor. Rates here run $6–10 s, $10–12 d, including private bath, hot water, and TV.

Food

Dozens of *comedores* and cheap restaurants line Atahualpa as well as 24 de Mayo between 27 de Febrero and 9 de Octubre. The **Chifa Oriental,** next to the Hotel Araucano, serves passable, filling plates in the $1.50 range, as does the **Restaurant Unicorno** down the block, with a *menú del día* for less than $1.

Steak with garlic sauce is $1.50 at the **Rincon de Suecia,** which is run by an amiable Swedish chap. They also serve vegetarian spaghetti and pizzas for $1.50 and up. For more refined (and

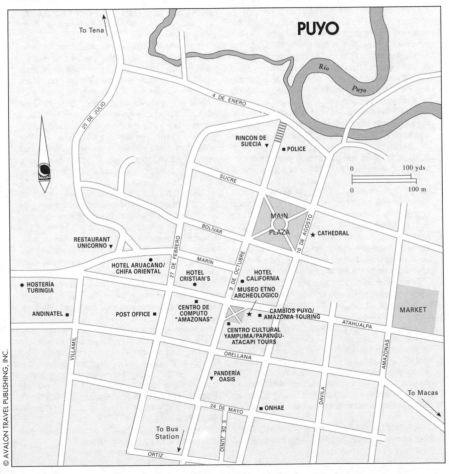

expensive) fare, stop by the restaurant at the Hostería Turingia, where almost every entrée, from chili to trout, is around $2. There's good bread to be had at the **Panadería Oasis** on 9 de Octubre and Orellana.

Sights

For a taste of Puyo's past, stop by the **Museo Etno Arqueologico** on the third floor of the old Municipio building, open 10 A.M.–12:30 P.M. and 1:30–5 P.M., free. Two km from Puyo is the 15.6-

KAPAWI ECOLODGE

Deep in a remote corner of the southern Oriente is a truly special place: a lodge that combines luxurious accommodations and service with the highest principles of ecotourism, in the middle of some of the most pristine rainforest in the country.

The Kapawi Ecolodge was begun in 1993, far down the Río Pastaza within a stone's throw of the Perúvian border. This is the heart of Ecuadorian Achuar territory, so before Kapawi's parent company broke ground, approval had to be secured from OINAE, the indigenous group's political organization. Three years later, the lodge was able to provide local communities with jobs and ongoing economic support in the form of rent paid for the land. Most of the employees who work for the lodge are Achuar, and Kapawi will pass into Achuar management in the year 2011.

The lodge itself was built entirely with native materials and methods—incredibly, not a single metal nail was used in the construction. Walkways link bungalows with room for 40 people who may find it easy to forget they're more than 100 km from the nearest city of any size. Everything is first class and completely ecofriendly. One of the largest private solar projects in South America powers the lights, all trash is recycled, and even the soap is biodegradable. Bottled drinking water and a British-valet–style umbrella are provided free of charge.

Two main buildings house a small library, a boutique, a meeting room, and a dining hall, which specializes in exotic jungle fruits and local delicacies such as tender filets of river fish so large that one can feed the entire lodge for a week. Wandering back to your oh-so-comfy bed in the evening, you'll be reminded where you are as the moon and stars reflect in the black glass of the lagoon fronting each cabin's deck and the forest life drones on like an orchestra tuning up for a performance that never comes. You may even find a wide-eyed opossum or shy tarantula peeking at you from the thatched roof.

Activities begin after an early breakfast. Silent electric motors power dugout canoes that take you down narrow blackwater streams, where long-nosed bats and Amazon kingfishers launch from the waterside branches (five of six species of kingfishers in Ecuador can be seen here). Flocks of blue and yellow macaws claim sandbars in the wide Pastaza, and this is the only place in the country where you might spot an orinoco goose.

Hikes ranging from easy to difficult are led by indigenous and biologist guides. Electric-blue morpho butterflies dance down forest trails like living sparks, while troops of squirrel monkeys make huge leaps from branch to bending branch along the river. It's impossible to take in everything at once. Look down and you'll see a black poison-arrow frog with bright blue stripes and a red pate; glance up and a parrot is watching you from its nest in a hollow treetop. Your indigenous guide will show you how forest tribes knock on buttress roots to signal over long distances, or point out plant after plant put to countless uses by the Achuar.

One of the highlights of any stay is a visit to an Achuar settlement. After a traditional greeting by your guide and a brief chat with the owner, your group will be served *nijiamanch* by women in the *tankamash,* or male part of the house. Say *maketai* (thank you, pronounced mah-keh-TIE) and at least pretend to drink the sour beverage, made from chewed-up yucca fermented with human saliva—to refuse would be considered an insult. Your guide will translate the conversation, followed by a tour of the small *chakra* where various medicinal plants are cultivated.

Five days at Kapawi cost $720–900 pp depending on when you come, and packages of four and eight days are also available. This doesn't include $150 for the flight to the lodge and a $10 pp per-day tax to the local Achuar community. For more information and to book a visit, contact Canodros S.A. in Guayaquil, Urdanota 1418 and Av. del Ejercito, tel. 4/280-143 or 280-173, fax 4/287-651, or in Quito at Carrión 256 and Leonidas Plaza, Ed. Libertador, piso 6, tel. 2/220-947,tel./fax 2/222-203,e-mail:eco-tourism @canodros.com.ec, mia.lac. net/canodros.

An emerging ceiba tree towers above this riverside forest.

JULIAN SMITH

15.6-hectare **Pedagogical Ethnobotanical OMAERE Park,** a small botanical reserve described as "superb" for its collection of 1,500 different species of Amazonian plants used by indigenous cultures. A team of Shuar, Zaparo, Huaorani, and Quechua specialists provide environmental education that emphasizes traditional knowledge. One-third of the park is cultivated in nurseries and greenhouses. Open Thurs.–Mon. from 8:30 A.M.–5 P.M., $1.

Tours and Recreation

Run by the Organización de Pueblos Indígenas de Pastaza (OPIP), **Papanga-Atacapi Tours,** tel.6/883-875 or 883-832, e-mail: papango@ punto.net.ec, is on 9 de Octubre and Atahualpa above the Centro Cultural Yamapuma (see following listing) and has been recommended for tours to Quechua and Shuar communities near Puyo.

One option for this first-hand look into traditional native culture is a three-day visit to one of the villages closest to Puyo by car and foot ($25 pp per day, three-person minimum). The other, more adventurous trip heads farther into the jungle by canoe for a stay of 4–6 days. This option costs $40 pp per day for at least four people and can be shortened by a plane ride, which costs extra. Friendly director José Gualinga will tailor each tour to the group's wishes. Guides speak Spanish and French and some English.

Santiago Peralta Cordero runs **Amazonia Touring** out of the Cambios Puyo office at Atahualpa y 9 de Octubre, tel. 3/883-866 or 883-219, fax 3/883-064, with trips from one to many

days starting at $25 pp per day. English-speaking guides are available; Patricio Garces is especially recommended. **Mentor Marino,** 27 de Febrero and 4 de Enero, tel. 6/885-500, is reported to be a good local guide. Inquire at the **Organización de Nacionalidades Huarani de la Amazonia Ecuatoriana (ONHAE)** about trips to their reserve, which they were in the process of organizing in 2000.

Shopping

The **Centro Cultural Yamapuma** has a good selection of *artesanía* and souvenirs plus a small café.

For odds and ends from clothes to hardware, try the vendors on Atahualpa east of 9 de Octubre or the handful of stores on Martín. The main **market** is open daily on the east end of town along Atahualpa.

Nightlife and Festivals

Several small **discos** are scattered around town, led by the huge **Sabor Latino** discotec across the street from the bus station. There are a couple of **pool halls** on 9 de Octubre just south of the main plaza.

The anniversary of the city's founding coincides with a **farming and industrial fair** the first few weeks in May. The **provincialization of Pastaza** is celebrated on 10 November.

Information and Services

Cambios Puyo on Atahualpa next to the museum changes travelers' checks and sells souvenirs,

venirs, and **Orientravel** on 9 de Octubre at Orellana reportedly also changes travelers' checks. The **Ministerio de Turismo** on the plaza offers a slim selection of maps of the area; and there's a police station one block north of the main plaza on 9 de Octubre.

Andinatel has an office on the corner of Villamil and Orellana and a booth at the bus station, and the **post office** is on 27 de Febrero and Atahualpa. The **Centro de Computo "Amazonas"** has public Internet access, open daily.

Transportation

The main **bus terminal** is south of the town center, reached by buses marked Terminal running down 9 de Octubre every 15 minutes. Direct lines run to most major cities in the highlands and the coast, including Quito ($2.50, 6–8 hours), Baños ($1, two hours), Tena ($1.50, three hours), Macas ($2.50, five hours), Riobamba ($2, four hours), Guayaquil ($4.75, eight hours), and Ambato ($1.50, three hours).

A taxi trip within the city limits, including out to the bus station, runs 40 cents.

MACAS

Half the fun of the southernmost major city in the Oriente (pop. 20,000) is getting there. Coming from either direction, you'll pass scattered Shuar settlements and catch quick glimpses of the forest to the east and mountains to the west. Almost exactly halfway along the road south from Puyo, your bus will grind to a stop at the bank of the Río Pastaza, where everyone has to get out and lug their bags over a rickety footbridge to another bus waiting on the other side.

The other half of Macas' fun is a combination

When I die
You will look for young men
But while I live
Put more chicha
In this beautiful bowl
Let us dance, my little wife.

—Shuar festival song

THE ORIGIN OF FIRE

Many years ago, they say, the Shuar didn't have fire. The only way they could heat their food was by the sun. In all the jungle, only a huge *hombronazo* had fire, and he guarded it jealously in his house. The few Shuar who had tried to steal it from him had been caught and crushed between the monster's huge hands. These fierce blows could be heard in the jungle far away—*tac, tac, tac*—which is why the Shuar called this particular *hombronazo* Takea.

Early one morning, Takea's wife was wandering through her orchard when she found a hummingbird, nearly frozen from the night's cold. The gentle woman took pity on the tiny bird and brought it home and sat it next to the fire. Revived by the heat, the hummingbird suddenly sprang up, grabbed a bit of the fire with his tail, and fled. The bird gave the ember to a Shuar woman, who distributed it to the rest of her village, enabling the Shuar to cook their food, warm their bodies, and light the darkness from that day forth.

—Shuar myth

---

of the beautiful setting, mild climate, and friendly inhabitants. Flowers in a riot of colors decorate the surprisingly clean town. To the east, the Río Upano meanders through a wide valley separating the Cordillera de Cutucú from the Andes, which loom to the west beyond the airport and the small Río Surumbaino. It's worth a walk to the quiet, residential south end of Macas for the view of the hills and river.

Although not readily apparent, Macas has seen its share of action. The original settlement was destroyed at the turn of the 17th century in a Shuar uprising. It was rebuilt only to endure repeated attacks during the 17th–19th centuries—the price to pay for being the only settlement in the region occupied by the fierce tribe. A foot trail to Riobamba was Macas' only link to the outside world until well into the 19th century.

In this century, Macas was declared the capital of the nearly deserted Morona-Santiago province, which is gaining inhabitants with the recent discovery of oil. Border fighting in 1995 caused the evacuation of most of the city. Today the strong military presence is a thing of the past, thanks to the 1998 peace treaty that decided Ecuador and Perú's border once and for all. Macas has a more bearable climate than other, lower jungle cities, and the bird-watching is good in the valley of the Río Upano.

Sights

Macas' modern **cathedral** was finished in 1992 and boasts stained-glass windows worthy of a much larger temple. The hallowed image of La Purísima de Macas commemorates a vision of the Virgin that appeared to a local family in 1595, back when it was called Sevilla del Oro. Five blocks north along Don Bosco, a small ethnographic collection fills the **Museo Arqueologico**

Municipal, which sits at the entrance to a pleasant park filled with trees and orchids with good views over the Río Upano and beyond (if the sky is clear, that is). It's open weekdays—ask the librarian to let you in.

Accommodations

Budget travelers should check out the **Residencial Macas,** Sucre and 24 de Mayo, where spartan but clean beds with shared bath are $1 pp. Both the **Hotel Orquidea,** Sucre and 9 de Octubre, tel. 6/700-132 or 700-970, and the **Hostel Esmeralda,** Cuenca 6-12 and Soasti, tel. 6/700-130, are spotless and comfortable, with rooms featuring private bath, hot water, and TV for less than $3 pp.

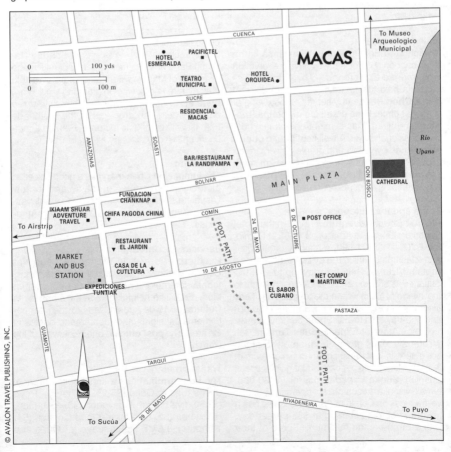

Food

Most of the best eateries in town are near the bus terminal. The **Cafe Pagoda China,** a jewel in the jungle, serves generous, tasty portions in the swankest spread this side of Baños. Basic plates like *chaulafans* and *tallarines* start at $1.25, whereas any of the nine ways they prepare shrimp will set you back $3.25. Within one block, the **Restaurant/Cafe El Jardin** also comes recommended, with nothing on the menu, including filet mignon, over $2.

Ecuadorian and Cuban dishes are less than $1 at the **Bar/Resturant Randimpa,** which also has pizzas for around $2. The **Bar/Restaurant El Sabor Cubano,** on 24 de Mayo south of 10 de Agosto, also does delicious Cuban plates for around $2.

Entertainment

At night, the Bar/Restaurant Randimpa is the most happening spot in town, playing everything from reggae to merengue. The **Rumba Discotec** is next to El Jardin on Amazonas, and **Ten's Chop Bar** nearby serves a frosty mug at a decent price. If the grand old **municipal theater** is repaired, Macas might once again host the occasional movie. A well-kept **public pool** is surrounded by yellow and purple flowers in the COEPRO children's school, about one km south of town on 24 de Mayo. It's open daily 10 A.M.–6 P.M. and costs 40 cents pp to use.

Tours and the Outdoors

IKIAAM Shuar Adventure Travel, in the Hotel Peñon del Oriente at Amazonas 15-05 at Comín, tel. 7/700-124, 701-690, e-mail: ikiaamjungle_tour@latinmail.com, is run by Bolívar Caita and Arhtam Vizuma. Their five-day trip to visit the Shuar costs $55 pp per day, including the flight to the village of Yaup where the tour begins. They also have three-day tours to Sangay ($90 pp) and one-day trips to visit Shuar communities.

Carlos Arcos of **Expediciones Tuntiak,** tel. 7/700-022, leads groups from an office at the bus station to visit Shuar communities on tours of 3–5 days for $50 pp per day. Shuar guides speak Spanish. **Sunka Expeditions,** tel. 7/700-088, e-mail: visunka@ecua.net.ec, operating out of a yellow kiosk on Comin at Amazonas, also has a full range of tours starting at $35 pp per day, with a three-person minimum. Some of their

"You are a guest in Waorani [sic] territory. They expect you to show absolute respect for their customs, belongings, families and especially their women . . . You must respect the Waorani culture . . . Your life and your work depend on it. We and they are equals; our differences are in our respective cultures and histories. Maxus has confidence in you."

—From a manual issued by oil company Maxus Ecuador, Inc. to its employees who work in Huaorani territory.

guides speak English.

To reach the eastern slopes of **Sangay National Park,** head to the town of General Proaño just north of Macas, where guides are available both for hire and advice on planning trips. From there a 1.5-hour bus ride (twice a day, three days a week) can drop you at the trailheads near the village of 9 de Octubre. Plan on a minimum of 3–4 days for any excursion.

Shopping

The **Fundacion Chanknap** has a good selection of indigenous crafts for sale, and a few Otavaleños sell artisan works in the small passageway next to the bus station along Amazonas.

Services and Information

Pacifictel sits next to the theater, and **Net Compu Martinez,** 9 de Octubre and 10 de Agosto, has Internet service for $2 per hour (open Mon.–Fri.). The helpful folks at the **Casa de la Cultura,** on 10 de Agosto, can provide information on local sights and recommend guides in the area. The **post office** is one block west of the church.

Transportation

The **bus terminal** has a small police branch. Buses runs to Quito ($5.25, 18 hours), Puyo ($2.50, five hours), Guayaquil ($8, 13 hours), Riobamba ($5, nine hours), and Cuenca ($4, 10 hours). **TAME** flights leave for Quito and

Guayaquil on Monday, Wednesday, and Friday for around $55 one-way, and **Austro** has planes bound for Cuenca on Monday, Wednesday, and Thursday. Ask at the airport about flights to small jungle outposts such as Yaupi, Taisha, and Pambantsa.

SOUTH FROM MACAS

Twenty-three km south of Macas sits the village of **Sucúa,** the center of the Shuar Federation. Vendors sell traditional crafts, and visits to Shuar villages can be arranged through the office of the Shuar Federation, three blocks south of the park on Domingo Comín 17-38. A few meager hotels and restaurants cluster near the central plaza—try the **Hotel Gyna,** tel. 7/740-926, and the **Oasis Restaurant,** both on Domingo Comín, for budget prices—and buses leave for Macas every hour from dawn to dusk (40 cents, one hour).

The Río Upano guides the road southward to the town of **Méndez,** an attractive and peaceful town with a circular main plaza (much easier for the evening stroll) near the juncture of the Ríos Paute and Zapote. From here a side road heads south along the Río Namangoza, then east along the Río Santiago to the remote outpost of **Morona.**

Sixty-four km before Morona is the settlement of **Santiago,** on the shore of the river of the same name, where canoes and guides can be hired to visit **La Cueva de los Tayos** (The Cave of the Oilbirds). These strange nocturnal birds use echolocation—like the clicks of bats and dolphins, except audible to humans—to find fruit by night and locate their nests deep within the earth. The high oil content of the birds' abdominal fat (a side effect of the oily palm fruits they favor) led early settlers and *indígenas* to boil the poor creatures down into an effective lamp fuel. Because it's 85 meters deep and black as night, you should only venture into the cave with a guide. Tour companies in Macas can organize visits.

The main road southwest from Méndez reaches **Limón** after 43 km, where itinerant wanderers can find budget quarters at the **Hotel Dreamhouse,** tel. 7/770-166, and the **Rediencial Limón,** tel. 7/770-114. A road (saddled with the official name General Leonidas Plaza Gutierrez) climbs west from the town to more than 4,000 meters before descending to Gualaco and Cuenca. Two more roads to the highlands leave west from **Gualaquiza,** 80 km farther south, where you can stay at the **Hostal Guadalupe,** tel. 7/780-113, and eat at the bamboo-walled **Cabaña Los Helechos.** The more westerly track follows the Río Cuyes upstream, whereas the other heads more northwest up the Río Cuchipamba to Sígsig, 68 km and 1,000 meters up into the Eastern Cordillera.

BOB RACE

NORTH COAST AND LOWLANDS
INTRODUCTION

The coast is Ecuador's forgotten quarter, squeezed in by most visitors only if there's time left over after the Galápagos, Oriente, and Sierra. Granted, it may be the least distinctive part of the country, and most of the larger cities aren't particularly inviting; but tiny, isolated fishing villages have a charm of their own, and with a little effort it's still possible to find deserted beaches washed by warm currents stretching for unbroken kilometers.

If flying direct from Quito to Manta, Bahía de Caráquez, Portoviejo, or Esmeraldas is beyond your budget, you're stuck with a lengthy but scenic bus trip down from the Andes. Santo Domingo de los Colorados is the major gateway west of Quito, with alternate routes connecting Latacunga with Quevedo, Ambato with Babahoyo, and Riobamba with Guayaquil by way of Milagro.

History
Ecuador's earliest advanced cultures got their start by the sea, beginning with the Valdivia culture along the central coast as early as 3500 B.C. The next major culture were the Manteña-

Huancavilca, who counted 20,000 members by the time Pizarro landed near Esmeraldas in 1526. Repeated pirate attacks during the 17th and 18th centuries left a legacy of non-Spanish surnames in pockets throughout the region.

The Land
Humid subtropical forests fed by Andean rivers blanket the small portion of the western lowlands that hasn't been cleared for farmland. Mangroves have a similar toehold on the northern coast. The wettest part of Ecuador's shore, this area receives three meters of rain annually, which makes it one big, wildly successful mosquito-breeding experiment.

The central coast is drier, although not as barren as the area near Guayaquil and farther south. Low, thorny hills rise a short distance inland behind Mulsne and Cojimíes and near Machalilla National Park.

Along with the Sierra, Ecuador's Coast seems to be one of the regions hit hardest by natural disasters. The torrential 1997–1998 El Niño season washed out many coastal roads, especially between Pedernales and Manta. On top of that,

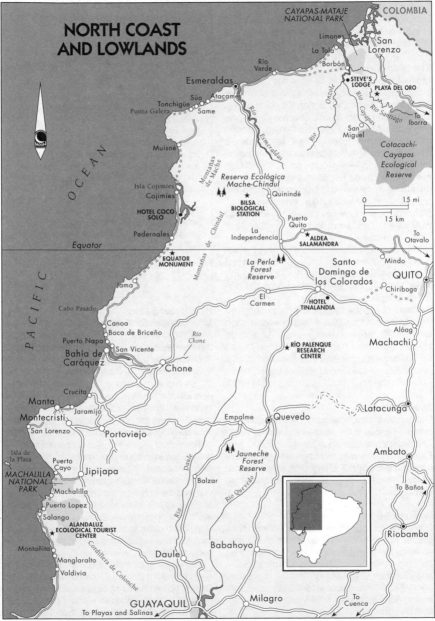

NORTH COAST AND LOWLANDS

COLOMBIA

CAYAPAS-MATAJE NATIONAL PARK

Limones
La Tola
Borbón
San Lorenzo

Río Verde
STEVE'S LODGE
PLAYA DEL ORO

Esmeraldas

Súa Atacames
Tonchigüe Same
Punta Galera

Río Esmeraldas
Onzole
Río Cayapas
Río Santiago
To Ibarra

San Miguel

Muisné

Montañas de Mache

Reserva Ecológica Mache-Chindul

Quinindé

Cotacachi-Cayapas Ecological Reserve

Isla Cojimíes
Cojimíes

HOTEL COCO SOLO

BILSA BIOLOGICAL STATION

Puerto Quito

La Independencia

ALDEA SALAMANDRA

Pedernales

0   15 mi

0   15 km

To Otavalo

Equator

EQUATOR MONUMENT

La Perla Forest Reserve

Santo Domingo de los Colorados

Mindo

QUITO

Jama

Cabo Pasado

Canoa
Boca de Briceño
Puerto Napo
San Vicente
Bahía de Caráquez

Chone

El Carmen

HOTEL TINALANDIA

Río Chone

RÍO PALENQUE RESEARCH CENTER

Chiriboga

Alóag

Machachi

Crucita

Manta
Montecristi
San Lorenzo
Jaramijó
Portoviejo

Empalme

Quevedo

Latacunga

Río Daule

Jauneche Forest Reserve

Ambato

Isla de la Plata

MACHALILLA NATIONAL PARK

Puerto Cayo
Jipijapa
Machalilla
Puerto López
Salango
ALANDALUZ ECOLOGICAL TOURIST CENTER

Balzar

Río Quevedo

To Baños

Montañita
Manglaralto
Valdivia

Cordillera de Colonche

Daule

Río Daule

Babahoyo

Riobamba

GUAYAQUIL

Milagro

To Cuenca

To Playas and Salinas

OCEAN

PACIFIC

MooN

the damage from the earthquake that hit near Bahía de Caráquez in August 1998 made travel in the region almost impossible for a time. (The infrastructure has since been mostly rebuilt.)

The People

Most of the population of Ecuador's northern coast descended from black slaves who were either freed or escaped during the colonial era. The Maroon culture, as it's become known, remains closely tied to its African heritage through music, dance, and folktales. As the story goes, a Spanish slave ship that foundered off the northern coast in 1553—ironically, the same year the official slave trade began in the Americas—is said to have released 23 slaves to settle the area. At this time in Ecuador, even free blacks were considered below *indígenas,* who could wear jewelry, bear arms, and walk unescorted at night.

With its comparatively lenient policies, the *audencia* of Quito became a haven for escaped slaves from as far away as Brazil, Chile, and Argentina. Still, frequent uprisings occurred during the colonial period, including the Autonomous Territory of Gentle Mulattos, which controlled the coast from Canoa to Atacames for a short while. One former slave named Alonso de Illescas governed from Esmeraldas to Manta for five decades, creating a near-nation almost completely beyond the control of the Spanish. Slavery in the New World was abolished in 1850.

Economy

Farms growing everything from rice and coffee to corn and citrus fruits keep the lowlands busy. The oil pipeline from the Oriente dead-ends at Esmeraldas, where lines of tankers wait to carry it around the world. Fishing, both industrial and private, is another major source of income, along with tourism.

When to Go

During the hot, rainy season of Dec.–June, many coastal roads turn into impassable mud bogs. As far as the tourist season goes, holidays bring the largest crowds: especially Carnival, Semana Santa, and the Christmas holidays. June–Sept. is also considered high season, when prices in the few hotels with rooms available can double.

UNCLE TIGER AND RABBIT

One day Uncle Tiger, Tío Tigre, was walking home with a basket full of fruit and bread. Conejo the rabbit saw him and decided he'd like that food for himself. He hopped through the woods to come out on the road ahead of Tío Tigre, and lay down pretending to be dead. When Tío Tigre came upon the rabbit in the road, he slowed but kept going, clutching his basket tightly.

Undaunted, Conejo jumped up and took a shortcut that brought him out ahead of Tío Tigre again, where he lay down as before. Once again Tío Tigre passed by the lifeless body without pausing.

But when Conejo tried his trick a third time, Tío Tigre stopped. Deciding that *three* dead rabbits were too good to pass up, he set down his basket and went back to pick up the first two. And so Conejo tricked Tío Tigre out of his food.

—Maroon folktale

Health and Safety

Mosquito repellent, water, and suntan lotion are essential to any North Coast beach getaway. At the very least, be well aware of the health risks from food—a particular problem in the land of shaved-ice treats and half-cooked seafood. Because the coast has one of the highest incidences of malaria in the country, insist on mosquito nets *(mosquiteros* or *toldos)* in hotels, especially along the northern coast. Better yet, buy your own net and string it up.

The poverty-stricken coast is one of Ecuador's dicier areas in terms of personal safety. Try to avoid night buses: in 1997, a private bus carrying a group of American university students, traveling between Guayaquil and Salinas well after dark, was robbed at gunpoint and sprayed with bullets. Carry as little of value as possible. and don't trust the lock on your beach cabin to stop even a mildly determined thief. Women especially should not walk alone on secluded beaches, even during the day.

The coast sees most of Ecuador's drug traffic on its way from Perú to Colombia and the United States, so be careful of drug setups and—if you must do it at all—do your serious partying with people you've known for more than 15 minutes.

WESTERN LOWLANDS

Ecuador's breadbasket (and banana-basket, and cacao-basket, and palm-oil-basket) stretches between the steep western slope of the Andes and the scrubby coastal mountain ranges just before the ocean. Huge agricultural plantations take advantage of the region's rich volcanic soil and abundant water from the highlands. Profits from this fertile region have traditionally flowed south to Guayaquil.

In this case, however, the cost of development was particularly steep. By the end of the 20th century, more than 95 percent of Ecuador's lowland forests—which easily rival the Amazon in sheer biological diversity—had been leveled as farms expanded. Add the fact that none of the cities are particularly noteworthy, and you have a region that is usually bypassed or sped through by tourists on their way to the beach. A few small forest reserves provide some respite from the monotonous cultivated fields.

SANTO DOMINGO DE LOS COLORADOS AND VICINITY

Descending into the western lowlands from Alóag (south of Quito) is a balancing act of fascination and fear: the views toward the ocean are stunning, but you're never quite sure that your bus will make it around the next hairpin corner. It's no surprise that the road itself, winding down a lush subtropical river valley, wasn't completed into 1960.

Santo Domingo (pop. 190,000) comes as both a relief (we made it!) and a disappointment (this is it?) to the tired traveler crawling off a bus from Quito or Esmeraldas. This humid, cramped, unbecoming city is one of the fastest-growing in the country, thanks to its position as the main gateway from Quito to the coast and transport hub for roads in every direction. Claustrophobes won't like it here, but it can be a good place to watch the bustle of life go by for an afternoon.

Otherwise, there's not much else to Santo Domingo. The Colorado *indígenas,* whose name the city commandeered, seldom put in their tra-

ditional red *achiote* hair paste except when someone is paying them (which is not recommended). Still, Santo Domingo is a popular destination for Quiteños looking for a leafy weekend getaway and for *narcotrafficantes* (drug dealers) from Colombia.

Accommodations and Food

Hotels in Santo Domingo are often full, regardless of what day it is. A whole slew of budget hotels congregate on the noisy main drag of 29 de Mayo. Of these the **Hotel Ejecutivo,** tel. 2/752-892 or 763-305, is the best deal at $2 s, $3.20 d with private bath and cable TV. The *cafetería* in the second-floor lobby serves a good, cheap breakfast. The **Hotel Caleta,** tel. 2/750-277, is also a deal at $2 pp with private bath, even without hot water.

The **Hostal Jennifer,** tel. 2/750-577, has rooms for $2.50 with hot water, private bath, and good showers (the sauna costs extra). If these places are full, the **Hotel Amambay,** tel. 2/750-696, will also do for $1.40 with private bath. Lots of basic restaurants along 29 de Mayo serve economical *platos del día,* and **La Fornacella Pizzeria** on the same street tosses a good wood-oven pie for $1 and up.

More luxury, in both accommodations and food, can be found out of town on Avenida Quito. The first hotel you'll pass is the **Hotel La Siesta,** Quito 12-26 and Pallatanga, tel. 2/751-013 or 751-860, about half a kilometer out of town. Classy in a rustic sort of way, La Siesta offers a bar and restaurant, along with rooms for $5 s, $6 d with shared bath, $7 s, $8 d private. The doubles are a particularly good deal. **Parrilladas Argentinas,** just past the Hotel La Siesta, is recommended for the quality of its cuts of beef. A full plate is $3. The obligatory **Chifa China** is behind the Hostal Jennifer.

Next comes the **Hotel de Toachi,** kilometer 1, tel. 2/754-688 or 754-689. It may look just like a U.S.-style motel from the street, but at least the pool is large enough to do laps in. For one night you'll pay $5 s, $7 d. Adjoining the hotel, **Ch' Farina** serves a great pizza with lots of sauce for about $1.50

SANTO DOMINGO DE LOS COLORADOS

GUAYAQUIL
BABAHOYO
MACHALA
MARKET
CINE AMBATO
LA FORNACELLA PIZZERIA
LATACUNGA
TULCÁN
BARRA
TSÁCHILAS
MONTECRISTI
FACES DISCOTEC ▼
DISCOTEC IGUANA ▼
ZARACAY TOURS/ METROPOLITAN TOURING
NET EXPRESS
MARKET
HOTEL EJECUTIVO
HOTEL AMAMBAY
HOSTAL JENNIFER
HOTEL CALETA
29 DE MAYO
CHURCH ★
PLAZA SARACAY
FILANBANCO
CUENCA
RIOBAMBA
AMBATO
3 DE JULIO

To Bus Terminal and Post Office
To More Santo Domingo Accommodations and Quito
RÍO TOACHI
QUITO
PACIFICTEL
RÍO POVE

0   100 yds
0   100 m

© AVALON TRAVEL PUBLISHING, INC.

Last but not cheapest, the **Hotel Zaracay,** just past the Hotel de Toachi, tel. 2/751-023, 370-914, fax 2/754-535, is built in a country-estate style with thatched roofs, pleasant land-scaping, tennis courts, and a tiny pool. The 70 rooms at this oasis run $25 s, $36 d with phone, TV, and air-conditioning ($13 s, $19 d without air-conditioning), including breakfast in the open-air bar/restaurant. Advance booking is advised.

Entertainment and Events
So what will you do with all the time you're not paying the Colorado *indígenas* to dress up and pose for photos? Two city **markets** cram the center: one between Guayaquil and Machala along Ambato, and another on the opposite side of 29 de Mayo between Cuenca and Ambato. Both spill into the surrounding streets. Calle 3 de Julio is one long market.

Both **Turismo Zaracay/Metropolitan Touring,** 29 de Mayo and Montecristi, tel. 2/750-546 or 750-874, fax 2/750-873, e-mail: tzaracay@ sd.pro.ec, and **Colorado Tours,** Tsachila 436 and Guayaquil, tel. 2/757-914 or 757-132, fax 2/757-942, organize tours of the area.

The **Cine Ambato** shows relatively new films on the big screen, or you can choose your own video for a private screening. Dancers can try the **Discotec Iguana** on Tsáchilas, or the more ex-clusive, neon-lit **Faces Discotec** farther north on the way to the bus terminal. Santo Domin-go's **Canonization Anniversary** festival takes place on 3 July.

Services and Information
The chaotic **Filanbanco** on the Plaza Saracay somehow manages to exchange travelers' checks. The **post office** is a few blocks north of the plaza along Tsáchilas on the right, and **Paci-fictel** (signed Andinatel) sits upstairs at the in-tersection of Quito and Toachi. Several Internet cafés, including **Net Express,** are scattered about the city center.

Transportation
Santo Domingo's **bus terminal** is located three km north of the center of town. Buses run to and from regularly, passing north on Tsácihlas and returning west down 29 de Mayo.

From here buses head to every city connect-ed to Santo Domingo by road, meaning every coastal city and then some. Major destinations in-clude Quito ($1.25, three hours), Guayaquil ($2.25, 5.5 hours), Esmeraldas ($1.50, four hours), Machala ($4, eight hours), Bahía de

Caráquez ($2.25, six hours), and Manta ($3, seven hours), but buses run to most highland cities as well.

Hacienda Tinalandia

Alfredo Garcon named this hotel and estate after his Russian wife Tina when the couple opened it together in the 1950s. Today it's considered one of the hottest birding spots in the country, with more than 350 species identified to date. Ornithological mouthfuls like the rufous-tailed hummingbird, pale-legged hornero, and rustic margin flycatcher flit through 240 acres of protected land along the Río Toachi, and another 600 acres are protected adjacent to the reserve.

Numerous hiking trails branch out from the main cabin complex on the south side of the river toward bird-feeding stations among the trees. Rafting, hiking, and horseback-riding trips can be arranged, and a seldom-used golf course is marked by flags and untended sand traps.

Meals on the porch overlooking the river include homemade delicacies such as naranjilla ice cream. Temperatures hover around 22°C, and May–Sept. are the driest months.

To reach Tinalandia, take a southbound turn onto a poorly marked track about 16 km east of Santo Domingo. Rooms are $80 s, $104 d, and the staff can arrange birding guides and transportation from Quito. Make reservations through the hacienda's office in Quito at Urb. El Bosque, Segunda Etapa, Av. Del Parque, Calle 3, Lote 98 #43-78, tel./fax 2/449-028, www.ecuador-explorer.com/tinalandia.

SANTO DOMINGO TO GUAYAQUIL

Río Palenque Science Center

This combination reserve and research center contains one of the largest swatches of lowland forest in Ecuador. Less than 200 protected hectares in a crook of the Río Palenque are surrounded by endless expanses of African palm and banana fields.

Resident botanist Calaway Dodson has documented one of the highest concentrations of plant diversity—1,200 species in 100 hectares—on the planet at Río Palenque. The reserve's primary forest includes a few stands of Río Palenque mahogany, which used to be the area's most valuable timber tree until overcutting left it one of the 10 most endangered plant species in the world. Three hundred sixty species of birds are the other main draw: the forest rings with the raucous cries of rufous-fronted wood quail and the liquid tones of the southern nightingale wren. More than 300 species of butterflies have also been identified here.

Facilities are more geared toward researchers than casual visitors. The small field station has a kitchen, generator electricity by day, and private bathrooms with cold showers. Guests pay $2 to visit for the day and $5 to spend the night.

The reserve is located about 40 km southwest of Santo Domingo, shortly past the village of Patricia Pilar. A sign points the way; it's 1.5 km down a side road. For information, contact the Centro Cientifico Río Palenque, tel. 9/745-790, or the Wong Foundation in Guayaquil, tel. 4/208-670 or 208-680.

CALI OF THE SOUTH

So much Colombian drug money has been invested in Santo Domingo de los Colorados that locals half-seriously refer to it as "Santo Domingo de los Colombianos." Investment is one thing, but what worries residents and officials is the purchase of huge expanses of prime agricultural land. One businessman recalled how several of his friends made a quick *sucre* when they sold land to Colombians for 30–100 percent above its market value, and were paid the entire amount in cash.

Not only are the *narcotraficantes* buying up the good land, but they're also putting it to shady uses. A May 1986 raid on a drug lab just outside Santo Domingo yielded US$4 million in cash, cars, and property, 33 defendants, and more than 800 kg of processed cocoa paste.

Ecuadorian drug barons are following suit. One good example is the 5,600-hectare hacienda owned by the alleged leader of the largest cartel in the country. In 1995 Ecuador's largest drug raid ever landed US$100 million in assets and left 51 people in jail.

Quevedo

Resting on the banks of the wide, brown Río Quevedo, Quevedo is a muggy, bustling settlement known as the Chinatown of Ecuador for its large Asian population. Most travelers just pass through, stopping off for a meal at one of the many *chifas* before continuing to Guayaquil or Santo Domingo.

The noisy main street 7 de Octubre parallels the river, divided by numbered cross streets. (Although Quevedo is not an especially dangerous place, it's a good idea to stick to 7 de Octubre after dark.) The **main plaza** and **church** are on 7 de Octubre between Calles 5 and 6. There are three **markets** on Calle 7 off 7 de Octubre—one to the west and two to the east, and 7 de Octubre is basically one long market in itself.

The **Hotel Ejecutivo International,** 7 de Octubre and 4a 214, tel. 3/751-780 or 751-781, fax 3/750-596, is a good value at $4 per room with air-conditioning and TV. Their restaurant is recommended as one of the best in town. An Olympic-sized pool and disco wait at the northeast end of town at the **Hotel Olimpico,** Calle 19 117 and Roldos, Ciudadela San José, tel. 3/750-455 or 750-965. Rooms start at $33.50, and the pool is open to the public for $1 pp. On the whole, Quevedo's *chifas* are dependable and cheap. The **Chifa Pekin,** 7 de Octubre and Calle 3, serves a better-than-average *chaulafan* for about one dollar.

You'll find **Pacifictel** on La Y, a small triangular intersection at the west end of 7 de Octubre with a white statue of a mother and child. The **post office** is one block north of Pacifictel on 7 de Octubre, and you can check your e-mail at **Mango Clubnet,** hidden away on the lower level of the corner of Bolívar and Calle 6 (open Mon.–Sat., $1.50 per hour).

Like most cities in the western lowlands, Quevedo is a crossroads between the Sierra and the coast. Most bus companies are located on 7 de Octubre and Bolívar (the next street toward the river) near the bridge; major cities served include Quito ($2.25, 4–5 hours), Santo Domingo ($1, 1.5 hours), Guayaquil ($1.50, 3.5 hours), and Portoviejo ($3, five hours). Many buses pass La Y on their way out of town.

SANTO DOMINGO TO ESMERALDAS

La Perla Forest Reserve

West Virginian Suzanne Sheppard came here in 1949 to start a farm with her husband. After discovering the sad state of Ecuador's coastal forests, the pair decided to set aside 250 hectares for the future benefit of visitors and local youth. Since then, they've struggled successfully against environmental laws dictating that land must be "improved" to secure ownership.

The reserve, 41 km north of Santo Domingo, has minimal facilities, but guides are available by prior appointment. Contact the Bosque Protector La Perla, Casilla 17-24-128, Santo Domingo, tel. 2/725-344 or 759-115.

Aldea Salamandra

This tranquil retreat, opened in 1994, was conceived with education in mind. Fees collected from guests not only keep the place open but also help support sustainable agriculture demonstrations in local communities and regular weekend visits by Quito schoolchildren. Hopeful, earthy phrases such as "responsible attitude" and "dignified and full life" keep cropping up in the hotel's literature and conversations with the owners.

Rustic bamboo cabins with thatched roofs sit on the edge of the Río Caoni. One room is set up in a tree over the water. Guests share composting toilets, and there aren't any showers, so bathing in the river is a daily ritual. Camping and hammock areas are also available. No red meats cross the kitchen doorway: on the menu here are chicken, fish, or vegetarian dishes.

Well-marked trails wind into the lush hills, providing getaways ranging from a few hours to a few days. Guided hikes head to waterfalls and a nearby ecological farm, and volunteer opportunities can easily turn a weekend stay into a week or longer. Guests can roast and grind their own cacao beans into chocolate, make tagua-nut jewelry, and find an opossum in the roof of their cabin, all on the same day. Rooms, all meals, and guided excursions cost $21 pp per day. Dec.–June is hot and rainy, averaging 30°C during the day. It's drier and cooler July–Nov.

Aldea Salamandra is two km east of Puerto

Quito, branching off the Santo Domingo-Esmeraldas road at La Independencia. Three bus companies (Kennedy, San Pedrito, and Alóag) send three to four buses each from Quito to Puerto Quito daily; the drivers know the Aldea Salamandra turnoff. If you're driving yourself, look for the "Hostería La Isla" signs, a small *tienda* (shop), and a sizable roadside shrine, all on your right if you're coming from Puerto Quito. From the turnoff, it's a 10-minute walk down the dirt road to the gate.

The reserve has an office in Quito at Calama E6-06 and Juan Leon Mera, tel. 2/228-151, 821-816; you can also find information at Los Shyris 3941 and Rio Coca, Edif. Montecarlo, piso 3, tel. 2/253-967, e-mail: aldeasalamandra@yahoo.com, www.aldeasalamandra.com.

Bilsa Biological Station

Fundación Jatun Sacha opened this field station in 1994 in the middle of what would become the **Reserva Ecologica Mache-Chindul,** which was set aside two years later by the director of the Ecuadorian National Park Service as he left office. Less than 1 percent of this type of coastal tropical wet forest remains in Ecuador, and you'll find most of it here in the low, rugged Mache and Chindul Mountains. Jatun Sacha adds land every year to their original 2,500-hectare holding, but only time will tell if pressures from logging and colonization will win out.

Elevations up to 800 meters lift an island of foggy ridges and muggy forest above the surrounding scrubland. The ecosystem is isolated from the Andes but rugged enough to trap a dense fog that supports cloud forest flora and fauna that are usually restricted to higher, wetter elevations. The impressive species list includes small rare jungle cats, jaguars, and mantled howler monkeys, along with 305 recorded species of birds. More than 20,000 plant seedlings are cared for in Bilsa's Center for the Conservation of Western Forest Plants, and an ongoing botanical inventory has uncovered 20 plant species new to science.

Three rustic cabins provide shelter for researchers, students, and natural history tour groups. Individual visitors should contact the Fundación ahead of time for permission to enter. Foreign visitors pay $5 to enter the reserve and $15 pp per day for room and board at Bilsa. Researchers and interns are expected to contribute $200 pp per month to offset lodging and meals. Volunteer opportunities are also possible.

Getting to Bilsa can be an adventure. Quinindé is the nearest town, where you'll want to find or hire a truck going to the village of Herrera, 25 km from the reserve. In the wet season (Jan.–May), you'll probably be able to get only as far as the intersection known as "La Y," but during the rest of the year you might be able to drive all the way to the reserve. Otherwise it's a three- to four-hour walk. Contact the Fundación Jatun Sacha, Pasaje Eugenio de Santillán N34-28 and Maurián, Urb. Rumipamba, Casilla 17-12-867, Quito, tel./fax 2/432-240, 432-173, 432-246, e-mail: jatsacha@ecuanex.net.ec, www.jatunsacha.org, for details on access and reservations.

NORTH COAST

The northern coast has traditionally been one of Ecuador's forgotten regions, lagging behind the rest of the country's economy because of its geographical and political isolation as well as its proximity to Colombia. Esmeraldas didn't receive electricity until 1932, and it wasn't until 1957 that a rail line finally linked San Lorenzo to the outside world (recently replaced by a road). Countless small fishing villages, unchanged for decades, go about their seaside business, as pollution, overcrowding, and disease take their toll on the larger cities. The region calls to mind a peculiar version of the Wild West by way of Africa, from the dark-skinned residents carrying machetes and living in stilt houses to the general air of disrepair and lawlessness—it's not for everyone but definitely distinctive.

Neglect by the national government has also been a sticking point since colonial times: when a 1976 Esmeraldas fire burned out of control because the local fire department didn't have the equipment to fight it, the resulting general strike and riots led the city government to impose martial law and a curfew.

Ecuador fought with its northern neighbor over the border in 1831 and 1916, when the Treaty of Muñoz Vernaza-Suarez established the current boundary. Today the main sources of friction are smuggling, drugs, and immigration (or the occasional smuggling of drugs by immigrants).

Visitors to the area should be inoculated against malaria and yellow fever.

ESMERALDAS AND VICINITY

You won't see pictures of Esmeraldas (pop. 120,000) gracing brochures about Ecuador's coast. With a large chunk of the country's entire coastal population scrambling to make a life within its boundaries, the capital of Esmeraldas province hustles and bustles but certainly doesn't sparkle.

After short rubber booms during the two World Wars, in the late 1970s Esmeraldas expanded into the main port city on Ecuador's northern coast. A deepwater port that was opened in 1979 allows large tankers to feed off the western terminus of the trans-Andean oil pipeline. The country's largest oil refinery erupts from the fertile river valley in nearby Puerto Balao like a smoking metal wart.

In the city center, a lush central park sidles up to the Orwellian concrete Santuario Nuestra Señora de La Merced. The city's seaside roots poke through in the occasional weathered coastal-style building with precarious balconies. Vendors on every corner do a good job of ignoring the garbage in the streets as they hawk every conceivable item necessary to life by the sea. The riverside Malecón brims with fruit and clothing stands, while shoreward you'll find *batido* sellers armed with fruit and blender.

Esmeraldas is a very poor city, making theft a distinct problem. Be especially careful along the Malecón, even during the day. Thieves typically make a quick grab for your belongings and hightail it toward the river islands, where they can disappear in a matter of seconds.

Accommodations

Many basic hotels are located in the center. With seagoing artifacts, flowers, and construction debris in the lobby, the **Hostal El Galeón,** Piedrahita and Olmedo, tel. 6/723-820, fax 6/725-924, is a mixed bag. So-so rooms with fan, phone, and private bath run $2 pp, or $3.25 for rooms with air-conditioning and TV. Similar to the Galeón in terms of room quality, the **Hostal Americano,** 7-05 Sucre, tel. 6/723-768 or 723-769, has accommodations for less than $3 with fan or air-conditioning.

Noises from the Malecón drift up to the **Hotel Asia,** tel. 6/714-594, 710-648, $2 pp with private bath and fan (some rooms have TV as well), and the **Hotel Turismo,** Bolívar 843, tel. 6/723-050, costs $2.25 pp with private bath and fan. At the **Hotel Miraflores,** tel. 6/723-077, $1 gets you a clean, brightly colored room with shared bath and fan.

The **Apart Hotel Esmeraldas,** tel. 6/728-700 or 728-703, tel./fax 6/728-704, is by far the best hotel in the center, but at $15 s, $19 d, it isn't a particularly good deal. Rooms have air-condi-

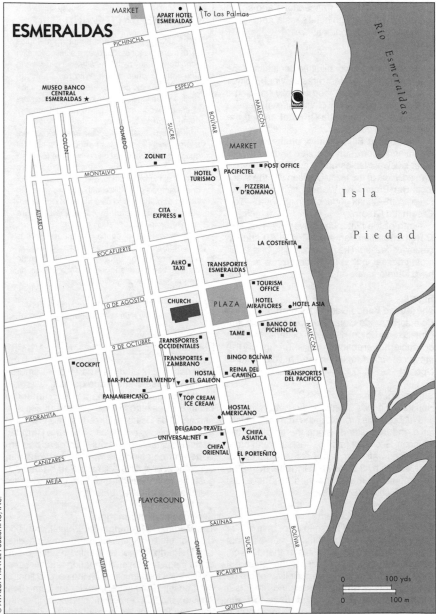

ESMERALDAS

To Las Palmas

MARKET
APART HOTEL
ESMERALDAS

PICHINCHA

ESPEJO

MUSEO BANCO
CENTRAL
ESMERALDAS ★

Rio Esmeraldas

MARKET

ZOLNET

MONTALVO

HOTEL
TURISMO

PACIFICTEL

POST OFFICE

PIZZERIA
D'ROMANO

CITA
EXPRESS

Isla

Piedad

ROCAFUERTE

LA COSTEÑITA

AERO
TAXI

TRANSPORTES
ESMERALDAS

10 DE AGOSTO

CHURCH

PLAZA

TOURISM
OFFICE

HOTEL
MIRAFLORES

HOTEL ASIA

9 DE OCTUBRE

TRANSPORTES
OCCIDENTALES

TAME

BANCO DE
PICHINCHA

COCKPIT

TRANSPORTES
ZAMBRANO

BINGO BOLÍVAR

HOSTAL
EL GALEÓN

REINA DEL
CAMINO

TRANSPORTES
DEL PACIFICO

BAR-PICANTERÍA WENDY

PANAMERICANO

TOP CREAM
ICE CREAM

HOSTAL
AMERICANO

PIEDRAHITA

DELGADO TRAVEL

UNIVERSAL.NET

CHIFA
ASIATICA

CHIFA
ORIENTAL

EL PORTEÑITO

CANIZARES

MEJIA

PLAYGROUND

SALINAS

RICAURTE

QUITO

0   100 yds

0   100 m

tioning, cable TV, and refrigerators, and suites are also available. The hotel's restaurant is the poshest in the city center as well.

Food
You'll relish the air-conditioned coolness of the **Chifa Asiatica,** on Mañizares between Bolívar and Sucre, where the food actually has some taste compared to many other *chifas;* plates are $1.50 and up. The **Chifa Oriental** around the corner is also passable.

The popular **El Porteñito,** on the corner of Mehía and Sucre, serves coffee and sandwiches at sidewalk tables under a green and white awning. Next to the Hostal Galeón sits the lively, local **Bar-Picantería Wendy,** right across the street from—thank goodness in this heat—**Top Cream Ice Cream.**

North of the plaza on Bolívar, the **Pizzeria D'Romano** offers large pies for $1.50 and ice cream for dessert. The ambience is so bad it's almost comical, but at least the pizzas actually have tomato sauce on them.

Sights
The **Museo Banco Central Esmeraldas,** in the Colegio Sagrado Corazón on Espejo between Olmedo and Colón, displays a decent collection of ancient ceramics from throughout the province, with a focus on the La Tola culture. Open Mon.–Sat. 9 A.M.–4 P.M., 40 cents pp.

Shopping
Household goods like mosquito nets, sandals, and rubber boots are sold in the **market** off Montalvo and from stands along the length of the Malecón. Scents of (mostly) fresh fish and other local foods waft from stands at the south end of the Malecón by Salinas and Ricaurte. In 1998 a new municipal market opened on Sucre just north of Pichincha.

Entertainment and Events
Esmeraldas is called the "capital of rhythm" for the prevailing African rhythms of marimba, but music halls open and close faster than tropical flowers. Ask your bartender for the latest hot spot. The former Cine Bolívar, Bolívar and 9 de Octubre, is now **Bingo Bolívar** and attracts a much more wholesome crowd. **Face to Face Discotec,** one block from the plaza, is a popular

---

SHAKE, RATTLE, AND FLIRT

The looping rhythms and bouncing melodies of marimba (or *currulao,* as it's called locally) echo down many nighttime alleys in cities along Ecuador's northern coast. With roots firmly in Africa, the music centers around the marimba itself, a xylophone-like instrument with large keys of *chonta* wood mounted over hanging ringers made from split bamboo.

Marimba's heartbeat comes from the *bombo,* a large bass drum made of wood with a head of goatskin or leather that gives its name to a particular variety of dance. Familiar maracas are shaken along with *guasas,* which are made out of dried bamboo stalks filled with *achira* seeds and closed at both ends to give a sound like a rainstick. Small tambourines called *cununos* are spanked with vigor.

Many varieties of dance and chanting songs accompany the lilting tunes. Watch for the coquettish exchange between male and female dancers before the shaking starts: a sample dialogue has the woman singing:

Bolívar with his sword conquered five nations
And me with my hips I conquer all hearts.

---

local dance spot, and the Apart-Hotel Esmeraldas has a **casino** and **video games.**

Various hapless avians flail each other to death on weekends in the **cockpit** at Eloy Alfaro and 9 de Octubre. Three festivals break the muggy monotony every year: **Bolívar's Birthday** packs the streets on 24 July; **Esmeraldas' Independence** coincides with an **Agricultural, Livestock, and Arts & Crafts Fair** on 3–5 August; and the **Founding of Esmeraldas** is remembered on 21 September.

Services and Information
The **Banco de Pichincha** at Bolívar and 9 de Octubre efficiently changes travelers' checks, and **Delgado Travel** on Cañizares and Sucre offers the usual travel information and services.

There's a tourism office on the second floor of the Consejal Provincial office (enter from 10 de Agosto), but don't expect much help or information. The **Colombian consulate** is in Las Palmas (see following section). Both **Pacifictel** and the **post office** are located by the *mercado* on Montalvo.

For Internet access, head to **Zolnet** or **Universal.net**, both of which are open Mon.–Sat. **PuntoNet**, above the Occidentales office, is open daily, but it only had one computer in 2000.

Transportation

Luckily (say some visitors), there are lots of ways to leave this city. TAME flights to Quito (Mon., Wed., Fri., and Sun., $14 one-way) and Guayaquil (Mon., Wed., Fri., and Sun., $25 one-way) leave from the **General Rivadeneria Airport,** across the mouth of the river. To get there, it's a 15-km trip upstream to San Mateo, where you cross the river and descend to Tachina. A taxi costs $3 and takes half an hour. Buses to San Lorenzo or other towns to the north pass the airport, but make sure to allow enough time to get there.

There's no main bus terminal to make life easier, so travelers are left with a smattering of *cooperativa* offices around the town center. Buses to Muisne ($1, 2–5 hours) and Borbón ($3, 4–5 hours) leave from **La Costeñita**, Malecón between Rocafuerte and 10 de Agosto. They also sell bus tickets to La Tola ($3, 4–5 hours), where it's easy to catch a boat to San Lorenzo. La Costeñita controls the frequent runs to Atacames (40 cents, 45 minutes), Súa (50 cents, 50 minutes), and Same (60 cents, one hour).

Panamericano, Piedrahita at Colón, sends the best luxury buses to Quito at 11:45 A.M. and 11:15 P.M. ($6), and to Guayaquil at 11 P.M. ($6). To reach Manta, book with **Reina del Camino,** Piedrahita at Sucre, with regular service for $4.50 and an *exclusivo* for $6.

Transportes Esmeraldas, on the north side of the main plaza, has numerous buses, both regular and luxury service, to Quito ($4.50, 5–6 hours) and Guayaquil ($5.25, eight hours). They also run a 5:35 P.M. bus to Huaquillas ($6.50, 12 hours) and an 8:40 P.M. bus to Machala ($5.50, 11 hours).

Transportes del Pacifico on the Malecón goes to San Lorenzo ($3.25, 5–6 hours) a few times every morning, and **Transportes Zambrano** has frequent departure to Santo Domingo, plus five a day to Muisne and two to Pedernales.

Trans Occidental, Sucre and 9 de Octubre, has a few each day to Quito, Guayaquil, Santo Domingo, and Machala. Sucre near Rocafuerte is home to **Cita Express,** going to Ambato ($3.50, seven hours) and Santo Domingo, and **Aerotaxi** (Guayaquil, Quito, and Ibarra).

Las Palmas

Esmeraldas' seaside suburb is scattered with hotels, restaurants, and discos, but suffers from the clamor of a busy international port and a littered beach you don't want to be caught on at night. This is the nicest part of the city, which isn't saying much. Avenida Kennedy is the main drag parallel to the shore, connected with the center of Esmeraldas by bus number 1 that runs regularly up and down Bolívar until late at night.

The **Colombian consulate** in Las Palmas is one block from the Hotel Cayapas off Kennedy. It's a good idea to stop here if you plan to cross into Colombia by boat at San Lorenzo. Open Mon.–Fri. 8:15 A.M.–12:15 P.M. and 2:15–5 P.M. **Accommodations:** The **Hotel Cayapas,** Kennedy and Valdez, tel. 6/721-318 or 721-319, fax 6/721-320, is particularly recommended— it's probably the nicest hotel in the city. Rooms with TVs go for $11 s, $15 d with air-conditioning, and their open-air La Tolita restaurant is also the best in town. An extensive menu of pastas, seafood, and meats starts at $2.50, although prices climb as high as $12 for shrimp or paellas.

At the far end of Kennedy, the **Hotel del Mar,** tel. 6/723-707 or 723-708, is the only accommodation in Las Palmas that actually has a view of the beach. Rooms with TV, phone, and private bath are a great deal at $4.50 s, $7 d (some have air-conditioning), and the Fenix Restaurant spills out onto the patio. A neon sign advertising Chic's Burger marks the modest **Hotel Ambato,** Kennedy and Guerra, tel. 6/721-144. Rooms feature private bath, fan, and TV and cost $4 s, $7 d.

Food: On the Kennedy block, the **Bar/Restaurant/Pizzeria La Cascada** has an open second story where pizzas start at $2. The **Parillada Los Helechos,** down by the Hotel Ambato, hides behind a wall of foliage. A full *parillada* served under their immense thatched roof is $3.25 for one person. Cheaper local food can be found off the main plaza one block back from Kennedy, by the Hotel Ambato.

Nightlife: Follow the thumping bass and flashing lights to a short strip of **discos** along the beach at the far end of Kennedy (Rock Julian's, of course, being my favorite). Discos situated away from the beach go a step or two up in quality, including Banana Disco Bar behind the Hotel del Mar, and the Arena Blanca Discotec down Kennedy by the main plaza. A few smaller bars at the end of Kennedy, such as Villakapi, even have some character.

ESMERALDAS TO THE BORDER

Ecuador's northernmost coastline dissolves into a tangle of mangroves as it reaches Colombia. Nearly three-quarters of the population in the farthest towns has immigrated—often illegally—from Colombia, bringing problems with smuggling and drugs.

North of Esmeraldas
The road hugs the coast to and past the Río Verde lighthouse, providing ample access to acres of undeveloped sand. Just south in the fishing village of Río Verde is the **Hostería Pura Vida,** tel. 6/744-203, a wonderful beachfront getaway that receives repeat praise. Comfy cabañas with private bath go for $12 pp. Twenty-two km past the point, the road splits toward **La Tola,** on the seaward point across from **Limones,** and **Borbón** inland.

Upriver into Cotacachi-Cayapas
Not many visitors enter this sprawling reserve from its downhill side via Borbón. It's a shame, too, because the brave few who do not only enjoy an incredible lowland jungle but can also visit the indigenous Cayapas tribes in nearby villages. (For more information on the Cotacachi-Cayapas Reserve, see the Northern Sierra chapter.)

If you have to spend the night in the riverside town of **Borbón,** pray that a room is available at the **Hostal Costa Norte,** because all of the other hotels in town maintain, shall we say, a very low standard. Sparkling clean rooms with fan and TV are $2.50, or $3 with private bath.

Hungarian Steve Tarjanyi and his wife Laura opened **Steve's Lodge** in the early 1970s, 45 minutes upriver from Borbón by motorized canoe. Three-day package tours, including a lo-

cally trained guide and excursions to the La Tola archaeological site and upriver into the forest (one overnight), run $250 pp, but you have to find your own way there. Waterskiing and canoe lessons within sight of the lodge also keep guests busy. For information, contact the current managers Antonio and Judy Nagy, Casilla 5148 C.C.I., Quito, tel. 2/431-555 or 447-709, fax 2/431-556, e-mail: nagy@pi.pro.ec.

Visitors to the tiny, quiet village of **Santa Maria de los Cayapas** can choose between the *pensión* of Señora Pastora, dormitory lodging in the local mission, or camping among the trees. Walter Quintero Torres is a recommended guide for day trips to nearby Cayapas villages and longer journeys into Cotacachi-Cayapas.

Lodgings become even sketchier farther upriver; ask the local pastor in the mission settlement of **Zapallo Grande** to point you in the direction of the local *pensión* or campsite. **San Miguel,** which is four hours by motorized canoe from Borbón, blends African, Ecuadorian, and indigenous cultures. The village, almost inside the Cotacachi-Cayapas reserve, is the main base for excursions into the reserve. Check in at the guardpost up on the hill for details, and be sure to arrange a spot on the predawn boat downriver the night before leaving. In San Miguel, you can stay at the **SUBIR Lodge,** although it has become a bit run down because of a lack of visitors. Rooms are $1.25 pp ($5 with three meals), and guides are available for tours into the reserve, but you still have to pay the park fee.

Transportation: Occasional motor launches connect the various settlements up the Río Cayapas. From Borbón, one daily boat heads to San Miguel around 11 A.M. ($8, four hours). Check locally for the latest word on connecting services between other villages such as Santa Maria and Zapallo Grande—the pattern seems to be that they go when they go.

SAN LORENZO

One of the least attractive cities on the coast sits in the mouth of the mangroves in Cayapas-Mataje National Park. Travelers used to come through this town, which was founded in the 17th and 18th centuries by escaped slaves, because it was the destination of the train from

Ibarra. Now that the train isn't running, a visit to San Lorenzo is usually warranted only by the festival of Santos Reyes and Santos Innocentes near the beginning of the year, or as the starting or ending point of a trip into the lower regions of the Cotocachi-Cayapas Reserve.

Roads connecting San Lorenzo to Borbón and Ibarra were finally completed near the turn of the millennium; expect to encounter passport checks and luggage searches because this city sees more than its share of illicit border traffic. Boats can be rented to visit completely undeveloped beaches on the seaward side of the mangrove islands offshore—most notably **San Pedro.** Otherwise, get ready to slap a few thousand mosquitoes as you wait for your boat.

Accommodations and Food
A few budget hotels are bearable for a night or two—the **Hotel Puerto Azul,** tel. 6/780-220, is the best in town and is right next to the train station. Rooms with private bath, fan, mosquito nets, and satellite TV are $2.50. If that's full, try the **Hotel Tolita Pampa de Oro,** tel. 6/780-240, just off Imbabura halfway between the train station and the jetty ($3 pp with private bath, fan, and mosquito net), or the **Hotel Imperial,** tel. 6/780-242, at the far end of Imbabura almost to the jetty, where rooms with mosquito nets, private bath, and TVs are less than $3.

Another option for longer stays in San Lorenzo is with a group of English teachers who offer room and board in exchange for a few hours of English instruction per day. This is a great way to get beneath the skin of life on the coast. Ask at the Pampa de Oro Hotel, or simply ask for the English teachers ("Donde están los profesores de Inglés?"). Luis Valencia has a cabin for visitors behind Andinatel and can arrange volunteer projects with disadvantaged children or local permaculture projects.

No restaurants stand out, but there's a good chance you'll be having **seafood** for dinner.

Entertainment and Events
A small **artesanía** shop on Imbabura a few blocks north of the train station sells locally woven baskets. Inquire locally about *salons* where musicians gather in the muggy weekend evenings and beat out *marimba* music until the wee hours.

These lilting rhythms are also a significant part of celebrations during the first week in January, when the festival of **Santos Reyes and Santos Innocentes** rolls into town. This event is reason in itself to visit San Lorenzo: garishly painted residents barely old enough to walk roam the streets hooting to the Macumba (voodoo) spirits of Africa and the Caribbean, and crossroads are commandeered by *cucuruchos,* self-appointed guardians who collect mock taxes to buy booze.

Information and Services
For information on the Cotacachi-Cayapas Reserve, drop by the **Ministerio de Ambiente** office, tel. 6/780-184, on the main plaza by the jetty. **Andinatel** is a few blocks north of the train station (look for the metal tower), and the post office is down a side street off the main plaza. If you plan on entering or leaving Colombia, you can get your passport stamped at the Capitania del Puerto (harbormaster's office) or the police station.

As of 2000, the Internet hadn't yet made any inroads to San Lorenzo, but the proprietor of the Copy-Compu Papelería across the tracks from the train station said that when it does, he would be the first to offer access.

Transportation
Now that the long-awaited road connecting San Lorenzo with Borbón has been completed, a smattering of bus companies have sprung up around the train station, which is slowly falling into disuse. The **train** still leaves daily at 7 A.M. for Progreso (three hours)—don't worry, you can still ride on the roof for kicks—and you can return to San Lorenzo at 2 P.M. ($2 round-trip).

The bus ride from Ibarra pales in comparison to the train but is still quite scenic. **Transportes del Valle** has buses leaving on the hour for Ibarra ($3) from 4 A.M.–2 P.M. **Transportes Espejo** also sends buses to Ibarra until 3 P.M., and **Transportes Esmeraldas** sends comfortable coaches all the way to Quito and Guayaquil. All buses out of town either start at or pass the crumbling monument in front of the train station.

If you're into coastal scenery, the boat ride into or out of San Lorenzo can be reason enough to visit. Two boat/bus companies have offices at the pier. **Transportes San Lorenzo de Pailon** has boats to Limones leaving at 6:30 A.M., 12:30 P.M., and 3:30 P.M. ($2), from where you can catch another boat to get to La Tola ($1.50), which is connected by road to Esmeraldas. **Transportes Pacifico** does boat/bus combinations all the way to Esmeraldas leaving every two hours from 5:30 A.M.–1:30 P.M. ($6 for the bus, with the same prices as above for the boat sections.) They also have departures to Colombia at 7 A.M. and 2 P.M. Transportes Pacifico is also a good place to get information on San Lorenzo and the surrounding area; they can arrange visits to mangrove swamps and deserted beaches nearby, although the prices can add up unless you have a group.

WEST OF ESMERALDAS

This stretch of coast, extending around Punta Galera down to Muisne, starts out as one of the more popular beach destinations in the country thanks to its proximity to the capital. Resort hotels and Greek-island vacation homes are deserted off-season and jammed during holidays. The towns themselves remain small and modest, and by the time you've passed Tonchigüe, you're well out into the boonies. An ant column of buses plies the coastal road.

Atacames

The first resort town west of Esmeraldas sports bright colors, loud music, and on the whole is surprisingly clean. This is the place to have a good time and party with Ecuadorian tourists, especially during the high season and holidays—if you can find space. The wide beach lines a spit of land that is separated from the town by a rank canal. To hit the ocean, take the diagonal road from the main bus stop in town, cross the footbridge, zig right, and follow the sound of surf. Three-wheeled "ecological" taxis cost less than 50 cents from the beach to the bus stop.

Umbrella-hawkers and kids balancing plates of sliced watermelon on their heads ply the Malecón parallel to the ocean. Hotels and restaurants line the strip, with prices dropping in direct proportion to their distance from the beach. Vendors hawk fruit, *ceviches,* and ice cream, and round thatched-hut bars each blare a different kind of music on the seaward side.

Take care when walking along the beach, especially at night and on the stretch between Atacames and Súa, because many thefts and assaults have been reported. If you run into problems, there's a police outpost at the west end of the bridge in town, half a block toward the beach on the west side. Also beware of the powerful undertow off the beach.

Accommodations: Low-end accommodations here can get pretty low—from brackish water and ravenous mosquitoes (bring your own net) to rats in the cheapest huts. On the road to the beach after crossing the footbridge, you'll find the **Cabañas Los Bohios,** tel. 6/731-089, 2/552-511, where two- to four-person cabins in a walled compound run $4 pp with fan and TV. The nearby **Hostal Maria Co.,** tel. 6/731-302, rents entire four-person apartments with kitchens for $20. The **Hotel Rodelu,** tel. 6/731-033, has rooms and cabañas comparable to Los Bohios (but without TVs) for $3 pp with private bath.

Head right (east) on the Malecón for about one km to the end of the pavement to reach the **Villas Arco Iris,** tel./fax 6/731-069, e-mail: arcoiris@waccom.net.ec. Nineteen plush cabins with front porches and hammocks line a sandy lane shaded by palm trees and accented with flowers and a pool. Accommodations, which include refrigerators, minibar, kitchen, air-conditioning, and an optional TV, cost $20–58 during the high season for up to six people, dropping to $12–38 in the low season.

More generic hotels anchor the Malecón back toward the center of town, such as the **Hotel Mediterraneo,** tel. 6/731-254, 2/240-445, with two- to six-person rooms for $4 pp with private bath and fan. More than a dozen cheap hotels cluster at the west end of the Malecón; the **Hotel Miravalle,** tel. 6/731-138, and the **Hotel Guajira,** tel. 6/731-278, are two of the better ones.

Food: A dozen stands under one thatched roof on the sand serve *ceviche* made fresh in front of you for less than $2 a plate. Choose from *concha* (conch), *langostino* (shrimp), or a *mixto* of the two, and wash it down with a fresh-squeezed orange juice. **Gabilos** sells *helados* and a coconut and milk sweet called *cocadas manjar.*

Across the street from the Hotel Rodelu, the **Restaurant Juan Griego** has a wide selection of seafood and meats for less than $2, and an excellent *menestra.* The **Ristaurante No Name**

PLAYA DEL ORO

Instead of a palm-fringed beach where sunbathers sip piña coladas, Playa del Oro (Golden Beach) is a remote village of 65 Afro-Ecuadorian families who live a largely subsistence lifestyle. A visit to this tight-knit community is a wonderful way to combine a visit to the rainforest with a chance to experience and help support a unique, fragile culture.

The tiny settlement is surrounded by roughly 10,000 hectares of community land, mostly primary forest, tucked up against the Cotacachi-Cayapas Ecological Reserve. This stretch of forest between northwest Ecuador and southern Panama, known as the Chocó, is one of the biologically richest and most threatened bioregions in the world.

In 1992 the Sustainable Uses for Biological Resources (SUBIR) Project helped the community build a traditional-style lodge near the village. The thatched-roof cabañas, completely renovated in 2000, have four-person rooms with private hot water bathrooms, electricity provided by solar cells, and mattresses so comfortable they deserve special mention. Meals combine typical Ecuadorian fare and ingredients from an impressive list of local specialties.

The residents of Playa del Oro run every aspect of the operation, from administration to cooking, under the guidance of the town's youthful president. It's hoped that the income will provide not only an economic alternative to forestry, but will also be able to pay for regular visits from a doctor and to hire a teacher for the local children. A few families have opened tiny craft shops in their homes to sell drums, woodcarvings, and children's toys to visitors to supplement their meager incomes.

Residents also serve as knowledgeable guides to take visitors upriver past an endless succession of waterfalls and into the surrounding forest. Birders can add as many as 250 species to their life lists in the subtropical woodlands, including the endemic scarlet-breasted dacnis and long-wattled umbrellabird. Popular destinations include a primate feeding ground, where monkeys are almost always seen, and a small stream where river otters are often spotted. Eight other species of mammals inhabit the surrounding forest and rivers, including all six neotropical cats indigenous to the area: jaguars, pumas, ocelots, margays, oncilas, and jaguarundis. (The village recently signed an agreement with the U.S. environmental group Touch the Jungle to protect their communal lands as a wild cat reserve.)

A research station is located a short way upstream in an abandoned army barracks, and a wildlife interpretive center was in the works in late 2000. If all goes according to plan, this center will serve as a release site for cats that have been confiscated from the illegal wild animal trade. When not out in the forest, the friendly villagers will soon make you feel like a part of the community. You can join the men for a bit of fishing or football, or tag along with their wives to go panning for gold—the declining but still profitable activity that gave the village its name. At night, local musicians sometimes turn the lodge's dining room into a dance hall.

The easiest way to visit Playa del Oro is through Angermeyer's Enchanted Expeditions (see "Tour Operators" in the Quito chapter). They offer complete, professionally run packages including lodging, meals, excursions with local guides and professional translators, and transport from the airport in Esmeraldas. Their four-day program costs $420 pp, and five days is $525 pp. (Add $50 for a round-trip flight from Quito to Esmeraldas.)

If you want to visit Playa del Oro on your own, you should let the community know at least one day in advance because food may need to be bought in Borbón, and a motorized canoe will have to be sent to pick you up in Selva Alegre about one hour downstream. Buses run to Selva Alegre from Borbón, and private transport can easily be arranged. A visit costs $10 pp per day for a bed and three meals, plus $18 for the boat ride from Selva Alegre. Tours with Spanish-speaking local guides cost extra (be sure to discuss this ahead of time) but are reasonably priced. For more information, you can contact EcoCiencia in Quito at San Cristóbal N44-495 and Seymour, tel. 2/242-417 or 242-422, fax 249-334, or stop by the Proyecto SUBIR/CARE office in Borbón.

Pizzeria, on the Malecón, has been recommended for pizza, and the prosaically named **Mexican Restaurant,** on the Malecón just east of the entrance road, has vegetarian burritos for $1 and shrimp fajitas for $3.

Entertainment: Look no further than the Malecón for *discotecas* such as Sambayo and Scala. For a quieter drink, head to the homey, unnamed bar with the thatch and green metal roof just before the Hotel Arco Iris.

Tours and Services: Tours Ecologiques "Le Petit," tel. 6/730-108 or 730-223, e-mail: lepetitbaños@yahoo.com, has a full platter of tours in the surrounding area, from horseback-riding trips ($22 pp per day) and mountain bike rentals to longer jungle ventures, Spanish classes, and whale-watching in the summer. They're on the Malecón just east of the entrance road.

To change travelers' checks, hit the **Banco del Pichincha** on the main plaza (weekdays only). The **Farmacia "Su Economica"** by the bus stop also changes travelers' checks. **Andinatel** is on the main plaza, and the **post office** is two blocks northeast of the bus stop on Roberto Cervantes, the main road into town. For Internet access, head to the **Librería y Papelería** on the main plaza, open daily.

Transportation: Trans Esmeraldas runs several buses to Quito ($5.25) and a couple to Guayaquil ($5.50) from their office on the main plaza. **Aerotaxi,** on Roberto Cervantes by the main bus stop in town, goes to Quito in the evening.

Súa

Just down the road from the fraternity-house vibe of Atacames is a different world—a small fishing town occupying a tranquil crescent bay. Súa is quieter, cheaper, and much less developed than its neighbors and has a welcome calming effect on visitors. (Still, hotel reservations are a good idea on weekends.)

Rolling green hills end in cliffs to the west, which can be skirted at low tide. One of these, called "Suicide Cliff," comes complete with a legend. A Spanish captain, so the story goes, fell in love with a princess named Súa, who on hearing that the captain had been killed in battle threw herself off the cliff. He hadn't, but when he returned and learned what happened, he took the same plunge. It's said that under the full moon you can see their ghosts wandering the rocks.

Development is coming to this very poor area, but there's still a long way to go. In the meantime, fishing barely keeps the town above water economically. The west side of town, near the muddy mouth of the Río Súa, still consists of nothing but rundown shacks where residents tie nets by hand (an expert using Japanese-made cord can knot 300 meters in a day).

Boats range from simple paddled dugout canoes to a few fiberglass launches with outboards. The fishing is done at night, when a bobbing flotilla drifts out under the light of homemade gasoline lanterns. Nighttime attacks by Colombian pirates who are after equipment and fish have prompted some fishermen to carry guns for protection. A good catch of 150 kg can bring as much as $75. Pregnant *langostinos* (crayfish) are sold to shrimp farms for up to $80.

The **Hotel Chagra Ramos,** tel. 6/731-006 or 731-070, in Quito tel. 2/443-822, is a friendly old favorite at the east end of town. Rooms with private bath and fan are $3.20; the newer cabins and villas spreading up the hill cost the same. Rent a jet ski for $48 per hour, or just relax with a cool drink in the restaurant.

A French couple runs the **Hotel Súa,** tel. 6/731-004, on the beachfront. Six double rooms go for $4 each. Their restaurant Chez Hélène offers seafood dishes for $1.50 and up, but save room for dessert: crêpe suzette and banana flambé are specialties, washed down with a cappuccino, espresso, or cognac. Next door the **Heladería/Pastelería San Luis** serves *batidos* and great fresh bread.

Farther down the short beachfront, the **Hostal Las Bouganvillas,** tel. 6/731-008, charges $2.75 pp for rooms with private bath and fan. Look for the sign a few blocks from the beach for the **Hotel El Peñon de Súa,** tel. 6/731-013, 2/657-502. Spacious rooms run $1.60 with private bath and fan, and the friendly owners will point out the TV room and a small bar where live *marimba* music is sometimes on the bill. At the **Coffe Bar,** a little west of Las Bouganvillas, you can find a great cup of coffee and some friendly conversation with the perpetually cheerful owner, who insists he uses only the best beans.

An **Andinatel** office is located near the entrance to Chagra Ramos, but the connections and hours are so erratic that residents say it's easier to go to Quito in person than to call there from here. A **police station** is opposite the Hotel El Shaman, half a block from the beach. **Buses** stop along the road beyond town.

Same

Same (pronounced SAHM-eh) offers the most pleasant developed beach in the area and is actually quieter than Súa—at least for the moment.

As the old hotels huddle in the center of the sand, an incredible amount of new building is going on, up to and including a Jack Nicklaus golf course and new highrise resorts in the hills to the east. In the future, this place may look more like Miami than Ecuador; in the meantime, enjoy the peace, gray sand, and surf. Same is very popular with gringos, so be prepared for higher prices than at Súa or even Atacames.

German artist Margaret Lehmann runs the **Seaflower Hostal/Restaurant,** tel. 9/455-038, 6/733-369, with her Chilean husband Luis. Their four rooms ($20), which are brimming with artwork and seashells, sleep up to five people and have private bath, hot water, fans, and mosquito nets. The homemade food in the restaurant is pricey but delicious, including homemade bread and jam for breakfast, and the owners are always looking for music to add to their collection in the sitting room.

The family-run **La Terraza,** tel. 9/476-949, 2/544-507, is a bit overpriced in comparison, but the four-person rooms ($22) are still comfy, with private baths and hammocks on the front porch with a view of the ocean. *Their* restaurant offers pizza, spaghetti, and seafood for $3–5. You'll have to walk a good ways toward the middle of the beach to find the **Hostal El Rampiral,** tel./fax 9/650-759, e-mail: rampiral@uio.satnet.net. Eleven cabins on stilts with hot water and refrigerators run $45.50 for up to four people, with prices slightly higher in the high season. The complex includes a pool and *cafetería.*

West of Same

The coastal road splits at **Tonchigüe,** a 20-minute walk from Same. The west branch leads to the lighthouse at **Punta Galera,** with a southern spur to Muisne. Several Trans Costañita buses per day run from Esmeraldas to Punta Galera, or you can take a bus to Muisne, get off at the junction and hitchhike.

Halfway to the lighthouse is the Canadian-run **Complejo Ecologico Playa Escondida,** tel. 6/733-368, 9/733-368, a secluded getaway on 34 hectares of semi-tropical forest against a cliff-backed beach. This place gets as many rave reviews—the word "paradise" is used a lot—as any destination on the coast. Cabins cost $12 pp including breakfast, and if you want to camp it's $5 pp, with three meals an addi-

tional $10–15. To get there, take a bus from Esmeraldas to Punta Galera and tell the driver to let you off at kilometer 14. From there it's a four-km walk, or you can hitchhike down the dirt road to the beach. You can also walk along the beach from Tonchigüe, but only at low tide.

Muisne

As far as beaches go, you can't do much better on Ecuador's northern coast than the seaward stretch on the tip of this stubby peninsula. Although most visitors usually head for the sea, the actual town of "Mui'ne" (lose the "s" to sound like a local) is on the inland side facing a muddy mangrove estuary at the mouth of the Río Repartadero. The road from Tonchigüe ends at a jetty, where you'll take one of the frequent *lanchas* across to the town itself—far from the most picturesque in Ecuador. Luckily, *tricycletas* wait to pedal you the two km to the beach (20 cents pp one-way) past cows wading chest-deep in flooded fields. (Based on the construction underway along the road to the beach, they're expecting big things to develop here, but for now it remains *muy tranquilo.*)

Muisne's beach is as flat and wide as an airport runway, fading into the palm-fringed distance in either direction. Pelicans skim low over the waves in perfect formation, and the occasional dolphin, turtle, or whale shows its head offshore. An abundance of driftwood becomes bonfire fuel at night. With the edge of civilization at your back and the ocean in front, it's the kind of place some find excruciatingly dull and others can't bear to leave.

Sadly, it seems that you sometimes hear as many horror stories about crime in Muisne as you do raves about its tranquility. Plainclothes police stepped up patrols in 1996, but things are still sketchy; don't walk down the beach alone beyond the buildings in either direction, and never take anything of value with you.

To the left (south) of the road to town are the two best budget hotels. The rustic, friendly **Hostal Playa Paraíso,** tel. 6/480-192, has 24 beds in 11 rooms and supplies mosquito nets. Rates are $3 pp with shared bath. The vegetarian restaurant has plates for $1 and up (all veggies are purified), and a book exchange and hammocks make it hard to leave the main crashpad room. If you do, there's a volleyball court outside and a bar in back. The owners can arrange horseback-riding trips.

Otavalo *indígenas* own the blue and orange **Hotel Calade,** tel. 6/480-279, e-mail: vendras@hotmail.com, two doors to the south. Beds and rooms are clean and spacious with mosquito nets and cost $5 pp with private bath, $4 shared. They also have a vegetarian restaurant and can arrange fishing and snorkeling trips and provide information on their full-moon parties. Internet service is $1 per hour.

It's hard to miss the "Pizza and Spaghetti" graffiti on the front of the **Restaurant Suizo-Italiano,** half a block back from the beach on the road to town. Their pizzas are great ($2–4), and because the dining room is also the family's living room, it can make for a fun dining experience. They also have a book exchange with some English and German titles.

Chess seems to be the game of choice in these parts, but if you're looking for a more visceral diversion, try the Hotel Calade's **Robo-bar,** the **Discoteca Mai Tai** on the north end of the beach, or the **Zulu Bar** of the Hostal Playa Paraiso.

Boat trips through the mangroves are organized by FUNDECOL (Fundación Ecologica Muisne), tel. 6/480-201, 2/290-593, e-mail: fundecol@ecuanex.net.ec. Trips are best in the afternoon at high tide and cost $38 for two people for a half day (prices drop rapidly for larger groups). Even better than the fishing is the birding—there are enough frigatebirds, egrets, tanagers, and vermillion flycatchers to keep any enthusiast happy. Many other trips, as well as volunteer opportunities, are available. Their office is off the main street a few blocks beyond Andinatel, but it's hard to find, so take a tricycle taxi or ask around.

You'll find **Andinatel** one block from the dock and the **post office** in the municipal building on the main plaza one block farther down. Buses to and from Esmeraldas run often throughout the day. Heading farther south to **Cojimíes** used to be a half-day adventure by boat through the mangroves and out into the breakers, but frequent *camionetas* ($1, 90 minutes) get most of the business nowadays. It's still possible to hire a boat to do the trip; ask around on the dock, and expect to pay about $20 for the two-hour journey—a unique opportunity to get wet, seasick, and sunburnt all at once, yet fun in its own way.

Trans Esmeraldas runs direct buses to **Quito** ($5.50, nine hours) at 9:45 P.M. and to **Guayaquil** ($6, 10 hours) at 9 P.M.

CENTRAL COAST

SOUTH OF MUISNE

Cojimíes to Pedernales

Cojimíes, at the tip of a sandy peninsula slowly dissolving into the sea, is the northern end of one of Ecuador's great drives. Until the construction of an inland road, the only way down this stretch of the coast was a low-tide blitz down the flawless beach itself. It's still possible—and highly recommended—to take the sandy route, where endless ordered rows of coconut palms line the leeward side and rocky cliffs take over farther south. Your hell-for-leather driver will dodge rocks and plow through drifts of shells and sand until the breeze in your face makes you grin like a pilot in a wind tunnel. Along the way lie the rusted hulks of cars that weren't fast or surefooted enough. Toward the southern end, shrimp fishermen tow nets through the shallows.

About halfway down the peninsula, 20 km north of Pedernales near the village of Cañaveral, is the **Hotel Coco Solo,** an old museum of a place that would make the perfect setting for a romantic movie (*Night of the Iguana,* anyone?). They're rightfully proud of the fact that they have no TVs, and they can set you up with a guide to explore the surrounding forest and rivers or point you in the right direction to do it on your own. Bungalows on stilts run $8 pp with breakfast, and campsites are available for $2. Reserva tions can be made through Guacamayo Adventures in Bahía de Caráquez on Bolívar and Arenas, tel./fax 5/691-412, 690-597.

An **equator monument** just south of Pedernales was erected by the governments of Ecuador and France to commemorate the 250th anniversary of Le Condamine's expedition (see special topic "Measuring the Earth" in the Introduction chapter). It's called The Birthplace of the Meter, thanks to something about the distance a pendulum travels in one second at sea level on the equator—let me know if you understand it.

Canoa and Vicinity

This quiet fishing town sits on a wide stretch of sand—one of the few places on Ecuador's coast whose beach actually grew following the disastrous 1997–1998 El Niño season. With more hammocks per capita than any other coastal town, Canoa is a very *tranquilo* alternative to other louder beach spots, but it's steadily growing in popularity. The surfing is great, and there's a big contest here in November. During the new moon, you can see luminescent plankton swirl in the water.

The clean and friendly **Posada de Daniel,** tel. 9/475-591, 5/691-201, costs $4–6 pp with private bath and great views of the ocean, even though it's a few blocks from the beach. The décor mixes bamboo huts and red leather chairs, and there's a bar, restaurant, a pool, horses to ride, and a boat for snorkeling trips. Friendly owner Daniel Potosí speaks English and gives surfing lessons.

Cabins and rooms on the beach at the **Hotel Bambú,** tel. 9/753-696, cost $4 pp per night with shared bath and $6–8 with private bath. They offer a restaurant and surfboards and boogie boards for rent, along with a hair-raising wind car for the adventurous. Just off the beach, the friendly **Tronco Bar,** tel. 9/674 695, has a restaurant and rooms for $2 (some have private baths, available on a first-come, first-served basis).

A host of seafood stands line Canoa's beach. Costa Azul gets good reviews, but after a few rum-and-cokes they're all more or less identical. Just off the beach, the **Arena Bar** serves purified-water drinks, sandwiches, and pizzas for $1–2. **El Torbellino** restaurant in town serves good typical dishes popular with locals for $1 and up.

At low tide, head north up the beach (the widest in the country) to a series of natural caves frequented by blue-footed boobies and bats. According to legend, a huge emerald belonging to a queen of the Cara tribe was hidden here. Although the caves were somewhat damaged by the 1998 earthquake that hit Bahía de Caráquez,

they're still worth a visit. Buses to Canoa from San Vicente take half an hour (20 cents).

A ton of development is planned for the beaches between Canoa and San Vicente—multinational hotel chains, polo fields, the works—but for now it's 19 km of some of the prettiest sand on the entire coast. Bare-bones facilities can be found in the villages of **Boca de Briceño** and **Puerto Napo,** but otherwise you're on your own.

BAHÍA DE CARÁQUEZ

As far back as the 17th century, the Spanish were saying how Bahía de Caráquez would be "one of the most beautiful ports in the world," set on a tongue of sand in the mouth of the Río Chone. What started as a small port city has evolved into the most pleasant city on Ecuador's coast.

Bahía, as it's known for short, is an anomaly. Although many other cities on the coast are sweaty, dirty, and ill-tempered, Bahía (pop. 18,000) feels like a place you'd visit just to walk the streets. It's long been a retreat for Quiteños, who appreciate its cleanliness and easygoing pace.

The once-busy commercial port has given way to a mostly residential city, keeping the white buildings free of the smudges of industry. Generations of residents educated abroad (including ex-president Sixto Duran Ballén) have returned and invested their money and time into keeping their hometown vibrant through civic improvements such as the restoration of the waterside Malecón (a.k.a. Avenida Ratti).

A series of natural calamities just before the turn of the millennium almost brought Bahía to its knees. Six months of almost continuous rain during the 1997–1998 El Niño season caused widespread landslides, washing away many nearby roads. Then, in August 1998, an earthquake measuring over 7 on the Richter scale leveled a good portion of the city and left residents (at least those whose homes still stood) without electricity or water for months. At one point, 2,500 of the town's 18,000 residents were living in the streets. Most of the damage has since been repaired.

On a brighter note, Bahía officially declared itself an "eco-city" in 1999, initiating ambitious plans to recycle most of the city's waste and

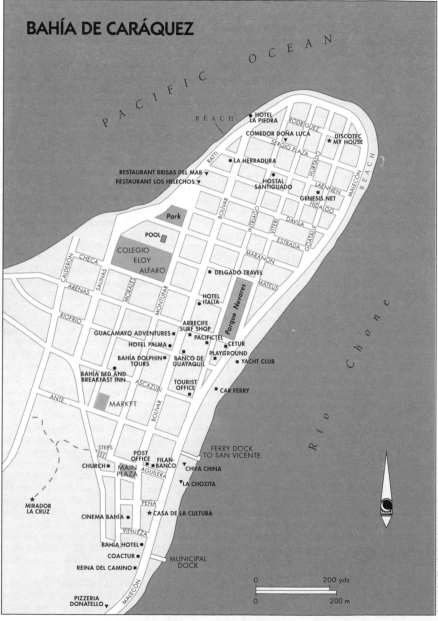

BAHÍA DE CARÁQUEZ

PACIFIC OCEAN

BEACH

- HOTEL LA PIEDRA
RODRÍGUEZ
COMEDOR DOÑA LUCA ▼
- DISCOTEC ★ MY HOUSE
SERGIO PLAZA
RAITI
- LA HERRADURA
HURTADO
BEACH
MALECÓN
LAENNEN
RESTAURANT BRISAS DEL MAR ▼
RESTAURANT LOS HELECHOS ▼
HOSTAL SANTIGUADO ■
- GENESIS.NET
HIDALGO
BOLÍVAR
INTRIAGO
VITERI
DÁVILA
GOZAIALE
Park
ESTRADA
POOL ■
COLEGIO ELOY ALFARO
MARAÑÓN
CHECA
SALINAS
CALDERÓN
MORALES
MONTUFAR
- DELGADO TRAVEL ■
MATEUS
ARENAS
HOTEL ITALIA ■
RIOFRÍO
Parque Nevares
ARRECIFE SURF SHOP ■
GUACAMAYO ADVENTURES ■
- PACIFICTEL ■
- CETUR
HOTEL PALMA ■
PLAYGROUND
BAHÍA DOLPHIN TOURS ■
BANCO DE GUAYAQUIL ■
- YACHT CLUB ■
BAHÍA BED AND BREAKFAST INN ■
ASCAZUBI
TOURIST OFFICE ■
ANTE
BOLÍVAR
MARKET ■
- CAR FERRY ■
Río Chone
STEPS ▦
POST OFFICE ■
FILAN- ■BANCO
FERRY DOCK TO SAN VICENTE
CHURCH ■
MAIN PLAZA
AGUILERA
- CHIFA CHINA ▼
- LA CHOZITA ▼
MIRADOR LA CRUZ ★
PEÑA
CINEMA BAHÍA ■
- CASA DE LA CULTURA ★
VINUEZA
BAHÍA HOTEL ●
COACTUR ■
REINA DEL CAMINO ■
MUNICIPAL DOCK
PIZZERIA DONATELLO ▼
MALECÓN

0   200 yds
0   200 m

© AVALON TRAVEL PUBLISHING, INC.

bring it into harmony with its surrounding bioregion.

Accommodations

The **Bahía Bed and Breakfast Inn,** Ascazubi 316 and Morales, tel. 5/690-146, typifies a great budget hotel: strong fans, comfortable beds, and cable TV in the lounge, all for $3 pp with shared bath ($5 pp private). Friendly owner Jacob Santos, who lived in Canada, speaks English and also runs Bahía Dolphin Tours (see under "Tours"). He offers Internet access and is happy to give advice on touring the area. Best of all, a real, *full* breakfast is included in the price.

If you're on a tight budget, the **Hotel Palma,** Bolívar 918 and Riofrio, tel. 5/690-467, is passable, starting at $2 pp with private bath. Rooms facing the Río Chone in the **Bahía Hotel,** tel. 5/690-509, fax 5/693-833, are $1.50 with ocean view and private bath ($3 with fan). It's on the south end of the Malecón at Vinueza. The homey **Hostal Santiguado,** Leannen 406 and Intriago, tel. 5/692-391, 690-597, has clean, high-ceilinged rooms for $4 pp with shared bath, $5 pp private, including breakfast.

At Hidalgo and Bolívar, you'll find the classy little **La Herradura,** tel. 5/690-446, fax 5/690-265. Wagon wheels and iron filigree evoke a snug country club, and the hotel's excellent restaurant facing the ocean has a wide selection of wines and surprisingly few dishes costing more than $6. Rooms with TV, private bath, and fan are a steal at $3.50 pp, and double that for air-conditioning and hot water.

Farther up the scale, the **Hotel Italia,** Bolívar and Checa, tel. 5/691-137, fax 5/691-092, offers the most comfortable accommodations in Bahía's center. Rooms with cable TV and private baths are $6 s, $14.50 d with fan, $14.50 s $19 d with air-conditioning.

Enjoy a sea breeze on the walkway over the rocks at the posh **Hotel La Piedra,** Ratti and Bolívar, tel. 5/690-780, fax 5/690-154, e-mail: apartec@uio.satnet.net. The hotel has a pool, a classy restaurant, and rents kayaks and bicycles to guests. Rates are $20 s, $30 d.

Bahía Dolphin Tours (see under "Tours") operates the **Casa Grande,** an intimately luxurious guesthouse on the Malecón near Piedra. A stay in one of the five double rooms costs $35 d including breakfast.

Food

Inexpensive meals draw locals and budget travelers to the **Parillada La Chozita** near the San Vicente ferry dock, where grilled meats range from $1–3, and to the **Comedor Doña Luca,** Sergio Plaza and Intriago, where a *plato del día* is just under $1. In accordance with national law, Bahía has a **Chifa China,** on the Malecón next to the San Vicente ferry dock. The inexpensive food tastes better than the décor would suggest. For a bit of Italian, head to the **Pizzeria Donatello** on the south end of the Malecón.

Itinerant gourmets frequent the restaurants in the more expensive hotels, along with a few others: the **Restaurant Brisas del Mar,** Ratti and Hidalgo, and the **Restaurant Los Helechos,** Ratti and Davila, both specialize in seafood for around $1.50 a plate. The latter is also a *discoteca.* As is to be expected, several other inexpensive seafood places line the Malecón.

Entertainment and Events

Grab your own snack and head to the **Cinema Bahía,** on Bolívar between Peña and Vineuza, for the nightly video at 8 P.M. The showings are almost always in English, and the variety is quite good. At other times you can watch your own movies in individual DVD rooms.

Drinks flow at the Hostal Santiguado's bar for less than $1, as locals get lubed up for one of Bahía's *discotecas:* Los Helechos (Ratti and Davila), My House (Hurtado and Rodríguez), and Eclipse, at the Yacht Club on the Malecón.

Bahía has a respectable schedule of annual festivals: **La Candelaria and Los Chiguales** (2 Feb.); **San Pedro and San Pablo** (28 June); **Virgen de La Merced** (24 Sept.); and the city's **cantonization** celebration (3 Nov.)

Recreation

There's not much in the way of beaches near Bahía (head to Canoa, or south to San Clemente or San Jacinto for sand), but the short hike up to the **Mirador La Cruz** is well worth it for the view of the bay. Cool off afterward with a dip in the **pool** at the Colegio Eloy Alfaro, which is open to the public. A small archaeology museum has found a home in the **Casa de la Cultura** on the Malecón at Peña. It's open Wed.–Sat. 10 A.M.–5 P.M., at least theoretically.

Bahía de Caráquez

Tours

The entire central coast is the domain of **Guacamayo Adventures,** Bolívar and Arenas, tel./fax 5/691-412, e-mail: ecopapel @ecuadorexplorer.com, www.qni.com/~mj /riomuchacho; if they can't set you up with information or a tour, they'll find someone who can. They'll recommend excursions to the Isla de Fragatas, an island in the river mouth inhabited by more than 40 species of birds. Try to go during low tide so you can walk on the island, and don't miss the private exotic animals collection. Trips to an ecological farm on the Río Muchacho also get repeat raves—you can stay in a treehouse, ride horses, harvest and roast your own coffee, and see plenty of wildlife. Tours start at $25 pp per day, and there are half-day tours to the mangrove-covered Islas Fragatas ($18 pp) and nearby tropical forests ($12 pp). They also rent 21-speed mountain bikes for $2 per day and have a free book exchange.

Bahía Dolphin Tours, tel. 5/692-097, 692-084, 692-086, fax 5/692-088, e-mail: archtour@telconet.net, has a similar roster of excursions. Trips to Isla Corazón, a protected mangrove forest, are their specialty. Prices for this ecotour (which employs local guides) depend on what you do—trips start as low as $5 pp, but consider paying more and taking their raft to the island. A full-day trip to the newly discovered Chirije archaeological site just south of the city runs $15–25 pp for 4–9 people.

Shopping and Services

Shoppers can find *artesanías* along the Malecón near the Yacht Club. The wife of the owner of Guacamayo Adventures sells beautiful handmade paper and envelopes with pressed flowers, and the office also stocks T-shirts and a goof selection of other handicrafts. The city **market** takes up the corner of Morales and Ante, and the **Arrecife Surf Shop** is on Arenas at Bolívar.

The **Banco de Guayaquil** on the corner of Bolívar and Riofrio changes travelers' checks, as does **Filanbanco** on Aguilera next to the **post office.** The **tourist information office** lends a helping hand from the corner of the playground park at Malecón and Arenas (open Mon.–Fri. 8:30 A.M.–1 P.M. and 2–5 P.M.), and **Pacifictel** is alongside the park on Intraigo. There's another tourist office just down the street from Pacifictel; it's run by university students studying tourism and is open on weekends.

Genesis.net, Gostale 402 and Laennen, offers Internet access, open daily.

Transportation

Bahía is an easy and pleasant city to walk around, but for a little diversion, try a *tricyclo* **ride.** These three-wheeled, rickshaw-type bicycles, also called "ecotaxis," can be found along the Malecón, especially in front of the local tourist office and the passenger ferry dock. A short hop shouldn't cost more than 50 cents.

Coactur next to the Hotel Bahía sends frequent buses to Manta ($1.50, three hours) and Guayaquil ($3.25, six hours). **Reina del Camino** a few doors down runs three buses per day to Quito ($4, 7–8 hours), Esmeraldas ($4.50, eight hours), Santo Domingo ($2, 3–4 hours), and Guayaquil. Buses and *rancheros* to nearby destinations also leave from the Malecón—ask around for details and destinations. You can rent a car at **Delgado Travel,** tel. 5/692-188, fax 5/692-192, on Bolívar at Mateus.

From the airport across the bay, **TAME** has flights to Quito on Thursday and Sunday at 5:30 P.M. ($25 one-way, 45 minutes). You can buy tickets at Multi-Agencias on Riofrio.

The **passenger ferry** to San Vicente leaves from the dock at Malecón and Ante when full (usually every few minutes) from about 6 A.M.–11 P.M. for 10 cents pp. A **car ferry** runs every half hour to the airport at low tide.

SOUTH TO MANTA

Crucita
This unremarkable fishing town is fast becoming a busy tourist destination, partly because of its wide and generally clean beach. Visitors come from around the globe to paraglide off the gentle dunes within sight of the sea (many competitions are held here). Diego Casto gives paragliding lessons; ask for him at the **Hotel Hipocampo,** tel. 5/676-167 or 676-165, on the south end of the beach, with rooms with private bath and fan for less than $3 pp. Hang gliding is also popular—ask at El Gordito Parapente Restaurant for details. Crucita has plenty of other restaurants, although none are particularly noteworthy. Buses run often to and from Manta (60 cents, 1.5 hours).

Jaramijo
According to archaeological evidence, residents of this fishing village have been hauling in the catch for more than 4,000 years. The festivities of St. Peter and St. Paul on 24 August include a unique "miniature U.N." celebration thought to have originated in feudal Spain. Ten "countries" are created and headed by "presidents" chosen from the populace. This honored position entails, among other things, giving speeches on the virtues of one's country and acknowledging pleasantries in return.

MANTA

Ecuador's second-most important shipping center sprawls across the mouth of the Río Manta. It's not the most pleasant city in itself—a faint fishy odor seems to hang around every other corner—but Manta can serve as a handy base or resupply point for excursions to nearby beaches.

A major port since pre-Inca times, Manta (pop. 160,000) was officially established by the Spanish in 1565 as a supply point between Panama and Perú. Repeated pirate attacks drove most inhabitants inland, leaving the city almost empty.

But times have changed, and today Manta is second only to Guayaquil in the volume of agricultural products exported and manufactured goods imported. It has become the center of the Ecuadorian tuna industry and home to a U.S. military base opened in the late 1990s. Sun-faded boats brighten the inner harbor, which empties at low tide, as the occasional cruise ship anchors farther out.

Orientation
Charlie Tuna welcomes you to Manta along the road from Montecristi, where warehouses and factories sport the logo of fish export companies. The town center and harbor are north of the Río Manta, with Murcielago beach another two km farther. Dirtier Tarquí beach fronts the tougher section of town east of the river (Calle 100 and higher), and the airport lies another three km beyond.

Safety
Although Murcielago beach is safe, Tarquí beach and the adjoining neighborhood are both questionable during the day and unsafe after dark (even though most of the budget lodgings are located here). Take a taxi here (and even in downtown Manta) if you have to get around after dark.

Sights and Activities
Of Manta's two beaches, **Murcielago** is cleaner and wider, with the Manta Surf Club providing lifeguard service and surfing lessons. **Tarquí** beach is seedier, lined with PVC-tube frames

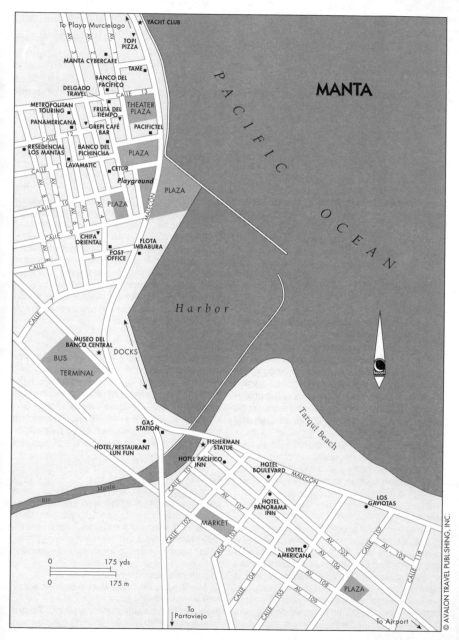

To Playa Murcielago

★ YACHT CLUB

TOPI PIZZA

MANTA CYBERCAFE

TAME

BANCO DEL PACÍFICO

DELGADO TRAVEL

CALLE 13

METROPOLITAN TOURING

FRUTA DEL TIEMPO

THEATER PLAZA

PANAMERICANA

GREPI CAFÉ BAR

PACIFICTEL

RESEDENCIAL LOS MANTAS

BANCO DEL PICHINCHA

PLAZA

LAVAMATIC

CETUR

Playground

PLAZA

PLAZA

PLAZA

CHIFA ORIENTAL

FLOTA IMBABURA

POST OFFICE

PACIFIC OCEAN

MANTA

Harbor

MUSEO DEL BANCO CENTRAL

DOCKS

BUS TERMINAL

Tarqui Beach

GAS STATION

HOTEL/RESTAURANT LUN FUN

FISHERMAN STATUE

HOTEL PACÍFICO INN

HOTEL BOULEVARD

MALECÓN

Río   Manta

HOTEL PANORAMA INN

LOS GAVIOTAS

MARKET

HOTEL AMERICANA

PLAZA

0   175 yds
0   175 m

To Portoviejo

To Airport

© AVALON TRAVEL PUBLISHING, INC.

that you can rent a cloth covering for to escape the sun. In the early morning, the night's catch is dragged onto the sand—look for sharks, swordfish, red snapper, and the occasional octopus. After dark, head inland (by taxi, of course) to one of the many *discotecas* in the area.

If you still have a few hours to kill, stop by the **Museo del Banco Central,** next to the bank at Malecón and Calle 7, which houses exhibits on the pre-Inca Manta culture. Enter by the bus terminal, and ask for the information sheet in English. Open 9 A.M.–4 P.M., $1 pp. The fact that Otavaleño *indígenas* manage to sell sweaters in this heat is a testament to their commercial prowess (next to Pacifictel).

The **Yacht Club,** under the striped blue awnings near the dock at Calle 15, has boats that can be chartered for deep-sea fishing. You can also take the 30-foot sailboat *Lorelei* out for a spin: a three-hour tour costs $100 for six people, including lunch. For other travel needs, stop by **Metropolitan Touring,** Av. 4 1239-1245, tel. 5/623-090, fax 5/611-277. The **Fería Agropecuaria** on 8–9 September draws loads of tourists, followed by an **International Theater Festival** in late September and **Manta Day** on 4 November.

Accommodations

Los Mantas is the only budget hotel in the center of town. Rooms are tiny and basic, but it's a clean and friendly place in a good location. Choose either a fan or a private shower (toilets are shared) for $2 pp. Rooms at the **Hotel Boulevard,** tel. 5/623-333, start at $6 with TV and tiny but clean private baths.

The neighborhood near Tarqui beach is filled with budget hotels. Two are particularly good deals: the **Hotel Americana,** Av. 106 and Calle 105, tel. 5/620-946, 625-112, has rooms for $3 pp with fan ($4 with air-conditioning); and the towering **Hotel Pacífico Inn,** Av. 106 and Calle 101, tel. 5/622-475, is $4 pp with private bath ($5 with air-conditioning).

Within sight of the sand, the **Hotel Panorama Inn,** Calle 103 and Av. 105, tel. 5/621-673, fax 5/611-552, has accommodations for $7 s, $13 d with fan ($13 s, $22 d with air-conditioning). The **Hotel Manta Imperial,** tel. 5/621-966, fax 5/610-601, sits right on Murcielago beach. Rooms with TVs run $18 with fans and $25 with air-conditioning and include access to a pool, gym, and

tennis courts. Roberto's disco and the restaurant are open to guests and the public.

Las Gaviotas, Malecón 1109 and Calle 106, tel. 5/620-140, fax 5/620-940, takes the prize for Tarquí's finest. Rooms are $18 s, $25 d, and the bar/cafeteria (with attached casino) is nice and cool. Near the bridges over the river is Manta's best, the **Hotel Lun Fun,** tel. 5/622-966, fax 5/610-601, e-mail: hotel_lun_fun@ecuabox.com. Chinese owners keep the place immaculate and run the highly praised restaurant. Rates are $36 s, $44 d.

Food

Both beaches are lined with the usual inexpensive, colorful seafood restaurant/bars, special-

---

A TOE IN THE DOOR?

The U.S. Southern Command, charged with helping end the Columbian drug trade, built an air and naval base near Manta in 1999 to the tune of $80 million. This "Forward Operating Location" will eventually support hundreds of personnel and five to eight P-3 surveillance aircraft flying anti-drug missions over Colombia. It is the first of ten planned for Ecuador.

Although Pentagon sources deny that funding for the base came from the $1.4 billion package set aside for "Plan Colombia," the Colombian defense minister and a retired Ecuadorian Army Colonel have both said otherwise. Opponents of the plan wonder if the U.S. is on its way to another situation similar to Vietnam and Cambodia in the 1970s, when "mission creep" dragged uninvolved countries into the fighting.

Crime and violence are already spilling over the 370-mile border between the countries as cocaine laboratories and rival forces in Colombia's mounting civil war flee to their more peaceful southern neighbor. The U.S. military has used the "Domino Theory" to justify sending troops, advisors, and money to Southeast Asia and Central America to prevent neighboring countries from toppling one after another into Communism, and the theory has been proven wrong repeatedly. It remains to be seen if the process will simply be repeated in South America.

shrimp with rice or a fried *corvina,* and a Pilsener or two to wash it down. The **Chifa Oriental** is your basic Chinese eatery, with *tallarines* for $1. For Japanese, try **Guen-Roku** at Calle 16 and the Malecón.

Topi Pizza, Malecón and Calle 15, serves pizza and Italian food in a faux-jungle hut on the way to Murcielago beach (the tasty pizzas actually have tomato sauce, a rarity in this country). A small pizza with everything is $2.25. Look for the creeper vines at the intersection of Av. 3 and Calle 12 to find the **Grepi Cafe Bar.** The pleasant open patio is good for a drink, with seafood plates for around $3. **Fruta del Tiempo,** on the corner of the theater plaza, has a good selection of sandwiches, juices, and salads. The extra-chunky fruit salad is a steal at 40 cents.

Services and Information
The **Banco del Pichincha,** Av. 2 between Calle 11 and 12, changes foreign currencies and travelers' checks on the second floor, and the **Banco del Pacifico** just up the street also changes travelers' checks. You can rent a car at **Delgado Travel** at Av. 12 and Calle 13.

To hop on the Internet, stop by **Puert@ Virtu@l,** Malecón and Calle 16, or **Manta CyberCafe** on Av. 1 at Calle 14. Both are open daily. Get the sea salt and beach sweat out of your clothes at **Lavamatic** on the corner of Av. 5 and Calle 11. You'll find the **tourist information office** down the pedestrian lane José Egas (Av. 3 between Calles 10 and 11), and **Pacifictel** overlooks the ocean at Malecón and Calle 11. The **post office** is at Av. 4 and Calle 8.

Transportation
Manta's main **bus terminal** occupies the southern end of the city center before the bridges to Tarquí. Buses run to Guayaquil ($2.25, four hours), Esmeraldas ($4, 10 hours), Santo Domingo ($3.50, seven hours), and Quito ($4, 9–10 hours). **Panamericana,** Calle 12 and Av. 4, runs comfortable buses with bathrooms to Quito and Santo Domingo ($6) at 11 A.M., 9:30 P.M., and 10:30 P.M. **Flota Imbabura,** on the Malecón at Calle 8, has similar bus service at noon and 10 P.M.

TAME, tel. 5/622-006, sells tickets on the Malecón just north of the theater park. Flights leave for Quito daily ($25 pp one-way).

Inland from Manta
Aside from Montecristi's hatmakers, none of the cities inland from Manta offer anything to the traveler besides a stopover on the way to or from the central coast. **Portoviejo,** one of the oldest cities in Ecuador, was founded in 1535 to mine emeralds and gold in the region (there are none). Today the capital of Manabí province is home to an Arts and Tourism fair in September and not much else besides a few sloths in the trees in the main plaza.

Along with having the most fun name to say in the country, **Jipijapa** ("hippy-happa") claims the title of "Sultana de Cafe" (Sultan of Coffee) because of its location in the middle of a fertile patchwork of coffee, cotton, cocoa, and kapok farms. Fine Panama hats woven in town are sold at the Sunday market.

Montecristi served repeatedly as an inland haven for coastal residents fleeing pirate attacks during the 17th century. That was before the *sombrero* industry came to town; as early as 1890 a French visitor noted that "in every hut of

roadside shrine

JULIAN SMITH

these towns were seen a man, woman, or young boy, and sometimes a child at work" weaving the soon-to-be-famous Panama hats. Although the craft is declining, the famous Montecristi *superfinos*—each one requiring up to three months' work—can still be bought directly from the weaving families.

From Jipijapa, you have the choice of heading straight southeast to Guayaquil or west over the hills to the coast, where the road makes a sharp turn south at **Puerto Cayo** toward the Santa Elena Peninsula.

PUERTO LOPEZ

The "Acapulco of Ecuador" enjoys a wide bay dotted with fishing boats and backed by green hills inland. Even though most people use Puerto Lopez only as a base for exploring the surrounding area, it's still an enjoyable town on average the hottest in Ecuador) with a lovely beach. In the morning, you can watch fishermen bring in and clean their catches, and in the afternoon see them cleaning and repairing their nets and boats. The coastal road serves as the long, dusty main street, where it's easy to picture a Wild West showdown taking place at high noon.

Accommodations
The **Villa Columbia**, tel. 5/604-105 or 604-189, tel./fax 2/482-724, e-mail: hostalvc@uio.satnet.net, gets repeat praise. They have rooms starting at $3 pp with private bath with hot water, along with hammock space and a kitchen. The friendly owners can point out the best beaches in the area, including Punto Los Frailes to the north. It's diagonal from the market, one block north and one block west of the church.

Dorm rooms at the **Cueva del Oso Youth Hostel**, tel. 5/604-124, just off the Malecón on Las Cano, can be a bit noisy, but for $2 pp they're hard to beat. The shared baths have hot water, and guests can use the kitchen. The friendly, spotless **Hotel Pacifico**, tel./fax 5/604-133, 624-064, is on the Malecón a few blocks north of the city center. Rooms are $4 pp with shared bath and $10 s, $16 d with private bath, including breakfast (all rooms have hot showers). Hammocks and trees fill the courtyard.

Food
If you've been traveling on the coast for more than a few days, you should be able to predict the string of cheap seafood restaurants on the Malecón with uncanny accuracy. **Carmita's** and **Spondlus** are both recommended. The latter serves some creative maritime breakfasts (try an octopus omelet). **Carmita's** on the beachfront is another option for a fresh seafood dinner, which you can follow with an evening stroll down the Malecón to walk it off.

Bellitalia on Moncayo is a bit out of the way and hard to find (follow the signs from the Hotel Pacifico), but it serves the city's best Italian for dinner Tues.–Sun. The friendly, American-owned **Cafe Ballena** on the south end of the Malecón has a large book exchange and several vegetarian options on the menu.

Sights and Activities
Understandably, most of Puerto Lopez's activities center around the ocean. **Whales** and **dolphins** can often be seen from the beach, and you can choose from about a dozen tour companies in town for close-up viewing from boats (best from July–Oct.). Most of these operations also offer tours to the Isla de la Plata and inland parts of nearby Machalilla National Park. All have roughly the same offerings and prices, and sometimes even share tour boats to ensure that the minimum group size is met.

Recommendations have come in for **Perfil Turistico,** tel. 5/604-147, at the Hotel Pacifico; **Sercapez,** tel. 5/604-130, on Córdova between the highway and the ocean; and **Machalilla Tours,** tel. 5/604-154, near Sercapez. Machalilla Tours also rents mountain bikes and organizes horseback-riding tours. For **scuba diving,** check out **Exploratur** on the Malecón.

Puerto Lopez hosts the **World of Whales Festival** in June. Ask at Machalilla Tours about Spanish lessons at the **Cosanita Spanish School,** tel. 5/604-154, fax 5/604-200, e-mail: schoolcosta@hotmail.com.

Services and Information
The **Machalilla National Park headquarters,** on the north side of the market, has information on the park and a tiny museum with displays of marine and land fauna. There aren't any banks in town, but the **Pacifictel** office is on the highway next to the market.

Transportation

All buses to and through Puerto Lopez stop on the main road by the market. Buses between La Libertad and Manta are fairly common, so you won't have to wait too long to head north or south along the coast. From the busy transport hub of Jipijapa, you can continue on to most of the country. **Transportes Carlos A Aray** has a daily 6 P.M. bus to Quito ($5, 11 hours).

MACHALILLA NATIONAL PARK AND VICINITY

Ecuador's only coastal park protects most of the country's tropical scrub desert and forest, along with a dramatic stretch of coastline and islands. This hot, arid plant zone once covered an estimated 25 percent of western Ecuador, but today only about 1 percent is left—most of it here. If you can't make it to the Galápagos, Machalilla's Isla de la Plata is the next best thing—not to be missed for its fauna above and below the water.

Flora and Fauna

Much of the tough-looking vegetation, including *opuntia* cactus and palo santo trees, will be familiar to anyone who's been to the Galápagos. The fat-trunked ceiba or kapok trees, whose bare branches look like upturned roots, produce a fine, downy fiber that was used in World War II life preservers. The algaroba tree can photosynthesize through its green bark even in the absence of leaves. Parakeets, armadillos, and two species of monkeys range from the lower elevations into the higher hills covered with deciduous and evergreen forests.

Isla de la Plata

Machalilla's offshore appendix was named for an alleged hoard of silver ingots left by Sir Francis Drake, who stopped here at the end of the 16th century after attacking a Spanish galleon. Today park rangers and a huge assortment of bird species make their home on the eight-square-mile island, 24 km out to sea west of Puerto Cayo.

The Isla de la Plata has been called the "poor man's Galápagos" because its count of frigate birds, albatrosses, and all three boobie species actually exceeds that of the famous archipelago. Swimming and snorkeling in Drake's Bay will bring you close to (if not face to face with) sea lions and sea turtles, along with the only coral areas off mainland Ecuador. Eleven species of whales pass by from June–October.

Archaeology

Traces of cultures up to 3,000 years old have been unearthed in the valley of the Río Buenavista. Agua Blanca, in the northern section of the park, is one of the richest archaeological sites in the country. About 200 stone sculptures show that the area, formerly called Salangome, served as the center of a trading network that sailed as far north as Mexico.

Many of the digs, including others at Los Frailes and San Sebastian, have been filled in to protect their contents from looters and the weather, but most of the artifacts have been moved to the museum in Salango.

Visiting the Park

After checking in at the administrative center in Puerto López, head north 6–7 km to the dirt track leading east through the gateway village of Agua Blanca. Tracks lead into the hills to other villages such as Las Peñas and San Sebastian, where accommodations can sometimes be arranged with local families. If you go by foot (as opposed to vehicle or rented animal), make sure to take enough water, especially for trips into the drier coastal scrub.

Machalilla extends three km seaward beyond beautiful beaches such as Los Frailes, near the town of Machalilla. Check in at the administrative center in Puerto López to enter the park and to visit the Isla de la Plata. The entrance fee to the park, including the Isla de la Plata, is $20 pp from July–Sept. and $15 otherwise, ($15/$10 for just the mainland section). Open daily 7 A.M.–5 P.M. Numerous tour companies in Puerto Lopez offer guided trips to the park's mainland and offshore sections. If you go to the Isla de la Plata, make sure your boat has two motors; it's a long way out there, and getting stranded is no fun.

Salango

This sleepy town is home to the small **Museo Salango,** housing archaeological displays on prehistoric coastal cultures taken from Machalilla National Park. Open daily 9 A.M.–12:30 P.M., 1:30–6 P.M., $1 pp. You can also hire a fishing boat to take you out to the hulking Isla Salango, two km offshore, to see the seabirds.

Private cabins for 2–5 people at the **Hostería Piqueros Patas Azules,** tel. 5/604-135, 4/386-881 or 386-928, are $10 pp. It's about three km south of the town and has a private archaeological museum highlighted by numerous in situ burial sites with skeletons encased in large clay jars. A $1 pp entrance fee will give you access to one of the loveliest beaches on the coast—never crowded and often deserted—as well as a peek at a sizable population of the endangered (and colorful) Cangrejo Azul (blue crabs). Reservations can be made through Guacamayo Tours in Bahía de Caráquez.

Octopus salad ($2) is only one of the seven ways they serve the aquatic cephalopods at the **Restaurante Delfin Magico.** Their tasty seafood is made leisurely to order, so you can visit the museum while you wait. Spondilus (spiny oyster) is another specialty.

Hotel Atamari

This luxury hotel was built in 1994 on a hilltop overlooking the ocean, two km south of Ayampe. Ten rooms and self-contained cabins (starting at $50 d and climbing well beyond that) enjoy a wide view of the Ocean and Ayampe Bay, as

ALANDALUZ ECOLOGICAL TOURIST CENTER

The most common complaint about Ecuador's coast is the lack of middle ground between grungy beach cabins and gleaming, expensive, polluting resort hotels. The Alandaluz Ecological Tourist Center fills the niche almost single-handedly, offering a beautiful and comfortable setting that you don't have to feel guilty about or go broke to afford.

Everything about this luxurious tree-house resort is designed to be as healthy, ecologically sound, and self-sustaining as possible. The thatched roofs are set at a 70-degree angle conducive to "inspiration, concentration, and clarity," and the cane and wood used in the traditional construction were cut during the new moon when the sap level is lowest, making the material more durable and less attractive to insects.

Organic gardens, composting toilets, and a full recycling program minimize the impact on the fragile coastal environment. The owners have even begun recycling programs in the village of Puerto Rico next door; every morning a man leads a horse-drawn cart to collect the hotel's bottles and cans.

Neon tropical flowers surround the sturdy bamboo, stone, and plaster cabins scattered in the bushes around the large main building. Only the infrequent car passing down the coastal road breaks the spell cast by the roar of the ocean, the occasional critter skittering off into the bushes, and the nocturnal hum of insects.

Once you've sampled the all-natural meals in the restaurant— try the *corvina* (sea bass) in peanut sauce or the pancakes with *mora* (blackberry) syrup—it's time for some serious lounging on the private beach, from which you can occasionally spot whales and dolphins on the horizon. Just watch out for the undertow and the surfers taking advantage of the waves.

If you're looking for a little more activity, Machalilla is only a short bus ride to the north, and the hotel's Pacarina Tour Agency organizes snorkeling excursions and overnight trips to experience daily life on a small coastal farm.

Small private cabins cost $22–30 s, $30–42 d. In the central building, rooms and cabins with shared bath are $12 s, $16 d, and space in the tree cabin is $16 s, $18 d. You can camp with your own gear for $2 pp or rent tents for $4–6 pp. Breakfast is $2, lunch and dinner $3 each.

Alandaluz offers a range of tours, including day trips to the mainland portion of Machalilla for $20–40 pp, and the Isla de la Plata for $30–60 pp, depending on how many people go. Transportation, lunch, and guides are included. Day-long fishing tours start at $34 pp.

Any bus traveling down the coastal road can drop you off at the entrance, just north of Ayampe. For more information, contact the Alandaluz Ecological Tourist Center in Quito at Baquedano 330 and Reina Victoria, tel. 2/505-084 or 543-042, e-mail: info@alandaluz.com, www.alandaluz.com.

does the acclaimed restaurant. Reservations are a good idea on weekends, tel. 2/228-470, fax 2/508-369.

South of Atamari, the coastal road winds through low green hills while keeping the ocean always in sight. As the road returns to the shore, elaborate vacation houses have staked out sections of beach. Fishing nets wound on poles lean against poor houses in between.

MONTAÑITA AND VICINITY

The small fishing town of Montañita owes its increasing popularity as a seaside hangout to the ocean, which beckons surfers—and surf-lifestylers—with the longest right break in Ecuador. Everyone here, it seems, has tan skin and long hair and is either carrying a board or gazing longingly at someone who is. It's not everyone's kind of place—to some, this dense collection of budget hotels, restaurants, surf shops, bars, and tattoo parlors seems sleazy, whereas to others it's party heaven. Many non-surfers still find themselves sucked in for weeks on end, even though the town lost much of its beach to the 1997–1998 El Niño.

Montañita is tourist-focused and often tourist-filled. Almost every building on the main street is a hotel, restaurant, or surf shop, and you're never more than a longboard's length from Internet access. Vegetarian food and seafood are both common, and you can find surfboards, boogie boards, and bikes for rent all over town. Many hotels rent surfboards, change travelers' checks, and offer Internet access and discounts for longer stays. New hotels are constantly shooting skyward like the bamboo thickets cut to build them. During Carnival, thousands of tourists descend for the Pan-American surf contest and bikini competition. Things are much more *tranquilo* at the north end of the beach near the break at Punta Montañita.

Montañita's famous main break skirts the rocks at the north end of the beach. High tides during February and May bring the best waves, but swells of 10 meters can come in June and July. Rip tides, jagged rocks, and occasional stingrays merit a watchful eye. The beach that remains is rocky and not particularly inviting (for swimming, head three km to Olon, a half-hour walk north of Punta Montañita), but as long as there are waves and enough sand to build a bonfire, Montañita's reputation will stay more or less intact.

Punta Montañita

At the entrance to the dirt lane near the break, you'll find the **Cabañas Vitos,** tel. 5/901-207, which are as much the sprawling house of a surfer and his family as a hotel. Surfboards and children's toys litter the yard, and there are pool tables inside and a bar on the beach. Surfboards cost $3 to rent for the day, and ragged boogie boards are free to guests. Basic rooms and raised cabins cost $3 pp, but you can pitch a tent for even less.

Down the lane on the left, **Tres Palmas Cabañas,** tel. 5/755-717, offers six rooms facing the ocean for $6 pp with private bath, fan, and hot water. David, the owner, is from San Antonio, Texas, so the Tex-Mex cantina on the beach (recommended for lunch and dinner) should come as no surprise. Across the lane, the balconies of the clean and pleasant **La Casa del Sol,** tel. 5/901-302, e-mail: casasol@ecua.net.ec, www.casasol.com, are covered with hammocks and drying laundry. Rooms sharing a bathroom are $5 ($8 with private bath and hot water), and dorm spaces are $2.

The family-run **Las Olas Restaurant** next door specializes, of course, in seafood. The portions are big and cheap—nothing is more than $2. They also have simple dorm rooms with shared bath for $2. Farther down the lane, you'll hit **Baja Montañita,** tel. 5/901-218 or 901-230, fax 5/901-228, a thoroughly modern hotel that seems a bit out of place here. Six-person cabins and rooms cost $18–24, with deluxe models starting at $73. A pool and restaurant face the rocky break.

In Town

A kilometer of empty beach separates the point break from Montañita proper. Here the three-story **Centro del Mundo** offers dorm rooms for $1.50 pp and private rooms for $3–4, so close to the beach you can practically fish from the balconies. Prices include breakfast and boogie boards to use. **La Casa Blanca,** tel. 5/901-340, e-mail: casablan@gu.pro.ec, a three-story building situated one block from the sand, is a pleasantly simple hostal with dorm rooms for $2 pp and private accommodations for $3–4. All bathrooms have hot water, and the restaurant has satellite TV.

Next door is the huge **Hotel Montañita**, tel. 5/901-269, with 36 rooms and 90 beds for $6 pp with fan and mosquito net. Some rooms have balconies and hot water, and hammocks and deck chairs abound. There's a great view of the ocean, satellite TV, and even a small pool. Another budget hotel on the same street is the surfer-recommended **Cabañas Tsunami,** which doubles as a surf shop. Dorm rooms are $2 pp.

The **Restaurant Doña Elenita,** on the main drag, garners repeat business for its exotic *empanadas* (banana and chocolate is a favorite). The **Restaurant Bellavista** serves a unique but tasty local version of pizza for $1.50, and **Blancas** has great *ceviche.*

Crafts are sold everywhere, but consider doing your shopping at the *artesanía* **shop** on the main road into town, which helps support local artisans. They have a good selection of basketry and tagua-nut carvings. **Pacifictel** has an office on the main square, and Montañita's **Festival de Arte** happens 31 Jan.–2 February.

South of Montañita

Fine beaches grace **Olon** and **Manglaralto,** north and south of Montañita, respectively. Both towns offer limited accommodations and food options. Surfers should keep going south to **Punta Brava,** where a consistent left breaks near an Air Force base (get permission to enter beforehand).

BOB RACE

GUAYAQUIL AND THE SOUTHERN COAST

Even though it boasts the largest city in the country, Ecuador's southern coast is considered by many to be the least interesting part of the country. For Ecuadorians the main draw is the ritzy resort towns of the Santa Elena Peninsula, whereas most travelers only see the peninsula out a window on their way to or from the Perúvian border.

Most of the original forest along this part of the coast has been cut in the last few decades to make room for banana and oil palm plantations, and almost all of the mangrove swamps outside of Manglares Churute Ecological Reserve have been sacrificed for shrimp farming. Still, a few protected areas preserve the tangled vegetation that once covered Ecuador's southern coast.

SANTA ELENA PENINSULA

The scrubby heel of Guayas province is hands down the most popular destination for Guayaquileños seeking sun and surf. Families in minivans zip past the cacti and kapok trees to stake out a spot on the sand, preferably within walking distance of the condo. In contrast to the north coast's empty stretches and mellow vibes, the Santa Elena peninsula bustles with jet skis, discos, and blinding glass highrises so close to the water that the high tide threatens to fill their lobbies. Any of the peninsula's major cities will be packed on major holidays and just about any weekend between January and April, so plan your visit accordingly.

Although the surfing is good at the tip of the peninsula and north of it, **deep-sea fishing** is the main sporting draw. Because the continental shelf is just offshore, the bottom drops out quickly and deepwater species are close at hand. The cool water brought by the Humboldt Current provides plenty of baitfish, which in turn attract billfish like Pacific sailfish, bigeye tuna, and striped, black, and blue marlin—some of which top 500 kg. Bonito, sailfish, and dolphin (not the mammal) are also popular. The best fishing months are July–Oct., but make reservations well in advance at any time of year.

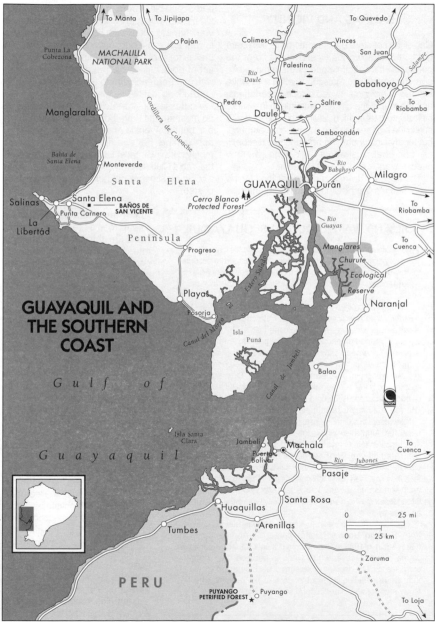

GUAYAQUIL AND THE SOUTHERN COAST

SALINAS AND VICINITY

One of the country's best resorts (by its own standards) holds down the westernmost tip of the peninsula. It's definitely one of the most exclusive: the beachfront Malecón bristles with white highrise apartments owned by rich Ecuadorians, and the rest of the city spreads inland in a more typically coastal fashion. Salinas can be crowded during the high season and overpriced year-round, but for stylish sunbathing and upscale discos, it can't be beat. Just about everything you may need or want is on the east Malecón.

The beach is divided into two sections by the posh Salinas Yacht Club, bulging out into the harbor one block from the main plaza. The west side, lined with apartments, is nicer; to the east you'll have to put up with boats and water-skiers in your horizon. Touts hawk car radios and umbrellas for rent on both sides. Watch for an old set of dock pilings on the eastern side, even with and perpendicular to the Banco de Pichincha, lurking just below the surface at high tide.

Addresses are confusing in Salinas; not only do most streets have both a name and a number, but the Avenida numbers also change without warning. For example, Avenida 3 is commonly called General Enrique, but only east of the Yacht Club (to the west it's Avenida 2). To top it off, in most cases neither number nor name is posted.

OIL AND WATER: QUITO VS. GUAYAQUIL

Like jealous siblings, Ecuador's two largest cities have a long history of sniping at each other over everything from economy to attitude. The rivalry embodies many of the differences—real and imagined—between the chilly Sierra and the sweltering coast.

Although both cities were founded near the middle of the 16th century, Quito remained the nexus of the country's economic, social, and political spheres well into the 1900s. Once Guayaquil got itself cleaned up enough, its crucial position in the country's economy became undeniable (although residents have always complained about how much of the money earned here ends up in Quiteño pockets). As the seat of government, Quito still runs the country and is the self-proclaimed cultural capital. But although the oil boom has refocused some economic light on the Andean city, Guayaquil is Ecuador's thumping coastal heart.

More pervasive differences can be found in the attitudes of the residents. After a few drinks, an outspoken Quiteño may let on how he considers Guayaquil a dirty, violent, crime-infested town populated by undisciplined *monos* (monkeys). For their part, Guayaquileños simply shrug and call it lack of pretense. Better that, they say, than going through life "polite, prompt, and dull" like their Andean neighbors. Life is short: stay out late, clean up later. Besides, who'd want to live in a city where the restaurants all close by 10 P.M.?

The disparity has been milked by presidential campaigns, from Rodrigo Borja's (Quito) defeat of Abdalá Bucarám (Guayaquil) in 1988 to Sixto Durán Ballen's (Quito) victory over Jaime Nebot (Guayaquil) in 1992. In addition, the economy promises to pit the feuding cities against each other in the near future: Quito is feeling the pinch of declining oil exports, whereas Guayaquil enjoys an agricultural and seafood export boom.

Accommodations

Cheap rooms are few and far between in this resort town, and rates can rise by as much as 20 percent in the high season. A double at the **Hotel Albita**, Av. 7 between Calles 22 and 23, tel. 4/773-211 or 773-042, costs $3.50 with private bath, fan, and a hammock on the balcony. During the low season, rooms at the **Hostal Las Rocas,** Calle 22 and Av. 3, tel. 4/774-219, go for as low as $3 pp. A second-floor balcony catches the sea breeze, but unfortunately the TV always seems to be on at full volume.

The **Hotel Yulee,** on the Malecón at Calle 16, tel. 4/772-028 is a family-oriented place that evokes an old mansion, with a courtyard opening onto a plant-filled plaza with umbrella tables. Rooms are $7 s, $9 d with shared bath, $10 s, $14 d with private bath, and $15 s, $18 d to add air-conditioning and cable TV. For a respite from the vacation hubbub, head to the far west end of the Malecón at Calle 2, where you'll find the **Hotel Florida**, tel. 4/772-780. Rooms here are $7 pp with private bath and fan. The **Residencial Rachel,** Av. 5 and Calle 17, tel. 4/772-526

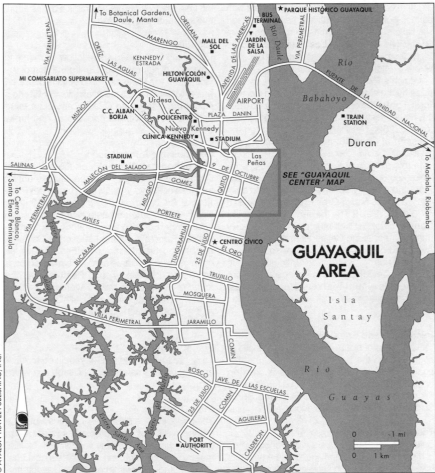

© AVALON TRAVEL PUBLISHING, INC.

GUAYAQUIL AREA

or 772-501, also has spotless habitations with private bath, TV, and fan for $6, $9 d.

For a bit more, the **Hotel Francisco 1,** Gallo and Calle 20, tel. 4/773-544 or 774-106, is small and tasteful. A pool and outdoor bar/restaurant compliment rooms with cable TV, air-conditioning, and phone for $20 s, $24 d. **El Carruaje,** Malecón 517, tel./fax 4/774-282, is known for its excellent restaurant. Fourteen rooms with sea view, air-conditioning, and cable TV run $36 s, $49 d ($30 s, $36 d without the view).

If you have a wider budget, look for the round gate of the **Hotel Calypsso,** tel. 4/773-605 or 773-736, fax 4/773-583, e-mail: calypsso@ gye.satnet.net, on the Malecón at Calle 30. Rooms in the luxury highrise, which includes a pool, gym, and sauna, are $73 s, $88 d.

Food

It should be no surprise that Salinas' Malecón teems with classy seafood restaurants. You can't miss **Mar y Tierra** at the intersection with Calle

37, decked out like a pirate ship complete with cannon ports, crow's nest, and servers dressed like sailors. Entrées such as pastas range from $3–11. The **Restaurant Los Helechos,** at Calle 23, is less upmarket but still a popular choice, where a whole meal won't cost more than $3.

Cozoli's Pizza, next to Mar y Tierra, serves pizza by the slice ($1 with a soda), and the **trattoria Tony Pizzeria,** on the Malecón at Calle 19, makes tasty wood-oven pizzas and pastas for about $2. The **Perla del Pacifico,** on the Malecón at Calle 20, is your basic *chifa* with meals for about $1.50

In this equatorial sun, ice cream has never looked so good, so **Il Gelato, Top Cream** and **Pingüino** on the Malecón all do a booming business, as does **Mardi Gras Frozen Daquiris** at Av. 3 and Calle 19. (By the same logic, **Dunkin Donuts** must not sell much coffee.) The **city market** area, along Calles 17 and 18 between Av. 3 and 5, features a dozen or so inexpensive eateries frequented by Salinas' working citizens—**Cevichelandia** is especially popular. Finally, a few **mini-markets** stock the usual beach supplies plus a few more edible odds and ends.

Recreation and Entertainment
Various types of **boats** can be rented to tootle or zoom around the harbor, from clunky paddleboats to small motorboats and jet skis. **Surfing** equipment and information can be found at the **Tropical Surf Shop** and the **Surf and Sport Surf Shop,** both on the Malecón.

Tours and Charters
Salinas occasionally hosts world sportfishing competitions, and several agencies are happy to take up the business in between. **Pesca Tours,** on the Malecón at Calle 20, tel. 4/772-391, fax 4/443-142, e-mail: fishing@pescatours.com.ec, www.pescatours.com.ec, has an office to make Papa Hemingway proud, plastered with hundreds of photos of grinning, sunburned clients next to fish larger than they are. Day charters start at $350, with lunch or drinks extra.

Seretur, on the Malecón between Calles 36 and 37, tel. 4/772-065, also offers fishing charters, plus whale-watching trips from July–Sept. for $40 pp. This outfit also offers birding tours to see the shorebirds that gather at the lagoons

left from the Ecuasal salt-extraction plants about five km southwest of town.

Nightlife
During the high season, just follow your ears to the disco of your choice. During the rest of the year, there are fewer weekend options. **El Zafari** on the Malecón is a current favorite. **Flintstone's Rockabar,** Gallo and Cuadra, attracts a more eclectic crowd with its pool tables and funky decor.

Services and Information
The **Banco del Pichincha** on the Malecón at Calle 29 will change travelers' checks until 2 P.M. on weekdays. Also try the **Banco del Pacífico,** at Av. 3 between Calles 18 and 19, for a slightly better rate and help with some foreign currencies. For incoming boaters, the **Capitania del Puerto** is on the Malecón at Calle 30, and the **tourist information office** has a semiopen office in the same area. The **post office** is on Av. 2 and Calle 17, and **Pacifictel** can be found on Calle 21 between Avenidas 3 and 4. Both **CafePlanet,** Ave 3 and Calle 25, and **Salinas.net,** on Calle 19 just off the Malecón, offer daily Internet access.

Transportation
To get to La Libertád or Guayaquil, go to Av. 7 and flag down a *selectivo* or a *shared taxi,* which is quicker.

Punta Carnero
The opposite side of Salinas' coin lies along the southern side of the peninsula's western tip: crashing waves and empty sand stretch for kilometers in either direction. Two hotels next door to each other offer very comfortable accommodations overlooking the ocean: the **Hotel Punta Carnero,** tel. 4/775-450, and the **Hosteria del Mar,** tel. 4/775-370. Both have pools, restaurants, discos, and bars, and rooms for $15–20 s and $20–25 d (add $10 in the high season).

LA LIBERTÁD AND VICINITY

Only slightly more useful from the tourist's perspective than its neighbor Santa Elena, La Libertád still bears the scars of the 1982–1983 El

Niño season. Even though La Libertád is the largest city on the peninsula (pop. 55,000) and the transportation hub, it's still mainly used as a stopover. Although there are a few spots where you could swim, you probably wouldn't want to. On the whole, the city doesn't feel very safe and has somewhat of a reputation for crime. Fortunately, its busy port and thriving markets keep the economy going.

Accommodations
Decent budget lodgings are available at the **Turis Palm**, 9 de Octubre and Barreiro, tel. 4/785-159, where clean rooms with fan and private bath are $3 pp. Three blocks up Guayaquil from the shore, the **Hostal Viña del Mar,** tel. 4/785-979, is a much better value at $3 s, $5 d with fan and private bath. The owner is very friendly. One more block uphill, the quirky, antique-packed **Hotel Palatino,** tel. 4/786-770, gives you a TV and hot water for $8 s, $12 d. Share a bathroom for $5 s, $6 d, or luxuriate in air-conditioning for $10 s, $14 d. Some rooms have refrigerators.

Food
The thatched-roof **Restaurant La Isla,** on the Malecón at Bodero, gets at least the breeze off what used to be the beach. Basic Ecuadorian meals are less than $1. On Av. 2 is the inevitable **Chifa Taiwan,** with rice dishes for $2 and seafood for up to $6.

Transportation
Both CICA (Costa Azul) and CLP (Cooperativa Libertád Peninsular) run a few **buses** to Guayaquil every hour. CLP's are Brazilian-made and especially comfortable. Transportes Esmeraldas has evening buses to Quito ($6.50). To head north along the coast, go about one km south of the center to the "mini terminal terrestre" on Montenegro. *Selectivos* (small buses) with various companies drive west on 9 de Octubre toward Salinas.

Baños de San Vicente
If the beach doesn't leave you relaxed enough, try out this small complex of thermal baths a few kilometers east of La Libertád. For the full treatment, there's a pool, sauna, and therapeutic mud pit. Look for the billboard advertising the

Campo Magnetico de Salud between La Libertád and Montañita. It's open daily 9 A.M.–6 P.M., and admission is $3 pp. Massages are $1. Accommodations at the **Hotel Florida** are $6 d, including pool and hot tub, of course.

Museo "Los Amantes de Sumpa"
One km west of Santa Elena, this small complex has a wide variety of displays on five pre-Hispanic coastal cultures. Archaeological exhibits, a full-sized traditional *campesino* house, and a Manteño balsa sailboat are all part of the collection. Two hundred sets of skeletons were unearthed in the Las Vegas cemetery in the 1970s, including the "Lovers of Sumpa," the well-preserved skeletons of a man and woman in an 8,000-year-old embrace. Even though the descriptions are only in Spanish, it's an excellent museum and well worth a stop. A small gift shop sells traditional crafts such as tagua-nut carvings. Any bus or shared taxi heading east of La Libertád can drop you off close. Open daily except Wed., 9 A.M.–1:30 P.M. and 2:30–5 P.M., 40 cents pp.

PLAYAS AND VICINITY

The nearest resort destination to Guayaquil is still a fishing town at heart. Balsa rafts crafted in the ancient style still slip into the waves at dusk to ply the waters of the southern point and the Gulf of Guayaquil. Playas is a dusty, very Ecuadorian resort town, which is busiest Jan.–Apr. and on weekends year-round. It's less popular than its glitzy cousins to the west, but more bearable as a result. At night the gazebo in the triangular main plaza is softly lit by lanterns. Robberies and assaults have been reported on the beach at night, so head inland after sunset.

Accommodations
Playa's lodging options are slim. The clean rooms at the **Residencial El Galeón,** tel. 4/760-270, are a good value at $2 with fan, mosquito net, and private bathroom. The **Hotel Marianela,** tel. 4/761-507, have rooms with private bath, fan, and mosquito net for less than $2 in a building that looks as if it might topple at any minute. Until it does, it's one of the cheapest places in town.

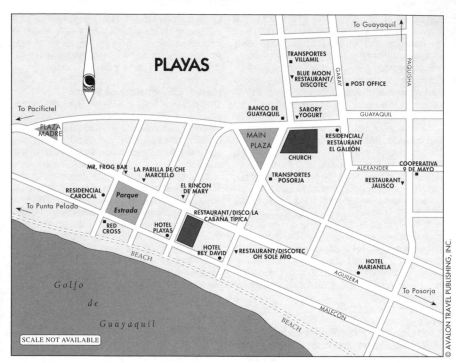

The **Hotel Playas,** tel. 4/760-121 or 760-611, offers pure drinking water and a restaurant facing the ocean; rates are $1.50 pp with private bath and fan. One block east along the Malecón brings you to the **Hotel Rey David,** tel. 4/760-024, where good rooms cost $5 pp with a fan, $7 pp with a TV, and $10 pp with air-conditioning.

Food

Don't pass through Playas without eating at one of the seafood cafés strung along the beach. Each is indistinguishable from its neighbors except for the address and the person it's named after, but at any one the fruits of the ocean can bo quite tasty—try the *ostras* (oysters) and *conchas* (conchs).

Back in town the **Restaurant Jalisco** is a local favorite, with simple Ecuadorian meals and ice-cold drinks for about $1. **La Parilla de Che Marcello** has grilled meats for around $3, and for snacks and fruit salads, try **Sabory Yogurt** near the church (their burgers are 50 cents). Vege-

tarians will appreciate the Middle Eastern options like falafel and tabouli for $1 at **El Rincon de Mary.**

Various *centros commerciales* on Guayaquil near the Hotel La Terraza cater to beachgoers, but some have a limited selection of groceries, along with a plethora of booze and T-shirts.

Recreation and Entertainment

The town's gently curving **beach** has showers and changing rooms available for a fee and is popular with surfers. For the real low-down on the local wave scene, stop by the Resturant Jalisco and ask for Juan Gutierrez, the president of the Playas Surf Club. He's a friendly guy with a wealth of knowledge, and he's very patient with those who speak little Spanish. For even less of a crowd, make your way about five km west along the dirt road to **Punta Pelada,** backed by cacti-studded cliffs.

The **Restaurant La Cabaña Tipica** has a disco, as does the **Blue Moon Resturant/Dis-**

cotec. On the northwest corner of the Parque Estrada, you'll find **Mr. Frog Bar,** which has been known to host an evening's fun. The **Restaurant/Discotec Oh Sole Mio** has live music nightly under a giant thatched roof, but it really hops on weekends.

Sunset beach rides on horseback are the specialty of **Cabalgatas Tours,** tel. 9/769-626, one km out the Data Highway toward Posorja..

Services and Information
Playas' tiny **post office** is on Garay, and if you head west from the small Plaza Madre for about one km you'll reach **Pacifictel.** If you're very patient, the **Banco de Guayaquil** will eventually change your travelers' checks.

Transportation
Frequent buses to **Guayaquil** ($1, two hours) leave with Transportes Villamil and Transportes Posorja. Cooperativa 9 de Marzo sends rattletraps to **Posorja** from the intersection of Guayaquil and Alexander. The easiest way to get between Playas and either Santa Elena, La Libertád, or Salinas is to take a Guayaquil-bound bus and change in Progreso.

East of Playas
The road down to the southern tip of the peninsula at Punta Arenas is known as the Data Highway because it passes through two towns called Data de Villamil and Data de Posorja. For the first 10 km along the coast, the highway is lined with hotel complexes and vacation homes on the shore side—an interesting contrast to the shacks and salt flats on the other side. Signs for public access lanes to the beach pop up every few kilometers.

Numerous *hosterías* have laid claim to a section of beach for the benefit of vacationers looking to get out of Playas. A good example is the **Estrella del Mar,** tel. 4/760-430, near kilometer 1.5. Doubles are $6–7 with private bath, ceiling fan, and hot water, and the hotel offers a restaurant and private parking. About one km farther, the Swiss-run **Hostería Bellavista,** tel. 4/760-600, is more comfortable at $16 s, $28 d, with phone, TV, and air-conditioning. This quiet, well-run place has a small pool, a squash court, a sauna, and horses for rent for $3 per hour.

The road elbows left at Data de Posorja, near the onion-dome Convento Santa Teresa, before reaching the fishing village of **Posorja.** Looking across the narrow Canal del Morro toward the Isla Puná, Posorja is a crusty, working-class town dependent on the whims of the sea. Surprisingly homey accommodations are available at the **Hostería Posorja,** tel. 4/764-115, on the point at the end of town. The terrace over the water and a bar that oozes character might be reason enough to come all the way out here. Rates are $2 pp with private bath and fans.

GUAYAQUIL AND VICINITY

The largest city in Ecuador has a bad rap. Just listen to Paul Theroux in *The Old Patagonian Express:* "Visitors to Guayaquil are urged to raise their eyes, for on a clear day it is possible to see the snowy hood of Mount Chimborazo from the humid streets of this stinking city; and if you look down, all you see is rats."

Sure, you do stand a good chance of seeing your first (but certainly not last) seaside rodent here, and it is humid, and some parts of the river don't smell so great, and crime is a problem. But really, it's not that bad. The fact is, things are different here on the coast. The humidity makes even a pleasant stroll along the Malecón an effort, and it appears to have an effect on the personalities of the inhabitants themselves. Here the vibe is Caribbean, not Andean—an interesting racial mix of *indígenas,* blacks, Asians, and mestizos seem more intent on enjoying their nights and enduring the climate than on keeping the streets scrubbed and the buildings clean. It takes some getting used to, so at least give Guayaquil the benefit of the doubt.

The city sits on the west side of where the Ríos Babahoyo and Daule meet to form the deep, stubby Río Guayas, only 56 km long before it empties into the Gulf of Guayaquil. Water in the streets is common because Guayaquil is only an average of four meters above sea level, and the Río Guayas rises and falls with the tides. Various *esteros* (estuaries) snake off into the salt flats to the west, outlining countless mangrove-bordered islands.

Guayaquil, whose population hovers somewhere near 4 million, has always been a prototypical port city, and today has evolved into the country's most important commercial center and the largest port on this side of South America. Close to half of the country's industry is based here, and almost all of its agricultural products depart from here for cities around the world. As with any city that sees this much traffic, Guayaquil has problems with smuggling, especially drugs from Colombia.

History

Guayaquil was founded in 1537 by Francisco de Orellana to replace an original settlement to the east that had been destroyed repeatedly by native tribes. Two versions of the origin of the town's name exist: according to some, the city was named for Santiago de Guayaquil (St. James) because it was refounded on his festival day, whereas the more romantic recall the story of the Huancavilca chief Guayas and his wife Quil, who killed themselves rather than fall into the hands of the Spanish.

From early on, Guayaquil was one of the most important ports in the Spanish South American empire during the 16th and 17th centuries, second only to El Callao near Lima. This fact didn't escape the notice of pirates like Captain Morgan, who obliged by sacking and pillaging almost at will. By the 18th century, the situation was really bad. The tropical climate made the area a breeding ground for almost every disease imaginable. Typhoid fever, dysentery, malaria, yellow fever, and even bubonic plague spread quickly through the population, helped by an almost complete lack of sanitary facilities and streets that flooded for months out of the year. Rats were as common as children in the streets and in many homes, and regular fires raged through the closely packed wooden buildings. One bad blaze in 1896 destroyed much of the colonial sector.

The turn of the century brought some relief when the United States threatened to withhold traffic from the newly completed Panama Canal if Guayaquil didn't clean up its act. A crack team of doctors sent by the Rockefeller Foundation organized municipal works and sanitation campaigns to make the place more livable.

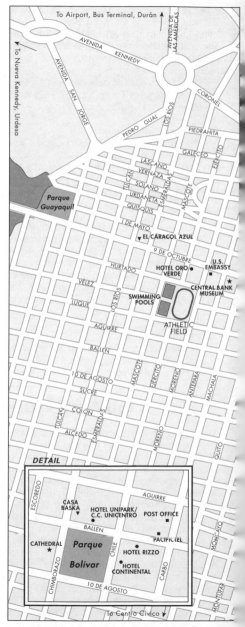

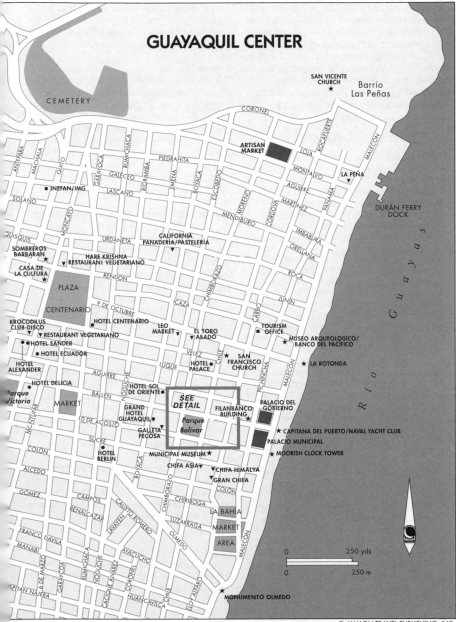

GUAYAQUIL CENTER

CEMETERY

SAN VICENTE CHURCH ★

Barrio Las Peñas

CORONEL

ARTISAN MARKET

LOJA

MONTALVO

LA PEÑA ▼

AGUIRRE

MARTINEZ

PANAMA

ROCAFUERTE

MALECÓN

DURÁN FERRY DOCK

ANTEPARA
MACHALA
QUITO
GARAYCOA
RUMICHACA

PIEDRAHITA

RICBAMBA
JIMENA
BOYACA
ESCOBEDO
MORENO
CORDOVA

IMBABURA

ORELLANA

ROCA

JUNIN

■ INEFAN/IMG

GALECEO

LASCANO

SOLANO
MONCAYO

URDANETA

CALIFORNIA PANADERIA/PASTELERÍA ▼

QUISQUIS
SOMBREROS BARBARAN ★
CASA DE LA CULTURA ★

HARE KRISHNA ▼ RESTAURANT VEGETARIANO

RENDON

MENDIBURO

CHIMBORAZO

ICAZA
CARBO

PLAZA CENTENARIO

9 DE OCTUBRE

HOTEL CENTENARIO ★

KROCODILUS CLUB-DISCO ●
▼ RESTAURANT VEGETARIANO
●●HOTEL SANDER
● HOTEL ECUADOR

LEO MARKET ▼

EL TORO ▼ ASADO

TOURISM OFFICE ★

MUSEO ARQUEOLOGICO/ BANCO DEL PACIFICO ★

HOTEL ALEXANDER
HOTEL DELICIA ●

VELEZ

HOTEL ● PALACE

CHILE

SAN FRANCISCO CHURCH ★

PICHINCHA
MALECÓN

★ LA ROTONDA

Rio Guayas

AGUIRRE

LUQUE

arque Victoria

MARKET

BALLEN

MCNTUFAR
ZOGUCHE

HOTEL SOL DE ORIENTE ●

SEE DETAIL

FILANBANCO BUILDING ★

PALACIO DEL GOBIERNO

10 DE ACOSTO

GRAND HOTEL GUAYAQUIL ●

Parque Bolivar

COLON

SUCRE
HOTEL BERLIN ●

GALLETA PECOSA ▼

MUNICIPAL MUSEUM ★

★ CAPITANA DEL PUERTO/NAVAL YACHT CLUB

PALACIO MUNICIPAL

★ MOORISH CLOCK TOWER

ALCEDO

BOYACA

CHIFA ASIA ▼

▼ CHIFA HIMALYA
▼ GRAN CHIFA

COLON

GOMEZ

CAMPOS

CALIXTO ROMERO

BENALCAZAR

CHIMBORAZO

CHIRIBOGA

LA BAHÍA

LAVAYEN

LUZARRAGA

MARKET AREA

FRANCO DAVILA

MANABI

GARAYCOA
RUMICHACA
NOGUCHE
CACIQUE ALVAREZ
CORONEL
CHILE

AYACUCHO

OLMEDO

MALECÓN

6 DE MARZO

APITAN NAJERA

HUANCAVILCA

ELOY ALFARO

★ MONUMENTO OLMEDO

0   250 yds

0   250 m

MooN

The second half of the 20th century has seen huge numbers of people flow into Guayaquil in response to various economic booms along the coast—most notably the banana blitz of the 1950s. All of these people had to find somewhere to live, and because Guayaquil is surrounded by nothing but marshes and salt flats, overcrowding has become a serious problem. Sprawling *suburbios,* poor and squalid settlements, have been staked out on quick-and-cheap landfills covering various estuaries and even part of the Río Guayas itself. Unsurprisingly, flooding is also a serious problem.

Orientation

The city center is all business, with executives crowding the sidewalks and gleaming highrises facing the river. Occasional colonial housefronts—more common in the barrio of Las Peñas—break this monotony with scrolled grillwork along pastel balconies and latticed windows. Traffic can be a nightmare, so walking is your best bet. Take note that some street names change partway, especially in the northeast section of Guayaquil's center near Las Peñas.

More swank residential suburbs spread north and east, including La Garzota, Sauces, and Alborada. Nueva Kennedy and Urdesa are the two most visited, offering plenty of restaurants, nightclubs, and shopping areas but no lodging. Most tourists come at night for the action, but the suburbs are a welcome relief any time from the chaos of the city center. East of the airport, the impressive Puente de la Unidad Nacional spans the Ríos Daule and Babahoyo over to Durán.

Climate

One hotel brochure describes Guayaquil's climate as "deliciously tropical." Tropical, agreed, but "deliciously" isn't exactly the modifier I'd have picked, but I guess "humid as hell" wouldn't sell many tour packages. Temperatures hover around 30°C year-round, so the important variable becomes the amount of moisture in the air. Jan.–March brings 12–15 days of precipitation per month on average. April and May are more bearable, until the sun comes out during the June–Dec. "dry" season. Still, no rain doesn't mean no water in the air; humidity is the rule, regardless of the season.

Safety

With some of the worst poverty in Ecuador, Guayaquil has a serious problem with crime. Attackers often work in pairs, especially around hotel and bank entrances and at the bus station. Don't walk around downtown at night any more than you have to (remember, taxis are

---

THE GENERALS MEET

The only time the two greatest leaders in Latin America's independence struggle met was in Guayaquil in 1822. Simón Bolívar and José de San Martín, both glorified generals, had corresponded during the battle but had never met face to face. Bolívar the Venezuelan operated in the north, whereas San Martín, from Argentina, fought to the south.

Each man had his own issues to settle. San Martín, who requested the meeting, was more concerned with immediate issues such as the fate of Guayaquil, fought over by Perú and Colombia. Bolívar's thoughts were focused on his precious idea of Gran Colombia, a united South America under one government.

True to style, Bolívar took charge of the meeting from the start. He reportedly rushed from Quito to reach Guayaquil before San Martín, who was on his way north from Perú. When San Martín arrived, Bolívar welcomed him warmly to "Gran Colombian soil," and at a banquet that night raised a toast to "the two greatest men in South America." What happened at the meeting itself, though, may never be known because the generals' private aides were not admitted. Because most accounts were written by Bolívar or his supporters, surviving versions of the encounter are probably skewed, but the general consensus is that San Martín, no match for El Libertador's fiery personality, yielded completely.

That night as Bolívar whirled the ladies at a grand ball, San Martín left the city quietly for Perú. There he resigned his official title of Protector and sailed to Europe, leaving the fate of South America in Bolívar's hands. Today the largest statue on Guayaquil's riverfront commemorates the meeting.

cheap), and consider taking company in Las Peñas at all times. Take care walking in the street market area of La Bahia, at the Christ Statue (Sagrado Corazon de Jesus) on Cerro del Carmen, and in the southern part of the city. Keep an eye on your bags at the airport, and be aware that some assaults and robberies have resulted from travelers being followed to or from the airport, even by day. Never carry anything valuable in plain sight.

On the brighter side, Guayaquil's Malecón— once a crime zone of the highest order—has been hosed down and spruced up, and is now well-patrolled by police and completely safe.

SIGHTS

Malecón

Guayaquil's riverside avenue parallels the brown Río Guayas the entire length of the city center. Beginning as a small port in what is now the Las Pescas neighborhood, Guayaquil's waterfront gained a boost with the construction of its first wharf by president Vicente Rocafuerte. After the Maritime Port was constructed to the south in 1963, the riverfront area stopped being the city's economic and social center and slid into a period of deterioration.

Locals, then, are rightfully proud of the Malecón 2000, www.malecon2000.com, a monumental undertaking that aims to give the former heart of the city a complete facelift. If you've been here before, you probably won't even recognize it: the two-km pedestrian walkway has been extended out over the river and will be decorated with fountains, bridges, and modern sculptures representing land, water, fire, and air. Shoppping centers, crafts markets, restaurants, movie theaters, a hotel, and an ecological park are all in the works, and the Soth Market Building, built by famed French engineer Gustave Eiffel in 1907, will become the Malecón Museum. The Museum of the Banco Central will be moved here as well. Still under construction in 2000, the futuristic project already bustles in the evening. It's spotless and well-guarded, and is open 7 A.M.–midnight daily.

The southern end of the Malecón's central stretch is marked by the **Monumento Olmedo,** commemorating José Joaquín Olmedo, the city's first mayor and celebrated poet. Continuing north past the **United Nations Monument,** you'll reach the unmistakably ornate **Moorish Clock Tower.** The octagonal structure is the latest incarnation (1931) of an original tower that dated to 1770, and it is being refurbished as part of the Malecón 2000 project. The friendly caretaker inside will lead you—clucking all the way—up the spiral metal stairs to a view of the city and river from 23 meters up. Along the way, you'll pass the inner guts of the clock, which was made in London and whose weights need to be wound up by hand daily. The tower is open Mon.–Fri. 8:30 A.M.–12:30 P.M. and 1:30–4:30 P.M. Admission is free.

One of the prettiest sights from the tower is the three-masted sailboat *Guayas* parked at the Capitania del Puerto, which shares a berth with the Naval Yacht Club. The boat docks here occasionally between year-round training cruises for Ecuadorian Navy cadets. The boar statue in front of the building—razorback in repose— was a 1931 gift to the city by the local Chinese enclave.

The white-on-gray **Palacio Municipal** is beautiful in a way unlike most Ecuadorian government buildings: ornate but tasteful, with Corinthian columns supporting an arched interior passage with a glass ceiling. It was built from 1924–1928 in the Italian Renaissance style. The subdued design is echoed in the **Palacio del Gobierno** to the north, enclosing the model ship collection of the **Museo Naval,** open Mon.–Fri. 8–11 A.M. and 1–4 P.M., 10 cents. Between the two buildings, a pedestrian walkway is home to fountains and the pigeon-covered **Monumento Sucre.**

Although it's not actually on the Malecón, the Museo Nahim Isaias B., tel. 4/526-200 or 526-099, ext. 318, is easily reached from the avenue. It occupies the second floor of the Filanbanco building on Pichincha and Ballen (enter on Ballen) and houses well-presented exhibits on coastal archaeology and colonial art in its deliciously air-conditioned passages. It's open Mon.–Sat. 10 A.M.–5 P.M. and is free. The next stop along the river is **La Rotonda,** at the end of 9 de Octubre. The stately semicircular monument depicts Bolívar and San Martín's historic meeting (see the special topic, "The Generals Meet").

Las Peñas

Continue about 10 blocks north up the Malecón, just past the ferry to Durán and the La Peña music hall (not to be confused with the neighborhood), to reach this historic neighborhood on the slopes of Cerro El Carmen. It was part of the original Guayaquil settlement, and most of it appears unchanged: weathered houses line narrow, cobbled streets, as rotting balconies supported by bamboo poles look seaward.

Steps at the entrance lead up to the **Plaza Colón,** where two cannons point mutely at the water in commemoration of a 1624 raid by Dutch pirates. The winding **Calle Numa Pompillo Llona,** named after the author of the Ecuadorian national anthem, is lined by cafés and *galerías de arte.* The street, which is being restored as part of the Malecón 2000 project, dead-ends at the defunct National Brewery. Las Peñas' **Iglesia de San Vicente,** at Rocafuerte and Coronel, is the oldest church in the city, originally founded in 1548. After numerous fatal fires, this version was erected in 1938.

admiring the iguanas at Parque Bolivar

JULIAN SMITH

As a tourist attraction with plenty of isolated spots and claustrophobic lanes, it's natural that Las Peñas has had more than its share of crime. It's a good idea to limit your explorations to the church and Calle Llona. A police substation in the plaza at the entrance has made things safer, but keep your eyes open.

Plaza Centenario

Spanning four square blocks, Guayaquil's main plaza is among the largest in the country. A **Monument to the Heroes of Independence** includes four statues representing Heroism, Justice, Patriotism, and History. On the west side at 9 de Octubre, the **Casa de la Cultura,** tel. 4/300-500, features a museum of prehistoric art with an impressive collection of gold artifacts. Inside you'll also find a movie theater (with showings Mon., Wed., Thurs.), a school of the arts, and a café. The Casa de la Cultura is open Tues.–Fri. 10 A.M.–5:30 P.M., Sat. 9 A.M.–3 P.M., 20 cents.

Parque Bolívar

Not the biggest but certainly the most interesting park in Guayaquil, this pleasant plaza is presided over by a monument to Bolívar shaded by 30-meter trees. Here in the Parque de los Iguanas, as it's more popularly known, almost-tame reptiles slither down out of the branches to snap up lettuce and other goodies left by hotel workers around noon each day. Kids especially love the iguanas, squealing "¡Mira! ¡Mira!" ("Look! Look!") as the tiny reptiles joust for scraps and stride down the paths like they own the place. Look carefully and you might also spot a sloth among the leaves. A fish pond and dozens of turtles complete the menagerie.

The weathered gothic **cathedral** on the west side of the park replaces a wooden one built in 1547.

Other Museums

A huge relief of Atahualpa overlooking the intersection of Antepara and 9 de Octubre marks the entrance to the **Central Bank Museum,** tel. 4/327-402. The anthropology collection inside focuses on coastal cultures, featuring a life-sized reproduction of a Manteña Huancavilca balsa raft. A *videoteca* and *musiteca* have videos and recordings to peruse, respectively (open Mon.–Fri. 9 A.M.–4 P.M.). The main collection is open Tues.–Fri. 10 A.M.–6 P.M., Sat. and Sun. 1–4 P.M., $1 pp. Guides are available. (As of 2000, this museum was planned to be moved to the Malecón.)

The **Municipal Museum,** in the Biblioteca Municipal on Chile between Sucre and Carbo, tel. 4/524-100, focuses on the city's history. The collection inside features everything from archaeology to modern art and is open Tues.–Sat. 9 A.M.–5 P.M. for free. Every Saturday there's a free two-hour historical tour of the city starting at 10 A.M.

A collection of ancient ceramics from across Ecuador fills the **Museo Arqueologico Banco del Pacifico,** on Icaza and Pichincha, on the second floor. Temporary exhibits and an Internet café fill the third floor. Open Mon.–Fri. 8 A.M.–5 P.M., Sat. and Sun. 11 A.M.–1 P.M.

Other Sights

Guayaquil's **general cemetery** at the north end of the city center is also called the Ciudad Blanca (White City), and even a quick drive past will show you why. Blindingly clean mausolea make up an ornate city of the dead, sheltering the corpses of the wealthy in better housing than most of the city's living residents could ever hope for. This is another somewhat dodgy area, so try to go during the day and in a group, and don't wander too far from the entrance.

The Ecuadorian Orchid Society began the **Botanical Gardens,** tel. 4/416-975 or 416-004, in 1989. A significant percentage of Ecuador's lengthy orchid list is represented, planted among shady paths and artificial streams. The five-hectare plot, heading west out of town, lies in the Urbanización de Los Orchideas, most easily reached by a taxi ($2.50, 30 minutes) or through tours organized by most upscale hotels or Chasquitur. The gardens are open daily 8 A.M.–4 P.M., $5 pp.

On the eastern bank of the Río Daule in the Cantón Samborondón, the **Parque Historico Guayaquil,** tel. 4/833-807, re-creates life—both human and animal—near the turn of the 20th century. A raised walkway leads visitors through the endangered wildlife zone, where you might spot one of 50 species of birds, mammals, or reptiles. Deer, tapirs, monkeys, sloths, wild cats, and harpy eagles all avoid the midday sun, making morning and afternoon visits the best. Displays in the reconstructed rural hacienda and

19th-century suburb re-create the crafts and crops of the coastal zone a century ago. Tours are given in Spanish and English, and visitors can peruse the museum, restaurant, and cafeteria at their leisure. Open Tues.–Sun. 9 A.M.–5 P.M., $1 pp.

A statue to Independence by Guayasamin marks the entrance to the **Centro Cívico,** south of the city center on Av. Quito/25 de Julio. The Guayaquil city orchestra gives free concerts here, and the complex includes convention centers and exhibition halls.

ACCOMMODATIONS

Less Than $10

For the largest city in the country, Guayaquil has a sad dearth of decent budget hotels. The well-run **Hotel Delicia,** Ballen 11-05 and Montúfar, tel. 4/324-925, is one of the most popular, which explains why it's usually full. Clean rooms run $2 pp with shared bath, $5.50 with private bath, air-conditioning, and TV. At $1.50 pp with fan and private bath, it's hard to beat the clean, ship-shape **Hotel Berlin,** Rumichaca 15-03 and Sucre, tel. 4/524-648.

Rooms with private bath, TV, and fan at the **Hotel Sander,** Luque 11-01 and Moncayo, tel. 4/320-030 or 320-944, run $5.25. It's clean and well-run, but not quite the deal the **Hotel Ecuador** is. At Moncayo 117 between Luque and Aguirre, tel. 4/321-460, this place has rooms for $4 with fan and $5 with air-conditioning. All have TVs and private baths. The **Hotel Centenario,** Vélez 728 and Garaycoa, tel. 4/515-578, fax 4/328-772, overlooks the park of the same name. Rooms with air-conditioning and cable TV are $8 d. They have a popular restaurant and disco.

$10–25

A bit out of the center of town but worth the trip is the **Ecuahogar Youth Hostal,** tel. 4/248-357, fax 4/248-341, e-mail: youthost@telconet.net. Shared rooms in the four-floor building are $10 pp including breakfast (ISIC discount). Try to get a room on the top floor for the views. They have cable TV, a VCR, and run city tours. It's opposite the Banco Ecuatoriana de la Vivienda near the airport; to get there, take a taxi or bus 22 from the bus terminal.

The **Hotel Alexander,** Luque 11-07 between Moncayo and Quito, tel. 4/532-000 or 532-,651, is a good value at $17 s, $20 d with in-room phones, cable TV and air-conditioning. At the **Hotel Rizzo,** Ballen 319 and Chile, tel. 4/325-210, fax 4/326-209, e-mail: hrizzo@gye.satnet.net, all of the 60 rooms have air-conditioning, TV, and phone, and include a continental breakfast for $22.

$25–$50

The **Tangara Guest House,** Sáenz and O'Leary, Ciudadela Bolivariana, Bloque F, Casa 1, tel. 4/284-445 or 4/282-828, fax 4/284-039, is the first real standout in this midpriced category. Operating under the slogan "Budget Accommodations for Upmarket Travelers," the friendly Perrone family runs the tastefully appointed place as if guests were staying in their own home just next door. Six rooms run $33 s, $40 d (10 percent SAE discount), and a fully equipped kitchen is available. It's located between the airport and the bus station; tell your taxi driver to head for "Ciudadola Bolivariana."

An Asian motif winds through the **Hotel Sol de Oriente,** Aguirre 603 and Escobedo, tel. 4/325-601 or 325-702, fax 4/329-352. Accommodations ($26 s, $29 d) include use of a gym and sauna, but the Great Wall restaurant is open to all. The **Grand Hotel Guayaquil,** Boyacá 1600 and 10 de Agosto, tel. 4/329-690, fax 4/327-251, e-mail: grandhot@gye.satnet.net (reservations: reserghg@gye.satnet.enet), www.grand-hotelguayaquil.com, has it all: 180 luxury rooms with cable TV, a sports complex with two air-conditioned squash courts, a lushly landscaped pool, and two restaurants. Rates are $40–45 s, $45–50 d, $125 suites.

$50–75

The **Hotel Palace,** Chile 214-216 and Luque, tel. 4/321-080, fax 4/322-887, e-mail: hotpalsa@impsat.net.ec, provides good security and travel assistance for $56 s, $78 d. Its restaurant receives repeat applause.

$75–200

Guests at the elegant **Hotel Unipark,** Ballen 406 and Chile, tel. 4/327-100, fax 4/328-352, e-mail: ecuni@gye.satnet.net, can amuse themselves for days without ever leaving the building. It's attached to the Unicentro shopping mall, which features a casino and video arcade. They have the El Parque French restaurant, the Uni-cafe, and the upstairs Unibar, which specializes in sushi and sports a view of the Parque Bolívar. You'll also find a gym with hot tub and sauna. Reception is on the second floor. Rates for their 138 rooms are $146 s, $183 d. You can make reservations in the United States through Prima Hotels, 800/447-7462, 212/223-2848.

At Guayaquil's **Hotel Oro Verde,** 9 de Octubre and Moreno, tel. 4/327-999, fax 4/329-350, e-mail: ecovg@gyc.satnet.net, www.oroverdehotels.com, guests enjoy 192 rooms and 62 suites with air-conditioning, satellite TV, and VCRs. There's also a gourmet deli, a casino, three restaurants, a piano bar, a fitness center, and a partridge in a pear tree (not really). Rates start at $150. You can make reservations in the United States through **Leading Hotels of the World,** 800/223-6800, 212/515-5813, e-mail: info@ihw.com.

There are three top-notch restaurants at the **Hotel Continental,** Chile and 10 de Agosto, tel. 4/329-270, fax 4/325-454. One, El Fortin, has won international gourmet awards. Rooms go for $90–105 s, $115 d. Reservations are also available in the United States and Canada through Golden Tulip Hotels, 800/333-1212.

More Than $200

A ten-story atrium is only the beginning of Guayaquil's newest luxury digs, the **Hilton Colón Guayaquil,** tel. 4/689-900, fax 4/689-149, five minutes from the airport on Orellana in the Ciudadela Kennedy Norte, the city's sparkling new financial zone. They also have 274 rooms and 20 suites with climate control and noise-insulated windows, cable TV, and phones. Downstairs there's a casino, a gym, a pool, five restaurants, and a 24-hour café. Rates are $240 s, $260 d, and reservations can be made in the United States at 800/445-8667, in the U.K. at tel. 800/298-303, and in Germany at tel. 0130-2345.

FOOD

Most of Guayaquil's best restaurants are in the ritzy suburbs and the more expensive hotels in the city center. Breakfast can be difficult to locate: the most popular morning meal in the city seems to be an *empanada* and carrot juice from a sidewalk vendor. You can also try the extensive breakfast buffet at the Pepe de Oro in the Grand Hotel Guayaquil ($3.75), or one of the small places on 9 de Octubre across from the U.S. Embassy.

Ecuadorian

The **Restaurant 1822** of the Grand Hotel Guayaquil comes recommended as a within-reason splurge, with a classy atmosphere and fantastic plates, including steak and seafood starting at $5. **Lo Nuestro,** Estrada 903 and Higueras, Urdesa, offers midpriced Ecuadorian fare for $3–15, with Italian entrées on the inexpensive side. **La Canoa** at the Hotel Continental and the Oro Verde's **El Patio** also offer Ecuadorian fare for slightly more.

Steak Houses

The huge **La Parillada del ñato,** Estrada 1219 and Laureles, Urdesa, is famous throughout Ecuador for its mammoth portions and always packed. Filet mignon is $4.50, but vegetarians can get a great pizza for 60 cents. Carnivores also head to **El Toro Asado,** Chimborazo 124 and Vélez, where all kinds of grilled flesh averages $2.

Lunch and Snacks

On the ground floor of the Unicentro mall, the cheerful **Unicafe** has lunch plates in the $3–4 range. If you want, you can choose your own *trucha* from the live tank. **El Buen Sabor,** 4-05 Pichincha, serves a wide range of juices and empanadas, as does the **Pepa de Oro** coffee shop/cafeteria in the Grand Hotel Guayaquil. Fruit salads and sandwiches make up the menus at **Leo Market,** on Escobedo just south of 9 de Octubre, all for about 50 cents.

Vegetarian

For a healthy, inexpensive meal, try the **Restaurant Vegetariano,** Luque and Moncayo, where all meals (including the faux *seco de chivo*) are less than $1. The **Hare Krishna Restaurant Vegetariano,** on the northwest corner of the Parque Centenario, serves a variety of Ecuadorian, Chinese, and Western plates for $1. Build your own salad at the offbeat **Afrodita Restaurant Vegetarian Gourmet,** Estrada and Ficus in Urdesa, or try the basmati rice with mango chutney. Prices range from $3–4.

A *shawarma* is just over $1 at **Maalik Al Shawarma,** 811-B Estrada in Urdesa, and falafels are only 60 cents. Almost across the street is the **Café al Sindibad,** Estrada and Guayacanes, with *shawarmas* ($1.50) and water pipes with apple tobacco.

Seafood

Gourmets swear by one of Guayaquil's most expensive eateries, the Chilean **El Caracol Azul,** 9 de Octubre 1918 and Los Ríos. Here on the coast, **crab houses** *(casas de cangrejo)* are a way of life, brimming with beer and hungry patrons up to their elbows in crustacean parts. Ask at your hotel for the current favorites. The **Red Crab,** Estrada and Laureles in Urdesa, is a high-class place with prices to match, but you can still get ceviches for just $3.

Even though it doesn't look fit for fish itself, the river was once lined with many inexpensive seafood restaurants worth a visit. When the Malecón 2000 project is finished, many eateries will once again overlook the water, but odds are they won't be nearly as cheap.

Asian

Sucre and Chile is Guayaquil's *chifa* corner. The **Chifa Himalya** and **Chifa Asia** on Sucre are your usual budget eateries with nothing on the menu more than $2, but for slightly more money you can't top the ambience—shark-fin soup and cats in the potted plants—at the **Gran Chifa,** Carbo 1016 near Sucre. Entrées here are $1–3. You'll spot lots more *chifas* in this area. **Tsuji,** Estrada 813 and Guayacanes, Urdesa, is the classiest—and only—Japanese establishment in town. A meal will set you back around $10, and you can stick around for karaoke afterward.

Other International

The **Trattoria da Enrico,** Balsamos 504 and Ebanos, Urdesa, has received repeat awards as the best restaurant in the country by a national gastronomic club. Don't be scared off by the waterfall and fish ponds at the entrance—you can get pasta here for as little as $4.50, although an entire meal can run up to $20. Less intimate but easier on the wallet is **Tratoria da Pasquale,**

Estrada 7-27 and Guayacanes, also in Urdesa. Their extensive menu averages around $3.

A good wine selection and reasonably priced Spanish delicacies set apart the **Casa Baska** (formerly La Tasa Vasca), a restaurant and tapas bar at Ballen 4-22 and Chimborazo. A *Paella de Vallencia* goes for $4, as do most other dishes on their constantly evolving menu. Fans of French cooking should inspect the award-winning **Le Gourmet** at the Hotel Oro Verde, where a dinner will set you back about $15. A wide selection of Mexican favorites at **Rosa Mexicano,** Estrada 7-12 and Ficus, include the recommended enchiladas ($2.50).

Sweets and Fast Food

The **Galleta Pecosa** bakery at 10 de Agosto and Boyacá turns out some of the best pastries you'll find in Ecuador; try a 25-cent *borrachita* ("little drunkard"), a chocolate truffle-style pastry moist with raisins and liquor. For breads and other treats, stop by the **California Panadería/Pastelería** on Urdaneta between Jimena and Boyacá.

Many gringo fast-food joints along 9 de Octubre between Boyacá and Carbo have tapped into Guayaquil's executive lunch crowd. Satisfy your grease fix at **Dunkin' Donuts, Kentucky Fried Chicken, Burger King,** or **Pizza Hut.** Most of these and more, including a **Baskin-Robbins,** line Estrada in Urdesa.

SHOPPING

Guayaquil's **main market** is technically bordered by 10 de Agosto, Ballen, 6 de Marzo, and Garzacocha, but in reality it sprawls for blocks in a throng of tables of fish, colorful stacked fruit, and an overpowering mixture of smells and yells. **Las Bahías,** near the Malecón north of Olmedo, is more of a black market. All kinds of goods, from shoes to refrigerators, arrive in a tax-free, semi-legal way.

Various **shopping centers** cater to more choosy browsers. Unicentro is north of the Parque Bolívar in the city center. Urdesa has the Centro Commercial Río Centro and Nueva Kennedy has two, named Policentro and Plaza Quil. The popular C.C. Alban Borja is north of Urdesa. The only thing more exciting to

Guayaquileños than the Malecón 2000 is the **Mall del Sol,** a gigantic American-style mall with 150 shops, a food court, and a 10-screen cinema.

For *artesanías* like paintings and sculpture, try the Las Peñas district. An **artisan market** occupies the block south of Loja between Chile and Chimborazo. Out of 250 or so shops, a handful sell quality items, including woven hats and bags and leather work. It's not Otavalo, but the selection is good. It's open daily 9:30 A.M.–6:30 P.M. Other Otavalan goods are sold in many shops and stalls around the San Francisco church.

Sombreros Barbaran, on 1 de Mayo half a block west of the Parque Centenario, sells Panama hats made in Montecristi. If you'd like to pick up a Guayasamin painting while you're here, head to the **Man-Ging Art Gallery,** 111 Cedros, just off Estrada. It's worth a visit even if you're just browsing because all the work is excellent.

ENTERTAINMENT AND EVENTS

Nightlife

Guayaquil offers plenty to keep locals and visitors busy after-hours. Countless **discos and bars** hum into the early hours with every kind of crowd imaginable.

Things are a bit rough in the local establishments downtown, concentrated at the west end of Icaza and on Luque south of the Parque Centenario. The **Krocodilus Club-Disco** is near the southwest corner of the park. **La Peña Rincón Folclórico,** at Malecón 206 and Montalvo, features live music. (Take a taxi because the area around La Peña is unsafe at night.) Many larger hotels like the Oro Verde and Unihotel have discos and **casinos.**

The **Jardín de la Salsa,** on Avenida de las Americas north of the airport, can and sometimes does hold 5,000 gyrating dancers. Other popular discos include **Acústica,** on Orellana close to the Hilton Colón; **Chapos,** at Estrada and Las Monjas, and **Santé,** on Orellana next to the Banco del Progreso. **Studio Bar** is on Av. de las Americas, and **TV Bar** is in Ciudadela La Garzote in front of El Cantonés restaurant. Of course, the best way to find out where the current hot spots are is to make friends with a

Guayaquil Movie Theaters

Albocines . . . . .C.C. Plaza Mayor 4/244-986
Cinemark . . . . .Mall del Sol 4/692-013
Maya . . . . .Las Lomas and Dátiles 4/386-456
Metro . . . . .Boyacá 4/322-301
9 de Octubre . . .9 de Octubre and Rumichaca . . .4/531-788
Supercines . . . .Riocentro Entre Ríos 4/831-234
Supercines . . . .Riocentro Los Ceibos 4/852-790

Guayaquileño, but just about any of the above are a sure bet.

Listings for the close to 20 **movie theaters** appear in *El Telegrafo* and *El Universo*, Guayaquil's two major papers. This is where you'll also find information on theatrical presentations performed at the **Centro Cívico**, along 25 de Julio south of the city center.

Festivals
Carnival in Guayaquil includes the usual melee of flying water, paint, and mud. On 24–25 July, **Bolivar's Birthday** combines with the **Foundation of Guayaquil** for one of the city's largest celebrations, including the Pearl of the Pacific beauty contest and various cultural events. Another combination celebration occurs 9–12 October in the **Independence of Guayaquil** and **Columbus Day/Día de La Raza.**

TOURS

In addition to Galápagos trips, **Canodros S.A.,** Urb. Santa Leonor, Solar 10, via al Terminal Terrestre, tel. 4/280-143, 280-164, 280-173, fax 4/287-651, e-mail: eco-tourism1@canodros.com.ec, arranges visits to its celebrated Kapawi Ecolodge in the southern Oriente (see the special topic, "Kapawi Ecolodge" in the Oriente chapter).

Galasam Economic Galápagos Tours, 9 de Octubre 424 and Córdova, Ed. Gran Pasaje, tel. 4/304-488, 566-286, fax 4/311-485, e-mail: galaplus@gye.satnet.net, www.galapagos-islands.com, sells some of the least expensive tours to the Galápagos in the city. They can also take you around the city, deep-sea fishing, scuba diving, and to the Manglares Churute Reserve.

Chasquitur, Urdaneta 1418 and Av. del Ejérci to, tel. 4/281-084 or 281-085, fax 4/285-872, e-mail: galapago@galasam.com.ec, is recommended for earth-friendly junkets, including visits to Manglares Churute Ecological Park and bird-watching in several locations around Guayaquil, as well as whale-watching from July–Sept.

Several other companies offer the usual mix of Galápagos, Sierra, and Oriente ventures: **Kleintours,** Alcivar, Mz. 410, Solar 11, Kennedy Norte, tel. 4/681-700, fax 4/681-705; **Ecuadorean Tours,** 9 de Octubre 1900 and Esmeraldas, tel. 4/287-111, fax 4/280-851; and **Metropolitan Touring,** Antepara 915 and 9 de Octubre, tel. 4/320-300, fax 4/323-050.

You can book half-day tours of the Botanical Gardens and the Parque Histórico Guayaquil through the Hotel Sol de Oriente for just $10. **Pesca Tours,** tel. 4/443-365, e-mail: fishing@pescatours.com.ec, www.pescatours.com.ec, sends deep-sea fishing boats out from the Santa Elena peninsula.

SERVICES AND INFORMATION

Money
Exchange rates in Guayaquil are as high as any in the country. **Filanbanco,** 9 de Octubre between Pichincha and Carbo, advances cash on Visa cards, as does the **Banco del Guayaquil** at Pichincha 105 and **Lloyds Bank** at Pichincha 107. The **Banco del Pichincha** on the north side of Parque Centenario changes travelers' checks and a good selection of foreign currencies. All these banks have ATMs. **Cambiosa,** 9 de Octubre 113 and Malecón, will change travelers' checks at a high commission (although it's better than what you'll get at the airport). You can also change money at **Delgado Casa de Cambio** between Chimborazo and Chile.

The **Western Union** office is at Pichincha and Luque, tel. 4/322-700. Most major credit cards have offices in the center of town: **Visa Filanbanco,** Luque 121 and Carbo, tel. 4/513-180; **MasterCard,** Carbo and 9 de Octubre, Ed. San Francisco 300, tel. 4/561-730; and **Diners**

500 or 884-500, fax 4/889-464.

Communications
Both **Pacifictel** and the **post office** have their offices in the building bordered by Ballen, Aguirre, Carbo, and Chile. For courier services, look up **DHL,** 8va Oeste 100 and San Jorge, or **World Courier,** on the 8th floor of Chile 303, tel. 4/326-050 or 326-553.

Internet cafés are everywhere in Guayaquil, especially in malls like Unicentro and along Estrada in Urdesa. Most charge $1–1.50 per hour and are open daily. Two worth trying are **Laware,** 9 de Octubre 1309 between Quito and Machala, and **Officenet** at 801-C Rumichaca.

Health
The **Clínica Kennedy,** San Jorge between 9a and 10a in Nueva Kennedy, tel. 4/286-963, is the hands-down choice among Guayaquil's foreign community for its specialists and emergency services. Also recommended is the **Clínica Santa Marianita,** Boyacá 1915 between Colón and Olmedo, tel. 4/322-500; for emergencies, call 4/516-444. Dental services are provided at the **Clínica Dental Urdesa Central** in Urdesa.

Other Services
The **immigration office** out by the bus terminal, tel. 4/297-004, 297-197, 297-198, can give extensions on visas and answer other border-related questions. The **tourist information office,** Iraza 203 and Pichincha, tel. 4/568-764, e-mail: infotour@telconet.net, is staffed by helpful English-speaking employees. It's up on the sixth floor (turn left out of the elevator). They also have an office at the airport. For maps, stop by the **Instituto Geográfico Militar** at Quito 402 and Solano, tel. 4/393-351.

TRANSPORTATION

Land
If you're feeling left out because you haven't been ripped off by an Ecuadorian **taxi** driver yet, that should be solved within a few hours in Guayaquil. Trips within the downtown area *should* cost about 50 cents, and don't pay more than $2 to go to Urdesa, the airport, or the bus terminal, except at night. Ask at your hotel about how much you should expect to pay to your destination before hopping aboard.

Traffic downtown makes **local buses** only worth it for journeys out of the downtown area. All have fares (usually about 10 cents) and numbers posted in the front window, and most post their destination in the window. Bus number 52 heads north up the Malecón to Urdesa frequently, and number 2 passes the same way for the airport and bus terminal. Numerous buses pass the Centros Commerciales Policentro and Alban Borja and the Mall del Sol. Bus number 13 also goes to the malls.

Guayaquil's **bus terminal** is just north of the

Malecon 2000, a new parkway along Rio Guayas

TIM BEWER

GUAYAQUIL AIRLINE NUMBERS

AIRLINE	INFORMATION	RESERVATIONS
Aeca	4/288-110	288-110
Aerocontinente	4/303-404	303-408
Aerolineas Argentinas	4/690-012	690-013
Air Canada	4/560-572	563-982
Air France	4/687-198	687-149
American Airlines	4/564-111	564-111
Avensa	4/327-085	327-082
Avianca	4/320-313	287-850
British Airways	4/325-080	323-834
Continental Airlines	2/567-241	567-241
Copa	4/883-752	883-753
Cubana	4/390-727	390-727
Iberia	4/329-558	329-382
Japan Airlines	4/889-789	385-108
KLM	4/288-451	692-876
LanChile	4/324-360	328-360
Lufthansa	4/324-360	328-475
TACA/Lacsa	4/562-950	562-950
TAME	4/560-778	565-806
United Airlines	4/566-311	566-311
Varig	4/327-082	327-085

airport. For such a monstrosity, it's actually pretty efficient; buy your ticket at one of the 50 or so windows and head upstairs to the roof to catch your bus. Rides leave for just about every city in the country. Quito is eight hours and $5 away.

Renting a car in Guayaquil is expensive. If you find it's absolutely necessary, however, some major companies include:

Avis, Av. de las Americas, C. C. Olimpico, tel. 4/285-498 or 285-519

Budget, García Moreno and Hurtado, tel. 4/328-571, 320-668, 329-898

Delgado, García Moreno and Hurtado, tel. 4/523-004

Ecuacars, Ciudadela Adace, tel. 4/285-533

Air

Head north of the city center on Quito to Avenida de las Americas to reach the Simón Bolívar International Airport, tel. 4/282-100. Tickets for international flights are available from any of the many travel agencies in the city or at the airline offices themselves. The international departure tax is $25 pp.

TAME flies to Quito about five times daily

($27 one-way), to Cuenca Sun.–Fri. ($21 one-way), to Esmeraldas Mon., Wed., Fri., and Sun. ($25 one-way), to Lago Agrio Mon.–Sat ($38 one-way), to Loja Mon., Thur., and Fri. ($21 one-way), to Macas Mon., Wed., and Fri. ($28 one-way), to Machala Mon.–Fri. ($18), to Tulcán Mon.–Fri. ($45 one-way), and to Baltra (daily) and San Cristóbal in the Galápagos Wed. and Sat. four times daily ($167 one-way).

About one km south of the main airport is the small aircraft terminal, where other airlines, air taxis, and charters leave for coastal cities such as Bahía de Caráquez, Manta, and Esmeraldas. **Icaro Express** flies to Quito Mon.–Fri. ($55 one-way), and to Cuenca Tues.–Fri. ($33 one-way), and **Austro Aereo,** near the airport, tel. 4/296-687, 284-048, heads to Cuenca Mon.–Sat. at 9 A.M. and Mon.–Fri. at 5 P.M. for $29 pp one-way.

Water

The ferry for **Durán** from the north end of the Malecón was suspended during the construction of Malecón 2000 but should be running again soon for about 20 cents. The **Port Authority** is all the way south on 25 de Julio, near the mouth of the Estero de Muerto.

NEAR GUAYAQUIL

Cerro Blanco Protected Forest

This may well be the only nature reserve you'll ever encounter that owes its existence to the enlightened attitude and conservation efforts of a cement plant. Only 15 minutes from Guayaquil, Cerro Blanco protects 3,500 hectares of tropical dry forest in the Chongón-Colonche hills under the auspices of the El Cemento Nacional, which in turn profits off the plentiful limestone in the area.

GUAYAQUIL CONSULATES AND EMBASSIES

Most Guayaquil consulates and embassies are open Mon.–Fri. 9 A.M.–noon or 1 P.M.

Argentina: Aguirre 104 and Malecón, piso 4, tel./fax 4/323-574

Australia: Nahin Isaías and Luis Orrarte, Ed. Tecniseguros, Kennedy Norte, 4/680-823 or 680-700, fax 4/682-030

Austria: 9 de Octubre 1312 and Quito, tel./fax 4/282-303

Belgium: García 301 and Vélez, tel. 4/454-429, fax 4/454-234

Bolivia: Cedros 100 and Estrada, Urdesa, tel. 4/885-790 or 885-791, fax 4/885-789

Brazil: Av. del Periodista 312 and 3 Este, Nueva Kennedy, tel. 4/283-825, tel./fax 4/293-046

Canada: Córdova 810 and Rendón, Ed. Torres de la Merced, piso 4, tel. 4/563-580

Chile: 9 de Octubre 100 and Malecón, Ed. San Francisco, piso 23, of. 3, tel. 4/562-995, fax 4/565-151

Colombia: Córdova 1021 and 9 de Octubre, Ed. San Francisco 300, piso 22, of. 2, tel. 4/568-752 or 568-753, fax 4/568-749

Denmark: Córdova 604 and Mendiburu, tel. 4/308-020, fax 4/204-591

Finland: Urdaneta 212 and Córdova, tel. 4/564-268 or 564-381, fax 4/566-291

France: José Mascote and Hurtado, tel./fax 4/328-442

Germany: Las Monjas and Arosemena, kilometer 2.5, Ed. Berlin, tel. 4/200-500, fax 4/206-869

Holland: Ycaza 454 and Baquerizo Moreno, piso 2, tel. 4/563-857, fax 4/563-964

Israel: 9 de Octubre 729, piso 4, tel. 4/322-555 or 322-000, fax 4/328-196

Italy: 9 de Octubre 100 and Malecón, piso 23, of. 5, tel. 4/563-136, fax 4/563-140

Japan: Km. 11.5 via a Daule, tel. 4/253-055 or 253-600, fax 4/250-151

Mexico: Tulcán 1600 and Colón, tel./fax 4/372-928

Norway: 9 de Octubre 109 and Malecón, piso 4, tel. 4/329-661, fax 4/329-253

Panama: Aguirre 509 and Chimborazo, piso 9, of. 901, tel./fax 4/512-158

Peru: 9 de Octubre 411 and Chile, piso 6, tel. 4/322-738, fax 4/325-679

Spain: Circunvalación Sur 118 and Calle Unica, Urdesa, tel. 4/881-691

Sweden: Km 6.5 via a Daule, tel. 4/254-111, fax 4/254-244

Switzerland: 9 de Octubre 2101 and Tulcán, tel. 4/453-607, fax 4/435-289

United Kingdom: Córdova 623 and Solano, tel. 4/560-400, fax 4/562-641

United States: 9 de Octubre 1571 and García Moreno, tel. 4/323-570, fax 4/325-286

Venezuela: Chile 329 and Aguirre, piso 2, tel. 4/326-579 or 326-566, fax 4/320-751

Almost 200 species of birds include many waterfowl and the endangered great green macaw, the symbol of the reserve. Its nests (the first of which was found only in 1994) are closely guarded by park personnel. Morpho butterflies flash their turquoise wings by day, howler monkeys earn their name in the evenings, and crab-eating raccoons dip into water pools by night.

An interpretive center stands next to well-furnished campgrounds and the starting point for two trails: the short loop Quebrada Canoa and the longer, scenic Buenavista path. Natural-history guides are required on the trails. The center is open Sat. and Sun. 8:30 A.M.–3:30 P.M. It's possible to visit during the week, but you need to call ahead for reservations. Entrance to the reserve is $1.25 pp and about $5 to camp.

To get to Cerro Blanco on your own, take a "Transportes Chongón" bus from Parque Victoria, or any bus toward the Santa Elena Peninsula. In either case, look for the large sign just before the cement plant about 15 km from Guayaquil, near the community of Puerto Hondo. It's a short walk from there to the information center. For more information and mid-week reservations, contact the Fundación Pro-Bosque in Guayaquil, Cuenca and Eloy Alfaro, Ed. Multicomercio, piso 2, office 91, tel. 4/416-975, 417-004, fax 4/872-236.

Manglares Churute Ecological Reserve

This coastal reserve south of Guayaquil was created in 1979 to protect 34,985 hectares of mangroves from the ravages of shrimp farming. The tangled plants cover 67 percent of the park's area, and along with the surrounding salt flats provide shelter for a wide range of shorebirds, such as laughing gulls, roseate spoonbills, ospreys, herons, egrets, and ibis.

Manglares Churute is one of the few places in Ecuador to see horned screamers (the feathered kind). January, when water levels in the many shallow *lagunas* are highest, is the best time to view waterfowl. Inland stretches of dry tropical forest in the coastal Cordillera de Churute shelter white-fronted capuchin and mantled howler monkeys, along with the occasional agouti, tigrillo, and armadillo.

The road between Guayaquil and Machala passes the entrance to the reserve. Look (or ask) for the administrative center on the west side, near the pueblo of Churete, 26 km south of where the road splits at Boliche (itself 26 km east of Durán). Not all drivers know it, so make

sure yours knows exactly where you want to go or you may get dropped off in the middle of nowhere. Here you can pay the entrance fee ($10 for foreigners), view videos, and arrange for maps and guides for walks into the reserve. Trails lead downhill to the mangroves and up into the dry peaks of the Cerros El Mirador and Masvale. Boats to explore the mangroves, with room for 20 people, can be hired for $12 per day.

South to Machala
The route south from Guayaquil to the Perúvian border passes through the least interesting section of Ecuador's coast. It's drier here than it is farther north, giving southbound travelers a taste of northern Perú's coastal desert. Thorny scrub and cactus survive on 25 cm of rain per year, dropped during a rainy season that is two months shorter than usual. Even so, plantations of coffee, citrus fruits, and bananas thrive along the way.

MACHALA AND VICINITY

Sometimes it seems as if every major human settlement has its claim to fame, from the City of Brotherly Love to the Largest Ball of Twine East of the Mississippi. The capital of El Oro province proclaims itself Banana Capital of the World, and it's easy to see why, with acre after acre of neatly planted fronds waving in the coastal breeze in every direction. Every morning the beach writhes with fresh-caught fish, and it seems as if everyone in town is helping clean them.

After its founding in 1758, Machala (pop. 200,000) enjoyed a cacao boom in the early 20th century that resulted in most of the economic development of the southern coast before the yellow torpedo took over in the 1930s. Even the rise of shrimp farming in the 1980s didn't shake the banana's hold—more than one million tons a year leave through Puerto Bolívar, seven km west. Over the decades, these agricultural bonanzas have made El Oro's capital one of the most prosperous—and well-kept—cities on Ecuador's coast.

Orientation
Machala's streets are oriented diagonally, running northeast-southwest and northwest-south-

east. The main thoroughfare, 9 de Octubre, runs along the northeast side of the **Parque Central** and the city's **cathedral.** North one block along 9 de Mayo, you'll find the main **outdoor market.** About five blocks southeast of the market on Olmedo is the **Parque Colón,** and you'll hit the **Parque de los Héroes** five blocks northwest of the Parque Central.

Accommodations
Many travelers crossing the border prefer to spend the night here rather than in Huaquillas, and for good reason—Machala is a much more pleasant place. Budget rooms with private bath and air-conditioning have been recommended at the friendly **Hostal Mercy,** Junín between Olmedo and Sucre, tel. 7/920-116 ($2 pp), and at the **Hotel Mosquera Internacional,** Olmedo between Guayas and Ayacucho, tel. 7/931-140 ($6 pp). The **Hotel Ecuatoriano,** 9 de Octubre and Colón, tel. 7/930-197, 962-077, has large rooms with private bath and air-conditioning for $2.50 pp.

Rooms with private bath, cable TV, and air-conditioning at the **Hotel Marsella,** Las Palmeras and 9 de Octubre, tel. 7/935-577 or 932-460,

peace painting, Huaquillas

TIM BEWER

cost $8 s, $12.50 d. Even better accommodations at the **Hotel Rizzo,** Guayas 2123 and Bolívar, tel. 7/921-511, run $13.50 s, $18.50 d. They have a pool, disco, restaurant, casino, and private parking.

Luxury travelers should steer toward the **Hotel Oro Verde,** Circunvalación Norte and Calle Vehicular V7, tel. 7/933-140, fax 7/933-150, in the suburbs 10 minutes out of town. It has 58 rooms and 12 suites for $138 s, $162 d. Gourmands can sample the La Fondue Swiss restaurant, as well as a café and gourmet deli. Reservations can be made in the United States through Prime Hotels, 800/447-7462, 212/223-2848, e-mail: ecovm@gye.satnet.net.

Food
The short hop to **Puerto Bolívar** is well worth it for the wide selection of fresh seafood. It can be hard to choose when three places right next to each other all advertise the "best ceviche in the world," but hey—that makes it hard to go wrong, doesn't it?

In Machala itself, **Don Angelo** on 9 de Mayo at Rocafuerte, scores points for its breakfasts, large portions, and for being open 24 hours. Seafood and pastas average around $1.50. Also try the **Chifa Central** on Tarquí between 9 de Octubre and Sucre, where the air-conditioning is set on "arctic" and nothing will cost you more than $2, and the **Cafetería Americana,** on Olmedo between Guayas and Ayacucho, which serves reasonably priced Ecuadorian food (go figure).

Chesco Pizzeria, on Guayas half a block north of the Parque Central, has good pizzas starting at $1.25 (call 7/936-418 for delivery). Full *almuerzos* are only $1 at **El Paraiso de la Vida,** a vegetarian restaurant on Ayacucho at 9 de Octubre.

Entertainment and Events
Machala's **Banana World Fair** slides into town the third week in September, but movies happen all year round at the **Cine Popular** on Sucre between Guayas and 9 de Mayo. Their film selection varies, so you'll probably find better pickings at the **Unioro Mall** on the northeast edge of town, where relatively recent movies are often shown with Spanish subtitles. Take bus number 1 from the Parque Central, or a taxi for less than $1. The **Peña de Machala,** on Guayas just north of the Parque Central, has live music every night.

Services and Information
Exchange travelers' checks at **Delgado Travel** on 9 de Mayo near the plaza. There's also a **Banco del Pacífico,** Rocafuerte and Junín, and half a dozen other banks along the Parque Central. The **post office** is at Bolívar and Montalvo, and **Pacifictel** sits on 9 de Octubre between Palmeras and Vélez.

For border matters, stop by the **Perúvian consulate,** tel. 7/930-680, on the second floor of the north corner of Bolívar and Colón. For questions about Manglares Churute, the **Ministry of** the **Interior** has an office on 9 de Mayo and Pichincha, tel. 7/932-106.

Medical emergencies are handled 24 hours a day by the **Hospital Teófilo Dávila**, tel. 7/937-581, on the Parque Colón.

Both **Ciber@yogur**, on 9 de Mayo half a block down from the Ministry of the Interior, and **C@quí.net**, 1324 9 de Octubre at Ayacucho, offer public Internet access.

Transportation

Machala's airport is about one km southwest of the center along Montalvo. From there you can fly with **TAME**, Montalvo between Pichincha and Bolívar, tel. 7/930-139 or 932-710, to Guayaquil (Mon.–Fri., $17.50 pp) and Quito (Mon.–Fri., $25 pp). **Icaro Express** has flights to the capital Monday mornings and Thursday afternoons.

There's no main long-distance bus terminal—just pick your destination and head to the respective *cooperativa* office. CIFA, on Bolívar and Guayas, leaves every 20 minutes throughout the day for **Huaquillas** ($1, 75 minutes). For buses to **Guayaquil** ($2.25, four hours), visit Ecuatoriano Pullman, 9 de Octubre and Colón, or Rutas Orenses, 9 de Octubre and Tarquí. CIFA also goes to Guayauil from 9 de Octubre and Tarquí. Transportes Occidentales, Buenavista and Olmedo, and Panamericana, Colón and Bolívar, go to **Quito** ($6.50, 10 hours), and Transportes Cooperativa Loja, Tarquí and Rocafuerte, heads for **Loja** ($3.50, six hours).

Cuenca ($2.25, 4.5 hours) is also a destination for Rutas Orensas plus Transportes Pullman Sucre and Azuay, both on Sucre between Junín and Tarquí. Cooperativa TAC, on Colón between Rocafuerte and Bolívar, sends buses hourly throughout the day to **Zaruma** ($1.50, three hours).

Jambelí

Facing the Gulf of Guayaquil from the northern tip of the Archipelago de Jambelí, this popular beach resort becomes crammed with Machala's hard-working residents during weekends and holidays. Inexpensive restaurants and hotels cater to local beachgoers and the few foreign tourists who visit. You'll find plenty of cabañas and tents for rent, which is good because there's little shade on the beach. The place is almost deserted midweek, and many businesses close.

Motorized canoes leave Mon.–Fri. every few hours from the old pier in Puerto Bolívar until 4 P.M., returning until 6 P.M. ($1 round-trip), and on weekends when full, which is often. The trip through the estuary affords birders some small relief from the brackish heat, with the chance to view rufous-necked wood rail or yellow-crowned night heron.

Huaquillas

Ecuador's busiest southern border town sits across the Río Zarumilla from Perú, with plenty of signs celebrating the recent peace accords. Perúvians cross here regularly to take advantage of lower prices on the Ecuadorian side. Many residents work as *hormigas* (ants) by carrying contraband across or under the bridge on their backs.

Facilities are marginal, but at least everything's on or near Av. La Republica, the main street. For budget rooms, the **Hotel Guayaquil**, behind the customs office, is endured more than enjoyed by travelers arriving too late to cross the border the same day. Private rooms are $3 pp with fans. You'll find much more of the same one block west on Cordóvez. The **post office** is in the customs building, and **Pacifictel** sits across the street. Money changers line the main street, so it's easy (if sketchy) to find someone to change your travelers' checks.

To cross the border, get your exit stamp at the Ecuadorian immigration office 4–5 km outside of town. From here you can cross freely into Aguas Verdes, as the Perúvian side is called. Complete the entrance formalities in the Perúvian immigration office a few kilometers beyond the bridge; taxis waiting to take you farther into Perú will stop here.

Panamericana runs a handful of direct buses to Quito daily ($7, 14 hours), and **Ecuatoriana Pullman** leaves regularly to Guayaquil ($1, four hours). **CIFA** has frequent departures direct to Machala ($1, 75 minutes).

Puyango Petrified Forest

The largest petrified forest outside of Arizona hides in a small section of the Río Puyango valley. Trunks of the *Auracaria* trees, whose cellulose has been replaced over millennia by water-soluble minerals, can reach over 10 meters long and 1.5 meters around. Worm holes are clearly visible in the stone giants, and if you look hard you can find many other species of plants and ferns trapped in surrounding rocks.

A dirt road runs south from Arenillas through Palmales and La Victoria before reaching the village of Puyango after 50 km. Loja buses from Machala make the trip, although you'll have to change buses along the way. There's a visitors center in the village where you can pay the $5 entrance fee before crossing the bridge to the reserve. Ask there for directions to a good campsite near the Río Chirimoya. For more information, contact the Puyango Petrified Forest Administrative Commission, Ciudadela Las Brisas, Mazana B-6, Villa 2, Apto. 5, Machala, tel./fax 7/937-655, tel. 7/930-012.

Up Into the Hills

Heading east toward Loja and the southernmost Sierra, a short detour via Piñas to the mining country around **Zaruma** provides a glimpse into the southern Sierra's ancient heart of ore. Spanish King Felipe II decreed the establishment of Zaruma in 1549 to serve as a base for gold extraction, which provided an easy choice of the eventual name for the province itself—El Oro.

By now the lodes have been picked almost clean, but visits to the mines can still be arranged (you'll marvel and cringe at the almost prehistoric equipment). Locals can point out a set of **thermal baths** in the nearby hills, and the usual smattering of basic *residenciales* and restaurants anchor the town itself. Buses run to Machala often.

BOB RACE

SOUTHERN SIERRA
INTRODUCTION

The highland provinces of Cañar, Azuay, and Loja contain few peaks higher than 4,000 meters but still enclose some of the most rugged topography in the country. Ecuador's long-running border dispute with Perú (settled in 1998) centered around the forbidding Cordillera del Condor in the southernmost Amazonian province of Zamora-Chinchipe. It was the region's inaccessibility (one river was discovered only in 1947) that, along with decades of political posturing, made it almost impossible to determine where one country ended and the other began.

Because of its historical isolation from the rest of the country—major highways didn't connect Cuenca to Quito and Guayaquil until the 1960s—the entire area has held firmly onto it roots. Cuenca's colonial heart beats strongly after centuries, and older ruins within the city tie it to its pre-Columbian past. Indigenous groups such as the Saraguros and descendants of the Cañaris retain traditions that predate the Inca.

Although the southern Sierra lacks the immense national park lands of its northern neighbors, outdoor enthusiasts can still get their fill here. Vistas of lakes and misty hills in El Cajas National Recreation Area rival any in the country, and intrepid hikers will uncover unique treasures in Podocarpus National Park. The three-day hike along the lofty Inca Trail, south from Achupallas, ends at Ingapirca, Ecuador's premiere set of Inca ruins.

Most tours of the region begin in Cuenca, which can be reached by bus from Riobamba (quite a haul, albeit scenic) or on the less popular uphill route from Machala. The road connecting Loja with the Oriente via Zamora is used even less but passes through some of the least-visited areas in the country. Daily flights connect Cuenca with Quito and Guayaquil.

The southern Sierra is usually your first or last glimpse of Ecuador if you're traveling overland via Perú. Huaquillas on the coast and Macará south of Loja are the main places to cross the border, and there are smaller, infrequently used border posts at Zapotillo, Amaluza, and Zumba.

SOUTHERN SIERRA

GUAYAQUIL Durán

Alausi To Riobamba
Achupallas
INCA TRAIL
LOS PAREDONES RUINS
Tambo
Cañar
INGAPIRCA RUINS
Rio Paute

Manglares
Churute
Ecological
Reserve

Naranjal

LAGUNA TOREADORA VISITORS' CENTER

Biblián
Azogues
Paute
Bulcay
Gualaceo
Chordeleg
Rio Gualaceo

ANGAS GUARDPOST

Cuenca

EL CAJAS NATIONAL RECREATION AREA

SOLDADOS GUARDPOST

Isla Puná

Golfo de Guayaquil

Girón

Sígsig

Jambeli
Puerto Bolívar
Machala
Pasaje

Oña

Gualaquiza

PANAMERICANA

Santa Rosa

Huaquillas
To Tumbes, Peru
Arenillas

Saraguro

Zaruma

Yantzaza Rio Zamora

Puyango
PUYANGO PETRIFIED FOREST Alamar
Celica
Catacocha
Rio Catamayo

El Cisne

Nambija

Catamayo Loja

Zamora
CAJANUMA GUARDPOST
BOMBUSCARA GUARDPOST
ROMERILLOS GUARDPOST

PODOCARPUS NATIONAL PARK

Zapotillo
Macará
La Tina

Vilcabamba

Cariamanga

Rio Mayo

To Sullana

Amaluza

PERU

Las Lomas

PERU

Zumba

0   15 mi
0   15 km

© AVALON TRAVEL PUBLISHING, INC.

CUENCA AND VICINITY

Like a trio of siblings, Ecuador's three largest cities have distinct personalities. Eldest Quito is the successful one, dressed up and ready for business (though with a wild side that comes out at night). Guayaquil lazes on the coast, can never keep its bedroom clean, but somehow makes more money than anyone. Cuenca takes its studies seriously, keeps its pants creased, and always makes the grandparents proud. The latter, the capital of Azuay province, is a pious, dignified city with the most intact colonial character in the country. What some would call stuffy, others call stately—either way, Cuenca seeps reverence from every pore. To dispel any lingering doubt, the city's municipal motto is *Primero Díos, Después Vos:* "First God, Then You."

With more than 400,000 inhabitants, Cuenca still has a surprisingly small-town feel—nuns stroll down narrow cobbled streets and everyone seems to know everyone else. The "Athens of Ecuador" also boasts three universities and was the first regular meeting place of poets in Latin America.

Things close early, and there's not much to do after dark, but that leaves the early evenings free for wandering and enjoying the play of sun-set light on the famous New Cathedral—entertainment enough for the poetically inclined.

Cuenca has become popular with travelers looking for a quiet, scenic city to settle down and study Spanish for a few weeks or months. It's an ideal city for strolling, whether along the banks of a river or among its many outstanding churches, theaters, and museums.

History

Cuenca began as a Cañari settlement called Guapondelig, meaning "plain and wide as the sky." The Incas moved in against fierce resistance in the 15th century and transformed the site into the palatial Tomebamba, favorite residence of Huanya Capac and ruling hub of the Quitosuyo, the northern reaches of the Inca empire. Its grounds and buildings, suitably fit for a king, were said to rival Cuzco itself.

In the civil war after the sudden death of the ruling Inca, his son Atahualpa was briefly imprisoned here by his half-brother with the help of the local Cañari *indígenas.* After a narrow escape (by supposedly turning into a snake), Atahualpa defeated his brother and razed the city in revenge, putting its entire population to death.

Spanish lieutenant Gil Ramirez Dávalos refounded the city in 1557. Alongside Quito and Guayaquil, it served as a capital of one of the three provinces that made up the territory of Ecuador. Growth over the following centuries was slow because of Cuenca's isolation from the northern Sierra. The 1739 French equator-measuring expedition provided the most excitement in years. It wasn't until the mid-20th century that decent roads connecting Cuenca to the rest of the country were completed, transforming it from a sleepy market center into a modern city with the requisite factories, suburbs, and clamor. Luckily for visitors, it still retained enough of its colonial character that its historical center was declared a World Cultural Heritage Site by UNESCO.

Orientation

Four rivers feed the fertile Paucarabamba Valley that cradles Cuenca, originally named Santa

---

CONSULATES IN CUENCA

Brazil: Ordõnez Lazo, tel. 7/844-932

Chile: Tomás Ordõnez 3-27, tel. 7/840-061

Colombia: 12 de Abril and Peralta, Ed. Paseo del Puente, piso 2, tel. 7/830-185

France: Torres 1-92 and Solano, tel. 7/848-314

Germany: Bolívar 9-18, tel. 7/835-980

United Kingdom: Plazoleta de San Alfoso, pta. baja 9A, tel. 7/831-996

Italy: Jaime Roldós 4-80 and Huayna Capac, Ed. El Consorcio, piso 3, tel. 7/861-679

Spain: Estadio 3-40 and Calle, ed. El Ejido 3-40, tel. 7/810-211

U.S.: Borrero 5-18, Centro Abraham Lincoln, tel. 7/823-898

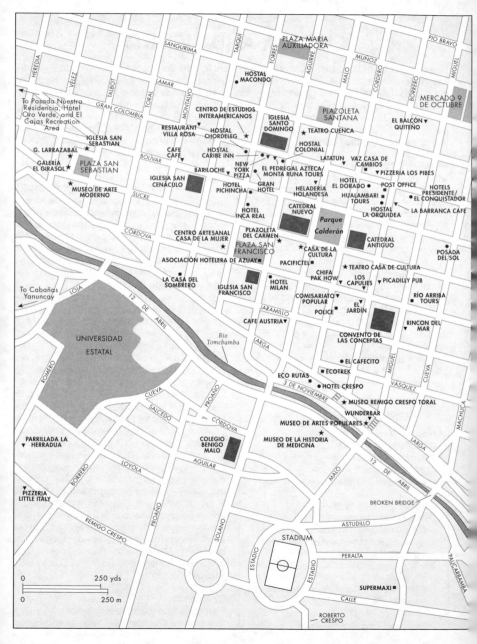

SANGURIMA

TARQUI

PLAZA MARIA
AUXILIADORA

PIO BRAVO

HEREDIA

VÉLEZ

TALBOT

LAMAR

MONTALVO

TORRES

AGUIRRE

MUÑOZ

MALO

CORDERO

BORRERO

MIGUEL

HOSTAL
MACONDO

GRAN COLOMBIA

TORAL

MERCADO 9
DE OCTUBRE

To Posada Nuestra
Residencia, Hotel
Oro Verde, and El
Cajas Recreation
Area

CENTRO DE ESTUDIOS
INTERAMERICANOS

PLAZOLETA
SANTANA

EL BALCÓN
QUITEÑO

RESTAURANT
VILLA ROSA

HOSTAL
CHORDELEG ★

IGLESIA
SANTO
DOMINGO

★ TEATRO CUENCA

IGLESIA SAN
SEBASTIÁN

CAFE
CAFE ▼

HOSTAL
CARIBE INN ★

HOSTAL
COLONIAL

G. LARRAZÁBAL

BOLÍVAR

LATATUN

VAZ CASA DE
CAMBIOS

GALERÍA
EL GIRASOL ★

PLAZA SAN
SEBASTIÁN

BARILOCHE ▼

NEW
YORK
PIZZA

EL PEDREGAL AZTECA/
MONTA RUNA TOURS

▼ PIZZERIA LOS PIBES

★ MUSEO DE ARTE
MODERNO

IGLESIA SAN
CENÁCULO

HOTEL
PICHINCHA

GRAN
HOTEL

HELADERÍA
HOLANDESA

HOTEL
EL DORADO ●

POST OFFICE

HOTELS
PRESIDENTE/
EL CONQUISTADOR

SUCRE

HOTEL
INCA REAL

CATEDRAL
NUEVO

HUALAMBARI
TOURS

HOSTAL
LA ORQUIDEA

LA BARRANCA CAFE

CÓRDOVA

Parque
Calderón

CENTRO ARTESANAL
CASA DE LA MUJER

PLAZOLETA
DEL CARMEN

CATEDRAL
ANTIGUO

POSADA
DEL SOL

PLAZA SAN
FRANCISCO

★ CASA DE LA
CULTURA

ASOCIACIÓN HOTELERA DE AZUAY ■

PACIFICTEL ▼

★ TEATRO CASA DE CULTURA

LA CASA DEL
SOMBRERO ■

CHIFA
PAK HOW

LOS
CAPULIES

▼ PICADILLY PUB

To Cabañas
Yanuncay

LOJA

IGLESIA SAN
FRANCISCO

HOTEL
MILAN

COMISARIATO
POPULAR ▼

EL
JARDIN

RÍO ARRIBA
TOURS

JARAMILLO

POLICE ■

RINCON DEL
MAR

CAFE AUSTRIA ▼

LARGA

CONVENTO DE
LAS CONCEPTAS

UNIVERSIDAD
ESTATAL

Río
Tomebamba

ROMERO

● EL CAFECITO

MIGUEL

12 DE ABRIL

CUEVA

■ ECOTREK

ECO RUTAS ●

VÁSQUEZ

CUEVA

SALCEDO

PROANO

CÓRDOVA

3 DE NOVIEMBRE

● HOTEL CRESPO

★ MUSEO REMIGO CRESPO TORAL

MACHUCA

WUNDERBAR

PARRILLADA LA
HERRADUA ▼

COLEGIO
BENIGO
MALO

MUSEO DE ARTES POPULARES ★

MUSEO DE LA HISTORIA
DE MEDICINA

LARGA

LOYOLA

AGUILAR

MALO

12 DE ABRIL

BORRERO

PROANO

▼ PIZZERIA
LITTLE ITALY

REMIGO CRESPO

SOLANO

BROKEN BRIDGE

ASTUDILLO

PALCARBAMBA

ESTADIO

STADIUM

ESTADIO

PERALTA

0 — 250 yds
0 — 250 m

SUPERMAXI ■

CALLE

ROBERTO
CRESPO

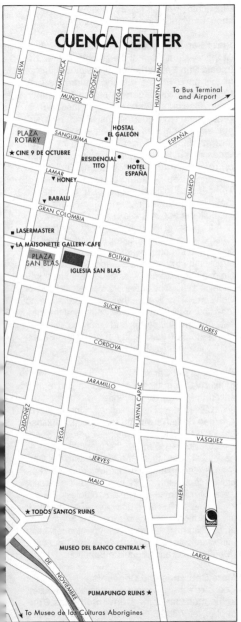

CUENCA CENTER

CUEVA

MACHUCA

ORDONEZ

VEGA

HUAYNA CAPAC

MUNOZ

To Bus Terminal
and Airport

PLAZA
ROTARY

SANGURIMA

HOSTAL
EL GALEÓN

ESPAÑA

★ CINE 9 DE OCTUBRE

RESIDENCIAL
TITO

HOTEL
ESPAÑA

OLMEDO

LAMAR

▼ HONEY

▼ BABALU

GRAN COLOMBIA

■ LASERMASTER

▼ LA MAISONETTE GALLERY CAFE

PLAZA
SAN BLAS

BOLÍVAR

IGLESIA SAN BLAS

SUCRE

FLORES

CÓRDOVA

JARAMILLO

H JAYNA CAPAC

ORDONEZ

VEGA

VÁSQUEZ

JERVES

MALO

MERA

★ TODOS SANTOS RUINS

MUSEO DEL BANCO CENTRAL ★

LARGA

3 DE NOVIEMBRE

PUMAPUNGO RUINS ★

To Museo de las Culturas Aborigines

© AVALON TRAVEL PUBLISHING, INC.

Ana de los Cuatro Ríos de Cuenca by the Spanish (*cuenca* means "river basin"). The Ríos Tomebamba and Yanuncay drain El Cajas National Recreation Area to the west, joining with the Ríos Tarquí and Machángara to form the Río Cuenca on their way east to the jungle. The Tomebamba divides the city center into two sections: to the north the historical center is little changed since colonial times, whereas gleaming glass buildings and modern suburbs are visible to the south.

Safety

On the whole, central Cuenca is safe to walk around in until 10 P.M. or so, although it's wise to take care in the market areas, particularly the Mercado 9 de Octubre. As in most large cities, visitors afoot are always best off in a group.

Reports once came in regularly about a pudgy local man who befriended female travelers by asking them to write letters for him, then raped them. Sightings of this man have become less and less frequent over the years, but it never hurts to be on guard. Hopefully this character has entered the realms of urban myth.

SIGHTS

Cuenca's wealth of religious architecture makes it easy to believe the saying that the city has 52 **churches**—one for every Sunday of the year. Many are attached to **convents,** self-contained worlds of sacrifice and austere beauty that have changed little in centuries. The churches of San Francisco and San Blas once marked the city's boundaries.

Parque Calderón

Tall palms and taller pines fill Cuenca's central park. On the west side sits one of Ecuador's architectural wonders—the massive Catedral de la Inmaculada, usually called simply the **Catedral Nuevo** (New Cathedral). Begun in 1880 by an ambitious local bishop who decided the old cathedral wasn't big enough, it was originally planned to be South America's largest church, with room for 10,000 worshippers. Work stopped in 1908 because of "architectural miscalculations," leaving the twin square towers unfinished. The pink marble facade and blue domes (cov-

JULIAN SMITH

Cuenca features a wealth of religious architecture.

domes (covered with tiles imported from Czechoslovakia) are unmistakable.

Inside, the Catedral Nuevo is even more awe-inspiring, humbling patrons into reverence with its pink shadows and stained glass from Belgium and Germany. Services fill the nave with keening voices chanting prayers in Latin and Spanish. Even if you're feeling burned-out on churches, this one is not to be missed.

The Catedral El Sagrario, also known as the **Catedral Antiguo** (Old Cathedral) is the city's oldest building, begun in 1567 with stones from the ruins of the Inca palace of Pumapungo. The steeple was used by La Condamine's group as one of the fixed points in the measurements of tho equator, inspiring a Spanish scientist visiting in 1804 to comment that this spire was more famous than the pyramids. Religious services were held here until the construction of the Catedral Nuevo. As of 2000, the structure was under renovation.

Opposite the Catedral Nuevo, at the intersection of Sucre and Malo, the **Casa de la Cul-tura** contains an art gallery, museum, and bookshop. Exhibits by local artists change often.

Plaza San Sebastian

At the western edge of the colonial center, the **Iglesia San Sebastian** occupies the north side of this park. Facing it is the **Museo de Arte Moderno,** which began as a Casa de Temperancia (House of Temperance). In the late 19th century, the story goes, a local bishop returning home one night was said to have come across a victim of the Devil's drink laid out in the street. When the sot turned out to be a priest, the bishop decided that Cuenca's drunks needed a place to sleep it off and began the House of Temperance in 1876. Cells used to house the inebriated were later used for criminals when the building became a jail.

After passing through various incarnations as a home for beggars, children, and the insane, the stately old structure was barely saved from destruction by the famous Ecuadorian painter Luis Crespo Ordoñez and was inaugurated as a museum in 1981. The setup is excellent, with lots of white space (notice the thick colonial walls) and long flower-filled courtyards setting off the intricate modern sculptures and paintings. It's open Mon.–Fri. 8:30 A.M.–6:30 P.M., Sat. and Sun. 9 A.M.–1 P.M.; admission is free.

Plazoleta del Carmen

Flower vendors fill this tiny square plaza, also called the Plaza de las Flores, with colors and scents every day. The twin spires of the **Iglesia El Carmen de la Asunción,** founded in 1682, rise behind a small fountain. Stones carved in Spanish baroque style frame the main entrance. A handful of nuns inhabit the **Monasterio del Carmen,** spending their days in prayer and contemplation completely cut off from the outside world, except for a small festival on 16 July in the adjoining plaza. The nuns do not even accept medical attention, but locals can leave offerings in an opening near the entrance. A painted refractory includes colonial masterworks by Caspicara (Manuel Chili) and Miguel de Santiago.

More Churches and Convents

Cuenca's richest religious art collection is housed in the museum of the **Convento de las Conceptas,** tel. 7/830-625, occupying the whole block between Córdova, Jaramillo, Borrero, and Miguel (the entrance is on Miguel). In the late 17th century, one Doña Ordóñez dedicated one of the finest houses in the city to serve as the convent, on the condition that her three daughters would be accepted (the house also served as their down payment to enter, a common practice in colonial times). The doors were shut in 1682, leaving a holiday on 8 December as one of the few times the Carmelite nuns are allowed to glimpse the outside world. Twenty-two rooms of sculpture and painting include many treasures from the Sangurima school of colonial art, along with crucifixes dating to the 17th century. Open Mon. 9 A.M.–noon and 2:30–5:30 P.M., Tues.–Fri. 9:30 A.M.–5:30 P.M., Sat. 10 A.M.–1 P.M. for $2 pp.

The Virgen del Rosario is the most precious icon in the **Iglesia Santo Domingo,** on Colombia between Torres and Aguirre. Gold and jewels donated by Cuenca's wealthiest women encrust the Virgin's crown. The modest exterior of the **Iglesia San Francisco,** on the plaza of the same name, belies a lavish baroque altarpiece inside, which is intricately carved and covered with gold leaf.

If you haven't hit your church limit quite yet, take a peek at the **Iglesia San Cenáculo,** on Bolívar and Tarquí, or the **Iglesia San Blas** on Ordóñez and Bolívar, built in 1575 with stones from the Inca palace of Pumapungo.

More Museums

At the bottom of the steps of Escalinata (a continuation of Miguel) along the river is the **Museo de Artes Populares,** tel. 7/828-878, with a museum of folk art, library, and excellent crafts shop all run by the Interamerican Center for the Development of Popular Arts (CIDAP). They have a very good collection of crafts and clothing from across Latin America; the display on how Panama hats are woven is particularly interesting. Visit the museum Mon.–Fri. 9:30 A.M.–1 P.M. and 2:30–6 P.M., Sat. 10 A.M.–1 P.M.

Even fans of the macabre will consider the **Museo de la Historia de la Medicina** (Medical History Museum) one of the most bizarre collections they have ever seen. Anything that had anything to do with the old military hospital whose grounds it occupies is on display, from ledger books and bed pans to an X-ray machine that would make Dr. Frankenstein proud. As if to make the collection even more unsettling, everything is displayed in stark white rooms either in bright yellow cases or just laying on the floor—that's including the corpses. (Fans of hip modern art will notice an uncanny similarity to the works of Damien Hirst.) This is one place that really needs to be seen to be believed. It's across the river on 12 de Octubre, open 8:30 A.M.–noon, 2:30–5 P.M., 20 cents pp.

Slightly downstream, you can't miss the smoked-glass edifice of the Banco Central, with the best archaeological collection in the southern Sierra next door in its **Museo del Banco Central,** tel. 7/835-255. Much of the pre-Columbian pottery and figurines were collected by Padre Carlos Crespi, a local friar who believed devoutly in the theory that coastal Ecuador was settled by the Phonecians. Antique musical instruments, local art, time-faded photos of Cuenca, and libraries share the building, and the entrance fee includes access to the Pumapungo ruins out back. It's open Mon.–Fri. 9 A.M.–6 P.M., Sat. 9 A.M.–1 P.M. and costs $1 pp.

The **Museo Remigo Crespo Toral,** Larga 7-07 and Borrero, tel. 7/830-499, contains a sparse but high-quality collection. Religious sculptures, paintings, archaeological relics, and *artesanías* fill the creaking wooden building overlooking the Río Tomebamba. It's open Mon.–Fri. 8:30 A.M.–1 P.M. and 3–6 P.M., Sat. and Sun. 9 A.M.–1 P.M.; free admission.

A short taxi ride can drop you off at the **Museo de las Culturas Aborigines,** tel. 7/880-010, a little more than one km south at 10 de Agosto 4-70 between Moscoso and Sánchez. The private collection displayed in the house of the Cordero-López family was recently opened to the public and includes 5,000 pre-Columbian pieces spanning every Ecuadorian culture up to the Spanish conquest. Optional guides speak English, Spanish, and French. Hours are Mon.–Fri. 8:30 A.M.–1 P.M. and 3–6:30 P.M., Sat. and Sun. 10 A.M.–3 P.M.; admission is $2 pp.

Pumapungo Ruins

Huayna Capac's palace-away-from-home had already fallen into ruin in 1547 when Spanish chronicler Pedro Cieza de León rode through. "These famous lodgings," he wrote, "were among the finest and richest to be found in all [the viceroyalty of] Perú, and the buildings the largest and best . . . . Today all is cast down and in ruins, but still it can be seen how great they were." Many Pumapungo stones were used to build the foundations and walls of buildings in Cuenca's colonial center.

German archaeologist Max Uhle rediscovered the ruins in 1922. Along with a temple to Viracocha, the Inca creator-god, Uhle uncovered the skeleton of a man in a specially widened section of wall: evidence of the pre-Columbian custom of burying a man alive in the foundation of a new wall to give it strength. Shattered jars, widespread scorching, and rooms filled with ash gave silent witness to Pumapungo's violent end.

The history of Pumapungo is more interesting than the ruins themselves—all that remains today are a series of low walls and niches still under excavation. The site, part of the Banco Central Museum, is open Mon.–Fri. 9 A.M.–6 P.M., Sat. 9 A.M.–1 P.M.

Todos Santos Ruins

In 1970, workers clearing a small park between Larga and Avenida Todos Santos unearthed a confusing jumble of rocks. Careful digging revealed layers of cultures: large, crude blocks of Cañari origin, finer Inca stonework with characteristic trapezoidal niches, and a Spanish watermill using both of the previous styles as a foundation. The site is now open to the public, along with a small site museum on Larga. For more information, call 7/832-639. The museum is open Mon.–Fri. 9 A.M.–1 P.M. and 3–6 P.M., Sat. 9 A.M.–1 P.M., 20 cents pp.

Architecture and Greenspace

The round portico of the **Banco del Azuay** at Bolívar and Borrero features Doric columns supporting a cupola of rose-colored marble. The same material decorates the imposing three-story facade of the **Palacio de Justicia** on the southeast corner of the Parque Calderón, originally built for use as the University of Cuenca.

The grassy slopes of the Río Tomebamba, known as **La Barranca,** make an afternoon meander down 3 de Noviembre one of the more enjoyable in the country. Colonial houses and modern apartments spill down from Larga almost to the river's bank, where indigenous women still lay out their colorful wash to dry.

ACCOMMODATIONS

Hotels in Cuenca are generally of a higher standard than those in the rest of the country. All have private bath and hot water unless noted otherwise. Cuenca's best rooms for the money fall into the midrange price categories. Many are converted colonial houses, with shady courtyards ringed by interior balconies.

Less than $10

The Swiss-run **El Cafecito,** Vásquez 7-36 and Cordero, tel. 7/832-337, e-mail: elcafe @ cue.satenet.net, is a funky little place that's often full. It's attached to a popular café that features live music on weekends. Rooms are $2 pp in the dorm and $4 pp with private bath. The **Hotel España,** Sangurima 1-17 and Huayna Capac, tel. 7/831-351 or 834-206, fax 7/846-442, has rooms with TV and phones for $5.50 s, $9.50 d, including breakfast.

At the **Hostal Caribe Inn,** Colombia 10-51 and Aguirre, tel. 7/835-175, tel./fax 7/826-227, rooms are a deal at $4 s, $7 d, with breakfast included. The **Hotel Milan,** Córdova 9-89 and Aguirre, tel. 7/831-104, is another good value, with the same prices as the Hostal Caribe Inn and balconies with views of the Plaza San Francisco to boot. They run day tours in the surrounding area and offer mountain bikes to rent for $4 per day, including helmets.

Rooms with TV are $4 pp at the **Residencial Tito,** Sangurima 1-49 and Vega, tel. 7/829-734 or 835-921, fax 7/843-577, and the **Hostal El Galeón,** Sangurima 2-42, tel. 7/831-827, has cavernous chambers for $3 pp. The secure **Hotel Pichincha,** Torres 8-82 and Bolívar, tel. 7/823-405 or 823-868, is an immense building run like clockwork by dueña Sara Muñoz. With rooms for only $2, it's justifiably popular with the backpacking set. The owners offer the same impeccable service in fancier surroundings at the **Hostal Pichincha Internacional,** Montalvo 9-78 between Colombia and Bolívar, tel./fax 7/833-695, where $6 pp gets you a room with TV and telephone.

At the **Hostal Colonial,** Gran Colombia 10-13 and Aguirre, tel./fax 7/841-644, 823-793, e-mail: hcolonial@cue.satnet.net, rooms around a pleasant courtyard are $8 pp, including TV and refrigerator. The restored colonial home also houses a good restaurant. Finally, the **Gran Hotel,** Torres 9-70 between Bolívar and Gran Colombia, tel. 7/831-934, fax 7/831-819, has 33 spotless quarters with TVs around a covered courtyard for $6 s, $9 d.

$10–25

The colonial **Macondo Hostal,** Tarquí 11-64 and Lamar, tel. 7/840-697, fax 7/833-593, e-mail: macondo@redei.org, offers kitchen facilities for guests near its interior garden. Rates are $9.50 s, $14.50 d for shared bath and $14.50 s, $19.50 d with private bath—some consider this overpriced, but that doesn't keep it from being popular. The owners offer city tours and day trips.

Numerous travelers recommend the **Posada Nuestra Residencia,** Los Pinos 1-1004 and Ordoñez Lazo, tel. 7/831-702, fax 7/835-576, a bed-and-breakfast just west of the city center. Bilingual owners Rafael and Lucía Carrión are gracious hosts and offer guests eight comfortable rooms with cable TV for $15 s, $25 d (including breakfast, of course). One room has a kitchenette, and there's a garden, fireplace, and outdoor barbecue for everyone to enjoy.

If you stay at the **Hotel Presidente,** Colombia 6-59 and Miguel, tel. 7/831-066 or 831-341, e-mail: hotelpresidente@yahoo.com, try to get a room on one of the upper floors for the best views. Rates are $15.50 s, $20.50 d up high, or $12 s, $15.50 d on the bottom floors, including breakfast. The **Hotel El Conquistador,** Colombia 6-65 and Borrero, tel. 7/831-788, fax 7/831-291, is slightly more expensive at $20 s, $24 d, including cable TV, refrigerators, breakfast buffet, and airport transportation.

For $7 s, $14 d, rooms at the **Hostal La Orquidea,** Borrero 9-31 and Bolívar, tel. 7/824-511, fax 7/835-844, are a bargain. Each has a TV and phone, and there's a good restaurant on the premises. The colonial **Hostal Chordeleg,** Colombia and Torres, tel. 7/824-611, fax 7/822-536, offers rooms with TV, phone, and private bath for $10 s, $14 d, including breakfast.

At the **Posada del Sol,** Bolívar 5-03 and Cueva, tel./fax 7/838-995, you'll find homemade jams, granola, and yogurt waiting at breakfast in the colorful courtyard. Twelve rooms make up the modest but very comfortable hotel, with a reading room for relaxing in

front of the fire. Rates run $18 s, $24 d, including a continental breakfast.

In a private house southwest of the city center are the **Cabañas Yanuncay,** Cantón Gualeco 2149, between Loja and Las Américas, tel. 7/819-681. Two cabins in a garden are yours for $12 d, including breakfast. Other homemade organic meals are available, and the owner speaks English. A taxi is the easiest way to get there, or else take a Baños-bound bus and get off at the "Arco La Luz" sign.

$25–50

Among other things, a seascape mural on the second floor of the glass-covered courtyard distinguishes the **Hotel Inca Real,** Torres 8-40, tel. 7/823-636, fax 7/840-699, e-mail: incareal @ cue.satnet.net. It's in a lovely colonial building, of course, and friendly service and all the amenities are included for $30 s, $36 d.

In the city center, the **Hotel El Dorado,** Colombia 7-87 and Cordero, tel. 7/831-390, fax 7/831-663, e-mail: eldorado@cue.satnet.net, offers a disco, gym, and a piano bar up on the seventh floor. For $40–48 s, $48–58 d, guests enjoy satellite TV, mini-bars, a free continental breakfast, and transportation to and from the airport.

$50–75

Twelve of the 31 rooms in the **Hotel Crespo,** Larga 7-93, tel. 7/842-571, fax 7/839-473, overlook the Río Tomebamba, as does the dining room. The setting inside is dark and elegant, and rooms cost $46 s, $56 d, including breakfast.

$75–200

The **Hotel Oro Verde,** tel. 7/831-200, fax 7/832-849, e-mail: ecovc@gye.satnet.net, is three km west of the city center on the way to El Cajas, on Av. Lasso along the Río Tomebampa. For all the usual luxuries, along with a Swiss restaurant considered one of the best in the city, visitors pay $140 s, $165 d, including breakfast and airport transport. There's a more casual restaurant as well, along with a bar, deli, outdoor pool, gym, and sauna. Llamas, peacocks, and parrots grace the outdoor lagoon, near the trout stream and herb garden. Reservations can be made in the United States through Prima Hotels, 800/447-7462, 212/223-2848.

FOOD

Local Favorites

Reasonably authentic local meals can be had at **El Balcón Quiteño,** Sangurima 6-49 between Borerro and Miguel, where almost everything goes for $2, or **La Cantina y Fonda** at Borrero and Córdova, with live folkloric music on weekend evenings and dishes for $2.50–4. **Bariloche,** Bolívar 11-28 and Torres, also serves typical Ecuadorian food (and some not-so-typical dishes, such as Pollo Africano) for around $1.50. The intimate plant-filled courtyard is reason enough to come. **El Pavón Real,** Gran Colombia 8-33 and Cordero, has a fantastic $1 *almuerzo* occasionally accompanied by a live guitarist.

Raymipampa, under the arcade on the west side of Parque Calderón, is popular with tourists as well as locals for its view of the park and bright café-style atmosphere. Entrées, including crêpes, fall in the $1.50 range. **Honey,** Lamar 4-21 and Machuca, is a local institution serving American-style greasy-spoon fare. They make the bread for the grilled cheese and hamburgers themselves, along with the ice cream for the extra-thick milkshakes and banana splits. If they had any decorations, a hamburger would probably cost more than 80 cents.

You'll find *parriladas* aplenty on Remigio Crespo west of the stadium. Locals recommend **La Herradura,** on Romero just of Crespo. For seafood at local prices (mostly less than $1), try the **Rincon de Mar** on Miguel across from the Convento de la Conceptas. Their *trucha con menestra* is a tasty mix of the coast and the Sierra.

Pizza

When Cuencaños order their pies, chances are they call the **Pizzeria Little Italy,** tel. 7/885-674. You can also eat in at their place at Cueva 6-17 and Remigio Crespo, where a small cheese pie is $2.25. **New York Pizza,** Gran Colombia 10-43 across from the Iglesia Santo Domingo, is the real thing—slices are 60 cents, and family-size pizzas are $3.50. Everything else on the menu, from ravioli to *churrasco,* is less than $2. They will also deliver (tel. 7/842-792).

Health Food

Cuenca's health-conscious steer toward the **Restaurant Vegetariano La Primavera,** Miguel and Córdova, for the fruit salads, soy-meat sandwiches, and 60-cent set lunch.

International

El Pedregal Azteca, Colombia 10-33, has the most authentic Mexican fare this side of the Yucatán, down to a stained-glass likeness of Catinflas and the dish of *mole* on the table. Portions are tasty but not huge for $2. The beautiful 19th-century building, called La Casa Azul, can attract a boisterous crowd at night with patrons tossing down Dos Equis and tequila to live music. Live Andean music fills the place on Mon., Wed., and Fri. nights.

The **Chifa Pack How** is one of the city's best but still reasonably priced—plates average $1.50. The **Restaurant Gran Muralla,** Jaramillo 8-38 and Cordero, comes highly recommended for Chinese as well.

Something Special

Vying for the title of Best Restaurant in Cuenca are **El Jardin,** Córdova 7-23 and Borrero, where prices range from $3.50 for a *ceviche* to $18 for lobster, and the **Villa Rosa,** Colombia 12-22

RESTAURANT SPANISH

appetizer	apertivo, bocadillo
cold	frio (-a)
to cook, cooked (adj)	cocinar, cocinado (a)
cup	copa, taza
dessert	postre
fork	tenedor
glass	vaso
hot	caliente
knife	cuchillo
main course	plato fuerte
pepper	pimienta
plate	plato
salt	sal
seat	silla
spoon	cuchara
table	mesa
tip	propina
to order, order (n)	pedir, pedido
waiter	mesero

flower market

and Montalvo, with slightly lower prices and a more intimate setting. The **Restaurante El Mirador** earns its name from its spot on the ninth floor of the Hotel Presidente. It's fancy but affordable, with entrées like breaded sea bass and filet mignon in mushroom sauce around $2.20. Breakfast starts at $1. Great views of Cuenca are included.

Cafés and Sweets

A quiet coffee in a tranquil setting—maybe with something sweet on the side—can be had at the **Cafe Austria,** Jaramillo and Malo, **La Barranca Cafe,** Borrero 9-68 and Gran Colombia, and the **Casa Grande Cafe-Restaurant.** The latter, on Cordero between Colombia and Bolívar, has an open grassy courtyard surrounded with white brick walls desperately in need of a mural. The café at the **El Cafecito Hotel** is always packed, partly because the hamburgers, pastas, and Mexican entrées are all less than $1. Hip local youth prefer the **Cinema Cafe** at the Teatro Casa de la Cultura. All of these cafés offer the whole range of caffeinated potables, with few items more than $1.50.

The **Heladería Holandesa,** Malo 9-45, satisfies any sugar cravings with its cakes, fruit salad, and ice cream. You can find good bread and sweets at the **Delicatesen El Dorado,** at Cordero and Gran Colombia; and **Delicentro,** Gran Colombia and Balo, is a good bakery that also has ice cream. **Donut King** is a few doors down from La Herradura—fittingly, it's right be-

hind the larger-than-life likeness of Homer Simpson.

Supermarkets

To stock up for yourself, try the **Comisariato Popular** supermarket at Córdova and Cordero, or other **supermarkets,** one at Huayna Capac and Sucre and the other at Lamar and Cordero. There's a **Supermaxi** on Avenida de las Americas just north of Ordoñez Lazo, west of the center, and another on Calle east of the stadium.

SHOPPING

Coaches for the upcoming Leisure Olympics—main events Strolling and Shopping—couldn't ask for a better training camp than Cuenca. Vendors specialize in the unusual, the finely wrought, and the expensive: custom jewelry, handmade ceramics, pre-Columbian-style *ikat* textiles, and enough antiques and religious icons to stock a dozen castles.

On the Plaza San Sebastian are the **G. Larrazabal** art gallery and the **Galería El Girasol,** with a small but high-quality collection, including handmade indigenous shawl pins called *tupus.* Ceramic magician Eduardo Vega fills **Artesa,** Colombia and Cordero, with his works. **Galería Pulla,** Jaramillo 6-90 and Borrero, is named after another famous Ecuadorian artist whose paintings and sculptures fill the showroom. Pricey modern crafts with a traditional touch—primari-

primarily women's clothing made with indigenous fabrics—can be found at **Kinara,** Sucre 7-70 and Cordero.

Jewelry can also be expensive, but it's worth shopping around for the occasional deal. Most come from nearby crafts villages (see "East of Cuenca"). *Joyerías* (jewelry shops) are concentrated on Cordero near Colombia and along Colombia between Aguirre and Cordero , and jewelry stands fill the Plazoleta Santana on the corner of Lamar and Malo. Leonardo Crespo's Joyería Turismo, a Cuenca institution, has changed both location and name. It's now the **Relicario de las Artes,** at Borrero 9-64 and Gran Colombia, and carries jewelry as well as paintings. Another option is the **Galería Claudio Maldonado,** Bolívar 7-75.

Many antique stores surround Las Conceptas. The **Cafe Galería,** Córdova 7-54, and Laura's, Miguel 7-16, both have good selections. **Productos Andinos,** on Colombia between Malo and Cordero, sells the usual Andean artifacts. Both **El Tucán,** Borrero 7-35, and **Colecciones Jorge Moscoso,** Cordero and Córdova, have a little of everything—for the right price. The **Centro Artesanal Casa de la Mujer** is a mall with more than 100 vendors selling just about every type of *artesanía* imaginable, from baskets and balsa sculptures to Panama hats and paintings.

Some of Ecuador's finer Panama hats are made in the southern Sierra by families who have woven the *toquilla* straw for generations. **Homero Ortega Padre e Hijos,** tel. 7/801-288, have exported *sombreros* around the world from their shop on Dávalos 3-86 near the Terminal Terrestre. They also have another shop at Miguel 6-84. (You know Ecuador has entered the 21st century when Panama-hat weavers have websites: www.homero-ortega.com.ec, e-mail: ortega@etapa.com.ec.) **Aurelio Ortega** sells hats at Malo 10-78, as does a shop on Cordero next to La Cantina. You can also try Alberto Pulla and his store/workshop **La Casa del Sombrero,** Tarquí 6-91 and Córdova. For a wider selection, stop by the Thursday morning hat market at María Auxiliadora Plaza.

Markets

Cuenca's main market day is Thursday, with smaller spreads on Saturday and minimal vending the rest of the week. The **Mercado 9 de Octubre** sees the most goods changing hands, including crafts, clothes, and *cuyes* (guinea pigs). Witch doctors cure true believers and the gullible on Tuesdays and Fridays. The flower and plant market in the **Plazoleta del Carmen** is one of the most photogenic in the southern Sierra.

Otavalo textiles and daily goods are sold in the **Plaza de San Francisco** and the **Plaza Rotary,** and a local market fills in the small plaza fronting **Las Conceptas.** Panama hat weavers sell directly to wholesalers in the **Plaza María Auxiliadora.**

RECREATION

Hikes, Guides, and Equipment

Contact the **Club Andinismo Sangay** for information on climbing courses and hikes into El Cajas. Group hikes happen most Sundays, with a bus leaving the Parque Calderón at 8 A.M. ($3 trip fee). They have an office at Gran Colombia 7-39 and Cordero, tel./fax 7/836-758, tel. 7/823-932, e-mail: adinismosangay@yahoo.com. You can also ask at La Barraca Cafe, Borrero 9-68 and Gran Colombia, for information.

Eduardo Quito, Miguel 9-56, tel. 7/823-018, 827-594, fax 7/826-594, has been recommended as a private guide for outdoor activities near Cuenca. He speaks English, has his own 4WD vehicle, and can take groups to Ingapirca. **Eduardo Astudillo,** Sangurima 996, tel. 826-714, has also been recommended as a private guide. You can rent camping gear at **Acción Casa Deportiva,** Bolívar 12-70 and Montalvo, tel. 7/833-526.

Tours and Other Activities

Ecotrek, Calle Larga 7-108 and Cordero, tel. 7/841-927 or 834-677, fax 7/835-387, e-mail: ecotrek@az.pro.ec, is probably the best-known adventure travel operation in Cuenca. They lead mountaineering trips to Cotopaxi and Chimborazo and jungle trips into the Amazon. Their tours in custom vans aren't cheap—El Cajas for 2–3 people costs $240 pp for four days, and a city tour runs $25 pp—but the guides are knowledgeable and experienced.

A more economical option for trips to El Cajas, Ingapirca, and nearby crafts villages is **Río Ar-**

riba **Expediciones,** Miguel 7-14 and Córdova, tel. 7/840-031, e-mail: negro@az.pro.ec, with one-day El Cajas excursions for $30 pp. **Expediciones Apullacta,** tel. 7/837-815, e-mail: apullacta@cedei.org, is affiliated with the CEDEI Spanish school. They run day trips to El Cajas, Ingapirca, and surrounding villages for $35 pp, and will even go with only one person. **Roo Tours,** Cajas and Ingapirca, tel. 7/835-533 or 835-888, has also received favorable reports for their El Cajas and Ingapirca excursions ($45 pp) and their guides, who speak English, French, and German.

Hualambari Tours, Borrero 9-67 and Colombia, tel./fax 7/842-693, e-mail: hualamba @ cue.satnet.net, has day trips to El Cajas, Ingapirca, and nearby villages ($35 pp) that are reportedly excellent. Guides speak English, Spanish, German, French, and Italian. Ask about horseback riding at a nearby hacienda ($45–50 pp), a mule-supported three-day trek along the Inca Trail to Ingapirca ($215 pp), homestays in Cuenca, and budget Galápagos cruises.

Metropolitan Touring, 6-62 Sucre and Borrero, tel. 7/831-463, e-mail: metrocue @impsat.net.ec, offers city tours and trips to surrounding areas, including a private train ride through the famous Naríz del Diablo below Alausí, which, combined with a visit to Ingapirca, goes for $84 pp.

Horseback-riding trips can be arranged with **Monta Runa Tours,** Gran Colombia 10-29 and Aguirre, tel. 7/846-395, tel./fax 7/840-031, e-mail: montarun@az.pro.ec. They also organize trips of one or more days around Cuenca ($50 pp per day) and send guided groups along the Inca Trail to Ingapirca. Juan Diego, another horseback guide, speaks English and can be contacted by phone at 7/838-695. Mountain biking is the forte of **Eco Rutas,** operating out of an office on 3 de Noviembre next to the Hotel Crespo. They rent bikes for $8 per day, including helmets and goggles, and organize riding trips to El Cajas for $40 pp (minimum two people).

For information on an eight-day **paragliding course** for $250 pp, contact John Rivera, tel. 7/832-601, 840-402, e-mail: johnrivera25 @hotmail.com. If you'd prefer to organize your own trip, consider renting a taxi and driver through **Taximan,** tel. 7/857-663, or **Paisa,** tel. 7/863-774.

ENTERTAINMENT AND EVENTS

Nightlife

Cuenca's local paper *El Mercurio* lists what's showing at the various theaters in town, most of which show American movies with Spanish subtitles. Choices include the **Cine 9 de Octubre,** Lamar and Cueva; **Teatro Cuenca,** Aguirre 10-58 between Lamar and Colombia; and the **Teatro Casa de la Cultura,** on Cordero between Sucre and Córdova (not to be confused with the Casa de la Cultura itself on Sucre and Aguirre, which occasionally hosts movies as well). The **Multicines** near the stadium, under construction in 2000, will greatly increase Cuenca's cinematic options once it's open.

Head down the steps of Escalinata (south from Miguel) to reach **Wunderbar,** a small cave-like place with German beers and occasional live Andean music. Live Latin music is also on the weekend schedule at **La Moradora del Cantor,** out Colombia/Lazo in the direction of the Hotel Oro Verde, and at **Los Capulies Cantina,** at Córdova and Borrero, which has a pool table upstairs. Opposite Los Capulies is the **Picadilly Pub,** an upscale British-style tavern.

Next to El Cafecito is **Mayombe,** the most popular *salsateca* in town (although some prefer **Babalu** on the corner of Gran Colombia and Machuca). **Que Será** at Jaramillo and Huayna Capac is your standard *discoteca,* whereas **Azucar** under the broken bridge plays both salsa and modern dance music. Some of the better downtown hotels, including El Conquistador and El Dorado, have discos. If you'd like to polish up your gyrating, stop by the **Cachumbambe Tropical Dance Academy,** tel. 7/882-028, at Crespo 7-79 and Guayas. The Equinoccial Spanish school (see "Spanish Schools") offers salsa and merengue lessons for $3 per hour—the first one is free.

There's a small **casino** in the Hotel Cuenca at Borrero and Lamar.

Festivals

Cuenca's main festivals include **Corpus Cristi** in June, when firecracker-studded towers are ignited in Parque Calderón for nights on end as flocks of paper hot-air balloons rise toward the stars. The **Foundation of Cuenca** from 10–13

April is another excuse to cut loose, and the celebrations for **Cuenca's Independence** on 3 November are combined with All Souls' and All Saints' Days (1 and 2 November) for a three-day festival of theater, art, and dancing.

Cuenca's **Christmas** festival is one of the most famous in the country. The Paseo del Niño Viajero—said to be the best holiday parade in Ecuador—begins on the morning of Christmas Eve. Indígenas from villages for kilometers around throng the streets. Symbols of prosperity, including strings of banknotes, poultry, and bottles of alcohol, are both carried and worn (that's right, worn) in the hope of arranging for even more of the same over the next year from any spirits willing to oblige. The procession winds from the Iglesia San Sebastian to the Cathedral, and the festivities don't stop until everyone wakes up and—hey, it's next year!

SERVICES AND INFORMATION

Money Exchange
Most *casas de cambio* are found east of Parque Calderón. **Vaz Cambios** has a branch at Gran Colombia 7-98 and Cordero, with Western Union money-transfer service available. You'll find **Cambidex** at Cordero 9-77 between Colombia and Bolívar, **Cambistral** at Sucre 6-64 and Borrero, and **M.M. Jaramillo Arteaga** at Sucre and Bolívar. All four change travelers' checks.

If for some strange reason you'd rather deal with a bank, the **Banco del Pacífico** on Malo 9-75 between Gran Colombia and Bolívar gives cash advances on MasterCard. For Visa advances, go to either **Filanbanco,** Sucre between Torres and Aguirre; **Banco La Previsora,** Colombia and Malo; or the **Banco del Guayaquil,** on Sucre between Miguel and Borrero. Most of these banks also have **ATM machines** for cash withdrawals.

Communications
Cuenca's **post office** is in the center of town on Borrero and Colombia, and there's an **EMS** express mail office around the corner. **Pacifictel** is on Malo between Córdova and Sucre. And even stodgy old Cuenca has entered the information age: Internet cafés are popping up like daisies in springtime. Try **ExploreNet,** Aguirre and Lamar; **Bapu Cafe Net,** Córdova and Cordero; **Ve@internet,** Cueva and Bolívar; or **@If.net,** Borrero and Vazquez.

Spanish Schools
Cuenca is a popular place to study Spanish for extended periods, explaining the many high-quality language schools in town. The **Centro de Estudios Interamericanos** (CEDEI), Colombia 11-02 and Torres, Ed. Empleadeos de Azuay, piso 3, tel. 7/839-003, e-mail: interpro@cedei.org, offers Spanish classes for $6 per hour as well as courses in Quechua, colonial Latin America, and Andean literature. They can also arrange positions teaching English.

Nexus Lingua y Culturas, 12 de Abril 1-19, tel. 7/884-016 or 888-220, offers Spanish classes for $5 per hour as well as positions teaching English locally. The **Centro Cultural Ecuatoriano-Norteamericano Abraham Lincoln,** Borrero 5-18, tel. 7/823-898, tel./fax 7/841-737, e-mail: rboroto@cena.org.ec, is also recommended for $5 per hour. They can arrange homestays with local families.

Estudio International Sampere, Miguel 3-43 and Larga, tel./fax 7/841-986, e-mail: samperec@samperecen.com.ec, offers Spanish instruction that can be combined with cultural activities like ceramics classes. **Equinoccial,** Cordero 9-32, tel./fax 7/834-758, e-mail: eee@cue.satnet.net, www.equinoccial.edu.ed, has one-to-one instruction for $3–5 per hour. They also have an office at Solano 11-83 and offer dance lessons (see "Nightlife"). **Tere Hermida,** recommended as a private Spanish tutor, can be reached at night at 7/822-838.

Laundry
To get out those mud stains from the Inca Trail, take your dirty duds to **Fast Klin Lavandería,** Miguel 6-66 and Córdova; **La Química Lavandería,** on Borrero next to the Picadilly Pub; or **Lavahora,** just down Vazquez from El Cafecito.

Tourist Information
The **Ministerio de Turismo** has an office on the second floor of the Edificio San Agustin on Córdova between Aguirre and Malo. In the Terminal Terrestre, you'll find the **Camara de Tur-**

ismo del Azuay, with city maps and a waiting room (called the "Sala V.I.P.") with leather couches and cable TV. They're open daily 8 A.M.–10 P.M.

The Asociación Hotelera del Azuay, Córdova and Aguirre, tel. 7/836-925, can help with maps and information on all types of hotels in Cuenca. They can make hotel reservations and are very helpful with all tourist-type questions. For permits, information, and maps of El Cajas, stop by the office of the Ministerio del Ambiente on the third floor of the MAG office at Bolívar 5-33 and Miguel.

Police and Immigration

The main police office is on Cordero between Córdova and Jaramillo, open Mon.–Fri. 8 A.M.–noon and 3–6 P.M. Immigration matters are handled here, but you have to report crimes to the OID investigative division, tel. 7/864-924, at Turuhuayco and Calle Vieja out past the bus station. There's also a small police stand in the Plaza San Francisco.

Healthcare

The Hospital Santa Inés, on Córdova Toral 2-113 and Cueva, tel. 7/817-888, is just across the river and employs a few English-speaking doctors. Also recommended for quality healthcare is the Clinica Santa Ana, Manuel Calle 1-104, tel. 7/817-564, southeast of the river.

TRANSPORTATION

Buses

Cuenca's Terminal Terrestre is two blocks northeast of the traffic circle at España and Huayna Capac, and is probably the most orderly and pleasant in the country. Several bus companies have luxury service to Guayaquil ($4, five hours), as well as most cities in between and beyond, including Quito ($6, 9–10 hours) and Macas ($4, 9–10 hours). Panamericana has an office at 5-24 España, just beyond the bus station, and sends luxury buses to Quito daily at 10 P.M. ($6.75). Buses to Loja ($3.50, 5.5 hours) run via Saraguro, and Transportes Cañar has direct service daily to Ingapirca at 9 A.M. and at 1 P.M. every day except Sunday ($1). Local city buses cost about 10 cents.

Taxis and Car Rental

The minimum taxi fare in Cuenca is 80 cents, which will get you just about anywhere in town. The bus station and airport are each a $1 ride from the city center. To hire your own wheels, try Localiza, España 14-85, tel. 7/863-902. They also have an office at the airport (tel. 7/803-198), as does Inter Rent-a-Car, tel. 7/801-892.

Flights

Planes leave from Cuenca's Mariscal Lamar airport, two km northeast of the town center on Avenida España. It's a 10-minute walk from the Terminal Terrestre, or a short hop on a taxi or local bus.

The TAME office is on Malo 5-05 and Larga, tel. 7/843-222, and at the airport (tel. 7/866-400). Their flights leave for Quito Mon.–Sat. for $30 one-way, and for Guayaquil Mon.–Sat. for $18 one-way. Icaro Express flies to Quito Tues., Thurs., and Sun. for $68 one-way, and Austro Aero, Hermano Miguel 5-42 and Vázquez, tel. 7/832-677, leaves for Guayaquil Mon.–Sat. for $29 pp one-way.

VICINITY OF CUENCA

Not to be confused with the larger tourist mecca to the north, the *pueblito* of Baños sits eight km southwest of Cuenca. Similar to its eponymous

---

CUENCA AIRLINE OFFICES

American Airlines: Miguel 8-63 and
   Bolívar, tel. 7/831-699
AeroPeru: Cueva 8-81 and Bolívar,
   tel. 7/840-516
Avianca: Huayna Capac 7111 and Sucre, tel.
   7/835-916
Continental: Aguirre 10-96 and Lamar,
   tel. 7/847-374
Copa: Borrero 9-57 and Gran Colombia,
   tel. 7/842-970
KLM: Cueva 8-70, tel. 7/835-926
Iberia: Colombia 7-97 and Cordero,
   tel. 7/842-998
TACA: Sucre 7-70 and Cordero,
   tel. 7/837-360

sibling, hot springs are the draw here, burbling up from 3,000 meters to surface at more than 100°C. A few cheap *residenciales* provide lodging, as does the colonial-style **Hostería Durán,** tel. 7/892-485 or 892-486, fax 7/892-488. This full resort boasts tennis and racquetball courts, a gym, water slides, private hot springs, and plush rooms with all the amenities. Rates are $15 s, $20 d. The best hot springs are near the hostería; **Rodas** has the hottest thermals for $2 per day.

Take a taxi from Cuenca or catch a local bus at the intersection of 12 de Abril and Solano, south of the river, which then passes the Plaza San Francisco on Cordova. Buses also leave from outside the bus station and head down Muñoz.

Buses run from Cuenca to the top of the hill, where a baby-blue church with tiled domes is worth a look. The Hostería Durán is a short ways below, surrounded by a billiards hall, discos, and plenty of restaurants (if you're looking for *cuy,* this is the place). Just downhill from the Hostería Durán are two more lodgings options: the **Hostería El Ricón de Baños** and **Bohemia Drinks,** both of which have rooms with private bath for around $3. Neither, however, is a great value, and they each see a lot of short-term traffic (nudge, nudge), so budget travelers are better off staying in Cuenca.

Head four km south of Cuenca's center along Avenida Solano, and you'll crest at the **Mirador Turi,** a lookout with a view all the way to the peaks of El Cajas on a clear day. Processions from Cuenca on Good Friday lead to the white Iglesia de Turi. Buses leave from 12 de Abril and Solano on the hour, or a taxi will cost you about $1.50 (bargain hard).

EL CAJAS NATIONAL RECREATION AREA

Some of the most varied and spectacular scenery in the country fills this reserve, whose proximity to Cuenca—only one hour's drive west—helps make it one of the most popular outdoor destinations in the area. El Cajas' 70,000 acres shelter everything from cloud forest to rocky lunar landscapes, but lakes (more than 200 of them) scattered among jagged peaks characterize the reserve best.

Most of El Cajas lies above 3,000 meters, with *páramo* covering most of the rugged terrain. Frost and ice above 4,000 meters try their best to deter the thriving of hardy vegetation such as the tiny quinua tree, clinging to life higher than any other tree in the world. Look for these 200-year-old specimens tucked up against hillsides in pockets of primary forest, clothed in a green palette of mosses and ferns and fighting each other for sunlight. Visitors stand a good chance of seeing the 40 or so wild llamas that were reintroduced to the park in the late 1990s.

Archaeology
Fragments of Inca roads throughout the reserve link numerous *tambos,* ruins of waystations along the royal highway, which is said to have run through here all the way to the coast. Traces of the roads connect the Lagunas Luspa and Mamamag, and the Lagunas Ingacocha and Ingacarretero. The area near Molleturo hill has the highest concentration of ruins in El Cajas, where great views of Chimborazo and El Altar give evidence of the Inca skill at picking sites that were both scenic and easily defended. Other ruins can be found near the Lagunas Toreadora and Atugyacu.

llamas in the road, El Cajas National Recreation Area

Visiting the Park

The Aug.–Jan. dry season is the best time to visit El Cajas, promising the most sun and regular but short-lived rain showers. Nighttime temperatures can still drop below freezing. The rainy season from Feb.–July has the highest average temperature but more precipitation. High altitudes make acclimatization a good idea—hike high, sleep low.

Rubber boots, multiple layers of clothing, a tent, and warm sleeping bags are all essential because deaths from exposure have occurred here. Also consider fishing gear and a compass if you plan to wander far afield, which you certainly should. Four IGM 1:50,000 maps cover the area: *Cuenca, Chaucha, San Felipe de Molleturo,* and *Chiquintad.* Entrance to the park is $10 pp.

A two- to four-hour path leads around Laguna Toreadora, and Cerro San Luis (4,200 meters) on the opposite side can be climbed in a day. Head around counterclockwise to the Al San Luis sign soon after crossing the outflow. From there a series of black and yellow stakes leads to the summit. Another path passes the Cueva de los Muertos (Cave of the Dead), named for travelers in the previous century who died there.

For advice on multiple-day itineraries, ask the park rangers or any of the tour companies or guides in Cuenca, who will be glad to arrange a guided visit. Juan Diego at the Posada del Sol hotel leads horse trips into El Cajas. You can stay at the **Huagrahuma Páramo Lodge** run by Ecotrek in Cuenca (see under "Tours and Other Activities"). Opened in 1996 at 3,700 meters, the lodge has 26 rooms, a restaurant, and camping space.

Access

The main route to El Cajas from Cuenca begins as Gran Colombia before turning into Avenida Lasso as it nears the Hotel Oro Verde. After eight km, the road passes the village of Sayausi before reaching the Laguna Toreadora information center after 34 km. Make sure to tell the bus driver to let you off there, or you'll find yourself far beyond the reserve in the town of Molleturo before you know it.

Buses leave the Plaza San Sebastian at 6 A.M. daily except Thursday and take about 2.5 hours to reach the lake. The return buses are less predictable, passing back between two and four P.M. Not much traffic goes this way, making hitchhiking difficult, and taxis are expensive ($30–40 one-way).

Another route enters El Cajas from the south, via Baños and guardposts at the village of Soldado and Angas. Buses along this longer, bumpier road (four hours each way) leave from the park in Cuenca at the corner of Loja and El Vado at 6 A.M. on Monday, Wednesday, Friday, and Saturday.

EAST OF CUENCA

The hills above Cuenca to the east shelter several crafts villages that are well worth a detour. Sunday is market day, but it's possible to visit all the main ones in a day on any day of the week and be back in Cuenca by night. Buses run every few minutes between each town and its neighbors, usually from the main market plaza, and numerous tour companies in Cuenca offer tours by private bus or car. If you'd prefer to take your time, there are numerous lodging options and a network of trails connecting the towns, similar to the area around Otavalo (see the Northern Sierra chapter).

Paute

Set in the valley of the Río Paute northeast of Cuenca, the town of the same name is known for the wide variety of sweaters woven by its artisans. It's also the home of a Fruit Festival on 26 February, with folk dances and exhibits.

The most luxurious accommodations in the area are at the **Hosteria Uzhupud,** tel. 7/250-339 or 250-329. Almost 50 rooms include 11 suites and a pair of less expensive bunk rooms. The whole range of modern hacienda luxuries include a pool, sauna, steam room, and disco. Horseback rides can be arranged, and an orchidarium and gardens on the stately main grounds bring some of the area's 320 bird species—including the 19-cm giant hummingbird, the largest in the world—almost to your doorstep. Rates are $34 s, $44 d. Reservations can be made through offices in Quito (tel. 2/652-345) or Cuenca (tel. 7/831-390, fax 7/847-390, e-mail:huzhupud@cue.satnet.net), or in the United States through Holbrook Travel at 3540 N.W. 13th St., Gainesville, FL 32609-2196, 800/451-

7111, fax 352/371-3710, e-mail: advisor@holbrooktravel.com, www.holbrooktravel.com.

Taking the south branch of the road toward Gualaceo and Chordeleg will bring you past **Bulcay,** where textiles are woven on backstrap looms from hand-dyed thread and sold in a women's cooperative shop.

Gualaceo
Near the Río Santa Barbara, 34 km from Cuenca, this small town hosts the largest indigenous market in the area every Sunday. Three separate markets—fruits and vegetables, crafts and clothes, and produce and household goods—blend effectively into one. Tourists come for the fine woven and embroidered textiles, such as the *macana* shawls with macramé fringes.

The **Parador Turístico Gualaceo,** Loja and Parador, tel./fax 7/842-443 or 225-010, provides the best lodgings. Rooms and chalets with hot water and private bathrooms cost $30–40 pp; amenities include satellite TV, tennis courts, and a pool. The hotel is about one km south of the Plaza 10 de Agosto along Gran Colombia, up a long palm-lined drive. At the entrance to the hotel is the **Museo Artesanal de Gualaceo,** a combination craft museum and expensive gift sop. The small but interesting collection ranges from pottery to musical instruments. Open Tues.–Sat. 8 A.M.–noon and 2–5 P.M., Sun. 8 A.M.–1 P.M., free.

Near the Parador Turístico is the homey **Hostal Molino,** tel. 7/255-049, which in fact is a home with large comfortable rooms for $8 s, $12 d. Budget travelers recommend the basic but clean **Hostal Pachacama,** Rodríguez 3-49, tel. 7/256-547, on the southeast corner of the market. There's also the **Residencial Gualaceo,** tel. 7/823-454, a block north of the main plaza at Gran Colombia and Piedra, and the **Hostal Carlos Andres,** tel. 7/255-369, another block north on Gran Colombia. All three have rooms for about $2 with private bath, TV, and hot water.

The **Restaurant Don Q** on the northwest corner of the main plaza gets high marks for its food and ambience, serving typical Ecuadorian fare for about $1.50. **El Dragon Restaurant,** one block north of the bus station, serves Ecuadorian and Chinese food.

Vaz Casa de Cambio, on the corner of 3 de Noviembre and Colón, changes travelers' checks at good rates and is open on Sundays. Gualaceo's **Peach Festival,** 4–10 March, features exhibitions of flowers and crafts, and the anniversary of the **Canonization of Gualaceo** falls on 25 June.

The road from Cuenca to Gualaceo (45 minutes, 30 cents) is plied by buses that leave every 15 minutes from Cuenca's Terminal Terrestre. Gualaceo's bus station is on the east side of Roldos between Cordero and Reyes, southeast of the main market plaza. A shortcut down into the Amazon heads east through the Macas Pass (3,350 meters) after 24 km before dropping to Limón.

Chordeleg and South
This smaller village lies five km downhill from Gualaceo, a pretty one- to two-hour walk if you're so inclined. The Sunday market here is more oriented to tourists, with flashier merchandise and higher prices. Chordeleg has been a jewelry center since before the Inca arrived, and today a handful of *joyerías* (jewelry shops) around town turn out finely wrought silver and gold. A small community museum on the main plaza has displays on the history and techniques of this and other local crafts, including ceramics, hat weaving, and textiles.

A smaller, more indigenous Sunday market is held in **Sigsig,** 26 km south of Gualaceo. Panama hats made in town are usually for sale. The rough "road" southeast to Gualaquiza in the Amazon lowlands makes a good two- to three-day hike.

NORTH OF CUENCA

Azogues
The name of the Cañar province capital has roots in the Spanish translation of quicksilver, after the rich mercury ore deposits found in this part of the Sierra. With few sights in itself, Azogues is best visited as a base for trips to Biblián, Cañar, and Ingapirca. It's hard to miss the **Iglesia del San Francisco** perched on a hilltop at the southeast end of town, only slightly marred by an immense blue sign for Radio Santa Maria.

There's a small **religious museum** at the church, but special permission is needed to enter. More impressive is the **Museo Etnografico Regional** at the Casa de la Cultura, half a kilometer south of the market on Bolívar. One of the best of its kind in the country, this collection covers Cañar culture by taking visitors through mock-ups of an indigenous house and market, among other things. Upstairs is an archaeological display. Labels are in Spanish only, and the museum is open Mon.–Fri. 8 A.M.–noon and 2–6 P.M., free. Music, dance, and other cultural performances are occasionally held at the Casa de la Cultura.

If you're passing through on a Saturday or Sunday, stop by the busy **market,** southwest of the main plaza, bordered by Sucre, 3 de Noviembre, Rivera, and Matovalle. Panama hats are one of the most important commodities being bought and sold, and a quick amble through town will probably bring you to the door of a *sombreria,* where the straw lids are being blocked and woven.

The best of the scant lodging options in town is the **Hostal Rivera,** 24 de Mayo and 10 de Agosto, tel./fax 7/244-275, where comfy rooms with lots of decoration, TV, and private bath are $5 s, $9 d. They also have the best restaurant in town, where $2 gets you a tasty meal and good service. The new owners of the **Hotel Santa Maria,** Serrano and Abad, tel. 7/241-883, are eager to please, offering rooms with TV and private bath for $3 pp. Other acceptable budget options include the **Hotel Charles,** Rivera and Solano, tel. 7/241-364, and the **Hotel Chicago,** 3 de Noviembre and 24 de Mayo, tel. 7/241-040. Both have rooms for $2 or less.

Azogues has no shortage of restaurants serving standard Ecuadorian fare, but few stand out. The primary exception to the rule is **Pizza Ritza** on Sucre and Bolívar one block east of the market. The **Chifa Familiar** on the southwest corner of the market has just a few Chinese options for about $1, and the **Polleria 87,** on 3 de Noviembre between Cordero and 24 de Mayo, has the best chicken—for that matter some of the best food—in town.

Pacifictel and the **post office** are both on the main plaza, and you can exchange travelers' checks at **M.M. Jaramillo Arteaga** on Sucre, half a block east of the market. A short taxi ride (80 cents) up to the church will save you the steep walk, and the **bus terminal** on 24 de Mayo and Azuay is just a short bus ride away from the town center. From here buses leave for Cañar (40 cents, one hour) and Cuenca (35 cents, 45 minutes), among other destinations.

Biblián

More of a church with a town than a town with a church, Biblián is seven km farther north along the Pana. Here the ornate **Sanctuario de La Virgen del Rocío** (Sanctuary of the Virgin of the Dew) lives up to its once-upon-a-time label. It's well worth a brief stop on your way north or south and is the destination of a pilgrimage in late September, begun in 1893 when a miraculous rain answered local prayers to the Virgin to end a severe drought. Panama hats are sold in the Sunday market, and you can watch them being made the rest of the week.

Cañar

The nearest major town to the Ingapirca ruins is the home of descendants of the Cañari *indígenas,* who were defeated and assimilated by the Inca. The Cañari fill the streets with their brightly colored ponchos and white felt bowlers, chatting in Quechua sprinkled with a few words in their own ancient tongue. They're known for their double-sided weavings sold in town and at the vibrant Sunday market. The best place to buy them is at the local jail, half a block up Colón from the main plaza, where prisoners make and sell them from behind a metal fence. They don't come cheap and bargaining with the inmates isn't easy, as you can probably imagine. They will, however, happily tell you the stories of their incarceration—I bought one from a man serving five years for killing a thief.

Both the **Hostal Ingapirca,** tel. 7/235-201, and the **Residencial Monica,** tel. 7/235-486 or 235-564, offer rooms on the plaza for $2 pp with private bathrooms and hot water. Some of the most dilapidated **buses** in Ecuador leave every 20 minutes from the east side of town (ask for directions) for the village of Ingapirca (not the ruins), taking almost one hour (40 cents). **Trucks** will make the run to the ruins for $6 round-trip, including waiting for you; ask on the plaza or along 24 de Mayo. The owners of the Residencial Monica will do the same for $5, but they don't always have a truck available.

Transportes Cañar has departures every 15 minutes to Cuenca (80 cents, two hours) from their office on 24 de Mayo a few blocks east of the plaza. They also go to Ingapirca at 6:15, 6:40, and 10:45 A.M. and 2:50 P.M. A few buses head north from Cañar, but locals recommend going out to the Pana or El Tambo and flagging one down.

INGAPIRCA RUINS

They're billed as Ecuador's best set of pre-Columbian ruins, but to be honest, Ingapirca is the country's only true Incan structure that survived the Spanish invasion more or less intact. Still, the fine Inca masonry perched on a picturesque hillside make the 10-km detour from the Pana a worthwhile day trip, even from Cuenca.

History

The Cañari were the first to build here, calling their temple/observatory Cashaloma, meaning "place where the stars pour from the heavens." The Incas came steamrolling through at the end of the 15th century, erecting the current structure before being flattened themselves by the Spanish. Archaeologists are still unsure as to the site's specific function—most likely it was a religious settlement, with a distinctive oval temple and attached convent for ritual maidens (many female skeletons have been unearthed). Other guesses range from a military fortress and grain depository to a *tambo,* or rest spot along the Inca highway. Most likely, Ingapirca was a combination of all of the above because evidence for each theory is supported by the construction.

In the centuries since the Incas departed, many of Ingapirca's stones have been carted away to provide the foundations of buildings, especially churches, in the immediate area. In 1966, the site was opened to the public, and nine years later responsibility for the ruins' upkeep and administration fell into the hands of the local Cañari *indígenas.*

The Site

Just past the town of Ingapirca, five hectares of low stone walls and grassy slopes are anchored by the famous rounded temple. The requisite llamas add a picturesque touch to the scene, which besides the temple is mostly just a vague outline of what must have been. The small **Pilaloma** complex on the south side marks the original Cañari settlement, next to a pointy-roofed replica of an Incan house and round depressions called *colcas* that were used to store food.

A fragment of Inca road called the **Ingañan** (better engineered than many modern Ecuadorian highways—notice the drainage channel) leads past *bodegas,* which were also used for food storage, to an exterior plaza called **La Condamine** after the French scientist's visit in 1748.

temple of the sun at Ingapirca

JULIAN SMITH

These were the nobles' living quarters, including the *acllahuasi*—dwellings of ceremonial virgins. Don't miss the V-shaped rock at the entrance, which was supposedly used for beheadings. Next to it is a larger stone with 28 holes that was thought to be used as a lunar calendar; rainwater caught in the holes told the date by reflecting the moon's light differently throughout the month.

Across the **main plaza** sits the **Temple of the Sun,** also known as El Castillo (The Castle). If you've been to Perú, you'll recognize the usual mind-boggling Inca stonework that forms the two-story structure, too tight to fit even a piece of paper between the blocks. The elliptical shape, pocketed with trapezoidal niches, is unique in Inca ruins. The entire structure is exactly three times as long as it is wide, leading some archaeo-architects to envision three adjoining circles representing the three phases of the sun: *anti* (dawn), *inti* (noon), and *cunti* (sunset).

The collection in the well-done **site museum** includes a mummy, pottery, and ancient textile fragments set under a magnifying glass to show the amazing craftsmanship. Guidebooks to the site are available in different languages, and a room upstairs contains examples of traditional indigenous dress. An **artisan shop** next door sells regional crafts, *cafeterías* and public toilets are across the way, and there's even Internet service at the site (Oh, the irony!).

The $5 pp entrance fee for foreigners includes a free tour (tips, as always, are appreciated). Ingapirca is open daily 9 A.M.–5 P.M.

Practicalities

The ruins can be reached from the Pana via either El Tambo or Cañar, by car, bus, or foot (a scenic but uphill three-hour hike). About one

---

THE INCA TRAIL TO INGAPIRCA

One of Ecuador's most popular overnight hikes follows an ancient Inca road through the southern tip of the Avenue of the Volcanoes. Mountain vistas and great trout fishing make the three-day journey enjoyable, whereas campsite thieves can do the opposite. Keep in mind that you're hiking at about 3,000 meters the whole way, and that the trail follows a river, so it can get muddy—take it slow and bring rubber boots. The IGM 1:50,000 maps *Alausí, Juncal,* and *Cañar* cover the area, and with a compass should put the trip within range of even weekend hikers.

First make your way from Alausí to Achupallas-a one-hour, US$8 taxi ride or tiring 25-km hike. Leave Achupallas to the south past the elementary school, cross the Río Azuay, and reach the west bank of the Río Candrul after passing through a natural hole in the rock. From here the trail heads clearly south between the Cerros Mapahuña and Pucará. There's a good campsite on the south side of the Laguna Tres Cruces at 4,200 meters, 14 km, and 6–7 hours from Achuallas.

Day two takes you below the peak of Cerro Quilloloma to the west, which at 4,400 meters is the highest point along the hike. The Ríos Sansahuín and Espíndol join the Candrul near here. Although it would be possible to push to Ingapirca in one long second day, most hikers choose to spend the night among the graffiti of the Los Paredones (Big Walls) ruins, east of the Lago Culebrillas and 10 km from the Laguna Tres Cruces.

The worn stone path eventually disappears past Los Paredones, but luckily the rooftops of Tambo come into view soon after. Pass under a power line on the way down to and across the Río Silaute before ascending to Ingapirca.

---

km before the ruins is the village of Ingapirca, where the family-run **Residencial Inti Huasi,** tel. 7/290-767, has clean rooms with hot water and private bathrooms for $2 d and a popular restaurant where good Ecuadorian fare goes for about $1. If the restaurant is full, as it often is, the **Restaurant El Turista** a few doors down will do.

The new **Posada Ingapirca,** tel. 7/831-120 or 838-508, fax 7/832-340, e-mail: santaana @aracno.net, has eight fancy but still rustic rooms with private bath and hot water for $35 per room. Set in a restored farm building, this place can make you feel as if you've stepped back a century. The antique-filled dining room is the haunt of tour buses, but if you can come just for the $8 lunch, views of the Temple of the Sun and heat from the fireplace are included.

Trans-Cañar buses run direct from Cuenca's Terminal Terrestre at 9 A.M. daily and 1 P.M. Mon.–Sat. ($1, 2.5 hours), returning at 1 and 4 P.M. Most tour companies in Cuenca offer organized excursions.

SOUTH TO LOJA

The Pana splits 15 km south of Cuenca. On its way downhill to Machala, the west branch reaches **Girón** after 22 km, with great hikes in the surrounding cloud forest to waterfalls and rivers teeming with trout.

Saraguro

The eastern branch of the Pana threads the Tinajilla Pass (3,527 meters) before reaching this village, which is home to the *indígenas* of the same name.

Almost everything of import is located on the main square, including the post office, Pacifictel, several craft vendors, and the **Restaurant Reina Cisne,** where a filling *almuerzo* is less than $1. This is also the place to catch a bus to Loja (2 hours) or Cuenca (3.5 hours); they pass through roughly every half hour, stopping in front of their respective offices. Accommodation in town is very basic. The **Residencial Armijos,** tel. 7/200-306, and the **Residencial Saraguro,** tel. 7/200-286, are northeast of the plaza with rooms for about $1 and hot water in the mornings (or so they claim); the latter has a flower-filled courtyard.

For a small town high in the Andes, Saraguro has plenty to do. For starters, stop by the **Sunday market** (from 9–11 A.M.) or one of the many indigenous artisan shops. **Maria Alegría Quizpe,** who lives in Barrio Pucará, will teach you to make necklaces in the local style for a small contribution. Ask directions to the home workshop of **Manuel Encarracion Quizipe,** who weaves dozens of different kinds of textiles on 12 upright looms (his wife and daughters make jewelry). Along with all that, Saraguro is one of the better towns in Ecuador to just sit along the square and watch life go by.

After the religious ceremonies, Saraguro's **Christmas festival** is a jovial community gathering with heaping plates of food, drinking, and dancing. Suggested **hikes** nearby include the Sinincapa caves, the Virgencaca waterfall, Puglla Mountain, and the Huashapamba Cloud Forest.

As a matter of fact, many side tracks lead off into the hills all along this section of the Pana, into some of the most remote regions of the Ecuadorian Sierra (more suited to hiking boots or mountain bikes than cars). Try the route through **Nabón** from La Ramada north of Oña, or either of the east-west roads from Saraguro. From here the southbound Pana inches over four more passes before descending to Loja.

LOJA AND VICINITY

The gateway city to the southern Amazon enjoys the pleasant climate of the Cuxibamba Valley (meaning "cheerful flowery garden"), which helps account for its tranquil character. It's one of the oldest cities in the country, founded in 1546 near Catamayo to the west before being moved to its present location two years later. The only event of note in Loja's history occurred in 1897, when a small hydroelectric project just west of the city center lit the first light bulbs in Ecuador.

Today Loja (pop. 120,000) is a quiet, pretty city of little distinction. Gold finds to the east and west have brought in money over the years, but the city still has a very middle-class air, enjoyable and relaxed. Not all first impressions are positive, though: in our first 12 hours in Loja, a friend and I witnessed a backpack snatching at the bus terminal, were woken at 3 A.M. by drunken cabdrivers blasting dance music across the street from our hotel, had a purse slashed by a little old woman in a crowded street, and were teargassed over lunch by police trying to break up a student demonstration. Nevertheless, most visitors who get beyond the bus terminal find Loja an affable and enjoyable place.

A National University, two technical colleges, a music conservatory, and a law school make the capital of Loja province a center of learning on Ecuador's southernmost tip. The Ríos Zamora and Malacatus bracket the city center, intersecting just north of it before heading east to add more water to the jungle. Ecuadorians consider the Loja accent to be the best in the country, claiming the city's inhabitants almost sing when they speak Spanish.

SIGHTS

City Center

At the north end of the city center where the rivers intersect, the castlelike **Portón de la Ciudad** (City Gate) is handsomely lit up at night. On the east side of Loja's **Parque Central** is the city **cathedral**, which hosts the Virgen del Cisne icon (see "West of Loja") from late August to the beginning of November. Opposite the Municipalidad building is the **Museo del Banco Central**, tel. 7/573-004, with small exhibits of archaeology and works by local artists in a restored colonial building. It's open Mon.–Fri. 9 A.M.–noon and 2–4:30 P.M., $1 pp.

As in Cuenca, many of Loja's old buildings have recently been restored, making a random stroll through the city center a rewarding experience. The stretch along Lourdes between Sucre and Bolívar is particularly attractive. Loja's independence was declared on 18 November 1820 in the aptly named **Parque de la Independencia** (a.k.a. Plaza San Sebastian), five blocks south of the central plaza. All of the buildings around the plaza have been given facelifts, making it one of the most beautiful plazas in Ecuador. Dance and music performances are occasionally held here in the shadow of the clock tower during weekday evenings.

Loja's best views are from the **Virgen del Loja** statue, east and uphill on Rocafuerte, and the **Iglesia El Pedestal,** also called the Balcón de Loja (Balcony of Loja), west of the city center on 10 de Agosto.

Outside the Center

Head a few kilometers north of the center to reach the **Parque Jipiro,** a fantasy world for young and old on an island in the Río Zamora. The park's most famous landmark, a miniature, slide-filled Kremlin, is just part of a huge playground filled with equipment that would send American liability lawyers into convulsions. Other diversions include a pool with waterslides, a skate park, paddleboats, a small avian zoo, and a planetarium inside a miniature mosque. Open daily 8 A.M.–noon and 2–6 P.M.

South of the center spreads the campus of the **Universidad Nacional de Loja.** Go just to see the **Jardín Botánico "Reindaldo Espinosa,"** tel. 7/582-764, a large botanical collection with more than enough flowers and bizarre plants to make it worth the trip for floraholics and bird-watchers alike. Open Mon.–Fri. 9 A.M.–4 P.M. (The actual entrance is 150 meters south of where you will surely assume it is.) Across the highway is the **Parque Universitario La**

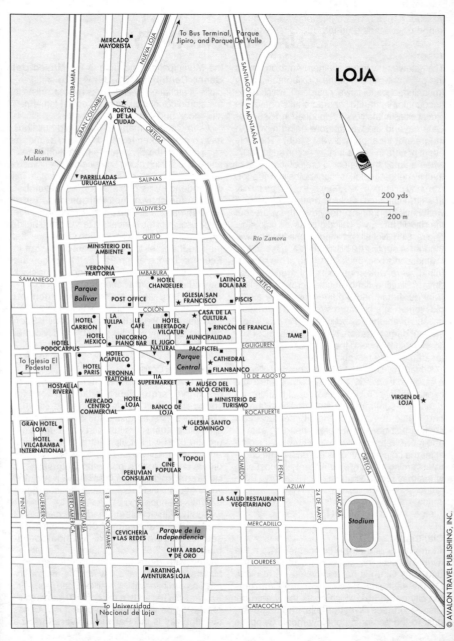

LOJA

To Bus Terminal, Parque Jipiro, and Parque Del Valle

MERCADO MAYORISTA

PORTÓN DE LA CIUDAD

Río Malacatus

PARRILLADAS URUGUAYAS

MINISTERIO DEL AMBIENTE

VERONNA TRATTORIA

Parque Bolívar

POST OFFICE

HOTEL CHANDELIER

IGLESIA SAN FRANCISCO

LATINO'S BOLA BAR

PISCIS

Río Zamora

HOTEL CARRIÓN

LA TULLPA

LE CAFÉ

HOTEL MÉXICO

UNICORNO PIANO BAR

HOTEL LIBERTADOR/ VILCATUR

CASA DE LA CULTURA

RINCÓN DE FRANCIA

EL JUGO NATURAL

MUNICIPALIDAD

PACIFICTEL

HOTEL PODOCARPUS

To Iglesia El Pedestal

HOTEL ACAPULCO

HOTEL PARIS

VERONNA TRATTORIA

TIA SUPERMARKET

Parque Central

CATHEDRAL

FILANBANCO

HOSTAL LA RIVERA

MERCADO CENTRO COMMERCIAL

HOTEL LOJA

BANCO DE LOJA

MUSEO DEL BANCO CENTRAL

MINISTERIO DE TURISMO

GRAN HOTEL LOJA

HOTEL VILCABAMBA INTERNATIONAL

IGLESIA SANTO DOMINGO

VIRGEN DE LOJA

TAME

CINE POPULAR

TOPOLI

PERUVIAN CONSULATE

CEVICHERIA LAS REDES

Parque de la Independencia

CHIFA ARBOL DE ORO

ARATINGA AVENTURAS LOJA

LA SALUD RESTAURANTE VEGETARIANO

Stadium

To Universidad Nacional de Loja

0   200 yds
0   200 m

NUEVA LOJA
CUXIBAMBA
GRAN COLOMBIA
ORTEGA
SANTIAGO DE LA MONTAÑAS
SALINAS
VALDIVIESO
QUITO
IMBABURA
SAMANIEGO
COLÓN
EGUIGUREN
ORTEGA
10 DE AGOSTO
ROCAFUERTE
RIOFRIO
OLMEDO
J.J. PEÑA
AZUAY
24 DE MAYO
MACARA
ORTEGA
PINTO
GUERRERO
IBEROAMERICA
UNIVERSITARIA
18 DE NOVIEMBRE
SUCRE
BOLIVAR
VALDIVIEZO
MERCADILLO
LOURDES
CATACOCHA

© AVALON TRAVEL PUBLISHING, INC.

tario **La Argelia,** with a network of well-maintained trails leading up into the piney woods. The park is open from dawn to dusk, but it's hit or miss when the visitors center will be open. Southbound buses marked "Argelia Capuli" pass the garden and park.

ACCOMMODATIONS

Less Than $10
Rooms with private bath, cable TV, and phone are only $5 pp at the **Hostal La Riviera,** Universitaria and 10 de Agosto, tel. 7/572-863, tel./fax 7/577-302. The same owners operate the **Hotel Quinara,** tel. 7/570-785, next door, with similar prices and almost the same level of quality.

Several other recommended budget hotels have good deals on rooms with private bath for less than $5 pp. Try the **Hotel Paris,** 10 de Agosto 16-49 between 18 de Noviembre and Universitaria, tel. 7/561-639; the **Hotel Carrión,** Colón 16-36 and 18 de Noviembre, tel. 7/584-548; the colonial **Hotel Loja,** Rocafuerte 15-27 and Sucre, tel. 7/570-241; or the newer **Hotel Chandelier,** Imbabura 14-82 and Sucre, tel./fax 7/578-233. All of these places also have shared rooms for $2 or less.

For a small increase in price, you can get a much nicer room at the **Hotel Acapulco,** Sucre 7-61 and 10 de Agosto, tel. 7/570-651 or 570-199, for $8 s, $12 d, with cable TV, private bath, and phone. Expect the same prices and spotless accommodations at the **Hotel Podocarpus,** Eguiguren 16-50 between 18 de Noviembre and Universitaria, tel. 7/581-428 or 579-776.

$10–25
The **Hotel Libertador,** Colón 14-30 and Bolívar, tel. 7/560-779, fax 7/572-119, is Loja's most upscale accommodation, offering guest racquetball courts, a gym, and a pool. Rooms cost $19 s, $21 d, with a presidential suite for $26. Right next door, the **Gran Hotel Loja,** Aguirre and Rocafuerte, tel. 7/575-200 or 575-201, fax 7/575-202, has rooms of comparable quality (although without the extra facilities) for $8 s, $14 d, as does the **Hotel Vilcabamba Internacional,** Iberoamérica and Riofrio, tel. 7/573-393 or 573-645, fax 7/561-483, along with its own La Bastilla Restaurant.

FOOD

Typical Food and Seafood
José Antonio's, in the "Centro Exclusivo de Compras Vallto," on 10 de Agosto between Sucre and 18 de Noviembre, serves Loja's best seafood starting at $3 in a setting worthy of a much larger city. The **Cevichería Las Redes,** 18 de Noviembre and Mercadillo, is more modest but also good.

Hotel restaurants range from the generous, economical **Hotel Mexico,** Eguiruren 15-89 and Sucre, with a heaping *almuerzo* for $1, to **La Castelanna** of the Hotel Libertador, one of the fanciest in the city. Beef tenderloin in "caviar sauce" (go figure) is $2.20. Locals frequent **La Tullpa,** 18 de Noviembre and Colón, for a little bit of everything for $1–3.

International
Visit the **Chifa China** next to the Hotel Paris for a taste of the Orient, southern-Sierra style, or the **Chifa Arbol de Oro,** on the corner of Lourdes and Bolívar, with slightly higher prices. **Parilladas Uruguayas,** Universitaria and Salinas, is a good, inexpensive grill, and **Veronna Trattoria,** Imbabura 15-46 and 18 de Noviembre, has good food and service. (Cook Miguel Saldago learned to make Italian food in Nebraska, of all places.) Pastas average $2 and medium pizzas $4.

In the spirit of variety, the **Rincón de Francia** does a little French, a little Italian, and a little Ecuadorian served in a funky courtyard or one of the small rooms surrounding it ($2–3). It's a half block north of the cathedral on Valdivieso.

Cafés, Health Food, and Supermarkets
La Salud Restaurante Vegetariano, Azuay 12-08 and Olmedo, satisfies vegetarians in the south end of town with a $1 *almuerzo,* and the **Restaurant Vegetariano El Paraiso,** on Sucre near the Ministrerio de Ambiente, does the same for patrons in the north with their $1.25 *menú del día.*

Juices and healthy snacks fill the short menu at **El Jugo Natural,** on Eguirren between Sucre and Bolívar, and the corner café **Topoli,** on Riofrio and Bolívar, features tasty breakfasts and yogurt in the morning and burgers, hot dogs, and falafel in the afternoon—all for less than $1.

Le Café, a quiet place for coffee or fruit juice and a quick empanada, is at Colón 14-96 and Sucre. An **ice cream parlor** holds down the corner of Azuay and 18 de Noviembre, and there's a **Tia Supermarket** half a block west of the Parque Central on 10 de Agosto.

ENTERTAINMENT AND EVENTS

Nightlife

The "Musical Capital of Southern Ecuador" has a depressingly limited range of evening options. Most are of the drinks-and-taped-music variety, such as the **Unicorno Piano Bar,** with live music on Fridays and a dim red velvet interior on the west side of the Parque Central. **Latino's Bola Bar,** on Imbabura 12-76 and Valdivieso, has pool tables.

Of Loja's two movie theaters, only the **Cine Popular** gets big-time Hollywood films in which people keep their clothes on (for the most part). **Cabañitas Peña Bar,** Sucre 10-90 and Azuay, has live music, and you can stop by the **Casa de la Cultura,** Colón and Valdivieso, to see if anything interesting is on the schedule. Choose your diversion at **Piscis,** on the corner of Olmedo and Colón, where options include pool tables, ping-pong, chess, and foosball.

Festivals

Loja comes alive during the first few weeks in September when the **Virgen del Cisne** rolls into town. Huge processions and a produce fair in the Parques Del Valle and Jipiro liven up this otherwise Mildville. The **Independence of Loja** is celebrated on 18 November, and the **Feast of San Sebastian** on 8 December coincides with the *fiesta* commemorating the **Foundation of Loja.**

SHOPPING AND SERVICES

Unlike its larger neighbor to the north, Loja is not a great shopping city. The **Mercado Centro Commercial** was rebuilt in 1991 into perhaps the cleanest and best-organized indoor market in Ecuador. It's a good place to spot visiting Saraguro *indígenas,* as is the **Mercado Mayorista** on Nueva Loja just north of the river confluence.

A workshop on Azuay 14-13 and Bolívar belongs to one of the town's several guitar makers. Ceramic vases are the specialty of a shop on Colón between Sucre and Bolívar. Several art galleries and craft sops have opened up on the restored section of Lourdes, and odds are more will follow. Otavalan goods are sold at 10 de Agosto 14-79 and Sucre.

Tour Companies

Vilcatur, tel./fax 7/588-014, tel. 7/571-443, e-mail: vilcatur@impsat.net.ec, operates out of the Hotel Libertador, offering tours to Puyango Petrified Forest for $30 pp (two-person minimum) and bird-watching in Podocarpus for $22 pp. They also go to Saraguro, El Cisne, and other nearby destinations. English-speaking guides are available, and they have cars for rent. **Aratinga Aventuras Loja,** Lourdes 14-80 and Sucre, tel./fax 7/582-434, e-mail: jatavent@cue.satnet.net, specializes in bird-watching tours to Podocarpus ($33 pp with two people), but owner/guide Pablo Andrado can also set up trekking and camping trips. **Biotours,** Eguiguren and Olmedo, tel./fax 7/578-398, 597-387, e-mail: biotours@cue.satnet.net, also does tours in the area.

Services and Information

Filanbanco on the Parque Central and the **Banco de Loja** at Bolívar and Rocafuerte will both change travelers' checks. Assorted money shops will change Perúvian soles; ask at your hotel for one nearby.

Loja's **post office** is at Colón and Sucre, and **Pacifictel** sits half a block east of the central park on Eguiguren. There's another Pacifictel office and Internet access at the bus terminal. Information on entering the country to the south can be found at the **Perúvian consulate,** Sucre 10-64 and Azuay, tel. 7/571-668. The **Ministerio de Turismo** has an office at Valdiviezo 8-30 and 10 de Agosto, and the **municipal police** are in a castlelike building on the corner of Imbabura and Valdivieso.

If you're thinking of visiting Podocarpus National Park, check in with the **Ministerio del Ambiente,** on Sucre between Quito and Imbabura, tel. 7/571-534 or 577-125, or the **Fundación Arco Iris,** Guerrero 12-09 between Olmedo and Riofrio, tel. 7/572-926.

Colón between Bolívar and 18 de Noviembre is Loja's Internet alley, with three **web cafés** and more undoubtedly to follow. Other options include **Planet Cyber,** 18 de Noviembre 6-56 and Eguiguren (open daily), and **Cyber C@fe** at Bolívar and Rocafuerte.

TRANSPORTATION

Like its market, Loja's **terminal terrestre** is clean, modern, and organized. It's a 10-minute bus ride north of the city center at Gran Colombia and Isidro Ayora. Local buses run north on Universitaria and back down Iberoamerica/Aguirre every few minutes. Panamericana has luxury overnight buses for Quito leaving at 5:15 P.M. for $9 (14–15 hours). Normal buses to Quito are $7, and you can also get to Cuenca ($3.50, five hours) and Zamora ($1, two hours). **Transportes Loja** goes to Piura, Perú, at 7 and 10 A.M. and 11 P.M. ($7.25, eight hours).

Vilcabamba Turis buses leave for Vilcabamba every half hour from the terminal. Just as convenient, quicker, and less inexpensive—albeit less comfortable—are the **taxi rutas** leaving from Iberoamérica and Chile, half a kilometer south of the city center. Local buses heading south on Iberoamérica pass nearby; just tell the driver where you are going. They cost 60 cents pp and leave when full; it's 45 minutes to Vilcabamba.

Flights with **TAME,** 24 de Mayo and Ortega,

tel. 7/573-030 or 570-248, and **Icaro Express** leave from the airport in nearby Catamayo (see "West of Loja").

EAST FROM LOJA

The southern gateway to the Ecuadorian Amazon follows the Río Zamora northeast from the town of Zamora. This little-used back door to the Oriente is perfect if you like to go where none of your friends have been. The road from Loja to Zamora is one of the most scenic in the country, making the bus ride to Zamora alone worthy of a day trip. Leaving Loja, the route twists and turns so much that you'll find yourself still staring down at the city half an hour after you've left. It climbs up to a 2,500-meter pass before snaking through deep wooded valleys and past waterfalls. The road is in good condition most of the way, so it would make an excellent bike ride (even if you cheat and have a bus take you up to the pass!)

Zamora

The powerful sun that hits you as you step off the bus reminds you that Zamora, at 1,000 meters elevation, is definitely on the tropical side of the country both geographically and culturally. This rough-and-tumble frontier town 65 km east of Loja succumbed to continual raids by local indigenous tribes after its founding in 1550. Rebuilt in the 19th century, it became the cap-

Zamora

ital of the newly founded (and similarly unde-veloped) province of Zamora-Chinchipe in 1953; it was another decade before the city saw its first motor vehicle. The rediscovery of gold in nearby Nambija has injected some life into the dusty streets, but Zamora still seems like the kind of town where the mail arrives by stagecoach and the bars don't serve drinks with umbrellas.

Zamora's lodging options serve as a reminder that this isn't a tourist town. The **Hotel Gimyfa,** on Diego de Vaca one block east of the plaza, is the best in town for $6 s, $8 d, with TV, private bath, and hot water. There's even a **Tropy Burger** on the ground floor. Almost as nice is the **Hotel Internacional Torres,** tel. 7/605-195, for $4 pp. Both hotels have discos, which is as much activity as you'll find around here at night. The **Hotel Seyma,** tel. 7/605-583, is cheaper and barely passable a block and a half from the plaza on 24 de Mayo. Rooms are $2 with shared cold-water baths.

Ceviche is $2.50 at the open-air **Cevicheria Bart's Cave** on the northwest corner of the plaza. More than a dozen restaurants in and around the bus station serve basic Ecuadorian fare. One block south of the bus station on Sevilla de Oro is **Cheers,** a good place for a beer (although nobody will know your name).

On the northeast corner of the plaza, you'll find a sign for **Yanknam,** advertising handicrafts and tourist information. This is now the office of a shipping company, but as of 2000, there were still a few dozen craft items left, and the friendly staff will still answer questions about the area. If you're looking for a guide for hiking or horse-back riding in the surrounding hills, they'll send you to the furniture store around the corner at 4-103 Diego de Vaca.

Pacifictel is one block north of the main plaza. The **post office** sits a few doors east of the plaza on Sevilla de Oro, although you would hardly know it from the faded sign (look for "al de Correos"). You can check your e-mail for $2 per hour right in front of the bus station. For information on Podocarpus, stop by the **Ministerio del Ambiente** office across the cemetery a short distance out the road to Loja.

The **bus terminal** is a few blocks east of the plaza alongside the **market.** Buses and rancheros head out to various small towns where

locals will stare at you as if you fell out of the sky—even more than in Zamora. Gualaquiza is $1.60 and five hours away.

Northeast into the Jungle

The Río Zamora valley leads the way from Zamora through the squalid mining boomtown of **Nambija,** from which a primitive track winds north along the Río Yacuambi toward remote **24 de Mayo.** Further downhill from Nambija are **Yantzaza** and **Gualaquiza.**

PODOCARPUS NATIONAL PARK

Ecuador's southernmost national park is a hidden gem. Large tracts of virgin forest shelter a bewildering array of climates and residents; some of the most spectacular scenery lies within easy access of Loja and Vilcabamba. Even as poaching, illegal colonizing, and especially mining take their toll on Podocarpus, the relatively few tourists who visit come away knowing they've seen something special—whether it's the fairy-tale high-altitude forest or one of the flashier of the park's hundreds of bird species.

Habitats

The park ranges from 1,000 meters in the river valleys to 3,600 meters in the higher reaches of the Nudo de Sabanilla mountain range, part of the larger Cordillera Real. Stretching unbroken from the high Andes to low-altitude rainforest, Podocarpus' 360,000 dripping hectares encompass countless microclimates, many found nowhere else in Ecuador.

Most of the park lies between 2,000 and 3,000 meters, consisting of hillsides covered with moist cloud forest. Four separate watersheds, including that of Loja, depend on Podocarpus for their moisture. More than 100 small Andean lakes left in glacial depressions dot the landscape, fed and drained by waterfalls and rushing streams.

Flora and Fauna

More than 40 percent of the park's 3,000–4,000 plant species are endemic. Podocarpus takes its name from having the country's largest contingent of the Podocarpus or romerillo tree, the only conifer native to Ecuador. Although many of these trees have been cut down for their high-quality wood, some old 40-meter giants can still be appreciated in remote tracts of cloud forest. Once the world's only source of quinine to fight malaria, the Cascarilla tree, *Chinchona succirubra,* is common on the western slopes. Other common plants include orchids, bromeliads, palms, and tree ferns.

Podocarpus is by far the most important animal sanctuary in Ecuador's southern Andes. Along with attractive but seldom-seen species such as the spectacled bear, mountain tapir, ocelot, puma, and deer, the park is home to an avian variety to make a birder drool: 600 species have been recorded so far and many more are on the way.

The main entrance at Cajanuma has been called one of the best spots in the world, in terms of variety and easy access, for viewing Andean birds. The list goes on and on: 61 species of hummingbirds, 81 different tanagers, the Andean cock-of-the-rock, and the endangered bearded guan *(Penelope barbata),* are only the beginning. Endemic species such as the neblina metaltail *(Matallura odomae)* and the white-breasted parakeet *(Phyrrura albipectus)* also make a strong showing. In 1988, a new species of antpitta was discovered in the park, with a call like a cross between an owl's hoot and a dog's bark. At 10 inches high, it's the second-largest known antpitta in the world.

Visiting the Park

For most of the park, Oct.–Dec. are the driest overall months, with Feb.–Apr. seeing the most rain. Temperatures vary from a 12°C average in the high Andes to 18°C in the rainforest. Raingear is a must. The west side of Podocarpus is covered by the IGM 1:50,000 maps *Río Sabanilla* and *Vilcabamba* (or the 1:100,000 *Gonzanamá*), and the east side falls within the 1:50,000 *Zamora* and *Cordillera de Tzunantza.* The Ministerio del Ambiente and Arco Iris in Loja (see "Loja and Vicinity") have information on the park, and tours run from both Loja and Vilcabamba. Entrance to the park is $5 pp.

Western Access

The turnoff for the main park entrance at Cajanuma is 23 km south of Loja on the road to Vilcabamba. From here it's nine km uphill to the **Cajanuma refuge,** opened in 1995 with the help of The Nature Conservancy, the World Wildlife Fund, and the Peace Corps. It has space and facilities for up to 20 people—book with the Ministerio del Ambiente in Loja beforehand. Grab a map, and hit one of the many marked *senderos* (trails) that wind off into the woods, ranging from the 400-meter-loop Sendero Oso de Anteojos (Spectacled Bear Trail) to the two-day hike to the Lagunas del Compadre.

Eastern Access

The lower-altitude reaches of Podocarpus can be accessed more directly by way of Zamora. A 40-minute journey down the west side of the Río Bombuscara—half drive, half walk—brings you to the **Bombuscara interpretive center.** After a dip in the river, try the one-hour trail to a cliff lookout, and keep your eyes open. Maybe you'll see a gray tinamou, coppery-chested jackamar, Ecuadorian piedtail hummer, or one of a whole spectrum of tanagers (paradise, orange-eared, blue-necked, bay-headed, green and gold, and spotted).

Even more remote is the **Romerillos guardpost** along the Río Jamboe, reached by heading 18 km down the east side of the Río Bombuscara. Both of the eastern entrances are best reached by taxi or *ranchero* from Zamora.

WEST OF LOJA

Catamayo, 31 km west of Loja, is the site of the **La Tola Airport.** TAME has flights to Quito Mon.–Sat. for $30 one-way, and to Guayaquil Mon., Thurs., and Fri. for $15 one-way. **Icaro Express** flies to Quito Wed., Fri., and Sun. for $68 one-way. Reserve your seats beforehand in Cuenca if possible. If you find yourself stuck here overnight, the **Hotel Turis,** 24 de Mayo and Ayora, tel. 7/677-126, or the **Hotel Rosasanna,** tel. 7/677-066, next door offer decent budget rooms for less than $3. While away an afternoon waiting for your plane next to the pool at the **Centro Recreacional Popular Eliseo Arias Carrión,** five km from the center of town.

A short spur north from Catamayo ends at **El Cisne,** where the **Sanctuario de La Virgen del Cisne** is kept in a grand old church. The icon was carved in the late 16th century and is one of the most venerated in the Ecuadorian Andes. A five-day festival starting 15 August clogs the road to Loja with crowds of pilgrims bearing the image on their shoulders. Some make the entire trek on foot. The Virgin arrives in Loja on the 20th, where it stays until 20 November.

Macará

In 1995, Ecuador's second-largest gateway to Perú saw gunfire across the 2.5-km bridge over the Río Macará. With the signing of the border agreement in 1998, though, things have quieted down, which is always a good thing in a border town. Because fewer tourists come this far out, the border crossing at Macará (pop. 15,000) is simpler than at Huaquillas to the north.

The **Hotel Paradero Turístico,** tel. 7/694-099, is about 500 meters southwest of the town center along the road toward the border, and rooms with private bath and hot water cost about $5 d. For other budget accommodations, try the clean and friendly **Hotel Amazonas,** Rengel 4-18 and Valdivieso, or the **Hotel Espiga de Oro** just north of the market, with a slow and pricey restaurant. The seafood at the **Dragón Dorado** on Calderón is said to be good. **Cooperativa Loja** and **Cariamanga** both send buses to Loja ($3, 7–8 hours).

Crossing the Border: The Pana rolls southwest from the center of town for 2.5 km to the Perúvian border. Taxis and trucks make the trip often, or you can walk it in less than one hour. Get your exit stamp at the **Ecuadorian Immigration** office—open daily 8 A.M.–noon and 2–6 P.M.—then cross the bridge into La Tina, Perú, where you can get your entry stamp in the building on your right. *Collectivos* run from the Perú side to the larger cities of Sullana and Piura.

VILCABAMBA

This small town, nestled in one of Ecuador's most pristine corners, gained some notoriety when word began to spread that residents lived longer—sometimes *much* longer—than usual. Although further study has somewhat debunked the "Valley of Longevity" theory, Vilcabamba's gorgeous setting and tranquil pace of life have taken over as its main draw. Set at the intersection of five valleys, Vilcabamba enjoys clean air,

mild weather, and hiking, biking, and horseback-riding options in every direction.

From the days of hippie guru Johnny Love Wisdom's failed University of Life, Vilcabamba (pop. 4,000) has had to make room for legions of wanderers drawn by the undeniably healthy atmosphere. The 20th century arrived a little late here—horses are still as common as cars in the streets—and as a result the town has had to cope with significant changes in the last few decades. Along with electricity, running water, and sewage systems, Vilcabamba has seen crime rise, along with health problems such as cancer and heart disease. In a sad irony, residents of Ecuador's "Valley of Eternal Youth" are dying younger than ever before.

Add to that the legions of backpackers who scribble Vilcabamba next to Otavalo, Baños, and Montañita on their Must-See lists, and you have a beautiful place balanced on the edge. It's one of those places travel writers hesitate to describe too lovingly, lest it become loved to death. Reports are already coming back that Vilcabamba isn't as *tranquilo* as it once was. By all means come, inhale the air, ride a horse, leave a little healthier—just please, tread lightly.

Accommodations in Town

Vilcabamba's cheapest rooms can be found at the **Hotel Valle Sagrado,** tel. 7/580-686, on Calle Sucre on the main plaza. The **Hostal Mandango,** Huilcopamba and Montalvo, is a close runner-up for budget lodgings. It has an inner courtyard with hammocks and an open-air rooftop bar. Both places see a lot of traffic and are comfortable for $2 pp or less. Carmita of the Commercial Carmita on the plaza has a furnished apartment for rent in town, with two bedrooms, three double beds, a kitchen, and hot water for $3 pp per night. Ask at the store or call the Pole House (see following entry).

Just off the main plaza is the newer, cheerful **Hidden Garden Pensión,** tel./fax 7/580-281, tel. 7/580-286, e-mail: vilca@srv8.telconet.net. Bright, simple rooms cost $4 pp with shared bath and $5 pp with private bath, including breakfast, and guests can use the pool and kitchen facilities and wash their own laundry or have it done. E-mail and fax services are open to guests. The **Hosteria La Posada Real,** tel.

VILCABAMBA'S CENTENARIANS

What is also important is to avoid drinking cold water when you are sweating. And keep in motion. Those who just sit around die early.

—Ernesto Inigu, reportedly 118 years old (1988), when asked the secret of his longevity

Vilcabamba's reputation as the Valley of Eternal Youth has been around a long time—but not nearly as long as some of its residents. If there is indeed something special here that scares off the Reaper, the jury's still out—but, even scientists agree, you could choose a much worse place to live out a long, healthy life.

Since scientists began visiting the area in the 1970s, reports have conflicted concerning if, how many, and why Vilcabamba has more than its share of very old residents. While there is a large population of sprightly seniors, exact numbers are few and far between. A 1971 survey found 819 townspeople over 100—a little over 1 percent, or one per 100. In comparison, the United States at the time had one per 330,000.

Seven years later, on the other hand, an anthropological research team from American universities in Wisconsin and California concluded that nobody in Vilcabamba was over 96. In 1988, a local hospital administrator claimed that there were 39 Vilcabambans alive who were born in the 19th century. Theories for the overestimations include lying for higher social status (age is revered in Latin America), the exodus of younger residents leaving an age-heavy population, and the use of identical names by a few interrelated people.

In rural Ecuador, the most reliable way to confirm age is through birth, baptismal, and marriage records kept by the Catholic Church. Passports and letters, although few, also come in handy. More suspect are memories of historic events—which, although fascinating if true, are easily fabricated—and word of mouth. Visiting in 1970, a Harvard researcher was introduced to Miguel Carpio as the oldest person in the village at 121. Four years later, the same scientist returned and was introduced once again to Carpio—then said to be 132.

I'll Have What He's Having

Scientists have long lists of theories of how those who are over 100 pull it off. All agree that clean water and air are two fundamental building blocks. Next comes lots of physical activity well into old age, increasing cardiovascular fitness. Heart attacks may still strike a grandpa in good shape, but they may be "silent" and go unfelt and ineffectual. Diet is crucial. The average Vilcabamban over 50 eats a daily diet of 1,200 calories (versus the 2,400 suggested in the United States for folks over 55), including 35–38 grams of primarily animal protein (versus 65 suggested in the United States) and 12–19 grams of fat, mostly from vegetables. Such healthy, spartan fare may head off atherosclerosis (fatty buildup in the arteries).

Next step: stay happily married. Along with the companionship and psychological support of a healthy relationship, researchers have concluded that the benefits of marriage don't stop at the dinner table. A Japanese TV team filming in Vilcabamba in 1980 reported that one citizen was still having sex at 117. Locals still tell with reverence the story of one man in the 1950s who allegedly married for the third time at 105 and went on to father two more children. "A good bed is the secret of longevity," said Albertano Roa, 119 in 1994.

Geneticists point to the "unhealthy" lifestyles led by some over 100—smoking, drinking, and raising (limited) hell—in espousing their version. Lack of "bad" genes that lead to fatal disease may also be a key. Perhaps a small group of individuals genetically predisposed to longevity settled here long ago, starting a pocket of descendants who would reap the benefits of long life for generations to come. Then there's always the theory of naturist guru Johnny Love Wisdom, who said the secret is that Vilcabamba is bombarded with "toxin-killing radiation from magnetic sun storms." Whatever the cause, Vilcabamba's semi-true reputation has caught on abroad—Texas-based Youngevity, Inc. markets a "Vilcabamba formula" multivitamin modeled on the mineral content of the local water—because at least part of the town seems to be doing something right.

7/580-904, sits on the edge of the fields at the northeast corner of town on Agua del Hierro. A wide balcony around the raised first floor gives it an almost Victorian feel, by way of the Amazon. Seven large rooms are $5 pp with private bath and hot water, and limited *cafetería* and kitchen facilities are available.

Accommodations Outside of Town

Vilcabamba's most luxurious lodgings, in the traditional sense, are at the **Hostería Vilcabamba,** tel. 7/580-272, fax 7/580-273, a short distance before the town center on the road to Loja. You'll find guests sunning on the terrace facing the great mountain view after enjoying the elegant pool and spa (also open to the public for $1.50 pp). Rooms are $12 s, $16 d, and have private baths with bathtubs. The Hostería has a bar and a small café.

A whole different kind of crowd congregates at the **Hostal Madre Tierra,** tel./fax 7/580-269, tel. 7/580-687, e-mail: hmtierra@ecua.net.ec, www.ecuadorexplorer.com/madretierra, one of my favorite places to stay in Ecuador. For $6–9 pp with shared bath and $10–25 pp with private bath, guests can choose between the small rock pool, steam room, nightly videos, or the hammock strung up among the birds and flowers. Prices include a delicious communal breakfast and dinner. Shared cabins are rustic but comfortable, with bunk beds and mosquito nets. The owners recently opened a spa uphill from the main building, where you can immerse yourself in every bodily luxury from massages and mud baths to herbal wraps and . . . ah . . . colon treatment. Horse hire with a guide costs $10 for four hours, and the staff can arrange all-inclusive tours of Podocarpus National Park for $255 per day for 1–3 days.

The latest addition to Vilcabamba's accommodation lineup is the **Hostería Las Ruinas de Quinara,** tel./fax 7/580-301 or 580-314, e-mail: ruinsaqui@hotmail.com, www.lasruinasdequinara.com, about 10 minutes outside of town on the road southwest to Yamburara. For $9 pp, guests can enjoy rooms with shared bath ($11 pp private), the heated swimming pool, sauna, hot tub, steam room, and cable TV and a selection of videos. If that's not enough, Internet access, massage, bike and horse rental, and dance classes are extra.

Farther out into the countryside you'll find the **Cabañas Río Yambala,** also simply known as **Charlie's Cabañas.** Rooms and cabins in a beautiful riverside setting five km east of town range from $2–6 pp, with hot showers and a restaurant with cooking facilities open to guests. Charlie's is a favorite retreat for budget-conscious travelers looking to relax in solitude (many cabins are isolated among the trees) and quiet—the only sounds are running water from the nearby river, birdcalls, and the wind in the trees. Owners Charlie and Sarah also rent a refuge in the foothills of Podocarpus National Park with space for 12 people, gas stove, and fireplace. They've set up a marked trail system nearby and run guided day trips on horseback. The cabins are a one-hour walk from the town center, but a free taxi shuttle runs from the bus station for guests. To arrange a visit and ride, call 7/580-299 in town and leave a message if they're not there, www.vilcabamba.org/charlie.

Alicia and Orlando Falco, naturalist guides with experience in the Galápagos and the Amazon, run the **Pole House Lodge,** tel. 7/673-186, e-mail: ofalcoecolodge@yahoo.com, a 10-minute walk from town. It's a rustic, secluded place set up on stilts at the edge of the Río Chambo, with cooking facilities and rooms with private baths for $7.50 d. Adobe and bamboo cabins can hold 24 people for $3–7 each. There's a kitchen, hot showers, and room for bonfires next to the river. A fridge and blender mean you can make fresh *jugos* from the fruits in the garden. The lodge is a seriously relaxing place, but if you're up for some activity, try the hiking trails in their 40-hectare Rumi-Huilco Nature Reserve. The Falcos also organize nature walks in Podocarpus (see "Entertainment and activities"). Ask at the Primavera handicraft shop on the plaza in town for information on the lodge and the walks.

Food

The small **Huilcopamba** restaurant, on the northwest corner of the park, serves a good selection of fresh juices to accompany plates in the $1 range (some vegetarian options). For an Italian menu, go next door to the restaurant of the **Hotel Valle Sagrado,** which also has some vegetarian dishes. Although Vilcabamba is far from the ocean, the **Primus Interpares Cevichería,** next to the bus terminal, turns out some decent seafood. **La Terraza Madre Tierra** (not to be confused with the hotel) serves excellent Mexican food on the plaza for $2–3 per meal—the chicken fajitas are the best. A friendly French couple runs the **Rendez-vous** restaurant in town, with tasty crêpes, a good pancake breakfast, and happy hour daily from 6–7 P.M.

Recreation

The best and cheapest recreation option in Vilcabamba is exploring on foot. A good place to start is one of the three drinking-water plants in town, where Vilcabamba's reputation for longevity is bottled for those unfortunates in less balmy climes. Along with Vilca Vida and Kastal, the Vilcagua spring water is said to have beaten out Perrier and Evian in an international tasting competition.

Maps and trail descriptions for various hikes, including a day hike along the Río Uchima, are available at Hostal Madre Tierra. That odd-shaped peak that dominates the valley to the west is called **Cerro Mandango** (Tripe Mountain). To climb it, head south out of town past the bus station and the *cooperativa* sign. A trail leads uphill to the right—you're on the right track if you have to pass through a gate; just ask for the *sendero al cumbre de Mandango* (trail to Mandango peak). One hour uphill through forest and cow pastures brings you to a hilltop cross overlooking the town, but the real summit isn't for another hour.

Of the Mandango's three peaks, only numbers two and three (2,026 meters) can be scaled safely—nearly vertical walls of crumbling dirt separate the tops from their bases. Be careful crossing between one and two, and don't scramble so high (speaking from experience) that you can't get down without an airlift. Afterward, it's possible to descend north into the valley of the Río Vilcabamba, then head east toward Madre Tierra and the main road.

A longer journey east of Vilcabamba is also possible, along the Río Yambala valley through spectacular scenery to the edge of Podocarpus. Ask at Charlie's for maps and information on using one of their *refugios* just inside the park boundary. The IGM 1:50,000 *Vilcabamba* map covers the area.

Something about the Vilcabamba valley soothes the soul, so it seems only natural to let someone soothe your body with a **massage.** The masseuses at the Hostal Madre Tierra's spa will knead away your cares for $22 per hour ($19 for guests).

Shopping

Jewelry and **trinket** vendors in the plaza compete with **Artesanias Primavera** for tourists' souvenir dollars. The small shop stocks everything you'd need for the true Vilcabamba Experience—granola, medicinal herbs, horsehair massage gloves—along with crafts such as the Saraguro *indígenas'* double shoulder bags, called *prededores.*

Entertainment and Activities

After two decades guiding in the Galápagos, **Orlando Falco** moved to Vilcabamba and began leading trips into the wilds of the southern Sierra. He's an ecologically minded, knowledgeable naturalist guide who leads trips of different lengths and difficulty into the rainforest and Podocarpus National Park. He provides English-speaking guides and transportation for $25 pp per day, including lunch and the park entrance fee.

Day-long horse rides are one of the most popular diversions in Vilcabamba. They usually cost between $3–7 pp for a four-hour trip up to $75 per day for three-day excursions and should be arranged at least the day before. Trips can be set up through most hotels or through one of the many private guides in town. Resettled Kiwi Gavin Moore runs **Gavilan Horse Tours** and offers excursions ranging from 1–3 days for about $25 pp per day. His tours have received enthusiastic kudos. Ask for Gavin in town at the Tienda de Pancho on the main plaza by the Huilcopamba restaurant. Also recommended as private guides in Vilcabamba are **Rogelio Toledo, Ernesto Avila,** and **Wilson Carpio.**

Vilcabamba isn't the nightlife center of southern Ecuador. Wherever you find yourself after hours, though, that glazed look in the eyes of your fellow partiers might not just be too much *aguardiente,* but rather the hallucinogenic (and illegal) effects of the endemic **San Pedro cactus,** one of the town's main attractions for the mood-altering inclined. In late February, Vilcabamba's annual **festival** brings visitors from throughout southern Ecuador for a long weekend of music, dancing, horse-riding competitions, and general revelry.

Services and Information
The **tourist office** on the main plaza is said to be helpful and stock information on what to do in the valley. (**AVETUR,** Vilcabamba's local tourism association, maintains a general information website at www.vilcabamba.org, e-mail: info@vilcabamba.org.) **Andinatel** is on the same corner at the tourist office, and the **post office** shares the **police** building one block north.

There's no place in town to exchange travelers' checks, but many hotels accept them (try to make sure first).

Transportation
Two **bus** companies go to Loja: Cooperativa Sur Oriente and Vicabamba Turis. Both leave roughly every hour from the terminal and pass the plaza (90 minutes, 60 cents). Taxi Ruta Avenida 24 de Mayo crams half a dozen people into one car for the run to Loja, which costs a bit more but takes half the time.

BOB RACE

THE GALÁPAGOS ISLANDS
INTRODUCTION

It's not often that you come across a place that's unique in the world. All too many must-sees, no matter how glowingly described by guidebooks and friends, seem to pale in the harsh light of reality. But the Galápagos Islands exist truly without parallel, huddled far out in the Pacific Ocean in the center of a bubble of life like nowhere else on earth.

Initial impressions of the islands certainly don't promise much—the bleak, plant-stubbled landscape carries all the impact of a cheap movie set at first glance. But within a day or two of beginning your tour, you'll have seen things you'd never have believed existed. Tortoises the size of armchairs, iguanas that swim, schools of hammerhead sharks, and birds with huge blue feet are all, at most, slightly curious at your presence. By the end of your stay, you'll have gotten a taste of what the earth was like well before the human race showed up and started throwing its weight around. Hopefully, you'll be able to understand how a short visit to the islands more than a century ago sparked one of the greatest scientific insights in history.

The Galápagos wildlife is often described as tame, but I disagree. It's not that the animals are tame; it's that they just *don't care* that you're there. In a world that has existed for millennia with no major predators, human beings become just another large, curious-looking thing, about as threatening as a tree. The feeling of looking at acres of wild animals that don't flee at your arrival—a place where you actually have to be careful not to step on anyone as you walk down the trail—is nothing short of amazing.

You'll hear the Galápagos described as a "laboratory of evolution," which, along with all

IMPORTANT GALÁPAGOS PHONE NUMBERS

	SANTA CRUZ	SAN CRISTÓBAL
National Park Service	5/526-189 or 526-511	520-138
Police	5/526-101	520-101
Hospital	5/526-103	520-318
TAME	5/526-165 or 526-527	
INGALA	5/526-151	520-171
Charles Darwin Station	5/526-146 or 526-147	

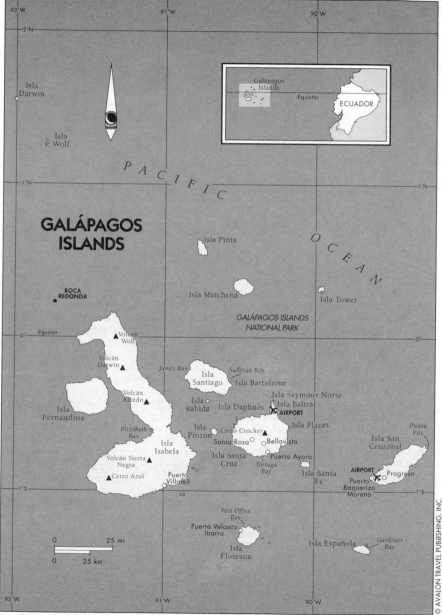

PACIFIC

OCEAN

Isla Darwin

Isla Wolf

GALÁPAGOS ISLANDS

ROCA REDONDA

Isla Pinta

Isla Marchena

Isla Tower

GALÁPAGOS ISLANDS NATIONAL PARK

Equator

Volcán Wolf

Volcán Darwin

James Bay

Sullivan Bay

Isla Santiago

Isla Bartolomé

Volcán Alcedo

Isla Rabida

Isla Daphnes

Isla Seymour Norte

Isla Baltra

AIRPORT

Isla Fernandina

Isla Pinzon

Cerro Crocker

Isla Plazas

Punta Pitt

Elizabeth Bay

Santa Rosa

Bellavista

Isla San Cristóbal

Volcán Sierra Negra

Isla Isabela

Isla Santa Cruz

Puerto Ayora

Tortuga Bay

Isla Santa Fé

AIRPORT

Progreso

Cerro Azul

Puerto Villamil

Puerto Baquerizo Moreno

Post Office Bay

Puerto Velasco Ibarra

Isla Floreana

Isla Española

Gardener Bay

0   25 mi

0   25 km

Galápagos Islands

Equator

ECUADOR

© AVALON TRAVEL PUBLISHING, INC.

ISLAND NAMES

Almost every island in the Galápagos boasts at least two names, and some have three or more, counting the English, Spanish, and nicknames. I've followed the lead of Michael Jackson (the author, not the singer) in selecting the names used in this book, listed here alphabetically followed by any variations. All names are official, except Floreana and Santiago, whose official names follow in boldface.

Cowley
Baltra (South Seymour)
Bartolomé (Bartholomew)
Beagle
Enderby
Española (Hood)
Fernandina (Narborough)
Floreana (**Santa María;** Charles)
Isabela (Albemarle)
Marchena (Bindloe)
Pinta (Abingdon)
Pinzón (Duncan)
Plazas
Rábida (Jervis)
San Cristóbal (Chatham)
Santa Cruz (Indefatigable)
Santa Fé (Barrington)
Santiago (**San Salvador;** James)
Seymour Norte (North Seymour)
Sin Nombre (Nameless)
Tower (Genovesa)
Tortuga (Brattle)
Wolf (Wenman)

the other talk about species, adaptations, and 19th-century naturalists, is enough to make any nonscientist's head spin. What's going on? Simply, the Galápagos Islands are as close to a perfect laboratory experiment on evolution as any place ever discovered. Nobel laureates couldn't have designed a better test if they tried—take a few species, stick them out in the middle of nowhere for a few million years, and see what happens. The result is many unique species found nowhere else on earth, perfectly adapted to their difficult environment, and a few only halfway through the evolutionary process thrown in for good measure.

In part because of how special they are, the Galápagos Islands face a host of problems that threaten the ecosystems that make them unique. The causes are nothing new—human overcrowding, exploitation of resources, too much tourism "loving" the islands to death—but the results could be tragic. If you're interested in helping, tax-deductible **donations** for research, conservation, and environmental education can be sent to the **Charles Darwin Foundation,** P.O. Box 96609, Washington, DC 20077-7174. Donors of $25 or more will receive the bilingual publications "Noticias de Galápagos." For more information on the Foundation and its efforts, contact the CDF Secretary General Office, Casilla 17-01-3891, Quito, tel. 2/244-803, 241-573, fax 2/443-935, e-mail: cdrs@cdarwin@org.ec, www.galapagos.org.

THE LAND

Take five-and-twenty heaps of cinders dumped here and there in an outside city lot; imagine some of them magnified into mountains, and the vacant lot the sea; and you will have a fit idea of the general aspect of the Encantadas, or Enchanted Isles.

—Herman Melville, "Las Encantadas," 1854

The 13 volcanic islands of the province of Galápagos lie scattered over 60,000 square km in the eastern Pacific ocean. Actually the tips of underwater volcanoes, the islands become younger and higher to the west. Isabela, the largest island of the group (4,275 square km), consists of six volcanic peaks joined by old lava flows. One of these, Cerro Azul, is the highest point in the archipelago at 1,689 meters. Sixteen tiny islets and almost 50 rocks complete the archipelago's 8,000 square km of land. Land and sea meet in more than 1,350 km of coastline.

Puerto Villamil on Isabela is one of the islands' three largest towns. Most residents live on Santa Cruz Island, where Puerto Ayora is the largest city, while sleepy Puerto Baquerizo Moreno on San Cristóbal serves as the provincial capital.

A MELANCHOLY ACCOUNT

May 19th: Yesterday in the afternoon the Boat return'd with a melancholy Account, that no Water was to be found . . ."

"May 20: They tell me the Island is nothing but loose Rocks, like Cynders, very rotten and heavy, and the Earth so parch'd, that it will not bear a Man, but break into Holes under his Feet, which makes me suppose there has been a Vulcano here . . ."

"May 23: [We] resolv'd to leave these unfortunate Islands . . . We pity's our 5 Men in the Bark that is missing, who if in being have a melancholy Life without Water, having no more but for 2 Days, when they parted from us."

"May 30: Had we supplied outselves well at Point Arena, we should, no doubt, have had time enough to find the Island . . . reported to be one of the Gallapagos, where there is Plenty of good water, Timber, Land and Sea Turtle, and a Safe Road for Ships . . . but . . . I shall say no more of these Islands, since by what I saw of 'em, they don't at all answer the Description that those Men have given us."

—Captain Woodes Rogers,
from ships' log during
1707 visit to Galápagos

Volcanic Origins

The Galápagos are the result of one of the most volcanically active regions in the world. The islands sit directly over a hot spot in the Pacific crust plate, where underlying magma bulges much closer to the surface than usual. Millions of years ago, molten rock began to bubble up through the crust, cooling in the seawater and piling into mountains that eventually poked above the surface.

As the Pacific crust plate slowly grinds its way southeast under the Nazca plate, which supports the South American mainland (a billion-year nudge that gave birth to the Andes mountains), the volcanoes over the hot spot were carried along as well. New volcanoes quickly formed to take the place of older ones and were slowly worn away by the sea and weather, resulting in a rough chain of islands trailing off toward the mainland. (Comparatively, the U.S. state of Hawaii is also a chain of hot spot volcanoes.)

All of this slow bubbling and sliding produced a few interesting side effects. The islands that currently make up the archipelago are about 3.5 million years old—geologic newborns—but the entire process has been going on for much longer. This means that many more volcanoes have come and gone, weathered away to nothing beneath the seas to the east, than remain visible today (a crucial clue in an evolutionary puzzle concerning the iguana). The islands will eventually disappear as the Nazca plate drives them under Perú faster than the hot spot can push out new ones. Don't worry, though—we're only talking a few centimeters per year, and the whole process will take about 50 million years.

Volcanic Activity

Clues to the islands' volcanic origins are everywhere, and new scars form daily. Beaches of volcanic minerals and jagged spires of tuff (compacted volcanic ash and debris) dot the coast, whereas farther up in the highlands you can visit collapsed calderas and lava tunnels, which formed when lava continued flowing within a hardened outer layer.

On more recent flows such as the one in Sullivan Bay, it's possible to distinguish the two main types of basaltic lava found in the islands. Ropy pahoehoe (pa-HOY-hoy) lava, from the Polynesian word for "calm sea," is formed when a cooled surface layer wrinkles over a liquid base like the skin on cooling hot chocolate. Jagged a'a (AH-ah) lava contains more silicates and starts out stickier, cooling quickly and completely into a super-stucco surface that's tricky to negotiate on foot. The name comes from the Polynesian word for "choppy sea," but it's more easily remembered as the sound you'd make walking over it in bare feet.

The islands of Marchena, Pinta, Isabela, and Fernandina, farthest north and west, are the youngest and most geologically active. Isabela and Fernandina have been blowing off steam, and occasionally much more, well into the 20th century. In 1954, a passing film crew noticed a strange new white beach in Urvina Bay on the west coast of Isabela. On closer investigation they found that an entire stretch of shoreline—coral, fish, and all—had just been raised six meters above sea level by volcanic pressure underneath. Fernandina's latest eruption in 1995 lasted three months and sent a 100-meter-wide flow of lava five km into the sea.

THE SEA

The islands are pushed and pulled by several ocean currents, stirred by trade winds dragging over the water's surface, and intensified by the earth's rotation. The Perúvian (or Humboldt) Current, one of the world's grandest, sweeps north along the coast of Chile and Perú. Subdivided into coastal and oceanic currents, the Perúvian Current parts from the coast near the equator to flow west and wash the Galápagos with its cool waters. The Panama Current flows down from Central America, turning west toward the archipelago near the coast of mainland Ecuador.

West of the islands, the warm Equatorial Current (split into northern and southern sections) continues the surface thrust of the Perúvian Current west into the Pacific. Deep beneath the water's surface, meanwhile, the Equatorial Countercurrent—also called the Cromwell Current—rushes toward the Galápagos from the west. Upon encountering the westernmost islands in the archipelago, the Countercurrent is deflected upward, bringing with it cool, nutrient-rich water from the depths of the Pacific.

The Countercurrent isn't as constant as the other currents—it flows more during the dry season—but it's possibly the most important current of all. The western upwelling, from 5–10°C cooler than the surface waters, is crucial to the marine habitat of the islands. Algae thrive on the nutrients, attracting fish and marine invertebrates that are more suited to the tropics than the middle of the Pacific. Larger marine mammals, such as whales and dolphins, follow these fish, and terrestrial animals and birds depend on the bounty of the surrounding sea. Galápagos penguins and flightless cormorants wait for the Countercurrent to begin their breeding season.

CLIMATE

The climate of the Galápagos Islands is almost completely determined by sea currents, whose varying temperatures bring seasons that differ only in cloud cover and the amount and type of precipitation. The islands enjoy 12 hours of sunlight throughout the year.

Seasons
The hot or rainy season from Jan.–Apr. arrives when the Panama Current warms the nearby waters to 26°C. Daily showers bring 6–10 cm of precipitation per month. Although there is less chance of a completely dry day during the hot season, you'll encounter more warm, sunny days per month than you will in the cool season. Average temperatures climb into the 30s, with Feb-

JULIAN SMITH

hanging out on the shore

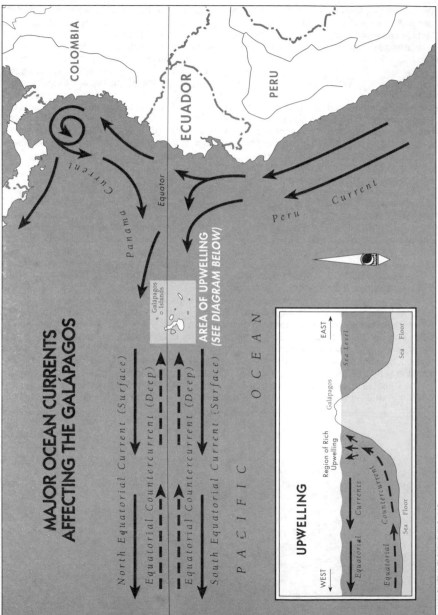

MAJOR OCEAN CURRENTS AFFECTING THE GALÁPAGOS

COLOMBIA

ECUADOR

PERU

Panama Current

Equator

Peru Current

Galápagos Islands

AREA OF UPWELLING
(SEE DIAGRAM BELOW)

PACIFIC OCEAN

North Equatorial Current (Surface)

Equatorial Countercurrent (Deep)

Equatorial Countercurrent (Deep)

South Equatorial Current (Surface)

UPWELLING

WEST

EAST

Sea Level

Sea Floor

Galápagos

Region of Rich Upwelling

Equatorial Currents

Equatorial Countercurrent

Sea Floor

© AVALON TRAVEL PUBLISHING, INC.

ruary and March the warmest and sunniest months.

The Jun.–Nov. cool season arrives with the colder (20°C) waters from the Perúvian Current. Average temperatures drop to less than 27°C, and any precipitation that falls is usually in the form of *garúa*, a misty drizzle that gathers in the highlands. This lingering fog forms at the inversion layer—the intersection between lower ocean-cooled air and warmer air above it— at around 400–600 meters. There are fewer chances of outright rain, but foggy days are common. Lower elevations remain dry and dead-looking, especially from August to November. December and May are transition months.

THE INCREDIBLE SHRINKING IGUANAS

Although the 1997–1998 El Niño didn't hit the Galápagos as hard as it did mainland Ecuador, it still had a big effect on the island's inhabitants. One of the most curious results was reported in *Nature* by Martin Wikelski, professor of Ecology, Ethology, and Evolution at the University of Illinois at Urbana-Champaign.

In examining data collected since 1987, Wikelski and his co-workers noticed that marine iguanas shrank when the marine algae they feed on died during the El Niño season and then regrew to their original size when food became plentiful again. The study was the first conclusive finding of a shrinking adult mammal and countered an unofficial dogma among scientists that, well, animals just don't do that.

On one island, Wikelski found that some iguanas lost not only half their body weight but also one quarter of their length during the 1997–1998 El Niño season. They're not sure how exactly the iguanas managed it, but they hypothesize that the animals may have somehow absorbed part of their skeletons. By becoming smaller, an iguana would increase its chances of survival by making it easier to forage and be warmed by the sun. When food became plentiful again, the iguanas started growing back to their original size to increase their odds of winning territories and reproducing. "You want to be the largest one during the non-El Niño years," summed up the report, "and then you want to be the smallest one during the El Niño years."

The ability to control the loss and recovery of bone mass may eventually have significant implications in human health care. The U.S. national expenditures for osteoporosis—a medical condition in which bones become brittle and break easily, especially in the elderly—were estimated at $10 billion in 1987. Astronauts are also known to lose bone density during extended periods in space.

Altitudinal Variations

The climate at sea level can be hot and arid. Rain is scarce, with minor drizzles and mist during the cool season. Average temperatures drop into the teens as you climb to 500 meters, where the climate begins to resemble subtropical and temperate zones. The highlands on the larger islands (Fernandina, Isabela, Santa Cruz, and San Cristóbal) bear a distinctive type of cloud forest, complete with mist, mosses, lichens, grass, and trees. Temperatures up here, amplified by the dampness, can get downright cold.

A climatic effect known as **rain shadow** occurs on the higher islands and results in different amounts of rain—and hence different vegetation at different elevations—on opposite sides of the islands. Stratus clouds borne by warm, dry trade winds approach the islands from the southeast (windward) at about 600 meters. As the clouds brush up and over the islands, they cool and dump their moisture in the form of rain or mist, leaving little or no precipitation for the trip down the northwestern sides away from the wind (leeward). As a result, cooler, wetter habitats begin at lower altitudes on the windward sides of the islands, whereas the leeward sides remain relatively dry to higher elevations. Fernandina, in the rain shadow of Isabela, illustrates this phenomenon well. The smaller island receives much less moisture than its larger neighbor's high volcanic peaks.

El Niño

There was a time toward the end of the 20th century when it seemed as if everything from heat spells to failed marriages was being blamed on this mysterious climatic phenomenon. Named for the Christ child for its tendency to appear near the Christmas holidays, El Niño (and its climatic cousin La Niña) arrives periodically to create havoc throughout the Pacific basin.

When El Niño is in town, warm waters from the north surge suddenly and force the Perúvian Current south for anywhere from 6–18 months. Ocean temperatures rise, clouds gather, and 6–10 cm more rain falls per month than average. The extra moisture is welcomed by the thirsty islands, but occasionally El Niño brings too much of a good thing.

During the El Niño of 1982–1983, sea temperatures rose by as much as 10°C above normal, wreaking havoc on the islands' delicate ecological balance. Fish and surface algae disappeared almost overnight, leaving marine mammals, reptiles, and seabirds to die of starvation. Not a single waved albatross hatched in 1983, and only half of the 800 flightless cormorant pairs and about 25 percent of the Galápagos penguins survived. Vegetation thrived briefly, then vanished in a subsequent drought, spelling disaster for herbivores.

The worst was yet to come. In 1997 and 1998, an especially extreme El Niño season hit the islands with a crippling blow. December 1997 saw a foot of rain fall on some islands that usually get that much in a year, and sea temperatures rose to 30°C. Terrestrial plant and animal life thrived with the increase in precipitation, including many exotic species such as rats and mice.

Under the surface, however, things quickly became desperate. Although some species, especially fish, could migrate to cooler waters, land-based animals could only go so far. Cool-water marine organisms like plankton and algae, which are vulnerable even to slight temperature changes, started to die off, and soon the animals that depended on them for food followed. Up to 90 percent of the marine iguanas on North Seymour may have died, partly because some were driven to eat poisonous brown algae when their normal diet of green algae was gone. Sharks and fish moved to different locations and depths as the water temperatures shifted. When the sardines left, the sea lions had little left to eat. Approximately 90 percent of sea lion births failed in 1997, and 76 percent of dominant adult males are estimated to have perished.

Galápagos penguins couldn't follow prey species driven to deeper, cooler water, and as a result penguin populations fell by 65 percent.

Boobie chicks drowned in nests filled with rainwater, and rats ate penguin eggs and chicks. No penguin reproductive activity was observed at all in 1997–1998.

By late 1998, surface ocean temperatures were back down to 20°C. Sea lion and marine iguana populations were slowly recovering, and boobies were having chicks again. Coral, bleached when the algae that lived within it died, began to show signs of color.

HISTORY

Ironically, the Galápagos Islands' own inhospitable nature has saved them for much of their history. In the middle of the ocean, with hardly a drop of fresh water, the islands underwhelmed visitors for centuries before permanent settlers managed to scrape a toehold in the volcanic soil. The world eventually became aware of the treasure secreted among the barren-looking islands, just as early visitors were beginning to permanently alter the islands' natural balance.

Pre-Inca *indígenas* from the coast of Ecuador were probably the first to visit the islands, as evidenced by fish bones and food remains uncovered in various spots. Blown out to sea by storms and swept west by the Humboldt Current, these hapless sailors often made one-way journeys of discovery. In 1572, the Spanish chronicler Miguel Sarmiento de Gamboa reported that the Inca Tupac Yupanki had visited the archipelago on the advice of a seer who flew ahead to scout the way. This account is thought to be a legend only, though, because the Incas weren't seagoing people.

In 1535, a ship carrying Tomás de Berlanga, Bishop of Panama, stood becalmed off the coast of what would become Colombia on its way to the Spanish settlements in Perú. The Panama Current pushed the helpless vessel southwest for weeks before washing it among the Galápagos. There the thirst-maddened crew chewed cactus pads for moisture before slumbling across pools of rainwater. Setting sail once more, the ship and crew spent almost a month at sea before the Bahía de Caraquez came into sight.

In a subsequent letter to the Spanish King, Berlanga described the islands' unique and fearless wildlife, but concluded that they weren't fit for

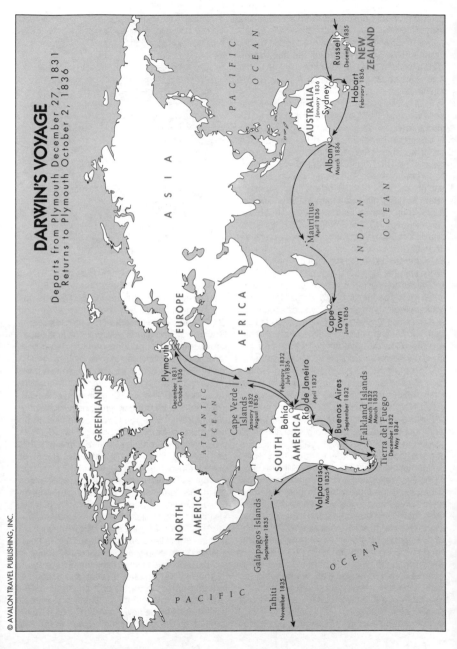

© AVALON TRAVEL PUBLISHING, INC.

DARWIN'S VOYAGE

Departs from Plymouth December 27, 1831
Returns to Plymouth October 2, 1836

PACIFIC OCEAN

ASIA

NEW ZEALAND
Russell December 1835

AUSTRALIA
Sydney January 1836
Hobart February 1836

Albany March 1836

Mauritius April 1836

INDIAN OCEAN

EUROPE

AFRICA

Cape Town June 1836

GREENLAND

Plymouth
December 1831
October 1836

ATLANTIC OCEAN

Cape Verde Islands
January 1832
August 1836

Bahia February 1832 July 1836
Rio de Janeiro April 1832

SOUTH AMERICA

Buenos Aires September 1832

Falkland Islands March 1832 March 1833

Tierra del Fuego December 1832 May 1834

NORTH AMERICA

Valparaiso March 1835

Galápagos Islands September 1835

Tahiti November 1835

PACIFIC OCEAN

colonization. He described the giant tortoises as having shells like riding saddles (called *galápagos* in Spanish), and the description stuck. On the 1574 *Orbis Terrarum,* the map of the known world, a small cluster of dots off the South American coast bore the label *Insulae de los Galopegos.*

That same century, the Spanish conquistador Diego de Rivadeneira landed in the Galápagos after 25 days at sea. On his return to Guatemala, Rivadeneira tried to claim discovery of the islands, calling them Las Islas Encantadas (The Enchanted Islands) after their supposed tendency to drift on the ocean, coming and going in the enshrouding mist. Half a century later, English pilot Sir John Hawkins wrote: "Some fourscore leagues to the westward of the Cape lyeth a heape of Ilands the Spaniards call Illas de los Galápagos; they are desert and beare no fruite."

During the 17th century, Dutch, English, and French pirates turned the Galápagos into a base for attacks on coastal ports and Spanish galleons laden with treasure for Madrid. Captain Cook was among the buccaneers who attacked rich port cities like Guayaquil before retreating to the islands to escape pursuers. The pirate William Ambrose Cowley made the first working map of the Galápagos, naming them after British royalty. Floreana and Santiago Islands were originally dubbed Charles and James, respectively, after British monarchs, and Isabela was once called Albemarle after a duke of the same title.

Pirates were the first to realize that the islands' giant tortoises could be stored aboard to provide fresh meat for long voyages, a practice that was honed to deadly perfection by 18th-century whalers. In 1841, Herman Melville visited the Galápagos on one of hundreds of whaling ships plying the rich waters around the archipelago, inspiring his account entitled "Las Encantadas." By then it was apparent that the Galápagos were worth something, so on 12 February 1832, Ecuador beat out halfhearted attempts by the United States and Great Britain to claim the archipelago officially. ("A harmless and even comical opinion," muses Kurt Vonnegut in his novel *Galápagos,* about as significant as if the country "had annexed to its territory a passing cloud of asteroids.")

An isolated penal colony established on Flo-

Charles Darwin

reana in the 1830s began a proud Galápagos tradition that continued throughout the 19th and 20th centuries. The brainchild of Galápagos Governor-General José Villamil, the first colony was home to Ecuadorians whose death sentences were commuted to a life of toil on the islands. Almost 300 convicts made a meager living growing a native lichen for dyes and selling produce to passing ships. Englishman Colonel J. Wiliams, the infamously cruel governor of the colony from 1839–1841, was driven out in an uprising that left only 80 convicts behind. Other penal colonies, on San Cristóbal in the 1890s and Isabela in the 1960s, have also begun to enter the realm of legend.

Charles Darwin's visit aboard the H.M.S. *Beagle* in 1835 gained notoriety with the publication of *The Origin of Species* in 1859. Although the visit itself didn't actually give the budding naturalist an instant lightning-strike of inspiration, it did provide crucial evidence to Darwin's later theories and culture-shaking publications. ("See special topic, Charles Darwin and the Galápagos.")

The islands' strategic location stirred serious foreign interest in the early 20th century. The U.S. offered to lease the Galápagos to protect the entrance to the new Panama Canal, finished in 1914, and the U.S. Navy trained in the waters of the archipelago during World War I. During World War II, the Ecuadorian government allowed the U.S. Sixth Air Force to set up a station on Baltra and a few other islands to protect the Panama Canal and to monitor Japanese activity in the South Pacific. The airport built on Baltra was given to Ecuador after the war.

William Beebe's book *Galapagos: World's End,* published in 1924, helped change the public's image of the islands from a strange, forbidding place to a starkly beautiful sanctuary with an ecology unique in the world. A healthy dose of weirdness remained, though, and seemed to attract outcasts and settlers with more fancy than practicality, especially on Floreana. Norwegians arrived to catch and smoke fish, whereas others came simply for the isolation and freedom.

Serious conservation efforts began when the islands were declared a national park in 1959. The Charles Darwin Research Station in Puerto Ayora, opened in 1964, was followed four years later by the Galápagos National Park Service, signaling the start of an earnest effort to study the islands and exhibit them to the world. Tourism began in the 1960s when wealthy boaters stopped off for a few days to paint their ships' names on the rocks and admire the giant tortoises over martinis and paté. A monthly ship from Guayaquil was the only other way to reach the Galápagos until regularly scheduled air service began in the early '70s.

Meanwhile, unrestricted immigration to the is-lands increased the discontent of island residents toward their situation and the government on the mainland. Friction continues to this day, as settlers led by false preconceptions pour in and find much less than they expected. Water and electricity are scarce and money is tight; the government is accused of concentrating on tourism to the expense of its own citizens. For its part, the government, in the uniform of the National Park Service, struggles to protect a fragile ecological balance from a 10 percent annual immigration rate and 50,000–60,000 visitors per year.

The 1986 Galápagos Marine Resources Reserve, which bestowed national park status on the waters around the islands as well, was received particularly poorly since it included a ban on unrestricted fishing in the local waters. Resulting strikes and threats came to a head in January 1995 when 30 machete-wielding *pepineros* (sea cucumber fishermen) seized the Darwin Station and threatened the life of tortoise Lonesome George. The Ecuadorian government backpedaled in response, opening the waters around the archipelago to large commercial fisheries in 1995. The controversy over sea cucumbers continued; in 1997, a park warden was shot by poachers, and several dozen tortoises on Isabela were killed by fishermen in protest of government restrictions.

The latest installment in the saga occurred in March 1998 when the Ecuadorian National Congress approved the long-awaited Special Law for the Galápagos. Aimed at conserving

giant tortoise

TIM BEWER

CHARLES DARWIN AND THE GALÁPAGOS

We will now discuss in a little more detail the struggle for existence.

—Charles Darwin,
On the Origin of Species
by Natural Selection.

The man who would make the Galápagos famous with what some have called "the greatest idea anyone has ever had, anywhere" was born in 1809 into an upper-middle-class British family. Throughout his comfortable childhood, Darwin was fascinated by the natural world. After unsuccessful stints at medical school and the priesthood, where he preferred collecting specimens to studying, Darwin was thrilled to accept the post of unpaid naturalist onboard the H.M.S. *Beagle.* The stout 26-meter vessel sailed from Plymouth, England, on 27 December 1831, on the first leg of a round-the-world voyage to map the South American coastline.

During the voyage, Darwin befriended Captain Robert Fitzroy, who shared his cabin and saw the young landlubber through the seasickness that plagued him the entire trip. The *Beagle* stopped at Cape Verde and the Canary Islands off the coast of Africa before crossing the Atlantic and beginning a two-year exploration of South America's eastern coast. Darwin soaked it all in, roaming the Amazon near Bahia, Brazil, and riding alongside *gauchos* in the high plains of Uruguay. In 1834, the *Beagle* rounded Cape Horn and headed up the western coast of Chile and Perú.

Darwin had already noticed things along the way that challenged the Biblical theory of creation. Dinosaur bones in Argentina were explained by devout Fitzroy as leftovers from the Great Flood. High in the Andes above Valparaíso, Chile, Darwin came across fossilized sea shells at 4,000 meters, proving to him the theories of slowly changing land masses put forth in Charles Lyell's groundbreaking *Principles of Geology,* a hefty tome he had been given to read on the trip.

Out of a five-week stay in the islands, Darwin managed to spend 19 days ashore. In his visits to San Cristóbal, Floreana, Santiago, and Isabela, the naturalist filled his days by collecting samples, observing the animals, and taking notes. What he discovered provided crucial clues that led to the gradual birth over the next two decades of the theory of evolution through natural selection. From the tortoise shells and finch beaks, shaped differently from island to island, Darwin began to ponder the idea of separate species evolving from a common ancestor. The fearlessness and beneficial adaptations of the iguanas, cormorants, and penguins all added pieces to the puzzle.

Before returning home to England, the *Beagle* crossed the Pacific and Indian Oceans, stopping at New Zealand, Australia, and Mauritus before rounding the tip of Africa. After crossing and recrossing the Atlantic again, the ship sailed into Falmouth Harbor on 2 October 1836. Darwin was never the same after the voyage. His studies took on an intensity they never had before, prompting his father to remark, "Why, the shape of his head is quite altered."

In *The Journal of the Voyage of the Beagle,* (1839) and especially its chapter on the Galápagos, one can almost watch Darwin's theories unfold. When the *Beagle* set sail, he was still a firm believer in the Biblical story of creation and the immutability of life on earth. But after witnessing the animals on different islands, similar enough to be related but different enough to be separate species, he slowly began to change his mind.

It would take another two decades, though, before Darwin was ready to publish his theories. Along with collecting information and writing, he spent much of his time worrying about the impact his work would have on England's highly evangelical society. Not only did he fear that he would be "murdering God," but he also could have potentially faced criminal charges of sedition and blasphemy. In the end, only the threat of someone else publishing a theory of evolution first—which Alfred Russel Wallace was about to do in 1858—finally spurred Darwin to act. That same year, friends arranged for Darwin and Wallace to read a joint paper to the Linnean Society of London, formally presenting evolution to the public for the first time.

On 24 November 1859, Darwin published *On the Origin of Species by Means of Natural Selection,* a work that would forever change the way we view ourselves, our world, and our place in it. Amid the controversy this watershed work caused, many readers lost sight of what Darwin was actually saying. In a nutshell, he proposed a **theory of evolution,** in which separate groups of animals change over time in response to their environment.

Up until that point, the fact that certain animals seemed "well-designed" for the places they lived and the food they ate was explained as just that—the result of an omnipresent God designing animals and setting them together on the Earth like pieces in a puzzle only a few thousand years ago. Grass was made to grow, gazelles to eat the grass and run, lions to chase gazelles and roar—each in its own specific role for which it was designed and to which it would always be suited.

Darwin had been intrigued by the Galápagos finches, which displayed a wide array of beak shapes and sizes to take advantage of many different types of food but still resembled each other closely. He began to wonder if one group of finches had arrived at the islands long ago and somehow become all these different kinds since then.

After two decades of mulling this theory over, in the *Origin of Species* Darwin proposed an idea so simple that it was almost sublime: perhaps groups of organisms actually *changed* over time in response to the challenges their members faced every day. Perhaps gazelles hadn't always been fleet of foot—perhaps they hadn't even always been gazelles! The ability to run, along with countless other qualities, such as a long neck to reach high tree leaves, thick fur to stay warm in winter, or a nervous disposition to make an animal bolt when danger threatened, could have developed over time in response to pressures from the surrounding world. Perhaps, Darwin suggested, these traits—called **adaptations**—were not the whims of an almighty being but rather the result of some spontaneous natural process that could be quantified and studied.

To explain the process, Darwin proposed a mechanism called **descent with modification.** He based it on observations of animals and plants in captivity, which produced many more offspring than could possibly survive, given the limited amounts of space or food in the environmental "niche" they occupied. Sooner or later, no matter how many babies you have, they're going to bump up against the limits of their surroundings—whether it's by eating all the food or taking up all the space—and then it's every hippo (or beetle, or weed, or bacteria) for itself.

Some of these offspring might be better suited to survive and reproduce—which, in the end, is the only way to measure an organism's "success" in the grand scheme of things—than their siblings, perhaps even than their parents. Only the ones most well-suited to their environment, Darwin concluded, would survive, an idea that became the cornerstone of the process of **natural selection:**

As many more individuals of each species are born than can possibly survive; and as, consequently, there is a frequently recurring struggle for exis-

tence, it follows that any being, if it vary however slightly in any manner profitable to itself, under the complex and sometimes varying conditions of life, will have a better chance of surviving, and thus be naturally selected.

If somehow these "selected" organisms could pass on the qualities that made them successful to their offspring by some as-yet mysterious process (the idea of genes would have to wait nearly another century), then the members of that particular line, logically, would eventually outreproduce their less "fit" competitors and spread their successful selves over the landscape (hence the book's subtitle, *The Preservation of Favoured Races in the Struggle for Life*). Maybe gazelles's ability to run quickly had come about because their ancestors had been chased, and the ones that didn't run quickly enough hadn't lived to reproduce and pass their quick legs onto their progeny.

The process could even work in "reverse," leading to the loss of adaptations that were suddenly no longer beneficial. On an island with no predators, and hence no need to fly to safety, wings might eventually just get in the way. Birds that could somehow forego growing them would be able to swim after fish more efficiently and have more energy left over for other things—such as reproducing—than their fellows. Hence the flightless cormorant.

Darwin was the first to admit that his theory was still full of holes and that he was not the first to suggest this concept, having drawn on the work of a long list of scientists, including Jean-Baptiste Lamark, Charles Lyell, Thomas Malthus, and Darwin's own grandfather Erasmus. Huge gaps in ancient lineages made the fossil record far from perfect. Most of all, in Darwin's words, this process of **evolution** was "clumsy, wasteful, blundering, low and horribly cruel," characterized by inefficiency, lifelong struggle, and probable extinction—surely not the method employed by sublime Nature.

Although it is accepted today as the scientific theory with the most experimental support in history, the ideas in the *Origin* caused an uproar in Victorian England just as their creator had feared. (Monkeys in the family tree? I *beg* your pardon!) Darwin's closing remark that: "Light will be thrown on the origin of man and his history" ranks as a pinnacle of British understatement. The clergy especially had a problem with it. In saying that life on earth grew and changed like living organisms themselves did over the course of their lives, the theory implied that what

(continued on next page)

the islands' biodiversity while encouraging and regulating sustainable development, the law addresses the threat of introduced species through eradication and quarantine programs. The law also restricts immigration and promotes local environmental education programs. The percentage of tourist revenue going to the park itself has been increased to 40 percent, and other badly needed monies are being redirected to the islands' inhabitants, earmarked for public works and payment of overdue salaries.

The law's most controversial section is proving to be the expansion of the Galápagos Marine Reserve from 15 to 40 nautical miles into the waters around the islands. Within these new boundaries—at 140,000 square km, the country's second-largest marine reserve—only tourism and "artesanal" (i.e., local tradi-tional) fishing are permitted. If fishing is not limited, argue scientists, marine life will eventually be fatally depleted. Eight million sea cucumbers have been harvested in the last two years, and commercial long-time fishing systems, which catch just about anything, are particularly hard on sensitive shark populations that are a major drawn for tourist divers (and whose fins fetch up to US$50 per pound in Asian markets).

Already, industrial fishing interests are contesting the declaration as unconstitutional, demanding that 10 percent of the area be opened to large fishing vessels. By 2000, four ships had been caught fishing illegally and impounded. On the islands, things became even more serious. Unwilling to accept further limits to their catch, local fishermen on Isabela destroyed the National Park and Darwin Station offices in protest, including sacking the private homes of the park and station directors. Protestors kidnapped the giant tortoises at the Isabela breeding center and prevented tourist boats from landing at other islands. The Ecuadorian Marines had to be flown in, and park employees were forced to hide among the mangroves and swim out to boats sent to rescue them. Luckily no injuries were reported.

The fishermen argue that the government is trying to destroy their livelihood and that they don't want to become tour guides or craftsmen instead. They resent the amount of money spent on research and conservation and point out how the lights of industrial fishing ships—owned by powerful Manta fishing interests supposedly in collusion with corrupt government officials—are still visible offshore at night.

As a result, the Ecuadorian government backed down somewhat, increasing lobster quotas and extending the fishing

CHARLES DARWIN AND THE GALÁPAGOS
(continued)

might have once been created by God must have been in need of improvement. Even if He was still in the equation somewhere, the Creator became imperfect. (But then again, one could argue, perhaps the imperfections were part of a heavenly plan as well—food for after-dinner tour-boat debate for the philosophically inclined.)

But Darwin's evidence was overwhelming, and his argument fit the 19th-century spirit of exploration and discovery (and, conveniently, the contemporary attitude of more "advanced" cultures colonizing and dominating more "primitive" ones). Darwin tried his best to stay out of the furor his theory caused, preferring to leave that to other scientists, such as Darwin's friend and "bulldog," English biologist Thomas Henry Huxley (who said upon reading the *Origin,* "How extremely stupid of me not to have thought of that.").

Darwin's theories gradually became accepted among scientists and the general public, even when in *The Descent of Man and Selection in Relation to Sex* (1871) he examined mankind's moral and spiritual evolution alongside its physical development. Even human beings, he wrote, practiced sexual selection, with females selecting males based on promising attributes and vice versa.

The naturalist who was now known around the world spent the last decades of his life writing up his notes, studying plants, and living in the Downe countryside with his wife (and cousin) Emma and their 10 children. He died on 19 April 1902 and was buried in honor next to Sir Isaac Newton in Westminster Abbey in London. The last sentence of *The Origin of Species* would be a fitting epitaph for the man and the blinding truth he exposed to the world:

We should never have sought either solace or moral instruction in nature.

seasons. Emboldened fishermen are now pushing for a complete revision of the statute, demanding a year-round fishing calendar, the permission to use long-line methods, and the reopening of the closed sea cucumber harvest.

These events passed mostly unnoticed in the eyes of the rest of the world, but that soon changed. On 16 January 2001, the captain of the Ecuadorian-registered tanker *Jessica* misjudged his entry into Shipwreck Bay on San Cristóbal Island, ran aground, and began leaking diesel fuel. Despite international cleanup efforts, approximately two-thirds of the ship's 240,000-gallon cargo, originally meant for tour boats, found their way into the pristine waters.

Then nature intervened: favorable winds and tides carried much of the fuel to the north and away from the islands. Small stretches of beach and a handful of animals were contaminated, but on the whole shoreline damage was kept to a minimum. The long-term effects of the spill on ocean-floor algae, the foundation of the islands' entire food chain, have yet to be determined, but the director of the National Park said he expected the ecosystem to recover fully within 3–4 years.

CHARLES, LEAVE THE IGUANAS ALONE

The father of evolutionary theory would have been booted from the Royal Society for the Prevention of Cruelty to Animals by his own accounts of tormenting, eating, and general negativity toward the Galápagos's inhabitants during his visit. In the *Voyage of the Beagle*, he wrote of dining on giant tortoises: "The breast-plate roasted . . . with the flesh on it, is very good; and the young tortoises make excellent soup; but otherwise the meat to my taste is indifferent."

He went on to describe the marine iguana as "a hideous-looking creature, of a dirty black colour, stupid, and sluggish in its movements." One hapless iguana Darwin repeatedly threw into the ocean kept returning to the same place on shore. This "singular piece of apparent stupidity" caused the naturalist to wonder about the animal's response to predators: "Urged by a fixed and hereditary instinct that the shore is its place of safety, whatever emergency there may be, it there takes refuge"—meddling naturalist or not.

Land iguanas fared little better. "Like their brothers the sea-kind," he noted, "they are ugly animals, of a yellowish orange beneath, and of a brownish red colour above: from their low facial angle they have a singularly stupid appearance." Even in the dinner pot, the land iguana just couldn't measure up: "These lizards, when cooked, yield a white meat, which is liked by those whose stomachs soar above all prejudices." After watching one land iguana dig a nest hole "for a long time," Darwin proceeded to yank it back out by the tail.

"At this it was greatly astonished," he wrote, "and stared me in the face, as much as to say, 'What made you pull my tail?' " Indeed.

THE NATURAL WORLD

The natural history of these islands is eminently curious, and well deserves attention.

—*Charles Darwin,*
The Journal of the Voyage of the Beagle

Life in the Galápagos is a study in extremes. These parched, rocky islands spread out under the equatorial sun are surprisingly rich in life. The only way to survive here, it seems, is to adapt, which means a high level of **endemic species**— those found nowhere else on earth. The Galápagos has 1,900 endemic species out of 5,000 total: 32 percent of the plants, almost half of all birds, half of all shore fish and insects, and 90 percent of the reptiles have become so specifically adapted to life in the islands that they hardly resemble their original mainland ancestors at all.

In contrast, the fragility of the Galápagos ecosystem shows itself in a low level of **diversity:** there aren't as many *different* species as one would expect. This paucity of species has created a delicate balance—certain species are completely dependent on others, both plant and animal, and cannot survive without each other.

Colonization

By now you've probably asked yourself the most obvious question about the islands' inhabitants: How did they get there? The Galápagos were never connected to the mainland, and 1,000 km of open water is a long swim. As impressive as it seems, though, most species arrived more or less under their own power. Fish and marine mammals cruising the currents might have bumped into the islands and decided to stay, whereas land birds blown off course wouldn't have known the way back to the mainland even if they had wanted to leave. Sea birds and migrant species, knowing a good fishing spot when they saw one, might have returned to breed year after year. Insects and plant seeds could also have been carried from the South American continent by high winds, whereas other seeds were probably excreted by birds or arrived stuck to their feet.

As for terrestrial reptiles and rats, the generally accepted explanation involves the large rafts of vegetation that can still be seen washing down Ecuador's ocean-bound rivers. Any animals or plants that happened to be aboard, provided they could survive the journey, stood a slim chance of riding the currents all the way to the Galápagos. (Some rafts are even large enough to support living trees—another colonization possibility.) With their ability to slow their own metabolism, reptiles are particularly suited for such a long, difficult journey. On the other hand, large mammals would tend to die of dehydration, and amphibians would dry up during the trip, which explains why there weren't any of either group on the islands before the arrival of man.

Marine Life

The Galápagos are every bit as spectacular beneath the water's surface as above it. A staggering diversity of life inhabits a wide range of marine habitats, from mangrove estuaries to lava-rocky tide pools, volcanic beaches to sandy bottom. About 50 marine species are endemic, in a percentage comparable to endemic numbers on land. All of this is a result of a few climatic factors—a combination of warm and cold currents and the El Niño phenomenon, which periodically warms things drastically—that have turned the Galápagos into a natural marine reserve in the middle of the Pacific.

Because the ravages of hunting have not, for the most part, reached far below the surface, the same fearlessness is found beneath the waves as on land. Sea turtles sleeping near the surface will only steer casually away upon being awakened. Sea lions almost treat you like one of the pack—just stay out of the way of the territorial bulls. And in the deep, it's almost as if you weren't there at all, as huge schools of fish engulf divers in living clouds of silver.

Taxonomy

A brief explanation of taxonomy (the scientific classification of living things) should help neophytes better appreciate the natural history of the islands. All organisms are categorized according to seven major taxonomic divisions, which in order from general to specific are kingdom (i.e., plant or animal), phylum, class, order, family, genus, and species (what particular *kind* of short spiny anteater). Every single organism ever discovered has been given a unique spot in this hierarchy, pinpointed by a lengthy label of Latin and Greek terms.

The term you'll hear over and over again in talk of the Galápagos ecology is **species,** the fundamental taxonomic unit that's loosely defined as a group of organisms sharing many common characteristics. Species usually live in a specific area and are only able to successfully reproduce with each other.

Plants and animals are most often referred to by their **common name** as well as their **scientific name,** usually written as the genus (capitalized) and species. Animals in the Galápagos also have Spanish names, of course—only some of which are related to their common (English) names. For example, the blue-footed boobie (common name) is called the *piquero patas azules* in Spanish (blue-footed lancer) and saddled with the scientific name *Sula nebuoxii.*

MAMMALS

Only six species of mammals originally called the Galápagos home, and four of those arrived by swimming or flying. The long ocean crossing (at least two weeks by floating raft) is too long for most mammals to survive; in fact, Galápagos rice rats set a world record in long-distance colonization.

Galápagos Sea Lion

Somehow feline and canine at the same time, the Galápagos sea lion *(Zalophus californianus wollebacki)* is a smaller cousin of the California sea lion. (Males in the Galápagos reach only 250 kg.) Their charming snout, whiskers, and dark eyes belie a voice that sounds like the winner of a belching contest—even a newborn pup can bleat like a Billy goat coughing up a hairball.

Some 50,000 sea lions sprawl over beaches and rocks throughout the islands; prolonged snoozing helps replenish oxygen used up during long, deep dives after fish. Sharks and killer whales are the sea lion's chief predators. Sea lion bulls defend beach harems—short stretches of sand filled with females and pups—by patrolling loudly just offshore. Any male who is careless enough to approach the boundary is confronted immediately; the winner is usually the one who can raise his snout higher. Although most of this posturing is harmless, sea lion attacks are the most common cause of animal injury in the Galápagos. Steer well clear of patrolling males, especially when snorkeling.

Galápagos Fur Seal

With its small external ears and strong propulsive forward flippers, the Galápagos fur seal *(Arctocephalus galapagoensis)* isn't really a true seal (family Phocidae) at all. Like the larger Galápagos sea lion, the fur seal is a member of the eared-seal family Otaridae. Fur seals are smaller than sea lions, with a thick, furry coat that traces their ancestry to the cold coasts of Perú and Chile.

This luxurious coat almost led to the fur seal's extinction in the 19th century. The warm, two-layered pelt was in high demand in Europe and the United States, leading to unchecked slaughter at the hands of hunters. One ship in 1823 reported a take of 5,000 skins in two months. By the turn of the century, the seal was thought to be extinct—a California Academy of Sciences expedition in 1905 found only one seal in an entire year.

Fortunately the fur seal has made a comeback, despite a low birth rate of one pup every two years. Today 30,000–40,000 fur seals inhabit the northern and western islands of Pinta, Marchena, Santiago, Isabela, and Fernandina.

Whales and Dolphins

Several cetaceans (completely aquatic mammals) can be seen around the islands. Those without teeth use hairy plates of baleen in their jaws to strain gallons of tiny creatures from the water. The **blue whale,** the largest animal in the world, is an occasional visitor to the archipelago, and the more common **humpback whale** *(Megaptera novaeangliae)* can reach 16 meters. The sight of one of these giants breaching completely out of the water—most often seen west of Isabela and Fernandina—is awe-inspiring. Smaller baleen species include finback, sei, Bryde's, and minke whales.

Toothed cetaceans eat larger prey, including fish and squid. Black and white **killer whales** *(Orcinus orca)* are the true lions of the sea. The sight of a tall, black dorsal fin is enough to clear a beach of sea lions in an instant. A population of **sperm whales** *(Physete macrocephalus)* is slowly recovering from the depredations of 19th-century whalers. Three resident species of **dolphin** surf the bow waves of cruising ships with an unmistakable glee. Schools of up to 100 can be seen leaping in unison through the waves.

Bats and Rats

Two endemic species of **bats** made the long crossing—probably by accident—to make their home in the Galápagos. The **hoary bat** *(Lasiurus cinereus)* wears a soft brown coat frosted with white on the tips of its wings. The other species, *Lasiurus brachyotis,* is abundant on the central and western islands.

Two species of **rice rats** are left from an original seven. The rest were driven to extinction by the Norwegian black rat *(Rattus rattus),* which was introduced by visiting ships. The remaining rice rats endemic to Santa Fe *(Oryzomys bauri)* and Fernandina *(Nesoryzomys narboroughii)* are nocturnal vegetarians, feeding on young lava cacti and seeds.

REPTILES

The reptiles of the Galápagos define the islands more than any other group of animals. Here reptiles still rule the earth, giving a taste of what the rest of the planet may have been like tens of millions of years ago. More than 90 percent of the reptile species in the Galápagos are endemic, a testament to their ability to enter a state of hibernation-like torpor that would have allowed their ancestors to survive the long ocean crossing. In addition to the reptiles described as follows, the Galápagos harbor five endemic species of **gecko** and three species of **Galápagos snake.**

Giant Tortoise

These creaking giants, with skin like the world's oldest leather jacket, are the largest in the world.

THE SAD TALE OF LONESOME GEORGE

The only surviving representative of Pinta's giant tortoise species was taken to the Darwin Center in 1971. Although approximately 2,000 tortoises have been bred at the station and re-released into the wild, George would have none of it. One scientist spent six months trying unsuccessfully to get sperm from the reluctant reptile. Scientists couldn't figure out why George wouldn't mate, until a DNA analysis revealed that George's closest relatives weren't from neighboring Isabela, as they had thought, but from Española and San Cristíbal. There are female tortoises from both islands at the center, but researchers first want to try and find a real Pinta female to keep the subspecies genetically pure.

They're found only here and in the Seychelle Islands, 650 km off the coast of Tanzania. The Galápagos species, *Geochelone elephantopus,* can reach 250 kg and nobody knows how old. Dependable records top out at 100 years, but some stories have turtles lasting more than 200 years. During your visit to the Darwin Center in Puerto Ayora, notice the smooth domes of the tortoises in captivity, and think how long it must have taken to wear those huge shells down by rubbing against nothing but branches.

The shell of a giant tortoise reveals which island, or at least what type of island, its owner hails from. Saddle-shaped shells, high in front and the back, evolved on low, arid islands where tortoises must be able to lift their head as high as possible to browse tall vegetation. (The tortoises' necks and legs are also longer on these islands.) Semicircular domed shells come from higher, lusher islands with vegetation that grows low to the ground. Males have larger and longer tails, with a concave plastron (bottom plate) that helps them mount females during mating.

During mating season, the only time tortoises make any noise, unearthly groans echo for kilometers as males joust for dominance—a relatively simple showdown in which the higher head wins. When her eggs are ready to hatch, the female softens hard soil with urine before digging a nest for as long as five hours. A single layer of tennis-ball-sized eggs is then covered with six inches of packed earth that soon dries hard. The nest is a surprisingly delicate system: the top layer of mud must keep the heat and moisture levels within a narrow range because a temperature difference of a few degrees Celsius decides whether the offspring will be male, female, or stillborn. Broods hatch during the first months of the year.

Tortoises spend much of their lives in a state of torpor, when their metabolism and body temperature slow significantly. This ability allows them to survive dry periods on the island with a minimum of food and water. But when the rains do come, look out—on Alcedo Volcano on Isabela the wet season is greeted by a slow-motion orgy of eating, drinking, mating, and wallowing in new pools of water. By nighttime everyone ends up in the mud, snoozing contentedly in large groups.

When the islands were first discovered, there were as many as 250,000 tortoises, and 14 islands each had their own species. Today there are only about 15,000 left, and three of those species (Santa Fe, Floreana, and Fernandina) are extinct. The Pinta species is represented by one surviving member named Lonesome George. Whalers were once the tortoises' main enemy, but today the danger comes from introduced animal species. Pigs can dig up dozens of nests in no time, hatchlings fall prey to cats and rats, and larger tortoises can be killed by dogs. Even if they do survive to adulthood, tortoises often have to compete with burros, goats, and cattle for food.

Marine Iguana

The only true marine lizard in the world, *Amblyrhynchus cristatus* evolved from a terrestrial species that took to the water to survive. In short evolutionary time (only 2–3 million years), marine iguanas have adapted well to feed on coastal seaweed. A flattened snout allows closer munching, a vertically flattened tail propels better in the water, long claws grab underwater rocks firmly, and a pair of salt-eliminating glands in the nostrils cleanse sea salt from their system. As a result, they're prodigious divers that are able to stay under for well more than an hour by lowering their heart rate by one-half.

Anywhere from 200,000–300,000 marine iguanas inhabit the Galápagos. Males can reach a little more than one meter in length and weigh up to 20 kg, with the average size increasing toward the western islands. Bright colorings attract females during the dry season; Española's iguanas are particularly colorful. Despite their prehistoric appearance (and the fact that one was used as a model for the updated version of *Godzilla*), the iguanas are harmless—Kurt Vonnegut accurately describes the scaly swimmers as "no more dangerous to life forms of any sort, with the exceptions of seaweed, than a liverwurst."

Marine iguanas feed on shallow-growing seaweed, shunning the tough, brown stuff for tender green and red morsels. This inconspic-

marine iguanas

TIM BEWER

uous but surprisingly nutritious plant grows like, well, a weed—a one-km patch can quintuple its mass in less than two weeks and support up to 3,000 iguanas at once, who gobble it as if there's no tomorrow. Marine iguanas feed like clockwork for a certain amount of time every day, usually about one hour, and they always know to go at low tide. Basking in the sun helps each iguana generate enough heat to digest a bellyful of cellulose.

Regulating body heat is a prime concern, especially after a long dive. Like all reptiles, marine iguanas are ectotherms, meaning their internal body temperatures are at the mercy of outside temperatures. Males prefer to dive during the hottest part of the day to keep cool. Once back on shore, the trick becomes not warming back up *too* much: lava-rock temperatures can climb more than 40°C, and iguanas die if their body temperature rises above 45°C. To remedy this problem, iguanas face the sun, exposing as little surface area as possible, and raise their bodies off the ground to allow air to circulate underneath. On cold days and at night, iguanas congregate into huge piles to conserve heat.

Marine iguana populations fell slightly over the years as a result of hunting by early visitors, but recent El Niño seasons in the 1980s and 1990s struck much more deeply. Abnormally warm waters killed the shallow-growing algae, spelling doom for those iguanas not strong enough to reach deeper algae. Since then, in a handy example of evolution in action, marine iguanas have become slightly larger, and females breed every year instead of every two as before.

Land Iguana

The seven subspecies of land iguana (genus *Conolophus*) in the Galápagos have evolved a pale yellow coloring in contrast to their mainland ancestors' arboreal green. Land iguanas evolved from a similar species as their seagoing relatives— the difference being that by the time land iguanas' ancestors arrived at the islands, enough ground vegetation had grown that they didn't have to take to the water to survive.

Land iguanas live in dry areas, where they spend the night in dugout burrows to conserve heat. Their menu is mostly vegetarian; any plant within reach gets chomped, including berries,

AN IGUANA MYSTERY SOLVED

Scientist Vincent Sarich raised an interesting question in his 1983 scientific paper, "Are the Galápagos Iguanas Older Than the Galápagos?" While the current estimate for the age of the archipelago is between two and three million years, naturalists were sure that marine and land iguanas must have needed at least 15 million years to diverge so completely from their common mainland ancestor. In short, the islands weren't nearly old enough to have given endemic species enough time to evolve into their present state.

Careful analysis of the ocean floor to the east yielded an answer. Six hundred km from the mainland to the east of the archipelago were found the remains of old, sunken islands, formerly part of the Galápagos group. Before plate drift had carried them east and erosion had reduced them to undersea nubs, these islands may have been around for as long as the Galápagos hotspot has been active (more than 80 million years). Present species would then have had ample time to arrive, evolve, and move to the present islands.

flowers, fruits, and cactus pads, spines and all. Land iguanas get much of their water from food. After digging their way out of the nest, tiny newborn iguanas must avoid hawks, owls, and introduced predators until they're large enough to defend themselves. Males can reach 13 kg and live more than 60 years. Maturity comes between ages 10 and 15, when adult males begin a career of vigorously defending a specific territory, with head-nodding threats that often end in battle.

As a result of hunting and introduced species, the land iguana species on Santiago and Baltra have become extinct, and those on other islands are in trouble. A captive-breeding program at the Darwin Center attempts to maintain threatened populations at viable levels. Only Fernandina's iguanas have avoided outside intrusion, and they're among the largest in the islands.

Sea Turtles

The eastern **Pacific green turtle** *(Chelonia mydas agassisi)* is the most common species in the islands. Called *tortugas negras* (black turtles) in Spanish, Pacific greens depend on the Galápagos for nesting beaches. Beyond that, it's not known whether they live here year-round or migrate periodically to the mainland. Green sea turtles average around 100 kg and can often be spotted sleeping on shallow sandy bottoms or mating in open water. Awkward at or above the surface, sea turtles glide gorgeously beneath, where they can hold their breath for hours. They're often seen coming up for air alongside anchored boats.

Also present in the islands, although rarely seen, are the **Pacific leatherback** *(Dermochelys coriacea)* and the **Indo-Pacific hawksbill** *(Eretmochely imbricata).*

Lava Lizard

Seven species of the ubiquitous lava lizard *(Tropidurus albemarlensis)* scurry over sand and rock on almost every island. The larger males can reach 30 cm, and females can be identified by red throat patches. Lava lizards feed democratically, gulping down insects, plants, and even each other. In turn, they're pursued by many larger birds, who are only occasionally fooled by the lizards' break-away tails.

Like soldiers at boot camp, lava lizards do push-ups constantly, to the point that their Spanish name *(lagartija)* has become a slang term for push-up. The pattern of ups and downs is different for different island species and is thought to defend territory as well as regulate body temperature.

SEABIRDS

With nothing but water in every direction, the Galápagos are a perfect stopover for wide-ranging seabirds. Estimates range as high as 750,000 in the islands at any one time. Because they can come and go freely, seabirds have evolved less endemic species in the Galápagos compared to other types of birds. Out of the 19 species of seabirds on the islands, only five are endemic: the Galápagos penguin, flightless cormorant, waved albatross, lava gull, and swallow-tailed gull. Of these, only the last three can fly.

Boobies

Aptly named from the Spanish *bobo* (clown), boobies are the awkward but endearing mascots of the Galápagos. They belong to the same family as gannets (Sulidae), whom they resemble with their large webbed feet, round heads, and long pointed beaks. All boobies catch fish with awe-inspiring plunges into the water from midair. You'll see blue-footed boobies doing this most often near the shore—a crash into the water inches from the base of rocky cliffs, a second of silence, then a pop to the surface and *gulp* goes a fish. Air sacs in their skulls diffuse the shock of impact, and closed-beak nostrils keep salt water out. Boobies typically lay two or three eggs to ensure that at least one (and often only one) chick survives to adolescence. This brutally effective evolutionary insurance policy often involves larger chicks killing their smaller siblings.

Blue-footed boobies *(Sula nebouxii)* symbolize the Galápagos in the minds of much of the world (helped by countless T-shirts, hats, postcards, and posters). About 30 percent of

blue-footed boobies

THE BOOBIE DANCE

[It] seems to have absolutely no connection with the elements of booby survival, with nesting or fish. What does it have to do with, then? Dare we call it 'religion'? Or, if we lack that sort of courage, might we at least call it 'art'?

—Kurt Vonnegut, Galápagos

the world's population nest in the islands—close to 10,000 pairs—where they feed close to shore. Males and females both have the famous neon-blue feet; actually, the only way to tell the sexes apart is by the size of the pupil (smaller in males) and the sound of the call (females honk, males whistle). Males show off their feet during the courtship dance, a high-stepping ritual designed to show off sexual maturity and good genes—the bluer the better.

Blue-foots nest on the ground, where they scrape a shallow hole that becomes surrounded by a white ring of guano. Lacking the usual avian incubating pouch, parents keep the eggs warm on top of their feet, which are richly veined with warm blood vessels. After hatching, any chick that ends up outside the nest ring is as good as dead, ignored by its parents and pecked at by its siblings if it tries to re-enter.

There are more **red-footed boobies** (*Sula sula*) in the Galápagos than any other booby species (a quarter of a million pairs), but they're also the least often seen. Although the world's largest colony of red-foots nests on Tower Island, its inhabitants are usually feeding far out to sea. Red-footed boobies are the smallest on the islands and have blue bills and brown plumage (a few have white feathers). Their relatively small feet, tipped with small claws, allow them to nest in trees.

The beautiful **masked boobies** (*Sula dactylatra*) nest on cliff edges because, as the largest booby species, they have a harder time taking off from level ground. Most of the masked boobies in the world nest in the Galápagos, giving you a good opportunity to see their stunning plumage: one of the purest whites in the animal kingdom,

with a black eye mask and black wing edges.

Waved Albatross

Nearly the entire world population of the waved albatross (*Diomedea irrorata*)—some 12,000 pairs—nest on Española Island. Bulging white eyebrows atop cream-colored feathers give albatrosses a refined yet slightly comical appearance (think Groucho Marx in a nice suit). As graceful as it is soaring on its two-meter wings, the waved albatross is a duck out of water on land, waddling around like a sailor after too long at sea. The air-to-land transition seems to be a bit of a problem, too, as many landings end up a flailing tumble of feathers and squawks. Granted, many albatrosses have been cruising the thermals of the South Pacific for as long as 3–4 years without landing. The most successful albatross launch is a seaward leap off a cliff into a headwind.

Waved albatross couples mate for life, which can mean a 50-year commitment. The pair bond is reinforced through an elaborate courtship display, an ecstatic ritual that peaks in October and is worth scheduling a visit around. Bills clatter, circle, and point at the sky as participants perform an exaggerated version of their normal swaying walk. Practices such as adoption, adultery, and even rape have been observed among the graceful seabirds.

After going on long hunting junkets, parents stuff chicks to bursting with up to two liters of a predigested mixture of fish and squid. Researcher Bryan Nelson described the result: "For the first four months of its life the chick is hardly more than a great, oil-filled skin, covered in matted brown down. It is grotesque with the fascination of the truly ugly."

Galápagos Penguin

Short-listed for the Cutest Endemic Species award, the Galápagos penguin (*Sheniscus mendiculus*) seems as out of place in the hot, dry islands as a polar bear at a beach party. At 35 cm high, it's one of the smallest penguin species. Having evolved from the Humboldt penguins that inhabit the Patagonian coasts of Perú and Chile, the Galápagos penguin is the only penguin found north of the equator. Because they still retain much of their original insulation, Galápagos penguins have to struggle to stay cool in the hot sun. The classic wings-out pose lowers a bird's temperature, but it occasionally comes down to a choice between the cooking of the nest eggs (which must be continually shaded by day) or the parents (who are forced to jump into the water). With only 3,000–5,000 breeding pairs, Galápagos penguins are one of the rarest species of seabirds in the world.

Frigatebirds

The bad boys of the Galápagos are notorious for making a living stealing food from other species. This type of feeding, called kleptoparasitism, is the reason frigatebirds were named after fast colonial-era warships. A forked tail, backswept wings, and extremely low weight for their size make them faster and more maneuverable then anyone else in the air. They can often be seen harassing a boobie returning with fish for a chick until the parent disgorges its meal; the frigatebird will then scoop its pilfered food out of the air. They're not above stealing food right out of a chick's mouth on the ground, either. This light-fingered lifestyle has evolved partly because frigatebirds can't dive for their own food; with only vestigial preening glands, a frigatebird can't waterproof its feathers and sinks like a stone if it becomes waterlogged.

The males' distinctive red throat pouch is inflated to attract females. Once they go to the bother of pumping it up with air, they'll leave it inflated all day. A female drifting over a group of males during the mating season elicits waves of pouch-waving, bill-rattling, and calling meant to attract her to particular nests. Pairs mate for life, and chicks take up to one year to learn the thieving acrobatics of survival.

The male magnificent frigatebird *(Fregata magnificens)* has a purple-tinged nape and a white patch on the breast conveniently shaped like an M. An all-white breast and greenish neck and chest distinguish the male great frigatebird *(Fregata minor)*. (Biologists talk in hushed tones about the rarely seen "pretty nifty frigatebird," but no one has been able to capture one yet. Just kidding.)

Flightless Cormorant

You'll have to make it out to Fernandina and western Isabela to see some of the 2,000 pairs of flightless cormorants *(Nannopterum harrisi)*, one

of the few bird species in the world that has lost the ability to fly. The aquatic birds are a study of evolution in action from their steel blue eyes to their asymmetrical feet. Millenia of diving after fish, eels, and octopi on the near-shore bottom, combined with a lack of predators on land, have allowed the cormorants' wings and tail to atrophy to vestigial nubs. The typical avian keeled breastbone—a solid anchor for strong flying muscles—has vanished in flightless cormorants, whereas their long snakelike neck, strong kicking legs, and huge webbed feet make them experts at pursuing fish underwater. Flightless cormorants still haven't forgotten their roots, though, and they stand patiently to dry their ragged wings every time they emerge from the water.

Cormorant nests are an impressive conglomeration of flotsam and twigs that are in use year-round by breeding pairs. The nests are often set precariously close to the waterline, and many eggs are washed away by high spring tides.

Endemic Gulls

Close to 15,000 pairs of **swallow-tailed gulls** *(Creagrus furcatus)* nest throughout the islands. They're one of the prettier gulls around, with a charcoal-colored head and white and gray body highlighted by red feet and a distinctive red eye ring. Unlike most other gulls, swallow-tails feed out to sea at night, pointing boat captains the way toward land in the morning. The **lava gull** *(Larus fuliginosus)* is thought to be the rarest gull in the world, consisting of only about 400 mating pairs nesting in the Galápagos. Their dark gray plumage blends into the lava rocks they prefer, but their obnoxious chortle gives them away immediately.

Other Species

A distinctive chattering call signals the return of the **red-billed tropicbird** *(Phaethon aethereus)* from feeding far out to sea. If they make it past the frigatebirds, their next task is to pull off a swooping landing into the windy cliffside nests they prefer. Tropicbirds have a fragile beauty, with a gray body and long, flowing white pintails capped by a red bill and a black mask.

If you've spent any time near the coast, you'll undoubtedly recognize the **brown pelican** *(Pelecanus occidentalis)*, which are often seen at sunset skimming regally in formation, inches above the water. It's one of the largest and most commonly seen Galápagos seabirds, but actually one of the smaller species of pelican. It may not seem designed for it, but this ungainly looking seabird plunges into the ocean over and over to capture food. After filling its 14-liter beak pouch with water on impact, the pelican filters out the fish and gulps them down.

The western cliffs of Isabela are home to the **brown noddy** *(Anous stolidus)*, a ternlike bird that nests in caves and dark niches. Noddies bring a classic beauty to the Galápagos, with an avian tuxedo of smart gray plumage punctuated by a white forehead and eye patches. You'll occasionally see them waiting on pelicans' heads for scraps.

If you happen to see a small black bird skimming the water for fish, it could be one of a few species. Both the **Audubon's shearwater** *(Puffinus l'herminieri)* and the larger **dark-rumped petrel** *(Pterodroma pharopygia)* have a black back and white front. The latter, also called the Hawaiian petrel, is nocturnal and highly endangered—more so in Hawaii than the Galápagos, although for the same reason.

White rump patches decorate three types of storm petrels: the **white-vented** or **Eliot's storm petrel** *(Oceanites gracilis);* the nocturnal **Madeiran storm petrel** *(Oceanodroma castro);* and the day-feeding **Galápagos storm petrel** *(Oceanodroma tethys).*

COASTAL BIRDS

Herons and Egrets
Five species of herons inhabit the islands. All hunt small reptiles, mammals, insects, and fish by waiting motionless and then spearing their prey with a quick jab of their long beak. The **great blue heron** *(Adrea herodias)* stands 1.5 meters high as it poses one-legged among the mangroves. You might be surprised by one standing silent and fearless in a Puerto Ayora back alley. The smaller **yellow-crowned night heron** *(Nyctanassa violacea)* feeds by night. Its hunched shoulder and furtive, yellow-eyed glance gives it a cloak-and-dagger look, capped by a bright yellow sweep of feathers on top of the head. Lava rocks hide the small, gray **lava heron** *(Butorides*

sundevalli), the only endemic species. They hunt fish, crabs, and lizards in rocky tide pools.

Greater Flamingos
About 500 of these pink, leggy birds *(Phoenicopters ruber)* wade through brackish lagoons around the archipelago. Punta Cormorant on Floreana and Dragon Hill on Santa Cruz are two good places to see them feeding on brine shrimp by filtering through the salty ooze. Listen closely and you can hear the quiet splooshes as the birds, head upside down, push the water through their hairy beak filters similar to whale's baleen. Here's a cocktail-party fact for you: flamingos are actually white but turn pink from the carotene pigments in the shrimp they eat.

Waders, Paddlers, and Beach Stalkers
The **American oystercatcher** *(Haematopus ostralegus)* looks like a bad drawing of a bird: head too small, red bill too large. Only 150 or so pairs of these bright-eyed birds live in the islands, where they comb intertidal areas for food. Along with flamingos, inland bodies of water are home to the **white-cheeked pintail duck** *(Anas bahamensis),* also known as the Bahamas duck, along with the **common stilt** *(Himantopus mexicanus).*

Galápagos shorelines and beaches are patrolled by **whimbrels** *(Numenius phaeopus),* **sanderlings** *(Crocethia alba),* **ruddy turnstones** *(Arenaria interpres),* **northern phalaropes** *(Lobipes lobatus),* and **semipalmated plovers** *(Charadrius semipalmatus).*

LAND BIRDS

The only way that land birds could have reached the Galápagos was to have been blown far out to sea by a storm—the reason only 29 species inhabit the islands today. Those that arrived survived by adapting, eventually dividing into 22 endemic species. Higher islands with more vegetation zones (and hence more ecological niches) support more endemic species.

Darwin's Finches
The Galápagos' 13 species of finches, made famous by Charles Darwin's work, all look more or less alike. Don't worry about trying to tell

TOO MANY

Thomas Malthus's 18th-century social science theories were actually based in part on reports of goats in the Galápagos. After hearing how the hoofed marauders died in droves when a particular island had been stripped bare, Malthus reasoned that humans were in danger of doing the same thing—to the entire earth.

them apart; just being aware of their significance is enough. After all, as one researcher noted, "it is only a very wise man or a fool who thinks he is able to identify all the finches which he sees."

The key to the finches, as Darwin quickly noticed, is the beak. Different types of finches have beaks of different sizes and shapes, allowing them to gobble many different kinds of food. Short, thick beaks enable ground finches to crack hard seeds, whereas longer, slimmer bills allow other species to probe crevices for insects and munch cacti or flowers. The finches, it seems, evolved to fill a wide range of ecological niches left vacant by the lack of other terrestrial birds—a process ecologists call *adaptive radiation*. At the same time, they remained similar enough to have obviously come from a common ancestor. Darwin noticed all this, writing: "The most curious fact is the perfect gradation in the size of the beaks in the different species. One might really fancy that from an original paucity of birds in this archipelago, one species had been taken and modified for different ends."

The eating habits of a few finches are worth special mention. Woodpecker and mangrove finches use a cactus spine or small twig to get at a fat, tasty grub burrowed deep in a tree branch, making them one of the few animals to use and modify tools. The sharp-billed ground finch goes one step farther—this unremarkable brown bird pecks at the base of a boobie's tail until a trickle of blood starts flowing, which the finch drinks without much protest from its victim. These "vampire finches," as they have been nicknamed, also roll other birds' eggs—some nearly as big as themselves—over lava rocks until they crack, and then eat the insides.

Mockingbirds

Like the finches, the four species of mockingbirds endemic to the Galápagos seem to have filled a niche usually taken by other animals. In this case, small land mammals were absent, leaving the mockingbirds free to pick up insects, small reptiles, and various scraps. Galápagos mockingbirds exhibit an interesting family bonding, in which related groups guard territory and share in the responsibilities of raising juveniles.

The ranges of the four species are separated onto different islands. The **Galápagos mockingbird** *(Nesomimus parvulus)* is the most widespread, found on Isabela, Floreana, Santa Cruz, Santiago, and Santa Fe. San Cristóbal is home to the **Chatham mockingbird** *(Nesomimus melanotis)*, and on Española you'll find the inquisitive **Hood mockingbird** *(Nesomimus macdonaldi)*, with its long, curved beak. The **Charles mockingbird** *(Nesomimus trifasciatus)* once ranged over the Floreana area but today is limited to a few nearby islets.

Other Land Birds

Because it has no natural enemies, the **Galápagos hawk** *(Buteo galapagoensis)* is known for its fearlessness. Darwin noted that "a gun here is almost superfluous; for with the muzzle I pushed a hawk out of the branch of a tree." This endemic scavenger is actually a type of buzzard. Through an unusual mating system known as *cooperative polyandry,* up to four males may mate with a single female and cooperate to help her raise the young, regardless (and ignorant) of whose offspring they are.

It's a toss-up as to which land bird is the prettiest. In the running is the **Galápagos dove** *(Zenaida galapagoensis),* whose plumage combines pink, gray, and white with red feet, an aqua-blue eye ring, and green iridescent patches on either side of the neck. Because many of these birds were hunted for food by early visitors, Galápagos doves aren't as tame as they once were, hiding under bushes and eating the *opuntia* cactus. The male **vermillion flycatcher** *(Pyrocephalus rubinus)* looks like a small fireball in the trees with its brilliant red coloring set off by a black eye stripe, wing, and tail. It typically catches insects in the highlands along with the bright **yellow warbler** *(Dendroica petechia),* whose liquid song echoes on most islands.

Early morning and evening are the best times to catch the **short-eared owl** *(Asio flameus)* out after chicks, rodents, and insects. The endemic **Galápagos barn owl** *(Tyto punctissima)* is nocturnal, so there's less chance you'll glimpse this moon-faced bird on the prowl.

INSECTS AND ARTHROPODS

Few insects make their home in the Galápagos because of the islands' isolation and short growing season. Those that do live here are usually dull-colored and come out only at night to escape the heat. As a result, many flowers are light-colored, so their insect pollinators can find them even in low light.

The **carpenter bee** *(Xylocopa darwini)* is one of the most important pollinators in the archipelago. Rocks and sand hide the endemic **Galápagos scorpion** *(Centruroides exsul),* a favorite prey of lava lizards. Also hunted by lava lizards, the bright **painted locust** *(Shistocerca melanocera)* wears a carapace decorated with red, yellow, green, and black. All of these insects are abundant in the lowlands.

FISH

Waters around the Galápagos shelter a strange mix of cold and warm-water species. The variety varies depending on where and when you're in the water. Currents and seasons bring water as cold as 15°C and as warm as 30°C to the islands, and the waters on different sides of the same island at the same time can vary as much as 2–3 degrees. Lava rocks serve as aquatic condos in place of coral reefs. Such a wide range of habitats allows more than 300 regular

INTRODUCED SPECIES

By far the most serious threat to the ecosystems of the Galápagos is the descendants of the animals and plants left by settlers and visitors over the centuries. Only two of the major islands are free of exotic species, while the plants and animals on the rest of the islands are largely defenseless against the feral intruders. Introductions still occur: the Norway rat arrived as recently as 1983 and has spread to at least two islands already.

Introduced Animals

Most introduced species began as domestic animals that escaped into the wild. **Donkeys** can exist in lower, drier elevations, where they eat through cactus-tree trunks to get at the juicy pulp, killing the plant in the process. Scattered **horses** and **cattle** roam the highlands, and feral **pigs** gobble down turtle eggs, sometimes as quickly as the turtle lays them. Groups of wild **dogs** have been reported to stage inexplicable, blood-thirsty attacks on land iguana colonies. Hundreds of corpses have been left to rot on both Isabela and Santa Cruz.

Cats can revert to the wild almost instantly (just ask any cat owner) and are a major threat to bird chicks on many islands. **Rats** and **mice**, present since the first whaling ship came ashore, are among the most difficult species to control, as well as the most destructive. Almost every giant tortoise hatchling on Pinzon in the last century has fallen prey to black rats, leaving an age-heavy population with little hope of reproducing. House mice began in settlers' homes and soon spread to many islands.

Because their permeable skin makes it impossible to survive a long, dry ocean voyage, amphibians were the only one of five classes of vertebrates that hadn't colonized the Galápagos—that is, until 1998, when a small species of **tree frog** was first captured on Isabela and Santa Cruz. Scientists think the frogs arrived in cargo ships and were able to establish sustainable breeding populations during the particularly wet 1997–1998 El Niño season.

Of all the introduced animals, **goats** are the most serious threat. Thanks to their ability to eat almost anything (they survive on seawater during droughts), goats can bulldoze their way across an island in no time. They eat native plants down to the ground, leaving nothing for native animals to eat and causing severe erosion as the plants die and release their hold on the soil. Add to this mix the reproductive capabilities of a copying machine and you have a recipe for disaster; three goats left on Pinta in the late 1950s had generated more than 40,000 descendants by 1970.

fish species to inhabit the surrounding ocean. Almost one-quarter of these are endemic—every one of the 15 fish Darwin caught and brought back to England was identified as a new species.

Even snorkelers can enjoy a colorful show in the shallows. The **moorish idol** *(Zanclus cornutus)* trails a long dorsal fin over a body banded with black, yellow, and white, and the **blue parrotfish** *(Scarus ghobban)* wears pastel green, blue, and pink. The **harlequin wrasse** *(Bodianus eclancheri)* is one of the most colorful fish around, covered with spatters of orange, red, black, and white. This type of wrasse is called a protogynus hermaphrodite, meaning it can spontaneously change sex from female to male.

Lava rocks hide the **heiroglyphic hawkfish** *(Cirrhitus rivulatus)*, colored in complicated patterns of brown, yellow, and gray. It seems as if the **red-lipped batfish** *(Ogcocephalus darwini)* was made from leftover parts, with a forehead horn, long snout, and stiff pectoral fins it uses as makeshift legs. True to its name, the bizarre-looking batfish sports a bright-red mouth. Even stranger is the mottled **four-eyed blenny** *(Dialommus fuscus)*, which can breathe air temporarily as it travels up to 30 meters from the water in search of insects and crabs. Its eyes are each split into two parts, enabling it to see above and below the surface simultaneously.

One of the biggest thrills while diving in the Galápagos is to be engulfed by an opaque school of fish that seems to go on forever—veteran divers describe being blinded by fish for 20 minutes or more. Deep-sea schoolers include **amberjacks** *(Seriola rivoliana)*, **yellow-tailed surgeonfish** *(Prionurus laticlavius)*, **steel pompanos** *(Trachinotus stilbe)*, and **barracudas** *(Sphyraena idiastes)*.

Introduced Plants

Not as obvious but just as deadly, introduced plants steal sun, water, and nutrients from native species. Introduced species have skyrocketed from 77 in 1971—many brought by early settlers for food, medicine, and building materials—to almost 500 in 1997 (compared to only 560 native species). Today, vines such as the passionfruit and blackberry grow quickly into impenetrable thickets, and trees such as the guava and red quinine take over entire hillsides. It's estimated that the guava species *Psidium guajava* alone covers 50,000 hectares in the Galápagos.

Solutions

The Ministry of the Environment, the Ecuadorian National Park Service, and the Charles Darwin Research Center are joining efforts to rid the islands of introduced species. Each method has its drawbacks: hunting, the simplest solution, is difficult in the broken terrain; traps and poison could kill native species as well; and fencing is expensive and effective only on larger animals.

But the hard work has paid off. Goats and black rats have been eliminated from a few small islands, and wild dog populations are being controlled. The disastrous El Niño of 1982–1983 actually helped an eradication campaign on Santiago against goats and pigs by weakening the animals. Park employees were able to kill 20,000 out of 100,000 goats and half of nearly 10,000 pigs.

Goat eradication efforts have eliminated the animals from Española, Plaza Sur, Santa Fe, Marchena, and Rábida in the last three decades, but Santiago and Isabela are each still estimated to have up to 100,000 goats. The National Park Service and the Charles Darwin Research Center are hoping to kill close to 200,000 feral goats on Isabela and Santiago using armed wardens and trained dogs. A promising program called Operation Judas Goat, developed in New Zealand, uses a radio-tagged goat with brightly painted horns to reveal the location of its herd. This technique has helped park wardens reduce Pinta's goat population from 30,000 to 200.

Floreana's dark-rumped petrel is an encouraging success story. Formerly, large populations of petrels had been decimated by dogs, cats, rats, and pigs. (Pigs ate so many petrels at one time that farmers noticed their pork tasted faintly of fish from the contents of the seabirds' stomachs.) One study in the 1960s showed that only four out of 92 nests produced young. A predator-control program involving poisoned bait and traps turned things around—today four out of five petrels survive chickhood, instead of one out of five as before.

Sharks and Rays

Stingrays frequent sandy beaches—your guide should warn you when it's wise to shuffle your feet to keep from stepping on one and getting stung. Formations of **golden rays** *(Rhinoptera steindachneri)*, and the beautiful **leopard spotted eagle ray** *(Aetobatus narinari)*, often slip through the shallow waters of mangrove lagoons. These last two, as well as **manta rays** up to six meters across, frequent open water as well.

White-tipped sharks and **black-tipped sharks** are also seen near shore. Both have dorsal fins tipped with the respective color. Farther out to sea, large schools of **hammerhead sharks** provide divers with enough excitement or terror (or both) for a week of normal diving. **Whale sharks** up to 20 meters long drift after schools of plankton, trailing remoras from their flanks.

MARINE INVERTEBRATES

No slideshow of a Galápagos trip is complete without at least a handful of pictures of the **Sally lightfoot crab** *(Grapsus grapsus)*, which are so-called for their ability to skip across water for short distances. The crabs' brilliant reds and yellows stand out perfectly against dark volcanic rocks, making for countless irresistible photo opportunities.

In shallow waters, snorkelers come across **golden sand dollars** while foraging along sandy bottoms dotted with **pencil-spined sea urchins** and many species of **starfish**. Gulf stars have bright red and/or white spiny backs, whereas the blood star is, naturally, pure red. Black sun stars fold their legs under their body during the day, and fragile stars seldom have five legs of equal length.

Many divers consider **scallops** to be the most beautiful marine invertebrate. The 15-cm shells of the magnificent scallop *(Lyropecten magnificus)* snap shut when divers approach, so you'll have to sneak up slowly to see the beautiful crimson and violet of the inner mantle, lined with golden tentacles and blue eye spots. **Slipper lobsters** *(Lyropecten magnificus)* venture out at night to avoid predators—an option the heavily hunted and less mobile **sea cucumber** doesn't have.

The waters off the islands are too cold for true reef-building coral, but other types are found in the depths. **Pebble coral** *(Cycloseris mexicana)* lays loose on the bottom beneath masses of endemic **yellow-black coral** *(Antipathes galapagensis)*. The electric-orange **cup coral** *(Tubastraea tagusensis)* is thought to have been wiped out by the 1982–1983 El Niño.

On the makeshift reefs, you'll find the **leopard-spotted sea anemone** *(Antiparactis)*, along with **golden sea fans** *(Muricea)*, made up of thousands of tiny individual polyps held together by their eight arms. In the shadows lurk **squid** and **octopus**, blending in perfectly with their surroundings by expanding and contracting colored skin cells called *chromatophores*. **Nudibrachs**, shell-less members of the snail family Gastropoda who have taken to the water, come in a range of bright colors. These beautiful floating slugs eat other invertebrates, such as anemones and jellyfish, each of which probably dies surprised that its stinging cells (nematocysts) didn't protect it. The nudibrachs digest their prey and store the stinging cells for their own use later on.

FLORA

"All the plants have a wretched, weedy appearance," wrote Darwin in *The Voyage of the Beagle*, "and I did not see one beautiful flower." Although it may be uninspiring, the flora of the Galápagos is worth a second look. True, most of it is desert or semi-desert vegetation, and in certain seasons the lower parts of the islands look about as lush as a vacant lot. But they're *unique* dead-looking plants—of the Galápagos' 550 native species (compared to mainland Ecuador's 20,000), about 34 percent are endemic. The fraction jumps to 42 percent when all subspecies and varieties are included.

Many species, such as *opuntia* and *scalesia*, have evolved from a single original colonizer species on one island to more than a dozen species endemic to different islands today. And there are even regions of true, wet green in the upper altitudes of the higher islands, distinguished from their tropical mainland counterparts only by an abundance of endemic species.

Vegetation in the Galápagos is divided into three areas by altitude and climate. The coastal or littoral area surrounds each shoreline, at the delicate intersection of fresh and salt water. The semi-deserts of the dry areas receive the most visitors, whereas the lush, humid area is the smallest, continually dampened by the *garúa* mist.

Coastal Areas

Tangled walls of **mangroves,** ringing many islands like a woody mat of uncombed hair, are good examples of plants' adaptations to salty conditions. Able to grow only in brackish waters, mangroves weave themselves into the sand and marshes by sending down prop roots from limbs and sending up small breathing roots called *pneumatophores.* Long, pendant seedlings drop into the water, where they either stick vertically into the bottom or float until they lodge somewhere suitable for sprouting.

Mangrove species can usually be distinguished by their leaves. The red mangrove *(Rhizophora mangle)* has larger, pointier, shinier leaves than those of the white mangrove *(Languncularia racemosa).* Also found in the archipelago are the black mangrove *(Avicennia germinans)* and the less common button mangrove *(Conocarpus erectus).*

The creeping stems of the **beach morning glory** *(Ipomoea pes-caprae)* support the plant's beautiful, funnel-shaped flowers. The lavender blossoms are among the largest in the islands, and the vine is important in stabilizing shifting sands along the coast. The **lava morning glory** *(Ipomoea habeliona)* also has long, tubular blossoms. The fleshy leaves of the *sesuvium* species, common throughout the archipelago, change from bright red in the dry season to green in the wet season. Land iguanas love them, despite their salty taste. Leaves of the **saltbush** *(Cryptocarpus puriformis)* are even brinier.

Dry Areas

Most of the shrubs in this intermediate region are usually prickly and uninviting (the better to ward off predators), and almost all are tolerant of dry conditions (xerophytic). The **palo santo** *(Bursera graveolens)* is the most visible species, blanketing entire hillsides with its lifeless gray forms during the dry season. The tree, a relative of frankincense and myrrh, is burned as incense in churches for its fragrant (and insect-repelling) smoke. Its name, meaning "holy stick," comes

from its habit of flowering near Christmas.

The other plants you'll remember best from your visit are the **cacti,** the most distinctive flora of the islands. Like their mainland cousins, Galápagos cacti bristle with protective spines (actually leaves adapted for defense and water retention) and fat stems to store water. The prickly pear cactus, *Opuntia,* provides a lesson in evolution in itself. Fourteen separate species have evolved on different islands from a common ancestor. All have large, flat pads but vary widely in height and armor. On islands with land iguanas and tortoises, the plant's major predators, *opuntia* species have evolved a tall, woody trunk and tough spines for protection. *Opuntia* on Santa Cruz, for example, can grow 12 meters high. On islands with no large predators, on the other hand, *opuntia* cacti grow low to the ground. These species have spines that are soft enough to allow birds to nest among them—and with luck to pollinate the cactus in return.

Other Galápagos cactus species include the endemic lava cactus *(Brachycereus nesioticus),* a small, chunky plant that's often the first thing to grow in new lava flows, and the candelabra cactus *(Jasminocereus thouarsii),* whose slim cylinders can grow up to seven meters across.

Members of the *scalesia* genus may not be as distinctive as their prickly neighbors, but they've got them beat in diversity, with 15 species and six subspecies spread throughout the islands. The woody shrubs, relatives of the daisy and sunflower, also stem from a single pioneer species and range up into the humid area. The newest species, *Scalesia gordilloi,* was discovered only in 1986 on Santa Cruz.

The thorny **palo verde** (green stick) grows 2–10 meters high. Its scientific name, *Parkinsonia genus,* refers to the plant's tendency to shake like someone with Parkinson's disease during periods of drought. This motion drops the plant's tiny leaves, which would otherwise let too much water evaporate. Four endemic species of *tiquilia* grow low, gray, and ugly in volcanic ash. Even more unappealing is the *amargo* (bitter) plant *(Castela galapageia),* a shrub so bitter that even goats won't touch it. The fruit of the nasty little **manzanillo** *(Hippomane mancinella)* are poisonous, and its sap can cause severe skin reactions. Steer clear of this 10-meter-high tree, also called the "poison apple," and its small green leaves and flowers.

It's hard to believe, but the fruit of the tiny, wild **Galápagos tomato** *(Lycopersicon cheesmanii)* contains about 40 times more vitamin A and beta-carotene than its supermarket cousin. Cross-bred varieties are being developed for commercial distribution.

Humid Areas

The moist highlands of Santiago, Santa Cruz, San Cristóbal, and Floreana support dense forests of *lechoso (Scalesia pedunculata)*. Garlands of mosses, ferns, and liverworts festoon the tall trees' branches, along with orchids and clumps of Galápagos mistletoe *(Phoradendron henslovii)*. Some 90 species of **ferns** are found in the higher reaches, including the three-meter fern tree *(Cyathea weatherbyana)* on Santa Cruz.

Cacotillo, or cat's claw *(Miconia robinsonia)*, gives its name to a humid area subregion. The shrub, which is endemic to Santa Cruz and San Cristóbal, sports colorful purple and pink flowers. Charles even had a flower named after him—the tiny white blossoms of the endemic **Darwin's aster** *(Darwiniothamnus tenuifolius)* peek from the highland grasses.

VISITING THE ISLANDS

When to Go

High tourist season in the Galápagos occurs near the holidays (Dec.–Jan.) and during the northern hemisphere's summer (Jun.–Aug.). In those months it can be hard to find space on a tour unless you book well ahead. Then again, fewer boats operate during the off-season, which can make spots scarce as well. Many boats are dry-docked for repairs and maintenance during September and October.

As far as weather is concerned, during the dry season (Jun.–Nov.) the islands become brown and sere as dormant vegetation waits for the rains. Skies are often cloudy but little rain falls, and the water is colder for swimming. Rains come during the wet season (Jan.–Apr.), alternating with hot and sunny days. The islands turn green, and sea turtles lay their eggs. November may well be the best overall month to visit—not too hot or cold and not too many tourists.

The Galápagos are one hour behind mainland Ecuador (six hours behind GMT).

What to Bring

There's no need to go shopping for your Galápagos clothes. Aside from shorts and T-shirts, just make sure to bring a light jacket or sweater and a pair of long pants for chilly mornings and evenings, and a rain jacket for visiting the damp highlands. Sturdy boots are essential for the rough lava, and a hat and sunglasses keep the equatorial glare to a minimum.

Sunblock and seasickness pills should go in with the toiletries. It's hard to overemphasize the importance of protection against seasickness. The open waters between the islands can be surprisingly rough, especially in smaller boats, and trips are occasionally canceled because passengers can't stand the constant nausea. You can buy medicine patches to stick behind your ear, and some people prefer an elastic acupressure band that fits around the wrist. A day pack and water bottle make shore visits easier, and good snorkeling equipment guarantees that you won't be caught with your trunks down in the water.

If you have any money left after buying your ticket, spend it on photography equipment. Even if you're only a casual photographer, you'll feel like a pro in this wildlife photographer's nirvana. Grab close-ups with a telephoto lens—at least 200 mm, preferably 300 or even larger—and bring UV and polarizing filters to help cut the midday glare. Water protection for your gear, even if only sturdy freezer bags, is a must for *panga* rides. Finally, bring twice as much film as you think you'll need, and a few rolls on top of that. You'll be surprised how quickly frames fly by in the Galápagos, and film prices on ships and in the islands are ridiculously high. I always plan on shooting at least one roll of film per day. It's possible to sell leftover film to others visitors just arriving.

GETTING THERE

By Air

Needless to say, if you booked your trip in Ecuador, make sure you're flying to the correct island to begin your tour. The ticket counter in Quito is a madhouse, with tour agents checking in large groups as everyone else waits in line. All flights originate in Quito and stop over in Guayaquil for at least one hour, where everyone has to get out for a security check. Tours

GALÁPAGOS NATIONAL PARK RULES

These rules are vitally important if the delicate natural balance of the Galápagos is going to survive an ever-increasing onslaught of tourism. You'll come across them over and over again during your trip to the islands, but it can't hurt to repeat them one more time for clarity's sake.

1. **No plant, animal, or remains of such (including shells, bones, and pieces of wood), or other natural objects should be removed or disturbed.** Imagine 60,000 tourists per year each taking home a shell or picking a flower.

2. **Be careful not to transport any live material to the islands, or from island to island.** Seeds and/or soil stuck to shoe bottoms are the main culprit. Your guide should administer this rule, making everyone wash their feet and/or shoes before returning to the boat.

3. **Do not take any food to the uninhabited islands.** As they say, the seed you drop may become a tree.

4. **Do not touch or handle the animals.** Believe me, I know how hard it is to resist those baby sea lions. But even casual human touch will inevitably lead to the animals becoming shy of people and may transmit disease.

5. **Do not feed the animals.** See rule number 4.

6. **Do not startle or chase any animal from its resting or nesting spot.** Breeding seabirds are especially at risk. Eggs can easily overheat if left unshaded, and an abandoned boobie egg is instant frigatebird food. Take special care when photographing: no picture is worth the death of its subject. Also, don't take flash pictures directly in the animal's faces. Birds' sharp eyesight can be easily damaged by repeated bursts.

7. **Stay within the areas designated as visitor sites.** The white-staked trails have been carefully mapped out not to interfere with the animals' breeding, courtship, and living areas. Stick to them.

8. **Do not leave any litter on the islands or throw any off your boat.** This should go without saying, but you'd be surprised. Animals, especially marine mammals and turtles, can hurt or even kill themselves by playing with or trying to eat discarded trash.

9. **Do not deface the rocks.** Even though so many visitors have already, refrain from doing so.

10. **Do not buy souvenirs or objects made of plants or animals from the islands.** Black coral, which began in short supply, is now highly endangered because of poaching for the jewelry trade. If anyone offers you illegal souvenirs, report them to your guide or the National Park Service.

11. **Do not visit the islands unless accompanied by a licensed National Park guide.** And obey your guide at all times.

12. **Restrict your visits to officially approved areas.** Some areas have been set aside for study or wildlife management, including Daphne Minor and parts of Santiago.

13. **Camping anywhere without a permit is against the law.** Check at the National Park office near the Darwin Center in Puerto Ayora for legal spots.

14. **Show your conservationist attitude.** If you see someone breaking the rules, first gently suggest that they don't. If they continue, tell your guide or a National Park Service employee.

cruising the islands

JULIAN SMITH

should reconfirm for you; otherwise, do it yourself a few days before departure, and make sure your name is on the passenger list, *not* the waiting list *(lista de espera)*.

TAME has two daily flights from Quito to Balta on Santa Cruz via Guayaquil. Quito to Baltra costs $378 pp round-trip ($324 pp in the low season from 1 Sept.–30 Nov. and 16 Jan.–14 June). Fares from Guayaquil are slightly lower. Student discounts are available during high season to full-time students under 26 years old with ISIC cards. The flight takes about three hours from Quito, and you're allowed to bring one piece of luggage up to 25 pounds.

Military flights known as *logisticos* leave from Quito every other Wednesday morning at 6:30 A.M. The Fuerza Aérea Ecuatoriana flight travels via Guayaquil to San Cristóbal, Balta,and Isabela. You'll have to reserve seats on the Monday morning the week of your flight between 9 A.M. and noon at 3570 Ave. de la Prensa (about six blocks north of the main airport entrance). They'll take your name and passport number and tell you to return the next morning to pay in cash (around $290 round-trip, depending on which island you fly to),

Other Options
Air travel isn't your thing? A berth on a **cargo ship** may be more your speed. The *Piquero* leaves Guayaquil near the end of each month, stopping by Santa Cruz, San Cristóbal, and Isabela. It isn't the most luxurious way to go,

and if you buy a round-trip ticket, you're limited to returning with that particular ship, meaning you can stay only 7–9 days on the islands. On the other hand, you can often find companions aboard to make up a tour group. One-way passage is about $150 pp. Inquire in Guayaquil at the **TRAMFSA office,** Baquerizo Moerno 1119 and 9 de Octubre, piso 6, Of. 602, or at the **capitanía del puerto** along the Malecón. Passage can also be booked through **Neptunotour** in Quito, 290 Gangotena Enrique and Orellana, and Guayaquil, Tulcan 1824 and Ayacucho, tel. 4/360-779, fax 4/450-441).

If you would like to visit on **your own ship,** consider this: not only do you have to pay a marine entry tax (around $200) and the park entrance fee (another $100), but you're also responsible for hiring a local guide and shelling out a fee of $200 pp per day for *everyone* on board, crew included. Still interested? Steer all questions and applications to the port captain in Puerto Ayora, tel. 5/526-163.

Entrance Fees
The National Park entry fee is $100 pp for foreigners, payable in cash dollars or travelers' checks at the airport upon arrival. Keep your receipt because your boat captain will need to record it. You'll also have to pay a port fee: $12 in Puerto Ayora on Santa Cruz or $30 in Puerto Baquerizo Moreno on San Cristóbal.

Galápagos Airports

Tour groups are met at both airports by smiling, sign-waving guides who will direct you to the bus to take you to the dock and your waiting boat. If you're arriving without being booked on a tour, the Baquerizo Moreno airport is within walking or taxi distance of town.

Getting from Baltra to Puerto Ayora is a bit more complicated. The journey is in three stages: a free bus ride to the Itabaca canal between Baltra and Santa Cruz, a short ferry across the channel, and another bus up and over the Santa Cruz highlands and down to Puerto Ayora. The whole trip takes about one hour, and you can buy bus tickets at the airport. To get back to the airport from town, catch the bus in front of the CITEG sign in Puerto Ayora in the morning.

CHOOSING A TOUR

The only way to visit the Galápagos is by boat with a tour group; beyond that, your choices are limited to what kind of boat and, for some, whether to sleep aboard or not. Prices vary widely, as does service: when shopping around for a tour, remember that in the Galápagos—perhaps more than most destinations—you get what you pay for. Visiting the Galápagos is probably the most expensive thing you'll do in Ecuador, but if you plan it right and luck out with good weather, a good guide, and friendly companions, it can easily be one of the most amazing things you ever do.

Tour boats are organized into three classes—Economic, Tourist, and First—and trips range from 4–8 days. Unless you're really strapped for cash and/or time, five days should be the minimum length of tour to consider. Prices range from less than $300 pp for a four-night Economy class trip to more than $2,000 for eight days on a First class vessel. (Days of arrival and departure are counted as full days.) It may lessen the sting to know that these prices include food, accommodation, transfers to and from your boat, trained guides, and all your shore visits. You'll have to pay extra for airfare to and from the islands (see previous discussion), insurance, gratuities, souvenirs, and alcoholic or soft drinks on board.

Itineraries are strictly controlled by the Na-

tional Park Service to regulate the impact of visitors on the delicate sites. This means sticking to a tight schedule, so if you feel at times as if you're being herded, well, you are—in theory, for the good of the islands. The only valid reasons on most boats for altering an itinerary are medical emergencies and bad weather.

Economy Boats

Prices for the least expensive boats range between $500–750 pp per week, and even less for special last-minute deals and tours that spend the nights ashore (check to see if food is included). Five-day tours are $325–500, and four-day tours are less than $300. Because much of the footwork is left up to the passengers—often including flying to the islands, finding a group, and buying food—you'll have more say in how things are run, including planning the itinerary.

On the other hand, there have been accounts of Economic class boats sinking, catching fire, or breaking down in the middle of the ocean. Guides are usually not as well trained as those on luxury boats and may speak only limited languages other than Spanish. Accommodations and food may likewise disappoint. Because most economy boats are small (8–12 passengers), you'll get to know your fellow travelers well—perhaps too well—and your boat will toss more on rough seas. In addition, many economy trips must be arranged in the islands, so you may well decide that waiting around up to a week to find a suitable group may not be worth the money.

Certain security measures should be heeded for any economy boat tour in the Galápagos (or Ecuador, for that matter). Be sure the boat has adequate safety equipment: fire extinguishers, life jackets, and flares. The South American Explorers' Quito clubhouse has a handy contract that's highly recommended for any budget tour to nail down expected service and itinerary details.

Economic class boats, on the whole, are the best (or only) option for those on a limited budget and/or time frame. If you plan and negotiate your dollars and days carefully, your trip can turn out great—even a bit of an adventure.

Galápagos Daily Departures

All tours begin with a morning flight from the mainland on the first day and end on the last day with an afternoon flight back to the mainland. Prices are pp unless otherwise noted.

BOAT	CLASS	PASSENGERS	ACCOMMODATIONS	PRICE
Sunday: 4 Days/3 Nights				
Amigo I	Tourist	16	8 double	$516
Lobo del Mar	Tourist	16	8 double	$408
San Juan	Tourist	12	6 double	$456
Rembrandt	Tourist Superior	30	15 double	$760
Delfin	First	36	21 double	$456
Sunday: 5 Days/4 Nights				
Mabel	Economic	10	5 double	$336
Merak	Economic	8	4 double	$504
Valiant	Economic	10	3 double, 1 quad	$336
Yolita	Economic	12	6 double	$360
Aida Maria	Tourist	16	8 double	$510
Angelique	Tourist	12	6 double	$432
Antartida	Tourist	10	5 double	$576
Darwin Explorer	Tourist	16	1 single, 1 triple, 6 double	$563
Sunday: 8 Days/7 Nights				
Cormorant	Economic	12	6 double	$480
Mabel	Economic	10	5 double	$504
Merak	Economic	8	4 double	$719
Pulsar	Economic	10	2 double	$748
Valiant	Economic	10	3 single, 1 quad	$492
Yolita	Economic	12	6 double	$516
Aida Maria	Tourist	16	8 double	$768
Amigo I	Tourist	16	8 double	$860
Angelique	Tourist	12	6 double	$780
Angelito	Tourist	16	8 double	$1,470
Antartida	Tourist	10	5 double	$840
Darwin Explorer	Tourist	16	1 single, 1 triple, 6 double	$900
Lobo de Mar	Tourist	16	8 double	$816
Pelikano	Tourist	16	8 double	$892
San Juan	Tourist	12	6 double	$768
Rembrandt	Tourist Superior	30	15 double	$1,525
Alta	First	16	8 double	$2,898
Ambassador I	First	86	62 cabins	$2,965 s, $2,372 d
Coral I & II	First	20/22	10 double/11 double	$2,350
Delfin	First	36	21 double	$1,610
Mondrian	First	16	8 double	$1,750
Parranda	First	16	8 double	$2,898
Monday: 4 Days/3 Nights				
Sullivan	Tourist	16	8 double	$360
Tropic Sun	Tourist Superior	48	18 double, 3 suites	$600 d, $1,600 suite
Corinthian	First	48	24 double	$750
Letty	First	20	10 double	$875
Santa Cruz	First	90	45 double	$1,122

BOAT	CLASS	PASSENGERS	ACCOMMODATIONS	PRICE
Monday: 5 Days/4 Nights				
Golondrina	Economic	8	2 double, 1 quad	$350
Gaby	Tourist	16	8 double	$455
Seaman	Tourist	16	8 double	$575
Tip Top II	Tourist	16	8 double	$900
Fragata	Tourist Superior	16	8 double	$510
Tip Top III	Tourist Superior	16	8 double	$1,000
Tropic Sun	Tourist Superior	48	18 double, 3 suites	$800 d, $2,140 suite
Monday: 8 Days/7 Nights				
Seaman	Tourist	16	8 double	$900
Cruz del Sur	Tourist Superior	16	8 double	$1,080
Dorado	Tourist Superior	16	8 double	$1,080
Estrella del Mar	Tourist Superior	16	8 double	$1,080
Fragata	Tourist Superior	16	8 double	$820
Tropic Sun	Tourist Superior	48	18 double, 3 suites	$1,400 d, $3,740 suite
Corinthian	First	48	24 double	$1,800
Letty	First	20	10 double	$2,050
Santa Cruz	First	90	45 double	$2,620
Tuesday: 4 Days/3 Nights				
Erick	First	20	10 double	$875
Flamingo	First	20	10 double	$875
Isabela II	First	40	20 double	$1270
Tuesday: 5 Days/4 Nights				
Discovery	Tourist	20	10 double	$504
Beagle III	Tourist Superior	10	5 double	$950
Tuesday: 8 Days/7 Nights				
Discovery	Tourist	20	10 double	$744
Gaby	Tourist	16	8 double	$624
Sulidae	Tourist	12	6 double	$1,250
Beagle III	Tourist Superior	10	5 double	$1,500
Samba	Tourist Superior	12	6 double	$1,500
Erick	First	20	10 double	$2,050
Flamingo	First	20	10 double	$2,050
Isabela II	First	40	20 double	$2,955
Wednesday: 4 Days/3 Nights				
New Flamingo	Economic	10	5 double	$312
Poseidon	Economic	10	5 double	$324
Darwin	Tourist	16	8 double	$540
Islas Plazas	Tourist Superior	16	8 double	$672
Galapagos Explorer II	First	100	50 double	$943
Wednesday: 5 Days/4 Nights				
Poseidon	Economic	10	5 double	$360
Amigo I	Tourist	16	8 double	$540
Lobo de Mar	Tourist	16	8 double	$510
New Daphne	Tourist	16	8 double	$540
Pelikano	Tourist	16	8 double	$630
San Juan	Tourist	12	6 double	$528
Rembrandt	Tourist Superior	30	15 double	$945

Galápagos Daily Departures
(continued)

BOAT	CLASS	PASSENGERS	ACCOMMODATIONS		PRICE
Delfin	First	36	21 double		$920
Freedom	First	12	6 double		$880
Wednesday: 8 Days/7 Nights					
New Flamingo	Economic	10	5 double		$576
Amigo I	Tourist	16	8 double		$860
Cachalote	Tourist	10	5 double		$1,250
Darwin	Tourist	16	8 double		$960
Lobo del Mar	Tourist	16	8 double		$816
New Daphne	Tourist	16	8 double		$864
Andando	Tourist Superior	12	6 double		$2,060
Islas Plazas	Tourist Superior	16	8 double		$1,080
Rembrandt	Tourist Superior	30	15 double		$1,525
Sagita	Tourist Superior	16	8 double		$1,975
Ambasador	First	86	62 double	$2,965 s,	$2,372 d
Delfin	First	36	21 double		$1,610
Freedom	First	12	6 double		$1,400
Galapagos Explorer II	First	100	50 double		$2,205
Thursday: 4 Nights/3 Days					
Mabel	Economic	10	5 double		$264
Yolita	Economic	12	6 double		$276
Valiant	Economic	10	3 double, 1 quad		$264
Aida Maria	Tourist	16	8 double		$384
Angelique	Tourist	12	6 double		$348
Antartida	Tourist	10	5 double		$480
Darwin Explorer	Tourist	16	1 single, 6 double, 1 triple		$450
Thursday: 5 Days/4 Nights					
Seaman	Tourist	16	8 double		$575
Sullivan	Tourist	16	8 double		$420
Tropic Sun	Tourist Superior	48	18 double, 3 suites	$800 d ,	$2,140 suite
Corinthian	First	48	24 double		$1,050
Letty	First	20	10 double		$1,175
Santa Cruz	First	90	45 double		$1,499
Thursday: 8 Days/7 Nights					
Mabel	Economic	10	5 double		$504
Merak	Economic	8	4 double		$719
Valiant	Economic	10	3 doubles, 1 quad		$492
Antartida	Tourist	10	5 double		$840
Seaman	Tourist	16	8 double		$900
Sullivan	Tourist	16	8 double		$672
Tropic Sun	Tourist Superior	40	9 double, 3 suites	$1,400 d,	$3,740 suite
Aggressor I	First	14	7 double		$2,964
Aggressor II	First	14	7 double		$2,964
Corinthian	First	48	24 double		$1,800
Letty	First	20	10 double		$2,050
Santa Cruz	First	90	45 double		$2,620

Friday: 4 Days/3 Nights

Golondrina	Economic	8	2 double,1 quad	$348
Galapagos Adventure I	Tourist	20	10 double	$630
Galapagos Adventure II	Tourist	16	8 double	$570
Sulidae	Tourist	12	6 double	$782
Tip Top II	Tourist	16	8 double	$900
Beluga	Tourist Superior	16	8 double	$1,232
Fragata	Tourist Superior	16	8 double	$520
Tip Top III	Tourist Superior	16	8 double	$1,000
Isabela II	First	40	20 double	$1,685

Friday: 5 Days/4 Nights

Discovery	Tourist	20	10 double	$504
Gaby	Tourist	16	8 double	$456
Erick	First	20	10 double	$1,175
Flamingo	First	20	10 double	$1,175

Friday: 8 Days/7 Nights

Golondrina	Economic	8	2 double, 1 quad	$552
Discovery	Tourist	20	10 double	$744
Gaby	Tourist	16	8 double	$624
Galapagos Adventure I	Tourist	20	10 double	$1,008
Galapagos Adventure II	Tourist	16	8 double	$912
Tip Top II	Tourist	16	8 double	$1,400
Beluga	Tourist Superior	16	8 double	$1,970
Fragata	Tourist Superior	16	8 double	$831
Tip Top III	Tourist Superior	16	8 double	$1,600
Erick	First	20	10 double	$2,050
Flamingo	First	20	10 double	$2,050

Saturday: 4 Days/3 Nights

Discovery	Tourist	20	10 double	$336

Saturday: 5 Days/4 Nights

New Flamingo	Economic	10	5 double	$432
Poseidon	Economic	10	5 double	$360
Cachalote	Tourist	10	5 double	$782
Darwin	Tourist	16	8 double	$660
Islas Plazas	Tourist Superior	16	8 double	$720
Galapagos Explorer	First	100	50 double	$1,354
Reina Silvia	First	16	8 double	$1,194

Saturday: 8 Days/7 Nights

Poseidon	Economic	10	5 double	$540
Islas Plazas	Tourist Superior	16	8 double	$1,080
Diamante	First	12	6 double	$2,310
Eclipse	First	48	2 single, 23 double	$2,670
Galapagos Explorer II	First	100	50 double	$2,200
Lammerlaw	First	16	8 double	$2,650
Mistral	First	12	6 double	$2,310
Nortada	First	10	5 double	$2,030
Rachel	First	8	4 double	$1,940
Reina Silvia	First	16	8 double	$1,910
Resting Cloud	First	8	4 double	$1,940

Moderately Priced Boats

Tourist class boats are the most common in the islands. (Boats at the high end of this range are also called Tourist Superior class.) They're usually medium-sized sailboats or motorboats holding 10–20 passengers. Accommodations are a step up from Economy class, but the cabins in some are still small and the toilets are still pumped by hand. Some would argue that the food in Tourist class is the best because the cooks are generally excellent and only have to cook for a small group. Some itinerary flexibility remains (by group vote), and guides can be outstanding.

Costs range between $750–$900 pp per week for Tourist class and $800–1,500 pp per week for Tourist Superior class. Shorter tours are less: expect to pay $400–800 pp for five days on a Tourist class boat ($500–1,000 pp for Tourist Superior class), and $300–500 pp for four days on a Tourist class boat ($550–750 for Tourist Superior).

Luxury/Cruise Ships

First class, the most expensive type of tour, starts at $1,400 pp per week and climbs to $3,000. Boats in this class maintain a standard of luxury matching the finest hotels on the mainland. Cabins, food, and service are impeccable. Everything is organized by loudspeaker announcement, from shore visits to buffet lunches and sit-down dinners. Guides are the cream of the crop, with multilingual fluency and university degrees the norm. Because these boats are the largest ones plying the archipelago, they're able to visit far islands like Fernandina, Isabela, and Hood beyond the range of smaller, slower boats. Sea rolling is minimized, although still a factor.

The short list of minuses includes a complete lack of itinerary flexibility—everything is planned to the minute—and larger shore groups, which can make keeping up and hearing the guide a chore.

Shore-Based Tours

Those especially troubled by seasickness will be glad to hear that a few options allow you to sleep on shore. Remember that hours will be wasted traveling to and from the islands every day, and some farther islands will remain completely out of reach. Budget travelers can find accommodations in Puerto Ayora or Baquerizo Moreno and arrange a string of day tours.

Guides

Next to a boat that doesn't sink, a good guide is the most important factor in your visit. Guides qualify in one of three classes: Class Three, usually on first-class boats; Class Two, on tourist class boats; and Class One on economic boats. All guides are supposed to speak at least two languages, but Class One guides often speak little besides Spanish. Every guide has to pass rigorous examinations every three years and complete a training course on the islands every six years to keep his or her certification.

When booking a tour, ask about your guide's specific qualifications and what language he or she speaks. In general, the more expensive the tour, the better the guide.

Booking

Tours can be arranged by phone from your kitchen table in your home country, but keep in mind that the farther from the boat you set things up, the more you're paying for legwork you could conceivably do yourself. Countless travel agencies in Quito advertise tours, so shopping around is the way to go. The best deals often come when agencies are desperate to fill the last few spaces on a tour, so some judicious holding out may work to your advantage. Beyond the list included here, Safari Tours in Quito and the South American Explorers' Quito clubhouse are the best sources for recommended boats and last-minute deals. Deposits range from 10–50 percent depending on the boat and tour operator. You are normally required to have paid in full 30 days before sailing unless you're getting a last-minute deal.

Puerto Ayora is the place to go for booking a tour in the Galápagos, although this applies mainly to budget tours. While you're negotiating the price and itinerary, keep a few things in mind: don't include sites you could visit yourself like the Darwin Center and the Santa Cruz highlands, get the entire agreement down on paper, and be ready to put down a food deposit ahead of time. Direct all complaints concerning tours, before or after, to the port captain (Capitanía del Puerto) if you booked in the islands, and to the agency directly if you booked in Quito or outside the country.

RECOMMENDED TOUR OPERATORS

Although dozens of tour operators throughout Ecuador offer trips to the Galápagos, only a handful earn consistently positive reviews. It's a sad fact that many agents are ill-informed and end up promising itineraries that don't hold and refunds that are slow in coming—when they do at all—if something goes wrong. When you're talking about this much money, it's best to go with the proven few.

Angermeyer's Enchanted Excursions, Foch 769 and Amazonas, tel. 2/569-960, 221-305, fax 2/569-956, e-mail: angermeyer@accessinet.net, www.angermeyer.com.ec, run the highly recommended motor sailers *Cachalote* and *Sulidae,* along with the motor yachts *Angelito* and *Beluga.* **Safari Tours,** Calama 380 and Juan León Mera, tel./fax 2/220-426, tel. 2/552-505, fax 2/223-381, e-mail: admin@safari.com.ec, www.safari.com.ec, has a database of last-minute tour vacancies that can save you a bundle, and they can be reached from the United States at 800/434-8182.

Metropolitan Touring was the first to organize high-quality Galápagos trips in the 1960s. The 90-passenger *Santa Cruz* is one of the largest vessels plying the islands, and they offer the more intimate 38-passenger *Isabella II.* Metropolitan Touring has offices throughout the country, with the main one in Quito at Republica de El Salvador N36-84, tel. 2/464-780, fax 2/464-702. Information and bookings are available in the United States through Adventure Associates, 13150 Coit Rd., Ste. 110, Dallas, TX 75240, 800/527-2500, 972/907-0414, fax 972/783-1286, e-mail: info@ecuadorable.com, www.ecuadorable.com.

Galasam (Economic Galápagos Tours), 9 de Octubre 424, Ed. Gran Pasaje, piso 11, Of. 1106, Guayaquil, tel. 4/306-289, 9/860-220, fax 4/301-759, e-mail: info@galasam.com.ec, www.galasam.com.ec, specializes in budget trips and operates the First-class yachts *Dorado, Cruz del Sur, Estrella del Mar,* and *Islas Plazas,* along with the Tourist-class yachts *Darwin* and *Antartida.* **Quasar Nautica,** Los Shyris 2447 and Villarroel, tel. 2/441-550, 446-996, fax 2/436-625, e-mail: qnautic1@ecnet.ec, www.quasarnauticatumbaco.com, just added the *Eclipse* to

their yacht roster, which already included the *Diamante, Mistral, Nortada, Parranda, Resting Cloud, Lammer Law,* and *Alta.* They can be contacted in the United States through Tumbaco Inc., Miami International Commerce Center, Suite 115, 7855 NW 12th Street, Miami, FL 33126, 305/599-9008, 800/247-2925, fax 305/592-7060, e-mail: tumbaco@gate.net.

LIFE ONBOARD

Daily Routine

The day of arrival in the islands, you'll be shown to your boat and cabin. Don't worry if it's small (and most are, except on the cruise ships). You'll have something to keep you busy during most of the day, and any spare minutes you'll probably want to spend on deck or socializing in the common area/dining room. Your guide will introduce him or herself and the rest of the crew and spend a few minutes explaining the park rules, your itinerary, and the day-to-day schedule during your stay.

Every day after that, you'll be rousted out of bed at about 8 A.M. to find breakfast waiting. Chances are the boat will be in a different location—maybe even a different island—than when you went to bed, after sailing or motoring most of the night. The morning visit takes between 2–3 hours, including the *panga* ride to shore. Your guide will direct the group along the path or down the beach, explaining what (and who) you're seeing and filling in relevant natural history details as you go.

If your guide seems overly concerned about keeping the group together and making everyone stick to the trail, try not to be perturbed. After all, these guides herd thousands of tourists a year past the same sites, and a surprising number of folks think that because they paid so much money to come here they shouldn't have to follow orders once they arrive. This is simply not true. Better too strict than too lax, for the sake of the islands. Stick together, listen to the guide's explanation, and you'll enjoy the visit without causing more than a minimal impact. The same sentiment applies when your guides insist that you wear a lifejacket during *panga* rides; they face two days in jail if they're caught with passengers not wearing one.

Back on board, you'll find your cabin clean and lunch ready. The midday meal is casual—a buffet on cruise ships and sandwiches or snacks on smaller vessels. Your guide will announce the departure time for the afternoon excursion; there's usually time for a short break of an hour or so to rest, digest, or update your journal. Occasionally the boat will travel between sites by day.

The afternoon visit runs much like the morning, except now the best light for photos comes with the setting sun. If you have the opportunity to **snorkel,** don't miss it. Snorkeling in the Galápagos is incomparable—where else can you swim with sea lions and turtles, along with the usual gorgeous fish and marine life? Bring your own equipment if you have it. It's even worth buying it for the trip. Much of the equipment on tour boats is substandard or lacking altogether, and you may have to pay extra to rent it. Snorkeling gear can be rented in Puerto Ayora at Galápagos Sub-Aqua and Scuba Iguana. Wetsuits are handy but not necessary; wearing just a swimsuit, most people can last about half an hour in the water before getting chilled.

There should be some time before dinner to wash up or perhaps even read a little. Dinner is the most significant meal of the day; on cruise ships it's a formal, sit-down affair with invitations to the captain's table and everything. Your crew might surprise you with fresh lobster or fish such as *pargo* (red snapper) or *bacalao* (cod). After the meal, your guide will give a talk on what you saw today and where you'll be visiting tomorrow.

An evening's post-dinner entertainment ranges from dancing on cruise ships to swapping tall tales over beers on sailboats. Remember that drinks are not included in the tour price, so be ready to pay the piper the day of departure. A day in the equatorial sun takes a lot out of you, though, so don't be embarrassed to make a beeline from the dinner table to bed.

Tipping

Giving a gratuity at the end of the voyage is customary; your crew and guide work hard (as they'll probably remind you) and aren't paid as much as you think. Beyond that, any tip should reflect the service, so use your best judgment. Cash dollars and travelers' checks are both welcome. The usual procedure is to tip the guide separately from the rest of the crew. Crew tipping should be done through a tip box or to the entire group at once to minimize the chances of anyone get-

ting shortchanged. The going rate for exceptional service is $1–2 per day per crewmember.

Safety

All this talk of natural history seems to fuel some biological urge to breed, or at least try to; there have always been numerous complaints of male guides hitting on female passengers. If an island tryst wasn't in your plans, decline politely, and if it persists, report him to the tour operator.

DIVING IN THE GALÁPAGOS

By now you must be getting tired of superlatives, but heed at least one more: the Galápagos are among the most spectacular dive destinations in the world. The islands' underwater riches have been known since 1925, the year the New York Zoological Society's Oceanographic Expedition sent divers with lead boots and hand-pumped air hoses to explore the archipelago's ocean bottom. In 1998, the long-awaited Special Law for the Galápagos extended the protected marine zone to 40 km from the shores of the islands. At last count there were 62 marine visitor sites spread throughout the archipelago, many on islands closed to visitors above the surface.

Diving in the Galápagos is not for beginners. Cold waters make a wetsuit essential, and the best marine life usually keeps to areas of strong currents—up to 3.5 knots in places. Visibility is poor, ranging from 10–25 meters (half that of the Caribbean). Many divers are in open water, making hang-off lines impossible, and the nearest decompression chambers are on the mainland, in Ecuador and Panama (an equal distance away).

If you can handle it, though, the Galápagos Islands offer a world-class diving experience, with schools of fish so thick that the water seems alive. Sea jacks arrive in boisterous groups, whereas docile cod wait farther down. Active volcanic vents keep things interesting, but not nearly as much as a school of a thousand hammerhead sharks circling in a tornado of teeth. The list goes on from there: whale sharks, manta rays, sperm whales, marine iguanas, and penguins all make appearances.

The best diving is during the hot season (roughly Dec.–May), with water temperatures between 20–25°C making a three-mm wetsuit adequate. Temperatures drop to 15°C in the cold season, when a six-mm wetsuit with hood becomes necessary. Other than your own wetsuit, you'll also want to bring a mask, gloves, dive alert whistle, and sausage or scuba tuba. Let your operator know ahead of time if you'll need any extra equipment. Accessories such as regulators and fins can be rented at Galápagos Sub-Aqua in Puerto Ayora, but there aren't any dive stores on the mainland.

Most dives don't exceed 40 meters, but a series of decompression stops is recommended. There is dangerous sea life to consider. Male sea lions guarding harems and territory are the most dangerous animals on the islands. Cone shells and scorpion fish should be avoided beneath the surface. Sharks usually approach out of curiosity; if they come too close for comfort, try exhaling noisily and abruptly, flashing a camera strobe, or feinting briefly in its direction. If these tactics fail, swim away slowly, keeping the animal in sight. *Never bolt.*

Because most visitors leave by plane, plan on leaving a day free at the end of your dive trip to avoid possible pressurization problems. The nearest decompression chamber is in Guayaquil.

Ecuadorian Dive Agencies

Day trips can be booked on the spot in Puerto Ayora, but longer trips should be arranged beforehand. Live-aboard charters are the usual way to go, with itineraries from 8–15 days available, although 10–12 days is suggested. Fernando Zambrano of **Galápagos Sub-Aqua** was the first guide on the islands and boasts two decades of diving experience. His outfit has the best reputation and a good safety record. They have an office in Quito at Pinto 439 and Amazonas, tel./fax 2/564-294, e-mail: sub_aqua@accessinter.net, www.Galápagos_sub_aqua.com.ec. They can also be contacted in the United States at 888/317-6333, 954/489-7749, e-mail: gsubaqua@diveres.com. Eight-day live-aboard trips are around $2,000 pp. They also have an office in Puerto Ayora, where they offer introductory dives for $75 pp per day and five-day diving courses for $350 pp.

Also in Puerto Ayora is **Scuba Iguana**, tel. 2/526-497 or 526-330, e-mail: info@scubaiguana.com, www.scubaiguna.com, run by Jack Nelson of the Hotel Galápagos and dive master Mattias Espinosa, who was featured in the Galá-pagos IMAX movie.

Daily dive prices start at $78 pp for two dives in Academy Bay and rise to $110 pp for other destinations. Five-day, seven-dive packages are $735 pp, and they have eight-day trips to Darwin and Wolf for $2,175 pp. Open-water certification courses are $577–939 pp, depending on your choice of accommodations. They also have an office in Quito with Scala Tours at Portugal 585 and 6 de Diciembre, Ed. Bello Monte, tel. 2/260-608 or 260-609, fax 2/258-655, e-mail: scalaviajes@andinanet.net, galapago.scuigua@scubadiving.com.

Because of numerous complaints, dive trips aboard the *Free Enterprise* are definitely to be avoided.

Foreign Dive Agencies

If you'd rather book a trip back home, **Aquatic Encounters** offers half a dozen dive packages per year that include four nights in Quito and seven nights aboard the 90-foot luxury motor yacht *Reina Silvia*. Rates are $3,355 pp, not including airfare to Ecuador or the islands. Contact them at 1966 Hardscrabble Place, Boulder, CO 80303, 303/494-8384, fax 303/494-1202, e-mail: Info@AquaticEncounters.com, www. aquaticencounters.com.

Named after a Scottish mountain, the 93-foot *Lammer Law* is one of the two largest trimarans in the world (the other is her sister ship the *Cuan Law*). It's fully air-conditioned and operates on a weekly schedule from Saturday to Saturday. Seven-night dive trips are $2,606 pp Dec.–Aug. and $2,350 pp the rest of the year, and nine nights cost $3,350 ($3,020 off-season). You and 15 of your best dive buddies can charter the whole boat for only $36,484 per week Dec.–Aug. ($32,900 Sept.–Nov.) Prices don't include airfare. Contact the Trimarine Boat Co., Box 4065, St. Thomas, U.S. Virgin Islands 00803-4065, 284/494-2490, fax 284/494-5774, e-mail: cuanlaw@surfbvi.com.

Dive Sites in the Central Islands

Within sight of Puerto Ayora, **Academy Bay** features a handful of sites recommended for beginners. Punta Estrada on the southwestern tip is home to sea turtles, golden rays, and white-tip sharks, and sea lions swim over to check you out at Caamaño Islet. The boulder walls and caves of the Punta Nuñez Cliffs are vivid with gorgonian sea fans; sea turtles and eels pass by on occasion. Santa Cruz Shoal also harbors gorgonians, sharks, and turtles.

Some of the islands' best diving surrounds Santa Cruz, only 1–2 hours by boat from Puerto Ayora. **Gordon Rock,** north of the Plazas, takes first place in this category. The difficult wall dive, swept by strong swells and currents, is well worth the trouble. It teems with large schooling fish, such as grouper, snapper, and amberjack, and huge moray eels peek out from the wall. Three types of rays and four kinds of sharks, including hammerheads and the Galápagos shark, are all often seen here.

Black coral and rays decorate the wall of **Daphne Minor,** and manta rays and schools of hammerheads slide by **North Seymour.** Both are highly recommended for experienced divers, along with **Mosquera** south of Seymour. The aggressive Galápagos shark frequents **Nameless Rock,** which is swept by strong currents off Santa Cruz's west shore. Beginners should try the **Islas Guy Fawkes** nearby, an easier dive with vibrant sponges and reef fish set against black coral. The wall dive at **Cousin Rock,** north of Bartolomé, features large moray eels, eagle rays, and hammerheads.

Other Dive Sites
Far to the north, the islets of **Wolf** and **Darwin** aren't even on most maps of the Galápagos. They should be, though, because the diving here is some of the best in the world. Schools of hundreds of hammerheads can be seen off Wolf's reef, and gigantic whale sharks cruise slowly by between June and November. Bottlenose dolphins are common at Darwin's Northern Arch.

The intermediate-level diving at Floreana usually requires an overnight stay on or near the island. Three dive sites are found just off the north shore. Playful sea lions are the main draw at **Campeón,** whereas exotic tropical fish such as the harlequin wrasse swim with barracudas and eagle rays at **Enderby.**

Tagus Cove on Isabela is great for night dives. At **Roca Redonda,** a short distance north of the island, volcanic gas seeps from the ocean floor in an area favored by grouper and sharks.

SANTA CRUZ AND NEARBY ISLANDS

The geographic and economic heart of the Galápagos is almost a visit in itself. Actually, if you're short on time or money (or both), that's not a bad idea—much of the island can be seen independently or with a guide hired in Puerto Ayora, and many of the best Galápagos sites are within day-trip range.

PUERTO AYORA AND VICINITY

The largest city in the Galápagos is more of a Caribbean speck of a town. Brightly colored houses line streets made of sole-scouring volcanic cobblestones, and front yards lined with flowering vines are more likely to have a boat up on blocks than a car.

With the highest standard of living in the Galápagos, Puerto Ayora is a tourist mecca where travel agencies, hotels, restaurants, and souvenir stores compete for the flood dollars released from cruise ships almost every weekend. Everything here is more expensive than on the mainland, especially film, food, and batteries—one and a half times normal prices and up. Residents will tell you that the only things lacking on Puerto Ayora are enough fresh water and a good hospital (most medical emergencies are handled in Quito).

Accommodations
Most of Puerto Ayora's budget hotels are afflicted with brackish water, and many don't have hot water. A friendly family runs the **Bed and Breakfast Peregrina,** Darwin and Indefategable, tel. 5/526-323, out of their home. Five rooms with private baths run $4 pp, including breakfast. There's a shady terrace and garden, and a laundry service is available.

Los Amigos, on Darwin and 12 de Febrero, tel. 5/526-265, has rooms with shared bath for $2 s, $3 d; and the small, friendly **Hotel Santa Cruz,** on Herrera and Indefategable, tel. 5/526-573, has six rooms with shared bath for $2 pp. The **Hotel Salinas,** Navaeda and Berlanga, tel./fax 5/526-107, is central and clean, with a small gar-

SURFING THE GALÁPAGOS

As any sea lion will tell you, the Galápagos has surf galore—so much so that board bags are becoming a common sight in the islands' airports. The beginning of the year (Jan.–April) is usually the best season, but waves can be good—or not—year-round. A wetsuit will make the cold water bearable, and keep an eye out for jagged volcanic rock bottoms, sharks, and male sea lions.

Choice spots are scattered thoughout the islands; many around Santa Cruz are within reach of a small boat from Puerto Ayora. For a detailed description of surfing in the Galápagos, order *Surf Report*, Vol. 10, #7 (July 1989) from Surfer Publications, P.O. Box 1028, Dana Point, CA 92629, 714/496-5922, fax 714/496-7849.

den, communal cable TV, a restaurant, and rooms for $3 s, $5 d with private bath. Rooms at the **Lobo de Mar,** 12 de Febrero and Darwin, tel. 5/526-188, fax 5/526-569, are $5 s, $6 d, with private bath, fans, and balconies.

Ten dollars pp will usually get you a private bath and hot water, except at the **Hotel Castro,** Los Colonos and Malecón, tel. 5/526-508, fax 5/526-113. Still, it's recommended as a clean, quiet place with fans, a terrace, a restaurant, and a bar. Prices are the same at the **Gran Hotel Fiesta,** Brito and Las Ninfas, tel./fax 5/526-440, with hammocks, cabins in a garden, and access to the Las Ninfas lagoon. The **Estrella del Mar.** on 12 de Febrero, tel. 5/526-427, is often recommended for its ocean views.

Muted orange path lights lead you through the mangroves to the **Red Mangrove Inn,** Darwin and Las Fragatas, tel./fax 5/526-564, e-mail: redmangrove@ecuadorexplorer.com, the hippest place in the islands. Opened in late 1994, the small hotel is as cozy as a California artist's weekend home (no shoes inside), with rose-colored walls decorated with batiks and tiles made by one of the owners. The dining room opens onto a patio and hot tub overlooking Darwin Bay. Rooms at the Red Mangrove cost $50 s, $80 d, with mountain bikes, sea kayaks, and windsurfers available on request. The owners also offer tours of Santa Cruz by mountain bike, kayak, and horseback.

Behind El Pelicano restaurant sits the **Hotel Angermeyer,** Darwin and Los Piqueros, tel./fax 5/526-277, a beautiful place surrounding a tropical courtyard. Every spacious room has a fan and private bath with solar-heated water, and those on the second floor open onto terraces over the swimming pool. The owners speak Spanish, English, and German and can arrange day tours. Rates are $55 s, $80 d. Jack Nelson inherited the **Hotel Galapagos,** tel./fax 5/526-296, fax 5/526-330, e-mail: hotelgps@pa.ga.pro.ec, from his father in 1967. The luxury hotel sprawls near the entrance to the Charles Darwin Center, with a large bar/dining area/sitting room overlooking the bay, perfect for a game of chess in the afternoon. The 14 cabins are simple and comfortable and have hot water, fans, and private baths. Shady gardens and bay views complete the picture. Rates are $60 s, $100 d.

Food
Start your day off with a filling breakfast of eggs, bread, yogurt, and granola at the **Cafeteria Sunrise** on Herrera, which also has good, inexpensive set lunches. Several small kiosks along Darwin east of Herrera are open in the evening (and some in the afternoons), serving traditional dishes that are prepared well and served fresh and cheap. The **Kiosco William** serves a tasty *encocado de langostino* (lobster in coconut sauce).

On the corner of Charles Darwin and Binford, the **Moonrise Cafe** (also a travel agency) is perfect for people-watching. Homemade cakes and breads are on the menu, with sandwiches and salads for $2–3. Another bakery opposite the telephone office opens early to serve hot bread and yogurt for anyone leaving on the early airport bus.

I like **La Trattoria del Pippo** near the Bed and Breakfast Peregrino for its open shaded patio, menu cartoons, and tasty tiramisú over an espresso after dinner. Pasta dishes such as the *spaghetti putanesca* with fish and black olives are $2–4. **Capricho,** at Floreana and Darwin, serves vegetarian food and organic salads; and **Media Luna Pizza** up the block offers good pies (which sell out quickly) and even better brownies. **Kathy's Kitchen** opens only during the high season, which is a shame because they have

PUERTO AYORA

To Darwin Center

CEMETERY

SCUBA IGUANA

ISLA FLOREANA

LAS PIQUEROS

SANCHEZ

LAS FRAGATAS

GALÁPAGOS GALLERY ★
HOTEL ANGERMEYER ●
MEDIA LUNA PIZZA ▼
CAPRICHO ■
GALÁPASON ★

RED MANGROVE INN
IGUANAS BANANAS ★
HOTEL GALÁPAGOS

12 DE NOVIEMBRE

RABIDA

GALÁPAGOS SUB-AQUA ■

AVE. CHARLES DARWIN

BOATBUILDING AREA

To INGALA Office, Highlands, and Ferry to Baltra

● MERCADO MUNICIPAL

LARA

NEVADA

LA TRATTORIA DEL PIPPO ▼
BED AND BREAKFAST PEREGRINA ●

● BANCO DEL PACÍFICO

AV. PADRE

INDEFATIGABLE

KATHY'S KITCHEN ▼
MOONRISE TRAVEL AGENCY AND CAFE
EL RECYCLADO ■

▼ LA GARRAPATA RESTAURANT
★ LA PANGA DISCOTECA

HOTEL SANTA CRUZ ■

JULIO HERRERA

LOS AMIGOS ■

★ ESTRELLA DEL MAR

12 DE FEBRERO

TAME ■

PACIFICTEL ■

RESIDENCIAL FLAMINGO ■

LOBO DEL MAR
● POLICE STATION

HOTEL SALINAS ■

MONTALVO

CHARLES BINFORD

HOTEL LIRIO DEL MAR ■
ENCANTOUR ●
EMETEBE ■

AVE. CHARLES DARWIN

MILITARY BASE

Academy

To Turtle Bay

CHARLES DINFOR

TOMAS DE BERLANGA

Bay

BRITO

CAFETERÍA SUNRISE ▼

LOS COLONOS

HOSPITAL ■

★ GALÁPAGOS DISCOVERY

Park

● PORT CAPTAIN

GRAN HOTEL FIESTA ●

HOTEL NINFAS ●

CHURCH ★

HOTEL CASTRO ●

RESTAURANT SALVAVIDAS ▼

▲ SUPERMERCADO PRO-INSULAR

CARGO DOCKS

TOURIST JETTY

| 0 | 500 yds |
| 0 | 500 m |

© AVALON TRAVEL PUBLISHING, INC.

good lunches and dinners that keep the crowds coming.

For seafood, try the **Restaurant Salvavidas** by the docks, the most authentically nautical in décor and location. It's popular with tourists and locals alike, who will tell you it's the best seafood place in town. Fish dishes are good and inexpensive at $3 and less. The open-air tables at **La Garrapata** are always packed after sundown because it's considered the best restaurant overall in Puerto Ayora. Good music and an attractive setting go well with the excellent *parillada de pescado*.

Shopping

Throw a rock in the air in Puerto Ayora and you'll probably hit a T-shirt or souvenir stand. There has to be a shop in Puerto Ayora named after every animal in the Galápagos—on one block sits the tortuga, vermillion (as in flycatcher), and cormorant boutiques. Most sell stamps, postcards, and T-shirts and offer mail services, but for the last, the post office is more dependable. A few shops, like the one in Capricho, have book exchanges. Remember to steer clear of buying anything made of endangered black coral.

The Charles Darwin center has two good gift

shops whose profits go to the National Park and the Darwin Foundation, making it the most ethical place to buy souvenirs. The **Galápagos Gallery** has a high-quality selection of souvenirs, including many wood carvings. You can watch artists hand-painting wildlife T-shirts in shops along Av. Darwin. **El Recyclado** at the corner of Berlanga and Darwin has a good selection of souvenirs, and the **Iguanas Bananas** gift shop stocks hand-painted wildlife tiles.

The best selection of food in town is at the **Supermercado Pro-Insular** near the docks. Produce is brought down from the highlands on Saturday to the **mercado municipal** on Herrera and Carrasco.

Recreation and Entertainment

Snorkeling gear is available for rent on almost every corner, but the best equipment comes from the dive shops. Two good spots in Darwin Bay are Las Grietas near the Hotel Delfín across from the docks, and off the beach near the Charles Darwin Station (watch for *pangas*). **Galápagos Discovery** rents mountain bikes, and the Red Mangrove Inn rents mountain bikes, sea kayaks, snorkel gear, and windsurfers. They even have a squash court.

La Panga, next to the Seventh Day Adventist church near the bend in Herrera, is probably the only discotec in the country with a painting of giant tortoises on the walls. **Galapasón** on Darwin and **Chique Macho** in the center of town are also popular for a night out. A handful of mellower bars are scattered around Puerto Ayora; try **Tambulero's Pub** near Galapasón.

Tours

Yenny and Steve Divine run the **Moonrise Travel Agency,** tel. 5/526-403 or 526-348, e-mail: sdivine@pa.ga.pro.ec. The agency is great for last-minute bookings aboard boats in the area. Tours of 3–8 days are available, and day tours to Santa Fé, South Plaza, Seymour Norte, and Bartolomé are available from $55 pp per day. **Galaven,** tel. 5/526-359, operates the *Galápagos Adventure I* and *II* and the *Esmeraldas III* for day tours; and Guayaquil-based **Galasam,** tel. 5/526-126, owns several boats and has a helpful office staff. **Gala Travel,** tel. 5/526-581, runs mostly smaller economic boats like the *Pulsar, Symbol,* and *Cormoran.* All are located on Darwin near the town park.

Services and Information

Puerto Ayora's **Banco del Pacífico** is probably one of the few in the country that actually overlooks the Pacific. They change travelers' checks, but lines are often long. **Western Union** has an office at Gala Travel, and **Pacifictel** is on Hererra near Indefategable. As of late 2000, they were working on new cable connections to the mainland, so services should be improving soon. **Internet access** is available at the bank and the Moonrise Travel Agency, and there is a small **hospital** with limited services on Herrera.

Transportation

Bus tickets to the highlands and Baltra airport are for sale at the ticket office marked "Muelle" near the park. The whole trip costs $1 one-way and is much quicker now that the road has been paved. Buses leave at 6:45, 7, and 11:30 A.M. to meet TAME's two daily flights.

INGALA, tel. 5/526-151 or 526-199, sends 24-person boats to Puerto Baquerizo Moreno on San Cristóbal on Friday at 8 A.M. ($15 pp one-way, 4 hours), returning on Tuesday, and to Floreana every other Wednesday at 8 A.M. ($15 pp one-way, 4 hours), returning the following Thursday. You're allowed 30 pounds of baggage (more costs extra) and are advised to buy tickets the day before at the office at the docks—the boat is often inoperable.

Water taxis wait at the dock to shuttle passengers to boats waiting in the harbor (20 cents pp by day, 40 cents at night). Just go down to the dock, yell "Taxi!", and tell the pilot what boat you're on; he'll know where it is. You can also wave them down from your boat to go into town.

Inter-island flights with **EMETEBE,** tel. 5/525-177, can get you to Isabela or San Cristóbal in half an hour for $70–80 pp one-way. They're in the same building as INGALA. **TAME** has an office at Darwin and 12 de Febrero, tel. 5/526-165, open Mon.–Fri.

Tortuga Bay

One of the most beautiful beaches in the Galápagos is a 45-minute walk from Puerto Ayora. Take Binford out of town to the west, up the steps, and past the National Park guardpost.

Follow the moderately rough trail straight to the beach. Tortuga Bay beach is wide, flat, and usually empty, and around the iguana-patrolled rocky point is a calm mangrove inlet that's perfect for swimming.

Charles Darwin Research Center

The main arm of the Charles Darwin Foundation for the Galápagos, the Darwin Center, tel. 5/526-146 or 526-147 (in Quito 2/244-803, 241-573, fax 2/443-935), e-mail: cdrs@fcdarwin@org.ec, www.galapagos.org, was begun in the 1960s as a research and breeding center for endangered native species. It's on every tour itinerary.

The visiting area (open daily 7 A.M.–6 P.M.) includes the tortoise breeding and rearing center, where endangered subspecies are hatched and cared for until they're old enough to protect themselves in the wild. The program started in 1965 with the Pinzón island tortoise and has since expanded to a goal of 50 per year of each subspecies.

Lonesome George, the last surviving member of the Pinta Island subspecies *(Geochelone elephantopus abindoni)* has been the most famous resident of the center since he arrived in 1971. Find a female Pinta tortoise and claim the $10,000 reward that's still standing. Farther down the trails are research facilities and offices, near an iguana rearing center that's closed to the public because of the animals' shyness. A beach is open daily 7 A.M.–6 P.M.

For those interested in keeping up with events on the islands, the foundation publishes the *Galápagos Bulletin* twice a year. Subscribe to the foundation in the United States at 100 N. Washington St., Ste. 232, Falls Church, VA 22046. If you're interested in **volunteering** with the Darwin center, be warned that spaces are few, so it helps if your talents and experience coincide with an ongoing project. Volunteers should have skills in biology and Spanish and are required to pay their own room and board ($9 per day in basic dorms) and reduced-rate airfare to the islands. Send a cover letter stating your interests and skills along with a curriculum vitae, letters of recommendation or references, and anything else you think might help make your case to the Head of External Relations, Charles Darwin Research Station, Casilla 17-01-3891, Quito, e-mail: vol@fcdarwin.org.ec.

SANTA CRUZ HIGHLANDS

Because 100 meters of altitude difference in the Galápagos has the same effect on the vegetation as a 600- to 700-meter variance on the mainland, your surroundings change quickly as you climb into the heights of Santa Cruz. Before you know it, you've left the dry, rocky coast for misty forests edging up against fields and pastures. Tours of the highlands can be arranged in Puerto Ayora, or many of the sites can be visited independently by bus, taxi, and foot. The CITTEG bus cooperative in Puerto Ayora rents trucks and drivers for flat day rates, or you can just hire one of the many *camionetas* (pickup trucks) around town. Contact the Moonrise Travel Agency or the Red Mangrove Inn in Puerto Ayora for horseback-riding tours of the highlands.

Seven km above Puerto Ayora is the small towns of **Bellavista** and **Santa Rosa,** from which several trails lead into the hills. The peaks of **Media Luna,** five km from Bellavista, can be climbed in 4–5 hours, and three km beyond it is **Cerro Crocker,** a journey of 7–8 hours. Guides are advised but not required.

You can also visit a few **lava tunnels** near Bellavista. Entered through collapsed roof sections, the tunnels stretch into the earth wide enough to drive a semi-trailer into and sometimes continue for miles. Admission is charged for tunnels on private land, such as those just east of Bellavista. Another set can be found about three km north of Puerto Ayora.

Steve Devine's Butterfly Farm, between Bellavista and Santa Rosa, is another regular stop on tours of the highlands. The combination cattle ranch/restaurant offers lunch and dinner with prior notice and has camping spaces. Giant tortoises graze in the wet grass among the cattle, while pure white cattle egrets *(Bubulcus ibis)* strike at bugs like feathered serpents. The tortoises plod through here from the Tortoise Reserve to the southwest, giving visitors perhaps their only chance to see the giant reptiles in a semi-wild setting. You'll know you've gotten too close when head and legs disappear with a hiss of escaping air. Yellow warblers follow the tortoises picking off parasites, and vermillion flycatchers frequent the trees. Visits to the farm can be arranged through the Moonrise Travel Agency in Puerto Ayora.

El Chato Tortoise Reserve claims the entire southeast corner of Santa Cruz island as a habitat for the endemic giant tortoise subspecies. The seven-km journey from **Santa Rosa** can be made by foot or horse. Up the road from Santa Rosa gape **Los Gemelos**, twin pit craters formed when large caverns left empty by flowing lava collapsed on themselves. Galápagos hawks, barn owls, and vermillion flycatchers flit through the damp *scalesia* forests surrounding the craters, which lie just off the road to Baltra a few kilometers past Santa Rosa.

OTHER SANTA CRUZ VISITOR SITES

Black Turtle Cove

Just west of the Canal de Itabaca between Santa Cruz and Baltra, this shallow mangrove lagoon extends far inland. The visit is just a slow *panga* float, leaving you free to admire the abundant bird life. Lava and great blue herons, lava gulls, frigatebirds, and boobies all nest in the tangled branches of red and white mangroves.

Life beneath the surface is just as active. Spotted eagles and golden rays glide by in slow, silent formation, and a watery snuff sound alerts you to green sea turtles coming up to breathe. Pencil-spined sea urchins and starfish litter the

bottom near a shallow rocky neck—navigable only by small craft—where white-tipped sharks sleep swimming against the current.

Cerro Dragon

This new visitor site on the west side of the island has a dry or wet landing depending on the tide. Within the first few minutes of landing, you'll pass blue-footed boobies propped on the rocks, marine iguanas sunning themselves on the beach, and two lagoons which, depending on the season, may be filled with flamingos. The two-km trail eventually leads to the top of Cerro Dragon, a modest climb with good views, which is named for the land iguanas that congregate nearby.

SEYMOUR NORTE

Volcanic uplift raised this small dot at the end of Baltra. It's a small, crowded island with a loop trail reached by a tricky dry landing. Walking the trail takes 1–2 hours, winding through gray groves of palo santo and *opuntia* cactus set low to the ground. Because many day trips from Santa Cruz come here, the island can become crowded with people.

Swallow-tailed gulls nest in the rocks near the landing, often with fuzzy chicks. A large colony of blue-footed boobies nests along the inland part of the loop. If you're lucky, you may see a courting display—just be careful not to step on an animal perched silently in the middle of the trail. Mag-

cactus trees on South Plaza

JULIAN SMITH

nificent frigatebirds, part of the largest colony in the Galápagos, nest farther in. Just about any time during the year, you can see the males displaying their bright red air sacs and chattering seductively to females soaring overhead. Marine iguanas and sea lions have claimed the beach along the coastal section of the walk.

DAPHNE MAJOR

Biologist Peter Grant spent decades studying finches' beak adaptations on Daphne Major, one-half of a pair of tiny islands between Santa Cruz and Santiago. The results, which are considered to be the first measured study of evolution in action, are described in his book *Beak of the Finch*. Daphne Minor is closed to the public, and visits to Daphne Major (considered a scientific research area more than a visitor site) are strictly limited by the Galápagos National Park Service.

If you're one of the select few, a difficult dry landing will lead you to a steep trail up to the rim of one of the island's two sunken craters. Masked boobies nest on the way up, and blue-footed boobies can be seen inside the crater. The trail continues along the rim to the lip of the second crater, with red-billed tropic birds visible along the way.

SOUTH PLAZA

Just off the east coast of Santiago, a pair of tiny uplift islands curve toward each other like horizontal parentheses. At only one km by two km, South Plaza is one of the smallest islands you'll visit. The distinctive bright yellow of the local land iguanas stands out among the cacti, as the lizards feed on cactus fruit and *opuntia* pads.

The loop trail begins near one of the largest sea lion colonies in the Galápagos—about 1,000 individuals—and climbs through a surprisingly colorful landscape. During the dry season, South Plaza's *sesuvium* turns bright red, contrasting to the gray and white rocks, green cacti, and turquoise ocean (*sesuvium* becomes bright green during the rainy season). Birds barnstorm the cliffs at the far end of the trail, sometimes trying to land three or four times before finally hitting the nest. Audubon's shearwaters, red-billed tropic birds, boobies, frigatebirds, and swallow-tailed gulls all live near South Plaza's cliffside.

SANTA FÉ

A short sail from Puerto Ayora (two hours) or Puerto Baquerizo Moreno on San Cristóbal (three hours) brings you to the beautiful anchorage off Santa Fé, a shallow bay where sea turtles and manta rays are dark shadows against the sandy bottom. After a wet landing, you'll begin a short loop trail starring a local variety of land iguanas. Members of this endemic species are pale yellow with well-defined scales and can grow more than 1.5 meters long. Santa Fé's species of *opuntia* cactus have grown up to 10 meters high in response and developed tough, woody stems. You'll also see the occasional Galápagos hawk or dove.

SAN CRISTÓBAL

Nothing could be less inviting than the first appearance. A broken field of black basaltic lava, thrown into the most rugged waves, and crossed by great fissures, is every where covered by stunted, sun-burnt brushwood, which shows little signs of life.

—*Charles Darwin,* **The Journal of the Voyage of the Beagle**

Darwin must have landed on San Cristóbal near its northern end, an area covered by lava and eroded volcanoes that give it away as one of the oldest islands in the archipelago. The bottom half of this easternmost island in the Galápagos shelters the provincial capital Puerto Baquerizo Moreno below green highland slopes, and even a freshwater lake.

History
Not to be outdone by its western neighbor Floreana, San Cristóbal boasts two infamous failed enterprises in recent times. Near the end of the 19th century, Ecuadorian entrepreneur Manuel J. Cobos began a penal colony in the highlands. The brutal settlement, ironically named El Progreso (Progress), was intended to make money

from sugarcane harvesting, but 14-hour workdays starting at 4 A.M. soon took their toll. For the slightest offenses, the 400 prisoners were lashed, executed, or marooned on deserted islands. The penal colony ended, perhaps inevitably, in an uprising in 1904. Cobos, who was 67 years old, was shot twice while standing on a porch in his underwear.

Six decades later, a group of more than 100 people from the northwestern United States tried to found a utopian fishing community near Puerto Baquerizo Moreno. The ill-conceived project collapsed within 14 months from a combination of disease, lack of skill, and poor planning. A scheme to catch lobsters and sell them to the U.S. market failed when it was discovered that no one knew how to catch the spiny crustaceans—in short supply to begin with—and the communal ship's refrigeration system had broken down beyond repair.

PUERTO BAQUERIZO MORENO

The capital of the Galápagos Islands is smaller and poorer than Puerto Ayora. It's also less dependent on (and receptive to) tourist dollars because most of the populace fishes for a living. Without having experienced a Santa Cruz- style

napping sea lion

SMITH

population explosion, Baquerizo Moreno remains small, even with the nearby airport and daily flights from the mainland. Sea lions sleep on dinghies at anchor in the amazingly clear harbor. Prices are generally lower here than in Puerto Ayora.

Sights

The high point of any visit to Baquerizo Moreno is a stop at the town's **interpretation center,** tel. 5/520-358, down Alsacio Northia past the Cabañas de Don Jorge. It's better than anything in Puerto Ayora outside the Darwin Center, with views of the ocean, wooden walkways, and exhibits on the human and geological history of the islands and, of course, the plants and animals. It's open daily 7 A.M.–6 P.M., $1 pp.

Interesting **murals** decorate both the Pacifictel building and the interior of the cathedral near the bay, whose aircraft-hanger ceiling and starry light fixtures give it a New Age atmosphere. Many of the wooden houses in the center of town were apparently moved and reassembled from the U.S. military base on Baltra.

Accommodations

Rooms at the **Hotel Chatham,** Northia and Armada Nacional, tel./fax 5/520-137, have fans, hot water, TVs, and private baths for $5 pp. It's a clean place with a central patio. The **Islas Galapagos,** Esmeraldas and Colon, tel. 5/520-203, fax 5/520-162, is also clean and relatively new. Rooms with the same amenities (except TVs) are $6 s, $10 d. The friendly folks at **Los Cactus** on Juan Jose Flores near the telephone office, tel. 5/520-078, have 13 rooms with private bath, hot water, and fans for $7 s, $10 d.

Baquerizo Moreno's most distinctive accommodations are found at the family-run **Cabanas Don Jorge,** on Alsacio Northia east of town, tel. 5/520-208, fax 5/520-100, e-mail: cabanasdonjorge@hotmail.com. It's popular with surfers for its crash-pad feol. Four unique cabins have lavastone walls, high ceilings, bunk beds and lofts, and one has a fridge and kitchenette. Each cabin has a fan and private bath with hot water for $12 s, $20 d (you can fit up to five people into one for $32). An eating area, bar, and living room fill the main house. All meals are available, and extended stays are possible.

Food

Grab a quick snack and a drink on the outdoor patio **Casa Blanca** by the gray whale on the pier. **Galapluz,** Hernandez and Quito, is a small place with coffee, snacks, and a gift shop. For dependable lunches, locals head to **Sabor Latino,** Hernandez and 12 de Febrero, and the **Cebicheria Langostino** at Melville and Hernandez. Rustic **Albacora,** Northia and Española, is recommended by locals for its seafood; and **La Palmera,** on Darwin and Ballena, is a hole in the wall with cheap lunches and dinners.

On Genoa next to the municipality building, **Genoa** has music in the evenings and a good atmosphere. **Miconia,** on del Armada by the Naval base, is a breezy place with pizza, Italian dishes, and views of the beach. A favorite of the international yacht crowd, the **Restaurant Rosita,** on Hernandez and Villamil, has been around for 50 years. Prices are higher than elsewhere in town, but it has lots of character and an extensive menu.

Entertainment

Baquerizo Moreno by night features the **Neptunus** discotec above the Casa Blanca Restaurant, competing with the **Blue Bay** near the tourist dock.

Tours and Excursions

Chalo's Tours, tel. 5/520-953, rents diving and snorkeling equipment, mountain bikes, and surfboards. They can organize day tours of the highlands ($15 pp, two-person minimum), Playa Chino ($20 pp, two-person minimum), Leon Dormida and Isla Lobos ($35 pp, three-person minimum), and Punta Pitt and the Galapaguera ($65 pp, three-person minimum).

You can reach **Playa Mann** in less than 10 minutes by foot; it's north of town near the interpretation center. **Playa Punta Carola** is 15 minutes past the lighthouse to the north. To reach **Frigatebird Hill,** pass the Cabañas Don Jorge and take a right through the stone wall at the end of the road after about five minutes. It should take about half an hour to reach the top of the hill from here, and once you get your breath back at the top, you'll be rewarded with views of beaches, bays, cliffs, and Baquerizo Moreno below. Magnificent and great frigatebirds both nest here at certain times of year.

Services and Information

There's a **tourist office** under the big concrete whale at the tourist dock, and **Pacifictel** has an office on Quito four blocks past Darwin. The **post office** is at the end of Darwin past the municipal building, and you can log on the **Internet** at a small place next to the Restaurant Rositas. It's expensive and the connection is bad, but new phone lines in the works should improve things dramatically. You can play **computer games** while you have your **laundry** done at a place beside the Hotel Northia on Alsacio Northia and 12 de Febrero.

Transportation

Buses leave from the Malecón half a dozen times daily for El Progreso in the highlands. **Taxis** to El Progreso cost about $1. **INGALA boats** leave for Puerto Ayora on Tuesday at 8 A.M. ($15 pp one-way, 4 hours). Space is limited, so buy tickets to El Progreso at the INGALA office a few kilometers up the road as early as possible. And remember that the sea between the island is still rocking and rolling, so don't eat a big breakfast before leaving, especially one involving *maracuya* (juice)—trust me on this one.

EMETEBE, tel./fax 5/520-036, has flights leaving most mornings at 8 A.M. for Baltra ($80 one-way, 30 minutes) and Isabela ($90 pp one-way, 45 minutes). San Cristóbal's **airport** is at the end of Alsacio Northia past the radio station.

SAN CRISTÓBAL HIGHLANDS

You don't need to be part of a tour group to visit San Cristóbal's highlands, although it does occasionally help with transportation. Avenida 12 de Febrero climbs north out of Baquerizo Moreno to El Progreso, a notorious former penal colony that's now a quiet farming village. Here you'll find the **Casa del Ceibo**, tel. 5/520-248, a treehouse in a huge ceibo tree you can rent for $2 pp per night. You'll have to provide your own food, but it's a good way to avoid the heat of the lowlands. They offer parilladas and other typical foods on weekends. The **Quinta D'Cristhi** also has food on weekends, along with football and volleyball games.

Tracks continue north from here to the settlement of Soledad, near an overlook at the southern end of the island, and east to Cerro Verde and Los Arroyos. On the way to Cerro Verde is the **Laguna El Junco**, one of the few freshwater lakes in the islands. The collapsed caldera is fed by rainwater and shelters wading birds and seven species of Darwin's finches. El Junco is 10 km past El Progreso; follow the highway and take a right onto a steep dirt track to get there. A narrow trail encircles the rim, offering views of almost the entire island.

Trails continue from Cerro Verde the length of the island. Destinations include **Puerto Chino**, a beach on the south coast 30 minutes downhill; **La Galapaguera** to the north, where San Cristóbal tortoises reside in the wild; and even Hobbs Bay and Punta Pitt at the far north end of the island.

OTHER VISITOR SITES

All sites on San Cristóbal are within day-trip range of Puerto Baquerizo Moreno. Around the western point of the island, directly south of the airport, is **La Lobería**. Half an hour by boat will bring you within sight of sea lions, blue-footed boobies, and the endemic San Cristóbal mockingbird. It's possible to walk here from Baquerizo Moreno in half an hour, or you can hire a taxi for $1. **Isla Lobos,** 30 minutes north of Baquerizo Moreno by boat, also takes its name from sea lions. Blue-footed boobies nest on the tiny islet, but because the dry landing and hike are both difficult, the site is not that popular.

Visits to sites on San Cristóbal's north coast are often combined with a stop at one of the beaches near Isla Lobos, including **Playa Ochoa, El Muerto,** and **Playa El Manglesito**. Farther north is **Puerto Grande** (also called Sapho Cove), a beach facing one of the Galápagos' most famous landmarks, **Kicker Rock.** Called León Dormido (Sleeping Lion) in Spanish, this leaning bolt of volcanic tuff stands 146 meters high a short distance from the coast. If your captain feels adventurous and sails through a narrow split in the rock, you'll see blue-footed and masked boobies nesting near frigatebirds on the rocks.

Just past Kicker Rock, the beach at **Cerro Brujo** provides a relaxing stop of swimming and snorkeling. The northeastern tip of San Cristóbal is named **Punta Pitt,** where a great visitor site was opened in 1989. A wet landing and long hike bring you inland to the only place you can see red-footed boobies in the Galápagos be-sides Tower Island. Other seabirds find the spot equally enticing, including masked and blue-footed boobies, frigatebirds, storm petrels, and swallow-tailed gulls.

SANTIAGO AND NEARBY ISLANDS

The Galápagos' fourth-largest island bears the distinction of harboring one of the archipelago's largest and most destructive herds of feral goats. Only four goats left on the island in the early 1800s multiplied to more than 100,000 by the middle of the 20th century. Recent backbreaking efforts by the Park Service and the Charles Darwin Center have reduced the population, but the herd is still a serious threat to the island's ecosystem. Many goats were shot and eaten by islanders, leading inevitably to gastronomic jokes aboard visiting boats—if you want to make your cook grin, ask him or her if the meat dish served for dinner is *chivo de Santiago* (Santiago goat).

Sullivan Bay
This site on the east end of Santiago near Bartolomé sounds like one of the dullest—an hour-long walk over bare lava—but can be one of the most enchanting. An eruption in 1897 left the area covered in mesmerizing patterns of black lava. Frozen blorps and squirts punctuate the endless expanse of smoky chaos frozen in stone, which is rough on the shoes but captivating to the eyes. This may have been one place Darwin had in mind when he described as follows:

"... immense deluges of black, naked lava, which have flowed either over the rims of the great caldrons, like pitch over the rim of a pot in which it has been boiled, or have burst forth from smaller orifices on the flanks."

If you brought black and white film, Sullivan Bay is the place to use it. The lava's glassy, almost ceramic feel comes from its high silicate content.

Buccaneer Cove
A freshwater source just inland made this cove a haven for pirates during the 17th and 18th centuries. Today, tour boats just sail past under impressive cliff faces spotted with the guano of millennia of nesting birds. Dark beaches lead to hillsides where you might be able to spot some of the island's famous goats.

James Bay
An easy wet landing sets you on the black beach of **Puerto Egas,** home to a dozing posse of sea lions. Snorkelers will enjoy exploring the rocks to the right. A two-km, three-hour loop trail leads inland past the rusted remains of a 1960s salt operation. Cruise ship crews have built a makeshift soccer field nearby. (Here your guide might tell you about a National Park guard who was forgotten in the 1950s on Santiago for nearly eight months instead of the usual three. Legend has it that he was taken off the island in a straightjacket.) Numerous donkey droppings are evidence of another introduced animal problem. Overhead soar Galápagos hawks, while on the ground you may spot Galápagos doves, mockingbirds, and even a Galápagos scorpion under a rock.

Farther down the trail are the famous fur seal grottoes, where the heaving ocean fills a series of pools and underwater caverns that are occupied by seals, sea lions, and crabs. It's a shame that visitors are no longer allowed to swim here, although understandable: the long trail is often crowded with as many as six tour groups at once. A wealth of marine life teems in the tidal pools. Bright Sally lightfoot crabs crawl over marine iguanas the color of lava, and yellow-crowned night herons, oystercatchers, and sandpipers hunt among the crevices. Four-eyed blennies and numerous marine invertebrates lurk underwater. Lavender sea-urchin spines blanket the beach near the end of the trail.

A second, little-used path from the landing ascends Sugarloaf Volcano, about 1,000 meters high. **Espumilla Beach,** a second beach slightly north of Puerto Egas, is the start of a trail through mangroves to a lagoon populated by Galápagos flamingos and other wading birds

Sea turtles nest on the sand near the mangroves, and snorkeling and swimming off the wide beach are possible.

BARTOLOMÉ

Most boats anchor under Pinnacle Rock on the southwestern end of Bartolomé Island. From here it's a short *panga* ride to the mangrove-fringed beach, one of the island's two visitor sites. This is a relatively relaxed site—most guides will let you do your own thing for an hour or two, then herd everyone onto the climb. Don't miss this opportunity to snorkel; besides the usual spectacular underwater sights, this is one of your best opportunities to swim with Galápagos penguins. Keep your eyes open and you'll probably see one of the stubby black torpedoes shooting past after a school of fish. It may not be able to fly, but the Galápagos penguin can sure swim, at speeds up to 40 km per hour.

Back on shore, a trail heads through the mangrove to a beach on the other side of the neck. You can't swim off this beach (whitetip sharks and stingrays aplenty), but between December and March you may glimpse female sea turtles waiting for night to come ashore and lay their eggs. Birders should keep their eyes open for Galápagos hawks, herons, and oystercatchers near the mangroves.

The other site on Bartolomé begins with a tricky dry landing on a rock jetty that is usually guarded by sea lions, sleeping as often as not. The 30-minute climb to the top of the island is made easier by a wooden staircase winding up the blasted volcanic face. It's a real moonscape up here, scarred by lava chutes and parasitic spatter cones (offshoots of the main lava tube). The incredibly light lava rocks come in a rainbow of pastel colors, from creams, grays, and browns to almost floral hues of rose and lime. Pioneer species such as *tiquilia* and lava cactus are only beginning to gain a foothold on the jagged landscape.

The view from the 108-meter summit is worth the hot climb. In front of you stretches the neck of Bartolomé, green with mangroves and punctuated by 40-meter Pinnacle Rock. Santiago Island covers most of the horizon—notice the Sullivan Bay lava flow to the left and how it enveloped offshore islands like viscous black water until they became welded to the mainland.

RABIDA

The exact geographic center of the Galápagos sits off the southern coast of Santiago. A wet landing drops you onto a rust-colored beach filled with dozens of sea lions stretched out moaning and snoring as if it were the morning after the world's biggest sea lion party. As you make your way down to the section of beach with grains the size and texture of Grape Nuts cereal, you'll come upon a colony of brown pelicans nesting in the salt bushes. Pelican chicks have a mortality rate of 60–70 percent during the first year of life; hence the numerous chick corpses scattering the sand. The live ones more than make up the difference, though, filling the air with their pterodactyl-like cries for food.

A salt pond on the other side of the bushes provides food for Galápagos flamingos and yellow-crowned night herons. It's a good spot to find a Galápagos hawk perched on a tree branch, stoically watching the assemblage of young and old sea lions who have claimed the shores of the lagoon as a combination nursery and retirement colony. Newborn pups suckle loudly and bleat for more between rolls in the shallow mud.

The snorkeling near the landing is excellent—just watch out for male sea lions. From here a trail leads up and over the hillside, for a view of the salt pond and the sleep cliffs on the other side of the spit. If you're visiting during the dry season, notice how the palo santo trees on the far hillside turn vaguely green at mist level, about halfway up.

SOMBRERO CHINO

The aptly named "Chinese Hat" island, off the east end of Santiago just south of Bartolomé, is open only to boats holding 12 people or fewer. A wet landing onto a rough coral beach begins a short walk through a broken volcanic landscape, ending above the ocean on the far side. The snorkeling off Sombrero Chino is excellent—just watch the strong current.

WESTERN ISLANDS

ISABELA

The largest island in the Galápagos consists of five different volcanoes joined together over the eons by repeated lava flows. From north to south they are Wolf (1,646 meters), Darwin (1,280 meters), Alcedo (1,097 meters), Sierra Negra (1,490 meters), and Cerro Azul (1,250 meters), and all remain at least partially active. The 130-km-long island harbors a wide range of habitats and a correspondingly large variety of animal species. It fits most people's mental image of a Pacific island: palm trees, pure white beaches, rocky cliffs, mangroves, and an easy pace of life in the settlements that's interrupted by few tourists. About 1,500 people live on the island, mostly in Puerto Villamil.

Isabela's moist higher altitudes provide an ideal habitat for giant tortoises, so it's no surprise that five separate subspecies of tortoise have evolved here, one on each volcano. Volcán Alcedo is home to the most—more than 35 percent of all the tortoises in the archipelago—and Darwin and Wolf together shelter another 15 percent. The cool upwelling waters off Isabela's west coast wash in enough nutrients to support large populations of flightless cormorants and Galápagos penguins, with whales and dolphins common offshore. With so much food available, Isabela's marine iguanas are the largest in the Galápagos.

Some of Isabela's older tortoises have seen the deadly days of the whalers replaced by several modern threats. Feral goats are rampant on the island, sparking half-serious talk of building a fence all the way across the island's narrowest point, between the Volcánes Alcedo and Sierra Negra, to stop further spreading. In 1984, an accidental fire on Sierra Negra raged for five months and destroyed much of the volcano's tortoise habitat. As if that weren't enough, the carapaces of more than 80 tortoises that had been killed and eaten by poachers were found around Isabela in 1994.

History

Isabela's traffic began arriving in the 18th century when whalers plied the rich waters to the west, stopping off to gather a few hundred tortoises along the way. The names of some of these ships are still etched into the rocks at Tagus Cove.

In 1946, a penal colony was built on the Sierra Negra's southern slopes, a brutal place filled with the worst offenders from the mainland. Hours were spent on pointless, dangerous tasks to fill the time: the lava-rock *muro de las lagrimas* (wall of tears), still standing near Puerto Villamil, was stacked by countless hands in the hot sun. Many prisoners are thought to have died at the hands of guards, although the truth may never be known. It's said that one police chief reported to a navy officer, upon receipt of a month's supplies: "Commander, nothing to report. Thirty prisoners fewer." The notorious jail was closed in 1959 after numerous escape attempts and campaigns by local residents to shut it down.

Puerto Villamil

About 1,200 people live in this settlement on the southern slope of the Sierra Negra Volcano. Various projects have kept the local populace busy since the towns were founded at the turn of the 19th century, including sulfur mining, lime production, coffee farming, and fishing. The tourist infrastructure here is still basic, but those who visit can enjoy the area's beautiful beaches, bird-filled lagoons, and highland hikes.

Accommodations: Budget rooms can be found at **San Vicente,** at Cormorant and Las Escalacias, tel. 5/529-140, for $3 s, $4 d, with private bath, fans, and cold water. It's often full of locals. **Tero Real,** Tero Real and Opuntia, tel. 5/529-195, has six cabins with private bath, fans, and refrigerators for $5 s, $8 d. Neither place has hot water, but meals are available at both on request. At the east end of town is **Isabela del Mar,** tel./fax 5/529-125, e-mail: isabela@hosteriaisabela.com.ec, www.hosteriaisabela.com, with a dozen rooms with private bath, solar-heated hot water, and fans for $7 pp. Some rooms face the beach. Keep going a little farther to **La Casa de Marita,** tel. 5/529-238, fax 5/529-201, e-mail: hcarmita@ga.pro.ec, a beautiful beachfront place that has seven rooms with kitchenettes, hot water, and private bath for $35 s, $50 d, including breakfast. It also has an elegant family-style restaurant.

Food: El Encanto de la Pepa is considered the best (and most expensive) restaurant in town, with good food in an attractive setting east of the plaza. Find good daily specials at the modern **Costa Azul** facing the *Capitania del Puerto,* and enjoy a pizza and a drink under the palm trees at **La Iguana** on the beach in the Parque Iguana. Several simple places in town offer good set meals: try **La Ruta** on the plaza and **Caracol** in the kiosk next to the police station.

Activities: Isabela Tours, tel. 5/529-207, is on the plaza and can arrange day trips. You can rent horses to explore the highlands for $5–10 pp through **Sr. Tenelema,** tel. 5/529-102, and **Modesto Tupiza,** tel. 5/529-217, who also has a truck for hire. It's a half-hour walk into the highlands west of town to reach the **Centro de Crianza** (La Galapaguera), where Galápagos tortoises are being bred and repopulated to their original islands. Farther up (three hours from town) is the *muro de las lagrimas* in the remains of the penal colony. The **beaches** west of town are good for surfing, and you can snorkel among the mangroves and rocky inlets east of town. Ask locally for details on trails leading from the town that were being constructed in 2000.

Services: The **police station** is on the plaza, and the **National Parks** office is one block away. **Pacifictel** is four blocks from the plaza. Bring cash because it's next to impossible to change travelers' checks here. If you must, try the panadería or the larger hotels.

Transportation: Buses leave daily on the 48-km round-trip into the highlands. They depart at 7 A.M. and noon by the market, returning about two hours later. **Trucks** can be rented to spots around town or in the highlands. **EMETEBE,** tel. 5/529-155, has flights to San Cristóbal ($90 pp one-way) and Baltra ($80 pp one-way). The *Estrella del Mar* sails for Puerto Ayora Thursday at 7 A.M. ($15 pp one-way, 4 hours). Buy tickets in the municipio building on the plaza the day before. Meet the incoming boat from Puerto Ayora at 4:30 P.M. Wednesday to get your name on the reservation list, or leave a message for the captain at the Hotel Salinas.

Isabela Highlands

High above the town of Santo Tomás towers the **Sierra Negra Volcano,** Isabela's oldest and highest. It can be climbed in 2–3 days, an option on longer tours or by special request on smaller boats. A three- to five-hour hike from Santo Tomás brings you to the edge of the 10-km caldera, where you'll spend the night amid fumaroles and mist. Volcán Chico, another four km, erupted as recently as 1979. **Alcedo Volcano** has been closed to visitors since 1995 because of the ongoing goat eradication program.

Punta García

The only visitors' site on the eastern side of Isabela isn't much of a thrill, but it provides an opportunity to see flightless cormorants and Galápagos penguins. Just south of here, though, is the landing point for the climb up **Volcán Alcedo,** one of the hardest to reach but most rewarding sites in the Galápagos. A sunrise landing on the beach is only the beginning of the overnight excursion; the 10-km uphill hike is hot, steep, and tiring, especially with a pack full of supplies (all gear must be carried in and out). Four to six hours later, though, you'll be soaking in the views over the 75-square-meter caldera. Among the steam vents and vegetation lives the largest population of giant tortoises in the Galápagos—more than 4,000 beasts who wallow in pools and mud puddles during the rainy season.

Punta Moreno

First stop here, north of Cerro Azul, is a *panga* ride along the sea cliffs and into a grove of mangroves in search of penguins and great blue herons. Then a three-hour hike takes you from the coast, with its penguins, flightless cormorants, and marine iguanas, to a handful of brackish ponds frequented in season by white-cheeked pintails and flamingos.

Elizabeth Bay

Slightly farther north in Isabela's elbow, Elizabeth Bay is explored only by *panga.* The scattering of islands at the mouth of the bay supports small populations of flightless cormorants, penguins, and marine iguanas. A peaceful drift brings you into shallow mangrove lagoons stocked with rays, turtles, and small sharks.

Urvina Bay

In 1954, a volcanic eruption lifted a sizable chunk of seabed six meters above the water's surface so suddenly that a visiting group of scientists found fish still flapping in puddles of seawater. Now visitors can get a slightly surreal look at a coral community, littered with the bones of marine animals and the shells of as many as 30 sea turtles. Flightless cormorants and marine iguanas have moved in already.

Tagus Cove

Centuries of graffiti decorate the rocks above this popular anchorage in the Bolívar Channel, directly across from Fernandina. The older records from whalers and sealers are carved into the rock (one reads 1836), whereas more recent crews have added the names of their vessels in paint. At three km, this is the longest walk (aside from volcano ascents) in the islands and strenuous in places.

The first 200 meters above the dry landing follows a steep gully that's fragrant with sea lion droppings up to the base of a wooden staircase. A short hike beyond the top of the stairs brings **Darwin Lake** into view, filling an eroded crater 12 meters deep in the center. A white ring around the edge is evidence of the lagoon's high salinity, which is too much for most creatures besides the occasional visiting Bahama duck.

Scientists once wondered how the lake filled with water because it was too saline for rainwater and too permanent to be filled by the occasional wave washing over the narrow wall between the lake and the bay. The answer? Seawater filters in through porous lava rocks beneath the surface, keeping the water level in the lagoon even with the ocean outside. The small round pebbles covering the trails began as raindrops that collected airborne volcanic ash and hardened before hitting the ground.

The trail peaks at a lookout over the entire extent of Isabela, including a large lava flow from the Darwin Volcano. Your guide should point out how new plant species began to appear near the top, forming thickets inhabited by the Galápagos flycatcher, finches, and mockingbirds.

A *panga* ride along the cliffs makes up the second half of the visit. Sea turtles swim past Galápagos penguins and sea lions, and handsome noddy terns nest in the caves and shadows. The ocean reaches into the rock itself, forming long caves where you might glimpse the so-called gringo fish—pink on the back like a sunburned tourist.

> *"Our ears were suddenly assailed by a sound that could only be equalled by ten thousand thunderers bursting upon the air at once; while the whole hemisphere was lighted up with a horrid glare that might have appalled the stoutest heart . . . At the time the mercury in the thermometer was at 147 [°F], but on immersing it into the water, it instantly rose to 150. Had the winds deserted us here, the consequences must have been horrible."*
>
> *—Benjamin Morrell, describing 1825 eruption of Fernandina*

FERNANDINA

The westernmost island in the Galápagos is one of the most pristine island ecosytems in the world. No foreign species have been introduced, despite heavy traffic nearby during the whaling heyday of the 19th century. Fernandina is many guides' favorite island, and for good reason: if your tour makes it out this far, you'll get to experience a very special place, where a lizard walking across the shattered fields of lava seems like a scene from the dawn of time.

Fernandina is the youngest volcanic island in the archipelago (only one million years old), as well as the most active. Eruptions in the wide caldera have continued well into the 20th century; one in 1968 collapsed the entire 30-square-km caldera more than 300 meters. Glowing plumes of lava from a 1991 eruption were captured on videotape by observers.

Punta Espinosa

Fernandina's only visitors' site lies on the island's northeast corner across from Isabela's Tagus Cove. After a dry landing in a grove of white mangroves, you'll come to a sandy point that's partly covered by rough lava from recent flows. The largest colony of marine iguanas in the Galápagos nests nearby, sneezing salt so loud that it sounds like the cold ward in a hospital. As you proceed single file down the beach (to avoid stepping on buried nests), you'll see shells and bleached mangrove trunks littering the sand, evidence of recent volcanic uplifts.

Sea lions fill the pools among the jagged rocks, females and pups playing while males patrol. At the tip of the point waits the highlight: the flightless cormorant nesting site. Each nest— a ragged witch's mop of seaweed and twigs—

supports a female sitting regally while her mate hunts for fish. Keep your eyes open for returning males, who offer a seaborne trinket to the female before drying their stubby wings in the ocean breeze.

Back near the landing site. you'll take a detour over the jagged lava, spotted with short, squat *brachycereus* lava cacti. Brilliant vermillion flycatchers often sit in the mangrove branches.

SOUTHERN ISLANDS

FLOREANA

History

Floreana's turgid story begins in the 18th century, when the island was bequeathed to an Ecuadorian officer in reward for bravery in battle. The officer soon held the island's 80 residents in a state of near-slavery, using giant mastiffs as police and bodyguards. An island-wide rebellion eventually forced the "Dog King of Charles Island" to flee to the mainland.

Life on Floreana got really interesting, though, in the early 20th century. William Beebe's book *Galapagos: World's End* captured the imagination of readers everywhere—particularly in the Old World—with its portrayal of the islands as a strangely beautiful "lost paradise." Among these readers were Dr. Friedrich Ritter, a holistic doc-

tor and philosopher, and his lover Dora Strauch, a former patient left crippled by multiple sclerosis. In 1929, the starry-eyed couple left their native Germany and respective spouses to start a new, natural, naked life in the Galápagos.

Ritter and Strauch chose Floreana for its reliable water supply and relatively rich soil, and named their settlement Friedo, a contraction of their first names. Ritter's accounts of gardening and nudism in the exotic islands caused a stir when published back in Germany, and the island began to attract passing yachters and more settlers. Friction between the two began early, though, as Ritter's cold personality and misogynistic Nietzschean philosophy began to take its toll on his no-longer-blushing bride.

Three years later, the Wittmer family arrived: father Heinz, pregnant wife Margaret, and their 12-year-old son Harry. Although inspired to come

post offiice bay,
Floreana Island

TIM BEWER

WHALING

When the British whaler *Rattler* began the first reconnaissance of the Galápagos in 1793, its crew quickly realized what a gold mine they had found. Between starting the Post Office barrel on Floreana and making the first workable charts of the islands, the *Rattler's* crew marveled at the pods of sperm, humpback, and fin whales on almost every horizon.

When word reached Europe and North America, the hunt began. The second whaler to visit the islands, the British ship *William,* took 42 sperm whales in 18 days—and that was just the beginning. The first half of the 19th century brought an onslaught of traffic to the islands. Besides the numerous whales themselves, the Galápagos were a perfect stopover on the way to the even richer grounds of the South Pacific Islands. The Galápagos provided a safe harbor where wood and water could be found inland.

Most important, the islands supported a seemingly endless supply of animals that did everything but hop into the pot and cook themselves. Giant tortoises in particular were almost wiped out because it was discovered that they could survive unaided for months in ships' holds, providing fresh meat well into a long ocean voyage. It became a wholesale slaughter: in nine days, the USS *Moss* took 350 tortoises, only to be outdone by the USS *Uncas,* which captured 416 in five days. More than 15,000 tortoises were taken from Floreana alone, leading to the extinction of that island's endemic species (later joined by those of Santa Fe and Rabida). Since an estimated 1,000 ships visited the archipelago during the 19th century—almost every one of which took between 60 and 90 tortoises—the total count is thought to approach 100,000.

As icing on the cake, whaling ships introduced black rats to the islands, a species that remains a major problem today. By the mid-1800s, though, the Galápagos earned the term "dry cruising" because most of the whales in the vicinity had been hunted out. The discovery of petroleum in the late 19th century spelled the end of the whaling industry; not a moment too soon for the islands' inhabitants.

by Ritter's articles, the staunch German family kept to themselves. Later that same year (1932) came the most colorful immigrants yet: Eloise Wagner de Bosquet, a self-styled "baroness" with a shady past, along with her two companions, Rudolf Lorenz and Robert Philipsson. Straight out of an S&M fantasy—complete with black boots, crop, riding britches, and pearl-handled revolver—the baroness settled her enclave in Post Office Bay, where she began causing trouble almost at once.

By now the inhabitants of Floreana were known around the world, and luxury yachts stopped by regularly to visit and deliver mail and supplies. From the start, the baroness acted as

if the entire island belonged to her, even to the point of bathing in the main water source, a large cistern near Post Office Bay. She talked of plans to build a luxury hotel on the island while rifling through mail and supplies intended for the Wittmers and Ritter and Strauch. Her relationship with Lorenz and Philipsson was the subject of much speculation; other residents began to see her as a vindictive, manipulative sex maniac who tormented her "love slaves" for the sheer fun of it. Lorenz began to show signs of physical abuse at the hands of the baroness and Philipsson, and Ritter and Strauch's relationship continued to sour.

A severe drought in March 1934, with temperatures soaring to 50°C, pushed things over the edge. One afternoon the baroness and Philipsson suddenly left by boat, saying only that they were headed for Tahiti—as if the island was next door instead of halfway across the Pacific. Almost all of their possessions were left behind in the abrupt departure, including the baroness' beloved copy of *The Portrait of Dorian Gray,* left on a night table. The pair were never seen again.

Eyebrows lifted during a search of the baroness' house when Ritter allegedly commented, "She won't return. You have my word on it." Lorenz also began exhibiting an ominous new calm, wandering off alone and breaking into abrupt fits of crying for no apparent reason. In July 1934, he left the islands aboard the small boat *Dinamita,* bound for Guayaquil. Within weeks the boat was reported missing.

Six months later Ritter—supposedly a vegetarian—became gravely ill from eating spoiled chicken cooked by Strauch. Later Margaret Wittmer recalled how he cursed Dora with his dying breath, trying to kick her when she approached his bedside. That same month the mummified bodies of Lorenz and the captain of the *Dinamita* were found on the parched beach of Marchena Island, dead of thirst and starvation. Lorenz's desiccated corpse weighed less than 10 kg.

Theories still simmer about what exactly happened among Floreana's unlucky colonizers. Dora Strauch returned to Germany, where she lived until 1942. The Wittmers alone remained to tell the tale. Margaret died at 95 in 2000, and her descendants still live in Puerto Velasco Ibarra and operate a small guesthouse. Margaret's son Harry was killed in a boating accident in 1951, but her other son Rolf (the first natural resident of the Galápagos) opened a successful tour company that still runs ships around the islands.

Several books tell the story of Floreana, including Margaret's own *Floreana, Isle of the Black Cats* and *Curse of the Giant Tortoise* (see "Books" for more information).

Puerto Velasco Ibarra

A dry pier landing welcomes you to this unofficial visitor site, a small settlement of 40 inhabitants near the original infamous colony. Floreana's isolation makes it ideal for anyone looking to escape the outside world, and agony for anyone addicted to a fast pace of life. There aren't any banks, the electricity is on only part of the day, and the only mail service is through the Post Office Bay barrel (see following section). On top of that, there's only one phone on the island, at the **Pensión Wittmer,** tel. 5/520-150. Rooms and bungalows all overlook the beach and cost $30 s, $50 d, with fans, private baths, and hot water. Three meals are $20 more pp. Buses leave for the highlands at 6 A.M. and 3 P.M. Mon.–Sat. and at 7 A.M. Sun. It's a half-hour bus ride or a three-hour walk eight km into the highlands to the **Asilo de la Paz,** the island's only water source. An **INGALA boat** leaves for Puerto Ayora every other Thursday at 8 A.M. ($15 pp one-way, 4 hours); if it's not running, which is often the case, be ready to entertain yourself and wait patiently for the **supply boat** *Paula* that arrives twice a month.

Punta Cormorant

After a wet landing at Punta Cormorant, you'll set foot on a beach with a noticeably greenish tinge.

Take a closer look and you'll see bits of olivine, a volcanic material, mixed with the dark sand. From here a trail leads up and over the neck of the point. Along the way you'll stop at an overlook above a brackish inland lagoon populated by occasional flamingos and other wading birds, such as white-cheeked pintails, stilts, and gallinules. Floreana's environment, slightly less forbidding than other islands its size, encourages several endemic plants. Along this trail you might happen across the velvet daisy *(Scalesia villosa)* or the cut-leaf daisy *(Lecocarpus pinnatifidus).*

At the end of the trail awaits the so-called organic beach, covered with an incredibly fine white sand straight out of a Caribbean advertising executive's dream. Powdery enough for an hourglass, the sand is said to be a byproduct of marine life nibbling away at coral (some scientists disagree). Stingrays and spotted eagle rays are common near the beach, so shuffle your feet if you walk in the water, which is stained the color of cream by the flourlike sand. Sea turtles nest here Nov.–Feb., but you might see a confused hatchling struggling toward the ocean even in the off-season. Bleached driftwood and the green vines of beach morning glory make this the most beautiful beach on the islands.

Post Office Bay

The practice of leaving mail in a barrel began in 1793, when ships bound for the Pacific whaling grounds would leave letters here to be picked up by homeward-bound ships whose crews would deliver the mail by hand. Today the barrel has evolved into a wooden box on a pole surrounded by a fascinating assortment of junk: driftwood, bones, T-shirts, business cards, luggage tags, even e-mail addresses scratched into the wood. Tradition dictates that if you find a letter addressed to someone near where you live, you are supposed to take it home with you and deliver it by hand, meeting the addressee in the process. Feel free to leave a postcard or letter yourself (no postage is necessary).

Just a few meters beyond the barrel are a lava tunnel and the rusted remains of a Norwegian fish operation dating to the 1920s.

Corona del Diablo

Actually a marine visitor site, the Devil's Crown is the unmistakable circle of jagged rocks situated offshore from Post Office Bay. The nooks and crannies of the forbidding islet offer great snorkeling, either outside the ring or in the shallow inner chamber, which is reached through a side opening or an underwater arch. Sea lions and the occasional hammerhead make things interesting from time to time, but you'll almost definitely see colorful tropical species like parrotfish, angelfish, and damselfish. The current on the seaward side can be strong and the water cold, so snorkel in carefully monitored groups.

ESPAÑOLA

The southernmost island in the Galápagos is also one of the oldest, weathered down until it pokes just above sea level. It's often the first stop for tours leaving from San Cristóbal, and what an introduction—many different seabirds use the island as a stopover or nesting site, making it a birder's dream. The visitor sites can be crowded because the island is within reach of day tours from San Cristóbal.

Gardener Bay
A wet landing deposits you on this beautiful, one-km-long crescent beach on the northeast side of Española. While the site is a bit mundane—no hikes, just beach—the snorkeling is excellent. Some of the dozens of sea lions sprawled on the sand might join you in the water, along with the occasional stingray or white-tipped shark. The beach is an important nesting site for marine turtles, so you might be lucky enough to come across one in the process. Turtle rock, a short *panga* ride offshore, shelters legions of bright topical fish like moorish idols, damselfish, and parrotfish.

Landlubbers can follow the guide's example and relax or read a book. Notice the endemic hood mockingbirds, inquisitive little buggers often found squabbling over territory on the beach. In this type of behavior, rare in land birds, two family groups face each other down over an invisible line in the sand and set about displaying—hend-

ing down to the ground with tails spread in the air—and screeching.

Punta Suárez
Almost one hour by boat from Gardener Bay on the western tip of Española waits one of the most outstanding visitor sites in the Galápagos. After a wet landing, you'll head out on a trail that loops toward cliffs on the south side of the point. Along the way you can't miss Boobieville, a major blue-footed boobie colony. In fact, you'll have to be careful not to step on any of the nests, parents, or young that sit in the middle of the trail like feathery toll attendants. Guano-stained rocks as far as the eye can see are peppered with boobies in all stages of life, from fuzzy newborns to mangy-looking teenage equivalents (adolescence is kind to no beast). Everyone who's not a parent is demanding to be fed.

Farther along the trail nest almost all of the waved albatrosses in the world. Between April and November, about 10,000 breeding pairs nest on Punta Suárez, one of only two breeding sites in the world. (The other is the Isla de la Plata off mainland Ecuador.) You might even be lucky enough to see the elaborate courtship dance, or at least hear the bill-clattering from behind a bush. You'll almost surely witness take-offs and landings, worth a wince or two at best. The soaring giants aren't all that graceful within range of the earth, making landings more an exercise in quick braking and luck. The nearby cliff face makes take-offs a little easier—the birds simply inch to the edge and leap.

Many other seabirds soar over the impressive cliffs at the end of the loop, including the Galápagos hawk, Galápagos dove, and swallow-tailed gulls. Down below, a blowhole sends spray 50 meters into the air with every crashing wave. Española's male marine iguanas, spread on the rocks at the base of the cliffs, boast brighter mating colors than anywhere else in the Galápagos. Neon turquoise spreads over their back and front legs, thought to be the result of eating algae particular to this island. Scientists also hypothesize that they may be a separate species.

NORTHERN ISLANDS

TOWER

Tower Island provides a jumping-off point for seabirds in the far northeast corner of the archipelago. It's eight hours by boat from its larger neighbors, meaning that a long, rolling crossing is usually done at night (stock up on seasickness remedies). The collapsed caldera that

JULIAN SMITH

a Galápagos penguin — the only species north of the equator

forms the low island opens to the sea to the south—boat captains navigate the tricky entrance to Darwin Bay by lining up the metal towers on shore.

Darwin Bay Beach
Keep an eye on the murky shallows on the way to the wet landing and you can spot white-tipped sharks. Graffiti recording the names of visiting ships decorates the rocks next to the organic beach. Trails from the beach head into the saltbushes filled with the nests of red-footed boobies and frigatebirds. Huge, hapless chicks stare out from the greenery on every side as their parents compete overhead for nest materials and food. Masked boobies and swallow-tailed gulls also nest here, and you may spot a storm petrel or its nemesis, the short-eared owl.

Another branch of the trail leads over rough rocks next to a series of tidal pools. Yellow-crowned night herons sit on the rocks, half-asleep by day, as lava gulls hover above. Notice how soft the *opuntia* cactus spines have become here because the plants don't have to defend against anything more dangerous than a bird's nest.

Prince Philip's Steps
Named in honor of a royal visit in the 1960s, this site near the tip of Darwin Bay's eastern arm is limited to boats of 12 people or fewer. First a *panga* ride along the bottom of the cliffs lets you look for frigatebirds and red-billed tropic birds. Next, a steep-railed stairway takes you to a trail along the top of the cliffs. Masked and red-footed boobies nest near great frigatebirds among the Palo Santo trees as storm petrels swoop overhead

RESOURCES

BOOKS

Many of the out-of-print books are available in libraries or from **Powell's Books,** 40 NW 10th Ave, Portland, OR 97209, e-mail: help@powells.com, website: www.powells.com. Titles published in Ecuador can often be found at Libri Mundi in Quito.

Description and Travel

Cárdenas, José-Germán, and Karen Marie Greiner. *Walking the Beaches of Ecuador.* Quito: J.G. Cárdenas and K.M. Greiner, 1988. An account of the authors' journey by foot down the entire coastline of Ecuador.

Clynes, Tom. *Wild Planet! 1,001 Extraordinary Events for the Inspired Traveler.* Gale Research, 1995. Festivals and celebrations from around the world, including many in South America.

Sienko, Walter. *Latin America by Bike.* Seattle: The Mountaineers, 1993. Excellent reference book on cycling in Central and South America.

Urrutia, Virginia. *Two Wheels & A Taxi: A Slightly Daft Adventure in the Andes.* Seattle: The Mountaineers, 1987. The author, a grandmother, rode through Ecuador with only her sense of humor and an Ecuadorian taxi driver as backup.

Wesche, Rolf. *The Ecotourist's Guide to the Ecuadorian Amazon.* Quito: CETUR, 1995. Covers Napo province and features excellent maps.

History

De la Vega, Garcilaso. *Royal Commentaries of the Incas & General History of Peru.* Out of print. First-hand account of the Incas at the time of the Spanish arrival and afterward.

De las Casas, Bartolomé. *A Short Account of the Destruction of the Indies.* Penguin USA, 1999. Originally written as a plea to Prince Philip of Spain in the 16th century, this is a searing indictment of European cruelty toward the native peoples of the New World.

Hemming, John. *The Conquest of the Incas.* San Diego: Harcourt Brace & Co., 1973. Probably the best account of the Spanish arrival in the New World and its aftermath. A long but surprisingly readable account that is exhaustively researched.

Ecuadorian Culture

Acosta-Solis, Basaglia, Bottasso, Hoeck, Ligabue, Marcos, Norton, Patzelt, Pallo, Rossi-Osmida, and Yost. *Ecuador: In the Shadow of the Volcanoes.* Quito: Ediciones Libri Mundi, 1991. General reference book on the country.

Anhalzer, Jorge. *Quito.* One of Anhalzer's many gorgeous coffee-table books available in Ecuador, filled with incredible photos. Other ones include *Amazonia, Llanganati, Galapagos, Ecuador: A Bird's Eye View,* and *Cotopaxi.*

Buchanan, Christy, and Cesar Franco. *The Ecuador Cookbook: Traditional Vegetarian and Seafood Recipes.* Christy Buchanan, 1998. A bilingual cookbook using easy-to-find ingredients.

Carvalho-Neto, Paulo. *Cuentos Folkloricos del Ecuador, Sierra y Costa, Vol. I-III.* Quito: Ediciones Abya-Yala. Folklore from the Andes and the coast. Written in Spanish.

Carvalho-Neto, Paulo. *Antologia del Folklore Ecuatoriano.* Quito: Ediciones Abya-Yala, 1994. Anthology of folklore from around the country. Spanish.

Cuvi, Pablo. *Crafts of Ecuador.* Quito: Dinediciones, 1994. Beautifully photographed book on Ecuadorian crafts.

González, Claudio Malo. *Cuenca Ecuador.* Quito: Ediciones Libri Mundi, 1991. Large-format book on Cuenca's historical treasures.

Paymal, Noemi, and Catalina Sosa. *Amazon Worlds.* Quito: Sinchi Sacha Foundation, 1993. A beautifully photographed coffee-table book on the indigenous cultures of the Ecuadorian Amazon.

Ecuadorian Literature

Adoum, Jorge Enrique, ed. *Poesia Viva del Ecuador, Siglo XX.* Out of print. Collection of 20th-century Ecuadorian poetry.

Beardsell, Peter R. *Winds of Exile: The Poetry of Jorge Carrera Andrade.* Out of print.

Izaca, Jorge Juan. *Huasipungo: the Villagers.* Carbondale, IL: Southern Illinois University Press, 1973. Landmark novel about peasant life in Ecuador that caused a furor when it was originally published in the 1930s. Brutally honest.

Spindler, Frank, trans. *Selections from Juan Montalvo.* Out of print.

General

Bemelmans, Ludwig. *The Donkey Inside.* Out of print. The French author of the famous *Madeline* series for children travels in Ecuador in the late '30s and early '40s. Subtle, always perceptive and sympathetic, at times scathing characterizations of Ecuadorians and their attitudes.

Buchet, Martine. *Panama: A Legendary Hat.* New York: St. Martin's Press.

Burroughs, William S. *Queer.* Viking Penguin, 1996. A companion piece to Burroughs's first novel *Junky* (1953), *Queer* describes a fictional addict's sexual escapades during a "hallucinated month of acute withdrawal" in Guayaquil and Mexico City.

Lourie, Peter. *Sweat of the Sun, Tears of the Moon.* University of Nebraska Press, 1998. First-hand account of an obsession with the treasure in the Llanganatis.

Michaux, Henri. *Ecuador: A Travel Journal.* Out of print. A short, quirky account of the Belgian-born author's travels in Ecuador in 1927. An interesting read, very philosophical, even spiritual at times.

Noble, Judith. *Introduction to Quechua: Language of the Andes.* NTC Publishing Group, 1999. A book and tape package that covers everyday phrases, grammar, and vocabulary.

Poole, Richard. *The Inca Smiled: The Growing Pains of an Aid Worker in Ecuador.* Out of print. The story of a British volunteer in Ecuador in the '60s, with interesting takes on the Andean indigenous personalities and third-world development.

Theroux, Paul. *The Old Patagonian Express: By Train Through the Americas.* Boston: Hougton Mifflin Co., 1997. The author travels from Canada to the tip of Chile by train. One chapter on the Quito-Guayaquil line, even though he didn't ride it.

Thompsen, Moritz. *Living Poor: A Peace Corps Chronicle.* Out of print. Two years on a farm in Esmeraldas in the 1960s, said to be one of the best books on the Peace Corps experience. The narrative of his life is continued in *The Farm on the River of Emeralds* (1979) and *The Saddest Pleasure: A Journey on Two Rivers* (Minnesota, Greywolf Press, 1990). All are eloquent, wrenching, and beautiful.

The Amazon

Forsyth, Adrian, and Ken Miyata. *Tropical Nature.* MacMillan, 1987. A great introduction for the layman, makes tropical ecology fascinating and understandable.

Kane, Joe. *Savages.* Vintage: 1996. Firsthand account of the Huaorani's fight against oil exploration, missionaries, and environmentalists.

Kricher, John. *A Neotropical Companion.* Princeton, NJ: Princeton University Press, 1999. Another good introduction to tropical ecology.

Emmons, Louise. *Neotropical Rainforest Mammals.* Chicago: University of Chicago Press, 1997. This scientific field guide has become the standard for studying these mammals.

Montgomery, Sy. *Journey of the Pink Dolphins: An Amazon Quest.* New York: Simon & Schuster, 2000. An exhaustive, lyrical account of the author's many trips to the Amazon in search of the elusive pink river dolphins. Contains color photos and discussions of the people, flora and fauna, politics, and ecology of the Amazon.

Oxford, Pete, and Renee Bush. *Amazon Images.* Quito: Dinediciones, 1995. Beautiful photos.

Smith, Randy. *Crisis Under the Canopy.* Quito: Abya Yala, 1993. Nonfiction work on tourism and the Huaorani.

The Galápagos

Angermeyer, Johanna. *My Father's Island: A Galápagos Quest.* Out of print. Life in the Galápagos through much of the 20th century.

Casto, Isabel. *A Guide to the Birds of the Galapagos Islands.* Princeton, NJ: Princeton University Press, 1996. Presents every species to have been recorded within the archipelago, including accidentals and vagrants. Thirty-two color plates.

Darwin, Charles. *The Voyage of the Beagle.* Penguin USA, 1999. A classic of early travel literature written by a wide-eyed, brilliant young man setting out to see the whole world. You can almost watch his theories bring born. One chapter out of 21 deals with the Galápagos.

Darwin, Charles. *The Origin of Species by Means of Natural Selection.* Gramercy, 1998. The book that shook the world—and as a bonus, it's one of the few groundbreaking scientific works that's truly readable.

Darwin, Charles, and Nora Barlow, ed. *The Autobiography of Charles Darwin, 1802–1882.* W.W. Norton & Co., 1993. A simple and straightforward look into Darwin's mind and the forces that shaped it.

Darwin, Charles, and Mark Ridley, ed. *The Darwin Reader.* W.W. Norton & Co., 1996. Selections from Darwin's works, including *The Voyage of the Beagle* and *Origin of Species.*

De Roy, Tui. *Spectacular Galapagos: Exploring an Extraordinary World.* Hugh Lauter Levin Associates, 1999. Text and breathtaking photographs by one of the islands's foremost advocates. Tui de Roy lived in the Galápagos for 35 years and also wrote of *Galapagos: Islands Born of Fire* (Warwick Publications, 2000).

Humann, Paul, ed., and Ned Deloach, ed. *Reef Fish Identification: Galápagos.* New World Publications, 1994.

Hurtado, Gustavo Vasconez. *Isle of the Black Cats.* Quito: Ediciones Libri Mundi, 1993. Novelized account of Floreana's soap operas.

Jackson, Michael. *Galápagos: A Natural History.* Calgary: University of Calgary Press, 1994. The definitive guide to the islands, a must-read for every visitor.

Latorre, Octavio. *The Curse of the Giant Tortoise.* Quito, 1990. Covers the strange history of the islands.

Vonnegut, Kurt, Jr. *Galápagos.* Delta, 1999. The emperor of irony's take on evolution, the human condition, and what would happen if the only people to survive a worldwide epidemic were a handful of passengers on a Galápagos cruise ship.

Weiner, Jonathan. *The Beak of the Finch: A Story of Evolution in Our Own Time.* Vintage Books, 1995. Describes the work of Rosemary and Peter Grant, who have studied 20 generations of finches on Daphne Major over two decades,

Wittmer, Margaret. *Floreana: A Woman's Pilgrimage to the Galápagos.* Wakefield, RI: Moyer Bell, 1990. First-hand account of early Floreana settlers.

Health

Bezruchka, Stephen M.D. *The Pocket Doctor.* Seattle: The Mountaineers, 1999. A handy travel health reference.

Forgey, William M.D. *Travelers' Medical Resource.* Merrillville: ICS Books, 1990. Absolutely comprehensive. Includes a toll-free computer database update service.

Rose, Stuart M.D. *International Travel Health Guide.* Northampton: Travel Medicine, Inc. Updated yearly.

Outdoor Recreation

Brain, Yossi. *Ecuador: A Climbing Guide.* Seattle: The Mountaineers, 2000. The most up-to-date and detailed guide to climbing Ecuador's major peaks.

Rachowiecki, Rob, Mark Thurber, and Betsy Wagenhauser. *Climbing & Hiking in Ecuador.* Bucks, England: Bradt, 1997. A wide-ranging books that covers mountaineering and hikes of various lengths throughout the country.

Birding

Rodner, Clemencia, Miguel Lentino, and Robin Restall. *A Checklist of the Birds of Northern South America.* New Haven: Yale University Press, 2001. Covers Ecuador, Colombia, and Venezuela.

Wheatley, Nigel. *Where to Watch Birds in South America.* Princeton, NJ: Princeton University Press, 2000. Site-specific, includes maps.

USEFUL WEBSITES

All Internet addresses should be proceeded by "http://"

General Ecuador Websites

www.ecuadorexplorer.com;EcuadorExplorer.com;complete online guide

www.ecuador.com;Ecuador.com;news, features, cultural, and business information

www.exploringecuador.com;Exploring Ecuador;tourism, business, arts, cultural organizations, and news

www.qni.com/~mj/; FunkyFish Ecuador Guide;offbeat travel info

www.latinworld.com/countries/ecuador/;LatinWorld: Ecuador

dir.yahoo.com/Regional/Countries/Ecuador/;Yahoo! Ecuador page;links to just about everything

The Galápagos

www.igtoa.org;International Galápagos Tour Operators Association

www.galapagos.org; Charles Darwin Research Station, Charles Darwin Foundation, and Galápagos Conservation Trust

www.terraquest.com/Galapagos;Terraquest's Virtual Galápagos site;photos, movies, and more

www.discovergalapagos.com/links.html;Discover Galapagos;natural history, conservation issues, and travel info

www.law.emory.edu/PI/GALAPAGOS;Galápagos Coalition;scientists and lawyers interested in Galápagos conservation and its relation to human activities

News and Media

www.hoy.com.ec;*Hoy* online; in Spanish

www.elcomercio.com; *El Comercio* online; in Spanish

www.eluniverso;*El Universo* online;in Spanish

www.washingtonpost.com/wp srv/inatl/longterm/worldref/country/ecuador.htm;*Washington Post* Ecuador coverage

www.herald.com/content/today/news/americas/content.htm;*Miami Herald* Latin America coverage;

dir.yahoo.com/Regional/Countries/Ecuador/News_and_Media/;Yahoo! Ecuador news and media page

Government

www.ecuador.org;Ecuadorian Embassy site

www.state.gov/www/background_notes/whabgnhp.html;U.S. Department of State background notes country index;choose Ecuador for most recent posting

www.odci.gov/cia/publications/factbook/geos/ec.html;CIA World Factbook: Ecuador

lcweb2.loc.gov/frd/cs/ectoc.html;U.S. Department of State's *Ecuador: A Country Study* online

travel.state.gov/ecuador.html;U.S. Department of State Ecuador consular information sheet for Ecuador

Weather and the Natural World

weather.yahoo.com/forecast/Quito_EQ_c.html;Yahoo! Quito weather forecast

www.weather.com/ins/countries_index/Ecuador.html;The Weather Channel Ecuador weather page

www.washingtonpost.com/wp srv/weather/south_america.htm;*Washington Post* South America weather

vulcan.wr.usgs.gov/Volcanoes/Ecuador;USGS Ecuador volcanoes page

www.volcano.si.edu/gvp;Smithsonian Institution Global Volcanism Program;includes recent worldwide activity

Other Websites

www.andes.org;Cultures of the Andes;Quechua language links, songs, and pictures

www.worldrevolution.org/Country.asp?CountryName=Ecuador;The World Revolution Ecuador page;human rights issues in Ecuador

www.survival.org.uk;Survival International;an organization that supports tribal peoples worldwide

Language

www.babelfish.com/Translations.shtml;Babel Fish translation site www.yupi.com/traductor;Yupi.com translation site

www.SpanishDICT.com;SpanishDICT.com;online Spanish dictionary

www.studyspanish.com;Learn Spanish;free award-winning online tutorial

www.geocities.com/Athens/Thebes/6177;Webspañol;links to online Spanish language resources

www.lenguaje.com/enlaces/Jergas/Guayaquilenismos.htm;Guayaquil slang

General Travel

www.planeta.com;Planeta.com:Eco Travels in Latin America

www.virtualtourist.com/South_America/Ecuador/?s=@971393433-32399;VirtualTourist.com Ecuador page;"real travelers sharing real info"

Newsgroups

For more news, views, and the odd bit of gibberish, drop in on the soc.culture.ecuador, soc.culture.latin-america and rec.travel.latin-america newsgroups

GLOSSARY

aguardiente—potent sugarcane liquor
arrope de mora—blackberry sweet
autoferro/autocarril—bus body on train chassis
barrio—neighborhood
basura—garbage
basurero—garbage can
batido—blended drink made with fruit and milk, like a thin milkshake
bolsita—small bag
botas de cuero—rubber boots
brujo—witch
bufanda—woven wool scarf
caliente—hot
callua—woven cloth belt
calzón—wide white pants worn by Salasca indígenas
cambio—change
camioneta—pickup truck
campesino—country-dweller (literally, "peasant"); often derogatory
canelazo—hot cinnamon drink made with aguardiente
cascada—waterfall
casilla—post office box
cerveza—beer
ceviche— dish made by marinating shrimp, fish, or crustacean parts in lime juice
chakra—a small agricultural plot often planted with numerous crops
chaulafan—inexpensive, filling fried rice dish served in chifas
chicha—mildly alcoholic drink made from fermented corn liquor (Sierra) or chewed yucca root (Oriente)
chifa—Chinese restaurant chirimoya—custard apple or sweetsop
chiva—motor home
chola— indigenous marsapan (marzipan) figure
cholo—intermediate racial category between indígena and mestizo (derogatory)
chompa—cold-weather jacket
cinta—woven cloth belt
ciudadela—neighborhood, suburb
cocha—lake

colibri—hummingbird
collectivo—small bus
conquistador—conqueror
cooperativa—cooperative; often a private bus company
cordillera—mountain range
correo electronico—e-mail
corvina—sea bass
costeño—resident of the coast region
criollo—full-blooded Spaniard born in the New World (colonial term)
cuba libre—rum and Coke
curandero—traditional medicine or faith healer
cuenta—bill for service
cuy—guinea pig (common food)
denuncia—crime report
encocado—seafood dish cooked with coconut milk
encomienda—colonial labor system in which indígenas were forced to work for Spanish settlers, who in turn agreed to convert them to Christianity and "protect" them
estrera—woven reed mat
faja—woven cloth strip used by indígenas in the Sierra to tie back long hair
ferretería—hardware store
flauta—reed flute used in Andean music
frio—cold
fútbol—soccer
guagua—Quechua for "baby"
guanabana—sweet paste made from guava
guardianía—guard post
hacienda—large country estate (colonial)
helado—ice cream (usually made with water, so technically sherbet)
indígena—member of an indigenous group (male or female)
ingacarretero—Inca highway
invierno—winter
joyería—jewelry shop
lahar—destructive volcanic landslide of mud, rocks, and water from lava-melted ice
lavaseca—dry cleaning service
marsapan—inedible dough used in crafts, primarily in Calderón (marzipan)

mestizo—of mixed European and indigenous heritage

mirador—balcony or vantage point

montuvio—a person of mixed indigenous, black, and white descent, often found along the coast

moreno—African-American (slang); also, dark-haired person

municipalidad—municipality (city government)

nogada—sweet nut candy (nougat)

obraje—colonial workshop in which indigenous workers were forced to weave textiles

páramo—high-altitude grasslands characterized low temperatures and abundant moisture

pannier—one of a pair of bags attached to a special frame on a bicycle

paredones—general term for pre-Columbian ruins (literally, "big walls")

paseo—stroll, usually taken in the evening

patrón—the owner of a hacienda (colonial); literally "boss" or "patron"

peña—nightclubs where live indigenous music is played

peninsulare—a person born in the Iberian Peninsula, i.e., Spain or Portugal (archaic) piedras escritas—written stones (petroglyphs)

piso—floor (in addresses)

poste restante—general delivery mail

propina—tip

pucará—Inca fortress

pueblo—village

pueblito—small village

ranchero—open-sided truck used as public transportation, especially on the coast and in the Oriente

residencial—inexpensive hotel

ronda—evening serenade

rondador—reed panpipes used in Andean music

saco—jacket, blazer

sastrería—tailor shop

sastrero—tailor

shigra—woven shoulder bag, often made of palm fiber

supermercado—grocery store

taller—workshop, often for crafts

tambo—thatched-roof shelter found in the Andes; also, rest stop along the ancient Inca highway

tapial—rammed-earth construction technique in which a mixture of earth and clay is compacted into walls

tapice—narrow tapestry

tienda—shop

tinku—ritualized rock-throwing battle during fiestas

tiple—Andean instrument

tullpa—indigenous shawl pin

verano—summer

viajera—female traveler

vúlcan—volcano

zapater—bootmaker

SPANISH PHRASEBOOK

PRONUNCIATION GUIDE

Consonants

c - as 'c' in "cat," before 'a', 'o', or 'u'; like 's' before 'e' or 'i'
d - as 'd' in "dog," except between vowels, then like 'th' in "that"
g - before 'e' or 'i,' like the 'ch' in Scottish "loch"; elsewhere like 'g' in "get"
h - always silent
j - like the English 'h' in "hotel," but stronger
ll - like the 'y' in "yellow"
ñ - like the 'ni' in "onion"
r - always pronounced as strong 'r'
rr - trilled 'r'
v - similar to the 'b' in "boy" (not as English 'v')
y - similar to English, but with a slight "j" sound. When y stands alone it is pronounced like the 'e' in "me".
z - like 's' in "same"
b, f, k, l, m, n, p, q, s, t, w, x, z as in English

Vowels

a - as in "father," but shorter
e - as in "hen"
i - as in "machine"
o - as in "phone"
u - usually as in "rule"; when it follows a 'q' the 'u' is silent; when it follows an 'h' or 'g' it's pronounced like 'w,' except when it comes between 'g' and 'e' or 'i', when it's also silent

NUMBERS

0 - *cero*	17 - *diecisiete*
1 (masculine) - *uno*, 1 (feminine) - *una*	18 - *dieciocho*
2 - *dos*	19 - *diecinueve*
3 - *tres*	20 - *veinte*
4 - *cuatro*	21 - *vientiuno*
5 - *cinco*	30 - *treinta*
6 - *seis*	40 - *cuarenta*
7 - *siete*	50 - *cincuenta*
8 - *ocho*	60 - *sesenta*
9 - *nueve*	70 - *setenta*
10 - *diez*	80 - *ochenta*
11 - *once*	90 - *noventa*
12 - *doce*	100 - *cien*
13 - *trece*	101 - *cientouno*
14 - *catorce*	200 - *doscientos*
15 - *quince*	1,000 - *mil*
16 - *dieciseis*	10,000 - *diez mil*

DAYS OF THE WEEK

Sunday - *domingo*
Monday - *lunes*
Tuesday - *martes*
Wednesday - *miércoles*
Thursday - *jueves*
Friday - *viernes*
Saturday - *sábado*

TIME

What time is it? - *¿Qué hora es?*
one o'clock - *la una*
two o'clock - *las dos*
at two o'clock - *a las dos*
ten past three - *las tres y diez*
six A.M. - *las seis de la mañana*
six P.M. - *las seis de la tarde*
today - *hoy*
tomorrow, morning - *mañana, la mañana*
yesterday - *ayer*
week - *semana*
month - *mes*
year - *año*
last night - *la noche pasada* or *anoche*
next day - *el próximo día* or *al día siguiente*

USEFUL WORDS AND PHRASES

Hello. - *Hola.*
Good morning. - *Buenos días.*
Good afternoon. - *Buenas tardes.*
Good evening. - *Buenas noches.*
How are you? - *¿Cómo está?*
Fine. - *Muy bien.*
And you? - *¿Y usted?* (formal) or *¿Y tú?* (familiar)
So-so. - *Así así.*
Thank you. - *Gracias.*
Thank you very much. - *Muchas gracias.*
You're very kind. - *Usted es muy amable.*
You're welcome; literally, "It's nothing." - *De nada.*
yes - *sí*
no - *no*
I don't know - *no sé* or *no lo sé*
it's fine; okay - *está bien*
good; okay - *bueno*
please - *por favor*
Pleased to meet you. - *Mucho gusto.*
excuse me (physical) - *perdóneme*
excuse me (speech) - *discúlpeme*
I'm sorry. - *Lo siento.*
Goodbye. - *Adiós.*
see you later; literally, "until later" - *hasta luego*
more - *más*
less - *menos*
better - *mejor*
much - *mucho*
a little - *un poco*
large - *grande*
small - *pequeño*
quick - *rápido*
slowly - *despacio*
bad - *malo*
difficult - *difícil*
easy - *fácil*
He/She/It is gone; as in "She left," "He's gone" - *Ya se fue.*
I don't speak Spanish well. - *No hablo bien español.*

I don't understand. - *No entiendo.*
How do you say . . . in Spanish? - *¿Cómo se dice . . . en español?*
Do you understand English? - *¿Entiende el inglés?*
Is English spoken here? (Does anyone here speak English?) - *¿Se habla inglés aquí?*
I'm sorry. - *Lo siento.*
Goodbye. - *Adiós.*
see you later; literally, "until later" - *hasta luego*
more - *más*
less - *menos*
better - *mejor*
much - *mucho*
a little - *un poco*
large - *grande*
small - *pequeño*
quick - *rápido*
slowly - *despacio*
bad - *malo*
difficult - *difícil*
easy - *fácil*
He/She/It is gone; as in "She left," "He's gone" - *Ya se fue.*
I don't speak Spanish well. - *No hablo bien español.*
I don't understand. - *No entiendo.*
How do you say . . . in Spanish? - *¿Cómo se dice . . . en español?*
Do you understand English? - *¿Entiende el inglés?*
Is English spoken here? (Does anyone here speak English?) - *¿Se habla inglés aquí?*

TERMS OF ADDRESS

I - *yo*
you (formal) - *usted*
you (familiar) - *tú*
he/him - *él*
she/her - *ella*
we/us - *nosotros*
you (plural) - *ustedes*
they/them (all males or mixed gender) - *ellos*
they/them (all females) - *ellas*
Mr., sir - *señor*
Mrs., madam - *señora*
Miss, young lady - *señorita*
wife - *esposa*
husband - *marido or esposo*
friend - *amigo (male), amiga (female)*
sweetheart - *novio (male), novia (female)*
son, daughter - *hijo, hija*
brother, sister - *hermano, hermana*
father, mother - *padre, madre*

GETTING AROUND

Where is . . . ? - *¿Dónde está . . . ?*
How far is it to . . . ? - *¿Qué tan lejos está a . . . ?*
from . . . to . . . - *de . . . a . . .*
highway - *la carretera*
road - *el camino*
street - *la calle*
block - *la cuadra*
kilometer - *kilómetro*

north - *el norte*
south - *el sur*
west - *el oeste*
east - *el este*
straight ahead - *al derecho or adelante*
to the right - *a la derecha*
to the left - *a la izquierda*

ACCOMMODATIONS

Can I (we) see a room? - *¿Puedo (podemos) ver una habitación?*
What is the rate? - *¿Cuál es el precio?*
a single room - *una habitación sencilla*
a double room - *una habitación doble*
key - *llave*
bathroom - *retrete or lavabo*
bath - *baño*
hot water - *agua caliente*
cold water - *agua fría*
towel - *toalla*
soap - *jabón*
toilet paper - *papel sanitario*
air conditioning - *aire acondicionado*
fan - *abanico, ventilador*
blanket - *cubierta or manta*

PUBLIC TRANSPORT

bus stop - *la parada de la guagua*
main bus terminal - *la central camionera*
airport - *el aeropuerto*
ferry terminal - *la terminal del transbordador*
I want a ticket to . . .- Quiero un tiqué a . . .
I want to get off at . . .- Quiero bajar en . . .
Here, please. - *Aquí, por favor.*
Where is this bus going? - *¿Dónde va este guagua?*
roundtrip - *ida y vuelta*
What do I owe? - *¿Cuánto le debo?*

FOOD

menu - *carta, menú*
glass - *taza*
fork - *tenedor*
knife - *cuchillo*
spoon - *cuchara, cucharita*
napkin - *servilleta*
soft drink - *refresco*
coffee, cream - *café, crema*
tea - *té*
sugar - *azúcar*
drinking water - *agua pura, agua potable*
bottled carbonated water - *club soda*
bottled uncarbonated water - *agua sin gas*
beer - *cerveza*
wine - *vino*
milk - *leche*
juice - *jugo*

eggs - *huevos*
bread - *pan*
watermelon - *patilla*
banana - *plátano*
apple - *manzana*
orange - *naranja*
meat (without) - *carne (sin)*
beef - *carne de res*
chicken - *pollo*
fish - *pescado*
shellfish - *camarones, mariscos*
fried - *frito*
roasted - *asado*
barbecue, barbecued - *barbacoa, al carbón, or a la parilla*
breakfast - *desayuno*
lunch - *almuerzo*
dinner (often eaten in late afternoon) - *comida*
dinner, or a late night snack - *cena*
the check - *la cuenta*

MAKING PURCHASES

I need . . . - *Necesito . . .*
I want . . . - *Deseo . . . or Quiero . . .*
I would like . . . (more polite) - *Quisiera . . .*
How much does it cost? - *¿Cuánto cuesta?*
What's the exchange rate? - *¿Cuál es el tipo de cambio?*
Can I see . . . ? - *¿Puedo ver . . . ?*
this one - *ésta/ésto*
expensive - *caro*
cheap - *barato*
cheaper - *más barato*
too much - *demasiado*

HEALTH

Help me please. - *Ayúdeme por favor.*
I am ill. - *Estoy enfermo.*
pain - *dolor*
fever - *fiebre*
stomache ache - *dolor de estómago*
vomiting - *vomitar*
diarrhea - *diarrea*
drugstore - *farmacia*
medicine - *medicina*
pill, tablet - *pastilla*
birth control pills - *pastillas contraceptivas*
condoms - *condomes, gomas*

ACCOMMODATIONS INDEX

RESTAURANTS INDEX

INDEX

CHURCHES

FESTIVALS AND HOLIDAYS

HIKING

INDIGENOUS GROUPS

MARKETS

MUSEUMS

VOLCANOES

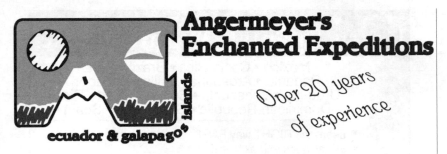

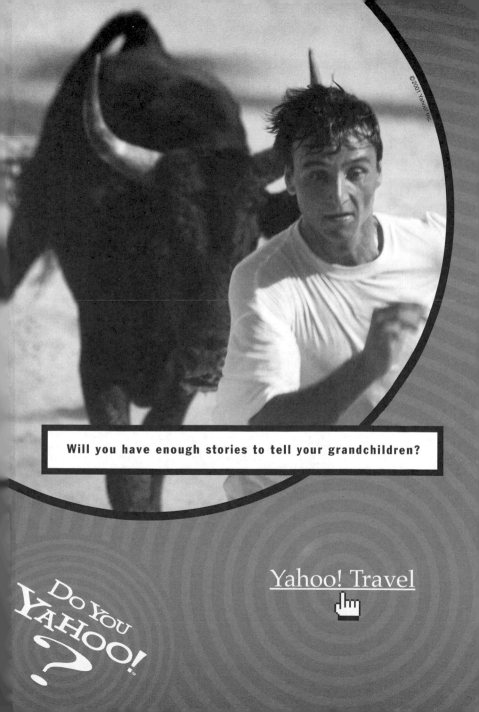

Will you have enough stories to tell your grandchildren?

Yahoo! Travel

DO YOU YAHOO!?

ABOUT THE AUTHOR

I travel a lot; I hate having my life disrupted by routine.

—Caskie Stinnett

Julian Smith has been writing since he could read and traveling since his first trip to Cape Cod with his parents as a child. A pre-college summer in Brazil sparked a love affair with (and in) Latin America, fueled by a stint studying the cloud forests of Costa Rica. Within days of receiving a B.A. in Biology from the University of Virginia, he found himself hopelessly entangled in a self-publishing venture that resulted nine months later in the one-pound, eight-ounce *On Your Own in El Salvador,* the first in-depth guide to the country. He's also the author of Moon's *Virginia Handbook* and has contributed to *Road Trip USA, Road Trip USA: California and the Southwest,* and *Online Travel Planning for Dummies.*

In addition to backpacking through much of South America, Julian has ranged from the top of Kilimanjaro to the bottom of the Grand Canyon. Along the way he's held jobs as varied as Canyonlands National Park Ranger and Asian Cuisine Public Outreach Coordina-

tor. When pointing out the bathroom or delivering Kung Pao Chicken fails to satisfy, there's always a desert tower to climb or some perfect Utah powder to snowboard.

He's currently working on a master's degree on grizzly bear ecotourism in the quiet, beautiful, pious mountains of northern Utah. If he's not in the hills, you'll find him back at home surrounded by great music, good books, mediocre cooking, and bad movies. The funk guitar may be gathering dust, but he still admits a fatal weakness for *The Simpsons.*

About the Updater

After studying political science at the University of Wisconsin at Madison and Spanish at the Universidad Laica Vicente Rocafuerte in Guayaquil, Tim Bewer settled down to a career as a legislative assistant. He gave up the desk job after just two years in order to travel and write full time, and since then his passport has been stamped in over 30 countries. His freelance articles have appeared in newspapers and magazines in the United States, Canada, and the U.K. He is also the author of *Wisconsin's Outdoor Treasures* and the *Acorn Guide to Northwest Wisconsin.*